Hi Emma

Another bril

work of art –

I maintain this is

the best cover for a

book on the methodology

of legal scholarship

in the history of the

world.

as always

Ed

RETHINKING LEGAL SCHOLARSHIP

Although American scholars sometimes consider European legal scholarship as old-fashioned and inward-looking and Europeans often perceive American legal scholarship as amateur social science, both traditions share a joint challenge. If legal scholarship will become too much separated from practice, legal scholars will ultimately make themselves superfluous. If legal scholars, on the other hand, cannot explain to other disciplines what is academic about their research, which methodologies are typical, and what separates proper research from mediocre or poor research, they will probably end up in a similar situation. Therefore we need a debate on what unites legal academics on both sides of the Atlantic. Should legal scholarship aspire to the status of a science and gradually adopt more and more of the methods, (quality) standards, and practices of other (social) sciences? What sort of methods do we need to study law in it social context and how should legal scholarship deal with the challenges posed by globalization?

ROB VAN GESTEL is Professor of Theory and Methods of Regulation at Tilburg University and Professor of Legal Research Methods at Leuven University.

HANS-W. MICKLITZ is Professor for Economic Law at the European University Institute, Florence.

EDWARD L. RUBIN is a Professor of Law and Political Science at Vanderbilt University, Nashville.

RETHINKING LEGAL SCHOLARSHIP

A Transatlantic Dialogue

Edited by

ROB VAN GESTEL

Tilburg University

HANS-W. MICKLITZ

European University Institute

EDWARD L. RUBIN

Vanderbilt University

CAMBRIDGE
UNIVERSITY PRESS

CAMBRIDGE
UNIVERSITY PRESS

One Liberty Plaza, 20th Floor, New York NY 10006, USA

Cambridge University Press is part of the University of Cambridge.

It furthers the University's mission by disseminating knowledge in the pursuit of education, learning, and research at the highest international levels of excellence.

www.cambridge.org
Information on this title: www.cambridge.org/9781107130920

First published 2017

A catalogue record for this publication is available from the British Library.

Library of Congress Cataloging-in-Publication Data
Names: Gestel, Rob van, editor. | Micklitz, Hans-W., editor. | Rubin, Edward L., 1948- editor.
Title: Rethinking scholarship : a transatlantic dialogue / edited by Rob van Gestel, University of Tilburg; Hans-W. Micklitz, University of Bamberg; Edward L. Rubin, Vanderbilt University.
Description: New York, NY : Cambridge University Press, 2017. | Includes bibliographical references and index.
Identifiers: LCCN 2016012708 | ISBN 9781107130920 (Hardback : alk. paper)
Subjects: LCSH: Jurisprudence–Europe. | Jurisprudence–United States. | Law–Europe–American influences. | Law–United States–European influences.
Classification: LCC K235 .R474 2017 | DDC 349.4–dc 3 LC record available at http://lccn.loc.gov/2016012708

ISBN 978-1-107-13092-0 Hardback

CONTENTS

CONTRIBUTORS

ROGER BROWNSWORD holds appointments at King's College London, where he was the founding director of TELOS (a research centre that focuses on technology, ethics, law and society) and at Bournemouth University. He is also an honorary professor at the University of Sheffield. He has published more than a dozen books, including (with Deryck Beyleveld) *Human Dignity in Bioethics and Biolaw* (2001); *Consent in the Law* (2007); *Contract Law: Themes for the Twenty-First Century* (2006); *Rights, Regulation and the Technological Revolution* (2008); *Regulating Technologies* (2008, coedited with Karen Yeung); *The Foundations of European Private Law* (2011, coedited with Hans Micklitz, Leone Niglia and Steven Weatherill); and *Law and the Technologies of the Twenty-First Century* (2012, coauthored with Morag Goodwin). He has more than 200 papers in edited collections and law reviews. Recently, he coedited both the *Cambridge Handbook on Human Dignity* (2014) and the *Oxford Handbook on Law, Regulation and Technology* (2016). Professor Brownsword has acted as a specialist adviser to parliamentary committees dealing with stems cells and hybrid embryos. From 2004 to 2010, he was a member of the Nuffield Council on Bioethics; from 2011 to 2015, he chaired the Ethics and Governance Council of UK Biobank; and currently, he is a member of the Royal Society working party on machine learning.

REZA DIBADJ is Professor of Law at the University of San Francisco. His research involves corporate and securities law as well as legal theory, international law and regulation. His writing focuses on two themes. The first involves the application of new tools, such as network theory, to legal analysis. The second is an exploration of different institutional choices the law has made: which methods are preferable, and under what circumstances? These two themes converge in an attempt to propose new, welfare-enhancing, institutional arrangements for the relationship between government and business. He has published one book and over thirty-five law review articles, book reviews and book chapters. He teaches a wide variety of business law classes, including Business Associations (Corporations), Securities Regulation (basic and advanced), International Business Transactions, Antitrust, and Mergers and Acquisitions. Dibadj is a graduate of Harvard College, Harvard Business School and Harvard Law School.

MATTHEW A. GASPERETTI attended the University of Notre Dame before completing an MPhil and PhD in anthropology at the University of Cambridge and enrolling at Stanford Law School. In his doctoral research, he used statistical methods to study biological change and social development in the prehistoric Middle East. Matthew is focusing his legal studies on international law, comparative law, development and conflict resolution. His recent research includes econometric analyses of the effects of different legislative frameworks for cultural patrimony preservation and the economic effects of bilateral investment treaties and arbitration conventions on foreign direct investment.

ROB VAN GESTEL is Professor of Theory and Methods of Regulation at Tilburg University and Professor of Legal Research Methods at Leuven University. He is a former Braudel fellow at the European University Institute in Florence and former TPR chair holder at the Academy for Legal Theory at KU Leuven Brussels. Van Gestel is the former chairman of the Dutch Association of legislation and member of the International Association of Legislation, former editor of the Journal for legislative studies *RegelMaat* and former editor of the Journal *Recht en Methode*. Van Gestel specializes in methods of regulation, judicial lawmaking and academic legal research. In 2007, he established the first research centre on methodology of law and legal research in Europe.

DEBORAH R. HENSLER is the Judge John W. Ford Professor of Dispute Resolution and Associate Dean for Graduate Studies at Stanford Law School. She was a cofounder of the RAND Institute for Civil Justice and served as its Director before leaving for Stanford. Trained as an empirical social scientist at the Massachusetts Institute of Technology from which she received a PhD in Political Science, over the past several decades she has conducted both qualitative and quantitative studies of the consequences of legal policy in the United States and the Netherlands, and she has taught research design for empirical legal studies at Stanford, the University of Chicago Law School and Catolica Universidade in Lisbon, Portugal. Hensler is a fellow of the American Academy of Arts and Sciences and the American Academy of Political and Social Science.

NILS JANSEN, serves as Professor for Civil Law and Director in the Institut for Legal History at the University of Münster. Jansen was a member in the Studienstiftung des deutschen Volkes studying law, philosophy and politics at the Universities of Passau, Kiel and Oxford. He graduated in 1994 and 1998 (Erstes and Zweites Staatsexamen) and achieved his doctorate in 1996 under the supervision of Robert Alexy; his Habilitation was in 2002 when he worked with Reinhard Zimmermann. Jansen has taught at the universities of Kiel, Regensburg, Cambridge, Augsburg and Düsseldorf. He has been a visiting professor at Duke Law School (2008), the University of Oxford (2009) and the Stellenbosch Institute for Advanced Study (2013 and 2015); since 2014 he is an extraordinary professor at the University of Stellenbosch. Jansen is a principal investigator and a member of the board of the Cluster of excellence 'religion and politics'. Jansen's main field of interest is the historical and theoretical foundations of European private law and in particular the law of noncontractual obligations. Monographs include *Binnenmarkt, Privatrecht und Europäische Identität* (2004), *The Making of Legal Authority* (2010) and *Theologie, Philosophie und Jurisprudenz in der Spätscholastischen Lehre von der Restitution* (2014).

PAUL W. KAHN is Robert W. Winner Professor of Law and the Humanities, and Director of the Orville H. Schell, Jr. Center for Human Rights at Yale Law School. He earned his PhD in Philosophy from Yale University and his JD from Yale Law School. He served as a law clerk to Justice White in the United States Supreme Court from 1980–1982. Before coming to Yale Law School in 1985, he practiced law in Washington, DC, during which time he was on the legal team representing Nicaragua before the International Court of Justice. From 1993 to 1999 he was Nicholas de B. Katzenbach Professor of Law. He teaches in the areas of constitutional law and theory, international law, cultural theory and philosophy. He is the author of *Legitimacy and History: Self-Government in American Constitutional Theory*; *The Reign of Law: Marbury v. Madison and the Construction of America*; *The Cultural Study of Law: Reconstructing Legal Scholarship*; *Law and Love: The Trials of King Lear*; *Putting Liberalism in its Place*; *Out of Eden: Adam and Eve and the Problem of Evil*; *Sacred Violence: Torture, Terror, and Sovereignty*; *Political Theology: Four New Chapters on the Concept of Sovereignty*; *Finding Ourselves at the Movies and Making the Case: The Art of the Judicial Opinion*; as well as numerous articles.

NEIL KOMESAR is the Miller Professor of Law Emeritus. During his career at the University of Wisconsin, he had been the Doyle-Bascom Professor, the Burrus-Bascom Professor, the Bosshard Professor and he held the Miller Chair. He teaches or has taught torts, property, land use, legal process, constitutional law, law and economics, and advanced legal analysis. He has also taught comparative institutional analysis at the European University Institute (EUI) in Florence. Professor Komesar has written on a wide variety of subjects, including constitutional theory, tort reform, land use, damages, criminal victimization, public interest law, law and economics, property rights, landlord-tenant law and class actions. He has developed an approach to the analysis of law and public policy called comparative institutional analysis and has authored two books on the subject, *Imperfect Alternatives: Choosing Institutions in Law, Economics, and Public Policy* (1994) and *Law's Limits: The Role of Courts, the Rule of Law and the Supply and Demand of Rights* (2001).

ORLY LOBEL is the Don Weckstein Professor of Employment and Labor Law at the University of San Diego and founding faculty of the Center of Intellectual Property and Markets. She teaches and writes in the areas of intellectual property law, employment law, innovation policy, regulatory and administrative law, behavioural economics, consumer law, and trade secrets. A graduate of Tel Aviv University and Harvard Law School, Lobel clerked on the Israeli Supreme Court. She taught at Yale Law School and served as a fellow at Harvard University Center for Ethics and the Professions, the Kennedy School of Government, and the Weatherhead Center for International Affairs. Lobel is the recipient of several prestigious research grants from the Robert Wood Johnson Foundation, the American Bar Association litigation Fund, the Searle-Kauffman Fellowship, the Southern California Innovation Project and Netspar, University of Tilburg. She is a member of the American Law Institute and serves on the advisory boards of the San Diego Lawyer Chapter of the American Constitution Society, the Employee Rights Center and the Oxford Handbook on Governance. Lobel is the author of several books; most recently, *Talent Wants to Be Free: Why We Should Learn to Love Leaks, Raids, and Free-Riding* (2014) and numerous articles. Her scholarship has won many awards including the Thorsnes Prize for Outstanding Legal Scholarship and the Irving Oberman Memorial Award.

DAITHÍ MAC SÍTHIGH is Reader in Law at Newcastle University. He previously held posts at the University of East Anglia (UEA, 2008–2012) and the University of Edinburgh (2012–2014), and studied at Trinity College Dublin, the Open University and UEA. He has research and teaching interests in law and technology and in public law. Daithí is a member of CREATe, the centre for copyright and new business models in the creative economy (funded by Research Councils UK), where he works on three projects. He is a member of the Open Data Governance Board (Ireland), and was the convenor of the Media and Communications subject section at the Society of Legal Scholars. Daithí is coeditor of the Dublin University Law Journal and a panelist for the EU alternative dispute resolution (ADR) system.

HANS-W. MICKLITZ is Professor for Economic Law at the European University Institute, Florence Italy, since 2007; Head of Department, 2012–2014; Director of Graduate Studies 2009–2011; Jean Monnet Chair of Private Law and European Economic Law at the University of Bamberg, Germany; Finish Distinguished Professor at the University of Helsinki, 2015–2020; and Head of the Institute of European and Consumer Law (VIEW) in Bamberg. He has also held or studied law and sociology in Mainz, Lausanne/Geneva (Switzerland), Giessen and Hamburg; consultancies for OECD in Paris, UNEP Geneva Switzerland/Nairobi Kenya and CI (Consumers International) Den Haag Netherlands/Penang Malaysia; study visits at the University of Michigan, Ann Arbor; Jean Monnet Fellow at the European University Institute Florence, Italy; and visiting professor at the Somerville College at the University of Oxford. He holds an ERC Grant 2011–2016 on European Regulatory Private Law, financed by the Academy of Finland on the Transformation of Private Law beyond and through the European Union, 2015–2020.

EDWARD L. RUBIN is University Professor of Law and Political Science at Vanderbilt University. He specializes in administrative law, constitutional law and legal theory. He is the author of *Soul, Self and Society: The New Morality and the Modern State* (2015); *Beyond Camelot: Rethinking Politics and Law for the Modern State* (2005) and two books with Malcolm Feeley, *Federalism: Political Identity and Tragic Compromise* (2011) and *Judicial Policy Making and the Modern State: How the Courts Reformed America's Prisons* (1998). In addition, he is the author of two casebooks, *The Regulatory State* (with Lisa Bressman and Kevin Stack, 2nd edn., 2013); *The Payments System* (with Robert Cooter, 1990), three edited volumes (one forthcoming) and *The Heatstroke Line* (2015), a science fiction novel about the fate of the United States if climate change is not brought under control. Professor Rubin joined Vanderbilt Law School as Dean and the first John Wade–Kent Syverud Professor of

Law in July 2005, serving a four-year term that ended in June 2009. Previously, he taught at the University of Pennsylvania Law School from 1998 to 2005, and at the Berkeley School of Law from 1982 to 1998, where he served as an associate dean. Professor Rubin has been chair of the Association of American Law Schools' sections on Administrative Law and Socioeconomics and of its Committee on the Curriculum. He has served as a consultant to the People's Republic of China on administrative law and to the Russian Federation on payments law. He received his undergraduate degree from Princeton and his law degree from Yale.

MATHIAS M. SIEMS is a Professor of Commercial Law at Durham University. He is also a Research Associate at the Centre for Business Research, University of Cambridge; a Research Associate at the London Centre for Corporate Governance and Ethics, Birkbeck, University of London; and an Invited Fellow at the Maastricht European Law Institute. He graduated from the Universities of Munich and Edinburgh and has held various visiting positions at universities in Europe, Asia and North America. He has published widely on topics of comparative law, company law and legal methods.

JAN M. SMITS is Professor of European Private Law and academic director of the Maastricht European Private Law Institute (MEPLI), both at Maastricht University, the Netherlands. He previously taught at the universities of Leiden, Tilburg and Helsinki.

NEIL WALKER has been the Regius Professor of Public Law and the Law of Nature and Nations at the University of Edinburgh since 2008. Before that he was Professor of European Law at the European University Institute, Florence 2000–2008. He has published widely on questions of subnational, national, European and transnational constitutional law and theory, and also on questions of policing and security. He is a Fellow of the British Academy and also a Fellow of the Royal Society of Edinburgh. His most recent book is ***Intimations of Global Law*** **(2015).**

ACKNOWLEDGEMENTS

Rob van Gestel wishes to thank Hans Micklitz and Jan Vranken for their helpful comments on an earlier draft of this contribution

Orly Lobel wishes to thank Keia Atkinson and Hani Farah for excellent research assistance. For generous support of her research in behavioral law and policy, Lobel acknowledges the Robert Wood Johnson Foundation and the Netspar Research Grant.

Hans Micklitz would like to thank Rob van Gestel, Dennis Patterson, Anna Beckers, Rónán Condon, Yane Svetiev, and the colleagues from the law department of the EUI for their critique and encouragement.

Mathias Siems and Daithí Mac Síthigh thank the staff members of the law schools at the Universities of Edinburgh, East Anglia, Trinity College Dublin and Düsseldorf, as well as Bucerius Law School, for their participation in the survey that formed the basis of the research reported in their chapter of this book.

Jan Smits would like to thank Anna Beckers, Anna Berlee, Rob van Gestel, Jaap Hage, Eve Meurgey and Daniel On for helpful comments.

Introduction

ROB VAN GESTEL, HANS-W. MICKLITZ AND
EDWARD RUBIN

I.1 The Premise of this Volume

European and American legal scholarship have tended to function as two self-contained traditions (mediated in some cases by Britain), but globalization renders this separation obsolete and, in fact, dysfunctional. Corporate law scholars find that the firms they study now operate internationally; administrative law scholars deal with regulations that are as often the product of treaties as they are of municipal legislation; environmentalists must be concerned with the damage that modern industry inflicts on the climate, the oceans and the jet stream as well as on their local streams and forests; and scholars focusing on human rights must draw on emerging moral norms that cross national frontiers. At the same time, they must provide answers to threats generated by private exposure carried by the World Wide Web and preserved in the Cloud, and by government surveillance or drone attacks coming from above the clouds.

While legal scholars on both sides of the Atlantic have devoted serious attention to the globalization of legal issues and legal systems, they have done so by relying on their separate methodological approaches.[1] What they have not done is to confront the challenge that globalization poses to these methodologies themselves. European and American scholars are not simply providing different answers to problems that they now inevitably share, but they are asking different questions, for example, with regard to the relationship between theory and practice.[2] Those questions,

[1] R.A.J. van Gestel, H.W. Micklitz and M. Maduro, Methodology in the New Legal World, EUI Working Papers LAW No. 2012/13. (http://papers.ssrn.com/sol3/papers.cfm?abstract_id=2069872).

[2] See for example: Brent E. Newton, Preaching What They Don't Practice: Why Law Faculties' Preoccupation with Impractical Scholarship and Devaluation of Practical Competencies Obstruct Reform in the Legal Academy, 62 *S.C. L. REV.* 105, 154 (2010); versus J.B.M. Vranken, Exciting Times for Legal Scholarship, 2, 2 *Recht en Methode in Onderzoek en Onderwijs* 42–62 (2012).

moreover, are drawn from separate intellectual traditions that have influenced each other at various times but then rebounded to continue along their individual trajectories. The pedagogic programs that these scholars provide have remained equally separate, and that separation, once again, is methodological. Their subject matter overlaps and their students often cross the ocean to extend their education, but the conception of a law school in Europe and America, and the basic approach to law that these institutions feature, remain strikingly distinct.[3]

Hans Kelsen, one of the most influential European legal theorists of the twentieth century, was welcomed by the University of California, Berkeley, when he fled from Nazi Germany. The university, aware of his stature and vaguely associating it with some form of science, named its newly built social science library in his honor. Kelsen, who possessed an active sense of irony, would point it out to friends who visited him at Berkeley: "Just look, an entire library named after me and not a single thing written by me is in it."

The purpose of this book is to bridge the methodological divide between European and American legal scholarship, to reach across the ocean that now truly merits its ironic nickname of the Pond. But the book does not aspire – and perhaps the proper word would be presume – to unify these separate scholarly and pedagogic methodologies. One reason for abjuring so grand, or grandiose, a project is that these two traditions are too well entrenched. A separate and possibly more compelling reason, however, is the converse; European and American scholarship have each become so varied and complex that any imaginable unity could only be achieved by resorting to inherited and counterproductive stereotypes. To put the matter bluntly, Americans often view European legal scholarship as old-fashioned and inward-looking due to its continued engagement with doctrine, whereas many Europeans see American scholarship as amateur social science that has lost contact with the realities of legal practice and judicial institutions. These are precisely the preconceptions that should be avoided in an enterprise of the sort that this book represents. We believe that American and European scholarship share a joint challenge. If legal scholarship becomes too much separated from practice, legal scholars will dig their own grave. If legal scholars, on the other hand, cannot explain to other disciplines what is academic about their research, which methodologies are typical for

[3] See for an overview of some of the differences: M. Reimann, The American Advantage in Global Lawyering, Dreizehnte Ernst-Rabel-Vorlesung 2012, 78 *RabelsZ* 2–36 (2014).

legal research, and what separates proper research from mediocre or poor research, we will probably end up in a similar situation.

Therefore, there is room and even a necessity for mutual learning and for interaction. This implies a generalization of US scholarship and European scholarship, as well as a generalization of the United States (a 200-year-old established democracy) and the European Union (EU) (a quasi-state, a laboratory of postnation-state building now for nearly sixty years). These generalizations, however, help us to identify overall trends on both sides of the Atlantic, trends which allow us to identify common denominators for discussion. Leading scholars from both Europe and the United States have been invited to think critically about the methodological premises and possibilities of their own tradition. They were asked to do so in light of the increasing intensity of transnational contacts between scholars due to the forces of globalization, and for the purpose of achieving mutual understanding regarding these premises and possibilities, but not to characterize the other methodology or to attempt a synthesis. The resulting collection of essays, therefore, represents a first step, a foundation on which we hope that both European and American scholars will be able to build a better understanding of each other's work and to develop collaborative research projects. Much more has to happen, though, in order to overcome American/European entrenchment. The contributions, originally written for a conference sponsored by the Global Governance Program of the European University Institute in Florence, Italy, are grouped around three themes: first, an institutionally grounded description of legal scholarship in Europe and the United States; second, a discussion of the role of doctrine in modern legal scholarship, from both the European and the American perspectives; and third, an account of the various interdisciplinary initiatives that are current in American legal scholarship and the way that they relate to pragmatic legal issues.

The contributors to this volume can speak for themselves, of course, and this Introduction will offer only very brief summaries of their essays as nothing more than a convenient guide for the reader. Before providing those summaries, however, the three of us, as editors of this volume, thought it might also be useful to the reader to locate the intensive and often detailed interaction that the contributions provide in the context of some of the general issues that have been raised by legal scholars who have previously addressed the methodological premises of legal scholarship, particularly as they differ in Europe and America. The three issues that unite the US/EU debate on the future of legal scholarship are: should legal scholarship aspire to the status of a science and gradually adopt more and more of the methods, (quality) standards, and practices of other (social) sciences?; should this scholarship play a pragmatic role in legal practice and legal institutions?; and finally, is legal scholarship undergoing a basic transition that will make it foreign, if not unrecognizable, to those trained in either the European or American traditions?

I.2 Should Legal Scholarship Be Regarded as a Science?

For a long time, European legal scholars have debated whether legal scholarship should be seen as a science, an art, a craft, or a form of applied theology. The inclination to treat it as a science was greatly enhanced in the early nineteenth century, when it turned out that science could not only explain how the Earth orbited and blood circulated, but could also produce steamboats and railroads. In 1847, Julius von Kirchmann, a German judge, delivered a famous speech to a society of legal scholars in which he accused his audience of doing nothing more than pointing out lacunae in case law and legislation, like the worms and insects that live off rotten wood. A few lines of new legislation would be enough to make entire legal libraries obsolete, he observed.[4] In the years following von Kirchmann's speech, many scholars who had been associated with the Historical School of German legal studies (with its founding father Fritz Karl von Savigny), such as Rudolf von Jhering, distanced themselves from the formalism that characterized this school and initiated the *Freirechtsschule*, or Free Law Movement. They argued that judges should be free to reach just and reasonable results, rather than being bound to the language of the Civil Code by chains of narrowly doctrinal reasoning. Under the influence of scholars such as Eugen Ehrlich and Herman Kantorowicz, the Free Law Movement morphed into the school of sociological jurisprudence (e.g. Roscoe Pound, Eugen Ehrlich, Max Weber), which claimed the mantle of science by attempting to develop decision rules from the systematic study of society.

Despite its willingness to draw on varied sources, the Free Law Movement was allied with the legal positivism that owed its origin to Jeremy Bentham and John Austin, two figures that reflected Britain's intermediate position between continental Europe and America. These positivist inclinations became dominant in Kelsen's jurisprudence, which explicitly

[4] J. von Kirchmann, *Die Wertlosigkeit der Jurisprudenz als Wissenschaft* (Berlin: Julius Springer Verlag, 1848), p. 29.

aspired to turn legal scholarship into a science. Kelsen was quite willing to view law as originating in social processes, but he insisted that the product of these processes, if it was to be considered law, must be a system of commands backed up by sanctions divorced from questions of morality. It might be important to ask whether the law was right or wrong, wise or foolish, but to regard those questions as elements of legal theory would be equivalent, in his view, to treating poems about the sweetness of flowers as botanical science, or accusing Albert Einstein of cultural relativism. Kelsen thus belonged to a long European tradition that associated a science of law with systematic thought based on clearly stated premises, and law's social origins as data for that approach to use, not as a challenge to its doctrinal integrity. That is perhaps the reason why the acquisitions staff of Berkeley's Kelsen Social Science Library could not find any of his works that corresponded to the American idea of social science. Kelsen wanted to underline the uniqueness of law as a discipline and therefore stressed the fundamental difference between *sein* and *sollen* or between normative and empirical questions as we would currently say.

The treatment of law as a science in the United States has been distinctly different. When C.C. Langdell, and his mentor, Charles Eliot, first established law as an intellectual discipline in American universities, they insisted that it was to be viewed as science, by which they meant natural science.[5] Like scientists, legal scholars must discern the underlying regularities that determine observed phenomena such as judicial decisions. The record of those decisions was the legal scholar's data and the law library was thus the equivalent of the chemist's laboratory.

As this view was becoming ensconced in American universities, a number of leading German legal scholars, including Kantorowicz and Kelsen, sought refuge in the United States. This produced one of the moments when the two traditions interacted only to rebound. Kantorowicz and other members of the Free Law Movement inspired the founders of American sociological jurisprudence, most notably Roscoe Pound, and the Legal Realists who followed, such as Karl Llewellyn, Jerome Frank, and Felix Cohen, to condemn Langdell and his followers as arid "formalists," whose idea that judges could apply the law "mechanically," without relying on judgment, was both an intellectual delusion and a threadbare apologia for the status quo. This sustained attack

[5] Edward Rubin, What's Wrong with Langdell's Method and What to Do About It, 60 *VAND. L. REV.* 609 (2007).

permanently, although perhaps unfairly,[6] destroyed the intellectual reputation of the so-called formalists and turned their attempt to characterize legal scholarship as science into an object of ridicule. The social basis of law that American scholars had learned from their contact with the European exiles was reinterpreted as politics rather than underlying cultural forces, and spawned the Legal Process movement.[7] Legal Process scholars, who were the dominant force in American legal academia for several decades after World War II, viewed law as a mechanism by which politically determined policies could be translated into governmental action. They also acknowledged the role of courts in enforcing constitutional constraints on the political process, but famously argued that this role being counter majoritarian, should be limited to situations where the political process had broken down due to racial prejudice, structural flaws or similarly delimited circumstances. Legal process scholars emphasized pragmatic judgment and institutional specificity, and did not contemplate any connection with natural science. Even when many American legal scholars turned to more technical, mathematical types of social science, such as economics and game theory, they shunned any claim that this constituted science.

One factor that may contribute to these divergent attitudes regarding the scientific nature of legal theory is the difference between a code law and a common law regime. If a legal system is based on comprehensive codes, the aspiration to draft those codes according to systematic and coherent principles will be strongly felt and sometimes associated with a "legal science" in which law is seen as a coherent system of written and unwritten rules. Common law, in contrast, is developed incrementally by judges, typically without central planning. For law to be a science in this context would mean that the common law displays underlying, comprehensive regularities that can be discerned by inductive reasoning from judicial decisions, which is exactly what Langdell and other formalists asserted. This is actually true at some level – judges are, after all, products

[6] See Brian Tamanaha, *Beyond the Formalist-Realist Divide: The Role of Politics in Judging* (Princeton, NJ: Princeton University Press, 2010).

[7] See Alexander M. Bickel, *The Least Dangerous Branch: The Supreme Court at the Bar of Politics* (Indianapolis, IN: Bobbs-Merrill, 1962); Charles Black, Jr., *The People and the Court: Judicial Review in a Democracy* (New York: Macmillan, 1960); Lon L. Fuller, *The Morality of Law* (New Haven, CT: Yale University Press, 1964); Lon L. Fuller, The Forms and Limits of Adjudication, 90 *Harv. L. Rev* 353 (1978) [written and circulated, but not published, in 1957]; Herbert Wechsler, Toward Neutral Principles of Constitutional Law, 73 *Harv. L. Rev.* 1 (1957).

of their culture – but implausible at the level of specificity that legal rules inhabit. Britain again serves as an intermediate case; it is a common law jurisdiction, but relies on centralized, law-making institutions typical of European nations, and has thus been less resistant than the United States to displace common law by legislation. Significantly, it was two British scholars, Pollack and Maitland, who exploded the myth that the common law ran back into the Anglo-Saxon past, and disclosed its forgotten origins in Angevin royal policy.[8] British scholars took their discovery to heart; American legal scholars, particularly in their role as legal educators, promptly forgot it again.

A second factor that separates Europe and America is a basic difference between the institutional contexts of legal scholarship. In both cases, legal scholars are primarily employed by universities, and teach as well as write. But European universities have existed for eight hundred years and law was regarded as an important element of their curricula from their inception.[9] Law-trained graduates played a crucial role in the process of state building and in the institutional consolidation of the Catholic Church. In contrast, there were virtually no law schools in the United States until after the Civil War. Lawyers were trained on the same apprenticeship model as shoemakers or blacksmiths, or through lectures provided by a practicing lawyer who, at most, rented space from a university in the same way that a university swimming pool might today be rented by a scuba diving school. Thus, when Langdell and Eliot decided to establish law as a degree program at Harvard – and indeed as an advanced degree for college graduates – they needed to demonstrate that legal studies possessed the intellectual content that would justify such a radical departure. The claim that law was a form of natural science served this purpose. It did so, however, in an instrumentalized and exaggerated way that could not be sustained or justified, and, for Americans, forever branded legal scholarship's claim to science as a chimera.

I.3 Should Legal Scholarship Serve Pragmatic Purposes?

Another ongoing issue is the extent to which legal scholarship should serve pragmatic purposes, that is, whether it should be addressed to

[8] Frederick Pollock and Frederic Maitland, *A History of English Law Before the Time of Edward I* (Cambridge: Cambridge University Press, 1968 [1895]).

[9] R.C van Caenegem, *Judges, Legislators and Professors: Chapters in European Legal History* (Cambridge: Cambridge University Press, 1992).

judges, legislators, and practicing lawyers. A scientific approach tends to see itself as studying these legal actors, rather than addressing them. But scientific investigation, even according to the strictest definition of the term, varies greatly in the extent of its pragmatic applications. It stands for itself and it is for the democratic powers to make use of legal science. Researching the origins of the universe and the topography of Pluto clearly count as science, but so does research on the tensile properties of steel or the effects of climate change. In other words, whether one adopts the view that legal scholarship should be scientific or not, the question of whether it should serve immediate, identifiable purposes will remain.

This issue has been intensely debated in the United States over the course of the past several decades.[10] One position, which recapitulates von Kirchmann's recommendation more than a century earlier, is that legal scholarship should move away from its close focus on what comes out of the courts or legislatures, an approach that Pierre Schlag has labeled as "case law journalism."[11] In the context of American scholarship, this move began by critiquing what it saw as the rotten wood of the then-dominant Legal Process School, combined with a political critique of the liberal consensus that this School was seen to both reflect and support. The Critical Legal Studies Movement, which drew heavily on European critical theory and deconstruction – in another momentary interaction between the two traditions – came from the political left. It argued that the common law's claim to be based upon neutral and enduring principles served as a means by which the governing elite could retain their power.[12] The Law and Economics movement was partially inspired by the Austrian School of Economics but was largely an American creation. It came from the political right, and argued that common law was efficient, and that regulatory statutes that displaced it were counter-productive efforts by overly intrusive interest groups and policy entrepreneurs. Despite this clear opposition of the two movements to each other, both agreed that the worms and insects of the Legal Process School misunderstood the essential nature of the legal system.

[10] See R. Feldman, *The Role of Science in Law* (Oxford: Oxford University Press, 2009).

[11] Pierre Schlag, Spam Jurisprudence, Air Law, and the Rank Anxiety of Nothing Happening (A Report on the State of the Art), 97 *Geo. L. J.* 803 (2009), p. 821ff.

[12] For a dialogue between leftist US and leftist German scholars, see Ch. Joerges, D. Trubek (ed.), *Critical Legal Thought: An American-German Debate* (Baden-Baden: Nomos, 1989).

These journeys into philosophy and microeconomics succeeded in detaching American legal scholarship from legal doctrine and in forging connections with the humanities and social sciences. For those who demanded a more theoretical approach, they represented a great advance, or perhaps a maturation, of the research that American law schools were producing. But many scholars and members of the legal profession generally remained committed to doctrinal scholarship. One of the best-known condemnations of the turn toward theory was an article by Judge Harry Edwards that declared: "While the schools are moving toward pure theory, the (law) firms are moving toward pure commerce, and the middle ground – ethical practice – has been deserted by both."[13]

Edwards' article signaled a growing bifurcation in American legal scholarship. The Critical Legal Studies Movement has faltered, perhaps because class consciousness in the academy, legal practice, and society at large is so much weaker in the United States than in Europe. But it has been succeeded by allied movements that possess more staying power in the American context, such as feminist and critical race theory. Law and economics has flourished, and while its claim to be the golden key that unlocks every legal issue is now widely disparaged, it has become the dominant methodology in many areas of business and commercial law. At the same time, other fields of social science, most notably political science, but also sociology and anthropology, have become important elements of America's academic landscape.

Doctrinal scholarship, despite Judge Edwards' lament, has displayed considerable continuity. In part, this is because it is so familiar to American academics, but also because this scholarship continues to find an audience among legal practitioners and judges. These institutional bases for doctrinal scholarship, moreover, find strong support from reflective scholars who feel that the essence of legal scholarship – its distinction from other disciplines – lies in its contact with the profession. Even one of the strongest defenders of multidisciplinarity in legal scholarship, Richard Posner, now argues that legal doctrine needs to remain dominant. In his book, *How Judges Think*, he insists that doctrinal research is vital for an understanding of American law, even in areas where common law has been replaced by statute.[14] Although he had

[13] H.T. Edwards, The Growing Disjunction Between Legal Education and the Legal Profession, 34 *Mich. L. Rev.* 34 (1992–1993).

[14] Richard Posner, *How Judges Think* (Cambridge, MA: Harvard University Press, 2008), p. 211.

previously called for the establishment of legal theory programs in US law schools to counterbalance the dominance of doctrinal scholarship, he is now arguing that doctrinal law should be emphasized as a counterweight to the dominance of legal theory.[15]

This challenge to interdisciplinary legal scholarship – the so-called "law and . . ." movement – is itself subject to challenge, however. Edwards and his allies have been charged with narrow-mindedness and a misplaced nostalgia for the value of doctrinal research.[16] Certainly, interdisciplinary scholarship in the US has continued to advance, particularly in first-tier law schools that provide extensive incentives and support for faculty research. It is quite possible that a majority of the new faculty being hired by these schools have, in addition to their law degree, an advanced degree in another field, most often in economics or political science, but also in philosophy, history, psychology, sociology, or anthropology. Empirical research, at a technical level that would qualify as valid scholarship in the non-legal discipline as well as in law, is becoming common in American law schools, and those who produce it garner increasing institutional support.

In Europe, the ups and downs of scholarship are less dynamic.[17] There is more continuity in the overall stable position of doctrinal legal scholarship. Just like in the United States, there was and is a challenge from leftist legal scholarship against dominant black letter law scholarship and there is a growing challenge from the rightist legal scholarship through

[15] Richard Posner, The State of Legal Scholarship Today: A Comment on Schlag, 97 *Geo. L.J.* 854–855 (2009).

[16] P.D. Reingold, Harry Edwards' Nostalgia, 91 *Mich. L. Rev.* 1998–2009 (1993); R.A. Posner, The Deprofessionalization of Legal Teaching and Scholarship, 91 *Mich. L. Rev.* 1921 (1993); J.M. Balkin and Sanford Levinson, Legal Historicism and Legal Academics: The Roles of Law Professors in the Wake of Bush v. Gore, 90 *Geo. L.J.* 173, 176–177 (2001). For Judge Edwards' surrebuttal, see H.T. Edwards, Another 'Postscript' to 'The Growing Disjunction Between Legal Education and the Legal Profession, 69 *Wash. L. Rev.* 561, 567 (1994). Later on the debate shifted to the use of empirical methods in assessing judicial decision making. See H.T. Edwards, Collegiality and Decision Making on the D.C. Circuit, 84 *Va. L. Rev.* 1335 (1998); v. R.L. Revez, Ideology, Collegiality, and the D.C. Circuit: A Reply to Chief Judge Harry T. Edwards, 85 *Va. L. Rev.* 805 (1999); K.M. Clermont and T. Eisenberg, Judge Harry Edwards: A case In Point, 80 *Wash. U. L.Q.* 1275 (2002), responding to Harry T. Edwards and L. Elliott, Beware of Numbers (and Unsupported Claims) of Judicial Bias, 80 *Wash. U. L.Q.* 723 (2002); H.T. Edwards and M.A. Livermore, Pitfalls of Empirical Studies that Attempt to Understand the Factors Affecting Appellate Decision-Making, 58 *Duke L.J.* 1895 (2009).

[17] For a helpful European reader: D. Kennedy, The Paradox of American Critical Legalism, 3 *Eur. L.J.* 359 (1997).

the law and economics movement which gradually gains ground in the Member States, particularly through the promotion of the OECD and the EU. The leftist legal scholarship in Europe fed on two sources: the revitalization of the early twentieth century critical legal thought and sociological jurisprudence.[18] The first shattered the conceptual foundations, the second the normative foundations through empirical research. Both leftist strands faltered gradually in line with the decline of social welfare thinking in Europe. So far the rightist movement has not gained a position which could be compared to the United States. This is particularly true for classical law and economics. This is different with regard to behavioral economics, which is strongly promoted through the EU and at least some Member States gradually introduce it into legal scholarship.[19] Overall, and this has to be underpinned, the pole position of legal doctrine over the last decades has remained largely untouched, despite two or three consecutive decades of irritation.

However, it seems as if the persistent dominance of doctrinal legal scholarship is increasingly coming under pressure nowadays. The reasons are manifold, but they have a lot to do with the changing role of the nation-state and the growing importance of the EU as a global actor – if there was ever something like a coherent system of law in the main fields of law (constitutional, criminal, private law). There appears to be a simultaneous trend away from doctrinal legal research and toward multidisciplinarity and theory building.[20] According to Jan Smits, doctrinal legal research is rapidly losing its status as the pinnacle of legal scholarship for a number of reasons. One is that the instrumentalization of law requires extralegal insights because doctrinal research alone cannot determine whether modern, purpose-driven laws will be effective and efficient. A second is the internationalization and digitization of law, which has led to a decline in the authority that is attached to national or state-made legal norms.[21] National constitutions, for example, today have to compete with in increasing amount of inter- and supranational human rights charters, and national highest courts start to look more for

[18] Ch. Joerges, D. Trubek (ed.), *Critical Legal Thought: An American-German Debate* (Baden-Baden: Nomos, 1989).

[19] A. Alemanno and A.-L. Sibony, *Nudging and the Law: A European Perspective* (Oxford: Hart Publishing, 2015).

[20] For an overview: B. van Klink and S. Taekema (eds.), *Law and Method: Interdisciplinary Research into Law* (Tübingen: Mohr Siebeck, 2011).

[21] J. Smits, Law and Interdisciplinarity: On the Inevitable Normativity of Legal Studies, 1 *Crit. An. of L.* 78 (2014).

decisions taken by other highest courts on the same or similar issues, simply because these decisions are more readily available.

As in the United States, however, this new approach has certainly not escaped criticism. Many European scholars agree with Judge Edwards' central argument that scholars should address their work to the legal community, specifically judges and practicing lawyers. This is even more important in Europe than in the United States, they argue, because of the EU's transformative effects on the legal systems of its member nations. While doctrine in basic legal areas such as contracts, torts, and property is relatively stable in the United States, thus requiring less attention and, incidentally, providing fewer opportunities for original research, entirely new bodies of doctrine have now become an essential part of the training and education of European lawyers. Miguel Maduro has argued that it is no longer possible to teach contract law, consumer law, or environmental law, to name just a few, without at least some basic knowledge about the nature and functions of EU law, its unique institutional framework, and its general principles and methods of interpretation developed by, among others, the General Court (EGC) and the European Court of Justice of the European Union (CJEU).[22] Because it cuts across traditional boundaries of private and public law, state-made law, and non-state law, EU legal doctrine is complex and challenging. Consequently, it demands scholarly attention and simultaneously creates opportunities for important intellectual contributions.

Ironically, this response to interdisciplinary and theoretical scholarship in Europe often looks to the United States for guidance, despite Judges Edwards' and Posner's jeremiads about the impracticality of current American scholarship. One obvious reason is the political and economic dominance of the United States during the second half of the twentieth century, the spread of mega American law firms to other continents, and the establishment of English as the new lingua franca. As this has occurred, American legal scholars have themselves devoted increased attention to the undeniable forces of globalization when looking at international trade, human rights law, commercial law (including lex mercatoria and Islamic financial law), global administrative law, and other areas. Moreover, as the EU evolves from an alliance to something that more resembles a loosely organized nation-state with a supranational outlook, the vast American

[22] M. Maduro, The Europeanization and Globalization of Law, *Contraditorio*, Policy Paper 10/1, February 2010, p. 5 (www.contraditorio.pt/admin/source/files/1276200432-PolicyPaper 10_01_LegalEducationandtheEuropeanizationandGlobalisationofLaw-Original.pdf).

literature on federalism and governance becomes relevant to Europe, particularly given this literature's recent trend away from constitutional law questions that are unique to American law and toward empirical and pragmatic analysis of actual federal–state relations, or "cooperative federalism," and "governmental experimentalism."[23] In his 2012 Ernst Rabel lecture, Mathias Reimann offers a more conceptual reason for national European doctrinalists to look toward American law, in particular those coming from continental Europe.[24] According to Reimann, American-trained jurists enjoy an advantage in global lawyering because their conception of law is "inherently more pluralistic, pragmatic, and political" and thus "fits the contemporary global legal order better than the continental European (and, more broadly, the civil law) understanding."[25] But he does not discuss the way in which the EU and European law – and just as genuinely European legal scholarship – is about to change the scenario. This type of European legal scholarship can in no way be equated to "the continental European understanding." It is a type of scholarship which uses the opportunities of a non-state bound legal order to engage in the type of discourse Miguel Maduro has in mind.

In short, both American and European scholars have been engaged in an intense debate, in the context of their own traditions, about the extent to which legal scholarship should serve pragmatic purposes. Despite many points of contact, the two debates have remained separate, in part because the idea of a pragmatic purpose differs in these two traditions. For Americans, pragmatic legal scholarship should serve the legal community; it should provide resources that judges, lawyers, and perhaps legislators and policy analysts can use to improve the quality of their decision making. For Europeans, pragmatism (also) involves leadership; it implies that legal scholars should generate ideas for political officials so that they can act in more thoughtful and visionary ways. In other words, legal pragmatism in the United States tends to mean the clarification and organization of legal doctrine; in Europe, it also implies the creation of legal doctrine.

Here again, both historical and institutional factors seem to account for the difference. In a common law regime, legal rules emerge gradually from incremental decisions by judges. There is no identifiable planning

[23] J. Zeitlin (ed.), *Extending Experimentalist Governance, The European Union and Transnational Regulation* (Oxford: Oxford University Press, 2015).

[24] M. Reimann, The American Advantage in Global Lawyering, Dreizehnte Ernst-Rabel-Vorlesung 2012, 78 *RabelsZ* 2–36 (2014).

[25] Ibid., p. 3.

process, and strict rules of evidence prohibit the judge from seeking advice from legal scholars outside the courtroom, or from asking their advice about domestic law under any circumstances. In a code law regime, legal doctrine is created in a planning process by professional drafters who are not bound by judicial rules of evidence and are expected to obtain advice and guidance from those with specialized knowledge. To be sure, this distinction between common law and code regimes has been largely effaced by the growth of the administrative state,[26] and the consequent turn toward positive, regulatory law, but the conceptual patterns that prior history established have remained. It is notable how infrequently Congress or the woefully understaffed American state legislatures make use of academic experts when drafting statutes. When the Contract with America Congress of the 1990s was looking for a sacrificial lamb to prove that it was willing to cut its own budget along with the budgets of federal agencies, it lighted upon the diminutive Office of Technology Assessment, a small, non-partisan group of experts who provided desperately needed technical advice to Congress' drafting committees.

Institutionally, European law schools, as stated above, are considerably older than modernity and played an important role in the creation of the modern state. Moreover, intellectuals and intellectual pursuits are generally well regarded, perhaps as a result of the role that the Catholic and later Protestant Churches played in the development of society. There is thus a long history of consulting legal experts on important legal matters, including the basic design of statutes and legal institutions. Again, and in line with the pressure on doctrinal legal scholarship, lawyers lose ground in politics and are gradually replaced by political scientists and economists. American law schools are recent creations, arriving well after federal and state governments had established their modes of operation. There is moreover, a strong undercurrent of anti-intellectualism in the United States, perhaps resulting from the ethos of the frontier (it is almost always helpful to invoke the Turner thesis to explain American exceptionalism). It would be a disadvantage for someone seeking to be Chancellor of Germany or Prime Minister of the Netherlands to lack knowledge of English, but Republican candidates for the Presidency, such

[26] There is ample discussion on the changing role and function of the nation-state in the US and the EU; however, there is no common language. Scholars might agree that the executive powers of nation-states have been considerably grown over the last century. This transformation is equated with "administrative state."

as, McCain and Romney, both tried to conceal the fact that they are fluent in French. Reimann's observation that American pragmatism serves as a basis for European legal theory is thus revealing as well as ironic.

I.4 Where Is Legal Scholarship Headed?

The third general issue raised by the contributions in this volume is whether either European or American legal scholarship can be adequately characterized at the present time, or whether both are undergoing such a significant transition that any definitive judgments must be treated with skepticism. Here the problem is not so much a matter of methodological differences as it is of the uncertainties than impede efforts to efface the differences generated by other issues, such as the scientific basis or pragmatic value of legal scholarship. However complicated it will be to establish and maintain communication between two different intellectual traditions, it will be more difficult still if neither one is quite sure where it is headed.

It would be impossible to give an accurate overview of all the transitions that are currently occurring in European and American legal scholarship at the present, given that many of the developments are fragmented, diffuse and more articulate in some areas than in others. Nevertheless, there are common threads that run through many of the contributions to this volume, including:

1) a shift from monodisciplinarity to multidisciplinarity and interdisciplinarity;
2) a move from a national focus on law and legal research toward a more transnational and global perspective;
3) a trend toward greater methodological awareness and accountability, together with the development of more explicit quality criteria and evaluation methods that demonstrate the value of legal scholarship to scholars in other disciplines and to the world in general; and
4) a preparedness to self-assurance (*Selbstvergewisserung*) of the foundations of law in the humanities and in the connection of law to legal philosophy.

Taken together, these trends point to the possibility, if not the likelihood, that legal scholarship is developing into something that is basically different from what it was before, that journal articles – the basic unit of academic production – will speak in a different scholarly discourse and be judged by different scholarly standards. But it is difficult to say what that discourse and those standards will be, whether either will emerge from the transition with their prior unity and whether that unity will continue to be distinct in Europe and America, or whether it will be transatlantic in character. Book-length monographs have always been more methodologically diverse, perhaps because they call for more reflection and are free from the constraints of either student editing (in the United States) or revise and resubmit peer review (in Europe). But they too, to the extent that they are seen by their authors as using legal methodology, can be expected to change, and their role relative to the journal article may change as well.

Comparative law provides a useful lens for considering these trends because it explicitly concerns itself with the differences in legal culture. One issue that comparativists have addressed is the translation problem, the difficulty of importing legal rules from one jurisdiction to another. While this sounds exceptional, and was certainly the bête noir of the German historical school, it is remarkably common in the real world. The whole European integration process over the last sixty years is built on the assumption that rules can be implanted into Member States' legal systems. By questioning the inherent value of legal rules, at least in their transferred form, the issue necessarily transcends traditional doctrinal approaches. At the same time it raises fundamental questions about the standards by which the quality and value of law is to be judged. The translation problem thus presents, in immediate and pragmatic form, questions that are often regarded as more abstract and remote from legal pragmatism in other areas. Using microeconomics for analyzing legal rules poses a translation problem of sorts, but it is of less immediate and practical concern than the question of whether German, Dutch, or American contract law will be effective for Japanese business people.

There has been a tendency for comparativists to condemn other legal scholars for being ignorant about the complexities of comparing legal systems, but they also need to reflect on their own role. Authoritative handbooks on comparative law may highlight the difficulties of "deep level comparative law," but often fail to explain when deep level consideration is necessary and, more importantly, how to do it. It is easy to say that researchers must not ignore the historical, political, and socioeconomic context in which legal solutions from other jurisdictions have taken shape, but how does one take all these particularities into account? And most people will immediately agree that it is important to avoid ethnocentricity and other biases while formulating research questions but how does one actually extract oneself from one's own mode of thought?

According to Gadamer,[27] the enterprise, like immortality, is both impossible and undesirable.

To generalize this point, it seems that the effort to determine where legal scholarship is headed by ascending to some empyrean level, above the clouds or the Cloud, is unlikely to succeed. The proposal implicit in the design of this book, and carried out by its contributors, is to achieve greater self-awareness of the methodology that informs current legal scholarship. Josef Esser termed it already in the 1970s as *Vorverständnis* (preconception), claiming that lawyers must undertake any effort to disclose the intellectual base, the implicit assumptions and values they start from. In other words, the approach is essentially procedural, something that not only sounds lawyerly, but also comports with much of contemporary epistemology. For comparative law, this would mean a greater attention to the meaning of comparison itself, an inquiry into the most useful ways to describe similarities, differences, and interactions between legal systems. As far as the integration between law and the social sciences is concerned, Epstein and King have shown that legal scholars often neglect the rules of inference while translating empirical findings into legal analysis and normative recommendations.[28]

The uncertainty about the direction of European and American legal scholarship, the sense that this is an era of transition rather than one where a generally accepted approach to scholarship prevails, demands that each scholar, or perhaps each affiliated group of scholars, do the work that would otherwise be done by the accepted approach. They need to identify the method they are using and the assumptions they are making as well as the conclusions they are reaching. In this sense, European and American legal scholarship are subject to a similar demand. Moreover, the response to this demand for methodological awareness should facilitate communication between the two, since it will disclose previously unstated differences. But the demand, being procedural, is no indication by itself that European and American scholarship will move in the same direction or toward the same goal.

The demand for methodological clarity has institutional as well as intellectual implications. To begin with, interdisciplinary scholarship places stress on law school research budgets. Smits observes that European law schools, which previously received earmarked budgets

[27] Hans-Georg Gadamer, *Truth and Method 235–74*. Garrett Barden and John Cumming, trans. (New York: Crossroad, 1988)

[28] L. Epstein and G. King, The Rules of Inference, 69 *U. of Chi. L.R.* 1 (2002).

for research, are now often required to compete with other disciplines on the basis of common performance indicators, such as the number of publications in peer-reviewed journals and the number of PhD theses produced.[29] American law schools have been spared this challenge thus far, but the countervailing factor is that their earmarked research funds typically do not provide for the increased costs of empirical data gathering. Second, a stronger emphasis on multidisciplinarity and interdisciplinarity in both Europe and America will lead legal research to be of greater interest to other disciplines, but also to being evaluated by those other disciplines. The political scientist whose eyes and mind glaze over when confronted with a doctrinal analysis of the procedure for challenging an administrative rule in court will be much more interested, but also much more capable of criticizing, an empirical study of the rule's effect upon its targets.

Such scrutiny from other university departments is likely to reveal that law schools are deficient in the evaluation and management of the scholarship that they produce. There is no international ranking of law journals or legal publishers, no generally accepted system of peer review, no international bibliometric databases that cover a large variety of law journals or books from different countries. It seems unlikely that law schools can continue to be so cavalier about the quality of their research without losing prestige and credibility. This does not mean that law should just copy and paste the research evaluation methods and procedures from other sciences, but it does imply that there will be increasing problems if legal scholars can say no more about the way they determine high quality legal research than to quote Justice Stewart Potter's test for pornography: "I know it when I see it." The more law becomes multidisciplinary and international the greater the need will be for more harmonized systems of quality management.

A second institutional implication of methodological awareness involves legal education. Law students on both sides of the Atlantic usually do not receive much training in research methods. As long as the law school curriculum was focused on training students to solve cases on the basis of existing case law and legislation, methodology courses were confined to finding relevant sources and writing briefs or office memos. The techniques of legal research were regarded as applications and extensions of these practice-oriented skills. An adventuresome

[29] Smits, Law and Interdisciplinarity, pp. 78–79.

student who wanted to learn more systematic approaches to research would need to trundle off to another department, and often end up being hassled by the registrar about getting credit for the course. However, as soon as the educational program begins to reflect scholarly research and consider law in its societal context, the story changes. It will no longer be possible to rely on an unstated and unreflective methodology derived from practice, or to refer law students to other faculties to receive the necessary methodological skills and research techniques, especially when students have received (almost) no prior training in how to set up and carry out different sorts of research.

A third one reaches even further. The globalization process has highlighted the boundaries of the amount of knowledge that a lawyer can master. In the past, legal education was primarily based on studying the national law, which means the law of the nation-state, whatever it looks like. In Europe, the rise of European law has introduced a new layer of knowledge which had to be integrated in the curricula. Globalization and technology, however, have dramatically increased the availability of knowledge over other legal systems, on transnational law-making, on all the huge quantity of rules produced by international organizations, international, semi-public, and semi-private bodies, often with an unclear legal status. So far, at least in Europe, legal education is still very much based on studying and learning the national legal system. There are some exceptions, mainly in Maastricht and Tilburg, but the dominant picture looks different. Taking globalization and the methodological challenges seriously, legal education at least in terms of global lawyering must shy away from knowledge transfer and should put emphasis on combining methodological training with legal theory and legal philosophy. It might very well be that legal education will split in the near future – into, for example, national education focusing on knowledge transfer and doctrinal legal scholarship, and global education focusing more on theoretical grounding and methodology.

I.5 Outline of the Book

The contributions to this book are spread over three major parts. The first part concerns the question of where legal scholarship is headed in the new legal world. The second part deals with the question of whether doctrinal legal scholarship deserves to be abandoned or needs to be revitalized, and the third part shows the intricacies of law and research.

I.5.1 Part I: Where Is Legal Scholarship Headed in the New Legal World?

Prediction is very difficult especially about the future, according to the well-known quote from Nobel Prize–winning physicist Niels Bohr. The authors in the first part of this book, nevertheless, do their best to look ahead in order to see in which direction legal scholarship is moving on both sides of the Atlantic. Is there a growing gap between the still-dominant European doctrinal tradition and the increasingly social science–oriented American legal scholarship, or are both strands of research bound to move closer toward each other looking for middle ground?

Legal research is currently viewed in three distinctly different ways: as part of humanities, as part of social sciences, and as akin to the analysis of law in legal practice. In Chapter 1, Mathias Siems and Daithí Mac Síthigh present the findings of a survey on the research methods in five law schools: two in Germany and one each in Ireland, England, and Scotland, as identified by scholars at those schools and analyzed using tools of both classical and compositional statistics. They asked the legal scholars to indicate to what extent they identify with legal research as part of humanities, as part of social sciences, and as akin to the analysis of law in legal practice. The main finding is that scholars of the German law schools have a relatively strong preference for practical legal research and scholars of the UK and Irish law schools seem to have a preference for law as humanities. Moreover, international legal scholars tend to be closer to the social sciences and younger scholars and private lawyers tend to be closer to practical legal research. Interestingly, there appear to be some signs of convergence since, across the five law schools, scholars tend to use practical legal research methods less often, and social sciences methods more often, than ten years ago.

In Chapter 2, Neil Walker examines how the development of an increasingly global outlook in law's normative ordering, as well as in its professional organization, underlines the significance of both humanist and social scientific methods and perspectives in legal education. The new global outlook also causes us to loosen or revise some of the distinctions – both of deep method and practical orientation – upon which our categorization of the variation of the juristic enterprise in a traditionally state-centered legal world is based. At the same time, Walker believes that the global jurist may remain no easier a category to pin down than that of the local jurist, no less controversial to specify, no less challenging a role in any such specification, and no less complex a curricular puzzle. With the emergence of the new global role some of the starker divisions and tensions inherent in the juristic approach, such as the traditional division between an internal (participants) perspective on law and legal research versus an external (observers) perspective, no longer seem to hold.

According to Roger Brownsword in Chapter 3, the new legal world that is developing right under our noses is not simply one that invites a more explicit engagement with methodology (because the horizons of legal inquiry are changing) but one that signifies a fundamental disturbance at the level of field, focus, and framing. It is not simply that the context or scope of inquiry is changing but that the ground is shifting under our feet. Not only is the Westphalian paradigm in which the nation-state is the most important source of law being replaced by an increasingly transnational or global paradigm inviting a deluge of thoughts concerning legal pluralism, but there is also another destabilization taking place due to the shift from law to regulation and, with that, to a more technological approach to managing human conduct. This contribution then explores the agenda for legal scholarship that this shift implies. Items on that agenda include the way we conceive of the regulatory environment, how Rule of Law values are to be applied where technologies are used as regulatory tools, the significance for liberal values of states using technological management as a means of social control and channeling, and what we now understand about the effectiveness of law.

Although globalization is increasingly affecting legal scholarship, it is interesting to see how big the differences between national publication cultures still are. In Chapter 4, Reza Dibadj presents a comparative empirical analysis of scholarly articles published in law journals, across three different jurisdictions – the United States, England, and France – between 2010 and 2014. Each article is coded along three dimensions: (i) author characteristics, (ii) analytical methods being deployed, and (iii) subject matter. Among the results generated by analysis of the data are that theoretical analysis is the most prevalent analytic method in the United States, and also in England, although not by as wide a margin. Doctrinal analysis ranks second while narrative and empirical approaches, although third, are fairly well represented. In France, however, doctrinal analysis predominates, with theoretical analysis second and narrative or empirical analysis a very distant third. In terms of subject matter, Constitutional Law is by far the leading subject in American law reviews, while the distribution of subjects in English journals is generally balanced, with no one predominating. Dibadj's study suggests that over 70 percent of articles in the top American journals are published by core faculty at elite US law schools, whereas in the United Kingdom and France there is a greater number of (foreign) authors from "non-elite" law schools suggesting perhaps that publications in those jurisdictions are more "democratic."

I.5.2 Part II: Should Doctrinal Legal Scholarship Be Abandoned?

Doctrinal legal scholarship nowadays has a rather negative image and is heavily associated with old-fashioned black letter law focused on the nation-state. As globalization continues and both practitioners and scholars require a "law in context" approach, it becomes clear that something needs to change. However, it is hard to imagine how legal scholarship could ever do without a normative orientation. Therefore it seems more likely that the future of legal doctrine lies more in making implicit methodological conventions more explicit and showing the added (theoretical) value toward other disciplines. This might also imply that a little less emphasis should be placed on coherence and perhaps a bit more on effects and values.

Jan Smits (Chapter 5) seeks to obtain a better understanding of the aims and methods of doctrinal legal scholarship. He argues that legal doctrine serves the three main goals of description, prescription, and justification, and makes clear that many methodological choices have to be made in order to pursue these goals. The first important finding is that legal doctrine reflects the normative complexity of the law: it offers detailed and sophisticated information about how to deal with conflicting arguments. Stripping the law from this practical knowledge by reducing it to general principles or policies, or by trading it in for economic or empirical analysis, is not helpful. In addition, the doctrinal approach is in many ways the necessary prerequisite for undertaking any other type of analysis of law (such as economic, comparative, empirical, or behavioral work). The second finding is that, despite the importance of legal-doctrinal work, its bad reputation is not entirely undeserved. According to Smits, doctrinalists pay too little attention to the choices they make when creating or developing a legal system. Doctrinal research can be highly original, but too often it is not. This calls for a change in attitude. It seems inevitable that legal doctrine must search for new foundations if it wants to compete with newer types of research in law.

Nils Jansen (Chapter 6) argues that European scholars should contribute to the making of a common doctrinal language (doctrine) for European law. Since the 1980s, an increasing number of scholars engaged in many projects aimed at developing such a legal language and thus participated in the making of a common European legal doctrine. Many of those projects, however, focused more on rule making than on its conceptual and doctrinal basis. Methodological reflection is rare in such projects. By studying the methodology of a case study on the law of assignment, Jansen shows that doctrinal legal research methods should be treated as a reflective, rather than a prescriptive, endeavor. There is no "ideal" method to be applied universally. Whether a particular methodological approach is convincing depends on the actual research question on the one hand, and on the shared knowledge and beliefs of a scientific community on the other. The purpose of methodological explanation can hence only be to elucidate a particular piece of scholarly work and thus enable others to assess its results.

In the 13th Ernst Rabel lecture (2012) M. Reimann stressed the "American Advantage in Global Lawyering." His argument is that continental legal systems in Europe remain bound to a classical understanding evinced through national uniformity, systematic structure, clear demarcations, authoritative rules, autonomous law, and law as decision making rules. Whether or not there is an American advantage in global lawyering should include, according to Hans-W. Micklitz in Chapter 7, a close analysis of the EU, EU law, and EU legal scholarship. Micklitz goes so far as to state that due to its openness and its incomplete – perhaps never to be completed – federal structure, the EU, EU law, and EU legal scholarship could serve as a counterpart to the American advantage, apt to trigger a mutual learning process as to the advantages and disadvantages of a distinct American and European style. This is what Micklitz calls the "European advantage." Its potential lies in the disclosure of its reality, but this requires a different view on Europe, one which changes perspective. Such a perspective would focus on the achievements of this unique construct called the EU which is not a state, which more than likely will never be a state or a federation of states in the Westphalian sense, but which is at the same time much more than an international organization. It is this success story (Barry Eichengreen) which has to be retold through the lenses of law and legal scholarship.

In the premodern era, law was primarily enforced, and often formulated, by judicial bodies (Chapter 8). Because it was regarded as an application of human reason to pragmatic issues of governance and commerce (the working principle that courts employed), great attention was paid to its conceptual and doctrinal coherence. Legislation was either assimilated to this basically judicial model or regarded as an act of will, and thus disfavored. Modernity's shift to administrative governance means that the legislature now takes the leading role in formulating law, and bureaucratic agencies take the leading role in enforcing it. Consequently, the standard of excellence for law has shifted from doctrinal coherence to instrumental effectiveness. If legal scholarship is to be accurate and useful, it must shift its focus to this new standard of excellence, and stop analyzing law in terms of a doctrinal coherence that is no longer either predominant or necessary in our legal system.

Finally, Rob van Gestel (Chapter 9) argues that, while doctrinal coherence might no longer be necessary in the modern legal world, more coherence and consistency is welcome in how we assess the quality of traditional (doctrinal) legal scholarship, especially if we want to stimulate transnational scholarly communication. Van Gestel suggests that law as a discipline has the advantage of lagging behind other social sciences when it comes to research assessment and quality management. From these other sciences we can learn that ranking, bibliometrics and even peer review have serious disadvantages when it comes to grasping what "quality" of (legal) scholarship entails. Therefore, van Gestel develops three alternative approaches: 1) shifting the emphasis from publication output control to the input side of training and socialization of research talent; 2) reducing publication pressure and increasing the attention for methodological accountability; and 3) more attention for theory building in doctrinal legal research. Building consensus with regard to what quality of legal scholarship entails and how we can recognize should not be seen as an administrative burden that we need to get rid of as soon as possible but as an important challenge that requires continuous debate.

I.5.3 Part III: The Interaction of Legal Scholarship with Other Disciplines

The value of incorporating other academic disciplines into legal scholarship is generally accepted. Few people would want to argue that the subject area departments into which European and American universities are divided represent some natural ordering of knowledge. The contested questions involve the choice of disciplines that should be regarded as most useful in understanding or improving the legal system and the particular ways in which the chosen disciplines are to be deployed. The answers to these questions will depend on matters that have been discussed in the first two sections of this volume: the extent to which law is seen as a body of doctrine or as an instrumentality for policy, and the conceptual and institutional structure through which the scholarly enterprise is carried out.

Neil Komesar (Chapter 10) argues that interdisciplinary scholarship is essential because the first question to be asked in any legal analysis is not what the proper rule should be but rather which institution should determine the applicable rule. Komesar identifies three basic alternatives that are available in our society – the judicial system, the political system, and the market. One possible conclusion to be drawn from this observation is that the choice among these alternatives determines the methodology that should be used; for example, choosing the judicial system implies the use of doctrinal analysis, choosing the political system implies the use of political science and policy analysis, while choosing the market implies that economic analysis should be employed. But the more basic conclusion is that institutional analysis, often considered a branch of sociology but more properly regarded as a discipline of its own, is the most basic approach. This approach should govern the way we design institutions and the way that courts decide whether to decide the merits of a particular case themselves, or whether they should defer that decision to another institution. Thus, for a court, institutional analysis should be the first consideration and should determine whether doctrinal analysis should be employed at all. Both courts and society should learn the language of institutional analysis. Komesar's contribution summarizes the basic contours of this mode of analysis: levels and scope of participation, including the role of interest groups, decisional resources, and transaction costs.

Deborah Hensler and Matthew Gasperetti (Chapter 11) discuss the broad area of empirical social science, including at least anthropology, economics, history, political science, psychology, and sociology, that has played an increasingly important role in legal scholarship. They show in their contribution that empirical legal scholarship is neither new nor peculiarly American: as long as societies have existed, they have created "law," and as long as positive social science has existed, law has been one of the topics of empirical inquiry. Over more than a century, the scope of empirical legal research in the United States has broadened to touch virtually every aspect of legal institutions and behavior and this approach is becoming more common elsewhere as well. Even though empirical findings are often ignored or discounted in high-stakes political debates, they argue, the demand for "data" to inform these debates are increasingly common. It is not unthinkable that in the future leaders of the bench and bar will call for "evidence-based" recommendations on proposed legal reforms as a matter of course. The popularity of empirical scholarship among law faculty may fade over time as other perspectives become more popular, but because of the law's centrality to society, the empirical study of legal behavior will inevitably continue.

Orly Lobel (Chapter 12) focuses on one area of interdisciplinary scholarship, but it is the area that has arguably been the single most influential one in recent decades: the use of microeconomics to model human behavior and legal rules. At first, this meant the use of a rational actor theory of human behavior, a somewhat antiquated understanding of economics that reveals some of the pitfalls of interdisciplinary scholarship. The problem with this approach, according to Lobel, is that human nature is too complex to reduce to the traditional rational actor. Microeconomic theory has long recognized this problem and has become interdisciplinary through the integration of behavioral and psychological studies into its model of human behavior. Behavioral studies show that humans are messy and often act in detriment to their stated goals. They suffer from biases that cloud their judgment and decision making, they have limited self-control, and they overestimate their own morality. The recognition of these non-rational modes of thought in interdisciplinary legal scholarship that relies on microeconomics can help both legal scholars and lawmakers develop a more modulated and fully informed methodology. At the same time, relying on this interdisciplinary approach to economics in interdisciplinary legal analysis may create pitfalls of its own. It may detract from the expressive character of law, induce over-confidence in findings from decontextualized laboratory experiments, encourage adoption solutions that are convenient to implement, and foster the belief that desirable social results can be achieved without regulatory intervention.

Paul Kahn (Chapter 13) argues that with respect to interpretation of the law, the embrace of social science, including microeconomics, reflects a misunderstanding of the interpretive process. Rather than treating this process as capable of being reduced to rules and carried out by a specified methodology, Kahn suggests, interpretation should be treated as a branch of the humanities. Between any legal rule and its application, there must be a decision. The rule must be interpreted under the circumstances of the particular case. Much of the law is a process of persuading and being persuaded with respect to the correct interpretation of a rule. This is a task for a humanist. The humanities can have no method because interpretation is a free, creative act. Creation cannot be subject to rules, and without rules there can be no method. The humanist scholar has no view on whether the law is trying to make us better or whether it is succeeding in such an effort. Kahn has no view on whether the law is or should be logically coherent; he has no concern with the outcome of any particular case. Rather, he focuses on what is the shape of the world of meaning within which legal claims are persuasive to particular communities.

PART I

Where Is Legal Scholarship Headed in the New Legal World?

1

Why Do We Do What We Do?

Comparing Legal Methods in Five Law Schools Through Survey Evidence

MATHIAS M. SIEMS AND DAITHÍ MAC SÍTHIGH

1.1 Introduction

Assume the following scenario: a law professor visits her university cafeteria and wants to sit at a table where she can get some useful comments on the method she plans to use in one of her papers. There are three tables: at the first table sit a historian, a philosopher and a theologian; at the second one an economist, a sociologist and a psychologist; and at the third one a judge, a solicitor and a public prosecutor. Assuming all else being equal (approachability, looks, gender, etc.), which table is our law professor likely to join?

This 'cafeteria test' aims to illustrate the multiple identities of legal research as part of humanities, as part of social sciences and as akin to the analysis of law in legal practice.[1] This chapter builds upon our previous work,[2] where we used this 'trichotomy' as a conceptual tool to explain the development of law schools and legal scholarship in the United Kingdom and suggested ways in which these concepts could be tested. By contrast, the current study has an empirical and comparative focus: here, we present the findings of a survey on the research methods identified by academic staff in five law schools, across Germany, Ireland and the United Kingdom (England and Scotland). The data was collected in autumn 2013 for the purpose of this chapter. In the survey we also collected contextual information (e.g., training, career stage). Thus, it is our aim to explore both the relevance of the jurisdiction and law school in which the scholar works and more general factors that may determine

[1] For a detailed explanation of these categories see Section 1.3.3.

[2] Mathias Siems and Daithí Mac Síthigh, 'Mapping Legal Research', 71 *Cambridge Law Journal* 651 (2012).

preference for one or the other research methods. We also address recent trends, such as the impact of interdisciplinary thinking and the possible 'globalization' of legal research.[3]

The collected survey data will be evaluated in a quantitative way. In addition, as we asked respondents to provide comments in free text, these more qualitative responses will also be considered in some detail, in particular in order to understand the role of determinants such as training (or lack of training). Throughout this chapter, we will also contextualize our findings with other primary and secondary materials. Thus, overall, our approach may be described as one of 'triangulation', namely, that we use multiple sources and methods in order to get a fuller picture of the legal scholar's preferences for or against particular methods.

The corresponding structure of this chapter is as follows: Section 2 explains the method and conceptual framework of this chapter, i.e., our survey method, the law schools studied, and the three categories of legal research. Section 3 presents the main results for the five law schools by way of ternary plots. It also interprets these results based on institutional and country differences. Section 4 explores possible further determinants of research preferences. Here we analyse factors such as gender, age, education and subject matter of research. We also identify dominant and changing paradigms in the five law schools. Section 5 addresses the implications of our findings and Section 6 concludes.

1.2 Method and Conceptual Framework

This chapter is based on a survey of academic staff at two German law schools (Heinrich-Heine University Düsseldorf and Bucerius Law School, Hamburg), two UK ones (University of East Anglia [UEA], Norwich, and University of Edinburgh) and one Irish one (Trinity College, University of Dublin[4]). The main survey question asked staff members to identify the frequency with which they use different methods

[3] See, e.g., Rob Van Gestel, Hans-Wolfgang Micklitz and Miguel Poiares Maduro, 'Methodology in the New Legal World', EUI Working Papers LAW No. 2012/13, available at http://ssrn.com/abstract=2069872.

[4] Trinity College is the single College of the University of Dublin, founded in 1592 by Charter as the 'mother of a university' (*mater universitatis*) with the relationship between the University and College the subject of subsequent debate and litigation. See further David Allardice Webb and Robert Brendan McDowell, *Trinity College Dublin: An Academic History* (Trinity College Dublin Press, 2004), 4.

of legal research. It is the aim of this section to explain our survey approach as well as its underlying conceptual framework.

1.2.1 Units of Comparison and Respondents

Our choice of universities and the corresponding countries has been based on substantive but also personal reasons. Analysing three European countries reflects the current debate about research methods in Europe.[5] It also has the advantage of a 'controlled comparison' as far as it can be assumed that European legal cultures are relatively similar, as compared to non-European countries. This may be an obvious statement if one considers differences between European traditions and African or Asian indigenous and religious legal cultures, but there is also the view that there are stark differences between legal research methods in Europe and the United States. For instance, it can be argued that in the continental European civil law countries as well as the islands of the common law (England and Wales, Ireland, Malta and Cyprus) and the mixed legal system of Scotland, a black letter approach to legal research is often still the dominant one. This is said to contrast with the US elite law schools where the interdisciplinary approach has won the day, in particular the economic analysis of law and other research associated with the social sciences.[6] In this chapter we contribute to this debate through providing empirical evidence for or against any similarity of research methods in four European jurisdictions.

In these jurisdictions we examined five law schools. This approach may be contrasted with one that would conduct a more general survey of all legal scholars. The justification for our method is that we aim for a relatively detailed understanding of particular law schools. Thus, this is

5 See, e.g., Martijn Hesselink, 'A European Legal Method? On European Private Law and Scientific Method', 15 *European Law Journal* 20 (2009); Rob van Gestel and Jan Vranken, 'Assessing Legal Research: Sense and Nonsense of Peer Review versus Bibliometrics and the Need for a European Approach', 12 *German Law Journal* 901 (2011); Rob van Gestel and Hans-Wolfgang Micklitz, 'Why Methods Matter in European Legal Scholarship', 20 *European Law Journal* 292 (2014).

6 See, e.g., Martijn W. Hesselink, *The New European Legal Culture* (Deventer: Kluwer, 2001); Karl Riesenhuber, 'English Common Law versus German *Systemdenken*? Internal versus External Approaches', 7 *Utrecht Law Review* 117 (2011); Kristoffel R. Grechenig and Martin Gelter, 'The Transatlantic Divergence in Legal Thought: American Law and Economics vs. German Doctrinalism', 31 *Hastings International and Comparative Law Review* 295 (2008). But see also Carroll Seron, Susan Bibler Coutin and Pauline White Meeusen, 'Is There a Canon of Law and Society?', 9 *Annual Review of Law and Social Science* 287, 298 (2013) (noting the difference between internal and external perceptions of US legal scholarship).

akin to 'cluster sampling' in statistics.[7] It is also related to ethnographic fieldwork as anthropologists may often study the population of specific locations in detail in order to understand the more general culture of a particular geographic area.

In the present case, we have not only collected quantitative data, but have also asked legal scholars to self-assess their research and invite them to tell us more about the reasons and influences, as well as changes over time.[8] This approach allows us to capture and explore different aspects of the academic career path and to use this evidence as the basis for highlighting the diversity of experiences and the degree of autonomy of individual scholars.

We chose these five law schools as they are research-focused, but not identical; for instance, in terms of age, size of the student body and esteem indicators.[9] In addition, because of the relevance of context, we choose institutions that are known to us (at least one of us has worked or studied in each of the five law schools). This also meant that we could get a relatively high response rate. Furthermore, our approach fits within an established practice of 'insider' research on academic life[10]

The respondents of our survey were the research-active core members of staff of these five law schools. In respect to the United Kingdom and Ireland, we include all those whose job title is lecturer/assistant professor, senior lecturer, reader, associate professor or professor, but exclude those designated as 'adjunct' or 'visiting', as well as any other title (e.g., teaching fellow, research fellow). In the case of Germany, we include professors as well as research assistants who either have a PhD or a substantial contract of employment (at least 50 per cent of full-time). This was done as to exclude PhD students who only have a minor involvement, say, in teaching tutorials, and who may therefore be regarded as equivalent to teaching fellows at UK universities. These rules were applied both at the point of inviting participation and at confirmation of the final dataset.

1.2.2 Procedure of Data Collection and Survey Method

The data discussed in this chapter were collected through a web-based survey, which was open during October 2013. The survey was first

[7] Claus A. Moser and Graham Kalton. *Survey Methods in Social Investigation* (Aldershot: Dartmouth, 2nd ed., 1979), 100–106.

[8] See also Appendix 1.2. [9] See Section 1.3.1.

[10] E.g., Pierre Bourdieu, *Homo Academicus* (Cambridge: Polity, 1988), 1–35 (justifying to study his own academic field, the French academia); Fiona Cownie, *Legal Academics: Culture and Identities* (Oxford: Hart Publishing, 2004), 22–25 (on insider research of legal academia).

piloted with a small number of testers (who did not participate in the full survey) and amended for clarity before full release. In the actual survey, subjects were identified through the use of publicly available staff listings (as of 30 September 2013) and the application of consistent criteria, and contacted through their institutional email address. Information on ethics and data protection was included and final explicit consent was sought at the point answers were submitted. In the invitation email and within the survey webpage we gave assurances that names would not be disclosed. Reminders were sent to those who had not responded and the survey was closed at the end of the month.

The survey was available in English for staff of the three institutions in the United Kingdom and Ireland and in German for the two German law schools. Minor customizations were made to reflect differences between jurisdictions and educational structure. For instance, two categories of 'senior' and 'junior' scholars were created, but expressed in language familiar to each higher education system, i.e. the ranks of lecturer, senior lecturer, and so forth for the UK and Irish universities and those of assistant and professor for the German ones. The precise text of both the invitation emails and the questionnaires is provided in the Appendix to this chapter.

In substance, the main aim was to identify the type of legal research method preferred by legal scholars. In this respect, we contemplated various options. First, we could have simply posed an open-ended question, i.e., asking the respondents to describe in a free text the methods that they use. This may have been appropriate given that some legal scholars suggest that 'legal science' is a 'sui generis' discipline,[11] distinct from the methods used in other parts of the university. In our questionnaire we provided a free text for further comments; however, we also felt that relying on unstructured responses alone may not have been very revealing. The responses may not have been easily comparable. Moreover, given the frequent lack of explicit recognition of methodology,[12] asking scholars to respond to one or more specific questions has the advantage that it encourages participation and reflection.

[11] See, e.g., Jan M. Smits, *The Mind and Method of the Legal Academic* (Cheltenham: Edward Elgar, 2012), 9 (suggesting that this should research what 'the law *should* be'); Jan M. Smits, 'Law and Interdisciplinarity: On the Inevitable Normativity of Legal Studies', 1 *Critical Analysis of Law* 75 (2014) ('question of what the law ought to be').

[12] Noted in van Gestel, Micklitz and Maduro, 'Methodology in the New Legal World', at 23. See also Hervé Tijssen, *De Juridische Dissertatie Onder de Loep: De Verantwoording van Methodologische Keuzes in Juridische Dissertaties* (PhD Thesis Tilburg, 2009), available at https://pure.uvt.nl/portal/files/1092488/Tijssen_dissertatie_090417.pdf (inter alia, examining the justification of methods in 90 Dutch PhD theses in law).

Second, it would have been possible to ask specific questions about 'objective' proxies and then construct an index according to these responses. For example, such questions could have asked the respondents in which journals they publish, which journals they read, which academic associations they have joined, which conferences they attend, and so forth. However, with this approach it would not have been easy to compare law schools across borders since legal journals, societies and other potential proxies are often specific to the jurisdiction or state in question. More fundamentally, such objective criteria suffer from the reverse problem as the first method, namely that they do not let the individual scholar self-assess the methods that they use.

As a result, we chose an intermediate approach, namely that we provided categories of legal research (based on our earlier work) and then asked respondents to indicate how far they felt that these reflected their own research methods. The respondents could also provide free text comments, which about 50 per cent of them did. This approach is in line with other studies. For example, in a recent study on property law, respondents were asked to self-assess their methods according to seven categories and to comment on 'influence or pressure' from their employing institution.[13] The categories that we used in the present chapter were already alluded to in the introduction and will now be explained further.

1.2.3 The Three Categories of Legal Research

There is more than just one way to classify different types of legal research. For example, it has been suggested to distinguish between internal and external methods of legal scholarship;[14] between doctrinal, reform-oriented and theoretical legal research;[15] between micro- and macro-legal research;[16] or between hard and soft, and between pure

[13] Sarah Blandy and Susan Bright, 'Property Law Research Now and into the Future', in Susan Bright and Sarah Blandy, *Researching Property Law* (London: Palgrave, 2015), 180.

[14] Richard L. Schwartz, 'Internal and External Method in the Study of Law', 11 *Law and Philosophy* 179 (1992); Christopher McCruddden, 'Legal Research and the Social Sciences', 122 *Law Quarterly Review* 632 (2006).

[15] Terry Hutchinson and Nigel Duncan, 'Defining and Describing what we Do: Doctrinal Legal Research', 71 *Deakin Law Review* 83, 101 (2012) (with reference to the classification of the Australian Pearce Committee in 1987).

[16] Mathias Siems, 'Legal Originality', 28 *Oxford Journal of Legal Studies* 147 (2008). See also Will Rhee, 'The Micro-Macro Legal Continuum and The Levels of Law', 8 *Socio-Legal Review* 1 (2012).

and applied approaches of legal research.[17] Following our previous research, this chapter uses the categories of 'law as humanities', 'law as social sciences' and 'law as a practical discipline'.[18]

The distinction between the humanities and the social sciences (in addition to the natural sciences) is common in the academic literature.[19] For this project, we are interested in legal research that makes use of the methods of humanities or social sciences, not the substance of the research; we reiterated this point on the face of the survey itself. This can be understood through distinguishing between the use of the methods of a historian (which would mean humanities) and the consideration of ancient cases (which would not necessarily mean this). A similar distinction is made in an article by Jane Baron where she distinguishes between 'humanist' and 'hermeneutic' law and literature.[20]

Furthermore, it is worth noting that our survey concerns the methods of humanities or social sciences as used by legal scholars. Thus, we have not surveyed whether and how other disciplines may also engage in legal research; for example, as it has sometimes been argued that the field of 'Law and Society' originated by social science scholarship outside the legal academia.[21] It also clear that the use of particular methods of humanities or social sciences does not necessarily mean collaboration across disciplines. For example, it has recently been argued that sociolegal studies and the welfare state literature share many characteristics but that there is 'a strange case of mutual neglect between these two scholarly traditions'.[22]

The category of 'law as a practical discipline' reflects that some legal academics may be 'academic lawyers' who share the ethics – and to some

[17] Paul Chynoweth, 'Legal research', in Andrew Knight and Les Ruddock (eds.), *Advanced Research Methods in the Built Environment* (Oxford: Wiley-Blackwell, 2008), 28. See also van Gestel and Micklitz, 'Why Methods Matter in European Legal Scholarship', at 305 (law as an instrument for social engineering versus intrinsic value of law).

[18] For details and further references see Siems and Mac Síthigh, 'Mapping Legal Research', at 653–656.

[19] See, e.g., Jerome Kagan, *The Three Cultures Natural Sciences, Social Sciences and the Humanities in the 21st Century* (Cambridge: Cambridge University Press, 2009).

[20] Jane B. Baron, 'Law, Literature and the Problems of Interdisciplinarity', 108 *Yale Law Journal* 1059, 1064–1065 (1999) ('While humanist law-and-lits argue that lawyers should read literature, others, whom I shall call 'hermeneutic' law-and-lits, argue that lawyers should read literary theory').

[21] For this discussion see Seron, Coutin and Meeusen, 'Is There a Canon of Law and Society?', at 290–291.

[22] Daniel Wincott, 'Images of Welfare in Law and Society: the British Welfare State in Comparative Perspective', 38 *Journal of Law and Society* 343, 349 (2011).

extent the methods, adjusted for the requirements of an academic post – of practicing lawyers.[23] Thus, these lawyers would mainly be interested in the substance and practical functioning of legal rules – as opposed to the scholarly 'why questions'.[24] This partly overlaps with doctrinal legal research, but the latter can also belong to 'law as humanities'. For example, Mark Van Hoecke identifies legal doctrine 'as a mainly hermeneutic discipline, with also empirical, argumentative, logical and normative elements'.[25] Some of these elements have a practical dimension but deep hermeneutical reflections are closer to the humanities.

In this respect, it is also clear that there can be differences between doctrinal scholars from different countries. Since the 'law as a practical discipline' category refers to practicing lawyers of the jurisdiction in question, for example, it may matter that in Germany legal practitioners tend to be more 'academic' than those in other countries (they often have a PhD in Law; they publish articles in law journals, contribute to books, etc.). Similarly, the 'humanities' dimension of doctrinal research may have different shades across countries: for example, in England, the long history of the common law may tend towards historical methods whereas the more conceptual thinking of civil law countries may invite the use of more philosophical methods.[26]

In the actual questionnaire we phrased the categories as follows:

Please assume that there are three main methods of legal research:

- *Legal research as part of humanities, i.e. analysis of legal texts (cases, statutes, etc.) using approaches similar to research in humanities (history, philosophy, literature, theology, etc.)*
- *Legal research as part of social sciences, i.e. analysis of law in its context, similar to research in social sciences (sociology, economics, psychology, etc.).*
- *Legal research as akin to the analysis of law in legal practice, i.e., similar to the approaches used by legal practitioners (judges, solicitors, etc.)*

[23] See Tony Becher, *Academic Tribes and Territories, Intellectual Enquiry and the Cultures of Disciplines* (Milton Keynes: Open University Press, 1989), 8, 30-31, 155.

[24] See van Gestel, Micklitz and Maduro, 'Methodology in the New Legal World', at 5 (difference between legal scholar and practitioner).

[25] Mark Van Hoecke, 'Legal Doctrine: Which Method(s) for What Kind of Discipline?', in Mark Van Hoecke (ed.), *Methodologies of Legal Research* (Oxford: Hart, 2011), 1, 17.

[26] For common and civil law see also Section 1.3.4.1, below. This may be tested with a so-called 'vignette study', i.e., to present respondents with hypotheticals and ask them to assess those in terms of the three categories. For such studies see generally, e.g., Christiane Atzmüller and Peter M. Steiner, 'Experimental Vignette Studies in Survey Research', 6 *European Journal of Research Methods for the Behavioral and Social Sciences* 128 (2010).

In your current research how frequently do you use one of these three approaches? Please allocate in total 10 points (e.g., something like 5/5/0 or 3/3/4).

Note that mixtures can be the result of a mix of these approaches in individual pieces or across various research outputs. Please also note that these categories refer to method not substance.

It can be seen that, on the one hand, the three categories are phrased in a generic language in order not to impose a particular view on how social science, humanities and practical-type legal research may be defined. On the other hand, the examples provided in brackets aim to ensure that all respondents will have sufficiently similar comparators, in terms of discipline (in the first two categories) and practitioners (in the third one) in mind when they answer the question.

The survey question asks respondents to categorize their current research. This approach has the aim to identify patterns of self-identification, namely that it can show who, subjectively, each scholars regards as his or her closest associates, as illustrated by the 'cafeteria test' of the introduction to this chapter. Asking for such a subjective stance is not uncommon in social surveys.[27] A possible objection can be that some respondents of such a survey may indicate a preference to a particular type of research because they perceive it to be of higher esteem. But even if that were to be the case, we contend that the aspirations and self-image of legal scholars, in terms of the research they would *like* to do, are relevant to a discussion of legal scholarship today.

Moreover, we believe that the neutral language of the questions and the anonymous nature of the survey (and it being carried out for an academic project rather than, say, an internal review of research quality) has reduced this risk of such merely aspirational responses as far as feasible. The questions were intended to provoke descriptive responses regarding the methods used, rather than an assessment of quality. We also focused on methods rather than outputs, which necessarily requires attention to how scholars report their own activities. The approach we took (of asking respondents to classify their own methods) is, however, not without risk. Experimental research in psychology and other disciplines suggests, unsurprisingly, a tendency for respondents to overstate positive characteristics when asked to classify or rate themselves (as compared with third parties), even when the risk of bias is specifically drawn to their

[27] See, e.g., Transparency International's Corruption Perception Indices, http://cpi.transparency.org.

attention.[28] There can also be understatement where the assessment is perceived as being of a 'difficult' task,[29] which could be a factor in relation to self-assessment of methods. We guarded against this through avoiding the use of language that suggests merit or virtue (or the opposites), and scrutinized free text comments for any evidence that this was a factor. It has also been argued that 'overplacement' by participants is not as problematic as initially thought,[30] that self-enhancing biases, while flawed, deserve study because of their contribution to behaviour,[31] and that study of 'possible selves' can be appropriate and rewarding.[32] As such, we contend that the results give a realistic depiction of methods used and believed to be used by the population studied.

The possibility of mixtures in the survey question can also be related to the 'cafeteria test'. For example, our law professor may work on various papers and for one paper she may like to get some feedback from social scientists, but for another one from legal practitioners or humanities scholars. It could also be the case that she responds that she would like to talk to a mixed group, say, one judge, one economist and one historian; again, this would indicate that this professor would presumably assign intermediate scores for each of the three categories.

1.3 Main Results for Five Law Schools in Four Jurisdictions

As the previous section explained, our empirical study focused on five law schools in Germany, the United Kingdom and Ireland. This section presents the main results. It starts with summary information on these law schools. We then present and interpret our results, based on institutional and country differences. The anonymized data collected in the survey are available at an accompanying project website.[33]

[28] Emily Pronin, Daniel Yin and Lee Ross, 'The Bias Blind Spot: Perceptions Of Bias In Self Versus Others', 28 *Personal and Social Psychology Bulletin* 369, 378 (2002).

[29] Don Moore, 'Not So Above Average After All: When People Believe They Are Worse Than Average and Its Implications for Theories of Bias in Social Comparison', 102 *Organizational Behavior and Human Decision Processes* 42 (2007).

[30] Jean-Pierre Benoit and Juan Dubra, 'Apparent Overconfidence', 79 *Econometrica* 1591 (2011).

[31] Constantine Sedikides and Aiden Gregg, 'Portraits Of The Self' in Michael Hogg and Joel Cooper (eds.), *SAGE Handbook of Social Psychology* (London: Sage, 2003).

[32] See contributions in Curtis Denkel and Jennifer Kerpelman (eds.), *Possible Selves: Theory, Research and Applications* (New York: Nova, 2006).

[33] See www.mappingmethods.blogspot.com/.

1.3.1 The Five Law Schools and Its Academic Staff

The schools vary in age, institutional mission, jurisdiction and other features. Table 1.1 provides an overview of these differences, identified at the time of the survey in October 2013.

In online surveys, it is often difficult to achieve a decent response rate.[34] In this respect, the information on the numbers of academic staff and their responses in Table 1.1 require further explanation. With respect to the two German law schools, we aimed to include professors as well as research assistants who either have a PhD or a substantial contract of employment (at least 50 per cent of full-time), in order to achieve reasonable comparability with the grade of Lecturer and above in the United Kingdom and Ireland.[35] However, the university websites do not indicate the type of employment contract; many of the research assistants that we contacted (the 'max.' numbers in Table 1.1) may not have been eligible for this study. If one considers only those who we knew to be eligible (the professors and assistants who already have a PhD), the response rates were 37 per cent and 32 per cent for the two German law schools.[36] With respect to other three law schools, the response rates were even higher: 70 per cent for Edinburgh and 59 per cent for Dublin and UEA. Thus, overall, the response rates werc very good, as compared with other studies in this field.[37] Half of the respondents also provided comments in the free text field of the survey.[38]

1.3.2 Visual Presentation of Main Results

There are different ways of presenting the data collected in our survey. A simple way of comparing the research preferences between the five law

[34] See, e.g., Mick P. Couper and Michael Bosnjak, 'Internet Surveys', in Peter V. Marsden and James D. Vright (eds.), *Handbook of Survey Research* (Bingley: Emerald, 2nd edn. 2010), 536–538 (noting the particular challenges of achieving high response rates for online surveys).

[35] See Section 1.2.1.

[36] The precise numbers are 11 out of 30 for Bucerius and 9 out of 28 for Düsseldorf.

[37] See, e.g., Duncan D. Nulty, 'The Adequacy of Response Rates to Online and Paper Surveys: What Can be Done?', 33 *Assessment & Evaluation in Higher Education* 301, 303 (2008) (citing eight studies with an average response rate of 33%); Willem van Boom and Rob van Gestel, 'Rechtswetenschappelijk onderzoek – Uitkomsten van een landelijke enquête', *Nederlands Juristenblad* (2015) web-version available at http://njb.nl/Uploads/2015/5/Van-Boom-en-Van-Gestel-2015.pdf (response rates between 13 and 29 per cent for survey at all ten Dutch law schools).

[38] These comments are also available on the project website, www.mappingmethods.blogspot.com/, and they reflect the diverse research preferences as discussed in the following.

Table 1.1 *Summary information on the law schools of this study.*

	Country	*Law school approx. student #*	*Law school academic staff # (and responses)*	*Institution (and law school) age*	*Structure of law school within university*	*Esteem indicators*[a]
Bucerius	Germany	960	max. 94 (14)	2000	Law-only private university	Top 10 in German law school rankings[b]
Düsseldorf	Germany	1200	max. 118 (23)	1965 (1993)	Faculty of Law	Above average in CHE ranking for German law schools[c]
Edinburgh	UK (Scotland)	1500	60 (42)	1583 (1707)	College of Humanities and Social Sciences	Member of Russell Group and Coimbra Group; law school ranked in top 10 of RAE 2008[d]
UEA	UK (England)	600	32 (19)	1963 (1977)	Faculty of Social Sciences	Top 20 in Times Higher Education 2013 global ranking of 'under 50' universities[e]
Dublin	Ireland	1000	22 (13)	1592 (1740)	Faculty of Arts, Humanities and Social Sciences	Highest ranked Irish university; member of Coimbra Group

[a] For the contentious role of rankings see Rob van Gestel, 'Sense and Non-sense of a European Ranking of Law Schools and Law Journals', 35 *Legal Studies* 165 (2015).

[b] www.law-school.de/rankings.html?&L=0.

[c] http://ranking.zeit.de/che2013/.

[d] www.ed.ac.uk/about/mission-governance/affiliations; www.ed.ac.uk/about/edinburgh-global/partnerships/global-networks; www2.law.ed.ac.uk/research/rae2008.aspx.

[e] www.timeshighereducation.co.uk/world-university-rankings/2013/one-hundred-under-fifty.

[f] www.tcd.ie/about/facts/; www.tcd.ie/globalrelations/global-reach/.

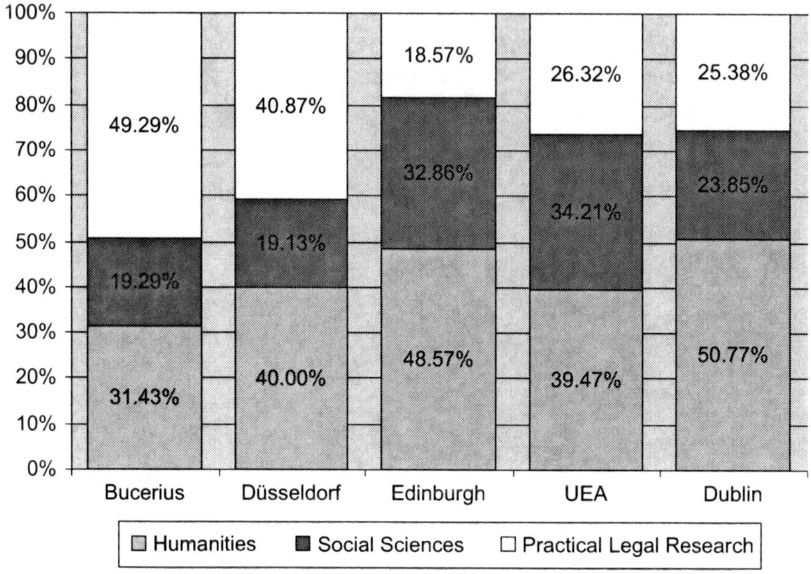

Figure 1.1 Research methods per university.

schools is to calculate the arithmetic means and present those in a bar chart: see the general preferences in Figure 1.1.

The problem with Figure 1.1 is, however, that it does not show the individual responses and the corresponding spread of the data. Thus, as already explained in our previous work, it is also useful to visually represent the relative presence of the three broad categories through 'ternary plots'.[39] The ternary plot, most familiar in the sciences, is an adaption of a Cartesian diagram for the particular circumstances of 'three dimensional' responses or observations. While we explore the data in more detail in this section (by institution) and in Section 1.4 (in terms of demographics), the ternary plot allows the reader to view the positioning of all respondents with ease, and assists with the identification of broad trends or themes.

The following diagrams of Figure 1.2 include all responses, with larger markings indicating more than one respondent with identical responses The arithmetic mean is identified as circles. We also highlight, in stars, the 'centre' of the dataset. The estimated centre, calculated with the compositional data analysis software CoDaPack, may be more appropriate than the mean for the particular data we have collected and the

[39] Siems and Mac Síthigh, 'Mapping Legal Research', at 668–669.

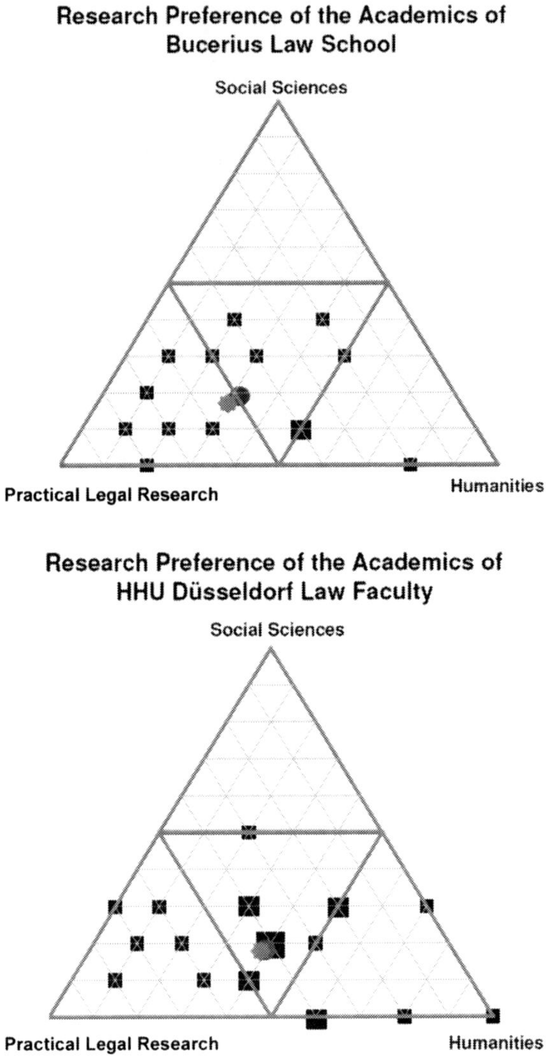

Figure 1.2 Research preferences of academics in five law schools.

geometric form in which it is presented.[40] Although the means and centres are closely aligned in our results, the mean is more affected

[40] John Aitchison, 'A concise guide to compositional data analysis' (2005), available at http://ima.udg.edu/activitats/codawork05/A_concise_guide_to_compositional_data_analysis.pdf at p. 49; Glòria Mateu-Figueras et al., 'The principle of working on coordinates', in Vera Pawlowsky-Glahn and Antonella Buccianti (eds.), *Compositional Data*

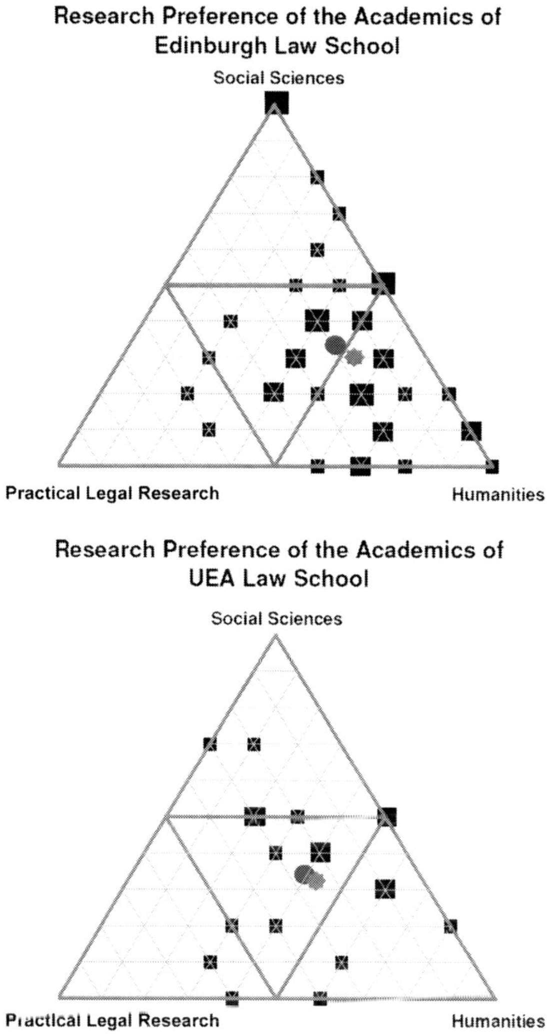

Figure 1.2 (*cont.*)

Analysis: Theory and Applications (Chichester: Wiley, 2011), 40. For these calculations some adjustment of the 'zero' responses was necessary. As in the present case those can be treated as 'rounded zeros', we replaced them with the value '0.25' (the average between 0.00..1 and 0.499..) and made corresponding changes to other values. This procedure is based on Josep A. Martin-Fernandez, Carles Barcelo-Vidal, and Vera Pawlowsky-Glahn, 'Dealing With Zeros and Missing Values in Compositional Data Sets Using Nonparametric Imputation', 35 *Mathematical Geology* 253 (2003).

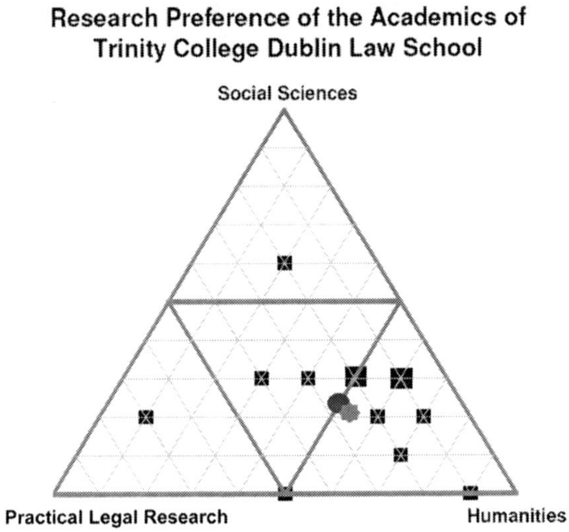

Figure 1.2 (*cont.*)

by outlying results – for instance, the cluster of 'social science only' respondents in Edinburgh pulled the mean away from the core of responses.

Compositional statistics also allows for the calculation of the spread of the data, known as the 'centred log-ratio transformation' (CLR) variance. This is the equivalent to calculating the standard deviations in classical statistics.

Table 1.2 shows that the two schools in the United Kingdom have 'more variance' – as we discuss below. The high value for social science variance in the same schools, as compared with the other three schools, reflects what is visible on the ternary plots – a group of respondents who identify strongly with social science (exclusively or to a very great extent). However, in all cases, the variance data demonstrates how the humanities category is more widely accepted (or less unusual) than that for social sciences.

1.3.3 *Interpretation Based on Institutional Differences*

The findings can be contextualized by considering the focus of the law schools we studied. This focus is identified, first and foremost, from the public documents of the school and (where relevant) the

Table 1.2 *Centred log-ratio transformation (CLR) variances for the five law schools.*

	Humanities	*Social sciences*	*Practical legal research*	*Total variance*
Bucerius	0.44	0.45	0.39	1.27
Düsseldorf	0.74	0.57	0.60	1.90
Edinburgh	0.75	1.03	0.79	2.57
UEA	0.71	0.80	0.79	2.31
Dublin	0.47	0.48	0.42	1.37
All law schools	0.73	0.84	0.79	2.37

institution in which it is located. Some of this information is presented in Table 1.1.

We note general consistency with the reputation or priorities of the schools. Starting with Germany, the traditional system of publicly funded universities means that German universities are relatively similar: all of them have decent resources but without some of them being 'global elite universities'.[41] Correspondingly, the law faculty of the University of Düsseldorf can be seen as a relatively typical German law school. The predominant mix of practical and humanities-influenced legal research is a general feature of German legal scholarship.[42] The law school's website shows, on the one hand, the traditional focus of a German law school on preparing students for the First Exam (which can mainly be associated with the practical dimension).[43] On the other hand, information on international collaborations, various research centres and specialized master degrees[44] indicates that the law school has also developed a wider range of activities.

[41] By way of illustration see U21 Ranking of National Higher Education Systems 2014, available at www.universitas21.com/RelatedFile/Download/589, where Germany ranks 14 out of 50 countries and the Times Higher Education World University Rankings, available at www.timeshighereducation.co.uk/world-university-rankings/2013-14/world-ranking where there is no German university in the top fifty.

[42] See Section 1.3.4. [43] www.jura.hhu.de/studium.html.

[44] See www.jura.hhu.de/internationales.html; www.jura.hhu.de/forschung/forschung-an-den-instituten.html; www.duslaw.de.

With respect to Bucerius Law School, our survey data show that the practical category is the main subject of emphasis. This is in line with the fact that Bucerius, as a private law school, collaborates closely with law firms, setting out in its mission statement how 'the course of studies is based on a unity of teaching and research, and merges the needs of the practicing legal community with an academic pervasion of the law' and acknowledging how 'donations from private sponsors are a sign of the society's confidence in the Law School';[45] some facilities are named after major law firms. It is also important to note that undergraduate students pay tuition fees at Bucerius, unlike students at most German public universities. As a result, students expect to receive an excellent and 'practical' legal education,[46] in order to get into the top jobs in legal practice after graduation. This may also have a side-effect on the practical research focus at Bucerius.[47]

The survey results for Edinburgh and UEA are relatively mixed as regards the preferences for particular research methods. This is in line with a statement on Edinburgh's website which identifies as its first core strategic objective the building of 'a research profile of depth and breadth which has demonstrable and transformative impact (academic, legal and social)'.[48] Yet, it is also worth noting that, according to our findings, Edinburgh only has a relatively small number of scholars who identify their research as falling within our 'practical' category. This may reflect the nature of one of the top ten UK law schools where practical legal research is often seen as not 'original' enough, in particular for the purposes of the UK Research Assessment Exercises (RAEs, now REFs).[49]

Furthermore, it is worth noting that, unlike the other three law schools, Edinburgh and UEA have a good number of scholars that associate themselves with the social sciences. This reflects the existence of clusters or centres explicitly framed in relation to the social sciences at both of these law schools.[50] It is also in line with some of the programs

[45] www.law-school.de/leitbild.html?&L=1.

[46] See also Christoph Luschin, 'A German Ivy? The Bucerius Law School', 19 *Southwestern Journal of International Law* 1 (2012).

[47] The relationship between teaching and research preferences is also discussed in Section 1.3.4.2.

[48] www.law.ed.ac.uk/other_areas_of_interest/about/about_edinburgh_law_school/strategy_and_vision.

[49] For the RAEs see also Section 1.3.4.2.

[50] At Edinburgh, the Criminology group since the 1970s (http://www.crg.law.ed.ac.uk/); at UEA, the ESRC-funded Centre for Competition Policy (www.competitionpolicy.ac.uk).

they offer: Edinburgh's interest in criminology supports an MSc in this field and UEA offers a Master of Research in 'social science research methods' as well as degrees in obviously interdisciplinary areas such as competition and media.

Social science methods appear less prominent in Dublin than in the two UK institutions. Although the response rate was lower here, the results are not entirely unexpected. Legal education in Ireland has long been closely linked with the small, self-employed Bar. In some universities, many full-time members of academic staff will continue to practice law, and the value of practical and clinical training within undergraduate legal education has been reasserted, although managerial approaches to workload are making it more difficult for full-time academic staff to practice law.[51] Trinity College itself is identified with performing particularly well in rankings that concentrate on 'arts and humanities'.[52]

1.3.4 Interpretation Based on Country Differences

It is also possible to relate our findings to differences between the countries of our study. The two German law schools show a mixture of practical and humanities-related legal research. Yet the humanities focus is strong across all the schools we studied, for instance also in Dublin, thus, possibly reflecting the European approach to law as humanities more generally. The two UK law schools show the greatest internal diversity, possibly due to the major changes that have happened across the UK universities in the last quarter-century, as the following will explain.

1.3.4.1 The Role of Legal Families

The most intuitive reason for these differences may be that legal systems and methods are very different, perhaps because there is a deep divide between common and civil law countries. The European scope of our study does not enable us to provide a general answer to the relevance of legal family classifications. Indeed, previous research[53] has found that

[51] Marie-Luce Paris and Lawrence Donnelly, 'Legal Education in Ireland: A Paradigm Shift to the Practical?', 11 *German Law Journal* 1067, 1079 (2010).

[52] http://www.tcd.ie/news_events/articles/trinity-ranked-among-top-100-universities-for-arts-humanities/1861.

[53] Hesselink, *The New European Legal Culture*; Riesenhuber, 'English Common Law versus German *Systemdenken*?'; Grechenig and Gelter, 'The Transatlantic Divergence in Legal Thought'; Seron, Coutin and Meeusen, 'Is There a Canon of Law and Society?'.

today US law and legal culture is very different from both the United Kingdom and continental Europe. Still, of course, there may also be differences within Europe. Although ideas do indeed travel, especially as joint projects are increasingly favoured in funding systems (e.g., requirements for cross-border collaboration in EU-funded schemes), differences in legal thinking persist.

For example, primers on legal research for postgraduate and doctoral students demonstrate how those groups are introduced to legal skills and aspects of (legal) philosophy in Germany.[54] On the contrary, similar texts for UK researchers include a mixture of methods: historical, comparative, doctrinal, sociolegal, and quantitative.[55] This itself is a development; as our respondents – in the free text of our survey – told us that the lack of social science training in the past continues to inhibit even successful, mid-career scholars from making use of these methods.[56]

We may also need to consider that the United Kingdom is not a uniform legal system, and that Scotland is sometimes seen as belonging to a separate 'mixed legal family'.[57] Having asked Edinburgh respondents whether they have received their undergraduate training in Scotland or elsewhere, we could calculate that the arithmetic means within the subcategory of Scots lawyers from Edinburgh (fifteen respondents) are 43 per cent for law as humanities, 36 per cent for law as social sciences and 15 per cent for practical legal research. This is fairly close to the overall Edinburgh data for all forty-two staff members:[58] thus, this suggests that, in terms of these three general

[54] E.g., Karl Larenz and Claus-Wilhelm Canaris, *Methodenlehre der Rechtswissenschaft* (Berlin: Springer 3rd ed. 1995); Bernd Rüthers, Christian Fischer and Axel Birk, *Rechtstheorie: mit Juristischer Methodenlehre* (Munich: Beck, 7th edn. 2013).

[55] E.g., Mike McConville and Wing Hong Chui (eds.), *Research Methods for Law* (Edinburgh: Edinburgh University Press 2007); Dawn Watkins and Mandy Burton (eds.), *Research Methods in Law* (London: Routledge 2013).

[56] Respondents EDI 15, EDI 21, TCD 9. For similar assessments see Michael Adler and Jonathan Simon, 'Stepwise Progression: The Past, Present, and Possible Future of Empirical Research on Law in the United States and the United Kingdom', 41 *Journal of Law and Society* 173, 188–191 (2014); Hazel Genn et al., *Law in the Real World: Improving our Understanding of How Law Works* (2006), available at www.nuffieldfoundation.org/nuffield-inquiry-empirical-legal-research-law-real-world. For the role of education see also Section 1.4.1.2.

[57] For the debate see, e.g., Sue Farran, 'Scots Law: A System in Search of a Family?', 61 *Northern Ireland Legal Quarterly* 311 (2010).

[58] See Section 1.3.2.

legal methods, Scotland is not very different from the rest of the United Kingdom.

1.3.4.2 Further Factors, in Particular, Higher Education

According to Tony Becher, even where the subject matter of particular fields appears to be global (e.g., in physics or engineering) 'geographical variation' of disciplines still exists as the methods of researchers may reflect 'identifiable features of a particular society, such as its education system or its level of economic development'.[59] Even more so, this is likely to be the case in legal scholarship where such factors may complement differences in legal culture and style. In the following, we cannot identify all cultural, psychological, social, political, economic or other factors which may determine why, say, the average English and German scholar do legal research in a different way. Rather, the following will focus on factors of higher education as these have been particularly controversial in recent years.

University structures do differ between institutions. In Germany, Immanuel Kant referred to law as being, along with medicine and theology, one of the three 'higher faculties'.[60] But in the United Kingdom, the 'predominant notion of academic lawyers is that they are not really academic'.[61] Is this still a fair summary, now that legal scholars are subject to the same research assessments and research-focused promotion criteria as other academics, and often share faculties and research council budgets with them?

Incentive structures have not converged. Differences between the governance and funding of institutions between countries may relate to research. In the United Kingdom, for example, both the funding and the reputation of an institution will be affected by the external review of the quality of the research outputs of its staff, in the Research Excellence Framework (REF; until 2014 called RAE, Research Assessment Exercise), where work is evaluated against criteria of significance, originality and rigour.[62] In the free text some of our respondents also made explicit reference to the importance of the REF for changes in legal scholarship,

[59] Becher, *Academic Tribes and Territories*, at 21–22.

[60] Immanuel Kant, *Der Streit der Fakultäten* (1789) – English translation by Mary J. Gregor, *The Conflict of the Faculties* (Lincoln: University of Nebraska Press 1992).

[61] Becher, *Academic Tribes and Territories*, at 30.

[62] www.ref.ac.uk/. See also Cownie, *Legal Academics*, at 135–138 (RAE effect, as 'increasingly important place of research in the culture of academic law').

appearing to assume that these criteria are more obviously met in the case of work in humanities and in particular social science: one of them proposed that approaches beyond 'black letter domestic' made it more likely that such work would be reviewed at the valued levels of 3* and 4* under the REF, and another pointed to the 'positive' impact of the REF in promoting quality and thus a move towards humanities and social science approaches over time.[63]

In Ireland, on the contrary, there is no equivalent system.[64] Nor is there one in Germany: academics are required to produce internal reports about research activity, but professors in publicly funded institutions enjoy strong protection against the termination of their employment. This is stronger than is the case in the United Kingdom, where the Education Reform Act 1988 provides for the amendment of university statutes so as to allow dismissal of academic staff on the grounds of redundancy or good cause (s. 203). More recently, institutions have made use of 'teaching-only contracts' and redeployed staff considered to be performing less effectively in research (especially with a view to the REF) to these contracts, or advertised more of these positions than before.[65]

Previous research has also pointed to variation between countries in the form and position of disciplinary boundaries. It is argued that, despite some convergence as a consequence of the Bologna Process and world and EU trade law, German and UK higher education systems still differ in their approach to the vocational dimension and to basic/applied research – and the fates of the social sciences and humanities are different as a result.[66] None of the countries we considered take the

63 Respondents UEA 16, EDI 23.

64 Key Perspectives Ltd, 'A Comparative Review of Research Assessment Regimes in Five Countries and the Role of Libraries in the Research Assessment Process' (2009), available at www.oclc.org/content/dam/research/publications/library/2009/2009-09.pdf, at pp. 23–26.

65 See, e.g., Paul Jump, 'Swansea's tough REF plans provoke disquiet' (*Times Higher Education* 5 September 2013) (commenting on the proposed move of staff without four 3* publications from a contract with six hours per week of teaching to one with eighteen hours); Anna Fazackerley, 'University Reputation: Will Teachers Pay the Price?' (*The Guardian*, 30 April 2013), available at www.theguardian.com/education/2013/apr/29/university-research-funding-harms-teaching (reviewing different positions taken by UK institutions on the consequences of nonsubmission to the REF for academic staff contracts).

66 Rebecca Krebs and Silke Wenk, 'Disciplinary Barriers Between the Social Sciences and Humanities' (2005), available at www.york.ac.uk/res/researchintegration/ComparativeReports/Comparative_Report_Construction_of_Knowledge.pdf at pp. 7–11.

Swedish approach of defining at a national level the disciplines that are part of the social sciences or humanities, and so the autonomy of German, UK and Irish institutions means that there can be variation across institutions, as well as across countries.[67]

Our focus in this chapter is on legal research. However, the approach of an institution to teaching also makes a difference – such as in choosing who to appoint and whether to promote a member of staff. The development of research methodologies, therefore, may compete for attention with responses to other incentives (e.g., the development of new courses, taking on administrative roles). There is clear potential for tension between research and teaching,[68] although the separation of function that has emerged in the United States (where much teaching may be 'outsourced', in some institutions, to adjunct professors and temporary staff) is less obvious in the countries we have considered in this study.[69]

The tension between teaching and research is likely to be more pronounced in the United Kingdom than in the other countries of this study. Due to the RAEs/REFs, the claim that 'in Common Law countries … most full-time professors think of themselves mainly as teachers rather than scholars',[70] is certainly not accurate any more for England and other parts of the United Kingdom. Thus, UK legal scholars may often feel that, for their research, they should not be 'too practical' as this may not help one's academic career, while in their teaching they should not be 'too theoretical' lest students complain that they do not get 'value for money' given the constant rise in student tuition fees.[71] In Germany, by contrast, the more practical research focus means that this tension is less

[67] Ursula Apitzsch and Irini Siouti, 'Comparative Report on the Infrastructural Definitions of the Humanities and Social Sciences in Eight European Countries' (2005), available at www.york.ac.uk/res/researchintegration/ComparativeReports/Comparative_Report_Infrastructural_Definitions.pdf.

[68] van Gestel and Micklitz, 'Why Methods Matter in European Legal Scholarship', at 300.

[69] For the discussion about such a split see Mathias Siems, 'A World Without Law Professors', in Mark Van Hoecke (ed.), *Methodologies of Legal Research* (Oxford: Hart Publishing, 2011), 71–86.

[70] David S. Clark, 'The Organization of Lawyers and Judges' in Mauro Cappelletti (ed.), *International Encyclopedia of Comparative Law*, volume 16 (Tübingen: Mohr 2002) para. 56.

[71] Similar the assessment by Hilary Somerlad et al., *The Futures of Legal Education and the Legal Profession* (Oxford: Hart Publishing 2015), 14 ('in essence the law school curriculum remains doctrinal and traditional'). For the fee structure in UK universities see www.ucas.com/how-it-all-works/student-finance/undergraduate-student-finance.

pronounced. Moreover, the fact that the Final Exam is predominantly managed by the Ministries of Justice (not the universities)[72] further stimulates the frequent emphasis on practical legal knowledge.

1.4 Possible Determinants of Research Preferences

The previous section highlighted the country and institutional differences between the law schools of our study. In this section, we consider the role of various themes that may shape the research preferences of individual academics. In particular, we analyse factors such as gender, age, education and subject matter of research (see Section 1.4.1). We also identify dominant and changing paradigms in the five law schools (see Section 1.4.2).

Despite the aim to identify possible determinants, this chapter does not use tools of inferential statistics, such as regression analysis. In the present context, it is often difficult to identify a clear unidirectional causal relationship; for example, if it were found that private lawyers had a preference for practical legal research, this would not necessarily mean that doing research on private law leads to a more practical approach, because it could also be the case that scholars who prefer to do a practical legal approach then decide to focus on topics of private law. There may also be cases where the decision to enter the academic career in law is dependent on whether one's preferred method of research is accepted in a particular market: for example, if persons with a degree from another discipline are less likely to associate with a practical approach, a market where the latter is dominant may see few of those academics.

As previously explained,[73] it is the general aim of this chapter to provide a nuanced picture of the situation in a small number of law schools familiar to us. In the following section we also present some aggregates of the five law schools. This may invite the response that these five units are not a representative sample, say, of law schools in Europe, or representative of the country in which they are located. To reflect this point, the following will also report to what extent a particular result holds for all of the five law schools, or whether there may be an outlier.

[72] According to §5d(2) of the German Judiciary Act (*Richtergesetz*) this concerns 70 per cent of the First Exam, while 30 per cent of this exam is set by the universities.

[73] See Section 1.2.1.

1.4.1 *Analysis of Possible General Determinants*

The survey, underlying this chapter, not only identified preferences in research methods, but asked respondents to provide information on a number of further personal characteristics.[74] Table 1.3 reports the results across the five law schools. The shadings highlight law schools that are 10 per cent above or below the percentages of the 'Total' column.

Table 1.3 shows some interesting differences. For example, the fact that there are relatively few female legal scholars in the two German law schools may reflect the fact that in Germany, until around ten years ago, men were considerably more likely to study law than women.[75] Given the different structure of universities,[76] the two German law schools also have more young staff members than the three other law schools. In terms of qualifications, it is notable that in the two UK law schools relatively few staff members have a qualification to practice law, possibly reflecting the impact of the RAEs,[77] and that in Dublin relatively few staff members have a degree in another discipline but more than in the other law schools a PhD in law (pointing, with due caution because of the response rate, to a shift towards an academic approach but not to the wider interdisciplinary changes visible in the neighbouring jurisdictions). With respect to the United Kingdom, it may be noted that almost all of the younger scholars tend to have a PhD (or are about to complete it), whereas some of the senior scholars entered legal academia at a time when it was still common to pursue a career in legal scholarship without a PhD.[78]

In terms of subject matter specialization, it can be seen that in the two German law schools almost all of the respondents clearly indicated that

[74] See Section 1.2.2 and Appendix 1.2. Although some of this information could have been gathered from university websites, we could not be certain that the websites were up to date, and important data was either unavailable (e.g., age) or incomplete (e.g., all qualifications).

[75] See data on law graduates, available at www.uni-due.de/isa/fg_wirtschaft_recht/rechtswiss/rechtswiss_mw_frm.htm.

[76] See academic career maps in Europe, at www.leru.org/index.php/public/extra/careermapseurope.

[77] See Section 1.3.4.2, above. See also Patricia Leighton, Tony Mortimer and Nicola Whatley, *Today's Law Teachers: Lawyers or Academics?* (London: Cavendish, 1995), 19–20 (large-scale study carried out by Anglia Polytechnic University in 1995 found that fewer than half of all law teachers, including university degrees and professional courses, in the United Kingdom had significant experience of legal practice).

[78] For the past situation see, e.g., Becher, *Academic Tribes and Territories*, at 108 (in the early 1980s in one of the leading law faculties only five out of thirty-two PhD graduates).

Table 1.3 *Variables (absolute counts, and per cent of respondents of each law school).*

		Bucerius	*Düsseldorf*	*Edinburgh*	*UEA*	*Dublin*	*Total*
Gender	Male	11	18	22	13	5	*69*
		78.6%	78.3%	52.4%	68.4%	38.5%	*62.2%*
	Female	3	5	20	6	8	*42*
		21.4%	21.7%	47.6%	31.6%	61.5%	*37.8%*
Age	≤35	7	14	12	8	3	*44*
		50.0%	60.9%	28.6%	42.1%	23.1%	*39.6%*
	36–49	5	5	19	8	8	*45*
		35.7%	21.7%	45.2%	42.1%	61.5%	*40.5%*
	≥50	2	4	11	3	2	*22*
		14.3%	17.4%	26.2%	15.8%	15.4%	*19.8%*
Rank	Junior staff	7	16	20	10	5	*58*
		50.0%	69.6%	47.6%	52.6%	38.5%	*52.3%*
	Senior staff	7	7	22	9	8	*53*
		50.0%	30.4%	52.4%	47.4%	61.5%	*47.7%*
Practice (domestic)	Yes	9	12	11	6	9	*47*
		64.3%	52.2%	26.2%	31.6%	69.2%	*42.3%*
	No	5	11	31	13	4	*64*
		35.7%	47.8%	73.8%	68.4%	30.8%	*57.7%*

Degree in other discipline	Yes	2	4	11	6	1	*24*
		14.3%	17.4%	26.2%	31.6%	7.7%	*21.6%*
	No	12	19	31	13	12	*87*
		85.7%	82.6%	73.8%	68.4%	92.3%	*78.4%*
PhD in law	Yes	9	13	27	13	11	*73*
		64.3%	56.5%	64.3%	68.4%	84.6%	*65.8%*
	No	5	10	15	6	2	*38*
		35.7%	43.5%	35.7%	31.6%	15.4%	*34.2%*
Type	Private law	8	10	12	8	4	*42*
		57.1%	43.5%	28.6%	42.1%	30.8%	*37.8%*
	Public law	5	12	20	6	5	*48*
		35.7%	52.2%	47.6%	31.6%	38.5%	*43.2%*
	Mixed	1	1	10	5	4	*21*
		7.1%	4.3%	23.8%	26.3%	30.8%	*18.9%*
Jurisdiction	Domestic law	6	17	6	6	6	*41*
		42.9%	73.9%	14.3%	31.6%	46.2%	*36.9%*
	Int'l, European or comparative law	4	1	19	6	4	*34*
		28.6%	4.3%	45.2%	31.6%	30.8%	*30.6%*
	Mixed	4	5	17	7	3	*36*
		28.6%	21.7%	40.5%	36.8%	23.1%	*32.4%*

they belong to either private or public law whereas in the three British and Irish law schools, mixtures are more common. The likely explanation is that in the common law world the divide between public and private law is of more recent origin.[79] Finally, there are some interesting differences in terms of domestic or international law focus. The two UK universities have the lowest number of 'pure' domestic scholars which is likely to be the result of a relatively open international market for academic appointments.[80] Edinburgh, in particular, contains few 'pure' domestic scholars which may also reflect the strong interest in comparative approaches in a small legal system sometimes considered as a mixture between common and civil law.[81] By contrast, Düsseldorf has a strong focus on domestic law, possibly reflecting the importance of the centralized final exam which mainly focuses on domestic law.[82]

The following presents the arithmetic means of the three research methods, distinguished by those variables. It would also be possible to display the 'centres' but, as we have seen previously, in our case this leads to similar results.[83]

1.4.1.1 Personal Characteristics

The ternary plot in Figure 1.3 shows that, on average, female scholars are closer to the social sciences than male scholars, whereas male scholars are closer to the other two categories. What may explain this gender difference? It may matter that, in the past, 'law' has been a discipline where a clear majority of scholars were men.[84] Thus, women who joined law schools may have felt the need to find a 'niche', since it may have been difficult to get into the existing male networks of traditional doctrinal scholars, i.e., those predominantly associated with practical legal scholarship and law as humanities.[85]

[79] See, e.g., Mathias Siems, *Comparative Law* (Cambridge: Cambridge University Press 2014), 49.

[80] See Chistopher McCrudden, 'A Comment on the Use of Foreign Professors in the German Council of Science and Humanities Report' (20 February 2014), available at http://verfassungsblog.de/a-comment-on-the-use-of-foreign-professors-in-the-german-council-of-science-and-humanities-report-prospects-of-legal-scholarship-in-germany-current-situation-analyses-recommendations-2/.

[81] See Section 1.3.4.1. [82] See Section 1.3.3. [83] See Section 1.3.2.

[84] See, e.g., for the United Kingdom, Cownie, *Legal Academics*, at 168–175; Clare McGlynn, *The Woman Lawyer: Making the Difference* (London: Butterworths, 1998). For Germany, Section 1.2.2 and Appendix 1.2.

[85] For the trend towards law as a social science, see also Section 1.4.2.2.

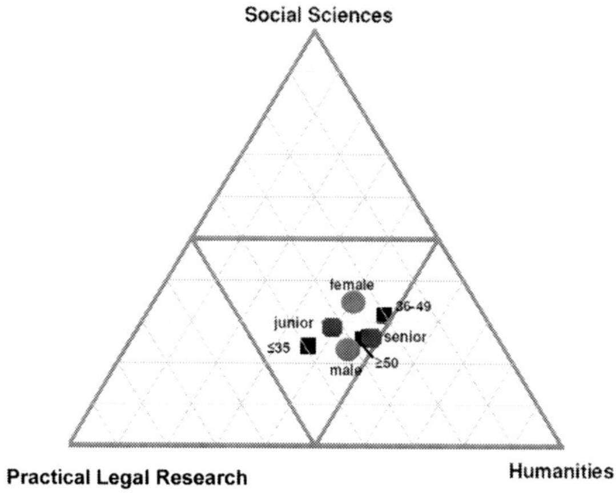

Figure 1.3 Research preferences per gender, age and rank.

In terms of age and rank, it is most interesting to see that younger and early-career scholars tend to be more 'practical'. This may be counter-intuitive given evidence from the United States that new fields, such as 'law and' scholarship, are preferred by younger academics.[86] Yet in our case it may reflect that younger scholars received their legal training recently and that this is usually of a black letter nature in the United Kingdom, Ireland and Germany. Thus, legal scholars may only adopt a more interdisciplinary perspective later on in their academic career. This can also be seen in some of the comments we received in our survey. Those included the lack of formal training in social science and how this inhibits the use of such methods (respondents from Scotland and Germany),[87] even though 'there might be occasions where it might be helpful' (respondent from Ireland).[88] Several respondents indicated how the influence of interdisciplinary collaboration, for example in a research centre, has accounted for a later shift towards social sciences.[89] A respondent from Germany also explained that classical methods tend to become less exciting as you progress with your research, and, similarly,

[86] William Landes and Richard Posner, 'Heavily Cited Articles in Law', 71 *Chicago-Kent Law Review* 825, 836 (1996).

[87] Respondents EDI 15, EDI 21, BUC 9.

[88] Respondent TCD 2.

[89] Respondents HHU 4, EDI 9, UEA 12.

one respondent from England indicated that he 'increasingly found "pure" doctrinal law a little dull – and limiting in so far as there is a finite stock of material, albeit changing over time'.[90]

The fact that Figure 1.3 shows differences between junior and senior academics may, in the words of Tony Becher, show the 'familiar contest of the Young Turks against the Old Guard'.[91] Here, then, the senior academics may be in a stronger position, as discussed in Pierre Bourdieu's study dealing with the 'power and prestige' in the 'academic field' in France. In particular, Bourdieu uses the notion of 'academic capital' being 'obtained and maintained by holding a position enabling domination of other positions and their holders', which he also links to age.[92]

In the present context, however, it also needs to be considered that the differences between the categories in the ternary plot may be regarded as relatively small, and that the age group of fifty or older is positioned between the other two groups. In addition, the ternary plot just indicated the mean, not the spread of the data. To identify the latter, it is possible to calculate the confidence intervals of the categories.[93]

Figure 1.4(a) shows that two of the circles do not overlap. Thus, we may say that we are 95 per cent confident about the difference between the age groups ≤ 35 and 36–49 years but we cannot be sure about the difference between ≥ 50 and the other two age groups. A problem with this result may be that the difference between the age groups could be driven by the differences between law schools: for example, we have received relatively many responses from young German legal scholars and German law schools tend to be more 'practical', i.e., this could actually account for the age effect. The same could be the case for gender since we received relatively many responses from male German scholars, and the two German law schools also tend to be more practical.

Yet, further analysis does not confirm this suspicion. Checking the precise differences between the five law schools, there are similar age and gender effects in all but one of them (Dublin, whereas already stated the response rate is low). Moreover, it is possible to conduct a more structured calculation, controlling for differences between law schools. For this purpose, we scaled the responses of each respondent according to the average of his or her university as compared to the overall average. Then,

[90] Respondents BUC 13, UEA 18 [91] Becher, *Academic Tribes and Territories*, at 72.

[92] Bourdieu, *Homo Academicus*, at 84, 87. See also Becher, *Academic Tribes and Territories*, at 58 (with the heading 'Great men, gatekeepers and the exercise of power').

[93] This uses a function provided by CoDaPack (see Section 1.3.2).

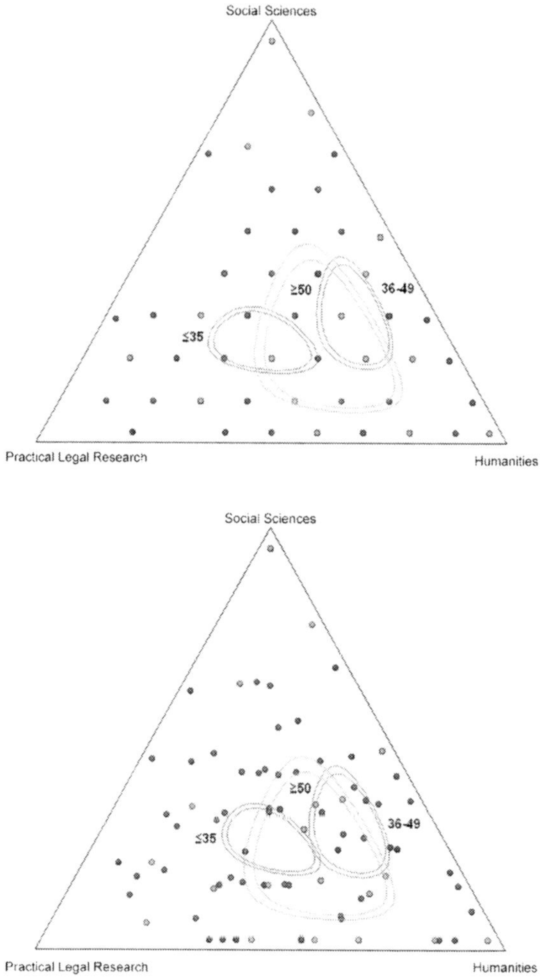

Figure 1.4 90 per cent and 95 per cent centre confidence intervals for age differences.

these transformed data can also be used to produce a ternary plot with centre confidence intervals. With respect to age, it can be seen that the Figure 1.4(b) looks similar to the original data; for example, younger scholars have indeed a tendency to be more practical, and we can say with 90 per cent confidence that there is a difference between the ≤35 and 36–49 age groups. With respect to the other variables of this section – as well as the two subsequent ones – the group differences of the original data also show up if we use the transformed data. Thus, we can assume that differences between the law schools do not drive the results of our determinants, and in the following sections we will only report the unaltered data.

We did not find that the centre confidence intervals of the other variables, both of this section and the two subsequent ones, were significant at the 90 per cent level: for example, the gender difference is only significant at the 70 per cent level for the original and at the 65 per cent level for the transformed data. This should not be a surprise given that often we only have a relatively low number of observations: for example, the age group ≥50 are just twenty-two respondents. It means that the findings of this section need to be interpreted with caution. For this reason we also provide frequent references to qualitative information (free text comments) in this section.

1.4.1.2 Education and Training

In their comments, many of our respondents indicated that training is a key facilitator of, and lack of training an important barrier to, methodological evolution.[94] In particular, this is relevant for the social science methods – lest, legal scholars who want to engage in these methods just become 'amateur social scientists'.[95] The quantitative data of Figure 1.5 confirm this observation for the aggregate level. It can also be checked that in all five law schools respondents with a non-law degree are more likely to associate with the view of law as a social science. In this respect, it is also notable that seventeen of these twenty-four respondents have a non-law degree which can be classified as being part of the social sciences – mainly, business, sociology or criminology[96] – while five have degrees from the humanities and two from the natural sciences.

Scholars who were formerly or continue to be legal practitioners are subject to a complex range of influences. While it might be assumed that such a scholar would have extensive knowledge of the interpretation methods that practitioners apply, and that these competences would have been highlighted and emphasized in their appointment by a university, it is not necessarily the case that a scholar of this nature would

[94] Respondents EDI 39, UEA 2; cf. respondents EDI 15, EDI 21, TCD 9

[95] Cf. also van Gestel, Micklitz and Maduro, 'Methodology in the New Legal World', at 14.

[96] This is line with Mathias Siems, 'How close is 'law' to other academic disciplines?', available at http://siemslegal.blogspot.co.uk/2012/06/how-close-is-law-to-other-academic.html (examining the interdisciplinary papers of legal scholars in the U.K.'s Research Assessment Exercise 2008).

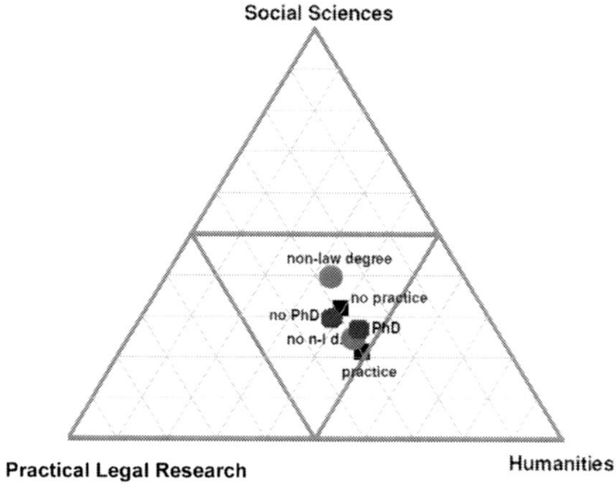

Figure 1.5 Research preferences per qualifications.

continue to focus on this method. Indeed, Figure 1.5 does not show that legal scholars who have a domestic qualification to practice law are more inclined to practical legal research than those who do not have such a qualification. In the free comments, respondents who had formerly practiced law also often explained how this change in professional status was reflected, over time, in a move towards methods other than practical. For example, three comments from English and Scottish legal scholars argued that the need to substantiate a practical perspective through theory prompted a gradual move from practical towards humanities or pointed to new perspectives gained after leaving practice, although past experience of practice also encouraged research that analysed this sector.[97]

A related question is whether a PhD in law makes a difference. In the UK context, it has been suggested that 'in the mid-1990s, the rise of the PhD as an entry-level qualification changed the nature of some, even very traditional, law schools'.[98] Yet, Figure 1.5 does not show such impact on the preferred type of research. Here, too, the plausible explanation is that legal scholars who do not have a PhD immerse themselves into the academic environment, not least since research of high quality

[97] Respondents EDI 2, UEA 11, UEA 13.
[98] SLSA discussion, 64 *Socio-Legal Newsletter* 4, 5 (2011) (quoting Sally Wheeler).

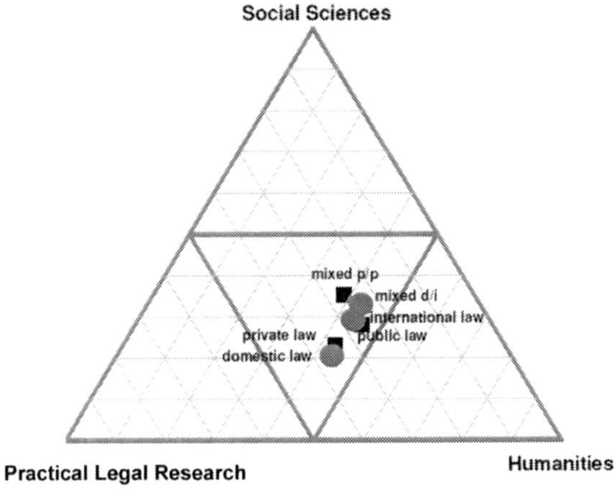

Figure 1.6 Research preferences per area of law and jurisdiction.

(e.g., submitted for the REF)[99] helps them in their academic career (in terms of promotion, research grants etc).

1.4.1.3 Subject Matter of Research

It may be expected that there is a relationship between working in a given area of law and the use of a method.[100] Both our quantitative and qualitative data tend to confirm a number of possible differences.[101] In our survey, we distinguished between public law (including criminal law), private law, and mixtures between public and private law. Figure 1.6 shows that, on average, private lawyers are closer to practical legal research than public lawyers. This may reflect that the core areas of private law – contract, tort and property law – can be studied in a relatively apolitical way (i.e., accepting the common [private] law as a fair, efficient system rather than interrogating its underlying political

[99] See Section 1.3.4.2.

[100] For instance, Becher, *Academic Tribes and Territories*, at 133, makes the claim that jurisprudence is 'pure' and family law is 'nothing if not applied', although this may not reflect the methodological pluralism of present-day legal research.

[101] The following quantitative observations hold for four of the law schools, not Dublin; but note that for the latter law school we only have a small number of observations in the three areas-of-law categories (4, 5, and 4 observations); thus, this non-result for Dublin should not be overinterpreted.

basis) and can therefore be subject to a relatively positivist understanding.[102] By contrast, there is a more 'natural' link between research in public law and other disciplines (e.g., political science for constitutional law, economics for competition law and sectoral regulation). The relatively high social science affiliation of scholars who mix public and private law is also plausible since a scholar adopting a social science approach may often be interested in the way a particular aim is achieved, be it with tools of public or private law, rather than primarily interested in the doctrinal features of, for example, contract law.

Comments provided by our respondents on their areas of interest point to a similar direction. For example, one of them mentioned that his research on 'property law theory' is bound to be 'very much humanities-like'.[103] Another respondent indicated that in researching the law of protest, most other research came from nonlegal disciplines, such as sociology and political science.[104]

The second distinction is between domestic law, international law (including comparative and European law) and mixtures between them. In the literature, Geoffrey Samuel suggests that comparative legal thinking challenges the 'authority paradigm', and by doing so turns it into a social science.[105] Two comments in our survey also indicate that 'comparative law requires an interdisciplinary approach' and that 'international law/EU law [is] considerably determined by political/economic context'.[106] Likewise, the quantitative data of Figure 1.6 show that legal scholars who mainly do domestic law are more likely to be associated with practical legal research.

A related question is whether, across law schools and countries, scholars engaged in international law (including comparative and European law) may gradually adopt a parallel approach to legal research. We therefore also calculated the mean scores per university distinguishing those from pure domestic legal scholars.[107]

[102] This may be different in areas of private business law (such as company law) where there could be closer links to disciplines such as economics and business studies. See also Adler and Simon, 'Stepwise Progression', at 180–181 (on approaches to private law by scholars using different methods).

[103] Respondent UEA 19. [104] Respondent UEA 3.

[105] Geoffrey Samuel, 'Is Law Really a Social Science? A View from Comparative Law', 67 *Cambridge Law Journal* 288 (2008).

[106] Respondent EDI 2.

[107] Thus, here we combined the numbers for 'international' and 'mixed domestic / international' since 'just international' has low *n*'s for some of the universities (see Table 1.3, above: only 1 for Düsseldorf and only 4 for Bucerius and Dublin).

Table 1.4 *Mean scores for international and 'mixed' legal scholars (and how they differ from those of pure domestic legal scholars).*

	Humanities	*Social sciences*	*Practical legal research*
Bucerius (n: 8)	3.00 (-0.33)	2.38 (+1.04)	4.63 (-0.71)
Düsseldorf (n: 6)	3.67 (-0.45)	2.17 (+0.34)	4.17 (+0.11)
Edinburgh (n: 36)	4.64 (-1.53)	3.33 (+0.33)	2.03 (+1.19)
UEA (n: 13)	3.85 (-0.32)	3.85 (+1.35)	2.31 (-1.03)
Dublin (n: 7)	5.71 (+1.38)	2.43 (+0.10)	1.86 (-1.48)
All (n: 70)	4.33 (-0.01)	3.13 (+1.03)	2.54 (-1.02)

It can be seen that in all five law schools international legal scholars are more likely to use methods of social sciences.[108] In return, they are less likely to associate with practical legal research. The main exception is Edinburgh, although it needs to be noted that, here, few respondents have no interest in international law (or comparative/European law; see Table 1.3) and, on average, the international scholars from Edinburgh are still less likely to be associated with practical legal research than those in three of the four other law schools.

In terms of convergence, however, we do not observe a similar method for international legal scholars, for example, given the continuing differences in practical legal research between the two German and the three other law schools.[109] This may be seen as a problem if we think that uniform application of international (and EU) law requires a similar approach across countries.[110] Yet some 'global' trends may lead to further changes, as the following will explain.

1.4.2 Dominant and Shifting Paradigms

In higher education studies it is discussed to what extent an academic discipline needs to share a certain level of homogeneity.[111] This goes back

108 See also Gregory Shaffer and Tom Ginsburg, 'The Empirical Turn in International Legal Scholarship', 106 *American Journal of International Law* 1 (2012).

109 This is also evident if one compares German and English-language textbooks on topics of international law, EU law and comparative law; e.g., the former ones tend to put a stronger emphasis on conceptual thinking, while the latter ones are more often structured as 'cases and materials'.

110 See van Gestel and Micklitz, 'Why Methods Matter in European Legal Scholarship', at 297.

111 See, e.g., Paul Trowler, 'Depicting and Researching Disciplines: Strong and Moderate Essentialist Approaches', 39 *Studies in Higher Education* 1720 (2014) (rejecting the view of 'essential characteristics which are all necessarily present in every instance').

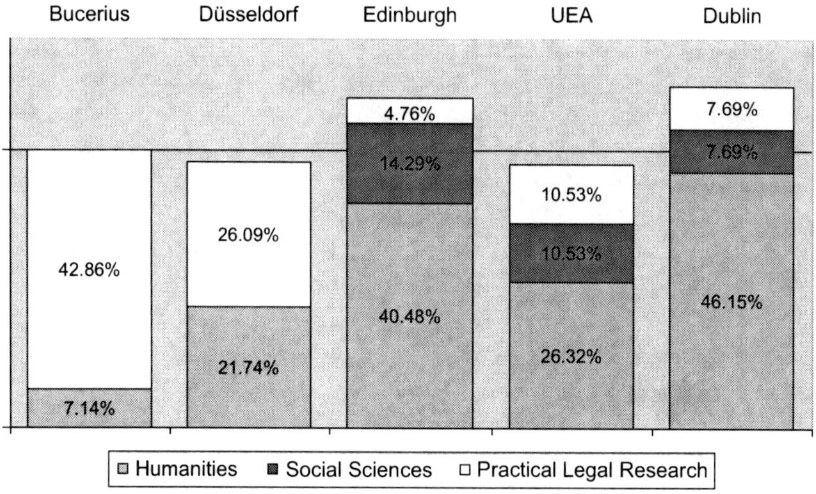

Figure 1.7 Frequency of a dominant paradigm.

to Thomas Kuhn who suggested that paradigms characterize 'coherent traditions of scientific research'.[112] While such coherence may indicate some stability, according to Kuhn, there can also be 'paradigm shifts' challenging current assumptions. Coherent traditions and corresponding shifts in legal research may also be identified with our survey approach. Yet, here, we will also have to consider that law is a diverse field,[113] in particular given the differences between countries and law schools.

1.4.2.1 Legal Scholars with a Clear Methodological Preference

Figure 1.7 presents the research preferences of those respondents who have assigned a score of six or higher (out of ten) to one of the three categories. Thus, these legal scholars seem to have a dominant research paradigm. Figure 1.7 shows that this is the case for around 50 per cent of the staff of each of the law schools, i.e., there is a roughly equal split between legal scholars who mix the three methods and those who predominantly use one of them.

[112] Thomas S. Kuhn, *The Structure of Scientific Revolutions* (Chicago: University of Chicago Press 3rd ed. 1996).

[113] Cf. Sanne Taekema and Bart van Klink, 'Legal Methods under Discussion', 1 *Recht en Methode* 1 (2011) ('In most sciences, generally accepted methods are the core of what constitutes the scientific discipline in question and what defines its scientific character. This is not the case for the discipline of law').

In three institutions more than 40 per cent of academics have the same dominant paradigm: humanities in Edinburgh and Dublin, and practical legal research at Bucerius. In such instances there may be some explicit or implicit pressure to follow this approach. The data also show that in the two German law schools practical legal research is the most frequent dominant method, whereas it is humanities in the three British and Irish law schools. Moreover, as noted previously,[114] only the three latter universities have some academic staff who consider themselves as 'full social scientists', for example, as they work as criminologists within a law school.

Overall, it can be seen that, at the levels of the law schools, there may be some support for a 'core of legal research'.[115] Such a position may extend to lawyers in legal practice: Pierre Bourdieu writes about the 'social cohesion' of scholars, 'designed to ensure the durable homogeneity of the habitus'. He then also mentions 'law' as a discipline as requiring a high level of cohesion, given that 'in the case of the jurists, a body of "authorities" cannot present itself in a state of disarray'.[116] Yet, this view of legal scholarship as supporting the need of legal practice may also have changed in recent years.

1.4.2.2 Changes of Research Methods

The respondents of our survey who were already academics ten years ago were also asked to indicate the methods they had used at that time. Figure 1.8 presents the result of these fifty-five respondents compared to the responses given by the same persons for their research preferences today. It can be seen that practical legal research has become less popular, and law as social sciences more popular, with a mixed development as regards law as humanities. This empirical finding shows a trend in line with our previous, more speculative, research about the developments in the United States, the United Kingdom and Germany.[117]

It is also possible to contextualize this trend within the wider debate about changes in legal research. Frequently, the question is raised whether Europe should follow US trends in legal scholarship and become

[114] See Section 1.3.3. See also Section 1.2.3 on the (possible) nonlegal origins of 'Law and Society'.

[115] Cf. Susan Bartie, 'The Lingering Core of Legal Scholarship', 30 *Legal Studies* 345 (2010).

[116] Bourdieu, *Homo Academicus*, at 65.

[117] Siems and Mac Síthigh, 'Mapping Legal Research', at 671–674. Similar for the Netherlands (based on an empirical study) van Boom and van Gestel, 'Rechtswetenschappelijk onderzoek'.

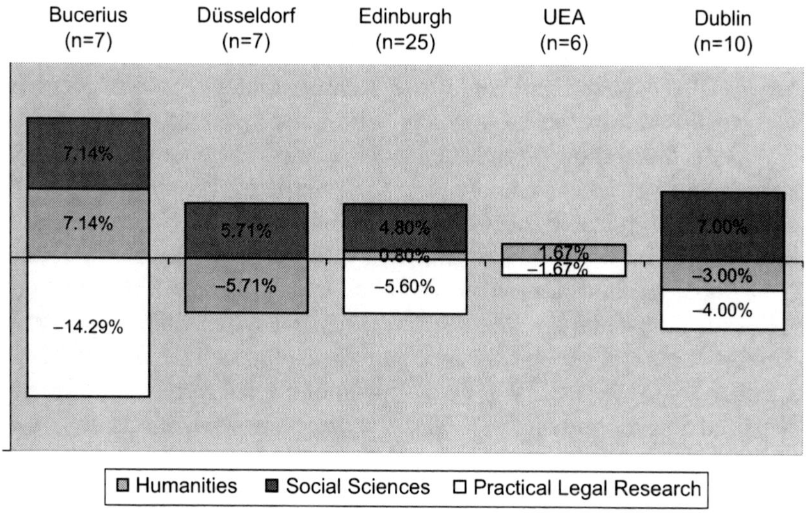

Figure 1.8 How did your methods change in the last ten years?

less focused on doctrinal legal scholarship.[118] Some even suggest that this is already reality. According to Mattias Kumm, there is a

> [S]alutary effect of American elite law school culture on European scholarship. It has encouraged European scholars to overcome the residual habits of a conceptually focused positivist complacency and more widely reembrace the study of law as a theoretically ambitious, internally multidisciplinary exercise.[119]

More cautiously, it may be said that, in Europe, legal scholarship is now a discipline in transition.[120] Of course, US legal scholarship is also a moving target.[121] In addition, the decline of doctrinal legal scholarship

[118] Cf. van Gestel and Micklitz, 'Why Methods Matter in European Legal Scholarship', at 292.

[119] Mattias Kumm, 'On the Past and Future of European Constitutional Scholarship', 7 *International Journal of Constitutional Law* 401 (2009).

[120] See van Gestel and Micklitz, 'Why Methods Matter in European Legal Scholarship', at 295 (on a recent Dutch research assessment exercise). See also Paul Chynoweth, 'Legal Scholarship: A Discipline in Transition', 1 *International Journal of Law in the Built Environment* 5 (2009); Cownie, *Legal Academics*, at 54 (discipline in transition).

[121] See, e.g., Victoria Nourse and Gregory Shaffer, 'Varieties of New Legal Realism: Can a New World Order Prompt a New Legal Theory', 95 *Cornell Law Review* 61 (2009) (on 'new legal realism' and 'cycles' with periods of more formalist and more socio-legal

may not be a matter of course: Rob van Gestel and Hans-Wolfgang Micklitz note the possible countertrend that the complex relationship between EU law and the law of the Member States requires 'doctrinal scholarship with its focus on interpretation and systematisation'.[122]

A good illustration of path-dependence and resistance is the discussion about a recent report by the German *Wissenschaftsrat*, a government-funded advisory body.[123] In line with the German tradition, this report notes the character of law as a 'professional discipline' (*Professionsfakultät*), seen as a discipline that is 'closely linked to both the academic system and the respective societal system'. The report also contains a modest support for more interdisciplinary legal scholarship at a subordinate level.[124] Yet even this modest suggestion is strongly criticized in a comment by a German professor who rejects any shift to 'law and' research, arguing that this would 'threaten what has made German legal science strong in the world: the dialogue between academia and judges, in particular the embedding of case law within legal doctrine'.[125]

It is also clear that the way legal research traditions change is often a complex one.[126] For example, while the individual researcher may follow a certain 'herd behaviour',[127] she is also able to find her own position within the academic field[128] – or even to shape the way paradigms may

approaches); Adam Liptak, 'The Lackluster Reviews That Lawyers Love To Hate' (*New York Times* 21 October 2013) available at www.nytimes.com/2013/10/22/us/law-scholarships-lackluster-reviews.html (discussing differences in peer review between law and other disciplines, and the impact of legal scholarship on judges and practitioners).

122 van Gestel and Micklitz, 'Why Methods Matter in European Legal Scholarship', at 294 (also ibid 310: revitalising doctrinal legal scholarship)

123 English version available at www.wissenschaftsrat.de/download/archiv/2558-12_engl.pdf

124 See Ralf Michaels, '"Law as the Study of Norms": Foundational Subjects and Interdisciplinarity in Germany and the United States' (19 February 2014), available at www.verfassungsblog.de/de/law-as-the-study-of-norms-foundational-subjects-and-interdisciplinarity-in-germany-and-the-united-states/ (interpreting the report as suggesting a 'subordinate role for interdisciplinarity').

125 Christian Wolf, 'Perspektiven der Rechtswissenschaft und der Juristenausbildung: Kritische Anmerkungen zu den Empfehlungen des Wissenschaftsrats', *Zeitschrift für Rechtspolitik* 20, 21 (2013) (own translation).

126 Cf. Brian R. Cheffins, 'The Trajectory of (Corporate Law) Scholarship', 63 *Cambridge Law Journal* 456, 458–477 (2004) (identifying five 'trajectories for legal research').

127 van Gestel and Micklitz, 'Why Methods Matter in European Legal Scholarship', at 305–307; van Gestel, Micklitz and Maduro, 'Methodology in the New Legal World', at 4.

128 Cf. also Cownie, *Legal Academics*, at 104–105 (autonomy as one of the advantages of academic life).

persist or be subject to change. This leads us to the more general questions about the implications of our findings.

1.5 Implications of Empirical Findings

It is often said that one cannot infer from 'is' to 'ought' statements.[129] Thus, our empirical study cannot, and did not aim to, establish that one particular method of legal research is 'better' than another one.[130] Yet, it is possible to draw the following implications from our empirical findings.

1.5.1 Thinking About Methods of Legal Research

The approach, underlying this chapter, suggests that one way of understanding methods is through surveys of self-identification supplemented by an analysis of the respective institutions. Thus, in the words of Rob van Gestel and colleagues, this is seen as a way of 'making the implicit explicit'.[131] We would suggest that the good response rate of our survey, as well as the observations made in the previous sections, also confirm the feasibility and value of such an approach, particularly when explicit consideration of methods is often absent from publications. But we also add a note of caution, from our experiences with carrying out the present project, that definitions and terms may not yet have a common understanding – and so, speaking the same language in a way that facilitates reasoned debate remains to be proven.

In substance, the fact that, according to our empirical findings, research methods in law differ considerably across countries can be considered as a major factor why we need to pay more attention to the

[129] The 'is/ought problem' goes back to David Hume, *A Treatise of Human Nature* (London: J. Noon 1739), 335.

[130] See also Siems, 'Legal Originality' (suggesting different ways of 'being original' in legal research); Jan Vranken, 'Exciting Times for Legal Scholarship', 2 *Recht en Methode* 42, 56 (2012) ('not to use the type of research as a quality indicator'); Ashish Kumar Singhal and Ikramuddin Malik, 'Doctrinal and Socio-legal Methods of Research: Merits and Demerits', 2 *Educational Research Journal* 252, 256 (2012) ('no hierarchy amongst methodologies').

[131] van Gestel and Micklitz, 'Why Methods Matter in European Legal Scholarship', at 313; van Gestel, Micklitz and Maduro, 'Methodology in the New Legal World', at 23. See also Smits, *The Mind and Method*, at 114–118 (on the merits and demerits of explicit research questions).

method of legal research, especially if a more transnational discussion is intended. Given these differences, legal scholars may find that they cannot simply take the method, predominant in their jurisdiction, for granted. This is most evident for comparative lawyers, as a meaningful comparative study not only requires familiarity with differences in legal rules but also with those in legal style, mentality and method. Moreover, as legal systems become more and more interconnected – due to international and European law but also due to soft factors – every legal scholar needs to have at least some familiarity with a 'foreign' understanding about the nature of legal scholarship. Awareness of these differences is particularly valuable for emerging scholars or potentially mobile researchers; recall that the mobility of academic researchers is a long-standing objective of EU projects and funding streams, as most recently restated in the Council Conclusions of 2012 on the European Research Area.[132]

Our empirical findings have shown that, in the law schools we studied, social science methods have become more and practical methods have become less popular in legal research. Growing interdisciplinarity suggests that legal scholars need to pay more explicit attention to methodological questions.[133] This is also in line with the finding of our survey as many of the respondents indicated that training (or lack of training!) is a key factor for the use of a particular method, and that understanding the diversity of methods facilitates other researchers in contextualizing published work and planning for collaborative efforts.[134]

Two further findings of this chapter are that there is often a split between legal teaching and research, as well as a divergence between the research preferences of more senior and more junior legal scholars.[135] It is suggested that greater awareness for the diversity of methods can reduce this split. In line with the practice in other academic disciplines, it would be plausible if legal education were to include more extensive training on diverse methodologies. This would then also be an advantage for more junior legal scholars as they would find it easier to choose and mix between different methods.

[132] www.consilium.europa.eu/uedocs/cms_data/docs/pressdata/en/intm/134168.pdf at paras 16–17. To be sure, this alone does not remove other institutional hurdles such as differences in research assessment procedures, see Section 1.3.4.2.

[133] See van Gestel, Micklitz and Maduro, 'Methodology in the New Legal World', at 8.

[134] See in particular Section 1.4.1.2.

[135] See Section 1.3.4.2 and Section 1.4.1.1.

1.5.2 *Preferences for One or the Other Research Methods*

This chapter argues that in order to understand different research preferences, the sources of influences upon the adoption of methods by an individual scholar, and by groups or institutions, must be observed and understood. We point towards possible determinants of preferences, and consider (from a range of sources) why these preferences exist. Such an understanding of the range of influences is a part of the overall shift towards the placing of methodology at the centre of the legal academic discourse.

For about half of the respondents of our study, these diverse sources of influence mean that they do not have a dominant method in terms of our three categories, but cluster in the 'inner triangle' of the ternary plots. More specifically, we found that in the two UK law schools there is considerable variety in the methods that legal scholars use. This may indicate that law is a discipline in transition, possibly because today 'we need more or other legal methods than in the past'.[136]

In particular, it is interesting to observe different preferences in and changes to 'practical legal research'. According to our data, legal scholars that focus on domestic law tend to engage in such research more frequently than comparative and international legal scholars. Thus, given the increased interaction between legal systems (as well as interactions between economies, cultures and societies), exclusive use of established, domestic legal methods can be seen as a barrier to the full realization of the potential of legal scholarship. As the audience for legal scholarship shifts,[137] so may methodologies. For those interested in promoting humanities and social science approaches, this is also an opportunity to highlight the benefits such approaches could bring; training and events could be targeted at the 'under-represented' group.

In four of the five law schools of our study academics answered that they use practical research methods less frequently than they did ten years ago. This may indicate a desire to shift towards more interdisciplinary approaches in the 'globalised world'. However, despite this trend, we

[136] van Gestel, Micklitz and Maduro, 'Methodology in the New Legal World', at 7.

[137] The question of the law school's relevant stakeholders has also been frequently discussed in the literature. See, e.g., Fiona Cownie (ed.), *Stakeholders in Legal Education* (Oxford: Hart Publishing 2009); Carel Stolker, *Rethinking the Law School: Education, Research, Outreach and Governance* (Cambridge: Cambridge University Press 2014), 290–324 ('Whose law school is it?'); Stefan PL de Jong et al., 'Evaluation of Research in Context: An Approach and Two Cases', 20 *Research Evaluation* 61, 68 (2011).

do not find a convergence in methods for legal scholars who, in our survey, indicate that they are engaged with research in international, European and/or comparative law. Thus, country differences are still more important for the choice of a particular method than the commonality of being an international scholar. This may be seen as a problem, for example, since EU law may be understood differently in different Member States.

1.5.3 Resistance and Complementarities

Parts of our empirical findings may be interpreted as verifying the existence of a dominant paradigm: at the country level, there are differences in particular between the two UK and the two German universities. In addition, at the level of individual scholars, we found the existence of a dominant model in respect of approximately half of the respondents. Both of these factors may prompt resistance against explicit legal methods which fall outside the 'preferred' category. This can be seen in particular in the controversies about the use of tools of New Public Management in universities, such as the RAEs in the United Kingdom.[138]

Criticism of our threefold categorization may also be some evidence of uncertainty in law schools on the approach to methods, with a related fear that categorization or identification is seen as a benchmark or a matter of 'right' and 'wrong'. For instance, some respondents argued that there was no distinction or were not clear on the difference between practical legal research and law as humanities, while others were content with this definition and happy to apportion work between these categories.[139]

In substance, a plausible reason for resistance may be that any shift towards one particular method may weaken the previous one: for example, as research in law becomes more closely aligned to (other) social sciences, it may lose its attractiveness to legal practice. It was already mentioned that in Germany such a line of criticism has been

[138] See, e.g., Richard Rutter, 'Margaret Thatcher Milk Snatcher: Higher Education and Universities', 12 April 2013, available at http://www.richierutter.com/margaret-thatcher-milk-snatcher-higher-education-and-universities/; Claire Shaw, 'Research That Doesn't Belong to Single Subject Area Is Deemed "Too Risky"' (*Guardian Professional* 21 November 2013), available at www.theguardian.com/higher-education-network/blog/2013/nov/21/interdisciplinary-research-ref-submission-university.

[139] Respondents BUC 4, EDI 18, UEA 10; cf HHU 19. See also Section 1.2.3 (explaining the categories).

directed against a recent report by the *Wissenschaftsrat*.[140] In the United States there has also been a lively debate about the apparent rise of 'impractical legal scholarship'.[141] Moreover, interdisciplinarity may – paradoxically – be criticized as reductionist far as it tells legal scholars to apply 'ready-made categories and logics of [another] discipline'.[142]

Reflecting on differences between legal research in civil and common law countries, it may therefore be tempting to suggest that one should achieve the 'best of all worlds' and mix the 'legal science' approach of the former with the interdisciplinarity of the latter countries.[143] Possibly, it could then be said that the two UK universities in our sample (in particular UEA) have already achieved such an equilibrium (including through staff turnover), given that all three categories carry some weight.[144]

However, it is not a matter of course that a mixed position is always the preferred one. The usefulness of such mixing may be limited by the 'institutional complementarities'[145] of academic structures, such as those we considered in our previous work on this topic regarding university governance and external funding of research.[146] This is not a new line of criticism. At a more philosophical level, Immanuel Kant noted that 'every science is in itself a system' and that therefore we should not simply treat it as 'part of another building' but 'must work with it architectonically, as

140 See Section 1.4.2.2.

141 E.g., Brent E. Newton, 'Preaching What They Don't Practice: Why Law Faculties' Preoccupation with Impractical Scholarship and Devaluation of Practical Competencies Obstruct Reform in the Legal Academy', 62 *South Carolina Law Review* 105 (2010); Harry T. Edwards, 'The Growing Disjunction between Legal Education and the Legal Profession', 91 *Michigan Law Review* 34 (1992). See also the recent discussion in blogs, e.g., http://balkin.blogspot.co.uk/2013/10/glass-houses-liptak-on-legal-scholarship.html and www.volokh.com/2011/07/23/chief-justice-roberts-and-current-legal-scholarship.

142 Mariana Valverde, 'Between a Rock and a Hard Place: Legal Studies Beyond Both Disciplinarity and Interdisciplinarity', 1 *Critical Analysis of Law* 51, 52 (2014) (in particular referring to economics). More generally see also Jerry Jacobs, *In Defense of Disciplines: Interdisciplinarity and Specialization in the Research University* (Chicago: Chicago University Press, 2014).

143 Markus D. Dubber, 'New Legal Science: Toward Law as a Global Discipline' (2014), available at http://ssrn.com/abstract=2462224.

144 See Section 1.3.2 as well as Figure 1.8 (showing little change in preferences over time).

145 For the general concept of 'institutional complementarities' see Peter A Hall and David Soskice, *Varieties of Capitalism: the institutional foundations of comparative advantage* (Oxford: Oxford University Press, 2001), 17.

146 See also Siems and Mac Síthigh, 'Mapping Legal Research', especially at 656–661 (faculties), 661–663 (research councils).

a building subsisting for itself'.[147] Thus, this may speak against any radical paradigm shifts in legal scholarship – especially given the existence, in some shape or form, of links between university law schools and the regulated legal professions.

Beyond these general trends, we would suggest that thinking about the direction of law as an academic discipline must not lose sight of the freedom of choice of individual scholars. For example, as there are more basic and more advanced forms of interdisciplinary legal research,[148] it should depend on one's own preferences and skills to what extent, say, a mere contextual legal analysis or a full-fledged empirical study is conducted. It is also clear – as it is reflected in some of the findings of our survey – that the choice of methods is closely related to the subject matter a legal scholar aims to research. Thus, overall, there are good reasons to welcome the growing diversity of modern forms of legal research.

1.6 Conclusion

The 'location' of an academic discipline is sometimes contentious. For example, while some medical researchers may consider themselves as part of the life sciences, others may emphasize the applied and practical nature of medical research.[149] Another contentious divide is between the social sciences and humanities; for example, in the United Kingdom, researchers in linguistics and media studies may either apply for funding to the research council for arts and humanities or the one for social sciences, depending on the specifics of their project.[150]

We suggest that legal scholarship is a field that is also torn between these dimensions of a practical discipline, the social sciences and

[147] Immanuel Kant, *Kritik der Urteilskraft* (1790), § 68 as translated by J.H. Bernard, *Kant's Critique of Judgement* (London: Macmillan, 1914).

[148] See, e.g., Mathias Siems, 'The Taxonomy of Interdisciplinary Legal Research: Finding the Way Out of the Desert', 7 *Journal of Commonwealth Law and Legal Education* 5 (2009).

[149] See, e.g., Thomas H. Broman, *The Transformation of German Academic Medicine, 1750–1820* (Cambridge: Cambridge University Press, 2002), 128; Robert E. Kohler, *From Medical Chemistry to Biochemistry: The Making of a Biomedical Discipline* (Cambridge: Cambridge University Press, 1982), ch. 6. See also the analogies between law and medicine in Stolker, *Rethinking the Law School*, at 139; John Flood, 'Doing Business: The Management of Uncertainty in Lawyers' Work', 25 *Law & Society Review* 41, 43–44 (1991).

[150] See www.ahrc.ac.uk/Funding-Opportunities/Research-funding/RFG/Additional-information/Pages/AHRC-and-ESRC-shared-interests.aspx.

humanities. For the purposes of this chapter, we conducted an empirical survey of five law schools across Germany, Ireland and the United Kingdom. We asked legal scholars to indicate to what extent they use the methods of 'legal research as part of humanities', of 'legal research as part of social sciences', and/or of 'legal research as akin to the analysis of law in legal practice'. Subsequently, we presented our results with ternary plots and other tools of classical and compositional statistics. Some of the differences in results can be explained by specific features of the respective law schools. But there is also a clear country effect since scholars of the two German law schools have a relatively strong preference for practical legal research and scholars of the three UK and Irish law schools a relatively strong preference for law as humanities, with law as social sciences also being relatively strong in the two UK law schools. Our analysis suggests that these differences are largely driven by institutional differences in higher education.

In the survey, we also collected information about possible determinants of research preferences at the individual level. We found that, for instance, international legal scholars (including EU and comparative lawyers) tend to be closer to the social sciences and that younger scholars and private lawyers tend to be closer to practical legal research. However, even within the group of international legal scholars, there are the profound country differences indicated in the previous paragraph. Still, our data show some signs of convergence since, across the five law schools, legal scholars told us that they tend to use practical legal research methods less often, and social sciences methods more often, than ten years ago. In the implications of our empirical findings we elaborated on these and other trends. While our study did not aim to establish that one particular method of legal research is 'better' than another one, we suggest that it shows that scholars need to pay attention to different methods, in particular the way these methods increasingly mix in order to achieve the 'best of all worlds'.

Future research could include content analysis of sample of papers and detailed interviews. This could enable researchers to identify differences between the (subjective) affinities or self-identification of scholars on one hand and the (objective) assessment of the use of methods by those same scholars.[151] We argue, however, that the views of the scholars we surveyed are deserving of consideration even without external review of their work as such self-identification may also have an aspirational dimension, thus indicating possible future developments in legal scholarship.

[151] See also Section 1.2.2.

Appendix 1.1

Email sent to legal scholars.

Survey on legal research methods	*Umfrage zu juristischen Methoden*
Dear [Name],	Sehr geehrter Herr / Sehr geehrte Frau [],
Mathias Siems and I are conducting a new study on research methods and it would be great if you could help us by responding to a few survey questions: it should not take more than three to five minutes!	ich hoffe, dass ich Sie um einen kurzen Gefallen bitten dürfte. Herr Dr. Mac Sithigh und ich arbeiten an einem Projekt zum Einsatz juristischer Methoden und es wäre toll, wenn sie uns dabei kurz unterstützen könnten: es sollte nicht mehr als drei bis fünf Minuten dauern!
We are studying legal research methods across a number of jurisdictions. The results will be presented at a workshop at the EUI in spring 2014 and subsequently published in a book, *Methodology in the New Legal World.*	Wir untersuchen, welche Methoden Rechtswissenschaftler in verschiedenen Ländern verwenden. Die Ergebnisse werden im nächsten Jahr auf einer Konferenz am Europäischen Hochschulinstitut (EUI) vorgestellt und anschließend in einem Buch zu „Methodology in the New Legal World'veröffentlicht.
Here is a link to the survey: [Link]	Die Umfrage findet sich auf [Link]
This link is uniquely tied to this survey and your email address. Please do not forward this message. Of course, the data will not be shared with anyone else - and in any subsequent publications we will only report the aggregate data per law school (and anonymize any free text comments).	Dieser Internetlink bezieht sich speziell auf Ihre Email-Adresse. Bitte leiten Sie ihn deshalb nicht weiter. Selbstverständlich werden Ihre Daten strikt vertraulich behandelt - und in den nachfolgen Publikationen werden wir nur die Aggregatdaten für jede Fakultät wiedergeben (und die Kommentare im Freitextfeld anonymisieren).

This project is being carried out in accordance with the University of Edinburgh College of Humanities and Social Science Code of Research Ethics. If you wish to withdraw from this project at any point after answering the survey, please contact us.

Many thanks!

Daithi and Mathias

Dr Daithi Mac Sithigh
Lecturer in Digital Media Law
Edinburgh Law School
University of Edinburgh
Old College, South Bridge
Edinburgh EH8 9YL
United Kingdom
www.law.ed.ac.uk/people/daithimacsithigh

Prof Mathias Siems
Professor of Commercial Law
Durham Law School
Durham University
Stockton Road
Durham DH1 3LE
United Kingdom
www.dur.ac.uk/mathias.siems/.

Unser Projekt wird in Übereinstimmung mit dem Forschungskodex der Universität Edinburgh, UK, durchgeführt. Es ist Ihnen jederzeit gestattet, Ihre Beteiligung zurückzuziehen.

Vielen Dank und beste Grüße,

Mathias Siems und Daithi Mac Sithigh

Prof. Dr. Mathias Siems, LL.M.
Professor of Commercial Law
Durham Law School
Durham University
Stockton Road
Durham DH1 3LE
United Kingdom
www.dur.ac.uk/mathias.siems/

Dr. Daithi Mac Sithigh
Lecturer in Digital Media Law
Edinburgh Law School
University of Edinburgh
Old College, South Bridge
Edinburgh EH8 9YL
United Kingdom
www.law.ed.ac.uk/people/daithimacsithigh.

Appendix 1.2

Questionnaire/survey.

Part 1. Which method(s) do you use in your research?

Please assume that there are three main methods of legal research:

- Legal research as part of humanities, i.e., analysis of legal texts (cases, statutes, etc.) using approaches similar to research in humanities (history, philosophy, literature, theology, etc.).
- Legal research as part of social sciences, i.e., analysis of law in its context, similar to research in social sciences (sociology, economics, psychology, etc.).
- Legal research as akin to the analysis of law in legal practice, i.e., similar to the approaches used by legal practitioners (judges, solicitors, etc.).

1) In your current research how frequently do you use one of these three approaches?

   Please allocate in total 10 points (e.g., something like 5/5/0 or 3/3/4). Note that mixtures can be the result of a mix of these approaches in individual pieces or across various research outputs. Please also note that these categories refer to method not substance.

2) If you were engaged in legal research in the course of

Teil 1: Welche Methoden verwenden Sie in Ihrer Forschung?

Bitte nehmen Sie an, dass die juristische Forschung in die folgenden drei Methoden untergliedert werden kann:

- Juristische Forschung als Teil der Geisteswissenschaft, d. h. Forschung, die juristische Texte (Gesetze, Gerichtsentscheidungen etc.) mit Methoden analysiert, die denen der Geisteswissenschaften (Geschichte, Philosophie, Literatur, Theologie etc.). entsprechen.
- Juristische Forschung als Teil der Sozialwissenschaften, d. h. Forschung, die das Recht im Kontext mit Methoden untersucht, die denen der Sozialwissenschaften (Soziologie, Ökonomie, Psychologie etc.). entsprechen.
- Juristische Forschung als ähnlich der juristischen Vorgehensweise der Rechtspraxis, d. h. Forschung, die das Recht mit Methoden analysiert, die denen von Rechtspraktikern (Richtern, Anwälten etc.) entsprechen.

1) Wie häufig verwenden sie diese Methoden in Ihrer gegenwärtigen Forschung?

   Bitte verteilen Sie insgesamt 10 Punkte (z. B. so etwas wie 5/5/0 oder 3/3/4). Hinweis:

employment ten years ago (i.e., in autumn 2003), how frequently did you use one of these three approaches at that time? If you were not so engaged, please skip this question.

Mischungen können sich daraus ergeben, dass Publikationen verschiede Methoden verknüpfen oder dass in verschiedenen Publikationen unterschiedliche Methoden verwendet werden. Bitte beachten sie auch, dass sich die drei Kategorien auf Methoden und nicht den Inhalt der Publikationen beziehen.

2) Wenn Sie bereits vor zehn Jahren (also im Herbst 2003) beruflich mit juristischer Forschung beschäftigt waren, wie häufig haben sie diese drei Methoden zu dieser Zeit verwendet. Falls dies nicht der Fall war, überspringen Sie bitte diese Frage.

Part 2. Further questions

1) Gender: (a) male; (b) female
2) Age: (a) 35 or younger; (b) 36 to 49; (c) 50 or older
3) Current position – please choose one: (a) Lecturer; (b) Senior Lecturer, Reader, Professor; for Germany: (a) Professor (W2, W3 or equivalent); (b) any other position
4) Form of employment – please choose one: (a) full-time; (b) part-time (if yes, please indicate percentage)
5) Main area of research – please choose one: (a) predominantly public law (including criminal law); (b) predominantly private law; (c) mixed. Note: 'predominantly' means at least 60% (e.g., if you have a 55% / 45% split please choose (c))

Teil 2: Weitere Fragen

1) Geschlecht: männlich, weiblich
2) Alter: 35 oder jünger, 36 bis 49, 50 oder älter
3) Gegenwärtige Position: Professor (W2, W3 oder entsprechend), sonstige Position
4) Art des Anstellungsverhältnisses: Vollzeit, Teilzeit (wenn ja, bitte geben Sie die Prozentzahl an)
5) Hauptforschungsgebiet – bitte wählen Sie eines: hauptsächlich Öffentliches Recht (inklusive Strafrecht); hauptsächlich Privatrecht; gemischt. Hinweis: 'hauptsächlich' ist definiert als mindestens 60% (wenn also z. B. die Aufteilung 55% / 45% ist, wählen Sie bitte (c)).

6) Scope of your research – please choose one (a) predominantly concerned with UK and/or Scots law; (b) predominantly comparative, international and/or European; (c) mixed. Note: 'predominantly' means at least 60% (e.g., if you have a 55% / 45% split please choose (c))
7) Training – please choose as many as applicable:
   (a) undergraduate law degree or equivalent (e.g., State Exam in German, JD in the US): (i) domestic (with variation for Scotland/UK), (ii) overseas
   (b) masters degree in law (or equivalent): (i) domestic and/or (ii) abroad
   (c) doctoral degree in law: (i) domestic and/or (ii) abroad
   (d) eligibility to practice law following professional legal qualification: (i) domestic and/ or (ii) abroad
   (e) degree other than law [free text: if yes, please specify level – undergraduate, master or doctorate – and discipline]

6) Umfang Ihrer Forschung – bitte wählen Sie eines: hauptsächlich deutsches Recht, hauptsächlich vergleichendes, internationales und/oder Europäisches Recht; gemischt. Hinweis: 'hauptsächlich' ist definiert als mindestens 60% (wenn also z. B. die Aufteilung 55% / 45% ist, wählen Sie bitte (c)).
7) Ausbildung – bitte wählen so viele wie zutreffend:
   (a) Erstes juristischen (Staats-) examen oder Äquivalent (z. B. LLB oder JD) in Deutschland, im Ausland
   (b) Juristischer Masterabschluss (z. B. LL.M.) in Deutschland und/oder im Ausland
   (c) Juristische Promotion in Deutschland und/oder im Ausland
   (d) Zweites juristisches Staatsexamen oder Äquivalent in Deutschland und/oder im Ausland
   (e) Abschluss in einer anderen Fachrichtung (bitte geben Sie den genauen Abschluss – Grad und Disziplin - an)

Part 3: Further comments

1) Do you have any further comments about our project? In particular, we would be interested in the reasons why you have adopted, or not adopted, particular approaches (e.g., this may refer to the topics such as

Teil 3: Weitere Kommentare

1) Haben Sie weitere Kommentare haben zu unserem Project? Uns würde insbesondere interessieren, warum sie bestimmte Methoden verwenden – oder nicht verwenden (z. B. könnte dies auf die

training in particular methods, collaborations, institutional influences) – and as far as your methods have changed in recent years, the reasons why this has been the case.	Ausbildung in bestimmten Methoden, Kollaboration oder institutionelle Einflussfaktoren verweisen) – und soweit sich Ihre Methoden verändert haben, warum dies der Fall war.
2) Are you willing to be contacted for a follow-up interview?	2) Wären sie bereit, wenn wir Sie gegebenenfalls zu einem Folgeinterview kontaktieren würden?

2

The Jurist in a Global Age

NEIL WALKER

2.1 The Jurist in Question

Whom do we think we are talking to when we look out across the Law School lecture theatre or seminar room? Are we instructing trainees? Are we simply supplying apprentices with those basic tools of the trade, a knowledge of statutes, case-law, contractual forms and the like – their sources and location, their place within a broader system of law, their general content, the rudiments of their interpretation and the basics of their circumstances of application – that will equip them in due course to advise clients on the multifarious ways and means of the law? Surely that is at least part of what we are supposed to be doing. But are we also attempting something grander? Are we seeking in addition to cultivate 'jurists'?

The vagueness that surrounds the term 'jurist' is testimony to how unsure we are about what such a larger ambition would entail, if, indeed, such an ambition were at all feasible. But if 'jurist' is to mean anything of substance – if it is to be more than a mere 'honorific title'[1] by which we as professors and teachers seek to dignify others and (not least) ourselves – then its specification must begin from the premise that a life spent in or around the law involves more than offering ourselves as the uncritical instrument of our clients' wishes, whoever these clients are and whatever their wishes might be. Rather, the jurist, in this basic and most preliminary conception, assumes a broader responsibility to ponder the idea and practice of law in general as a potentially valuable, and, in any case, value-relevant form of human activity.

I will have much more to say about the idea of the jurist, and about different and sometimes competing conceptions of what it is to be and become a jurist today. But an initial concern, and one that will bring

[1] R. Cotterrell, 'The Role of the Jurist: Reflections around Radbruch' (2013) 26 *Ratio Juris* 510–523

some coherence to our discussion of its various candidate meanings, is one of categorisation. For I want to argue that the juristic impulse negatively conceived – the basic 'anxiety',[2] ambition and determination to move beyond the narrowly client-centred conception of the practice of law, and beyond the educational horizons appropriate to that conception, in turn generates a range of different approaches to law's wider value-relevance, and so also to teaching and learning about what might be valuable in the law. The first part of the chapter will be taken up with an elaboration of that variety of sometimes-contending forces and considerations informing the role of the jurist, positively conceived.

In particular, I want to develop two interlaced sets of distinguishing factors. First, I pursue the longstanding if imprecise division of deep purpose and method between humanistic and social scientific visions of legal study as an intellectual activity that runs beyond the narrow template of professional knowledge acquisition.[3] Whereas their very shared appreciation that there is more to legal learning than an elementary knowledge of the content and systemic structure of a particular legal order suggests that these two visions should be seen as complementary rather than conflicting, that point is often neglected in the everyday politics of resource allocation in legal educational circles where a more basic distinction between narrowly professional and 'other' priorities tends to supply the implicit frame of reference. And in any case, even where a more embracing perspective is taken, questions of relative priority still arise, and so the distinction remains salient. Second, I seek to argue that for each broader vision there is an important set of internal divisions cutting across the basic distinction between humanities and social sciences, and in so doing also qualifying that basic distinction. This second variation involves a range of different practical orientations towards the idea and practice of law, namely *service*, *detached*, and *critical* orientations. Overall, this produces a framework that indicates a number of different emphases within any more expansive conception of legal education and inquiry, in so doing exposing the various challenges and pressures and highlighting the conflicting considerations to which the juristic mind-set is subject.

[2] M. Del Mar and C. Michelon (eds.) *The Anxiety of the Jurist* (Farnham: Ashgate, 2013).

[3] See e.g., D. Howarth, 'Is Law a Humanity (or Is It More Like Engineering)?' (2004) 3 *Arts and Humanities in Higher Education* 9–28; see also his *Law as Engineering: Thinking About What Lawyers Do* (Cheltenham: Edward Elgar, 2013); and see Chapter 1 in this volume.

In the second part of the chapter, having made this preliminary diagnosis, I want to reassess the adequacy of this framework to changing conditions. I examine how the development of an increasingly global outlook in law's normative ordering (and in the contestation of that ordering), as well as in its professional organisation, underlines the significance of both humanist and social scientific methods and perspectives in legal education. And in so doing, the new global outlook also causes us to loosen or revise some of the distinctions – both of deep method and practical orientation – upon which our categorisation of the variation of the juristic enterprise in a traditionally state-centred legal world is based. The global jurist may, in the final analysis, remain no easier a category to pin down than that of the local jurist, no less controversial to specify, no less challenging a role in any such specification, and no less complex a curricular puzzle. Arguably, however, with the emergence of the new global role – or at least new role dimension – some of the starker divisions and tensions inherent in the juristic approach no longer hold, and we can discern certain avenues of convergence of previously quite disparate horizons of thought and practice. What is more, consideration of the problems, possibilities and educational priorities associated with the role of the jurist in a global setting provides us with a clear window and a fresh perspective through which to renew our contemplation of the role of the jurist in general.

2.2 Disciplining the Study of Law

2.2.1 Between the Humanities and the Social Sciences

There is no bright-line division between the contemporary humanities and the social sciences. Nor should we expect there to be. Neither approach to knowledge and understanding was developed in contradistinction to the other. The humanities have a classical lineage, originally understood as an outgrowth of the liberal arts – as the set of skills appropriate to the Roman *liber* or freeman.[4] But even in their recognisably modern form, as they gradually came to be understood as a predominantly scholarly rather than a practical pursuit, the humanities

[4] For a recent magisterial treatment, see R. Bods, *A New History of the Humanities: The Search for Principles from Antiquity to the Present*, L. Richard, trans. (Oxford: Oxford University Press, 2014).

significantly pre-date the social sciences. And when the social sciences began to emerge in the eighteenth and nineteenth centuries their primary point of departure was not the long tradition of the humanities. Rather, as their name suggests, they developed as a counterpart to the rapidly developing natural sciences. For the social sciences were born of the attempt to put our investigation and understanding of the workings of the social world on a comparable footing to that of the workings of the material world. This was an enterprise, then, that sought such continuities as it could with the master sciences, but one that also acknowledged and explored the fundamental difference between the investigation of natural forces and that of human agency.

The quite different trajectories of development of the humanities and social sciences have produced criteria of distinction that are neither complete nor uncontroversial. In the most basic terms, the humanities study the products of human thought and feeling – of human culture in the round, and often in deep historical contemplation – so as to reveal the internal meaning of these products and what that might tell us about the human condition more generally. Their methods tend to be speculative, interpretive and reflective; their goal and purpose enhanced appreciation of what it is to be human; and, in a more applied mode, greater wisdom in practical judgement born of that enhanced appreciation. The social sciences are concerned with accounting for patterns of social belief and action in different settings. Their methods tend to be observational, explanatory and dispassionate; their goal and purpose the acquisition of greater knowledge of the causes and motivations of human behaviour; and, in a more applied mode, consideration of how changes in the causal or motivational background might affect and alter human behaviour.

The humanities tend to include cultural anthropology and ethnography, and often history itself, languages and linguistics, religion, literature and philosophy. They also embrace theoretical reflection on creative writing, in the performing arts of music, dance and theatre, and in the visual arts of painting, sculpting and architecture. The social sciences normally include social anthropology, physical anthropology, archaeology, economics, geography, political science, psychology, sociology and international relations. They may also cover history, linguistics and more self-consciously applied behavioural disciplines such as industrial relations, social administration and public administration. There is much overlap between the two lists. Anthropology and history are as likely to be studied for what they tell us about human potentials, pathologies and predicaments in general as they are to generate objective knowledge of how particular groups of people generate and respond to particular constellations of social forces. Even sociology, the generally recognised queen of the social sciences, is marked by a pronounced internal distinction between a quantitative approach in search of generalisable causal explanations and a more qualitative approach whose methods and ambitions of deep interpretation are more resonant of the humanities.[5]

If we consider the study of law, expansively conceived, under the umbrella of the humanities–social sciences distinction, the picture becomes even untidier. Legal studies manifestly cross the boundary between the humanities and the social sciences. On the one hand, law is a cultural product – an artefact – its actual and its ideal meaning, both in its manifold particular applications and more generally, a matter of interpretive or speculative judgement and of reflection on deep tradition. To that extent the study of law is a fit subject for the humanities? It supplies both a window *outwards* to the nature and limits of the collective human capacity for practical reason in the face of the fragilities of the human condition, and a window *inwards* to a special living tradition and systemic resource for treating projects and problems of our common life. On the other hand, law traces or otherwise helps reveal or produce certain regularities – whether causalities or propensities – in social relationships. We may understand and theorise these regularities, and how they influence or are influenced by law, in terms of political power and preference, economic motivation and incentive, psychological disposition or historical pathway. And in a more practical vein, both lawmaking in general and the resolution of particular legal disputes often rely upon certain empirical findings, which in turn may involve the deployment of social scientific methods. To that extent the study of law is a fit subject for the social sciences.

Yet law is not a 'pure' subject of the humanities, and certainly not a 'pure' social science. This is already superficially evident from the uncertain place of legal studies within the contemporary bureaucratic politics of higher education. In the organisation and funding of teaching and research by governments, universities and other bodies, law is sometimes characterised as one of the humanities, sometimes as a social science and sometimes as intellectually *sui genesis* or as occupying an indistinct or

[5] An interpretive approach whose lineage can be traced directly to Max Weber, generally considered as one of the founding fathers of modern sociology.

intermediate position between the two.[6] And if we dig deeper, while the 'impurity' manifests itself quite differently in the two cases, it derives from the same underlying source; namely, the very orientation towards a professional body of knowledge and practice from whose limited focus and restrictive priorities the humanities and social sciences perspectives struggle to free themselves. What is more, some of the tensions and countercurrents that arise in consequence of that struggle, as we shall see, also run in a similar direction.

2.2.2 *The Prominence of the Service Orientation*

2.2.2.1 Law in the Perspective of the Humanities

Considered in the perspective of the humanities, the study of law as a source of insight into our collective capacity to manage the human condition and as a resource of that collective capacity has certain unusual and distinctive features. As already noted, many humanities are primarily concerned with reflection rather than practice. That is certainly true of history, of large areas of philosophy, of literary criticism and of the study of the performing and visual arts. Others, at least in part, although often a secondary part, may be conducive to participation in a general social practice. For example, theology or the study of language forms may cultivate and facilitate our participation in an independent living practice of religion or language.

The study of law goes further, involving a more intimate relationship to practical activity. As we have already observed, it relates to a specialist practice of 'lawyering', and, in many of its forms, *serves* participation in that specialist practice. That is to say, the study of law is often in the service of a practice that, unlike the practice of language or religion, is not general within the community but is particular to a special occupational group, or at least requires investment in and commitment towards a distinct form of craft, skill or expertise. The primary service given to

[6] The evidence of mixed treatment is all around us in our daily academic life. I work in a School of Law that is located in a College of Humanities and Social Science, but within that college, my school stands quite apart from the larger School of Social and Political Sciences. One of the learned societies I am associated with, The British Academy, categorizes law as a social science, whereas another, the Royal Society of Edinburgh, treats law under a general head of Arts, Humanities and Social Sciences. The main UK humanities funding source, the Arts and Humanities Research Council, regards law as one of the humanities, while the main social sciences funding body, the Economic and Social Research Council, considers sociolegal studies within its remit.

participation in such specialist legal practice by those dedicated to the study of law is, of course, the academy-based preparation and cultivation of the skills of the participants in the specialist practice. In addition, it involves contributing to the body of knowledge that is the object of the specialism. That is to say, as well as servicing those learning the practice of law, legal scholarship and research, as it tends in a humanist direction, also services the body of legal doctrine that is the focus of their learning. In so doing, scholarship provides aid to those, in particular legal professionals, judges and legislative drafters, who as senior practitioners in the law cultivate and apply legal doctrine.

The role of expert legal scholarship of this kind has ranged from the modest to the ambitious, from textbook writing to the crafting of treatises, from the deferential to the assertive and from the disinterested to the engaged – from reportage, commentary and exposition, through advocacy and constructive suggestion, to the very occupation of the role of authoritative source of particular doctrinal rules or as systematisers and keepers of a particular doctrinal canon, with which the term 'jurist' is most prestigiously associated.[7] In its more creative and engaged modes, then, we find the most distinctive feature of legal scholarship conceived of as a humanist activity; namely, that the practice it services – the cultivation and application of legal doctrine – is not only the object of its teaching and study but also in some measure the product of its learning.

Clearly, then, there is much continuity between law understood as a narrow form of professional training, in which the service role is front and centre, and law understood under the sign of the humanities, in which the pull of the service orientation nevertheless remains strong. There is also, certainly, much added value. A humanities-based conception of law must also include, first, second-order reflection on the distinct character of law as a first-order interpretive practice. It must deal explicitly and from a general vantage point with the special kind of cultural product law is and the broad human purposes it seeks to serves; with the ways in which, as we have noted, it offers a window outwards to our broader capacity for practical reason and a window inwards to these general and distinguishing features of law, evidenced by our common legal heritage, as a special form of practical reason. This inquiry obviously brings in many of the topics familiar from legal philosophy, legal

[7] See e.g., J. Gordley, *The Jurists* (Oxford: Oxford University Press, 2013).

theory or jurisprudence syllabuses – the terminological variety itself a sign of methodological uncertainties and tensions surrounding legal education and scholarship[8] – from the search for generic or universal features of law, to an examination of law's basic ethical structure or purpose and its distinction from and relationship with other forms of normative order. This second-order reflection may also draw upon other fields within the humanities, in particular literature and history, as a source of insight into these large questions about the nature of law as a cultural product.

Law in the perspective of the humanities must offer, second, the kind of education in engaged legal reasoning – in law as a first-order interpretive practice – that Paul Kahn talks about in Chapter 13 of this volume ('Freedom and Method'). The cue is the irreducibility of legal norms and their deployment to a 'covering-law'[9] conception of rules and rule application, and recognition of the unavoidable element of creative judgement in its ongoing practice that law shares with all other cultural accomplishments that form the subject matter of the humanities. The emphasis is upon teaching by example and analogy – the Langdellian case method remains perhaps the most prominent example – and upon creating an environment of 'practicing the practice' of deploying the normative sources of the law not as formulae in the production of predetermined conclusions but as resources of active legal argument, persuasion and decision making. The aim is the cultivation of *phronesis* or practical wisdom;[10] in other words, nurturing the 'prudence' of the jurist. And as we have seen, the humanist method of legal education and scholarship also involves exposure to and engagement in the 'master' juristic practice of doctrinal articulation, refinement and development, a productive activity and craft skill or method which itself is closely related to and

[8] See e.g., W. Twining, *General Jurisprudence: Understanding Law from a Global Perspective* (Cambridge: Cambridge University Press, 2009), ch.1; R. Cotterrell, 'Why Jurisprudence is not Legal Philosophy' (2014) 5 *Jurisprudence* 41–55; and see also his *The Politics of Jurisprudence: A Critical Introduction to Legal Philosophy*, 2nd edn. (Oxford: Oxford University Press, 2009).

[9] On the distinction between a deterministic 'covering-law universalism' and an open-textured 'reiterative universalism', and its applicability over a number of areas of intellectual inquiry and public culture, see M. Walzer, 'Nation and Universe', in *Thinking Politically: Essays in Political Theory* (New Haven: Yale University Press, 2007) 183–218.

[10] See e.g., C. Michelon, 'But to Live Inside the Law, You Must Be Honest' in Del Mar and Michelon (eds.) *The Anxiety of the Jurist*, 83–100; see also Z. Bankowski, *Living Lawfully* (Dordrecht: Kluwer, 2001).

cultivated through the teaching and learning of legal problem-solving as a first-order interpretive practice.

Yet in all these activities the mark of the service orientation remains clear. In studying law as one of the humanities we are either reflecting in the broadest sense on the place and purpose of such a specialist normative service in our common life, or we are developing the deepest skills and forms of reflection attendant upon engagement in such a service, or we are involved in a form of normative production that contributes to the very resource upon whose exploitation the service is based.

2.2.2.2 Law in the Perspective of the Social Sciences

That law is not a 'pure' social science is more obvious. Rather, since Durkheim, it has been the object of social scientific theory and research, whether sociology, social psychology, political science, international relations or behavioural economics. Unlike the social sciences, law understood as legal doctrine does not supply an intellectual method for understanding regularities or explaining causal relationships in the world. Instead, the materials of law supply data to be studied to help account for or reveal these regularities and causalities. That is why we have the sociology *of* law, or of the legal profession, or the economic analysis *of* law, or a court-focused political science or international relations. Law is merely the specifier – that which defines the particular domain of social scientific study.

This generates two types of impurity, aside from the basic 'impurity' of law being the object rather than a form of social science. First, the pretheoretical specification of something called 'law' as the focus of a theoretical discipline such as sociology or political science might seem to beg the question. One of the preliminary tasks of social science in its efforts to go beyond lay understandings of the social world is surely to apply social science techniques to deconstruct 'folk' concepts such as 'law' (or, say, 'crime' or 'the family') rather than simply accept them in their already socially mediated form as providing the relevant horizon of inquiry. The sociologist or the political scientist should be as interested in why social groups code and construct some modes of regulation or social control as law and not others, in why different social groups draw the law/nonlaw boundary differently, and in what regulatory modes coded on either side of the boundary might have in common, as she should be interested in whatever features those regulatory modes conventionally regarded as law might share.

Second, and more urgently, even if the epistemological difficulties of law's already socially constructed meaning and range can be overcome, or can be bracketed, the motivation to circumscribe the object of study in these terms (*of* law) is often connected to a tendency to accept the issue definition favoured by legal practitioners and other professionals, and by the powerful political and economic actors on whose behalf they may act. The discovery and analysis of social scientific data about law, then, may be linked to the framing and remedy of certain problems in accordance with certain conventional understandings favoured by dominant social strata. Much research in this area, in other words, is or at least aspires to be 'applied' in a quite focused sense. Often endowed with the loose generic label of 'sociolegal research' or 'empirical legal studies', its purpose is to illuminate the working of certain institutions or processes of lawmaking, law-interpretation, law-application and law-reception with a view to their improvement in accordance with a preconceived public policy specification of what counts as a desirable solution.[11] This applies across the range of social scientific disciplines, whether it be criminologists or sociologists of deviance addressing patterns of rule infraction in criminal organisations or their law enforcement equivalents, institutional sociologists or political scientists comparing the structure of decision-making in courts to other decision making institutions, or law and economics scholars analysing the effectiveness of penalties and rewards as behavioural incentives in contractual and other devices of common agreement.

Again, therefore, as within the humanities research perspective, we see a service orientation very strongly at work in the social sciences perspective within legal education. In one sense, the link to the service orientation is less direct than in the case of the humanities. The service-oriented socially scientifically aware jurist *borrows* from the social sciences – from its data sets and methodologies of knowledge creation – in preparation and refinement of her practice as a creator, interpreter, or applier of legally relevant materials. The jurist with a humanities-based sensibility goes further, seeking to *incorporate* that sensibility into her basic role – understanding – in particular, a critically self-reflective perspective upon the kind of ethical practice law is (as expressed through its creation,

[11] The tension between a 'pure' sociology of law and applied sociolegal research, and also contestation over what counts as useful 'applied' knowledge, have been long-standing themes within many national academic environments. See, e.g., C. M. Campbell and P. Wiles, 'The Study of Law in Society in Britain', in (1976) 10 *Law and Society Review* 547–578; and on the American scholarship, see C. Seron, S. B. Coutin and P.W. Meeusen, 'Is There a Canon of Law and Society?' (2013) 9 *Annual Review of Law and Social Science*, 287.

interpretation and application), and how we might best contribute to that practice. In another sense, however, the service orientation is even stronger in the social sciences perspective. For to the extent that the social sciences remain other than and outside of law as forms of knowledge, this also tends to reinforce their subsidiary role. That they are merely borrowed underlines how they are seen by many as nothing more than a tool for the service-oriented lawyer seeking to 'engineer'[12] solutions to problems of human order, rather than as a perspective that might challenge the basic adequacy of our understanding of these problems, or of the basic social technologies, including law itself in some or all of its modalities, through which we address them.

2.2.3 Beyond the Service Orientation

The prominence of the service orientation within both humanities-based and social-scientifically informed conceptions of legal education generates a deep tension. If both these broader visions anticipate or respond to the inadequacies of a narrow professional conception of legal education, with its highly instrumentalised understanding of law as a client-centred activity, then it is ironic, if understandable, that the fruit of these perspectives should continue to bear such a strong service imprint. Understandable, because of the defining character of law and legal expertise as a specialist form of practical knowledge, and the necessity for any scheme of legal education, however widely drawn, to acknowledge and accommodate the centrality of this practice. Ironic, because to the extent that such accommodation also encourages a basic acceptance of the existing conditions of legal practice in our society, and so of the underlying set of assumptions and arrangements that privileges the role of law and legal expertise in our frameworks of self-government, this is at odds with the sceptically inquiring attitude to any species of received knowledge we find in both the humanities and the social sciences – the very attitude which accounts for and justifies their recruitment in aid of a larger conception of legally relevant scholarship and education in the first place.

Yet because of this tension, we also witness a considerable and growing resistance to the service orientation – even under its more generous cross-disciplinary canopy – within legal studies and the legal academy. In part, the explanation of this trend requires its own sociology. This

[12] Howarth, 'Is Law a Humanity?'.

would make particular reference to the worldwide growth of an autonomous university-centred legal academy since the mid twentieth century, and how this has encouraged a certain type of legal scholarship that assumes a greater 'critical distance' from practice, sponsoring currents of thought that challenge law's central role in the expression and reinforcement of the prevailing social order. In part, however, the explanation incorporates an older vintage. For it speaks again, and more forcefully, to the deeper animating spirit behind both the humanities and the social sciences, which, as we have noted, refuses to take for granted any forms of conventional wisdom and practice on their own terms: and it recalls how this spirit has infused legal education and scholarship over a much longer period, reaching back to its mediaeval and early modern origins.[13]

This is complex terrain, and any general mapping of it is bound to oversimplify. But with that caveat in mind, we can see these alternative social and intellectual forces as producing 'critical' and 'detached' counter-orientations to the broader service approach. For both humanities-based and social science–based approaches to legal inquiry and education have also generated certain projects and movements that are deeply critical of extant legal practice and doctrine or of the underlying general legal order, and others that stress their detachment from service concerns and the controversial value preferences associated with these service concerns.

In the case of critical approaches, there is a tradition of humanities-based philosophical work and of social scientific inquiry, in either case with strong roots in Marxist and other social egalitarian thought, which examines and reveals the role of law and lawyers in the production and maintenance of systems of societal domination based on class or other forms of social and economic stratification. While much of this research is either within social and political philosophy, and so clearly humanities based, or is explicitly social scientific in methodology, we also see more overlap between the two approaches than in the mainstream service orientation. Normative critique aided by the tools of moral and political theory is often joined in the one analysis with empirical accounts of law as a product of embedded power and a vessel of ideology. This becomes more pronounced as we enter the contemporary phase of critical legal scholarship; in the growth of Critical Legal Studies in the United States, which develops the more radical aspects of the legal realism of the

[13] See e.g., Cotterrell, *The Politics of Jurisprudence*, and 'Why Jurisprudence Is Not Legal Philosophy'.

previous generation; and in similar critical law movements in other parts of the world; and in other self-conscious forms of 'outsider jurisprudence',[14] including the broad churches of feminist legal theory and critical race theory and the somewhat more contained perspectives of such research streams as queer theory or critical Latino/a theory.[15] In all these cases, moreover, the critique of the mainstream academy and the reaction to its service orientation becomes more directed and more explicit than previously. Legal education in its dominant mode, even as it purports to take a more expansive approach, is still viewed as a more or less sophisticated training in professional hierarchy,[16] and as a means to marginalise the broader political nature of law in favour of its reductive conception as a neutral set of skills blind to any agenda other than client needs.

If we turn to the 'detached' stream, again we can see how this connects to the deeper methodological premises of both the humanities and the social sciences. If one manifestation of their sceptical temper is a critical orientation towards their subject matter, another is a heightened sense of dispassionate inquiry – of an intellectual endeavour not so much critical of the service orientation as insistently uncompromised by its insider commitments. This is most obviously true of the social sciences, with their lasting debt to the scientific method of disinterested observation and investigation,[17] but it also characterises the search for an Archimedean vantage point of inquiry or for context-independent truths of the human condition that we sometimes find in the humanities.[18] The particular motivation behind such approaches may range from the purely epistemological – a search for a form of knowledge that escapes the bias of prior commitment – to the consciously ideological – the presentation of one's perspective as all the more intellectually privileged for somehow transcending particular concerns and limitations. And so the knowledge

[14] M. Matsuda, 'Public Response to Racist Speech; Considering the Victim's Story' (1989) 87 *Michigan Law Review* 2320, at 2323.

[15] For a good overview of CLS and associated or similar movements, see B. Bix, 'Modern Critical Perspectives', in *Jurisprudence: Theory and Context*, 6th ed. (London: Sweet & Maxwell, 2012) 235–256.

[16] See e.g., D. Kennedy, 'Legal Education as Training for Hierarchy' in D. Kairys (ed.) *The Politics of Law* (New York: Pantheon, 1990) 38–58.

[17] See Campbell and Wiles, 'The Study of Law in Society in Britain'; Seron, Coutin and Meeusen, 'Is There a Canon of Law and Society?' .

[18] For discussion and critique, see R. Dworkin, 'Hart's Postscript and the Point of Political Philosophy', in *Justice in Robes* (Cambridge, MA: Harvard University Press, 2006) 140–186.

claims may be more or less modest. On the one hand, certain strains of so-called 'descriptive'[19] legal positivism within legal philosophy, for example, make no evaluative claims or even 'thick' explanatory claims about the world. And certain types of empirical legal research, too, involve no commitment either to how the world should be (re)constructed or even, as a matter of broad social ontology, to how it is and could be fashioned across broad social structures, but merely limit themselves to narrowly institution-specific forms of observation and data documentation.[20] On the other hand, certain normative projects within legal philosophy, perhaps most explicitly and ambitiously in the natural law tradition, but also within a certain tradition of legal philosophy more broadly – including the normative strain of legal positivism, involve bolder context-independent claims about the place of law in the general scheme of things and the universal or broadly generalisable qualities it might possess.[21] Equally, certain more ambitious projects within the social sciences, from Weber onwards, have made very broad empirically grounded claims about the relationship of law to wider social structures, to world-historical patterns in the evolution of these structures, and as to the socially conditioned functions and limits of law more generally.[22]

The lines distinguishing the service orientation from the critical and detached orientations are often blurred. Some approaches can be highly critical of prevailing patterns of legal and broader political and economic order yet still focus on ways and means of improvement.[23] Equally, certain detached perspectives, though motivated by an aspiration to provide disinterested knowledge, can generate insights that may be and

19 See, e.g., J. Waldron, *Law and Disagreement* (Oxford: Oxford University Press, 1999) 166–168.

20 For a comprehensive overview of the wide range of contemporary empirical legal research, see P. Cane and H. Kritzer (eds.) *The Oxford Handbook of Empirical Legal Research* (Oxford: Oxford University Press, 2010).

21 For a thoughtful defence of this type of approach, see J. Gardner, 'Law in General', in *Law as a Leap of Faith* (Oxford: Oxford University Press, 2012) 270–302.

22 M. Weber, *Economy and Society*, G. Roth and C. Wittich (eds.) (New York: Bedminster, 1968).

23 A well-known contemporary example would be the post-Marxist critical approach of the late Frankfurt School centred around the work of Jürgen Habermas. Although deeply critical of the way in which law as a 'medium' sustains deep economic and other systemic inequalities, Habermas nevertheless also defends law, including certain concrete constitutional forms supplied by modern law, as a potentially emancipatory 'institution' – a means by which more progressive features of the cultural 'life-world' can be sustained and communicatively open democratic processes can be generated ; see e.g., his *Between Facts and Norms*, W. Rehg, trans. (Cambridge: MIT Press, 1996).

are sometimes used by scholars and teachers whose priorities and commitments lie in the area of informing and so servicing the existing needs of the legal system. In general, however, the boundaries remain significant. Much critical literature is committed to deconstruction rather than construction, to forms of challenge that would require transformation rather than amelioration of existing legal structures. And certain disinterested perspective located at the more abstract heights of analytical jurisprudence or in the broader historical tradition of the social sciences lack the purchase upon immediate patterns of law and legal thinking that would suit and facilitate a service orientation, and would resist any attempts to be invoked for these purposes

2.2.4 Juristic Fault-Lines

Earlier, we suggested that the responsibility of the jurist, in looking beyond a narrow client-centred conception of lawyerly practice, was to take seriously the ways in which the practice of law in its various forms was a deeply and pervasively value-relevant activity and, it follows, to take seriously the responsibility of the practicing lawyer to engage with law's broader ethical implications. In recent studies, Roger Cotterrell has aptly summed up this broader aspiration as embracing a commitment to 'analysing, protecting and enhancing the *general well-being or worth of law as a practical idea*'.[24] Prompted by the work of the German scholar Gustav Radbruch during and after the Weimar Republic, Cotterrell proceeds to explore the contending pressures faced and the precarious balancing required in pursuit of such a role. He argues that law can be thought of from this most broadly ethically sensitive perspective as involving a weighing amongst three separate but always contextually related values; namely justice, order or security and orientation to a sense of overall purpose framed by different social and historical conditions. The resulting triangle is one of 'variable geometry'[25] in two senses. First, the relationship between the three values is fluid, with the order of priority between justice, security and social purpose altering according to circumstances. Second, the actual content of the social purpose value varies according to cultural context, as does the way in which this value helps shape and constrain the other values of justice and order.

[24] Cotterrell, 'The Role of the Jurist', 510. [25] Ibid., 516.

Cotterrell's formulation is useful in capturing both the abiding significance of the juristic role and its perennial tensions. On the one hand, he identifies the key motivational impulse behind the juristic role, positively conceived: the striving to maintain and enable the flourishing of the idea of law as a special kind of practice. On the other hand, by placing two fundamental and universal legal values – justice and order – in a relationship of internal balance with a culturally particularistic idea of social purpose, he demonstrates why that striving can only ever deliver provisional and partial success. Provisional, because, as is obvious, social purposes and priorities both vary across cultures and change over time within particular cultures, as does the relationship of these purposes and priorities to justice and order. Partial, because in any case the reconciliation of certain universal and timeless values with other particular and context-sensitive ones will always be incomplete, involving both epistemic doubt as to the nature and precision of the universal values and a trade-off between the competing goods these different and perhaps incommensurable orders of value – universal and particular – represent.

The tensions identified by Cotterrell in the role of the jurist are reflected in the divisions within the structure of advanced legal thought identified above. On the one hand, humanities-based inquiry tends to be more interested in the general context-independent values of justice and order, while social scientific inquiry focuses on the cultural and temporal variety of social purpose. But, as with the humanities/social sciences distinction more generally, this is a crude and porous boundary. On the other hand, the difference in practical orientation between service, critical and detached approaches speaks to more fundamental fault-lines within the juristic guardianship of the law's well-being. The service orientation speaks to the primacy of purpose and the immediate social context. The critical orientation speaks against just that societal bias, and the law's role as a dominant expression of societal bias, often in the name of other and supposedly universal values. The detached approach may be wary of either commitment, its preference for disinterested observation and analysis a measure of its implicit or sometimes explicit[26] acceptance that the contending impulses within the triangle

[26] Cotterrell's own approach is one that accepts that the jurist's solution will ultimately be societally specific, but also one that continues to operate from a disinterested perspective which recognizes and seeks to emphasize the contingent nature of any such solutions.

cannot be resolved – that our observation of the law and all its works can expose the tension between universal and particular in a salutary fashion but never fully overcome that tension.

2.3 The Jurist in a Global Age

2.3.1 The Coming of Global Law

Over the last half-century or so, responding to and reinforcing the growth in nonstate legal forms, there has been a gradual yet cumulatively profound move away from the predominantly state-centred understanding of legal order of the modern age towards one in which transnational and global understandings of legal authority have begun to accompany and in some cases rival these state-centred conceptions. There is massive literature on these developments, and this is not the place to explore them in detail or explain their deep causes.[27] Instead, what I want to do is concentrate on certain features of this transformation in how law is distributed and how it is authorised that connect closely with possible changes in the juristic mind-set whose basic structure we have set out, and on the shifting educational and research priorities associated with these changes.

In other work I have sought to focus on one aspect of the move away from a state-centred conception of legal order which does not seek to capture all aspects of postnational law in its kaleidoscopic variety, but which nevertheless seems to go to the heart of what is distinctive about the new poststate phase and about the role of the academy in this.[28] My point of departure has been to investigate a deeper commonality beneath the variety that is present at the increasingly popular semantic surface of 'global law' (and its functional equivalents). In so doing I have sought to define global law as one particularly developed and significant subset of transnational law, embracing *any practical endorsement of or commitment to the universal or otherwise global-in-general warrant of some laws or some dimension of law.*[29]

The emphasis on a universal or at least global-in-general warrant is intended to convey the idea of a jurisdictionally unbound law; it is one that knows no direct or indirect (e.g., through citizenship) territorial

[27] See, e.g., Twining, *General Jurisprudence*; see also N. Walker, *Intimations of Global Law* (Cambridge: Cambridge University Press, 2015).
[28] Walker, *Intimations of Global Law*. [29] Ibid., 18.

limits but is instead, within its own material remit, planetary in extension. The 'globality' of global law, then, does not depend upon source or pedigree, but upon intended destination. Global law may be produced at the global institutional level (e.g., the United Nations) or in global conventions of rule formation (e.g., general international law), but it may equally be posited at the national or other local or site-specific level through notions such as 'universal jurisdiction'; or, more commonly, it may be found in the cross-site acknowledgement and development of a shared body of doctrine or general legal world view. In this broad perspective, we can point to a large number of contemporary trends under the auspices of global law.

Global law so defined, whether explicitly so-called or implicitly understood as such, involves various different ways of imagining – and indeed *imaging* – law on a global scale as somehow 'containing' and shaping a more expansive domain of national and transnational legal variety. Global law, therefore, in its jurisdictional generality, never operates in isolation but always 'acts upon' other laws in their jurisdictional particularity and diversity. We may group these different approaches to global law, depending upon how they treat that underlying world of legal variety, into either *convergence-promoting* approaches or *divergence-accommodating* approaches.[30]

The convergence-promoting approaches cover both *structural* and *formal* extensions of public international law beyond the traditional picture of a merely 'transactional' law of voluntary obligations between states. These candidates for global law are exemplified, respectively, by a UN Charter-centred institutional hierarchy sharpened through a non-consent based and so globally pervasive use-of-force capacity, and by the reconceptualisation of international law as a formally integrated, state-consent-independent planetary legal system complete with general principles, obligations *erga omnes*, *ius cogens*, and so forth. In both cases the prevailing juridical image is one of a *pyramid*. Also within the convergence-accommodating basket we find a variety of *abstract-normative approaches*. These range from general doctrinal perspectives, such as a global human rights catalogue with (all) persons rather than states as ultimate legal subjects, to prepositive or protopositive framing ideas, such as the cosmopolitan guiding principles (e.g., accountability, participation, public reason, subsidiarity and human rights protection) identified by

[30] Ibid., ch. 3

various commentators,[31] or the neo-Habermasian notion of a universal code of legality,[32] or various recent formulations of a global rule of law.[33] Here the defining image is of the container, either the overcontainer or *umbrella* of abstract doctrine or principle, or the undercontainer or *vessel* of pre-positive common code.

The divergence-accommodating perspective includes *laterally coordinate approaches* such as the emergence of a new global 'law of conflicts'[34] through broader nonstate centred interjurisdictional choice of law processes and mechanisms in what was traditionally called 'private international law', as well as the plethora of new transnational constitutional and other legal pluralisms. The image here is of links in a vertical *chain* – of thin principles of mutual accommodation between different legal orders[35] Another divergence-accommodating approach focuses on those *functionally specific regimes* concerned with thematically circumscribed public goods in which the entire planet is the relevant community of risk or fate, as is gradually and unevenly emergent in areas such as climate change, migration and nuclear nonproliferation. The image here is of the *segment* – the slice or section of which presupposes a global whole but, rather than looking for a common legal theme across the whole, is concerned with only one section of that whole.[36] In addition, there is a further divergence-accommodating approach to global law involving the merger of existing legal fields into new hybrids or composite fields. These include the so-called new 'law of peace'[37]

[31] See, e.g., M. Kumm 'The Cosmopolitan Turn in Constitutionalism', in Dunoff and Trachtmann (eds.) *Ruling the World* (Cambridge: Cambridge University Press, 2009) 258–325; R. Domingo *The New Global Law* (Cambridge: Cambridge University Press, 2010).

[32] Developed by Klaus Gunter; see, e.g., 'Legal Pluralism or Uniform Concept of Law?' (2008) 5 *Journal of Extreme Legal Positivism* 5.

[33] See, e.g., G. Palombella, 'The (re)Constitution of the Public' in C. MacAmhlaigh, C. Michelon and N. Walker (eds.) *After Public Law* (Oxford: Oxford University Press, 2013) pp.286–310.

[34] See e.g., C. Joerges, P. F. Kjaer and T. Ralli, 'A New Type of Conflicts Law as Constitutional Form in the Postnational Constellation' (2011) 2 *Transnational Legal Theory* 153; H. Muir Watt, 'Private International Law Beyond the Schism' (2011) 2 *Transnational Legal Theory* 347.

[35] See e.g., N. MacCormick, *Questioning Sovereignty* (Oxford: Oxford University Press, 1999); N. Walker, 'The Idea of Constitutional Pluralism' 65 *Modern Law Review* 315 (2002); N. Krisch, *Beyond Constitutionalism: The Pluralist Structure of Postnational Law* (Oxford: Oxford University Press, 2010).

[36] Walker, *Intimations of Global Law*, 118–125.

[37] C. Bell, *On The Law of Peace: Peace Agreements and the Lex Pacificatoria* (Oxford: Oxford University Press, 2008).

or 'humanity's law',[38] both models involving a fresh mix of international criminal law, human rights law and other cognate elements to provide a new conception of global justice in the area of conflict resolution. They also include the new global 'law of recognition',[39] vastly extended from the traditional state-centred international law of recognition to cover the dignitarian and participation dimensions of recognition for all active contemporary global constituencies, women, racial and religious minorities and so forth, previously denied them. Again, in all these framing initiatives, what is striking is the movement beyond the boundaries of international law as interstate law, or indeed constitutional law as intrapolity law, in search of a warrant that is genuinely global in its deep justification and in its jurisdictional reach. The image here is of law as *flow*, of a series of tributaries merging into a wider but still clearly embanked global legal river. In all cases, those who coin the relevant term are seeking to capture and reinforce what they already understand as an incipient trend.

A final group of global approaches to law also suggests a fluid movement, though here the idea of a common historical *thread* is key. These include themes such as global constitutional law or Global Administrative Law,[40] and revived interest in the concepts of *ius commune* and *ius gentium*,[41] rather than hybrids of disparate trends; however, these are merely adaptations of a venerable legal discourse to the new global stage. These tend, moreover, to be highly open-ended, capable of being either convergence-promoting or divergence-accommodating, and so overlapping heavily with the approaches already mentioned. For example, global constitutionalism can focus on the convergence-sponsoring 'global constitution' of the UN, but equally on the thin intersystemic links of constitutional pluralism, or on Gunther Teubner's functionally segmented 'societal constitutionalism' in which the regulatory world is divided up into a series of self-contained spheres (sport, science, the Internet, etc.), each with its own profoundly different steering logic.[42] Here the idea of global law reaches its limit of open texture, the common

[38] R. Teitel, *Humanity's Law* (Oxford: Oxford University Press, 2011).

[39] E. Tourme-Jouannet, 'International Law of Recognition' (2013) 24 *European Journal of International Law* 667–690.

[40] See, e.g., the signature article by B. Kingsbury, N. Krisch and R.B. Stewart, 'The Emergence of Global Administrative Law' (2005) 68 *Law and Contemporary Problems* 15.

[41] J. Waldron, *'Partly Laws Common to All Mankind': Foreign Law in American Courts* (New Haven, CT: Yale University Press, 2012)

[42] See e.g., G. Teubner, *Constitutional Fragments* (Oxford: Oxford University Press, 2012).

language as much a cue for disputation as the trace of a common code. It remains remarkable, however, that the common term of trade in this context of disputation remains law's potentially *global* warrant.

In all of these variants global law emerges in response to questions about the uncertain basis of legal authority in a world in which the 'box matrix' of mutually exclusive state sovereignty no longer provides a sufficient or even dominant meta-authoritative global principle and guide. In all spheres of social and economic life, globalisation, with its unprecedented compression of time and space and connection of far-flung processes and events,[43] creates and amplifies new territorially unbounded commonalities and also new territorially unbounded differences in respect of interests, identities and values. Law is no exception. Each of the global law models purports to answer to the ways in which transnational law, by introducing regimes and patterns of law that are nonstate-centred or nonstate-contained – typically in response to the intensification of political, military, economic or cultural forces that are similarly state-uncontained – unleashes and places in dynamic tension new patterns of legal commonality and difference. Both convergence-promoting approaches and divergence-accommodating approaches to global law, as already noted, set out in their different ways to contain and reorder 'unruly' elements in the transnational mix. They do so whether by focusing on continuity, unity and hierarchy, and advancing new forms of universal or general normative leverage, as in convergence-promoting approaches; or by focusing on difference, particularity and heterarchy, and so either connecting or delimiting the transnational fragments, as in divergence-accommodating approaches. In so unfolding, they may supplement one another, but equally, as in the relationship between the new legal cosmopolitanism and the new legal pluralism, or between a single postinternational global legal order and globally segmented and fragmented regimes, they may challenge and provoke each other in a relationship of productive tension.

Global law, then, involves the development of new if typically less pervasive meta-principles that challenge and moderate rather than replace the previously dominant meta-principle of state sovereignty. They do so by reframing and refashioning existing and emergent doctrinal and institutional tendencies in ways that are appropriate to the increasingly dense planetary interdependence of legal jurisdiction and

[43] See e.g., A. Giddens, *The Consequences of Modernity* (Stanford: Stanford University Press, 1990).

regulatory purpose. These different conceptions of global law, with their various images of the legal world – pyramid, umbrella, vessel, chain, segment, flow and thread – stand in a complex and shifting relationship, one that is as much about complementarity as conflict and in which there is no prospect of final settlement.

2.3.2 *Situating the Global Jurist*

A number of points stand out from this brief sketch of forms of global law as particularly significant for our understanding of the role of the jurist in a global age, and of what this implies for the place of legal education and research. First, and most basically, if, as Cotterrell suggests, the jurist should be concerned about the 'general well-being' of the law, then a legal education fit for a jurist must take close account of the new interdependencies of transnational and global law set out above. While it has never been the case that a lawyer could satisfy his juristic conscience by attending only to the domestic legal order and its ethical underpinnings, but was required also to be curious about the nature and effects of international law and the example of other legal orders, the need to look beyond the local is now more palpable. The jurist of the global age must perforce be interested in the rich diversity of transnational law, in the national legal orders with which transnational law interacts, and in the ways in which the universal or general claims of an increasingly influential body of global law draw upon different legal, ethical and philosophical traditions. The jurist of the global age must, therefore, engage in 'general jurisprudence' in the sense captured by William Twining, namely the study of the whole range of 'legal traditions, cultures, or orders . . . from the micro-comparative to the universal'.[44]

Second, the jurist in the global age also has a much more specific and active role to play in the generation and justification of the new legal forms we associate with global law. As we have noted, the jurist has always been involved in the production of the very material that is also the object of analysis. This role is amplified in the new global context. In part, the explanation for this is a matter of occupational sociology. Generally speaking, there is a much greater continuity and much greater fluidity of role specification and professional organisation within what we

[44] Twining, *General Jurisprudence*, 20–21.

may call the community of 'global law-craft'[45] between practitioners and scholars than one finds in the typical national context. Lacking the prominent and well-embedded official casting of the typical national system, the potential for role ubiquity and versatility within the global system, and for elite networking across the range of roles, is far greater. Executive, judicial, arbitration and advisory roles are more likely to overlap or be severally pursued; professional and scholarly elites are more likely to intermingle and to be engaged in the same fora, networks and associations, and to speak to the significance of the same globally ramified judicial and other legal events.[46]

However, this sociological shift is also in some measure merely a reflection – and reinforcement – of a deeper factor explaining the greater involvement of the jurist in the production of global law. For it is precisely the unsettled quality of legal ordering to which global law responds and which it in turn displays – the erosion of taken-for-granted frameworks of legal authority – which offers the global jurist an expanded jurisgenerative role. As we have seen from the catalogue of global law, the academic community are often the map makers and symbolic entrepreneurs of the new legal globality, and so are heavily implicated in the naming and framing. In some cases, as my definition suggested, the global law model is more about 'commitment' than 'endorsement', projection than refinement, construction than reconstruction, and in these areas, such as global constitutionalism, Global Administrative Law, many of the abstract-normative approaches, global legal pluralism and the new global hybrids, the academic community is particularly to the fore. In other cases – for example, the structural and formal models, or the functionally specific global regimes – it is more a question of the incremental extension and retailoring of existing practice, but even here the scholarly community is involved in the work of persuasive adaptation. Global law is never either purely speculative nor disinterestedly descriptive; it always has an element of 'practical' engagement, even if this may be at some level of abstraction from recognised doctrine (hence the definitional reference to 'some laws' or to 'some dimension of law'), and, indeed, is often as much concerned with the

45 Walker, *Intimations of Global Law*, 45–47.

46 The exponential growth of elite global networks of judges, lawyers, legal scholars and legal educational forms and institutions, and of overlapping terms and topics of global legal reference across and within these networks, is discussed at length in Walker, *Intimations of Global Law*, ch. 2.

framework of authority required for the articulation of that doctrine than the content of what is articulated. But even in its more concrete forms, global law remains in a process of fluid and, of course, normatively contested becoming – of 'intimation'[47] rather than final resolution.

The pervasiveness and versatility of juristic involvement in the making of global law leads to a third key point. In the developing profile of the global lawyer, both humanities and social scientific perspectives are important, often in fluid combination. On the one hand, it is striking how much the development of the new global law draws upon aspects of our legal heritage, whether from or before the state-centred modern age.[48] The tradition of constitutional law, administrative law, human rights law, *ius gentium* and more is examined as a set of resources for a new age. Ironically, it is the erosion of the specific and direct *authority* of many of these legal frameworks that has led to their reappraisal as a reservoir of normative *suggestion*. But in all of this, we see the methods and deep purpose of the humanities very much at work. We witness at an intense level of engagement the attempt to understand and refine our capacity for law's special form of practical reason by reference to the deep record of our past practice and past reflection on that practice.

On the other hand, the development of the new global law is also about our ability to extrapolate from the present and to understand the trends taking place in transnational legal development. A project such as Global Administrative Law, or the refinement of the idea of 'proportionality' as a judicial meta-value for a variety of transnational contexts, or the spread of rights 'mainstreaming', or the revival of the rule of law as an ethic of global relevance, requires a capacity to understand incipient movements in the global legal landscape – their causes, mobilising potential and long-term effects – that draws heavily on social scientific knowledge and sensibilities. Global Administrative Law, for example, emerges from a well-documented and increasingly closely observed appreciation of the growth of many transnational administrative-like agencies that lack a formal legal pedigree in either state constitutional law or international law, but which rely instead on constellations of interests in areas such as sporting competition, public health, environmental protection, technical production standards or information technology, and which are gradually, if very unevenly, putting in place many of the tools and

[47] *Ibid.*, ch. 5. [48] Ibid., ch. 5, 151–157.

mechanisms we have traditionally associated with administrative accountability (impartial decision making, the duty to give reasons, etc.).[49] And at the outer edges of this movement of observation and suggestive reconstruction, we also see the growth of a kind of 'emergent analytics'[50] in international and transnational law. Here we find bodies of research on compliance or collective learning in which 'real world' testing is closely linked to regulatory adaptation, and so where trendspotting becomes of directly normative as well as diagnostic value.[51] In all of these cases, the emphasis on regulatory projection acknowledges and underlines the tenuous authority of some of our legal traditions but also provides the focus for normative renewal. In many cases, moreover, the creative interpretation and refinement of fluid trends continues to draw on our inquiries into our heritage tools of legal design in a manner that requires a close blend of humanistic understanding and social scientific awareness.

A fourth and final key point returns us to the fault-lines we identified between service, critical and detached orientations towards legal practice in the state-centred juristic mind-set, and considers how the new global environment might affect these. Does the somewhat greater creative engagement and productive involvement of the jurist on the global stage suggest some way of moving beyond these fault-lines? Some might prefer to highlight the opposite danger. They might see the mingling of scholarly voice and institutional fact as tending towards confusion – even an illegitimate collapsing – of theory and doctrine. Yet it is important to appreciate the inevitability of the jurist's implication in the process of imagining and framing global law. Jurists by definition lack political or democratic authority to decide the frameworks of our common life; this is sometimes forgotten, but it is as true in the national as in the

[49] See Kingsbury, Krisch and Stewart, 'The Emergence of Global Administrative Law'.

[50] G. Shaffer and T. Ginsberg, 'The Empirical Turn in International Legal Scholarship' (2012) 106 *American Journal of International Law* 1. See also Walker, *Intimations of Global Law*, 157–162.

[51] Perhaps the most developed example of this is the experimental governance movement, or tendency. Tellingly, this has achieved notable success in those transnational contexts where the basis of legal authority is particularly tenuous; See, e.g., C. Sabel and J. Zeitlin (eds.), *Experimentalist Governance in the European Union: Towards a New Architecture* (Oxford: Oxford University Press, 2010). On experimentalism in the US see, e.g., M. Dorf and C. Sabel, 'A Constitution of Experimentalist Governance' 98 *Columbia Law Review* 267 (1998); C. Sabel and W. Simon, 'Minimalism and Experimentalism in American Public Law' 100 *Georgetown Law Review* 53 (2011). On experimentalism in the EU, see K. Armstrong, 'The Character of EU Law and Governance: From "Community Method" to New Modes of Governance' 64 *Current Legal Problems* 179 (2011).

transnational setting. Yet in the nonstate setting the more prominent framing role that jurists are gradually assuming is precisely due to the growing complexity of our thick transnational interdependence and *the absence* of mechanisms that provide or would generate political and democratic authority structures to resolve the terms of that thick interdependence. Jurists, then, have no choice but to get involved – to address hard questions about our 'disorder of orders'[52] that will not go away just because no one has clear standing to answer them. But if the authority of jurists is situationally contingent, and mostly epistemic, based upon their legal knowledge and know-how, then they have a responsibility to employ this as fully and with such serious regard for the well-being of law as possible.

There can be no place, here, for a narrowly self-interested or conceited service orientation, for championing the role of lawyers and the place of lawyers just because of who we are, the happenstance of our involvement at so many of the dense regulatory intersections of transnational law, and the pull of our insider knowledge. Equally, however, so fluid are the dynamics of transnational law that such detachment as we can bring to the task of understanding where we are in legal terms is unlikely to remain in the realm of disinterested observation. The very circumstance of law's involvement in the process of globalisation militates against the kind of inquiry that seeks universal or long-term juridical truths that somehow stand above the fray. Rather, as we have seen, the emphasis is upon the emergent and the disjunctive, on forms of humanistic reflection or social scientific understanding that capture trends and subject them to forms of creative interpretation and refinement that will unavoidably be in competition with other such constructive efforts.

What is more, within the perspective of global law the distinction between these first two approaches – service and detached – and the critical approach, also becomes less apparent. This is not to deny the profound gap that lies between the present possibilities of global law – and so too the service we might provide to its existing forms – and some people's ideas of global economic or political justice.[53] Rather, it is to acknowledge that however far removed the art of the possible remains from certain conceptions of the global good, a concern with global justice

[52] N. Walker, 'Beyond Boundary Disputes and Basic Grids: Mapping the Global Disorder of Normative Orders' (2008) 6 *International Journal of Constitutional Law* 373–396.

[53] Walker, *Intimations of Global Law*, ch. 6; see also S. R. Ratner, 'Ethics and International Law: Integrating the Global Justice Project(s) (2013) 5 *International Theory* 1.

is already built into the reflexive development of global law. For in responding to the decline of a historically dominant meta-principle of legal authority, and the absence of any functionally equivalent steering mechanism, global law in its various forms, both convergent and divergent, tends already to look more explicitly to general ethical principles and purposes in search of a legitimate grounding for its authority. The gulf between critique and the tracking of the authoritative pathway for a transformative legal practice is often deemed unbridgeable in a state-centred critical literature that may view existing authority structures as inimical to root and branch reform. Yet that chasm is narrowed in an environment where all existing frameworks of authority are seen as incomplete or unsettled, and where the very conceptualisation and design of new frameworks of authority and new ways of imagining the legal world is seen as no one's special prerogative.

2.4 Conclusion

We should be careful not to overstate the significance of the effects of globalisation on the juristic mind-set, or on our sense of how legal education and research might alter in consequence. Much of legal education, and much of the debate over what it is or for the legally educated to be concerned with law's overall worth as a practical idea, remains within the boundaries of the state, which is still of key importance if not the monopolistic institutional player of old in a global legal age.[54] Those of us who are persuaded, as I am, that law's contemporary transnational movement is nevertheless one of profound scale and importance, with significant consequences for legal education and the role of the jurist in general, will worry over a relative neglect of the world beyond the state – a lag in awareness and so inadequate appreciation in legal educational circles of what a proper understanding of law's global horizons requires. Certainly, there has been considerable growth in new self-labelled 'global' or otherwise cosmopolitan-styled law schools, and in territorially unanchored networks or associations offering new transnationally focused forms of legal learning or advanced research or research-support opportunities – especially at or between national elite educational centres, as well as a more general increase in international exchanges and in the transnational content and orientation of national professional curricula.[55]

[54] See, e.g., P Glenn, *The Cosmopolitan State* (Oxford: Oxford University Press, 2013).
[55] See, e.g., Walker, *Intimations of Global Law*, esp. 36–39.

But these developments remain somewhat fragmented and piecemeal, with limited reflection on how global legal trends in the round may be shifting the centre of gravity of what should count towards 'the general well-being' of the law. Yet to repeat a point, we should not push this criticism too far. For we should also recognise that just because the discipline of law remains at its core a practical discipline, and just because the organisation and pursuit of that practice remains predominantly local in its immediate context and consequences, there are good reasons why the local domain should also continue to be the primary point of reference of legal education for many.

But even if the global dimension of legal education remains secondary, and even if we (reasonably) disagree about how prominent it should be or become, its gradual inclusion in the basic legal curriculum as one level of inquiry, as well as its reflection in new transnational educational forms, is likely over time to have a broader salutary effect. For one supplementary consequence of its closer embrace may be to spread a greater awareness of the general responsibilities and opportunities of jurists, however we may situate ourselves. Wherever we might be located, and at whatever geographical level our priorities of involvement lie, exposure to the tensions, opportunities and dangers of global law should remind us that our engagement with the law *qua* jurists require us to have more than a basic knowledge of the professional tools of the trade, and should reinforce to us how much we stand to benefit from greater cross-disciplinary awareness. Such exposure should also caution us that detachment, whatever its many virtues, cannot provide refuge from the hardest questions about the well-being of law, and that we should strive to face these hard questions in a manner that does not treat commitments to service and to critique as mutually exclusive.

3

Field, Frame and Focus

Methodological Issues in the New Legal World

ROGER BROWNSWORD

3.1 Introduction

Traditionally, 'methodology' does not have a high profile either in law school education or in legal research. As students, we endeavour to follow the example of our professors – we try to do what they do (mainly dancing around the doctrine and showing some agility in the face of counterfactuals); and as members of the academy, we again try to follow the example set by our mentors and role models, trying to write the kind of papers that we already read in the law reviews. Only many years after publishing papers or books might we pause to reflect on what we were doing as well as how and why we did it.[1] If one of the features of the 'new legal world' is that we must take methodology more seriously, where should we begin in locating methodology within the landscape of legal education and research?

According to the conventional wisdom, the lowest common denominator for law schools is that they aspire to teach their students 'to think like lawyers'.[2] What this means is that students will be taught that, when they are asked to advise on 'the legal position' in relation to some facts, they should base their advice on the relevant source materials – the Constitution, the legislation, the case-law, the code provisions, or whatever – of the particular legal system whose laws are applicable to the matter. Students will also be taught about some of the flexibilities within these source materials and how they can be handled without this violating the

1 For my own confessional as a contract lawyer, see Roger Brownsword, 'Maps, Critiques, and Methodologies: Confessions of a Contract Lawyer' in Mark van Hoecke (ed.), *Methodologies of Legal Research* (Oxford: Hart, 2011) 133.

2 See, e.g., Peter Birks (ed.) *Examining the Law Syllabus: The Core* (Oxford: Oxford University Press, 1992).

conventions that set limits on 'thinking like a lawyer'.[3] If we treat law as a kind of practice with its own manual and code of conduct for practitioners, students are being introduced to some parts of the manual and to the code. They are being taught how to find the relevant legal materials and how to apply those materials. Yet, for the most part, law schools do not give solemn lectures about methodology; they simply get on with teaching students how to do the things that (at least some) lawyers in practice do.

For many law schools, though, and especially for the research communities within those law schools, there is an aspiration to do much more than master the art of thinking like a lawyer – which, after all, merely seems to qualify graduates to play a somewhat sophisticated kind of game.[4] In such law schools, the ambition of legal inquiry is to 'understand' more about the practice of law, to be able to explain how it works, or to evaluate its performance in some way and then to offer various recommendations for its improvement.[5] When legal inquiry is in this mode, some particular research questions or hypotheses are articulated and then there is a methodological choice to be made: how are the questions to be answered, and how are the hypotheses to be tested? By contrast with questions that simply require an interrogation and application of the source legal materials, the questions that we are now contemplating invite a highly explicit engagement with methodology. Inquirers who seek to explain some aspect of the practice of law will be faced with choices between quantitative and qualitative methods, structural and action-based approaches, overt or covert participant observation methods, and so on; inquirers who seek to evaluate some aspect of the practice will be faced with choices between various economic and philosophical theories, 'inside out' and 'outside in' approaches, and so on; and, for those who address conceptual issues, there are challenging questions in relation to the methodology of concept formation.[6] When

[3] In the common law world, the classic text is Karl N. Llewellyn, *The Bramble Bush* (New York: Oceana Publications, 1951).

[4] See, Roger Brownsword, 'Whither the Law and the Law Books: From Prescription to Possibility' (2012) 39 *Journal of Law and Society* 296.

[5] Applying such a manifesto to legal education, see John N. Adams and Roger Brownsword, *Understanding Law* (London: Fontana, 1992; London: Sweet and Maxwell, 1996); and Roger Brownsword, 'Teaching Contract: A Liberal Agenda' in Birks, *Examining the Law Syllabus*, 42.

[6] On the choice between empiricism, pragmatist-conventionalism and rationalist-foundationalism, see Deryck Beyleveld and Roger Brownsword, *Law as a Moral Judgment* (London: Sweet and Maxwell, 1986; Sheffield: Sheffield Academic Press, 1994), ch. 3.

research proposals of this nature are submitted to funding bodies, referees will typically take a hard look at the methodology section of the application and, quite frequently, rejection slips will be sent with critical comments concerning either the lack of attention to methodology or the inappropriate nature of the chosen methodology.

Given this context, we can repeat our opening question: how should we describe the place of methodology in the realm of legal inquiry? A plausible response runs as follows. First, there are questions to be posed, or hypotheses to be formulated, and then (but only then) there are methodological matters to be addressed. Unless and until inquirers have formulated their question (or their hypothesis), they do not need to concern themselves with matters of methodology. However, once such a question (or hypothesis) has been formulated, inquirers need to think about how they are going to try to answer it (or test it). Sometimes, the appropriate methodology will be settled, unquestioned and implicit; for example, if the question concerns the wording of a particular legislative provision, the only appropriate methodology is to go to the source (whether by the traditional method of checking the hard copy in the law library or by modern electronic search and retrieval). However, if the question is not just about the wording but about how a particular legislative provision should be interpreted, methodology is less straightforward. There will be competing views about the criteria to be employed in determining the 'best' interpretation of the law. In other cases, particularly where inquiry seeks to explain or evaluate some aspect of the practice of law, it will be apparent at once that there is no settled methodology and that whichever strategy is employed it will be contestable. In all cases, legal inquirers need to have a strategy for answering the question at hand but it is only when there are competing strategies that an explicit engagement with 'methodology' is likely to take place.

One of the limitations of this plausible response is that it does not speak to the genesis of the questions that generate the need for methodological reflection. Presumably, inquirers have a cognitive interest in the questions that they ask; but why *these* particular questions? Before we get to methodology, we need some questions; but, before we have questions, we need what? The answer is that we need some field of human action or activity that attracts our cognitive attention and interest; we need to frame the phenomena within the field so that we can articulate, at least in a general way, the questions for our inquiry; and, we need a focus, or a number of focal points, within the field for our inquiries. Already it is implicit in the conventional wisdom that the 'field' of law is some kind of (rule-based) practice (such as subjecting human conduct to the governance of rules); we frame our inquiry by reference to rule-based governance that exhibits certain formal or functional features; and, within the field and the framing, our focus might be on the rules, or the practitioners, or the institutions, and so on, reflecting the unquestioned starting points for legal inquiry.

So long as the field, the frame and the focus remain relatively stable, there can be many different lines of inquiry, together with many methodological approaches, but there is at least a common root for the projects. However, once the field, frame and focus are seriously disrupted, legal inquiry is radically fragmented and destabilised. My view is that 'the new legal world' that prompts the present discussions is not simply one that invites a more explicit engagement with methodology (because the horizons of legal inquiry are changing) but precisely one that signifies a fundamental disturbance at the level of field, frame and focus. It is not simply that the context or scope of inquiry is changing but that the ground is shifting under our feet. The immanent pressure created by this tectonic disturbance is to construct a new paradigm – indeed, to construct a new Methodology (with a capital M) for legal inquiry. If this assessment is correct, in our new legal world, it is not enough to pay more attention to methodological questions that arise within the old paradigm – that is to say, to pay more attention to the way in which the particular lines of inquiry within the current paradigm are to be addressed; rather, what we need to do is reinvent the paradigm for legal inquiry and, with that, operate with a new Methodology – that is to say, we need to redefine our operative field, frame and focus.

In my view, there are two ways in which this destabilisation is taking place. The first is represented by the alleged breakdown of 'the Westphalian paradigm' (inviting a deluge of thoughts concerning 'legal pluralism');[7] and the second is foreshadowed by the shift of focal interest from law to regulation and, with that, to an interest in the

[7] This is well represented by, among a host of others, Douglas Lewis (ed.), *Global Governance and the Quest for Justice Volume 1: International and Regional Organisations* (Hart: Oxford, 2006); Jan Klabbers, *Anne Peters, and Geir Ulfstein, The Constitutionalization of International Law* (Oxford: Oxford University Press, 2009); and Andrew Halpin and Volker Roeben (eds.), *Theorising the Global Legal Order* (Oxford: Hart, 2009). For a critical overview, see Simon Roberts, 'After Government? On Representing Without the State' (2005) 68 MLR 1.

employment of a more 'technological' approach to managing human conduct. It is the latter that is the main concern of this paper. Stated shortly, my proposal is that we need a new Methodology, one in which the field of our interest is extended to include regulation by technological means (technological management), in which we frame our inquiries by adopting a broad conception of 'the regulatory environment' for human action, and in which we focus, inter alia, on the distinction between the normative and nonnormative elements of the regulatory environment.

The chapter is in eight principal parts. Having sketched the two aforementioned destabilising forces (in Section 3.2), I identify six new research questions arising from the second of these forces (in Section 3.3). These questions, which are at the nexus of law, regulation and technology, are:

- How do we conceive of the 'regulatory environment'?
- How are the values of the 'Rule of Law' to be applied where technologies are used as regulatory tools?
- What is the significance for liberal values of States using technological management as a means of social control and channelling?
- What is the significance of the complexion of the regulatory environment?
- Within the larger framework of the regulatory environment, what do we now understand about the effectiveness of law?
- To what extent can we expect the signals that comprise the regulatory environment to be coherent?

Then, in the following sections of the chapter (Sections 3.4 to 3.9), I offer some reflections on, and responses to, each of these questions.

3.2 Two Destabilising Tendencies

Before legal inquiry can commence, there needs to be some settled understanding of which part of the social world is under investigation. What is the field of legal inquiry? If we identify 'law' or the 'practice of law' with the operations of high-level nation-state institutions, notably the Legislature and the Courts, we will miss the significant practices of channelling and dispute-resolution that take place elsewhere in society. And even if we extend the field so that it covers all enterprises of subjecting human conduct to the governance of rules, we will miss the way that technological management – set against a backcloth of transformative technologies[8] – threatens to replace normative legal direction as the primary mode of social ordering. In this part of the paper, I present a sketch of the two destabilising tendencies at work in our new legal world.

3.2.1 *Pluralism and the Breakdown of 'the Westphalian Paradigm'*

Once upon a time, as H. L. A. Hart famously put it, the educated understanding was 'that the laws in England form some sort of system, and that in France or the United States or Soviet Russia and, indeed, in almost every part of the world which is thought of as a separate "country" there are legal systems which are broadly similar in structure in spite of important differences'.[9] Beyond the nation-states, with their constitutionally architected normative orders, the conventional wisdom was that there was an embryonic and contractualised normative order (regulating transnational interactions and international transactions), all founded on a Westphalian understanding of international relations. Such is the traditional view of the field – a field that, of course, has limits but also that has a certain topography. If our inquiries stray beyond the boundaries, they are off legal limits; and if we neglect the topography, our inquiries are of reduced significance and interest.

Thus, according to the Hartian framing, first, nation-states and their legal systems are presented as the dominant feature of the legal landscape; second, the high-level (secondary rule structured) institutional apparatus of municipal legal systems, and the activities of such institutions, are prioritised for our explanatory and evaluative inquiries; and, third, beyond the nation-state, it is high-level agreements (treaties) and high-profile international agencies (such as the UN) that merit our attention. If we accept this framing – a framing that is both Westphalian and mainly Western – we will find that a great deal of the stuff of governance and dispute settlement is either placed off limits or pushed into the background.

[8] See, e.g., Will Hutton, *How Good We Can Be* (London: Little, Brown, 2015) who suggests (at 17) that we find ourselves at 'a dramatic moment in world history. Nothing will be left untouched. We will live in smart cities, achieve mobility in smart transport, be powered by smart energy, communicate with smart phones, organise our financial affairs with smart banks and socialise in ever smarter networks.' I agree with Hutton: nothing will be left untouched; we will live in smart (technologically managed) regulatory environments; and jurists need to be on top of these developments.

[9] H. L. A. Hart, *The Concept of Law* (Clarendon Press, 1961) 2–3.

This, however, is not the end of the influence of framing. Hart's essay aims to do much more than stabilise the field of inquiry; it is designed to embed a particular conceptualisation of legal order. If we accept the Hartian frame, we accept not only that there is, for theoretical purposes, a critical distinction between the legal and the non-legal but also a certain view about the paradigmatically legal (namely, that those orders that display a union of primary and secondary rules are the quintessentially legal); whatever else we find in the pretheoretical legal ballpark, it is only a certain ideal-typical arrangement of rules and institutions that is to be treated as the genuine legal article. The Hartian frame, thus, goes way beyond trying to avoid a primitive misunderstanding; it tries to fix inquiry so that a certain understanding of the legal is entrenched.

In an age of intense globalisation, this framing is challenged by the apparent fluidity and fragmentation of legal orders as well as by the multiple mechanisms for governance that simply are not captured by the Hartian view.[10] Even the setting of the ballpark boundaries is problematic. As William Twining has remarked:

> Today, a map of law in the world that leaves out religious law, important forms of indigenous, customary or chthonic law, or emerging orders (eg, the new *lex mercatoria)*, just leaves out too much. From a global perspective a reasonably inclusive picture of law in the world would encompass various forms of non-state law, especially different kinds of religious and customary law that fall outside 'the Westphalian duo'.[11]

Even if the frame is so extended, so long as nation-states, national legal systems and high-level international agreements are prioritised for inquiry (conveying the sense that little else is of legal interest), some elements of discontent will persist. For the discontents, it is not that we can dispense with any kind of framing but that we need to reframe legal

[10] Compare Brendan Edgeworth, *Law, Modernity, Postmodernity* (Aldershot: Ashgate, 2003). At 119, Edgeworth argues that jurists need to develop a paradigm that recognises 'the reconfigured power of the nation state, globalized economic and political institutions, postindustrialism, and a starkly reconstituted class system and civil society'. For the landscape of legal pluralism, coupled with a critique of its persistent 'essentialist' conceptualisation of law see Brian Z. Tamanaha, *A General Jurisprudence of Law and Society* (Oxford: Oxford University Press, 2001).

[11] William Twining, 'Implications of "Globalisation" for Law as a Discipline' in Halpin and Roeben, *Theorising the Global Legal Order*, 39, at 47.

inquiry in a way that facilitates getting to grips with the changing face of global law and governance.[12]

For those legal scholars whose cognitive interest lies in the emergence of global (transnational) governance, there are many questions to be pursued. However, perhaps the most pressing task, as Douglas Lewis puts it, is 'to map out the "constitution", which means in the first instance that we ask who is wielding the power. Then we must ask whether such power is being wielded legitimately'.[13] For Lewis, the legitimacy agenda involves checking whether the procedural virtues of accountability, participation, transparency and so on are being expressed as well as how far global players (particularly transnational corporations) respect human rights. Given such an agenda, it is no exaggeration to say that there is much work to be done[14] – and, if this work is to be done, there needs to be a major rethink about the field, frame and focus for legal inquiry.

3.2.2 Regulation and Technological Management

One of the objections to the Hartian frame is that it overstates the importance of the distinction between the legal and the nonlegal; or, to put this slightly differently, it misleads by focusing attention on those

[12] Whether we should do this by extending the concept of law is a moot point. As Simon Roberts pointed out in his important Chorley lecture ('After Government?'):

> We can probably all now go along with some general tenets of the legal pluralists. First, their insistence on the heterogeneity of the normative domain seems entirely uncontroversial. Practically any social field can be fairly represented as consisting of plural, interpenetrating normative orders/systems/discourses. Nor would many today wish to endorse fully the enormous claims to systemic qualities that state law has made for itself and that both lawyers and social scientists have in the past too often uncritically accepted. Beyond that, consensus is more difficult ... Will all the normative orders that the legal pluralists wish to embrace necessarily be comfortable with their rescue as 'legal' orders?

[13] Douglas Lewis, 'Global Governance and the Search for Justice' in Lewis, *Global Governance* 1, 3–4. Similarly, having redrawn the field of general jurisprudential inquiry, Tamanaha, in *A General Jurisprudence*, concludes that '[m]uch hard work remains to be done' (at 242).

[14] As Lewis, in 'Global Governance', puts it, at 18:

> As well as the fact that the charting exercise has hardly begun, we know relatively little about how this web of [global] alliances and networks operate; how far institutionally, how far informally and with what degree of pluralistic input and what degree of transparency.

modes of governance that fit what Hart treats as the ideal type of law. Today, there is much more interest in setting legal ordering in the broader context of what I would call the 'regulatory environment'.[15] If we frame our inquiries in this way, not only will we be able to bring in the many 'local' normative orderings that are associated with informal governance,[16] we will catch up with the burgeoning technological instruments of ordering (some of which are nonnormative) that are not yet captured by any kind of framing.

Before we get to the regulatory environment, however, we should consider the concept of 'regulation'. In the Westphalian world, if we paused to ponder the difference between 'law' and 'regulation', we might have assumed that they meant much the same; but, in our new world of law, 'regulation' has a more specific meaning. A useful anchoring point is Karl Llewellyn's law-jobs theory.[17] So secured, we can say that the general idea is that regulation is designed to perform what Llewellyn calls the channelling function by steering and guiding the conduct of regulatees. Typically, regulators do this by issuing guidance, monitoring the response of regulatees and taking steps to correct noncompliance. Hence, as Julia Black puts it, we think of regulation as:

> the sustained and focused attempt to alter the behaviour of others according to standards or goals with the intention of producing a broadly identified outcome or outcomes, which may involve mechanisms of standard-setting, information-gathering and behaviour-modification.[18]

However, this leaves many questions unanswered – for example, questions about the identity of the regulators and the regulatees, about the difference between regulation and 'governance' and 'soft law', and about whether regulation extends beyond interventions that are intended to correct market failures to policies that are not focused on the economy.[19]

[15] See, Roger Brownsword and Han Somsen, 'Law, Innovation and Technology: Before We Fast Forward – A Forum for Debate' (2009) 1 *Law Innovation and Technology* 1.

[16] For some examples (of farming and whaling communities), see Robert C. Ellickson, *Order Without Law* (Cambridge, MA: Harvard University Press, 1991).

[17] Karl. N. Llewellyn, 'The Normative, the Legal, and the Law-Jobs: The Problem of Juristic Method' (1940) 49 *Yale Law Journal* 1355.

[18] Julia Black, 'What is Regulatory Innovation?' in Julia Black, Martin Lodge, and Mark Thatcher (eds.), *Regulatory Innovation* (Cheltenham: Edward Elgar, 2005), 1, at 11.

[19] For two background visions of regulation (one as an infringement of private autonomy justified only by considerations of economic efficiency, the other as a much broader collaborative enterprise), see Tony Prosser, *The Regulatory Enterprise* (Oxford: Oxford University Press, 2010), ch.1.

Notwithstanding these potential difficulties, if we think of the 'field' as one in which attempts are made to channel the conduct of the group, this allows 'pluralists' to focus their inquiries on the less visible operations of law as well as the myriad standard-setting and standard-reflecting practices that go on around the law. In this way, we can begin to construct a more complex picture of the regulatory environment as a range of signals that guide our conduct. None of this, it should be emphasised, signifies that 'law' (in the Hartian sense) is irrelevant: law is one element in the regulatory array but it is just one signal in a larger regulatory environment. Given this field, what we aspire to is a regulatory environment that sends the right signals in the right kind of way and that actually functions as intended – in other words, the right kind of regulatory environment is one that passes muster whether we interrogate it for its legitimacy or for its effectiveness. And this is a framing that we can usefully employ whether our inquiries concern global or parochial social ordering.

Importantly, with this new framing, there is an opportunity to move legal inquiry in a direction that enables it to stay connected to a rapidly changing context of risk management and technological control. When Hart wrote *The Concept of Law*, it was generally assumed that the legal enterprise was normative (in the sense that it was concerned with subjecting human conduct to the governance of rules[20]) and that it was institutionalised. Although the institutional form of law has been well and truly problematised, we have not yet woken up to the possibility and implications of a shift away from normative regulatory strategies; that is to say, we have not yet woken up to the way in which regulatory environments might become less concerned with subjecting human conduct to the governance of rules and more reliant on designing in or designing out approved (or disapproved) patterns of behaviour.[21] To put this in other words, within regulatory theory, the common assumption is that the initial regulatory intervention will be in the form of setting a standard (with, concomitantly, a normative signal). However, unless the concept of regulation (possibly along with the concept of law) is to be limited to the use of normative signals, there is no reason why regulation should not also feature nonnormative technological signalling instruments. At all events, by framing our inquiries in terms of constructing the right kind of regulatory environment, there is the prospect of

[20] See Lon L. Fuller, *The Morality of Law* (New Haven: Yale University Press, 1969).

[21] In general, compare Roger Brownsword and Karen Yeung (eds.), *Regulating Technologies* (Oxford: Hart, 2008).

developing a better understanding of the operation of law as we have it today as well as of preparing ourselves for a future in which the technologies of the present century both facilitate and confine our agency.

In his seminal work, recognising important developments in information and communication technologies and, concomitantly, in the online world that progressively mediates our interactions and transactions, Lawrence Lessig points us in the right direction. Famously, according to Lessig, there are four principal channelling modalities (or modes of regulation): namely, the law, social norms, the market, and architecture (or code).[22] The wearing of seat belts is one of Lessig's illustrative examples, thus:

> The government may want citizens to wear seatbelts more often. It could pass a law to require the wearing of seatbelts (law regulating behavior directly). Or it could fund public education campaigns to create a stigma against those who do not wear seatbelts (law regulating social norms as a means to regulating behavior). Or it could subsidize insurance companies to offer reduced rates to seatbelt wearers (law regulating the market as a way of regulating behavior). Finally, the law could mandate automatic seatbelts, or ignition-locking systems (changing the code of the automobile as a means of regulating belting behavior). Each action might be said to have some effect on seatbelt use; each has some cost. The question for the government is how to get the most seatbelt use for the least cost.[23]

Smart regulators will seek out the optimal mix of the various instruments that they have in this extended repertoire. But, let us pause to emphasise one point. The law is just one possible element in this mix – no doubt, it is glaringly obvious that this is so; but in a community of lawyers (with a legal doctrinal gaze), it warrants repetition. There is more than one way of channelling behaviour; and in any particular case, the law does not have to bear all, or even any, of the regulatory burden.

Potentially, with Lessig's identification of architecture and 'code' as channelling instruments, we open up a new dimension of contestation, namely whether law is to be understood to be normative or also non-normative. If we limit the concept of law to a normative phenomenon, then law operates exclusively through signals that convey what ought, or ought not, to be done (whether as a matter of duty, or as the effective

[22] Lawrence Lessig, *Code and Other Laws of Cyberspace* (New York: Basic Books, 1999), ch. 7; and Lessig, 'The Law of the Horse: What Cyberlaw Might Teach' (1999) 113 *Harvard Law Review* 501, 507–514.

[23] Lessig, *Code and Other Laws*, at 93–94.

exercise of a legal power, such as the power to make an enforceable will or a contract). However, if we allow that law might also be instantiated where the signals channel behaviour in a nonnormative way, then it is possible that technological fixes (signalling what can and cannot be done) will also qualify as legal phenomena. However, disputes of this kind – particularly disputes about whether 'code' should be conceived of as 'law' – could prove a distraction from the main issues. If 'code' and other forms of technological management are to overtake 'legislation' as the primary regulatory instruments, the urgent question is not whether we should recognise them as a species of 'law'; rather, the imperative is that we adopt a 'field' that allows us to pursue the key lines of inquiry in what will be a dramatically different ordering of social life. The thought that guides this paper is that the concept of the 'regulatory environment', broadly understood, will facilitate the focusing of our inquiries and the framing of our questions.[24]

3.3 A New Agenda for Legal Inquiry

No doubt, there are many questions that arise for discussion once we take our field of inquiry to be the regulatory environment. And, these questions surely multiply once we add into the field the rapid development of a raft of modern technologies – as Kenneth Abbott succinctly puts it, our regulatory interest is in '[s]cientific discoveries and technological developments [that] are fueling explosive advances in biotechnology, personalized medicine and synthetic biology; applied neuroscience; nanotechnology; information technology and artificial intelligence; robotics; geoengineering and other fields'.[25] To varying degrees, these technologies 'carr[y] the possibility of significant risks to health, safety and the environment' as well as 'other potential impacts that raise broader social, economic and ethical concerns'.[26]

[24] See the drift of my discussion in Roger Brownsword, 'Post-Technique: *The New Social Contract* Today' in David Campbell, Linda Mulcahy and Sally Wheeler (eds.), *Changing Concepts of Contract* (Basingstoke: Palgrave Macmillan, 2013) 14; and 'Comparatively Speaking: "Law in its Regulatory Environment"', in Maurice Adams and Dirk Heirbaut (eds.), *The Method and Culture of Comparative Law* (Festschrift for Mark van Hoecke) (Oxford: Hart, 2014) 189.

[25] Kenneth W. Abbott, 'Introduction: the Challenges of Oversight for Emerging Technologies' in Gary E. Marchant, Kenneth W. Abbott and Braden Allenby (eds.), *Innovative Governance Models for Emerging Technologies* (Cheltenham: Edward Elgar, 2013) 1 at 1.

[26] Ibid.

Given such risks and concerns, we tend to be preoccupied with questions of effective and legitimate regulation that treat these technologies as 'targets' (to be subjected to regulatory control). For example, while there are significant concerns about the health and environmental hazards presented by nanotechnologies and synthetic biology, it is the impact of modern biotechnologies, as well as neurotechnologies, on our essential humanity that has led to a resurgence of interest in human dignity.[27] At the same time, we struggle to find acceptable ways of keeping law adequately connected to rapidly changing technologies – data protection and assisted conception are just two obvious examples;[28] and the development of information and communication technologies has posed a large question mark alongside the capacity of regulators (whether national, regional or global) to make effective interventions.[29] However, the premise of this paper is that, important though these questions are, it is the potential utilisation of these emerging technologies as regulatory instruments that is truly destabilising and that it is this phenomenon that should become our focus.[30]

Accordingly, in our new legal world, at the nexus of law, regulation and technology, let me suggest an agenda for legal scholars that comprises the following six nonexhaustive lines of inquiry:

- How should we conceive of the 'regulatory environment'?
- How are the values of the 'Rule of Law' to be applied where technologies are used as regulatory tools?
- What is the significance for liberal values of States using technological management as a means of social control and channelling?
- What is the significance of the complexion of the regulatory environment?

[27] See, further, the discussion in Section 3.9 of this chapter. Generally, see Deryck Beyleveld and Roger Brownsword, *Human Dignity in Bioethics and Biolaw* (Oxford: Oxford University Press, 2001).

[28] On the challenge of regulatory connection, see Roger Brownsword, *Rights, Regulation and the Technological Revolution* (Oxford: Oxford University Press, 2008) ch. 6; and Roger Brownsword and Morag Goodwin, *Law and the Technologies of the Twenty-First Century* (Cambridge: Cambridge University Press, 2012) chs. 15–16.

[29] See, Roger Brownsword and Morag Goodwin, *Law and the Technologies*, chs. 11–14.

[30] To this extent, I have some considerable sympathy with the excellent analysis in Lyria Bennett Moses, 'How to Think about Law, Regulation and Technology: Problems with "Technology" as a Regulatory Target' (2013) 5 *Law, Innovation and Technology* 1.

- Within the larger framework of the regulatory environment, what do we now understand about the effectiveness of law?
- To what extent can we expect the signals that comprise the regulatory environment to be coherent?

It should be emphasised that this list is not exhaustive. My guess is that, in our new legal world, each area of substantive law (whether criminal, contract or tort law) will feel the impact of technological management as coding and design increasingly structure the environments in which we interact and transact.[31] When, for example, transportation is fully automated, when robots have replaced humans in dangerous workplaces, and when the risk of much old-fashioned crime has been technologically managed, my guess is that swathes of regulatory criminal law will be rendered redundant and what remains of criminal law and tort law will be of either reduced or different practical significance. In the meantime, so long as technological management is not comprehensive – for example, while driverless cars and lorries share the roads with driven vehicles – there will be many lines of inquiry to be pursued within particular sectors of legal research.

In the present chapter, I will limit my further remarks to the six questions highlighted above. To be sure, each of these questions (collectively embodying a new Methodology) might invite its own set of methodological reflections. However, in the following sections, I will speak directly (and in a very preliminary way) to the substance of each of these questions.

3.4 How Should We Conceive of the 'Regulatory Environment'?

Notwithstanding some vagueness about the idea of regulation,[32] we talk quite comfortably and confidently about the importance of getting the 'regulatory environment' right – right for banking and financial services, right for innovation, right for health care and patient safety, right for the European single market, right for small businesses, and so on. But how should we conceive of the 'regulatory environment'? In this section, I will introduce the concept of the regulatory environment as a signalling

[31] See, further, Roger Brownsword, 'In the Year 2061: From Law to Technological Management' (2015) 7 *Law, Innovation and Technology* 1.

[32] Julia Black, 'De-centring Regulation: Understanding the Role of Regulation and Self-Regulation in a "Post-Regulatory" World' (2001) 54 *Current Legal Problems* 103.

environment, differentiate between the normative and the nonnormative signalling dimensions of such an environment and apply these ideas to sketch three generations of regulatory environment (moving away from law towards technological management), before tackling questions about the identity of both the regulators and regulatees as well as about where the boundaries of any particular regulatory environment are to be drawn.

3.4.1 The Regulatory Environment as a Signalling Environment

Perhaps the most helpful starting point is to think about the regulatory environment as a kind of signalling environment, much in the way that we think about the setting for road traffic or for the railways. On the roads and railways, red lights signal 'stop' and green lights signal 'go'; and in the same way, regulators may signal that certain conduct is prohibited (red light), permitted or required (green light always indicating at least permitted and, in some contexts, required). These signals may be legal or ethical, formal or informal; and, in the world that Hart and others contemplated, these signals were normative in character, speaking to regulatees in terms of what ought or ought not to be done.

Now, in modern transport settings, the rules of the road might be supported by various kinds of technologies. For example, technologies might be employed to advise drivers that they are either noncompliant or at risk of noncompliance – as when roadside signs might flash a warning that the vehicle is exceeding the speed limit, or an overhead motorway gantry might advise that it is time to take a break, or a vehicle equipped with the appropriate sensors might caution the driver against proceeding when affected by drink or drugs. In all these cases, the signals continue to be normative (various acts ought or ought not to be done).

It is a feature of technologically enabled regulatory environments, however, that they do not always stop at advice. Sometimes, the technology simply disables an act.[33] On modern railway trains, for example, it is not possible for passengers to open the carriage doors until the guard has released the central locking system.[34] Similarly, smart cars might be disabled on sensing alcohol or drugs in the driver; and they will be

[33] See, e.g., Mireille Hildebrandt, 'Legal and Technological Normativity: More (and Less) than Twin Sisters' (2008) 12.3 *TECHNE* 169; and Roger Brownsword, *Rights, Regulation and the Technological Revolution* (Oxford: Oxford University Press, 2008).

[34] See Jonathan Wolff, 'Five Types of Risky Situation' (2010) 2 *Law, Innovation and Technology* 151.

designed so that they always comply with what are safe speed limits.[35] In this vein, Pat O'Malley charts the different degrees of technological control applied to regulate the speed of motor vehicles:

> In the 'soft' versions of such technologies, a warning device advises drivers they are exceeding the speed limit or are approaching changed traffic regulatory conditions, but there are progressively more aggressive versions. If the driver ignores warnings, data – which include calculations of the excess speed at any moment, and the distance over which such speeding occurred (which may be considered an additional risk factor and *thus* an aggravation of the offence) – can be transmitted directly to a central registry. Finally, in a move that makes the leap from perfect detection to perfect prevention, the vehicle can be disabled or speed limits can be imposed by remote modulation of the braking system or accelerator.[36]

Where environments are technologically controlled in this way, the regulatory signal is no longer normative (the coding is no longer in terms of what ought or ought not to be done, what is permitted and what is not permitted); in technologically managed environments, we have a quite different regulatory register. This is the register of practicability or possibility. Here, regulators signal that it is not reasonably practicable to do some act, *x*, or even *that x* simply cannot be done (that is, it is impossible to do *x*) – in which case, regulatees reason, not that *x ought not* to be done, but that *x cannot* be done (either realistically or literally). In other words, in place of prescription, we have only possibility.[37]

3.4.2 Normative and Nonnormative Signals

Acknowledging a residual bias towards (legal) normative environments, we need to recognise the way in which modern technologies insinuate

[35] See Eric Schmidt and Jared Cohen, *The New Digital Age* (New York: Alfred A. Knopf, 2013) at 25: 'Google's fleet of driverless cars, built by a team of Google and Stanford University engineers, has logged hundreds of thousands of miles without incident . . .' Indeed, for the sake of 'safety', it seems that driverless cars will even have the capacity to exceed the legal speed limits by up to 10 mph: see James Dean, 'Driverless cars are hardwired to speed', *The Times*, August 22, 2014, at 11. For the regulatory challenges presented by environments in which driverless cars operate alongside driven cars, see Ronald Leenes and Federica Lucivero, 'Laws *on* Robots, Laws *by* Robots, Laws *in* Robots: Regulating Robots' Behaviour by Design' (2014) 6 *Law, Innovation and Technology* 193.

[36] Pat O'Malley, 'The Politics of Mass Preventive Justice' in Andrew Ashworth, Lucia Zedner and Patrick Tomlin (eds.), *Prevention and the Limits of the Criminal Law* (Oxford: Oxford University Press, 2013) 273, at 280.

[37] Brownsword, 'Whither the Law and the Law Books'.

themselves into such environments, sometimes complementing the traditional normative signals but, at other times, replacing them with non-normative management or control.

Applying this analysis, we can treat any particular regulatory environment as having (in principle) two dimensions. First, there is the normative dimension: here, regulators seek to guide the conduct of regulatees; standards are set; prohibitions, permissions and requirements are signalled; regulators employ prudential, moral or combined prudential-moral registers to engage the practical reason of regulatees; and various kinds of technology might be used to reinforce the normative standards and the signals – in our times, such reinforcement typically involves surveillance, tracking and identifying technologies that increase the likelihood of detection in the event of noncompliance. Second, there is the nonnormative dimension: here, regulators target a certain pattern of behaviour; various kinds of technology (product design, automation, architecture and the like) are used to channel regulatees in the desired way; and the only register employed is that of practicability/possibility. As this dimension becomes more sophisticated, the technologies that are employed are embedded in our physical surroundings (in the way, for example, that sensors detect a human presence in a room and switch on the lights) or possibly in our bodies and our genetic coding. Although in the technologically managed environments of the future, a regulatee might explore what can and cannot be done; in many respects, this will no longer seem like a signalling environment: for regulatees who are habituated to this kind of environment, it will just seem to be the way things are. What once was an 'ought' now presents as an 'is' (reflecting the dense and powerful technological infrastructures that support the managed environments that surely will be populated by future generations).

3.4.3 Three Generations of Regulatory Environment

Gathering up these strands, we might construct a typology highlighting three generations of regulatory environment. In a first-generation regulatory environment, regulators would rely exclusively on normative signals. This is not necessarily a technology-free environment; but the technology would signal in a normative register – for example, in the way that surveillance technologies signal that the likelihood of detection is increased and, hence, regulatees ought (if only for prudential reasons) to comply. In a second-generation regulatory environment, regulators would rely on both (first-generation) normative signals and second-generation design of products and places (architecture). Where regulators rely on such a design strategy, the signal is no longer normative; instead, the design features associated with technological management signal what is practicable or possible. Moreover, at this stage, the line between infrastructural hardwiring (that has regulatory effects) and actions to be regulated starts to shift dramatically. Finally, in a third-generation regulatory environment, regulators would go beyond traditional normative signals and design of products and places by incorporating the regulatory design within regulatees themselves (for example, by controlling their genetic coding). Where design is embedded in regulatees in such a way that it channels their behaviour, it is likely to be much less apparent to regulatees that they are being regulated – if the design is reliable, regulatees will simply behave (like products) in accordance with their specification. In these three generations, we see our regulatory past, present and future.

3.4.4 Who Are the Regulators, Who the Regulatees?

The idea of a regulatory environment evokes a picture of regulators issuing signals that direct the conduct of regulatees. In 'Type 1' regulatory environments, where the relationship between regulators and regulatees is hierarchical, there will be a clear distinction between those who are regulators and those who are regulatees; in 'Type 2' regulatory environments, where the relationship is flatter, and where self-regulation is instantiated, the distinction will be less clear; and in 'Type 3' (hybrid) regulatory environments, where there are elements of both hierarchical and nonhierarchical relationships, the distinct identity of regulators and regulatees will be occasional.

In all such articulations of a regulatory environment, the question remains whether the regulators are restricted to public functionaries – or whether the regulatory environment also encompasses private 'regulators'. For some purposes, it might be convenient to limit 'regulators' to public functionaries, so that 'regulation' is an activity that the State or its delegates carry out. However, in general, if we are interested in tracking, explaining, and evaluating the exercise of power, we should allow for regulators to be interpreted broadly as covering parties in both public and private positions; and, where our particular interest is in the use of technological management, and when so many of the relevant initiatives emanate from the private sector (for example, Monsanto's 'terminator gene' and the technologies of digital rights management), it makes little sense to confine the class of regulators to those who act in a public capacity.

3.4.5 The Boundaries of a Particular Regulatory Environment

One of the many (and more obvious) questions that we might ask about our embryonic concept of the regulatory environment is: how do we draw the limits or boundaries of any particular regulatory environment? Should we draw them from the perspective of would-be regulators or from the perspective of regulatees?[38] Or, is there some external vantage point from which we can draw them?

To start with the regulators' view, their standpoint will be that they want (1) a class of regulatees (it could be a broad class or quite a narrow one); (2) to act (or to desist from acting) in a certain way; and (3) in some defined zone (which again could be broad or narrow). For example, while regulators want their regulatees, whoever they are and wherever they are, to respect the physical well-being of one another, they will have more focused schemes for safety on the roads, for health and welfare at work, and for the safety of patients in hospitals, and so on. Accordingly, in many cases, the regulatory environment will be multi-level: in the normative dimension, there will be background standards of general application but, in many cases, the foreground standards will be specific to particular persons or particular places, or both; and, in the nonnormative dimension, technological management might be quite general (as when the State applies filters and blocks in relation to online content)[39] but often it will be local and particular. On this account, the limits of the regulatory environment are set by the sum of the signals given by the regulators.

If, however, we construct this same regulatory environment from the standpoint of regulatees, which of the regulators' signals are to count?

[38] Compare Chris Reed, *Making Laws for Cyberspace* (Oxford: Oxford University Press, 2012). One of the principal themes of Reed's critique of current (failed) attempts to legislate for cyberspace is that lawmakers need to put themselves in the position of regulatees in order to assess which interventions will gain the respect of the latter. Although Reed focuses on law rather than the larger regulatory environment, his discussion invites constructing the regulatory environment from the standpoint of regulatees.

[39] See, e.g., T.J. McIntyre, 'Child Abuse Images and Cleanfeeds: Assessing Internet Blocking Systems' in Ian Brown (ed.), *Research Handbook on Governance of the Internet* (Cheltenham: Edward Elgar, 2013) 277; and Ian Brown and Christopher T. Marsden, *Regulating Code* (Cambridge, Mass.: MIT Press, 2013) ch. 5.

Do regulatees need to be aware of the signals that the regulators have given? Do they need to regard the regulators as 'authorised' to give signals? Do regulatees need to act on the signals? Different criteria of knowledge, legitimacy and effectiveness will generate differently constituted regulatory environments, each with its own limits.[40] Moreover, regulatees might have their own rules and regulations. For example, some motorists develop their own unofficial rules of the road (such as using their headlights to signal a direction to fellow motorists) which then might present some drivers with a dilemma: do they follow the official rules and their signals or do they follow the unofficial code and its signals? What we have here is not a competition between two top-down regulators but an exercise in bottom-up self-regulation coming into tension with the background top-down standards and signals. This is a phenomenon that is far from uncommon: we see it, for example, whenever a regulatee community sets up its own rival code or culture (whether this is drivers, file-sharers, bankers, doctors or sports people).[41] In these cases, the limits of the regulatory environment are unclear and, depending on the balance of power and influence, there is likely to be a degree of top-down regulatory ineffectiveness.

How, then, might a detached observer capture the essence of a 'regulatory environment' (if, indeed, this is a meaningful question)? Although we can say that we are conceiving of a signalling environment that is designed to channel group conduct, it needs to be recognised that there is a great deal of variety in particular instantiations. Whilst some environments are regulated in a top-down law-like fashion (with regulators clearly distinguishable from regulatees), others are more bottom-up,

[40] Exactly in the way that Reed appreciates for cyberspace; see Reed, *Making Laws for Cyberspace*.

[41] On the last-mentioned, see Roger Brownsword, 'A Simple Regulatory Principle for Performance-Enhancing Technologies: Too Good to be True?' in Jan Tolleneer, Pieter Bonte, and Sigird Sterckx (eds.) *Athletic Enhancement, Human Nature and Ethics: Threats and Opportunities of Doping Technologies* (Dordrecht: Springer, 2012) 291; and, for a rare insight into the norms that actually operate in the world of professional cycling, see Tyler Hamilton and Daniel Coyle, *The Secret Race* (London: Bantam Books, 2012). For further examples of the working norms of regulatee communities, see Ellickson, *Order Without Law*; Orly Lobel, *Talent Wants to Be Free* (New Haven: Yale University Press, 2013); and for an illuminating analysis of the relationship between copying and innovation – with, in some contexts, imitation encouraging and supporting innovation to the advantage of both those who copy and those who are copied, Kal Raustiala and Christopher Sprigman, *The Knockoff Economy* (Oxford: Oxford University Press, 2012).

more self-regulatory (with regulators and regulatees much less sharply defined as such) and more reliant on informal standards. Moreover, while some regulatory environments are reasonably stable and well-formed, others are unstable, overlapping, conflictual and so on.

Perhaps the way to address the current question is to relate it to our particular cognitive interest. For example, if our cognitive interest is in the relative effectiveness of the exercise of top-down regulatory power, we will start with a notion of the regulatory environment that reflects the regulators' view; but, to account for a lack of effectiveness, we will almost certainly construct an account of the regulatory environment that reflects the practice of regulatees. However, if our interest is in the legitimate exercise of regulatory power, we might consider the issue from the standpoints of both regulators and regulatees before trying to develop a detached view that then offers an ideal-typical construct of the regulatory environment. This takes us deep into issues of conceptual methodology.

No doubt, there is a great deal more to be said about the concept of a regulatory environment; but for present purposes, this suffices.

3.5 How Are the Values of the 'Rule of Law' to Be Applied Where Technologies Are Used as Regulatory Tools?

One way of viewing the ideal of the Rule of Law is as a compact between, on the one hand, lawmakers, law-enforcers, law-interpreters and law-appliers, and on the other hand, the citizenry. The understanding is that the actions of those who are in the position of lawmakers, law-enforcers, law-interpreters and law-appliers should always be in accordance with the authorising constitutive rules; and that, provided that the relevant actions are in accordance with the constitutive rules, then citizens should respect the legal rules and decisions so made. Similarly, the acts of regulators – whether in setting standards, monitoring compliance or correcting noncompliance – should be respected provided that the constitutive rules are observed.[42] In this way, the Rule of Law imposes some constraints on the way in which the power of the Law is exercised by its institutions, its officers and its agents.

That said, if the only constraint on the power of the Law is whatever set of constitutive rules is adopted locally, then the commitment to the Rule of Law might be some, but no great, improvement on

[42] Compare Karen Yeung, *Securing Compliance* (Oxford: Hart, 2004).

unbridled power.[43] One concern, for example, is that the rules of law will be brokered in political institutions by powerful interest groups and elites, without any concern for the larger public interest or common good.[44] The same kind of concern might be raised about the influence of powerful interests on the activities of regulators; and once technological management rather than rules is employed for regulatory purposes, we should again ask whether this is compatible with the values and virtues of the Rule of Law. We should ask whether the use of technological management, by both public and private actors, involves an abuse of power; and we should ask how the generic ideal of legality that nests within the Rule of Law can be applied, and perhaps reinvented, where nonnormative technological management displaces normative regulation. We can say a few words about each of these questions.

3.5.1 *Abuse of Power*

One of the key concerns flagged by Lessig is that digital rights management technologies might be used in ways that overreach the proprietors' lawful interests – for example, by denying some uses that would fall within one of the exceptions recognised by copyright law.[45] No doubt, we could generalise this concern. For example, at the TELOS launch conference at King's College London in 2007, there was an anxious discussion about the private use of the 'Mosquito' (an antiloitering device emitting a piercing high-pitched sound that is audible only to teenagers) in order to discourage young people from congregating outside shops or in other public places where they might interfere with private interests. The principle that governs such cases is clear: private power should be exercised only in ways that are compatible with the protected legal interests of others. So, whether copyright holders try to protect their interests by contract or by technology, they should do so only to the extent that this is consistent with the protected legal interests of others; and the same applies to Mosquito-using shopkeepers who would prefer

43 For a compelling discussion, see Judith N. Shklar, *Legalism* (Cambridge, MA: Harvard University Press, 1964).

44 See, e.g., Brian Z. Tamanaha, *Law as a Means to an End* (Cambridge: Cambridge University Press, 2006); and n.b. my remarks in note 138 concerning the relationship between the Rule of Law, regulatory coherence, and technological management.

45 See Lawrence Lessig, *The Future of Ideas: The Fate of the Commons in a Connected World* (New York: Knopf Doubleday, 2002).

that, if teenagers have to congregate in some place, then they congregate somewhere else. However, the novelty of these issues together with the lack of transparency in some cases means that there is a practical challenge even if the governing principles are clear.

When we turn to the use of regulating technologies by public bodies, the principle is again clear. Public bodies should act within their lawful powers and in a way that is compatible with respect for fundamental values, such as respect for human rights and human dignity.[46] Currently, when the criminal justice agencies are increasingly relying on tracking, monitoring, identifying, and locating technologies (such as, CCTV, GPS, RFID, and DNA profiling) respect for the right to 'privacy' is the main restriction on unbridled use. In the *Marper* case,[47] the European Court of Human Rights has emphasised that the impingement on privacy must be 'proportionate'; and in *Jones*, the United States' Supreme Court has affirmed the relevance of constitutional limits, specifically the limits set by the Fourth Amendment, to chipping and tracking vehicles on public roads.[48] It is not altogether clear how public use of the 'Mosquito' might be limited; but again, the elastic concept of 'privacy' might be adequate; and presumably, it would be 'privacy' that would be the basis for challenging a disproportionate future use of brain imaging or other scanning (e.g., thermal imaging) technologies.[49] The problem, however, is that new technologies and new applications are being developed very quickly and our constitutional repertoires (which were largely articulated for low-technology societies) might not be fit for purpose. What would we say, for example, in response to the proposal that human prison officers should be replaced by robots – an idea that is already being piloted in South Korea?[50] Assuming that the robots function reliably, would this use of technology violate any constitutional principles? If privacy is not the issue, human dignity is the fallback; but this is such a contestable value that its application is unpredictable.[51]

[46] See Ben Bowling, Amber Marks and Cian Murphy, 'Crime Control Technologies: Toward an Analytical Framework and Research Agenda' in Roger Brownsword and Karen Yeung (eds.), *Regulating Technologies* (Oxford: Hart, 2008) 51.

[47] *S and Marper v United Kingdom* [2008] ECHR 1581.

[48] *United States v Jones* 132 S. Ct 945 (2012).

[49] See *Kyllo v United States* 533 US 27 (2001) (police use of heat-sensing technology to detect domestic cannabis growing).

[50] Lena Kim, 'Meet South Korea's New Robotic Prison Guards' Digital Trends (April 21, 2012): available at www.digitaltrends.com/international/meet-south-koreas-new-robotic-prison-guards/.

[51] See Beyleveld and Brownsword, *Human Dignity in Bioethics and Biolaw*; and Roger Brownsword, 'Human Dignity, Human Rights, and Simply Trying to Do the Right

Whilst respect for human rights and human dignity might appeal as a cosmopolitan standard to limit the exercise of regulatory power, local articulations of the Rule of Law might adopt other substantive constraints. For example, in the United Kingdom, the principle that coercive legal powers should not be exercised unless the conduct that is to be criminalised is plainly harmful to others, has a considerable grip on policy making. In Section 3.6, we will review the limitations of this principle both in relation to normative regulatory interventions (where the problems have been well-rehearsed) and nonnormative technological management (where there is a danger that the constraints might be thought to be inapplicable). However, before that, we must turn to the fundamental challenge of bringing ideals of legality that presuppose a normative enterprise to bear on nonnormative technological management.

3.5.2 *Displacement When Technological Management Is in Place*

In (what I have termed) a first-generation regulatory environment, regulators will rely entirely on normative signals, the standard set by the law being one such signal. This, of course, is the context in which we have crafted our understanding of the Rule of Law. However, as regulators begin to rely on nonnormative design and coding, our understanding of legality will surely need some modification.

In a classic discussion of the ideal of 'legalism', understood as a set of generic procedural requirements, Lon Fuller proposed that the standards set should be general, promulgated, prospective, clear, noncontradictory, (reasonably) constant and possible (of compliance).[52] He also suggested that it was of the essence of the Rule of Law that enforcement should be congruent with the standards so promulgated. Where the standards are not promulgated, prospective, clear, noncontradictory and (reasonably) constant, regulatees will simply not know where they stand; even if they wish to comply with the regulatory standard, they will not know what it is. If the standard set requires impossible acts of compliance, regulatees

Thing', in Christopher McCrudden (ed.), *Understanding Human Dignity* (Oxford: Proceedings of the British Academy and Oxford University Press, 2013) 470.

52 Lon L. Fuller, *The Morality of Law* (New Haven: Yale University Press, 1969). For an application of the Fullerian principles to particular instances of cyberlaw, see Reed, *Making Laws for Cyberspace*, esp. at 914–916. As Reed summarises it (at 927): 'Complexity makes laws hard to understand, contradictory rules make compliance impossible and frequent change compounds these difficulties'.

cannot comply. Reliance on highly specific regulations will drain most regulatory resources and, again, it will leave many regulatees unclear about their position. And if there is a disconnect between the standards set and the enforcement practice, not only will regulatees be unclear about their position, they will lose respect for the regulatory regime.

For many years, jurists have debated whether the Fullerian principles speak only to the conditions for effective regulation or whether, as Fuller insists, they go to the heart of distinctively *legal* forms of regulation.[53] According to Fuller, there is a critical distinction between legal direction and mere managerial direction. As he puts it, 'law is not, like management, a matter of directing other persons how to accomplish tasks set by a superior, but is basically a matter of providing the citizenry with a sound and stable framework for their interactions with one another, the role of the government being that of standing as a guardian of the integrity of this system'.[54] Although, in the context of debates concerning the essential nature (or concept) of law, there is a fundamental choice between a moralised idea of law (evincing a necessary connection between law and morals) and an idea of law as a by and large effective institution for the direction of social life, in the larger regulatory picture other distinctions loom large. In particular, as I have said, there is the choice between normative and nonnormative ordering, between rules (signalling ought and ought not) and design (signalling can and cannot). For Fuller, as for his critics, law and management alike operate with normative registers; they are traditional regulatory environments. However, what happens when we move into second- and third-generation regulatory environments, where nonnormative signals (speaking only to what is practicable or possible) predominate? In such environments, what would we make of the Fullerian criteria?

In nonnormative regulatory environments, regulators still need to communicate with their regulatees; crucially, they need to signal that only certain options are practically available. To this extent, *clarity* of transmission is still important. Of course, if the regulatory environment, even a regulatory environment in which the signals are not clear, is designed in such a way that regulatees have no option other than to do *x*, they will eventually do *x*. Even so, *x* should be done with less friction and confusion where the regulatory signal is clearly and decisively transmitted. Similarly,

[53] See, e.g., H. L. A. Hart's review of *The Morality of Law*, at (1964–65) 78 *Harvard Law Review* 1281.

[54] Fuller, *The Morality of Law*, 210.

we might think that *constancy* has some value even in a nonnormative regulatory environment. In other respects, though, the traditional Fullerian criteria no longer seem to be applicable – or, at any rate, their application takes on a new meaning. For example, the requirement that regulators respect the principle of 'ought implies can' by prescribing only the possible takes on a new significance where regulators are operating in a register that recognises only the possible (regulatory approved courses of action) and the impossible (courses of action that regulators have disallowed). Most strikingly, the Fullerian value of *congruence*, which assumes an inevitable gap between the standard as declared and as administered, takes on a quite different significance in a context in which regulators do not rely on standards that are set to be action-guiding; in such a context, there is no such gap. In an increasingly technological age, the threat to the Rule of Law is not so much regulators who engage in enforcement practices that deviate from the declared rules as the technological mistranslation of declared standards;[55] the loss of enforcement discretion and debate (the latter being the so-called problem of 'stasis');[56] the impact of technological management on conscientious objection and civil disobedience;[57] and, in future, regulators who respond to perceived risks by adopting undeclared technological strategies that necessarily enforce the desired, or exclude the undesired, pattern of behaviour.

Clearly, the complexion of the regulatory environment changes in a fundamental way once nonnormative strategies replace traditional normative signals. Quite apart from the challenges that this presents to the values of the Rule of Law, it also threatens to compromise the possibility of moral community. This latter matter is one to which we will return (in Section 3.7).

3.6 What Is the Significance of States Using Technological Management as a Means of Social Control and Channelling?

In the nineteenth century, John Stuart Mill famously laid down one of the cornerstones of liberal values by declaring that coercion (whether

[55] See Danielle Keats Citron, 'Technological Due Process' (2008) 85 *Washington University Law Review* 1249.

[56] See, e.g., Christina M. Mulligan, 'Perfect Enforcement of Law: When to Limit and When to Use Technology' (2008) 14 *Richmond Journal of Law and Technology* 1 http://law.richmond.edu/jolt/v14i4/article13.pdf.; and Danny Rosenthal, 'Assessing Digital Preemption (And the Future of Law Enforcement?)' (2011) 14 *New Criminal Law Review* 576.

[57] For an insightful discussion, see, Evgeny Morozov, *To Save Everything, Click Here* (London: Allen Lane, 2013).

legal or moral/social) cannot be justified unless the target conduct is harmful to others. Harm to others is a necessary condition before command and control regulation can be legitimately employed; harm to oneself, physical or moral, is not sufficient.[58]

Although Mill's harm principle has an almost magnetic effect on the British intelligentsia, everyone knows that it breaks down quite quickly – particularly where the notoriously contested notions of 'harm' or 'others' are in play, or where the harm is not directly or clearly caused by the act in question. For example, any attempt to square criminal prohibitions on smoking in public parks (as is now the case in New York City and in some other parts of the United States) will struggle to find a convincing kind of harm as well as a proximate cause. Generally, it is not convincing to argue that passive smoking is a risk in open spaces; and, even if discarded cigarette butts are a nuisance, the standard prohibition on litter surely suffices. This leaves the argument that smokers fail to meet their responsibilities as role models in public places. However, liberals will rightly ask how far this goes. When we are in public places, should we stop eating candy or high-calorie food, should we make a point of walking rather than riding on public transport, of using stairs rather than escalators or elevators, and so on? Public health enthusiasts might not like these liberal constraints; but, if we profess to be liberals, we need to respect the limits set by our commitments.[59]

Similarly, in debates about the use of technologies for the enhancement of human capacity or performance, we soon run into problems with the characterisation of competitive advantage and disadvantage (or 'positional harm'). One of the leading advocates of enhancement, John Harris, defines enhancement as necessarily bringing about some improvement in human functioning. Thus:

> Enhancements of course are good if and only if those things we call enhancements do good, and make us better, not perhaps simply by curing or ameliorating our ills, but because they make us better people. Enhancements will be *enhancements properly so-called* if they make us better at doing some of the things we want to do, better at experiencing the world through all of the senses, better at assimilating and processing what we

[58] J.S. Mill, 'On Liberty', in J. S. Mill, *Utilitarianism* (ed. Mary Warnock) (Glasgow: Collins/ Fontana, 1962 [first published 1859]).

[59] See, Roger Brownsword, 'Public Health Interventions: Liberal Limits and Stewardship Responsibilities' (2013) *Public Health Ethics* (special issue on NY City's public health programme) doi: 10.1093/phe/pht030.

> experience, better at remembering and understanding things, stronger, more competent, more of everything we want to be.[60]

On this view, postenhancement (properly so-called), there is an improvement in A's capacity to perform some task (that is, relative to A's preenhancement capacity). For example, postenhancement, A has significantly improved vision or hearing; or A is able to concentrate better or stay awake longer or train harder than was the case preenhancement. Given that A has these improved capacities, it follows not only that 'postenhancement A' can outperform 'preenhancement A' but also that A can now perform better relative to B, C, and D. This is not to say that A will be able to outperform others (this depends on the capacities of B, C, and D, and whether or not they, too, are enhanced in the relevant respect) but it does mean that, postenhancement, A gains some positional advantage. In the context assumed by Harris, it is not A's intention to gain such a positional advantage; it is a secondary effect.[61] Nevertheless, once we switch to, say, sporting, educational or employment contexts, the problem is that enhancement is intended precisely to gain positional advantage. Students and employees, like sportsmen, who use enhancers or enhancing technologies do so precisely for their competitive (positional) advantage; they cannot say, other than quite disingenuously, that they are happy for others to have access to the same enhancers. How does this sit with the harm principle?

Unless we already know the answer that we want to give, we can keep on repeating the question (is it harmful?) without making any progress. So much so familiar. However, there is also an equally serious, but much less well appreciated, deficit in relation to the harm principle – namely, that Mill's principle speaks only to coercive (and normative) regulatory interventions. When regulators try to guide conduct by using incentives rather than threats, or by setting defaults in a particular way,[62] it is not clear whether or how Millian liberalism is engaged. Similarly, when regulators focus on reducing the practical possibility of certain acts or use design, architecture, or coding so that such acts are not possible, it is

[60] John Harris, *Enhancing Evolution* (Princeton: Princeton University Press, 2007), at 2 (emphasis added).

[61] Ibid., 28 et seq.

[62] Seminally, see Richard H. Thaler and Cass R. Sunstein, *Nudge: Improving Decisions about Health, Wealth, and Happiness* (New Haven: Yale University Press, 2008); and compare Cass R. Sunstein, *Simpler: The Future of Government* (New York: Simon and Schuster, 2013), at 38–39 for an indicative list of possible 'nudges'.

again not clear how liberal principles should be applied. If we rely on a literal reading of the harm principle, many modern regulatory interventions might seem to escape liberal evaluation.

Prospective liberals might spend a long time debating the best reformulation of the liberal ethic. At minimum, however, any reformulation must engage with the full range of regulatory instruments and strategies that are likely to be utilised. No matter how regulators attempt to deliver on their objectives, irrespective of whether coercion is employed, the liberal ethic must have sufficient purchase to enable us to assess the legitimacy of the intervention. Let me suggest, therefore, that the spirit of liberalism (in line with Mill's objections to paternalism) is that regulators should respect the interest of competent adults in making their own prudential judgements. Or, in plain language, regulators should always try to leave room for individuals to make their own judgement of what is in their own best interest. This does not assume that individuals will do better than regulators in judging what is in their own interest. Nevertheless, liberals believe that we should be left to place our own bets, winners and losers alike – a sentiment, it seems, shared by the motoring lobby that resists technologies that compel the wearing of seat belts.[63]

It follows that, if regulators are bound by such a liberal ethic, they should not attempt to channel regulatees towards a particular (conformist) model of living. This holds regardless of whether regulators use coercion, financial disincentives, default-setting, or technological management. If regulators do use a confining design, this might well give rise to another strand of liberal objection.[64] However, for present purposes, the fundamental point is that, if regulators have illegitimate (paternalistic) objectives, they cannot escape accountability simply because, instead of using first-generation criminal law or moral sanctions,[65] they have relied on second or even third-generation nonnormative regulatory strategies.

[63] See Jerry L. Mashaw and David L. Harfst, *The Struggle for Auto Safety* (Cambridge, MA: Harvard University Press 1990) ch. 7. According to Mashaw and Harfst, although the (US) Department of Transportation estimated that the so-called interlock system would save 7,000 lives per annum and prevent 340,000 injuries, 'the rhetoric of prudent paternalism was no match for visions of technology and "big brotherism" gone mad' (at 135).

[64] See Roger Brownsword, 'Lost in Translation: Legality, Regulatory Margins, and Technological Management' (2011) 26 *Berkeley Technology Law Journal* 1321.

[65] See Roger Brownsword, 'Criminal Law, Regulatory Frameworks and Public Health' in A.M. Viens, John Coggon, and Anthony S. Kessel (eds.) *Criminal Law, Philosophy and Public Health Practice* (Cambridge: Cambridge University Press, 2013) 19.

3.7 What Is the Significance of the Complexion of the Regulatory Environment?

As we have conceded, there is a great deal of work to be done in refining our understanding of the regulatory environment; but, if we are interested in explaining how social orders channel conduct away from conflict and towards coordination and cooperation, then we need to put the spotlight on the three registers that are available to regulators and, with that, the changing 'complexion' of the regulatory environment. To develop this line of thinking, we can organise the discussion around five nodal points: the regulatory registers; the relevance of the registers; the moral significance of hard technological management; the legitimate application of hard technological management; and the special status of infrastructural regulation.

3.7.1 The Regulatory Registers

By a 'regulatory register', I mean the kind of signal that regulators employ in communicating with regulatees. There are three such registers, each of which represents a particular way in which regulators attempt to engage the practical reason (in the broad and inclusive sense of an agent's reasons for action)[66] of regulatees. Thus:

(i) In the first register (the moral register), the coding signals that some act, *x*, categorically ought or ought not to be done relative to standards of right action – regulators thus signal to regulatees that *x* is, or is not, the right thing to do.
(ii) In the second register (the prudential register), the coding signals that some act, *x*, ought or ought not to be done relative to the prudential interests of regulatees – regulators thus signal to regulatees that *x* is, or is not, in their (regulatees') self-interest.
(iii) In the third register (the register of practicability or possibility), the environment is designed in such a way that it is not reasonably practicable (or even possible) to do some act, *x* – in which case, regulatees reason, not that *x* ought not to be done, but that *x* cannot be done.

In an exclusively moral environment, the primary normative signal (in the sense of the reason for the norm) is always moral; but the secondary

[66] In this broad sense, 'practical reason' encompasses both moral and nonmoral reasons for action.

signal, depending upon the nature of the sanction, might be more prudential. In traditional criminal law environments, the signals are more complex. Whilst the primary normative signal to regulatees can be either moral (the particular act should not be done because this would be immoral) or paternalistically prudential (the act should not be done because it is contrary to the interests of the regulatee), the secondary signal represented by the deterrent threat of punishment is prudential.[67] As the regulatory environment relies more on technological interventions, the strength and significance of the moral signal fades; here, the signals to regulatees tend to accentuate that the doing of a particular act is contrary to the interests of regulatees, or that it is not reasonably practicable, or even that it is simply not possible.[68] Where the signal is that a particular act is no longer a possible option, regulatee compliance is, so to speak, fully determined; in all other cases, and especially so in the normative range, the conduct of regulatees is underdetermined.

3.7.2 *The Relevance of the Registers*

How does a framing of this kind assist our inquiries? Crucially, if we share the aspiration for legitimacy, then the framing of our inquiries by reference to the regulatory registers draws our attention to any technology-induced drift from the first to the second register (where moral reasons give way to prudence) and then from the second to the third register (where the signal is no longer normative). Sophisticated technologies of control surely will appeal to future classes of regulators in both the public and the private sectors; but communities with moral aspirations need to stay alert to the corrosion of the conditions that give

[67] Compare Alan Norrie, 'Citizenship, Authoritarianism and the Changing Shape of the Criminal Law' in Bernadette McSherry, Alan Norrie, and Simon Bronitt (eds.), *Regulating Deviance* (Oxford: Hart, 2009) 13. Ibid., at 15, Norrie highlights three broad developments in recent British criminal law and justice, namely: (1) an increasing emphasis on notions of moral right and wrong and, concomitantly, on individual responsibility ('responsibilisation'); (2) an increasing emphasis on dangerousness and, concomitantly, on the need for exceptional forms of punishment or control ('dangerousness'); and (3) an increasing reliance on preventative orders and new forms of control ('regulation'). While the first of these developments is in line with the aspirations of moral community, it is the second and the third that such a community needs to monitor with care. In this light, see, in particular, Lucia Zedner, 'Fixing the Future? The Pre-emptive Turn in Criminal Justice' in McSherry, Norrie, and Bronitt (eds.), *Regulating Deviance*, 35.

[68] Compare Bert-Jaap Koops, 'Technology and the Crime Society: Rethinking Legal Protection' (2009) 1 *Law, Innovation and Technology* 93.

meaning to their way of life.[69] The key point is that, in moral communities, and in all walks of life, the aspiration is to do the right thing; respecting persons is doing the right thing; and it matters to moral communities that such respect is shown freely and for the right reason – not because we know that we are being observed or because we have no practical option other than the one that the regulators have left for us.

Whilst surveillance technologies leave it to regulatees to decide how to act, technologies can be used in ways that harden the regulatory environment, by designing out or disallowing the choice that regulatees previously had, or by disabling or excluding particular individuals. Such hard technologies speak only to what can and cannot be done, not to what ought or ought not to be done; these are nonnormative regulatory interventions. When regulatory environments are hardened in this way, it is not quite accurate to say, as Zygmunt Baumann says of postpanopticon ordering, that it involves 'rendering the permissible obligatory';[70] rather such hardening signifies that the impermissible (but, hitherto, possible) becomes impossible – 'ought not' becomes 'cannot'.

3.7.3 *The Moral Significance of Hard Technological Management*

Where hard technologies are introduced, not to protect P against himself,[71] but in order to protect P against the potentially harmful acts of others, the pattern of 'respectful' nonharming conduct is not explained by the prudential choices of regulatees, even less by their moral judgements. In a moral community, it is when code and design leave regulatees with no option other than compliance that the legitimacy of the means employed by regulators needs urgent consideration. The problem here is that, even if we concede that the technology channels regulatees towards right action, the technologically secured pattern of right action is not at

69 Compare Mireille Hildebrandt, 'A Vision of Ambient Law', in Roger Brownsword and Karen Yeung (eds.), *Regulating Technologies* (Oxford: Hart, 2008) 175, and 'Legal and Technological Normativity: More (and Less) than Twin Sisters' (2008) 12.3 *TECHNE* 169.

70 Zygmunt Bauman and David Lyon, *Liquid Surveillance* (Cambridge: Polity Press, 2013) at 80.

71 For example, where surveillance (and disabling) technologies are employed in a paternalistic spirit, to prevent a person, P, from self-harming, the objections are limited where P consents to this management of his conduct. However, if the hard design has not been authorised in this way, then P (who might well be unaware of the technologies that are in operation to manage the risk) will simply find that his options are restricted from time to time.

all the same as freely opting to do the right thing.[72] P might be protected from the potentially harmful acts of others, but moral virtue, as Ian Kerr protests, cannot be automated.[73] Expressing this concern in relation to the use of 'digital locks', Kerr says:

> [A] generalized and unimpeded use of digital locks, further protected by the force of law, threatens not merely [various] legal rights and freedoms but also threatens to significantly impair our moral development. In particular, I express deep concern that digital locks could be used in a systematic attempt to 'automate human virtue' – programming people to 'do the right thing' by constraining and in some cases altogether eliminating moral behaviour through technology rather than ethics or law. Originally introduced to improve the human condition, digital locks and other automation technologies could, ironically, be used to control our virtual and physical environments in unprecedented ways, to eliminate the possibility for moral deliberation about certain kinds of action otherwise possible in these spaces by disabling the world in a way that ultimately disables the people who populate it. Not by eliminating their choices but by automating them – by removing people from the realm of moral action altogether, thereby impairing their future moral development.[74]

Applying this analysis to the case of honest action, Kerr detects the irony that

> a ubiquitous digital lock strategy meant to 'keep honest people honest' is a self-defeating goal since it impairs the development of *phronesis*, stunts moral maturity and thereby disables the cultivation of a deep-seated disposition for honesty. Woven into the fabric of everyday life, digital locks would ensure particular outcomes for property owners but would do so at the expense of the moral project of honesty.[75]

The point is that the shift from law (or ethics) to technological instruments changes the 'complexion' of the regulatory environment in a way that threatens to compromise the possibility of authentic moral action[76] –

[72] Compare Morozov, *To Save Everything*.

[73] Ian Kerr, 'Digital Locks and the Automation of Virtue' in Michael Geist (ed.), *From 'Radical Extremism' to 'Balanced Copyright': Canadian Copyright and the Digital Agenda* (Toronto: Irwin Law, 2010) 247.

[74] Ibid., at 254–255. [75] Ibid., at 292.

[76] See, further, Brownsword, 'Lost in Translation'. Compare Charles Taylor, *The Ethics of Authenticity* (Cambridge, MA: Harvard University Press, 1991), for a thoughtful critique of various strands of 'modernity' in relation to a supposed loss of 'authenticity'. Taylor argues persuasively that the real issue is not whether we are for or against authenticity, but '*about* it, defining its proper meaning' (at 73); and, for Taylor, authenticity is to be understood as a moral ideal that accords importance to agents fulfilling themselves by

whether we see this as an act for which we can claim 'authorship' or responsibility, or as an act of self-affirmation or signalling to others of one's capacity to eschew prudential advantage and, instead, do the right thing.[77]

3.7.4 *The Legitimate Application of Hard Technological Management*

That said, it surely cannot be right to condemn all applications of technological management as illegitimate. For example, modern transport systems incorporate safety features that are intended to design-out the possibility of human error or carelessness.[78] Should we object to this? Or, should we object to the proposal that we might turn to the use of regulating technologies to replace a failed normative strategy for securing the safety of patients who are taking medicines or being treated in hospitals?[79]

Let us suppose that safety measures of this kind have been publicly debated and voted on in an acceptable democratic way. On the face of it, there has been due process and there is no further objection. Deliberative democracy does not finally close the door but, for the time being, the technological fixes must be accepted. Nevertheless, cautions and concern, prudential as well as moral, might remain.

First, from a prudential perspective, we might object that caution should be exercised.[80] It is all very well to vote for the technology today, but what if preferences change? If the technology is irreversible (particularly, for example, where the controls are biotechnological and involve some rewriting of the human genetic code), or if the costs of disabling the technology are very high, precaution indicates that the community should go very slowly with this strategy. Perhaps a prudential rule of thumb would be that the technology should only be adopted where it is designed for cheap discontinuity.

being true to themselves – but without this 'excluding unconditional relationships and moral demands beyond the self' (at 72–73).

77 For some helpful suggestions on this point, I am grateful to Marcus Düwell and others who participated in a symposium on 'Human Dignity: A Major Concept in Ethics?' held at the University of Tübingen on October 24, 2014.

78 For a vivid example, see Wolff, 'Five Types of Risky Situation'.

79 See Roger Brownsword, 'Regulating Patient Safety: Is It Time for a Technological Response?' (2014) 6 *Law, Innovation and Technology* 1.

80 Some might fear, for example, that, in our quest for greater safety and well-being, we will develop and embed ever more intelligent devices to the point that there is a risk of the extinction of humans: compare Nick Bostrom, *Superintelligence* (Oxford: Oxford University Press, 2014).

Second, from a moral standpoint, there is more than one kind of residual concern. For example, unless there is an 'override', there might be exceptional circumstances in which it is not possible to do the right thing. However, the objection that needs to be highlighted (because it cuts deeper) is that a community can tolerate only a certain level of hard technological management; there must remain ample opportunities for humans to engage in moral reflection and then to do the right thing – indeed, to express their human dignity by doing the right thing for the right reason.[81] So, the cumulative effect of adopting hard technological fixes needs to be a standing item on the regulatory agenda.[82] If we knew just how much space a moral community needs to safeguard against the automation of virtue, and if we had some kind of barometer to measure for this, we might be able to draw some regulatory red lines. However, without knowing these things, a precautionary approach (according and protecting a generous margin for moral reflection and moral reason freely to operate) again looks prudent.

These exploratory remarks suggest that we might need to develop a jurisprudence that is more context-sensitive, differentiating between the use of technological management for the purpose of (1) classic crime control and (2) the improvement of the conditions for human health and safety as well as to protect the integrity of the environment. Where technological management is used for classic crime control purposes, our concerns about due process and the corrosion of the conditions for moral community are most acute. By contrast, where the purpose is to improve the conditions for human health and safety (on the roads, at work, in hospitals and so on) by replacing regulatory rules with technological management, our moral concerns are not so clearly provoked. To be sure, the use of technological management for either purpose will be disruptive (especially with regard to its impact on employment and the loss of some practical options previously available to humans).[83] However, it is tempting to think that the use of technological management for

[81] See, further, Düwell, 'Human Dignity'.

[82] Karen Yeung, 'Can We Employ Design-Based Regulation While Avoiding Brave New World?' (2011) 3 *Law, Innovation and Technology* 1.

[83] For example, the American Truckers Association estimates that with the introduction of driverless lorries, some 8.7 million trucking-related jobs could face some form of displacement; see Daniel Thomas, 'Driverless convoy: Will truckers lose out to software?' BBC News, May 26, 2015, available at www.bbc.com/news/business-32837071; generally, see Andrew Keen, *The Internet is Not the Answer* (London: Atlantic Books, 2015), and Jaron Lanier, *Who Owns the Future?* (London: Allen Lane, 2013).

at least some purposes will be truly progressive. The challenge will be, first, to work out when, and for what purpose, it is right to resort to technological management and when not to do so; second, to agree on the guidelines for the use of technological management; and third, to adhere to the guidelines in what might be a context that defaults very quickly and stubbornly to technological measures.

3.7.5 *The Special Status of Infrastructural Regulation*

Before leaving the question of regulatory complexion, it is worth remarking that we might frame the issues in a rather different way. The concerns that have been expressed assume that the regulatory interventions in question are directed at human interactions rather than at the infrastructure presupposed by such interactions. Although the drawing of the line between such interactions and the infrastructure itself is subject to debate, there is a view that regulators may legitimately use a technological fix where their intention is to protect the infrastructure.[84] The gist of this view is as follows.

First, while the deepest layer of the regulatory environment should be concerned with securing the generic infrastructure for agency itself, the remainder should set the ground rules for agents' on-stage interactions and transactions. While the former is foundational and universal, the latter can be more tuned to local cultural commitments and preferences. To put this in cosmopolitan terms, while all regulators share a responsibility for securing the essential infrastructural conditions, within each community there is room for some (legitimate) variation in the regulation of local (on-stage) activities.[85]

[84] See, e.g., David A. Wirth, 'Engineering the Climate: Geoengineering as a Challenge to International Governance' (2013) 40 *Boston College Environmental Affairs Law Review* 413, 437: 'Lawmakers, both domestic and international would be remiss not to seriously consider geoengineering proposals to mitigate the harm of global warming.' This view is also implicit in Gareth Davies, 'Law and Policy Issues of Unilateral Geoengineering: Moving to a Managed World', available at: http://papers.ssrn.com/sol3/papers.cfm?abstract_id=1334625 (last accessed on May 10, 2015). See, too, Roger Brownsword, 'Crimes Against Humanity, Simple Crime, and Human Dignity' in Britta van Beers, Luigi Corrias and Wouter Werner (eds.), *Humanity across International Law and Biolaw* (Cambridge University Press, 2013) 87, 106–109. And, for a sustained caution against our tendency to undervalue infrastructural resources, see Brett M. Frischmann, *Infrastructure* (New York: Oxford University Press, 2012).

[85] For further discussion, see Roger Brownsword, 'Regulatory Cosmopolitanism: Clubs, Commons, and Questions of Coherence' (TILT Working Paper series, University of Tilburg, 2010).

Second, if the infrastructure is to be secured, this implies a considerable degree of international coordination and shared responsibility. Moreover, because politics tends to operate with short-term horizons, it also implies that the regulatory stewards need to have some independence from the political branch.[86]

Third, although (after its initial honeymoon period) the precautionary principle has been severely criticised – for example, it has been accused of being 'an overly-simplistic and under-defined concept that seeks to circumvent the hard choices that must be faced in making any risk management decision'[87] – a form of precautionary reasoning might well be acceptable in defence of the infrastructure.[88] According to such reasoning, where regulators cannot rule out the possibility that some activity threatens the infrastructure (which, on any view, is potentially 'catastrophic'), then they should certainly engage a precautionary approach.[89] The range of precautionary measures is quite broad. At minimum, regulators should consider withdrawing any intellectual property (IP) encouragement (notably patents) for the relevant

[86] See, too, Roger Brownsword, 'Responsible Regulation: Prudence, Precaution and Stewardship' (2011) 62 *Northern Ireland Legal Quarterly* 573.

[87] Gary E. Marchant and Douglas J. Sylvester, 'Transnational Models for Regulation of Nanotechnology' (2006) 34 *Journal of Law, Medicine and Ethics* 714, at 722. For an extended critique, see Cass R. Sunstein, *Laws of Fear* (Cambridge: Cambridge University Press, 2005).

[88] Compare Deryck Beyleveld and Roger Brownsword, 'Complex Technology, Complex Calculations: Uses and Abuses of Precautionary Reasoning in Law' in Marcus Duwell and Paul Sollie (eds.), *Evaluating New Technologies: Methodological Problems for the Ethical Assessment of Technological Developments* (Dordrecht: Springer, 2009) 175; and 'Emerging Technologies, Extreme Uncertainty, and the Principle of Rational Precautionary Reasoning' (2012) 4 *Law Innovation and Technology* 35.

[89] Even Sunstein changes tack when catastrophic harms are in contemplation. See Cass R. Sunstein, *Worst-Case Scenarios* (Cambridge, MA: Harvard University Press, 2007), esp. ch. 3. At 167–168, Sunstein develops the following precautionary approach:

> In deciding whether to eliminate the worst-case scenario under circumstances of uncertainty, regulators should consider the losses imposed by eliminating that scenario, and the size of the difference between the worst-case scenario under one course of action and the worst-case scenario under alternative courses of action. If the worst-case scenario under one course of action is much worse than the worst-case scenario under another course of action, and if it is not extraordinarily burdensome to take the course of action that eliminates the worst-case scenario, regulators should take that course of action. But if the worst-case scenario under one course of action is not much worse than the worst-case scenario under another course of action, and if it is extraordinarily burdensome to take the course of action that eliminates the worst-case scenario, regulators should not take that course of action.

technology[90] and they may in good faith apply protective measures or prohibitions even though such measures involve some sacrifice of a valued activity (actual or anticipated).[91] It is true that, in conditions of uncertainty, a precautionary sacrifice might prove unnecessary. However, the alternative is to decline to make the sacrifice even when this was necessary to defend the generic conditions. If regulators gamble with the generic infrastructure, and if they get it wrong, it is not just the particular valued activity, but all human activities, that will be affected adversely.

Fourth, as our discussion of the regulatory complexion highlights, for communities that have moral aspirations or that value their individual autonomy, it is important that the regulatory environment does not design out (nonnormatively) the opportunities for acting freely or doing the right thing. Nevertheless, where the regulatory stewards are acting to protect the infrastructure, a resort to designed-in solutions may be more readily justified. For example, if humans will not comply with normative regulatory requirements that are designed to tackle global warming, a nonnormative geoengineering technical fix might be a legitimate way of dealing with the problem.[92]

If regulators are trying to stage the conditions for moral community, they need not worry about the complexion of the regulatory environment; for, quite simply, until the infrastructure is in place, there is no prospect of any kind of human community.[93] So long as our understanding of the infrastructure is restricted to the *essential* conditions for human existence (particularly to such vital matters as the availability of food and water, and the preservation of the environment), this framing will not impact greatly on debates about the corrosion of the context for the moral life. However, if each community adjusts the infrastructural

90 Compare Estelle Derclaye, 'Should Patent Law Help Cool the Plant? An Inquiry from the Point of View of Environmental Law – Part I' (2009) 31 *European Intellectual Property Review* 168, and 'Part II' (2009) 31 *European Intellectual Property Review* 227.

91 For some insightful remarks on the difference between dealing with technologies that are already in use and newly emerging technologies, see Alan Randall, *Risk and Precaution* (Cambridge: Cambridge University Press, 2011).

92 For an overview of such possible fixes, see Jesse Reynolds, 'The Regulation of Climate Engineering' (2011) 3 *Law, Innovation and Technology* 113; and, for an indication of the burgeoning literature as well as possible responses to transboundary liability issues, see Barbara Saxler, Jule Siegfried and Alexander Proelss, 'International Liability for Transboundary Damage Arising from Stratospheric Aerosol Injections' (2015) 7 *Law Innovation and Technology* 112.

93 See, further, Brownsword, 'Criminal Law'; Brownsword, 'Responsible Regulation'.

threshold in a way that reflects the stage of its technological development, this might involve characterising many safety features that are designed into, say, everyday transport and healthcare facilities, as 'infrastructural' – which, concomitantly, expands the zone of ostensibly legitimate reliance on hard technological management.[94] Clearly, for regulators in more complex societies, where infrastructural conditions are heavily engineered, there will be a temptation to add to the infrastructure as a means of bypassing concerns about the undermining of moral community. However, that is obviously no answer for a community that genuinely retains its moral aspirations.

3.8 Within the Larger Framework of the Regulatory Environment, What Do We Now Understand About the Effectiveness of the Law?

Technological management promises to be an effective form of regulation. Whether this promise will be fulfilled, we do not yet know. However, we do know that many traditional normative regulatory interventions are relatively ineffective; and we do have a stock of particular case-studies concerning the impact of particular laws that offer rich accounts of ineffective interventions or of unintended negative effects. Moreover, we also know that the cross-boundary effects of the online provision of goods and services have compounded the challenges faced by regulators. If we synthesise this body of knowledge, what do we understand about the conditions for regulatory effectiveness?

To begin with, we can agree with Francis Fukuyama[95] that:

> [N]o regulatory regime is ever fully leak-proof ... But this misses the point of social regulation: no law is ever fully enforced. Every country makes murder a crime and attaches severe penalties to homicide, and yet murders nonetheless occur. The fact that they do has never been a reason for giving up on the law or on attempts to enforce it.[96]

[94] Compare Council Directive 2008/114/EC (on the identification and designation of European critical infrastructures and the assessment of the need to improve their protection). Article 2(a) of the Directive defines 'critical infrastructure' as 'an asset, system or part thereof located in Member States which is essential for the maintenance of vital societal functions, health, safety, security, economic or social well-being of people, and the disruption or destruction of which would have a significant impact in a Member State as a result of the failure to maintain those functions.'

[95] Francis Fukuyama, *Our Posthuman Future* (London: Profile Books, 2002).

[96] Ibid., at 189.

It follows that, if we set the bar for regulatory effectiveness at the level of complete achievement of the regulators' objectives, we will judge that virtually all regulatory interventions are ineffective. However, we should be careful not to assume that it is only murderers, thieves, and vagabonds that stand between regulators and complete effectiveness. The keys to effective regulation are far more complex.

Placing our inquiries within the context of the regulatory environment, we can simplify the complexity by focusing on the three critical areas in which the effectiveness or ineffectiveness of an intervention will be determined. These are, respectively, the zone in which regulators operate, the zone in which regulatees act and all surrounding areas in which third parties operate.

3.8.1 Zone 1: Where Regulators Operate

In the first of these areas, we can identify a range of very well-documented regulator-side issues. Let me mention just three: corruption, capture and inadequate resources.

First, there is perhaps the most widespread reason for regulatory ineffectiveness: at some level, whether in setting the standards, in monitoring compliance or in responding to noncompliance, regulators are corrupt. For example, one might wonder why so few illegal drugs are intercepted as they pass through the Caribbean. Why is regulation so ineffective? According to Ben Bowling, the islands' illicit drug economy thrives on:

> widespread corruption, ranging from the junior Customs officer paid to 'look the other way' when baggage handlers are packing aircraft luggage holds with parcels of cocaine at the international airport, to the senior officials who take a cut of the cash generated on their watch.[97]

Second, even if regulators are not directly 'buyable' in this way, they might nevertheless be captured by influential regulatees. For example, in her excellent book, *Dispensing with the Truth*,[98] Alicia Mundy presents an extended account of how the Fen-Phen diet drug found its way into the marketplace where it took a heavy toll on its users. According to Mundy, the personal tragedies brought about by use of

[97] Ben Bowling, *Policing the Caribbean* (Oxford: Oxford University Press, 2010) at 5.
[98] (New York: St Martin's Press, 2001).

Fen-Phen might have been averted had American Home Products (AHP, through its Wyeth-Ayerst division) not been so economical with the truth in relation to the risks associated with the drug and had the prevailing culture at the regulatory agency (the US Food and Drug Administration [FDA]) been less concerned with assisting the pharmaceutical companies to bring their products to market and more concerned with product safety. Once the lawyers were able to make the right connections between the knowledge of the producers of Fen-Phen, the properties of the drug and the damage done to the complainants, AHP had little choice but to make massive compensatory settlements with individual and mass tort claimants. Generally speaking, the tort system comes out of Mundy's account rather well and public regulation rather badly. So far as the FDA is concerned we have a familiar tale of regulatory capture: put crudely, the agency is either not willing or not able to distance itself from the interests of the pharmaceutical companies (resulting in a failure to take a hard look at the companies' claims) and this arises, in part, from the influence that the companies exert directly over the agency and, in part, from the indirect influence that is exerted via the political branch over, inter alia, resourcing for the agency.

This cues in a third reason: quite simply, regulators lack the resources to discharge their responsibilities. Notoriously, regulators often have to make hard choices in deciding whether to prioritise strategic issues or to respond to individual cases. Even if noncompliance is detected, it might be on a scale that overwhelms those agencies that are responsible for correction. For example, according to Ian Walden, when the Internet Watch Foundation identified some 7,200 UK persons who were involved with 'Landslide' (a major child pornography site hosted in Texas), this was a level of offending with which the criminal justice system simply could not cope.[99] Moreover, although the authorities in Texas were able to close down the site, as fast as one site was closed many others were opened. If the criminal justice system cannot cope with the general run of crime, it is hardly surprising that underresourcing is a problem in relation to newer kinds of online criminality – and, indeed, we might expect to find a similar story where regulatory agencies have somewhat specialised roles and responsibilities.

[99] Ian Walden, 'Porn, Pipes and the State: Regulating Internet Content', inaugural lecture, delivered on February 3, 2010, at Queen Mary University London.

3.8.2 Zone 2: Where Regulatees Act

Turning to the second of the areas, commentators generally agree that regulators tend to do better when they act with the backing of regulatees (with a consensus rather than without it).[100] If regulatees do not perceive the purpose that underlies a particular regulatory intervention as being in either their prudential or their moral interests (let alone in both their prudential and moral interests), the motivation for compliance is weakened. The use of marijuana as a recreational drug is the textbook example. Thus:

> The fact remains ... that marijuana use continues to be illegal in most parts of the world, even as people continue to break these laws with apparent impunity. And there is no resolution in sight. The persistence of marijuana use remains a prime example of how our legal system is based on an implicit social contract, and how the laws on the books can cease to matter when a large percentage of people decide they want to do something that may not be acceptable under the law.[101]

Similarly, experience (especially in the United States) with regulatory prohibitions on alcohol suggests not only that legal interventions that overstep the mark will be ineffective but pregnant with corrupting and secondary criminalising effects. However, before we can make the most of this insight, we need to understand much more about the roots of regulatee resistance, whether it be economic, cultural, professional, or moral in nature.

One of the key factors that will determine the penetration of a law is whether there is any *economic* resistance: quite simply, if regulatees act like rational economic actors, they will tend to view law as a tax on certain kinds of conduct. If noncompliance (or possibly relocation) is the better economic option, the logic for such regulatees is to disobey and (sometimes) pay. For instance, in the days when Sunday trading in the UK was illegal, it made good business sense for large-scale DIY enterprises to open their doors on Sundays and occasionally pay a £2,000 fine. If Sunday trading had damaged the reputation of these businesses, this

[100] The idea that regulators do best when they 'work with the grain' is emphasised in Iredell Jenkins, *Social Order and the Limits of Law* (Princeton, NJ: Princeton University Press, 1980); see, too, Phillipe Sands, *Lawless World* (London: Penguin, 2005) at 56, for the eminently generalisable piece of regulatory wisdom that 'there exists in diplomatic circles a strongly held view that if a treaty cannot be adopted by consensus its long-term prospects are crippled'.

[101] Stuart Biegel, *Beyond Our Control?* (Cambridge MA: MIT Press, 2003) 105.

would have had to have been factored into the economic calculation; but, generally, the public supported the vanguard Sunday traders, and so there was no such risk. Putting the point rather generally, we can say that, where business people believe that compliance makes economic sense, they will comply; but, where compliance does not make economic sense, they will be less ready to comply.[102]

Another key element of resistance is often to be found in the culture of target regulatees, whether popular or professional, occupational or business. Regulators need to reckon with the attitudes of the professions: professional bodies (particularly the legal and the medical professions) tend to be extremely jealous of their autonomy and, not unreasonably, think that they know their own businesses best. Attempts to regulate the professions in a way that runs across the grain of professional culture will almost certainly be ineffective. Similarly, where there is a certain occupational culture ('cop culture', the culture of getting the policing job done, is one of the best examples), regulators will meet with resistance where they try to legislate across the received norms of that culture. And so long as the culture of business is to maximise profits, attempts by regulators to encourage corporate social responsibility will tend to be more effective where they channel businesses towards win–win practices.[103]

Occasionally, resistance to the law is required as a matter of conscience – witness, for example, the peace tax protesters; physicians who ignore what they see as unconscionable legal restrictions; members of religious groups who defy a legally supported dress code; and the like. Such persons and such examples are probably the exception rather than the rule; but where the law is up against a case of genuine conscientious objection, then it is truly up against it.

In all these cases, the critical point is that regulation does not act on an inert body of regulatees: regulatees will respond to regulation – sometimes by complying with it, sometimes by ignoring it, sometimes by

[102] To a considerable extent, rational economic man operates on both sides of the regulatory fence; for example, in both the licit and the illicit drugs market. Compare Nichola Dorn, Tom Bucke, and Chris Goulden, 'Traffick, Transit and Transaction: A Conceptual Framework for Action Against Drug Supply' (2003) 42 *Howard Journal of Criminal Justice* 348, at 363, according to whom, it seems likely that 'only interventions causing traffickers to perceive a significant risk of capture leading to imprisonment have a worthwhile deterrent effect, lower-impact interventions providing for traffickers no more than the expected "costs of doing business"'.

[103] See John Parkinson, 'Corporate Governance and the Regulation of Business Behaviour' in Sorcha MacLeod (ed.), *Corporate Governance* (Oxford: Hart, 2006) 1.

resisting or repositioning themselves, sometimes by relocating, and so on. Sometimes those who oppose the regulation will seek to overturn it by lawful means, sometimes by unlawful means; sometimes the response will be strategic and organised, and at other times it will be chaotic and spontaneous. But regulatees have minds and interests of their own; they will respond in their own way; and the nature of the response will be an important determinant of the effectiveness of the regulation.[104]

Tim Wu, in a helpful discussion, asks readers to imagine regulatees, faced by an unwelcome law (or by some other kind of regulatory intervention) as disciplined prudential calculators.[105] The basic choice for such calculating regulatees is between avoiding the law or trying to change it. Thus:

> [G]roups and individuals face a choice between avoidance and change mechanisms when deciding how to react to burdensome laws. Very simply, if a law is a cost on its subjects, then *avoidance* and *change* mechanisms, the subjects of the compliance and political choice literatures respectively, can be pictured as different directions of reaction . . .
>
> [W]ithin each broader category of mechanism, are specific subcategories, such as lobbying or litigation in the case of change mechanisms, and evasion and avoision (sic) in the case of avoidance mechanisms.[106]

By evasion, Wu means that regulatees break the law but invest in reducing the chances of being punished, for example, by obscuring their faces during the commission of a crime, by hiring lawyers, or by bribing officials. By 'avoision', he means acts that involve 'efforts to exploit the differences between a law's goals and its self defined limits'.[107] Some tax avoidance schemes might fit this description, as would an example that Wu gives of a pornographer who includes indecent photographs in a work that also includes serious essays about some aspects of sex in marriage; and, similarly, we might think about the case of car drivers

[104] For an illuminating account of the illicit GM seed trade in India, by-passing both the local bio-safety regulations and Mahyco-Monsanto's premium prices, see Ronald J. Herring and Milind Kandlikar, 'Illicit Seeds: Intellectual Property and the Underground Proliferation of Agricultural Biotechnologies' in Sebastian Haunss and Kenneth C. Shadlen (eds.), *Politics of Intellectual Property* (Cheltenham: Edward Elgar, 2009) 56. At 74, the authors remark:

> Stealth seeds reflect the same kind of agency as urban appropriation of pharmaceuticals and software, films and music – the same anarchic capitalism at the grass roots – with similar risks and rewards.

[105] Tim Wu, 'When Code Isn't Law' (2003) 89 *Virginia LR* 679. [106] Ibid., at 695–696.

[107] *Ibid.*, at 692.

('manipulators') who slow down at speed cameras but then accelerate away once they are clear of the camera-monitored stretch of road.[108]

3.8.3 Zone 3: Where Others Operate

In the third area, we can bring into the reckoning various kinds of distortion or interference with the regulatory signals. Some kinds of third-party interference are well-known – for example, regulatory arbitrage (which is a feature of company law and tax law) is nothing new. However, even where regulatory arbitrage is not being actively pursued, the effectiveness of local regulatory interventions can be reduced as regulatees take up more attractive options that are available elsewhere.[109] Somewhat unusually, in the case of *S.H. and Others v Austria*,[110] there was a suggestion that the restrictiveness of the Austrian IVF rules was *helpfully assisted* by the coexistence of less restrictive regulatory regimes in adjacent European countries. Generally, though, this kind of regulatory competition is unwelcome in the home country.

Although externalities of this kind continue to play their part in determining the fate of a regulatory intervention, it is the emergence of the Internet that has most dramatically highlighted the possibility of interference from third parties. Famously, David Johnson and David Post predicted that national regulators would have little success in controlling extraterritorial online activities, even though those activities have a local impact.[111] While national regulators are not entirely powerless, the development of the Internet has dramatically changed the regulatory environment, creating new vulnerabilities to cybercrime and cyberthreats, as well as new online community cultures. The net effect is that local regulators are left wondering how they can control access to drugs, alcohol, gambling or direct-to-consumer genetic testing services, when Internet pharmacies, or online drinks suppliers, casinos or the like, all of which are hosted on servers that are located beyond the national borders, direct their goods and services at local regulatees.

[108] For an interesting study of motorists' attitudes and behaviour, see Claire Corbett and Isabel Caramlau, 'Gender Difference in Response to Speed Cameras: Typology Findings and Implications for Road Safety' (2006) 4 *Criminology and Criminal Justice* 411.

[109] See, e.g., Arthur J. Cockfield, 'Towards a Law and Technology Theory' (2004) 30 *Manitoba Law Journal* 383, 391–395.

[110] Application no. 57813/00 (April 1, 2010).

[111] David R. Johnson and David Post, 'Law and Borders: The Rise of Law in Cyberspace' (1996) 48 *Stanford Law Review* 1367.

Having viewed the prospects for effective regulatory interventions from all three angles, we can see that the regulatory environment is thick with signals that point in different directions. The lesson that we might take from this is that, even if the regulators' performance is exemplary, there are too many variables in play for anyone to be confident that new laws will move things in the desired direction let alone be fully effective.

On the face of it, because technological management controls many of the variables that distort and obstruct compliance with rules, the thought is encouraged that social control might be more effective if new technologies are utilised as regulatory instruments. Here, after all, is the prospect of not only an end to regulatory corruption and capture (as human operatives are taken out of the equation) but also the rendering irrelevant of cultures of noncompliance (as potential offenders are disabled and excluded and potential offences designed out); here, indeed, is the prospect of 'perfect control'. On the other hand, until we have some experience of more general technological management, we do not know whether its promissory notes will be honoured. For example, we do not know whether a lack of regulatory resource might mean that the management systems prove to be inadequate and unreliable, leading to problems and pressure for their withdrawal; we do not know whether those who oppose the measures will be able to inflict physical damage on, or otherwise disable, the systems; and the more that smart environments rely on information technologies, we certainly do not know whether it will be possible to protect these systems against cyberattacks.[112] Even if technological management proves to be resilient and effective, there is then the further question – one that we have already flagged up – of how far we think that it is legitimate for regulators to implement their policies in this way. Legitimate regulatory environments, we might find, are not necessarily geared for effectiveness; and effective technological management is not compatible with the community's values or deep moral aspirations.

[112] Following the devastating DDoS attacks on Estonia in 2007, the question of the vulnerability of critical information infrastructures in Europe rapidly moved up the political agenda: see, House of Lords European Union Committee, *Protecting Europe Against Large-Scale Cyber-Attacks* (Fifth Report, Session 2009–2010); and *The UK Cyber Security Strategy* (Protecting and promoting the UK in a digital world) (London: Cabinet Office, November 2011). Generally, see Susan W. Brenner, *Cyberthreats: the Emerging Fault Lines of the Nation State* (Oxford: Oxford University Press, 2009).

3.9 To What Extent Can We Expect the Signals That Comprise the Regulatory Environment to Be Coherent?

Famously, Ronald Dworkin argued that one of the characteristic aspirations of legal (especially judicial) practice is that it should be principled in its approach, displaying a certain kind of integrity,[113] and concomitantly that the body of legal doctrine (together with its underlying jurisprudence) should be coherent.[114] Arguably, such concerns are closely linked to the values of the Rule of Law.[115]

Recently, English contract lawyers have been wrestling with the relationship between two streams of doctrine, one dealing with the interpretation (or construction) of contracts and the other with implied terms. Controversially, in *Attorney-General of Belize v Belize Telecom Ltd.*,[116] the Privy Council (led by Lord Hoffmann) sought to assimilate these two doctrinal streams and instate a single unifying test based on the reasonable expectations of the parties in the particular context of their transaction.[117] One of the points made by supporters of this assimilation is that it 'promotes the internal coherence of the law'; and this, it is said, is important 'because it enables the courts to identify the aims and values that underpin the law and to pursue those values and aims so as to achieve consistency in the structure of the law'.[118]

Turning from contracts to IP, the regulatory environment for patents in Europe is a particularly interesting test-case not only for our understanding of the ideal of legal coherence but also, of course, for its practical realisation. For some time, national patent law regimes have operated under the umbrella of the European Patent Convention, 1973 (the EPC). However, following the enactment of Directive 98/44/EC on the Legal Protection of Biotechnological Inventions, one major sector of innovation falls to be regulated under both the EPC and EU law. For most purposes, this is not problematic. However, the exclusion against patentability on moral grounds that is provided for in both regimes has given rise to major questions concerning the patentability of innovative stem

[113] Ronald Dworkin, *Law's Empire* (Cambridge: Harvard University Press, 1986).

[114] For an extended discussion of the particular issue introduced in this section, see Roger Brownsword, 'Regulatory Coherence: A European Challenge' in Kai Purnhagen and Peter Rott (eds.), *Varieties of European Economic Law and Regulation: Essays in Honour of Hans Micklitz* (New York: Springer, 2014) 235.

[115] Compare Tamanaha, *Law as a Means to an End*. [116] [2009] UKPC 10.

[117] See Richard Hooley, 'Implied Terms after *Belize Telecom*' (2014) 73 *CLJ* 315.

[118] Per Arden LJ in *Stena Line Ltd. v Merchant Navy Ratings Pension Fund Trustees Ltd.* [2011] EWCA Civ 543, at [36].

cell research – questions that have been raised for determination both at the European Patent Office (in relation to the EPC) and before the European Court of Justice (CJEU). The two leading cases, *Wisconsin Alumni Research Foundation* (*WARF*) at the European Patent Office,[119] and *Brüstle* at the CJEU,[120] have generated a storm of controversy about both the substance of the decisions and the coherence of the patent regime.

Briefly, in October 2011, the CJEU, responding to a reference from the German Federal Court of Justice, ruled that innovative stem cell research conducted by Oliver Brüstle was excluded from patentability by Article 6(2)(c) of Directive 98/44/EC on the Legal Protection of Biotechnological Inventions – or, at any rate, it was so excluded to the extent that Brüstle's research relied on the use of materials derived from human embryos which were, in the process, necessarily terminated. Although this judgement was, broadly speaking, in line with the decision of the Enlarged Board of Appeals at the European Patent Office in the *WARF* case (where, once again, the products of pioneering human embryonic stem cell research were excluded from patentability), the decision in *Brüstle* (like the decision in *WARF*) has attracted widespread criticism.[121]

[119] Case G 0002/06, November 25, 2008. Here, the Enlarged Board of Appeal at the EPO was asked by the Technical Board of Appeal (T 1374/04 (OJ EPO 2007, 313)) to rule on four questions of law – one of which was whether Article 6(2)(c), as incorporated in the EPC Rules, forbids the patenting of a human embryonic stem cell culture which, at the time of filing, could be prepared only by a method that necessarily involved the destruction of human embryos (even though the method in question is not part of the claim). Treating this as an exercise in the interpretation of a particular rule, rather than a more general essay in European morality, the EBA said (at para 18):

> On its face, the provision ... is straightforward and prohibits the patenting if a human embryo is used for industrial or commercial purposes. Such a reading is also in line with the concern of the legislator to prevent a misuse in the sense of a commodification of human embryos ... and with one of the essential objectives of the whole Directive to protect human dignity.

Rejecting the argument that human embryos were not actually being used for commercial or industrial purposes, the EBA held that, where the method of producing the claimed product necessarily involved the destruction of human embryos, then such destruction was 'an integral and essential part of the industrial or commercial exploitation of the claimed invention' (para 25); and, thus, the prohibition applied and precluded the patent.

[120] Case C-34/10, *Oliver Brüstle v Greenpeace e.V.* (Grand Chamber, 18 October 2011).

[121] On the *WARF* case, see e.g., Paul L.C. Torremans, 'The Construction of the Directive's Moral Exclusions under the EPC', in Aurora Plomer and Paul Torremans (eds.),

In essence, the basis of the CJEU's decision is that Brüstle's research crosses one of the moral red lines provided for by the Directive – in this case, a 'dignitarian' line,[122] set out in Article 6(2)(c), that protects human embryos against instrumentalisation, commodification and commercialisation by researchers (or, in the words of Article 6(2)(c), that protects human embryos against use for 'industrial or commercial purposes'). For many IP lawyers, the very idea of moral lines being embedded in European patent law is unacceptable:[123] such lines are not drawn in other major regional patent regimes;[124] and decisions such as those in *WARF* and *Brüstle* serve to underline both the limited moral competence of patent examiners and the uncertainty created once courts engage in moral deliberations. For others, especially for utilitarian consequentialists, the *Brüstle* decision is misguided because, not only does it make the European regulatory environment less attractive to leading-edge biotechnology companies, it impedes the prospects of developing stem cell–based therapies for major human diseases (such as Parkinson's disease which was the target of Brüstle's research). Moreover, these sentiments will be echoed by secularists who will see the *Brüstle* decision as an

Embryonic Stem Cell Patents (Oxford University Press, 2009), at 141. There is also the question of how coherently the *WARF* reading of the exclusion fits with other EC legal measures that license human embryonic stem cell research; see Aurora Plomer, 'Towards Systemic Legal Conflict: Article 6(2)(c) of the EU Directive on Biotechnological Inventions', in Plomer and Torremans, above, at 173. Nevertheless, this broad interpretation was foreshadowed in EDINBURGH/Animal Transgenic Stem Cells (Patent App. No. 94 913 174.2, July 21, 2002, Opposition Division), on which, see Shawn H. E. Harmon, 'From Engagement to Re-engagement: The Expression of Moral Values in European Patent Proceedings, Past and Future' (2006) 31 *E.L. Rev* 642.

122 Here, I use the term 'dignitarian' to capture a range of duty-based ethics, both secular and nonsecular, that highlight the importance of not compromising human dignity. See, further, Roger Brownsword, 'Bioethics Today, Bioethics Tomorrow: Stem Cell Research and the "Dignitarian Alliance"' (2003) 17 *University of Notre Dame Journal of Law, Ethics and Public Policy* 15, and 'Stem Cells and Cloning: Where the Regulatory Consensus Fails' (2005) 39 *New England Law Review* 535.

123 However, Article 27(2) of the GATT/TRIPs Agreement permits members to exclude inventions from patentability on grounds of *ordre public* or morality. In other words, the international view is that provisions such as Article 53(a) of the EPC and Article 6 of Directive 98/44/EC are optional.

124 For example, although there is some early jurisprudence in the USA that shows that the requirement that a patentable invention should have 'utility' can be deployed for regulatory purposes, Gregory Mandel reports that 'no [US] court has held an invention invalid for being immoral, deceptive, or illegal for almost 100 years': see Gregory N. Mandel, 'Regulating Nanotechnology through Intellectual Property Rights' in G. Hodge, D. M. Bowman, and A. D. Maynard (eds.), *International Handbook on Regulating Nanotechnologies* (Cheltenham: Edward Elgar, 2010) 388, at 395.

example of European courts being captured by conservative religious dogmas that stand in the way of the progressive improvement of the human condition.[125]

What, though, should we make of the accusation that the decision in *Brüstle* as well as the background Directive are lacking in 'coherence', both formal and substantive?

The charge that *Brüstle* lacks *formal* coherence runs as follows: German law is highly sensitised to dignitarian concerns about the instrumentalisation of human embryos – indeed, German embryo protection laws are amongst the strongest in Europe; yet even governed by these strict national standards, Brüstle's research was perfectly lawful in Germany; how, then, can it be coherent for the CJEU to exclude this same lawful research from patentability? In other words, if research is permitted by the background law and regulation, how can it be formally coherent for the patent regime to treat such research as excluded?

The short answer to this charge is that it is formally coherent to combine a permission to do *x* with a refusal to encourage *x*, the latter being the effect of the *Brüstle* decision. Of course, when *x* is permitted (as was the legal position in Germany in relation to Brüstle's research), some explanation for nonencouragement might be expected. Nevertheless, the conjunction of nonencouragement with permission, if sometimes puzzling, is not formally incoherent.

However, there is also the claim that *Brüstle* lacks *substantive* coherence. The thrust of this charge is that the CJEU, being bound by the provisions of the European Convention on Human Rights, should always decide in terms that are compatible with the jurisprudence of the European Court of Human Rights;[126] in that jurisprudence, it is clear that human embryos are not treated as bearers of human rights; and, in particular, it is clear that the treatment (including destruction) of human embryos does not directly engage the Convention right to life.[127]

[125] Notably, the views associated with the Catholic Church. But, for a view defending the 'deontological' approach of the CJEU against the general 'consequentialism' of patent courts, see Jessica Giles, 'The *Brüstle* and *Eli Lilly* Cases: Creation – God or Humankind' (2012) 1 *Oxford Journal of Law and Religion* 518.

[126] See, most explicitly, Article 6 (ex Article 6 TEU) of the Consolidated Version of the Treaty on European Union, *Official Journal of the European Union*, C 115/13, 9.5.2008. Generally, see Sionaidh Douglas-Scott, 'The European Union and Human Rights after the Treaty of Lisbon' (2011) 11 *Human Rights Law Review* 645.

[127] See, *Evans v United Kingdom* (Application no. 6339/05) Grand Chamber, April 10, 2007; *Vo v France* (Application no. 53924/00) Grand Chamber, July 8, 2004.

It follows that there is no support in European human rights law for the dignitarian moral concerns that underpin Article 6(2)(c) of the Directive; and, thus, no good reason for the exclusion of patentability in relation to Brüstle's research.

Again, a short answer is available, namely that the Strasbourg jurisprudence does no more than deny that human embryos hold rights *directly* under the Convention; human embryos are not themselves bearers of rights. Nevertheless, this leaves open the possibility that Contracting States may grant *indirect* protection to human embryos, just as in many places protection is afforded to nonhuman animals. Provided that these indirect protections (motivated by the desire to do the right thing) are not incompatible with the rights directly recognised by the Convention – and, it should be noted, there is no Convention right that explicitly protects the interests of researchers in having access to human embryos for their base materials – then no regulatory incoherence arises. In other words, if Contracting States may, without infringing Convention rights, adopt protective measures in relation to human embryos, this must also be an option for both the Member States of the EU and the CJEU.

That said, further charges of incoherence are conceivable: for example, that the CJEU violates a Rule of Law standard of impartiality; that its prescriptive approach fails to cohere with the margin of appreciation typically accorded by the Strasbourg court to Contracting States where moral consensus is lacking; and that it fails to cohere with a certain vision of a regional association of communities of rights. It also invites some clarification of the very idea that legal and regulatory decision making should be 'coherent'. After all, one very obvious thought is that the best defence of the CJEU is that the Court was simply articulating the agreed terms of the Directive and that such incoherence as there might be resides in the Directive itself. In the real world, we know that the political branch will generate legislation that will often involve compromises and accommodations that indicate a lack of coherent purpose. Indeed, in the case of the Directive, we know that it was all but lost in 1995 and that it was only because of compromise and accommodation that it was rescued – from a political perspective, perhaps an incoherent agreed Directive would seem better than no Directive at all. In any event, if we are to assess the activities of courts and legislators by reference to a standard of coherence, in the context of the pluralistic nation-state democracies that collectively comprise the European Union, we need to work out just how much, and what kind of coherence, we can insist upon.

The problem is that the premise of doctrinal coherence (whether in patents or elsewhere – in contracts, for example) is severely disrupted once the Commission adopts 'a regulatory mind-set' focused on harmonising the marketplace. From a regulatory perspective, the only idea of coherence is an instrumental one: provided that a regulatory intervention works relative to the regulator's purposes, then coherence is satisfied. Crucially, a regulator need not cross-check that the principle underlying the latest intervention is coherent with the principle underlying some other intervention; regulators are simply directing regulatees.[128] Of course, it is important that regulatory interventions do not interfere with one another's purposes (in the way, for example, that there are concerns about competition law interfering with the incentives for innovation offered by patent law),[129] but there is no problem of incoherence if the regulators take a pragmatic approach to the effective pursuit of their policies.

Moreover, even without the Brussels agenda, we should perhaps accept that, as legislation overtakes the case-law, there will be some incoherence. This is politics. Rival political constituencies seek to influence the policy and text of the law. Sometimes, compromises and accommodations indicate a lack of coherent purpose.[130] Directive 98/44/EC is surely a perfect example. On the one hand, the Directive secures the interests of the scientific research community by declaring that innovative work around the human genome (including work that replicates naturally occurring sequences) is in principle patentable.[131] On the other hand, Article 6 of the Directive sets limits on patentability that reflect some of the concerns of those various constituencies that

[128] This is drawn out very clearly in Hugh Collins, *Regulating Contracts* (Oxford University Press, 2002) at 8: 'The trajectory of legal evolution alters from the private law discourse of seeking the better coherence for its scheme of principles to one of learning about the need for fresh regulation by observations of the consequences of present regulation.' Compare, too, Edward Rubin, 'Empiricism's Crucial Question and the Transformation of the Legal System' in Jean Braucher, John Kidwell, and William C. Whitford (eds.), *Revisiting the Contracts Scholarship of Stewart Macaulay* (Oxford: Hart, 2013) 74 at 85 et seq. (on the new mode of managerial governance brought forth by the advent of bureaucratic government or the administrative state).

[129] For an extensive jurisprudence, see Richard Whish and David Bailey, *Competition Law* 7th edn. (Oxford University Press, 2012) ch. 19.

[130] For an excellent case study, albeit in a very different context, see Andrew Murray, 'The Reclassification of Extreme Pornographic Images' (2009) 72 MLR 73.

[131] See, e.g., Recitals 20 and 21, and Article 5(2).

oppose developments in modern biotechnologies (especially the use of human embryos as research tools).[132]

What, then, should we make of the apparent (and possibly inevitable) decline of coherence in the new legal world that is regulatory Europe?

First, we should hold on to the vision of a regional association of communities of rights. Perhaps we do not need to cross-check for coherence but we certainly need to check upwards to the fundamental rights commitments of the community. In all its phases, even if the legal enterprise becomes a regulatory enterprise, the regulatory environment should be compatible with respect for human rights and underlying human dignity.

Second, trade imperatives should not be permitted to 'collateralise' or displace or compromise moral imperatives (whether these are imperatives that relate directly to human rights or indirectly so as in the case of environmental protection).[133] Communities of rights, in a regional association of such communities, should value their (relative) moral autonomy. Moral subsidiarity is not simply a recognition that, on some matters, local decision making is more efficient; the point is that moral communities need to give their commitments their own best interpretation. Any weakening on these ideals is again a worrying case of incoherence.

Third, the values that seem to underpin Recital 38 and Article 6 of the Directive reflect a conservative conception of human dignity. With the development of modern biotechnologies, such dignitarian values have attracted considerable support.[134] However, there is a tension between this conception of human dignity and the autonomy-based conception that underlies the modern articulation of human rights. Elsewhere, I have termed this the tension between 'human dignity as empowerment' (a rights-based conception) and 'human dignity as constraint' (a duty-based conception).[135] For a community of rights to permit the latter conception of human dignity to intrude through moral gateways in the law is clearly incoherent. In this light, the moral exclusions of the Directive and the decision in *Brüstle* seem to be motivated by a value that does not cohere with human rights commitments.[136]

[132] See, e.g., Recitals 37, 38, and 42.

[133] Compare, Sheldon Leader, 'Collateralism', in Roger Brownsword (ed.), *Human Rights* (Oxford: Hart, 2004) 53.

[134] See Brownsword, 'Human Dignity'.

[135] Beyleveld and Brownsword, *Human Dignity in Bioethics and Biolaw.*

[136] For an even more worrying example, see the judgment of the Grand Chamber at the European Court of Human Rights in the case of *SH v Austria* (application no. 57813/00)

Fourth, to underscore the previous point, it should be appreciated that there is an important difference between Europe as a region (and project) of 'closed' pluralism, where human rights (together with 'human dignity as empowerment') represent the fundamental values, and Europe as a region (and project) of 'open' pluralism, where rights-based values are in competition with conservative dignitarianism.[137] In the latter, the moral bonds are relaxed; tolerance implies more than acceptance of margins of difference—there is an acceptable heterogeneity; and the demand for regulatory coherence is correspondingly weaker.

Finally, and most importantly for present purposes, where the direction of travel is not simply from private law to public regulation but to the use, by both private and public regulators, of technological management, then such use must cohere with the constitutive values of the community. At the deepest level, this means that the use of technological regulatory tools must be compatible with the aspiration to function as a moral community; and, underpinning the values of the Rule of Law, each particular use must cohere with the community's best interpretation of its collective commitment to respect for human rights and human dignity.[138]

3.10 Conclusion

In this chapter, I have tried to refocus jurisprudential inquiries, to direct our gaze to a new world in which technological management coexists with, or even supplants, rules – legal, moral, social, secular and

November 3, 2011. There, the Court seems to permit Austria to rely on conservative dignitarian values to justify its restrictive IVF laws (prohibiting third-party donation of gametes).

137 For the implications of the difference between 'open' and 'closed' value pluralism, see Roger Brownsword, 'Regulating the Life Sciences, Pluralism, and the Limits of Deliberative Democracy' (2010) 22 *Singapore Academy of Law Journal* 80; and 'Framers and Problematisers: Getting to Grips with Global Governance' (2010) 1 *Transnational Legal Theory* 287.

138 Compare the discussion in Tamanaha, *Law as a Means to an End*, at 249–250. Tamanaha highlights four ideals associated with the Rule of Law, namely: 'that the law is a principled preserver of justice, that the law serves the public good, that legal rules are binding on government officials (not only the public), and that judges must render decisions in an objective fashion based upon the law' (249). Provided that instrumental regulatory strategies are committed to respecting these ideals, there is no problem. However, the anchoring ideas of the public (or common) good have been compromised and this leaves instrumentalist regulation – especially, I would add, regulation of the kind exemplified by technological management – dangerously adrift.

nonsecular – as a mechanism to direct, channel and control human behaviour. However, even though this is a long paper, there are many questions that readers might have about the relationship between the old world of law and the new. Let me respond briefly to three such questions in these concluding remarks.

First, as we transition from the old to the new, what exactly is my position in relation to methodological debates? In my introductory remarks, I employed a distinction between 'Methodology' (with a capital M) and 'methodology' (in lower case). Methodology (with a capital M) concerns the defining features of the operative theoretical paradigm, identifying the field for inquiry, the way that the field is to be framed and the particular focus for inquiry within the field; methodology (in lower case) concerns the way in which the particular lines of inquiry within the operative paradigm (whatever that paradigm might be) are to be addressed. Methodology (with a capital M) identifies the field and focal points of our cognitive interest; and methodology (in lower case) determines how we are to engage with and respond to the questions that we pose as we pursue our cognitive interests. My position is that, at this juncture, we should be engaging with questions of Methodology rather than questions of methodology.

My suggestion in this chapter is that we need to change our Methodology (with a capital M), adopting a new paradigm that enables us to track and assess the use of technologies as regulatory instruments operating alongside legal, moral and social norms. The salient features of this new paradigm are that the field encompasses both normative and non-normative (technological) regulatory modalities; that the field is to be framed by a suitably broad conception of the regulatory environment; and that a central focus for inquiry is the impact of technological management on the complexion of the regulatory environment. Whether or not this has implications for methodology (in lower case) depends on the range of questions that we wish to answer in the new paradigm. I have identified just some of the questions that interest me. In addition to questions about the changing complexion of the regulatory environment, there are questions about the reengineering of ideals of legality and the Rule of Law; about liberal values and how technological management impacts on liberty;[139] about the promised effectiveness of technological management compared to normative interventions; and about how

[139] For the relationship between law, liberty and technological management, see Roger Brownsword, 'Liberty and Technology' in Roger Brownsword, Eloise Scotford, and

traditional bodies of criminal law, tort law and contract law are likely to be affected by a regulatory strategy that uses technologies to render it impossible to do wrong (whether by taking prospective human wrong-doers or victims out of the equation, or by otherwise disabling or excluding potential wrongdoers or by hardening targets). Some of these questions invite philosophical and legal analysis; others invite empirical study supported by sociological, psychological, and behavioural theory, and so on. Quite possibly, in order to respond to these questions, it will be necessary to reflect critically on the appropriate methodology. However, first things first: first, the new paradigm (the Methodology) has to be accepted, then the questions to be answered need to be formulated, and then we can talk about methodology.

The second question concerns the drawing of the line between the Legal (with its internal binary of legal/illegal) and the non-Legal. How, where and why would I draw this line? In traditional jurisprudential debates, the salient features of the Legal are drawn from a list that includes rules and norms (normativity), certain kinds of institutions, certain kinds of function, certain kinds of authority claim, certain kinds of scope and comprehensiveness, certain modes of enforcement, certain kinds of sanctions and certain degrees of efficacy or effectiveness, and so on. This list represents, so to speak, the standard criteria.[140] Where the Legal is restricted to national legal orders, a particular array of the standard criteria is employed; where the Legal is extended to include both national legal orders and international law, there is some adjustment to, or relaxation of, the initial defining characteristics; and where the Legal is extended beyond the prevailing Westphalian view, the defining characteristics are again modified or relaxed. In other words, the category of the Legal, and concomitantly the distinction between the Legal and the non-Legal, is shaped by the way in which the standard criteria are employed – by which criteria are taken to be necessary, which are taken to be sufficient, by whether formal or functional features are privileged, and so on. Accordingly, if I were to claim that the phenomena associated with (nonnormative) technological management of human conduct should be treated as within the Legal, this would be to downgrade the significance of normativity within the standard list – indeed, I imagine that my claim would be rejected by some as 'ridiculous',

Karen Yeung (eds.) *Oxford Handbook on Law, Regulation and Technology* (Oxford: Oxford University Press, 2016) (forthcoming).

[140] Compare Tamanaha, *A General Jurisprudence of Law and Society*, ch. 6.

'absurd', 'not to be taken seriously' and so on. But would my claim – a claim, I should emphasise, that I am not actually making – be defensible; and, for that matter, would those who argue for exclusively normative conceptions of the Legal be able to defend their positions any more convincingly?

Let me state my views on this question quite shortly. First, I take it that the defence of any particular conception of the Legal will appeal to either 'theoretical' or 'practical' considerations or both. Second, to defend a particular conception of the Legal on *theoretical* grounds is to claim that, given certain premises, that particular conception of the Legal is entailed. If the premises are conceded to be optional, the defence is conditional and limited; for, even if the conception of the Legal is entailed by the premises, it is only if one accepts the premises that the defence is compelling. To argue, by contrast, that the premises are not optional is to raise the stakes massively; this defence now has the form of a transcendental argument and many will (rightly or wrongly) simply reject such a claim out of hand. While I would argue (transcendentally) that from premises relating to the agency of humans the only coherent account of the Legal is as a Moral phenomenon[141] (the role of the Legal–Moral being to provide provisionally authoritative resolutions of contested Moral questions), I would not claim that the distinction between the Legal (Legal–Moral) and non-Legal (non-Legal–Moral) is entailed in the same way. Thirdly to defend a particular conception of the Legal on *practical* grounds is a much more modest project: the claim is simply that, for certain purposes, a particular conception of the Legal is required or best suited or the like. However, this defence allows that given different purposes, different conceptions of the Legal might be appropriate. Fourth, it follows from these remarks that if I were to claim that (nonnormative) technological management of human conduct should be treated as within the Legal, I would not be able to make out a compelling *theoretical* defence of this position but I might be able to make out an instrumentally rational case relative to my *practical* purposes – and my recasting of the distinction between the Legal and the non-Legal would be ridiculous or absurd only if it did not assist my particular purposes. Moreover, what my critics could say in defence of their Westphalian or pluralist conceptions of the Legal would be no

[141] For this claim, see Deryck Beyleveld and Roger Brownsword, *Law as a Moral Judgment* (London: Sweet and Maxwell, 1986; reprinted Sheffield: Sheffield Academic Press, 1994).

different; their defence, like mine, would be that, relative to their purposes, their conception of the Legal works.

I have emphasised that I have not claimed that technological management should be treated as part of the Legal. Why not? Why not bite the bullet and claim that technological code as much as the codes of civilian legal orders is part of the Legal? Rather than signing up to the petition that has it that 'Code is Law', I have avoided the issue; and, I have done this because I know that many lawyers and legal theorists (including legal pluralists) will reject the idea that nonnormative phenomena can qualify as Legal – on this view, it is only normative phenomena that can qualify as Legal.[142] Instead, I have suggested that we should frame our new field of interest by employing a broad concept of the regulatory environment. This does not eliminate resistance because those who insist that the Legal is normative might also insist that the Regulatory is normative, this entailing that technological management cannot be characterised as either Legal or Regulatory. So be it. As I have said, the line between the Legal and the non-Legal is conventional; and I also treat the line between the Regulatory and the non-Regulatory as conventional. We need to be conceptual foundationalists (or rationalists) in sticking with the deeply unfashionable idea that the Legal is necessarily Moral; but there is no need to observe conventional conceptual distinctions in otherwise determining the zone of the Legal. If it suits our purposes to deviate from the conventions, we can do so. However, I see no need to disrupt those conventions so long as I can frame the new field in terms of the regulatory environment and thereby bring it within the purview of jurisprudential inquiry.[143]

Nevertheless, this might be too sanguine; and, in case it is, I have to add an important caveat. If, in fact, the community of academic lawyers treats technological management as either irrelevant or unimportant because, although it concerns the control of human conduct, it is not a Legal (or even a Regulatory) phenomenon,[144] then I would need to reconsider my position. After all, my purpose is to direct the attention

[142] For legal pluralists, see Tamanaha (n 10), ch. 7.

[143] To similar effect, see Roger Brownsword, 'Law as a Moral Judgment, the Domain of Jurisprudence, and Technological Management' in Patrick Capps and Shaun Pattinson (eds.), *Ethical Rationalism and the Law* (Oxford: Hart, 2016) (forthcoming).

[144] Even conceiving of the Legal or the Regulatory as covering phenomena that we treat as being 'coded' in terms of what is legal and what illegal, or what is permitted and what is not permitted, technological management (where the coding is in terms of what is possible and what impossible) might seem to be of a radically different order.

of lawyers to the growing importance of technological management as a strategy for controlling, channelling and ordering human conduct. If my concession to conservative conceptual frameworks obstructs my purposes, then perhaps I would need to bite the bullet. That said, my opening gambit is to invite reflection on the emerging use of technological management and to do this within the enabling frame of a broad understanding of the regulatory environment.[145] No longer is our world captured by prescriptive human laws and the covering laws of the physical universe; humans are now deploying nonprescriptive instruments that function in a way that is analogous to covering laws, determining what is possible and what is impossible. To explore the significance of our changing world, we do not need to reconceptualise the Legal but we do need to extend and refocus the field of inquiry.

The third question takes us back to legal education. How might the new paradigm, with a new agenda of questions, be taken up in the academy? The answer will, no doubt vary from one place to another; but, in general, I would expect the answer to depend on five interrelated elements, namely: the extent to which, from the institutional perspective, it is thought that there is 'a business case' to be made for developing programmes around the new paradigm; the extent to which there is resistance from the traditional academic community (who still regard disputes, cases and courts as central to legal scholarship); the view of the legal profession; the demand from (and market for) prospective students; and the further transformative impact of information technologies on legal education.

Viewing the question specifically from a UK perspective, the importance of the link between university law degrees and professional legal qualification should not be underestimated. In the UK, there is no long tradition of university law programmes being delivered to large cohorts of students. The relentless upward trend in demand for university law degrees goes back only fifty years or so. At all events, so long as law programmes operate as a gateway to professional practice, there will be pressure to maintain a curriculum that serves (or, at any rate, that is perceived to serve) the needs of lawyers in practice; and, so long as the student demand for university law degrees is related to exemption from professional legal examinations, there will be pressure to supply courses that meet that demand. Even if the existing curriculum does not actually

[145] See, further, Brownsword, 'In the Year 2061'.

serve particularly well the needs of those who plan to train with big law firms, a curriculum that is based in the new paradigm would seem to be even less well-suited. Of course, if the link with the professions is weakened, new options might become available. For the time being, though, the most that one might expect is that the new paradigm might be recognised as some part of a Jurisprudence or Legal Theory module (students being introduced to a school of 'Law and Technology', perhaps), and similarly so in those modules that are sensitive to new issues raised by a shifting context of emerging regulatory technologies—for example, there might be a new interest in the old conundrum of whether it is a criminal offence to attempt to commit an offence that (because of technological management) it is actually impossible to commit, and questions about legal capacity, legal personality, legal responsibility, and legal liability will no doubt be addressed.[146] For some time, I would expect it to be at postgraduate level that law students are systematically introduced to the new Methodology and then encouraged to pursue their own lines of inquiry as doctoral candidates. It follows that, even though research-led teaching is currently the fashion, even though there is now a burgeoning 'law and technology' literature (including some textbooks), and even though those young academics whose doctoral research has been in the field of regulation and technology will want to teach to this interest, I suspect that the new paradigm will be nurtured and explored in a handful of vanguard law schools but mainly in research centres and clusters that might for some time operate at a distance from taught programmes. Legal education, like the law, and unlike technology, moves exceedingly slowly.

To conclude, I have suggested that the significance of the technological developments that are underway is not simply that they present novel and difficult targets for regulators but, far more importantly, that they offer themselves as regulatory tools or instruments. Given that technologies progressively intrude on almost all aspects of our lives (mediating the way that we communicate, how we transact, how we get from one place to another, even how we reproduce), it should be no surprise that technologies will also intrude on law-making, law-application, and so on. Law will be, first, enhanced by technological support before being overtaken by the technologies. While the direction of smart regulatory theory is away from 'command and control' (because it does not work),

[146] As, indeed, they already are: see, e.g., John Frank Weaver, *Robots are People Too* (Santa Barbara, CA: Praeger, 2014); and Leenes and Lucivero, 'Laws *on* Robots'.

technological management sets aside 'command' and focuses instead simply on 'control'.[147] The point to take from this is not so much the pluralist message that the Legal is to be found in many more places than the Westphalian model recognises; rather the point is that, in all places, technological management threatens to crowd out those forms of social ordering that our current conventions treat as Legal. If our new legal world presages a radically different world of technological management, lawyers – above all, lawyers[148] – need to be ready for it.

[147] Compare David Garland, *The Culture of Control* (Chicago: University of Chicago Press, 2001).

[148] Compare Ian Macneil's insightful (although, at the time, puzzling) warnings about the rise of Technical Man and the need for a Posttechnique settlement, in which we retain our essential humanity while enjoying the benefits of new technologies: see Ian R. Macneil, *The New Social Contract* (New Haven: Yale University Press, 1980).

4

Transatlantic Publication Fashions

In Search of Quality and Methodology in Law Journal Articles

REZA DIBADJ

> The predominant view of [academic] lawyers is that they are not really academic – "arcane, distant and alien: an appendage to the academic world." Their personal qualities are dubious: vociferous, untrustworthy, immoral, narrow, and arrogant: though kinder eyes see them as impressive and intelligent. The discipline is variously described as unexciting, uncreative, and comprising a series of intellectual puzzles scattered among "large areas of description."[1]

> Cutting-edge universities, top institutes, and research clusters shot up everywhere, and everyone wanted to be even more excellent than their already-excellent competitors.[2]

A book on legal methodology provides a rare treat to do "what legal scholars seldom do: reflect on the nature of their work."[3] More specifically, I attempt in this chapter to build on prior empirical work where I compared who and what was being published in top law reviews in three different jurisdictions: the United States, Britain, and France.[4]

[1] Tony Becher, *Toward a Definition of Disciplinary Cultures*, 6 *Studies in Higher Educ.* 109, 111 (1981) (citing from interviews with academics).

[2] Mathias Binswanger, *Excellence by Nonsense: The Competition for Publications in Modern Science*, *Opening Science* 49, 51 (2014) (S. Bartling & S. Friesike, eds.).

[3] C. J. J. M. Stolker, *Legal Journals: In Pursuit of a More Scientific Approach*, 2 *Eur. J. Legal Educ.* 77, 78 (2004). See also Paul Chynoweth, *Legal Research*, in Advanced Methods in the Built Environment 28 (Andrew Knight & Les Ruddock, eds.) (2008) ("There is dearth of theoretical literature on the nature of legal scholarship and a consequent lack of awareness about what legal scholars actually do.").

[4] See Reza Dibadj, *Comparative Fashions in Legal Research* in *L'évaluation de la recherché en droit: Enjeux et méthodes* 213 (Bruylant, Penser le droit, 2015) (Alexandre Flückiger & Thierry Tanquerel, eds.).

Section 4.1 begins by discussing the key empirical findings of a research project that analyzed a sample of legal publications in the United States, Britain, and France. As discussed, the work proceeded in two phases: first, identifying what "top" journal and "elite" law school might be in each jurisdiction; second, analyzing each article according to author characteristics, legal method employed, and subject matter. Section 4.2 then draws implications from this preliminary work, attempting to relate the empirical results to the academic legal culture in each jurisdiction. Put simply, can one try to find meaning in these results?

Some implications are relatively innocuous, such as the reality that top journals in the world are very different in many respects, and that Europeans and Americans may have different views on what legal publications should emphasize. Others are more pernicious, such as the herding effect and tendency of many top American journals almost exclusively to publish glamorous subject areas and authors from elite institutions. While I offer thoughts on each of the three jurisdictions, Section 4.2 emphasizes the United States somewhat over Britain and France for two principal reasons. First, as far as I have been able to research, academic legal culture seems to be discussed more openly in the United States, engendering a larger and more varied literature on the subject. A secondary reason – admittedly an idiosyncratic one – is that as an American legal academic my greatest familiarity is with US legal culture.

After having surveyed what is being published in "top" law journals across three different jurisdictions, as well as trying to explore links between these results and legal culture, Section 4.3 tries to draw some implications. At least two important points emerge. First, that as legal academics we need to pay more attention to quality and how to measure it. Yet existing quality metrics – journal rankings, peer review, bibliometric citations, and the like – are by themselves at best incomplete and at worst misleading. As such, I argue that quality cannot be understood without the threshold concept of methodology. Entering the dangerous territory of linking methodology with quality becomes all but inevitable if we hope to begin improving the state of legal research. Ironically, what is deeply missing in this literature is a focus on methodology. While it becomes extraordinarily difficult, if not impossible, to generalize across jurisdictions, there remains a central question: What might Americans learn from Europeans when it comes to legal research, and vice-versa? Methodology can begin to provide a framework to address this question.

4.1 Empirical Work

My recent empirical study compared what was published in top law journals in the United States, Britain, and France over a three-year timeframe. The goal, simply put, was to try to understand what is "fashionable" in current legal research. "Fashionable" in the sense of what the "top" legal journals are publishing: Who is writing, with what analytical methods, on what legal subjects?

4.1.1 Methodology

The study was prepared in two principal phases. The first was to create a sample of "top" journals and "elite" law schools in three jurisdictions. The second was to take a representative sample of five "top" legal journals in each jurisdiction and "code" it along three dimensions: (1) author characteristics, (2) analytical methods, and (3) subject matter.

4.1.1.1 Phase One

Methods to identify "elite" law schools and "top" journals differed by jurisdiction. For the United States, I simply took the top twenty (twenty-two due to ties among law schools) as indicated in the controversial rankings provided by *US News and World Report*.[5] To determine top American law journals, I used the top five journals as measured by the impact factors calculated by the law library at Washington and Lee Law Library based on citations in other law reviews and judicial opinions.[6] Perhaps unsurprisingly, this ranking of law reviews matches quite closely the *US News* rankings of the law schools.

Rankings, however, became considerably more complicated for Britain and France. To determine "elite" British law schools, I used an amalgam of rankings provided by the *Times*, *Independent*/University Guide, and *Guardian* – sixteen law schools in total.[7] For top law journals, I relied on

[5] Yale, Harvard, Stanford, Columbia, Chicago, New York University, University of Pennsylvania, University of Virginia, University of California–Berkeley, University of Michigan, Duke, Northwestern, Cornell, Georgetown, University of Texas-Austin, Vanderbilt, University of California–Los Angeles, University of Southern California, University of Minnesota, Washington University in St. Louis, George Washington University, and University of Alabama.

[6] *Harvard Law Review*, *Columbia Law Review*, *Yale Law Journal*, *Stanford Law Review*, and *Georgetown Law Journal*.

[7] Oxford, Cambridge, University College London, London School of Economics, Nottingham, Queen Mary, Aberdeen, Durham, Birmingham, King's College London, Glasgow, Bristol, Edinburgh, SOAS, Newcastle, and Warwick.

two articles focusing on journal reputation and impact by Kevin Campbell and coauthors – from which I selected a "short-list" of five journals.[8] To assess "elite" French law schools, I used a ranking provided by the French Ministry of Education: if a school was ranked A+ or A in at least one legal discipline, I included it in the list of fourteen schools.[9] Unfortunately, I was unable to find articles on the subject of French law journal impact and reputation; as such, I conferred with French academics and librarians and included a selection of five journals among those in the Salle des périodiques and the Salle de lecture at the Bibliothèque Cujas in Paris, generally considered to be France's leading law library.[10,11]

It goes without saying that my methods are necessarily imprecise and could be endlessly debated. My goal, however, was not some illusory mathematical precision, but rather to get a sense of what is in fashion in legal academia.

4.1.1.2 Phase Two

I assembled copies (paper or electronic) of each article that was published over a very recent three-year period in the five representative "top" journals per jurisdiction.[12] Author characteristics where determined along three subcategories: (1) affiliation with an "elite" school; (2) whether the author is a "core" or "noncore" academic,[13] student, lawyer in private

[8] *Modern Law Review, Law Quarterly Review, Oxford Journal of Legal Studies, Cambridge Law Journal*, and *Legal Studies*. To ensure compatibility with the US general-interest journals, I selected general-interest British journals.

[9] Aix-Marseille 3, Montpellier 1, Paris 1, Paris 2, Paris 10, Bordeaux 4, Clermont-Ferrand 1, Grenoble 2, Lille 2, Lyon 3, Nantes, Paris 5, Strasbourg 3, and Toulouse 1.

[10] The one exception is the *Archives de philosophie de droit*, which is shelved separately (Sous-sol) at Cujas.

[11] *Revue trimestrielle de droit commercial et de droit économique, Revue française de droit constitutionnel, Journal de droit international, Droit pénal, Archives de philosophie de droit.*

[12] 263 articles for the US, 345 for Britain, and 202 for France – for a total 810 articles. I included articles and essays. I excluded book reviews, symposium pieces, tributes, and other solicited pieces. My goal was to analyze articles that were accepted for publication through some putatively competitive process.

[13] In the United States, Core comprises Professors, Associate Professors, and Assistant Professors; in Britain, Professors, Readers, Associate Professors, and Assistant Professors; and in France, Professors and Maîtres de conferences. Noncore is composed of other faculty, including lecturers, fellows, visiting professors, adjunct professors in the United States; lecturers and fellows in Britain; Chargés d'enseignement, Enseignants-chercheurs, and Attachés temporaires à l'enseignement et la recherche (ATER), and Chargé de cours in France.

practice, or government lawyers;[14] and (3) whether the author was one affiliated with an institution outside the law journal's home country ("international"). Where there were multiple authors, I performed this analysis for the first (lead) author.

I then characterized the principal legal method of analysis employed in the article: theoretical, doctrinal, historical/narrative, or empirical. Finally, I assessed the principal subject matter of the article in the self-explanatory categories with which legal academics are familiar; for instance, constitutional law or criminal law or administrative law.[15]

4.1.2 Results

Several interesting findings emerged from the data, which I summarize below by jurisdiction.

4.1.2.1 United States

4.1.2.1.1 Author Characteristics While "elite" laws schools comprise only 11 percent (22 out of 203) law schools accredited by the American Bar Association (ABA) in the United States, 71 percent of articles in the sampled journals were written by academics at "elite" law schools. Within this, the vast majority were authored by "Core" faculty (63 percent), with very few "Noncore" authors (8 percent). Twenty percent of the authors were affiliated with the law school publishing the journal. By contrast, only 23 percent of the articles are written by academics at "non-elite" law schools – all of which was authored by "core" faculty at those schools. Only 6 percent of the articles were written by nonacademics and 2 percent of the authors were affiliated with institutions outside the United States.

Perhaps the most interesting finding was that over 70 percent of articles in "top" journals are written by authors from "elite" institutions. As high as this percentage is, it very likely underestimates the influence of the "elite" American law schools for at least three reasons. First, even a cursory glance suggests that the symposia and invited pieces that were excluded are written predominantly by scholars at "elite" law schools. Second, among those authors considered "non-elite," most were nonetheless from highly ranked law schools outside the top twenty; phrased

[14] Including judges and clerks.

[15] Given that the French journals are subject-matter focused, the subject-matter analysis was carried out for US and British journals only.

differently, there were vanishingly few authors from lower-ranked law schools. Third, many coauthored articles (e.g., by students) had academics at leading institutions as second or third authors; my analysis, however, only considers the first author.

4.1.2.1.2 Analytical Methods and Subject Matter The predominant mode of analysis in the US journals was theoretical (65 percent), followed by approaches focused on history and narrative (17 percent). By contrast, only 10 percent used empirical methodologies and only 8 percent were doctrinal.

Constitutional Law was by far the most popular subject matter comprising an astonishing 24 percent of the articles written. The other popular topics were Administrative Law (9 percent), Criminal Law (8 percent), Legal Theory (8 percent), and Business Law (6 percent). Overall, the subject matter chosen was quite scattered across twenty-eight subject areas.

4.1.2.2 Britain

4.1.2.2.1 Author Characteristics Authors in the "top" British journals were remarkably different than in the United States. Only 35 percent of the authors were affiliated with "elite" law schools, with Noncore faculty even authoring slightly more articles (19 percent) than Core faculty (15 percent). By contrast, 56 percent of articles were authored by faculty at "non-elite" law schools, divided roughly evenly between Core (32 percent) and Noncore (24 percent). Nine percent of articles were written by other authors, roughly in line with the US journals. Of the five British journals, only two were affiliated with a law school;[16] on average, 19 percent of the articles were written by authors affiliated with these two faculties, roughly in line with the US journals albeit on a small sample. The percentage of authors affiliated with institutions outside Britain varied widely, but averaged 26 percent, in marked difference to the US journals.

4.1.2.2.2 Analytical Methods and Subject Matter Theory was less dominant in British journals (48 percent) with a significantly higher influence of doctrinal modes of analysis (32 percent). Narrative and historical approaches were in line with the US journals (17 percent), and there were even fewer empirical pieces published than in the United States (2 percent).

One subject area did not dominate the British journals, which were overall more balanced than their US counterparts. Criminal Law

[16] *Oxford Journal of Legal Studies* and *Cambridge Law Journal.*

(12 percent), Torts (10 percent), Legal Theory (9 percent), Constitutional Law (8 percent) and Business Law (8 percent) were the most popular subjects. The remaining subject areas were, much like the US journals, scattered across twenty-seven areas.

4.1.2.3 France

4.1.2.3.1 Author Characteristics Thirty-two percent of the articles in the "top" French journals were published by faculty at "elite" law schools, a very similar percentage to that in the British journals. Yet this scholarship was authored mostly by Core rather than Noncore faculty (26 percent versus 6 percent), much like in the US journals. Forty-five percent of the articles were authored by academics at non-elite law schools, again mostly by Core (35 percent) rather than Noncore (10 percent) faculty. In marked contrast to both US and British journals, 23 percent of the articles were written by nonacademics, and authors affiliated with an institution outside France comprised 13 percent of the articles.

4.1.2.3.2 Analytical Methods and Subject Matter Though not overwhelming, doctrinal analysis was the most prevalent in the French journals (53 percent), followed by theory (36 percent). Narrative and empirical approaches were even rarer than in the US and British journals: 10 percent and 1 percent, respectively.

The French journals, in the continental tradition, are characterized by subject matter. Given the French journals are not general interest journals, there was no need to conduct a subject matter analysis.

4.2 Mapping Empirical Results to Academic Legal Culture

The empirical results not only confirm insights into the academic legal culture in these three different jurisdictions, but also raise a number of questions about the research we are producing as legal scholars and how we are producing it – some innocuous, some perhaps more troubling.

While it is a treacherous task to try to compare academic legal writing in different jurisdictions,[17] I offer below some observations

[17] *Cf.* Neil Duxbury, Jurists and Judges: An Essay on Influence 2 (2001) ("Is it not possible that there exists here a problem of incommensurability? If, from one jurisdiction to the next, academic influence rears its head in different ways, what are we comparing?"); ibid., at 115 ("comparisons of the significance accorded by courts to academic commentary often neglect the fact that influence tends to manifest itself differently from one jurisdiction to [the] next.").

based on my empirical work and subsequent research to try to find meaning in its results.

4.2.1 What Is Published?

As the data suggests, there is a focus on theory over doctrine in US legal journals (65 percent versus 9 percent) and some skewing in subject matter toward Constitutional Law (24 percent) with Administrative Law a distant second (9 percent). Intuitively, this is consistent with anecdotal evidence among American legal academics: student editors emphasize glamorous subject areas, and a heavy emphasis on theory and interdisciplinary scholarship at "elite" law schools beginning in the 1970s and 1980s,[18] when, as Richard Posner observes:

> [A] number of law professors, mainly but not only at the leading law schools, adopted a new model of legal scholarship. The model looked at the law from the outside, from perspectives shaped by other fields of scholarly inquiry, such as economics, political theory, moral philosophy, literary theory, Marxism, feminist theory, cultural studies, cultural anthropology, structuralism and poststructuralism.[19]

In American legal culture, a narrative has emerged over at least the past two decades that legal academics are out of touch with legal practice and churning out esoteric scholarship of virtually no importance to the bench and bar.[20] For instance, in a 2011 interview, US Supreme Court Chief Justice John Roberts famously observed:

[18] See, e.g., Richard A. Posner, *Legal Scholarship Today*, 115 *Harv. L. Rev.* 1314, 1314 (2001) (until the 1970s, "materials used in the research were legal, extralegal purposes and perspectives were tacit, and the research was oriented toward reform and hence sought its primary audience among those people – mainly legal professionals, including other law professors, judges, legislators, and practicing lawyers – who were interested in improving law and legal institutions."); Rob van Gestel & Hans-Wolfgang Micklitz, *Why Methods Matter in European Legal Scholarship*, 20 *Eur. L.J.* 292, 292 (2014) [hereinafter van Gestel & Micklitz, *Methods*] ("Before the 1980s, most American legal scholarship was doctrinal and descriptive, or theoretical and prescriptive; the ultimate purpose of legal research was usually to prescribe a better outcome to a judge.").

[19] Posner, *Legal Scholarship Today*, 1316–1317. According to Posner, this shift was fueled by a variety of factors, including the "rise of nonmarket economics," "revival of moral and political philosophy," "rise of regulatory state," and "rationalization and specialization." See ibid., at 1318–1819.

[20] See, e.g., Adam Liptak, *The Lackluster Reviews that Lawyers Love to Hate*, N.Y. Times, Oct. 22, 2013. The phenomenon, however, is far from new. See *also* Richard A. Posner, *The State of Legal Scholarship Today: A Comment on Schlag*, 97 *Geo. L.J.* 845, 850 (2009) [hereinafter Posner, *Legal Scholarship Today*] ("One sees this most vividly in constitutional law and constitutional theory, field in which elite scholarship circulates in a

> Pick up a copy of any law review that you see, and the first article is likely to be, you know, the influence of Immanuel Kant on evidentiary approaches in 18th Century Bulgaria or something, which I'm sure was of great interest to the academic that wrote it, but isn't of much help to the bar.[21]

The criticism is not new. Over twenty years ago, Judge Harry Edwards provocatively observed "that judges, administrators, legislators, and practitioners have little use for much of the scholarship that is now produced by members of the academy."[22] More recently, another federal appellate judge stated that "I haven't opened up a law review in years. No one speaks of them. No one relies on them."[23] And a former Solicitor General wryly notes that "at the Supreme Court, academic citations are viewed as largely irrelevant – only a true naïf would blunder to mention one at oral argument."[24] Recent scholarship suggests that 40 percent of US law review articles have never been cited,[25] and that the US Supreme Court is citing law reviews with decreasing frequency.[26] A recent survey of law professors, student editors, attorneys, and judges reveals widespread dissatisfaction with US law reviews.[27]

sealed academic medium with virtually no leakage into the world of legislation, adjudication, judicial appointments, legal practice, or public policy.").

21 Comment made during an interview at the 2011 Annual Fourth Circuit Court of Appeals Conference, *available at* www.c-span.org/Events/Annual-Fourth-Circuit-Court-of-Appeals-Conference/10737422476-1/.

22 H. T. Edwards, *The Growing Disjunction between Legal Education and the Legal Profession*, 91 *Mich. L. Rev.* 34 (1992). See also Harry T. Edwards, *The Growing Disjunction between Legal Education and the Legal Profession: A Postscript*, 91 *Mich. L. Rev.* 2191 (1993).

23 Quoted in Liptak, *The Lackluster Reviews.*

24 S. Waxman, *Rebuilding Bridges: The Bar, the Bench, and the Academy*, 150 *U. Pa. L. Rev.* 1905, 1909 (2002).

25 See, e.g., T. A. Smith, *The Web of Law* (San Diego Legal Studies Research Paper No. 0–11, 2005), http://papers.ssrn.com/abstract_id=6422863; P. L. Caron, *The Long Tail of Legal Scholarship*, 116 *Yale L.J. Pocket* Part 38 (2006), www.thepocketpart.org/2006/09/06/caron.html.

26 See B. E. Newton, *Law Review Scholarship in the Eyes of the Twenty-First-Century Supreme Court Justices: An Empirical Analysis*, 4 *Drexel L. Rev.* 399, 404 (2012) ("the Justices have cited law review articles less frequently since the apex of the 1970s and 1980s, when at least one Justice's opinion in approximately half of the Court's cases cited one or more law review articles. During the first decade of the twenty-first century, on average, one or more Justices cited articles in their opinions in 37.1% of the Court's cases and, on average, the Justices cited 0.52 articles per opinion compared to 0.87 articles per opinion in the early 1970s.").

27 See R. A. Wise et al., *Do Law Reviews Need Reform? A Survey of Law Professors, Student Editors, Attorneys, and Judges*, 59 *Loy. L. Rev.* 1 (2013) ("Law reviews are likely not

One commentator bluntly notes that:

> By the end of the twentieth century, legal scholarship in some of the most highly reputed American law journals was being condemned as self-indulgent, verbose, abstruse, excessively footnoted, unconstructive, methodologically jejune, jargon-laden and – as regards the concerns of practising lawyers – irrelevant. More often than not, the condemnations were being levelled by the legal scholars themselves.[28]

Part of this can be explained by herding, or what is called the "Matthew effect": the "elite journals show a preference for publishing non-doctrinal work, and those are the journals which attract the most attention: hence the apparent disjunction."[29] But does the emphasis on theory over doctrine and on subject areas such as constitutional law explain this phenomenon completely? After all, notwithstanding this Matthew effect, it is still possible to deploy a variety of legal methodologies across a range of subject areas. Perhaps there is something more going on, as I propose below.

France provides a useful counterpoint, where 53 percent of the articles in my sample of "top" law journals were squarely doctrinal. To understand French legal scholarship, one must appreciate the "distinctive critical function of the *note d'arrêt* or case note"[30] – what can be aptly described as "ground zero of judicial writing"[31] in France. The central importance of case notes can be traced to opinion writing in the civil tradition; after all, "[i]t is because French judicial decisions tend to be so brief, furthermore, that the *arrêtistes* can legitimately take it upon themselves to guide the reader of any particular decision through the relevant case law, this being a task which, in Anglo-American law, would normally be performed by the court."[32] Law journals showcasing case notes

meeting the needs of attorneys and judges; and law professors believe that they have a capricious, negative effect on their careers").

[28] Duxbury, Jurists and Judges, at 23. See, e.g., Pierre Schlag, *Spam Jurisprudence, Air Law, and the Rank Anxiety of Nothing Happening (A Report on the State of the Art)*, 97 *Geo. L.J.* 803, 804 (2009) ("American legal scholarship today is dead – totally dead, deader than at any time in the past thirty years. It is more dead, vastly and exponentially more dead, than critical legal studies was ever dead during its most dead period. Nothing's happening.").

[29] Duxbury, Jurists and Judges, at 43. [30] Ibid., at 48.

[31] Jacques Chevallier, *Doctrine Juridique et Science Juridique*, Droit et Société, 2002, n° 50, 103, 114 (author's translation).

[32] Duxbury, Jurists and Judges, at 53.

began emerging in the mid-nineteenth century,[33] and the tradition continues essentially unabated into the twenty-first century.[34]

A critical point here is that these doctrinal notes "provide legal commentators with the opportunity to operate as shadow-judges, to showcase their doctrinal skills and to try to influence judicial thinking in the future. It hardly seems surprising that the distinguished academic lawyer should normally revel in the role of *l'arrêtiste*."[35] As has been pointed out to me by French law professors, it also provides an entrée into lucrative consulting work with French lawyers.[36]

In sum, legal culture at least partially explains the differences in what is being published in France versus the United States:

> We have seen, however, that many American law professors produce scholarship which judges do not find particularly useful. Legal commentary in France, by contrast, tends to be less abstruse and more pertinent to judicial concerns. In particular, the value that French lawyers place on the pithy, analytical *note d'arrêt* which appears alongside the case report means that the legal academy is predominantly responsible for the production of a body of legal literature judges generally read and respect.[37]

This tendency in France is also consistent with an emerging discourse on the European continent that is the polar opposite of what has been going

[33] See ibid., at 50 ("The journals which began to appear in the 1840s were usually the joint ventures of academic and practising lawyers, and the case notes which they contained were the product of, and were intended to be of interest to, both constituencies."). As Max Radin noted in 1928:

> One of the three collections of French reports, the *Dalloz*, the *Sirey*, or the *Gazette de Palais*, is read by almost very lawyer in France and the brief decision would be unintelligible and useless to him without the notes which are attached to them.
>
> As to these notes, we must confess that they far surpass the notes in our cyclopedias or collections. They are written by the most eminent experts in their special field that can be obtained.

Max Radin, *Sources of Law—New and Old*, 1 S. Cal. L. Rev. 411, 419 (1928).

[34] See, e.g., Duxbury, *supra* note 17, at 54 ("At the beginning of the twenty-first century, case note writing in France appears to be more significant a form of legal commentary than it has ever been.").

[35] Ibid., at 57. See also Ibid., at 56 ("French case note writers are rarely legal novices. Case note writing tends to be a task of privilege, a mark of distinction. Part of the reason for this. . .is that French case notes are highly visible.").

[36] See also ibid., at 56 ("case note writing is a valuable marketing strategy for those French academics who seek to supplement their salaries by acting as *consultants* on behalf of *avocats*.").

[37] Ibid., at 58.

on in the United States: namely, that European legal scholarship is too practical and not theoretical enough.[38]

British legal scholarship, on the other hand, lies somewhere between these two extremes.[39] In terms of analytical method, 32 percent of the British scholarship was doctrinal (versus 53 percent in France and only 8 percent in the United States); similarly, the leading law journals in Britain are not subject-matter focused in the continental tradition, but neither are they as skewed toward a particular subject area as in the United States; for example, the two top subject areas in Britain were Criminal Law and Torts, at 12 percent and 10 percent, respectively.

What is one to make of this? First, though England does not have a case note tradition as in France, there is still apparently more room of doctrinal scholarship among academics in Britain than in the United States:

> In England the case note is commonly considered to be one of the lowliest forms of legal literature, not least because the case notes section of the law journal often provides a nursery slope for the tyro academic who has yet to find either the time or the confidence to engage in more sustained research. In the USA, the case commentaries, frequently article-length by English standards, which appear in certain of the law school journals are invariably written by student editors. Most American law professors would consider the writing of such commentaries to be rather beneath them.[40]

Second, even "top" publications are not as theoretical and interdisciplinary as in the United States,[41] likely driven in part by the fact that

[38] See Rob van Gestel, Ranking, Peer Review, Bibliometrics and Alternative Ways to Improve the Quality of Traditional Legal Scholarship 2 (2015) [hereinafter van Gestel, Ranking] (unpublished manuscript, on file with author; "in many European countries the debate now seems to go in the opposite direction [to that in the United States] . . . Not only do scholars from other (social) sciences accuse legal scholars of being unacademic, but lawyers themselves also appear to have growing doubts about the methodologies they apply and about the theoretical relevance of traditional legal research." (citations omitted)).

[39] See, e.g., Chapter 1 in this volume(showing greater mix in legal research methods at law schools sampled in the UK than those in Germany)

[40] Ibid., at 55–56.

[41] Which is not to suggest that British legal publications have not been subject to criticisms akin to those of Judge Edwards in the United States. See, e.g., Jack Beatson, Legal Academics: Forgotten Players or Interlopers?, Inner Temple Reader's Lecture Series (Nov. 12, 2012) 28, *available at* www.judiciary.gov.uk/announcements/justice-beatson-inner-temple-lecture-12112012/ (commenting on a book on law, society and popular culture "With chapters on 'Lord Denning, Cricket, Law and the Meaning of Life' and

academic law in Britain is apparently a relatively new phenomenon[42] – whereas, by contrast, law schools found their place within American research universities much earlier.[43] Legal education in Britain is also apparently strongly influenced by the organized bar,[44] as well as those of the legal publishers.[45]

Finally, British legal scholarship is also not immune from the broader realities of legal scholarship in Europe that tend toward doctrinal work:

> [W]e must realize that doctrinal research is not under attack so much across the Atlantic, at least not yet. A first reason for this is probably that most legal researchers in Europe are still trained as "black letter" lawyers and usually do not have a PhD in another (social) science as is increasingly the case at the elite law schools in the United States … Second, doctrinal legal scholarship in Europe has far deeper roots than in the

'Dante, Cricket, Law and the Meaning of Life' or for the more practically inclined, 'Leg Before Wicket, Causation and the Rule of Law' the attraction of this over, say, Smith and Hogan on Criminal Law or Anson on Contract is clear.").

42 See Duxbury, Jurists and Judges, at 71 ("Academic law remained a fairly moribund, amateurish profession throughout the first half of the twentieth century. Never mind that judges were disinclined to allow citation of academic writings in court; academics, what few there were, were often disinclined to write."). See *also* ibid., at 69 ("History attests to this image of the academic lawyer as under-achiever.").

43 See, e.g., David Neuberger, Judges and Professors—Ships Passing in the Night?, Max Planck Institute Hamburg (Jul. 9, 2012) 11, *available at* www.judiciary.gov.uk/announcements/mr-speech-hamburg-lecture-09072012/ ("And it wasn't until the mid 20th century that academic law really flourished."); Beatson, Legal Academics, at 8 ("But for the first sixty years of the twentieth century academic writing was, with a small number of notable exceptions, regarded as, at best, a guide to the current state of the authorities, rather than a contribution to the development of the common law."); Harry Woolf, *The Atlantic Divide*, 34 *Tulsa L.J.* 657, 658–59 (1999) ("It is only relatively recently in the 19th century that law has been taken seriously as an academic subject of any significance."). *Cf.* Michael Adler & Jonathan Simon, *Stepwise Progression: The Past, Present, and Possible Future of Empirical Research on Law in the United States and the United Kingdom*, 41 *J. L. & Soc.* 173, 178 (2014) ("The 1920s saw an increasing demand for legal realists in American law schools. Within the academy, law schools were only just beginning to take their place in the modern research university.").

44 See, e.g., H. Glenn et al., *Law in the Real World : Improving our Understanding of How the Law Works*, The Nuffield Inquiry on Empirical Legal Research, Nuffield Foundation, London, 2006, 29 *available at* www.ucl.ac.uk/laws/socio-legal/empirical/docs/inquiry_report.pdf ("the main task and the main income of [law] departments, requires teaching a curriculum that is heavily influenced by the demands of the professional bodies places real constraints on the treatment of law as a "social science" discipline or on interdisciplinary dialogue, much less research."); Woolf, *The Atlantic Divide*, at 659.

45 See Woolf, *The Atlantic Divide*, at 664 ("The publishers of British reviews are usually well aware that practitioners are an important part of their market and they take care to ensure that a fair proportion of their wares meet the professions pragmatic needs.").

> United States where the spread of C.C. Langdell's dialectical case method in legal education concentrating on deductive logic and systematic interpretation of judicial decisions is a fairly recent development compared to the focus on legal doctrine in Europe, dating back to the renaissance of Roman law. Third ... in a melting pot of currently 27 [now 28] legal systems and a variety of languages and legal cultures, doctrinal scholarship with its focus on interpretation and systematisation and comparative law, will remain extremely important for the evolution of European law.[46]

It is perhaps unsurprising that British legal scholarship would be influenced by these European realities.

4.2.2 Who Is Publishing?

My empirical study suggests that over 70 percent of articles in the top American journals are published by faculty at elite law schools. As even the popular press has observed, "almost all the cachet in legal academia goes to professors who produce law review [law journal] articles ... law reviews [are] the ticket to punch for any upwardly mobile scholar."[47] But if it is difficult for faculty at non-elite law schools to publish in top journals, then this perpetuates hierarchy rather than fosters upward mobility. There thus might be some reality to the assertion of critics that "articles selection is not primarily based on merit but rather on author prestige and other extraneous factors."[48] The point that legal scholarship may be selected for publication based on ameritocratic considerations is a very serious one which gets to the heart of the legitimacy of the scholarly enterprise.

The point above that 40 percent of law review articles are never cited is incomplete: work by Thomas Smith suggests that the top 0.5 percent of articles receive 18 percent of citations; the top 5.2 percent of articles receive 50 percent of citations; and the top 17 percent receive 79 percent of citations.[49] Download distributions from the Social Science Research Network (SSRN) are remarkably similar.[50] The law reviews in my

[46] van Gestel & Micklitz, *Methods*, at 294.

[47] D. Segal, *What They Don't Teach Law Students: Lawyering*, N.Y. Times, Nov. 19, 2011.

[48] See Wise et al., *Do Law Reviews Need Reform?*, at 21.

[49] See Smith, *The Web of Law*, at 6.

[50] See Caron, *The Long Tail of Legal Scholarship*, at 42. The top 0.5 percent of articles constitute 21 percent of total downloads; the top 5.2 percent, 57 percent; and the top 17 percent, 80 percent.

sample, by definition, are the highly cited ones[51] – and they are featuring predominantly work by academics from elite institutions.[52] The other 90 percent of law faculty are, to a disproportionate extent, being left out of the discourse. To the extent top law journals would contain authorship by a broader cross-section of the legal academy or legal profession more broadly, there might perhaps be a broader range of perspectives, with concomitant greater balance among the different analytical methods, with less emphasis on theory. As such, the law journals could maybe become more useful to practicing lawyers and judges.

There is a related problem which exacerbates the phenomenon: faculty at "elite" law schools publishing in their own "top" law review. On average, about 20 percent of the articles in the US law journals I have studied are by faculty members of the law school publishing the journal – interestingly, there is some evidence that these articles are less frequently cited and perhaps of lower quality.[53] One recent empirical study raises significant concerns about this phenomenon:

> Should we care about law reviews' bias in favor of their own faculty? Framed another way, what is the opportunity cost of this bias? The costs are borne in part by authors collectively, particularly those who teach outside the top decile of law schools. Given that citation rates decline as rankings decline. . ., this bias likely has a crowding out effect. Articles from outside authors that law reviews would otherwise publish (were they not publishing their own faculty) end up in lower-ranked journals.[54]

Of course, there might be other plausible explanations for the disparity. Perhaps faculty at elite law schools are disproportionately sending articles to top law journals, or perhaps the articles they are producing are

[51] See *also* A. H. Yoon, *Editorial Bias in Legal Academia*, 5 *J. Legal Analysis* 309, 315 (2013) ("The ranking of law schools and law journals are negatively correlated with citation count, meaning the lower the rank of the law review or the school, the fewer the citations").

[52] *Cf.* Michael J. Saks et al., *Is There a Growing Gap Among Law, Law Practice, and Legal Scholarship?: A Systematic Comparison of Law Review Articles One Generation Apart*, 30 *Suffolk U. L. Rev.* 352, 374 (1996) ("The differences seem to be concentrated largely in the top-quintile law reviews. If the interlocutors in this legal debate read these journals disproportionately, it would not be surprising if they developed a mistaken impression of legal scholarship.").

[53] See Yoon, *Editorial Bias*, at 330 ("Law reviews, when publishing their own faculty, generate articles that are cited less often than when they select faculty from other law schools . . . If citation counts are a credible measure for quality, law review editors, when selecting articles from their own professors, act to the detriment of the law review").

[54] Ibid., at 335.

significantly better than those being produced by everyone else. At the very least, though, the empirical pattern raises questions. To the extent that "the journal in which authors publish their articles serve[s] as a proxy for their quality,"[55] then does this mean that faculty at non-elite law schools produce lower quality, or are there more troubling phenomena at work?

By contrast, does the greater number of authors from non-elite law schools in Britain and France suggest that publications in those jurisdictions are more "democratic"? Or might there be other explanations: for instance, is there a greater disparity between elite and non-elite institutions in the United States, or do elite European academics prefer publication venues other than law journals?

4.3 Quality and Methodology

My initial inclination after surveying what is being published in "top" law journals across three jurisdictions, as well as trying to explore links between these results and legal culture, is that as legal academics we need to pay more attention to quality and how to measure it. To be sure, this is important and I discuss it first below.

Quality, however, cannot be completely conceptualized without a threshold concept – namely, methodology. Only by grappling with quality and methodology can we even hope to begin improving the state of legal research. Yet existing quality metrics – journal rankings, peer review, bibliometric citations, and the like – are by themselves at best incomplete and at worst misleading. As such, I argue that quality cannot be understood without the threshold concept of methodology. Entering the dangerous territory of linking methodology with quality becomes all but inevitable if we hope to begin improving the state of legal research.

4.3.1 Quality

4.3.1.1 The Status Quo, Especially in the United States

Even discussing quality in scholarship is extremely controversial. To belabor the obvious, quality is very difficult to measure.[56] Given

55 Ibid., at 309.

56 See, e.g., Posner, *Legal Scholarship Today*, at 1325 ("Unfortunately, quality of scholarship is very difficult to measure."); Dan Subotnik & Glen Lazar, *Deconstructing the Rejection Letter: A Look at Elitism in Article Selection*, 49 *J. Legal Educ.* 601, 605 (1999) ("In this

imperfect information, we search for proxies as I have done in this chapter; notably, institutional affiliation and rankings.

Consider what is colloquially referred to in the United States as the "letterhead problem": "looking at the author's name, institution, or background to help organize tiers, or which papers get first, serious, or possibly any, attention."[57] This, in essence, creates a self-perpetuating hierarchy: since "the quality of an article is often based solely on where the article gets accepted and published"[58] and authors from "elite" institutions are precisely those getting published in "top" law journals.[59]

This state of affairs is only accentuated by an obsession with rankings of law schools and universities generally. Pierre Schlag laments the

> [A]nxiety . . . perhaps best reflected in our obsessive fixation on rankings – rankings of law schools, ranking of law reviews, ranking of legal scholars, rankings of citations and impact, and soon to come . . . rankings of rankings. Quantification rules as the major parameter of academic excellence . . . We don't have to worry that the enterprise might be entirely worthless if we're totally fixated on how well or how badly we are doing it relative to everybody else.[60]

These forces have been even stronger with the "new managerialism"[61] and "corporatisation"[62] of universities, all within the "broader context of neo-liberalism and globalisation."[63] As Schlag continues:

postmodern age, no generally accepted way to measure quality is available because there is wide disagreement about appropriate standards.").

57 Kevin M. Yamamoto, *What's in a Name? The Letterhead Impact Project*, 22 *J. Legal Studies Educ.* 65, 69 (2004).

58 Ibid., at 70.

59 See, e.g., Subotnik & Lazar, *Deconstructing the Rejection Letter*, at 604 ("the top law reviews systematically favor articles from authors (whether majority or minority) at high-status institutions (HSIs) . . . Since articles by faculty at low-status institutions (LSIs) can ordinarily add little if any status value, one would expect such articles to be substantially disadvantaged in the evaluation process."); Yamamoto, *What's in a Name?*, at 81–82 ("Articles editors admit that it is their belief that publishing pieces by famous authors, or authors associated with more prestigious institutions, enhances the image of their law reviews.").

60 Schlag, *Spam Jurisprudence*, at 826–827.

61 Richard Collier, *The Changing University and the (Legal) Academic Career—Rethinking the Relationship between Women, Men and the "Private Live" of the Law School*, 22 *Legal Studies* 1, 14 (2002).

62 Ibid., at 15.

63 Ibid., at 16. See *also* Rob van Gestel, *Sense and Non-Sense of a European Ranking of Law Schools and Law Journals*, Legal Studies 35, 1, 165–185, (2015) [hereinafter, van Gestel, *Sense and Non-Sense*] ("Ranking appeals to the competitive ethos that has entered universities since the 1980s on the upsurge of a neo-liberal belief in more private responsibility for public goods. This has led to more emphasis on competition

> Ironically, it is at this very moment – the moment when legal scholarship seems so thoroughly compromised – that law schools have decided, seemingly en masse, to intensify the monitoring of scholarly quality and quantity as well as to enforce scholarly output maximization strategies. Law faculties and administration are all increasingly heavily invested in mentoring, career positioning, SSRN download rates, citation indices, article placement strategies, blog announcements, and glossy scholarship advertising. It's all a kind of massive "no professor left behind" scheme.[64]

The overall picture that emerges, at least in the United States, is an "artificially staged competition"[65] to create the illusion of excellence.

This state of affairs creates incentives for legal academics to churn what Schlag calls "legally cognizable material" (LCM)[66]—"[s]cholasticism—highly elaborated, carefully crafted mediocrity."[67] As Richard Posner observes:

> And then the question becomes how to decide whom to hire and promote to perform the essential teaching function. There is reluctance to do so on the basis of teaching evaluations. . .whereas scholarly publication will be noted in other institutions and so cast some glory on the institution at which the teacher is employed. Hence the pressure on faculty to publish even when the scholarship that is published has no value; hence he straining after novelty, the drive for specialization, the quest for rigor, the adoption of a technical vocabulary – all methods of signaling quality that may, however, have no effect except to turn off students and other readers.[68]

The problem, of course, is not limited to legal academics, as one economist observes:

> The major goal of academics has become to receive a good certification, while the content of their research often no longer seems to matter. Many

between universities and to public steering on output indicators in order to increase 'productivity.'").

64 Schlag, *Spam Jurisprudence*, at 830.

65 Binswanger, *Excellence by Nonsense*, at 51. As Rob van Gestel observes:

> Ranking of law journals can be done for different reasons, ranging from providing standardised information to authors with respect to where to submit their papers (what are the "best" journals) to helping research foundations to decide which legal scholars to sponsor (the ones writing in high-ranked journals). *In most cases, however, the underlying rationale is to enhance a "status competition" on the basis of the reputation of the authors, the rejection rate of journals or their impact factors.*

van Gestel, *Sense and Non-sense*, at 12.

66 Schlag, *Spam Jurisprudence*, at 809. 67 Ibid.

68 Posner, *Legal Scholarship Today*, at 849.

> scholars do not first identify an important issue and worthwhile problem, which they then will analyse; rather, they do the reverse. They only engage in the study of a subject if and when they can be assured beforehand that the data available are of such good quality that the advanced econometric methods can be applied.[69]

Scholars are reverse-engineering to respond to what is arguably an incorrect objective function; in other words, "[p]ublishing one's work in an A-journal is therefore the most important and often also the only aim of modern scientists."[70]

The supervening irony in all of this is the seeming simultaneous creation of a research bureaucracy[71] and increasing alienation. Alienation exists along at least two dimensions. First, around whether what is being published in "elite" venues adds meaningfully to our current knowledge[72] and whether work in "non-elite" venues will even be taken seriously.[73] Second, and relatedly, between academic "haves" and "have-nots" – one commentator, for example, worries about the "hundreds of LSI [low-status institution] teachers who have been beaten down by the current system."[74] As Rob van Gestel notes:

> Rankings of law schools and law journals are serious business. They guide students, faculty and employers in making choices with regard to where to study, who to hire and how to appreciate the teaching and research output of scholars. The prestige of a law school will, for example, influence the quality and number of students it attracts, in turn determining the school's revenues that can be used, among other purposes, to appoint better professors, thereby increasing the potential to attract research funding, and so on. *In short, people's lives and jobs are at stake here.*[75]

4.3.1.2 Beyond Rankings?

So what can be done? One cautionary word would be for the British and French perhaps not to follow the path we have taken in the United States

[69] Bruno S. Frey et al., *Editorial Ruminations: Publishing Kyklos*, 62 *Kyklos* 151, 152 (2009).
[70] Binswanger, *Excellence by Nonsense*, at 54. [71] See, e.g., ibid., at 68–70.
[72] See e.g., ibid., at 65 ("The overall effect of all these perverse incentives is that scientists produce more and more nonsense, which adds nothing to real scientific progress.").
[73] *Cf.* van Gestel, *Sense and Non-Sense*, at 16 ("Truly ground-breaking work may be more likely to appear from marginal, dissident or unexpected sources, rather than from a well-established and entrenched mainstream.").
[74] Subotnik & Lazar, *Deconstructing the Rejection Letter*, at 613.
[75] van Gestel, *Sense and Non-sense*, at 2 (emphasis added).

on rankings[76] – though a global trend toward ranking universities is well afoot,[77] and a US News–type ranking of law schools in other countries may come in time.

4.3.1.2.1 Peer Review Can, on the other hand, Americans learn from the peer-reviewed systems that the British and French law journals use? Are they more meritocratic? After all, about a third of the articles in the "top" journals were published by faculty at "elite" institutions in Britain and France – rather than 70 percent in the United States. Perhaps this is a direction one might consider, but with the understanding that peer review is far from a panacea:

> In the sciences, objections are regularly raised against publications in journals: the waiting times are (much) too long, the periodicals are too expensive, the limits placed on the size of publications are too strict; subscribers also pay for publications of no importance to them; editorial boards have become too dependent on their external referees; editors belong to an in-crowd, etc.[78]

The "in-crowd" point is particularly interesting:[79] review is seldom truly "blind,"[80] and at least one study of leading economics journals calculates that over 40 percent of articles were published by scholars from six elite universities.[81] There also remains the fundamental, and surprisingly unanswered, question of what peer review actually means:

[76] *Cf.* ibid., at 10 ("One can rank law schools on the basis of faculty reputation, student scores, job placement, SSRN downloads and so on, but it remains highly questionable whether these criteria can be meaningfully amalgamated into one overarching quality judgment.").

[77] See, e.g., van Gestel, *Sense and Non-sense*, at 5 ("Performance measurement in academia has developed rapidly since the 1970s. Today there are several worldwide rankings of universities, such as the 'Shanghai ranking,' the QS World University Ranking, the Times Higher Education World University Ranking and the Leiden Ranking.").

[78] Stolker, *Legal Journals*, at 86.

[79] See *also* Binswanger, *Excellence by Nonsense*, at 55 ("The peer-review process is thus a kind of insider procedure . . . which is not transparent for scientists outside the established circle of champions.").

[80] See, e.g., ibid., at 63 (noting the "dubious nature of anonymity within the peer-review process").

[81] See Frey et al., *Editorial Ruminations*, at 153 ("During 2007, the five leading journals in economics . . . published 275 papers. No less than 119 (or 43% of all papers) were scholars who are associated with the leading US universities (Harvard, Yale, Princeton, Chicago, Berkeley and Stanford).").

> There is no consensus as to the appropriateness of different kinds of peer review, how to select peer reviewers, what criteria reviewers should adopt to assess the quality of scholarly legal publications, and whether it is useful to combine peer review with other forms of quality control, such as citation scores.[82]

There is also the very real frustration of scholars from non-elite institutions who find it virtually impossible to publish in the elusive "A journal,"[83] and the fact that reviewers often have more important things to do than actually engage the work they are reviewing.[84] Perhaps most significantly, one wonders whether peer review rewards putative incremental improvements rather than path-breaking insights – not only because the latter tend to of necessity be less-polished,[85] but also because they can upset the status quo in which the reviewers have a vested interest.[86] As one critic summarizes the situation:

> The peer-review process causes potential authors ... to converge upon mainstream topics and approaches, as novel ideas and approaches get rarely published or financed. However, scientific geniuses were hardly ever mainstream before their theories or methods were accepted. They are often quite unconventional in their way of working and, therefore, do not perform well in assessments which are based upon the number of publications in professional journals, citations, or projects acquired. *Neither*

82 van Gestel, *Sense and Non-sense*, at 26. See *also* Rob van Gestel et al., Methodology in the New Legal World, European University Institute Working Papers 2012/13 at 19, *available at* http://ssrn.com/abstract=2069872 [hereinafter van Gestel et al., *Methodology*].

83 See e.g., Frey et al., *Editorial Ruminations*, at 153 ("The demand to 'publish in A journals' thus asks the impossible from most scholars. The situation may, of course, be considered a tournament where few win but all participants are given an incentive to work hard. But is may also happen that the actual and potential losers are demotivated and leave academia, or are deeply frustrated and resort to obstruction. This reaction may explain why referee reports written with respect to the work of other scholars are often devastatingly discouraging—provided referees may write the reports anonymously.").

84 See, e.g., Binswanger, *Excellence by Nonsense*, at 56 ("by no means do all peers, who are mostly preoccupied with their own publications, actually read, let alone understand, the articles to be evaluated. Time is far too short for this and usually it is not even worth it because there are much more interesting things to do.").

85 See, e.g., Frey et al., *Editorial Ruminations*, at 157 ("papers with standard ideas have a better chance than contributions with innovative ideas, which almost by necessity are less polished and thus more open to critique").

86 See, e.g., ibid., at 155 ("it is exactly those scholars, though, who have most to lose when a new idea that undermines the approaches and ideas they have championed over many years is promoted. Such reviewers knowingly or unknowingly introduce a marked conservative bias.").

> *Albert Einstein nor Friedrich Nietzsche would be able to pursue a scientific career under the current system.*[87]

Perhaps the best one can say, then, is that peer review should have some role to play in assessing quality. This statement, however, comes with at least two caveats: it must somehow be as close to actual "blind" peer review as possible, and some incentive must be given to reviewers to take their work seriously. Law reviews in the United States, who increasingly ask their faculty to serve as informal peer reviewers, might also consider disallowing their faculty to publish in their own law review.

4.3.1.2.2 Citation Counts Another, perhaps complementary, approach, would be to use citation counts as "a proxy for influence"[88] and hence quality. There are, however, several problems with this approach as well.

First, as far as I have been able to find, bibliometric databases of legal journals exist only in the United States and not in Europe or other jurisdictions; as such, it would require significant investment to build out beyond the United States.[89] Second, citation counts do not "capture all the different aspects of scholarly quality."[90] Nor does number of citations necessarily even correlate to influence,[91] especially in a jurisdiction such as Britain with a historic norm effectively discouraging the citation of legal scholars.[92] Third, it can exacerbate herding or the

[87] Binswanger, *Excellence by Nonsense*, at 66 (emphasis added).

[88] Duxbury, Jurists and Judges, at 9.

[89] See van Gestel & Micklitz, *Methods*, at 312 ("there is no such thing as a uniform ranking of law journals in Europe or a metrics-based system of measuring the impact of scholarly legal publications."); van Gestel, *Sense and Non-sense*, at 20 ("there is no uniform bibliometric database for European law journals").

[90] van Gestel, *Sense and Non-sense*, at 6. See *generally* Marta Bladek, *DORA: San Francisco Declaration on Research Assessment (May 2013)*, College & Research Library News, Apr. 2014, at 191 (questioning bibliometric evaluations, notably Journal Impact Factor (JIF)).

[91] See, e.g., Duxbury, Jurists and Judges, at 1 ("Citations to a work of scholarship are not necessarily indicative of its influence, just as absence of citations to that work does not compel the conclusion that it has had no influence."); Beatson, Legal Academics, at 17 ("Citation by a court or its absence is not necessarily indicative of influence or its absence. From the point of view of the academic, positive citation is good for morale.").

[92] See, e.g., Duxbury, Jurists and Judges, at 24 (discussing the "English convention against the citation of the works of living commentators as authority."); ibid., at 68 ("Being essentially an oral tradition, the English adjudicative process 'is not conducive to the more ample citation practices found in some civil law countries and in the United States.'" (citations omitted)).

Matthew effect where the already famous get the lion's share of citations,[93] thereby hindering the emergence of novel or dissident voices. Indeed, one of the unintended consequences of building bibliometric databases in other jurisdictions – especially if it is accompanied by rankings of law schools – may be to engender a status competition like we already have in the United States.

It might be particularly helpful to make bibliometric databases and studies of citations as granular as possible; notably, separating out the citations in law journals from those in judicial opinions and works designed for practicing lawyers. Perhaps methodologies, like US News and Washington and Lee, conflate two different audiences: other legal academics versus practicing lawyers and judges? Might rankings of "top" law reviews differ depending on who the audience is? For example, one recent intriguing study of US Supreme Court citations suggests that in the first decade of the twenty-first century "nearly four in ten cited law review articles were written by authors who were not full-time law professors"[94] and that the "Justices have cited articles from the full gamut of law reviews in the rankings, including many law reviews that are not deemed tenure-worthy, at least from the perspective of the hiring and promotion committees at many elite law schools."[95]

The bottom line on citation counts is similar to that for peer review: each probably has some role to play in assessing quality, but certainly cannot be the entire picture.[96] As Rob van Gestel and Hans-Wolfgang Micklitz summarize the situation:

> [B]oth substantive assessment of scholarly legal publications and employing bibliometric indicators (citation scores, impact factors) can have significant disadvantages and adverse effects. Peer review is often hindered by the obscurity of the assessment criteria, subjective beliefs and biases of reviewers, while metrics say little about the quality of individual publications from a substantive perspective (the level or originality is hard to catch in numbers).[97]

[93] See, e.g., ibid., at 11 ("Our general predilection for citing the great over and above the not-so-great is evidenced by what citation analysts have termed 'the Matthew effect.' Academic esteem tends to cultivate itself: rewards tend to be skewed towards those who are already highly reputed.") (citations omitted)

[94] Newton, *Law Review Scholarship*, at 405.

[95] Newton, *Law Review Scholarship*, at 416. These two findings seem intuitive if one accepts the premise that "[a]s a general rule, the lower a law review's ranking, the larger ... its percentage of authors other than full-time law professors" Ibid., at 411.

[96] *Cf.* Duxbury, Jurists and Judges, at 17 ("analyses of citations may prove helpful for the purpose of assessing influence, but they must always be treated with circumspection.").

[97] van Gestel & Micklitz, *Methods*, at 313.

So where do we stand on the seemingly intractable problem of quality? My own view is that as a first pass, we need to think about how some combination of existing output measures – namely, rankings, bibliometric citations, and peer review – can be combined into an overall more holistic measure. While I understand that this approach does have significant drawbacks—including its algorithmic nature and that fact that it could actually backfire and exacerbate a research bureaucracy[98] – it at least merits serious consideration before being dismissed outright.

A second, perhaps complementary, approach would be to "think outside the box" by deemphasizing output and going down other paths such as focusing on input (such as how academics are trained and recruited)[99] and, perhaps paradoxically creating incentives for quality over quantity.[100] While there is some very promising emerging work on these alternative approaches, they remain a work-in-process.[101]

Yet neither approach appears satisfactory at the moment. Might there be a way out of this conundrum?

4.3.2 Methodology

Traditional metrics (rankings, peer review, citations counts) as well as novel approaches (inputs, quality over quantity) can only do so much work in serving as proxies for research excellence. As I located and "coded" the 810 articles for my little empirical study, nagging questions kept on recurring vastly more fundamental than author characteristics or analytical methods or subject matter. For instance, what research

[98] See, e.g., van Gestel, Ranking, at 54 ("As a consequence, it might seem logical to opt for a combination of ranking, peer review, and metrics-based research assessment in order to attenuate the disadvantages of individual research evaluation methods. This could, however, easily result in 'evaluitis' or a bureaucracy, which will overshoot the mark and lead to a culture of distrust and lack of confidence in academics.").

[99] See, e.g., van Gestel, Ranking, at 55 ("The first one, shifts the emphasis from output control to the input side of training and socialization of research talent. Both in Europe and in the US more attention could be paid to the training and education of young scholars with a taste for science.")

[100] See ibid., at 44–45 ("Especially in countries where national research assessments play a major role it might be better to introduce a maximum number of publications allowed to be submitted to the research assessment exercise than working with a minimum number. . . [I]f researchers may only submit a few publications to a research assessment exercise and their performance is judged on the basis of these self-selected publications, scholars will realize they have to produce a few pieces that are really innovative instead of a lot of 'middle of the road' work.")

[101] See also van Gestel, Ranking.

questions are these works trying to address? What assumptions are they making? Is there a lurking normative agenda?

The difficult question of methodology becomes inevitable. By methodology, I do not mean "the ways to identify and locate primary and secondary resources,"[102] but rather "a broader approach in which methodology represents 'the application of a conceptual apparatus or framework.'"[103] This is an important question in all academic disciplines, but particularly acute in law – a discipline that Posner labels "an intellectually insecure field ... [that] lacks a theoretical gyroscope and therefore wobbles, grabbing at the methods and insights of other fields while buffeted by the political and ideological currents of the day."[104]

There is obvious intrinsic intellectual value to methodology: posing research questions, making assumptions explicit, and exposing normative agendas, to name a few.[105] Consider Rob van Gestel and Hans-Wolfgang Micklitz's perceptive critique of European legal scholarship:

> There is an endless list of dissertations, books, articles, papers, etc. which simply follow mainstream ideas and ideologies, such as: harmonisation of laws is good and legal diversity is bad, human rights are a blessing for EU law but economic rights are a curse, consulting stakeholders over new EU laws and policies is the right thing to do but listening to lobbyists is wrong, transparency in decision making is good, secrecy is bad and so on. *In many cases, the authors do not even bother to explain on whose shoulders they stand, where they deviate from fellow researchers or from mainstream beliefs or practice or, more in general, to what extent they really add something new to the body of knowledge.*[106]

[102] van Gestel et al., *Methodology*, at 1 (citations omitted).

[103] Ibid., (citations omitted) and at 9 ("methodology of law and legal research is associated with a very broad range of topics varying from epistemological issues about how facts or rules and principles are perceived, constructed or deconstructed, to methods of judicial interpretation and the skills needed for proper academic legal writing.").

[104] Richard A. Posner, *The Rise and Fall of Administrative Law*, 72 *Chi. Kent L. Rev.* 953, 953 (1997). Pierre Schlag even goes so far as to posit that "having no great texts, no sophisticated methodologies, no great questions, and nothing else of any fundamental intellectual value, the discipline of law is organized as a kind of mimesis – specifically, the imitation of judicial idioms, tasks, gestures, professional anxieties, and the like." Schlag, *Spam Jurisprudence*, at 812.

[105] See, e.g., van Gestel & Micklitz, *Methods*, at 308 ("the inherent preconceptions and the reasons lying behind our assumptions ... when we conduct scholarly legal research deserve to be disclosed, and the same goes for the methods ... that will be applied to find answers to the research questions that we have chosen to investigate.").

[106] Ibid., at 305 (emphasis added).

In many ways, without asking fundamental methodological questions we remain rudderless and prone to the Mathew effect. Consider how van Gestel and Micklitz's critique echoes Schlag's more general one:

> It's as if we were all working really hard on an imaginary bus schedule. Someone writes an article saying we need to optimize the number of buses. Another person can't resist pointing out that it might be preferable to start by optimizing the number of bus stops instead. Soon someone writes that we should reconstruct the entire schedule. Someone else will suggest that we should split the schedule along eight different parts. Someone says, the eight parts are really sixteen. Some truly original thinker says there are ten. And then, some ranker comes along and starts ranking whose law school has the best bus scheduling program going. And somebody else decides to hold a symposium on bus schedule rankings.
>
> Pretty soon, we've got a collective imaginary going and we're pushing buses and bus stops all across pages of the *Yale Law Journal* and it all feels kind of real and pretty important. And it's not hard to believe that it's important. For one thing people are getting real rewards – prestige jobs, chairs, program funding – for imaginary bus schedule breakthroughs.[107]

A focus on methodology could improve doctrinal scholarship, nondoctrinal scholarship, and even help find a balance between the two. Doctrinal scholars should strive to articulate their methodology beyond – often subconscious[108] – use of "[l]ogic, analogy, judicial decisions, a handful of principles such as stare decisis and common sense"[109] Where and how should a doctrinalist draw the line between description and normative argument?[110] How should legal academics deal with the proliferation of heterogeneous legal sources?[111]

[107] Schlag, *Spam Jurisprudence*, at 832–833.

[108] See Chynoweth, *Legal Research*, at 34–35 ("The process involves an exercise in reasoning and a variety of techniques are used, often at a subconscious level, with the aim of constructing an argument which is convincing according to accepted, and instinctive, conventions of discourse within the discipline.").

[109] Posner, *Legal Scholarship Today*, at 1316.

[110] See, e.g., van Gestel et al., *Methodology*, at 5 ("Especially the training of law students in the 'art of persuasion,' . . . is tricky from a methodological perspective since it can easily spur one-sidedness and may provide an impetus to leave aside sources, arguments, and opinions that do not fit with the claims one wants to make.")

[111] See, e.g., van Gestel & Micklitz, *Methods*, at 312 ("the best response to growing heterogeneity of legal sources should be matched with a strengthening of theoretical and methodological components, where possible drawn from the common European heritage in legal theory and spurred by transnational scholarly legal communities.").

The questions are arguably even more acute for interdisciplinary legal scholars. Are there common techniques and questions among the various "Law and" movements?[112] What differentiates interdisciplinary legal scholarship from that in the mainstream social sciences, notably in affecting social policy?[113] More generally, how to avoid being labeled "amateur social scientists"?[114] As Richard Posner observes:

> Interdisciplinary legal scholarship, however, has neither a broad, knowledgeable professional audience nor a systematic, well-structured institutional substitute for the standard academic career pattern, which depends on such an audience. Most law professors who engage in interdisciplinary legal scholarship have not gone through the graduate school Ph.D. mill; their only degree is a J.D. And whether they have two degrees or one, they will submit their articles to student-edited law reviews.[115]

In such a context, better methodology becomes all the more important.

Perhaps most importantly, inquiry into methodology could also ask what the right balance between doctrinal and nondoctrinal scholarship should be – between the "internal" and "external" perspectives, respectively.[116] In the process, such questions might help shed some light on the two different roles law schools must necessarily play: serving the profession on the one hand, and contributing to the intellectual life of the university on the other.[117] Consider the critiques that elite American

[112] *Cf.* Chynoweth, *Legal Research*, at 31 ("there is also a strong correlation between pure, fundamental research and the willingness (indeed, the motivation) of researchers in these areas to question not simply the operation of law, but also its underlying philosophical, moral, economic and political assumptions. Research of this nature takes many forms but would include the Sociology of Law as well as the (left wing) Critical Legal Studies and (right wing) Law and Economics movements."). For one attempt along these lines, see Reza Dibadj, *Beyond Facile Assumptions and Radical Assertions: A Case for "Critical Legal Economics"*, 2003 Utah L. Rev. 1155.

[113] *Cf.* Posner, *Legal Scholarship Today*, at 1317 ("I also argue that its future, which is threatened by problems of quality arising from the peculiar and inadequate institutional structure of interdisciplinary legal scholarship, depends on the ability of the practitioners of this scholarship to influence practice, rather than merely to circulate their ideas within the sealed network of a purely academic discourse.").

[114] van Gestel et al., *Methodology*, at 14.

[115] Posner, *Legal Scholarship Today*, at 1323.

[116] See, e.g., Chevallier, *Doctrine Juridique*, at 105 ("Legal doctrine is an integral part of the production of law: it does not place itself in an outside position vis-à-vis law but seeks to 'situate itself within law' and 'intervene in law.'" Juridical science, on the other hand, seeks to situate itself 'outside law': placing itself in an external position vis-à-vis law, it seeks to adopt a critical and reflective point of view.") (author's translation).

[117] See, e.g., Collier, *The Changing University*, at 5 ("It [the law school] is part of the legal profession, a vital component within a wider community in relation to which it plays a

legal scholarship is too removed from practice,[118] or that leading French legal scholarship is insufficiently open to nondoctrinal perspectives:[119] is there a balance somewhere in between?[120]

My suspicion is that it is likely that there will be significant variation among jurisdictions – consider, for example, the role of the *note d'arrêt* to fill gaps in sparse French judicial opinions.[121] Ideally, if the questions on methodology are properly asked, then the value of each type of scholarship, properly done, would be more likely to be recognized. As one British judge aptly comments:

> [T]he new forms of legal scholarship are undoubtedly important if done well. And there will be material which will be of great interest to practicing lawyers and judges ... But it is not a reason for undervaluing doctrinal research, and for seeking to distance academics from the work of the judges who remain an important primary source of law in a

key role in the production of future generations of lawyers ... And it is part of a university, having historically evolved, for some, in an uncertain intellectual and political relationship to other disciplines which have been concerned, perhaps more unambiguously it has been argued at times, with the disinterested pursuit of knowledge."); Posner, *Legal Scholarship Today*, at 1321 ("The contrast between the internal and external perspective in legal scholarship ... tracks the contrast I am now discussing between scholarship written for the bar (broadly defined) and scholarship written for the academy. The latter type tends to be external, that is, to use techniques, vocabulary, and insights from other fields. Economic analysis of law is a clear example.").

118 See notes 20–28 and accompanying text.

119 See, e.g., Chevallier, *Doctrine Juridique*, at 115 (advocating for "a better equilibrium between the two: the hypertrophy of the doctrinal function must be counter-balanced by an accent placed on legal science, both in research and in teaching" (author's translation); Jean-Yves Cherot, *La question du point de vue interne dans la science du droit, La question du point de vue interne dans la science du droit*, Actes des 2èmes rencontres de théorie du droit d'Aix, Revue Interdisciplinaire d'études juridiques, 2007, n° 59, 17, 32 ("The simple observation that, in the practice of law, formal reasoning, authority, precedent, logical deduction (the internal aspect) are never closed upon themselves but open and communicative with a larger argumentation." (author's translation)).

120 As Siems and Mac Síthigh aptly demonstrate using a very simple example:

> Assume the following scenario: a law professor visits her university cafeteria and wants to sit at a table where she can get some useful comments on the method she plans to use in one of her papers. There are three tables: at the first table sit a historian, a philosopher and a theologian, at the second one an economist, a sociologist and a psychologist, and at the third one a judge, a solicitor and a public prosecutor. Assuming all else being equal...which table is our law professor likely to join?"

Siems & Mac Síthigh in Chapter 1 of this volume.

121 See notes 30–37 and accompanying text.

> common law system ... It is as deplorable as distancing top medical academics from the work of the hospitals and the treatment of the sick.[122]

In an era of staged competition and commodification, it would be difficult to ask whether there is likely less of a hierarchy of quality among publication than our obsession with rankings recognizes. At least, though, it might force the legal academy to provide better justification for the various publication venues in our discipline.[123] It might also make "top" American law schools ask whether there should be greater incentives given to engage in doctrinal scholarship – or "top" French and British law schools ask whether they are doing enough to promote interdisciplinary perspectives.[124]

As legal scholars, we must focus on fundamental concepts in methodology. It is imperative that we ask what criteria we consider important and how to implement these preferences in various publication fora.[125] Today, our work "can all too easily be dismissed as lacking a methodology, as being based only on opinion, or even as being 'not research' by peers operating within a scientific, rather than a humanities

122 Beatson, Legal Academics, at 28. See *also* van Gestel et al., *Methodology*, at 23 ("We believe there is no longer room for only one dominant role model for scholarly legal research. Doctrinalists, empiricists, comparatists, legal historians, law and economists and others co-exist in the new legal world and the quality of their work should be judged according to the rules of the discipline and not be determined by preferences for a particular type of research that is en vogue at the time.").

123 *Cf.* van Gestel et al., *Methodology*, at 18 ("It will become increasingly difficult to explain to the outside world that in an international legal world double blind peer reviewed journals co-exist with student-edited journals and non-reviewed journals without much clarity about the consequences in terms of quality and reputation of both the journal itself and the articles published in it.").

124 See, e.g., Posner, *Legal Scholarship Today*, at 854 ("The problem with the new system of recruitment and promotion is that it tends to freeze out the type of person who is very good just at legal analysis—whose identification is with the legal profession rather than with one of the standard academic fields, such as economics or history, philosophy or statistics, psychology or sociology. That is the type of person who, entering law teaching after a few years of law practice, would be superbly equipped to do Langdellian scholarship ... The law schools *need* legal analysts, not merely as teachers, but also as scholars. Doctrinal analysis cannot be left to judges.")

125 See, e.g., van Gestel, *Sense and Non-sense*, at 8 ("What we need in order to fuel a serious debate on quality of both legal education and scholarship is more information with regard to what legal scholars themselves consider important for the quality of teaching and research ... Few legal scholars seem to be happy with the growing influence of rankings and performance indicators, yet there appears to be little enthusiasm for organised action to try to regain control.").

paradigm."[126] If we do not act, the rankings system already imposed upon American legal academics will be here to stay – and will almost certainly expand to other jurisdictions, beginning with Europe.[127]

4.4 Conclusion

There is, to be sure, much work that remains to be done, both empirically and theoretically. My small empirical study was focused on a three-year period ending in late 2013; as such, the time series could be expanded to go back in time and assess historical patterns. The number of journals or jurisdictions under consideration could be expanded. Peer-reviewed US law journals could be analyzed, even though there are relatively few of them and they are, overall, not very influential compared to student-edited law reviews.[128]

At least two more nuanced extensions of the research might also be contemplated. First, a more detailed analysis of each article might point to some understudied correlations. For example, might there be any patterns based on length of article, whether a Core faculty author is already tenured or tenure-track – or in the case of most British and all French journals whether there are patterns depending who the publisher is? What about the role of international authors? Finally, though it is very unlikely the data would be made available, it would be fascinating to compare the characteristics of articles submitted to those that are eventually accepted for publication. Such extensions would no doubt significantly improve the comprehensiveness of this initial study.

Notwithstanding its risks, it would also be an interesting exercise to try to come up with a way of combining using existing metrics – journal rankings, bibliometric data, and peer review – to attempt a more holistic

126 Chynoweth, *Legal Research*, at 37. See *also* Schlag, *Spam Jurisprudence*, at 813 ("The law review article is an imitation of the legal brief and the judicial opinion. There are, of course, some important differences. The law review article is typically more intricate, more thoroughly researched, more detached, and more abstract. It is also, interestingly, written on behalf of no client, in no pending case, without a court date and addressed to no one in particular. *We're talking air law here.*") (emphasis added).

127 See, e.g., van Gestel, *Sense and Non-sense*, at 15 ("Law as a discipline cannot afford to do nothing because then, sooner or later, others will impose their rankings and quality management systems. Moreover, there is nothing against thinking about ways for law schools and law journals to evaluate the quality of what they produce.").

128 Anecdotal evidence also suggests that the patterns are likely to be similar, with the notable difference that several peer-reviewed journals tend to emphasize empirical methods.

assessment of publication quality. The greater, significantly more ambitious, agenda that would follow from this initial foray is to try to articulate more specifically the methodological weaknesses in contemporary legal scholarship, how they might be addressed, and how these proposals map to an assessment of quality and what should appear in different publication fora. To the extent this project provides a starting point for this more consequential discussion, it will have achieved its goal.

PART II

Should Doctrinal Legal Scholarship Be Abandoned?

5

What Is Legal Doctrine?

On The Aims and Methods of Legal-Dogmatic Research

JAN M. SMITS

5.1 Introduction

Doctrinal legal scholarship finds itself in an uncertain state. On the one hand, legal doctrine and a focus on the systematic elaboration of rules and principles of the positive law are no longer very much en vogue and are looked upon with suspicion. This is not only true for the United States[1] but is increasingly also the case in various European countries.[2] On the other hand, this development has been lamented for being at odds with what legal scholarship should be really about. Even in American legal academia, so much characterised by theoretical and interdisciplinary work, there is a continuing concern about the decline of the doctrinal method, expressed by authors as diverse as Richard Posner and Harry T. Edwards.[3] In Europe, despite fierce criticism, traditional doctrinal

Professor of European Private Law and academic director of the Maastricht European Private Law Institute (MEPLI), Maastricht University. I would like to thank Anna Beckers, Anna Berlee, Rob van Gestel, Jaap Hage, Eve Meurgey and Daniel On for helpful comments.

[1] See e.g., A.W.B. Simpson, 'The Rise and Fall of the Legal Treatise: Legal Principles and the Forms of Legal Literature', *University of Chicago Law Review* 48 (1981), 632 and Richard A. Posner, 'The Decline of Law as an Autonomous Discipline: 1962–1987', *Harvard Law Review* 100 (1987), 761.

[2] See for Germany already Ulrich Meyer-Cording, *Kann der Jurist heute noch Dogmatiker sein?*, Tübingen (Mohr) 1973 and for a recent overview Matthias Jestaedt, 'Wissenschaft im Recht', *JuristenZeitung* 69 (2014), 1; for the UK, the oft-cited Tony Becher, *Academic Tribes and Territories: Intellectual Enquiry and the Cultures of Disciplines*, Buckingham (SRHE) 1989, 30: legal work would be 'unexciting and uncreative' and largely descriptive; and Susan Bartie, 'The Lingering Core of Legal Scholarship', *Legal Studies* 30 (2010), 345; for France, Youssef Guenzoui, 'Les querelles doctrinales', *Revue Trimestrielle du Droit Civil* 2013, 47.

[3] See resp. Posner, 'The Decline of Law', at 777 ('Disinterested legal-doctrinal analysis of the traditional kind remains the indispensable core of legal thought, and there is no surfeit of

work still seems to be the type of research that legal scholars most frequently engage with. Many even see the ability to do quality doctrinal work as the most distinctive feature of a good legal academic or lawyer.[4] The doctrinal approach has therefore been described as 'mother's milk to academic lawyers',[5] as the method through which students learn to 'think like a lawyer'[6] and even as the 'nerve centre' of legal science.[7]

The aim of this chapter is to obtain a better understanding of the aims and methods of doctrinal legal scholarship. It has been observed time and again that despite the persistence of this type of research, we are insufficiently aware of its exact nature.[8] There is little doubt that the doctrinal approach provides a separate mode of thinking about the law, but both its proponents and critics seem too little aware of its foundations. This calls for a better understanding of what doctrinal work in law is really about. The oft-heard counterargument that the only reason to do this would be for the benefit of outsiders, while legal academics themselves know very well what they are doing, cannot be accepted. Even if it were true that doctrinalists know what they do, this knowledge is only very implicit.[9] Hence, I also do not believe that it is impossible to 'demystify' doctrinal reasoning.[10]

such analysis today.'); Harry T. Edwards, 'The Growing Disjunction Between Legal Education and the Legal Profession', *Michigan Law Review* 91 (1992), 34, recently taken up again by Richard Brust, 'The High Bench vs. the Ivory Tower', *ABA Journal* 1 February 2012.

4 Cf. for shared modes of thinking among legal academics in France, Christian Atias, *Epistémologie juridique*, Paris (Dalloz) 2002; and Philippe Jestaz & Christophe Jamin, *La doctrine*, Paris (Dalloz) 2004.

5 Christopher McCrudden, 'Legal Research and the Social Sciences', *Law Quarterly Review* 122 (2006), 632, at 634.

6 See for the US, Edwards, 'The Growing Disjunction', at 58; and for Germany, Claus-Wilhelm Canaris & Reiner Schmidt, 'Schlechte Juristen erkennt man an ihrer mangelnden Fähigkeit zur überzeugenden Lösung von Fällen', *Frankfurter Allgemeine Zeitung* 7 April 2011 (Nr. 82).

7 Walter Krebs, 'Die juristische Methode im Verwaltungsrecht', in: Eberhard Schmidt-Assmann & Wolfgang Hoffmann-Riem (eds.), *Methoden der Verwaltungsrechtswissenschaft*, Baden-Baden (Nomos) 2004, at 220.

8 See, e.g., Edward L. Rubin, 'Legal scholarship', in Dennis Patterson (ed.), *A Companion to Philosophy of Law and Legal Theory*, 2nd edn., Oxford (Wiley-Blackwell) 2010, 548; Edward L. Rubin, 'The Practice and Discourse of Legal Scholarship', *Michigan Law Review* 86 (1988), 1835; and Rob van Gestel & Hans-Wolfgang Micklitz, 'Why Methods Matter in European Legal Scholarship', *European Law Journal* 20 (2014), 292.

9 Rightly so: Terry Hutchinson & Nigel Duncan, 'Defining and Describing What We Do: Doctrinal Legal Research', *Deakin Law Review* 17 (2012), 83, at 99.

10 Cf. Geoffrey Samuel, 'Can Legal Reasoning be Demystified?', *Legal Studies* 29 (2009), 181.

This is not the place to go at length into the reasons for the asserted decline of doctrinal work.[11] These reasons are complicated and not only have to do with changing perceptions of what legal research should be about, but also with changes in university governance.[12] It seems that doctrinal work is under attack from at least three different angles: it is considered too provincial from an international perspective, too narrow from an interdisciplinary perspective and not creative enough from an academic perspective. In other words, mainstream legal research should become less national, less one-sided and less old-fashioned. The consequence of giving in to these objections, leading to a decline of the importance of legal doctrine, will necessarily be that the intricate link between legal academia and legal practice weakens.

Although this may be self-evident, this contribution does not argue that the doctrinal approach is the only relevant, or even the most important, way of doing legal research. Legal scholarship can consist of much more than only doctrinal work. However, the following does not only show that the doctrinal approach is in many ways the necessary prerequisite for undertaking any other type of analysis of law (such as economic, comparative, empirical or behavioural work), it is also claimed that the bad reputation of doctrinal work is undeserved. This requires scrutiny of what we mean by legal doctrine (Section 5.2), as well as an investigation of its aims (Section 5.3) and methods (Section 5.4). Section 5.5 concludes.

5.2 Legal Doctrine: An Attempt at Definition

It is surprising that, while the nature of comparative, economic and empirical research in law is widely discussed, this is not the case for doctrinal work.[13] Although any jurist has some idea of what legal

[11] On which (for the US) Posner, 'The Decline of Law', at 766, (for Germany) Jestaedt, 'Wissenschaft im Recht', 1; and for the Netherlands, Jan M. Smits, *The Mind and Method of the Legal Academic*, Cheltenham (Edward Elgar) 2012.

[12] One important indicator of the declining importance of doctrinal work is the low esteem that textbooks, case notes and commentaries have in university funding models and in research assessment exercises, such as the RAE and REF in the UK and the VSNU assessments in the Netherlands. Cf. Fiona Cownie, 'The Death of the Textbook Tradition', *European Journal of Legal Education* 3 (2006), 75, at 76.

[13] Cf. Emerson H. Tiller & Frank B. Cross, 'What is legal doctrine?', *Northwestern University Law Review* 100 (2006), 517, arguing that the nature of legal doctrine has been 'woefully understudied'.

doctrine is about, it is more difficult to define it. Terms such as legal doctrine, black letter law, formalism, doctrinalism and legal-dogmatic research[14] are all used to denote (the product of) a similar approach towards the law, be it with some national variations.[15] It is probably best described as research that aims to give a systematic exposition of the principles, rules and concepts governing a particular legal field or institution and analyses the relationship between these principles, rules and concepts with a view to solving unclarities and gaps in the existing law. This doctrinal approach is largely identical among the various subfields of the law.[16] Although originally developed for private law, it was taken over by scholars working in constitutional and criminal law (and other fields).[17] Three elements in this description deserve separate attention.

First, it is an essential feature of the doctrinal approach that it adopts an internal perspective: the doctrinalist places himself *inside* the legal system. This was already noted by Oliver Wendell Holmes[18] and repeated time and again by others in both the common law and the civil law tradition.[19] The legal system is not only the subject of the inquiry, it also provides the normative framework for analysis. The separate discourse that results from this does not need anything outside of the law to be carried out.[20] Put in another way, in the doctrinal approach the law is intelligible in its own terms. This remarkable feature of doctrinal work allows legal scholars to speak as if they are judges or legislators and to address these official lawmakers on their own terms, suggesting alternatives for the outcomes they reach. It is also reflected in the law

[14] J.B.M. Vranken, 'Exciting Times for Legal Scholarship', *Recht & Methode in onderzoek en onderwijs* 2012, 42.

[15] What German academics call *Rechtsdogmatik* is not entirely similar to what the French describe as 'la doctrine.' Cf. Nils Jansen, 'Rechtsdogmatik im Zivilrecht', *online Enzyklopädie zur Rechtsphilosophie* (2011), available at www.enzyklopaedie-rechtsphilosophie.net.

[16] For a different view: Jestaedt, 'Wissenschaft im Recht', at 7, who speaks of the 'three pillars architecture of jurisprudence', consisting of private, criminal and constitutional law.

[17] Unfortunately with little interaction between the three: there is a need for more *intra*-disciplinary comparison. See also Jestaedt, 'Wissenschaft im Recht', at 7.

[18] Oliver Wendell Holmes, *The Common Law* (Barnes & Noble) 2004, at 163: 'The business of the jurist is to make known the content of the law; that is, to work upon it from within'.

[19] As recently in the report of the German Wissenschaftsrat, *Perpektiven der Rechtswissenschaft in Deutschland*, 2012, at 5, on which, e.g., Stephan Lorenz, 'Forschung, Praxis und Lehre im Bericht des Wissenschaftsrats', *JuristenZeitung* 68 (2013), 704; Christian Atias, 'Ce que savent les jurists: les états du droit', *Revue Trimestrielle de Droit Civil* 2013, 315, no. 3; Pauline C. Westerman, 'Open or Autonomous?', in: Mark Van Hoecke (ed.), *Which Kind of Method for What Kind of Discipline?*, Oxford (Hart) 2011, 87.

[20] See e.g., Posner, 'The Decline of Law', 763.

curriculum, which is essentially about teaching students to work as a judge, legislator or lawyer and in fact *make a decision* in concrete disputes. This 'unity of discourse'[21] does not exist in other disciplines, where it would be unthinkable that the academic would make use of exactly the same terminology as the object of his study. Thus, the biologist describing the behaviour of the manatee does so in his own academic language and not in that of the manatee itself. Likewise, the sociologist studying the banking profession does not have to know how to make (or lose) money himself.[22] It can well be argued that it is exactly this internal perspective that turns legal scholarship into an autonomous discipline: as soon as it starts to adopt an external (economic, sociological, historical, etc.) viewpoint, there is no longer a legal approach to the problem in question.[23]

It must be emphasised that this does not mean that we cannot debate about the sources that should be taken into account in this internal discourse.[24] There will be consensus about the need to incorporate the 'official' sources of national legislation and case law, but not about the need to also involve, e.g., European and international sources, private regulation, and so forth.[25] Many choices need to be made in order to select the relevant sources. It will be seen in Section 5.4 that it is *inter alia* these choices that affect the extent to which doctrinal research is original or not.

Second, it is crucial for the doctrinal approach that the law is seen as a *system*. It would be a grave misunderstanding to regard legal doctrine as a mere description of existing legislation and case law.[26] It requires the organisation and reorganisation of the products of the institutions officially tasked with creating law into coherent principles, rules and concepts before we can speak of doctrine.[27] Or, as the Council of Australian

21 Rubin, 'The Practice and Discourse of Legal Scholarship', at 1859.

22 See Smits, *Mind and Method*, no. 10.

23 See Ernest J. Weinrib, *The Idea of Private Law*, Cambridge, MA (Harvard University Press) 1995.

24 Cf. McCrudden, 'Legal Research and the Social Sciences', at 635.

25 McCrudden, 'Legal Research and the Social Sciences', at 635, also looks at the potential use of economic or policy analysis as a matter of how open the system is. However, this seems to confuse *sources* and *methods*: if the official sources of law are investigated using economic analysis, this is no longer doctrinal work.

26 Cf. Grant Lamond, 'Analogical Reasoning in the Common Law', *Oxford Journal of Legal Studies* 34 (2014), 567, at 581: 'law is not simply a body of rules: it is a body of reasoned doctrines that are interconnected and interrelated.'

27 Cf. Martha Minow, 'Archetypical Legal Scholarship: A Field Guide', *Journal of Legal Education* 63 (2013), 65 and McCrudden, 'Legal Research and the Social Sciences', at 633: 'constructing logically coherent conclusions from elementary principles'.

Law Deans states: 'Doctrinal research, at its best, involves rigorous analysis and creative synthesis, the making of connections between seemingly disparate doctrinal strands, and the challenge of extracting general principles from an inchoate mass of primary materials.'[28] All relevant elements are thus fitted together into one working whole, resolving internal inconsistencies among seemingly contradictory materials. The law is only a system because of the explicit choice to consider it as such, by treating principles, cases and concepts as signs of an internal intelligibility.[29]

It will be seen in Section 5.3 that this systematising approach can serve different goals, including the intelligible description of law and the steering of its application. Here it must already be accentuated that, again, doctrinalists have to make many choices regarding the method of systematisation. There is not one way of doing this. For example, an important question is how many 'coherent' systems have to be construed.

The third essential feature of the doctrinal approach is that it systematises the *present* law.[30] It is surely possible to systematise law that is not applicable, such as the law of the past or a foreign law, but this would not qualify as legal doctrine. Crucial for the legal-dogmatic approach is that it is able to accommodate new developments such as recent case law and legislation against the background of societal change. This engagement with legal practice by reacting to changes to the law by legislators and courts turns legal doctrine into a living system that aims to achieve both constancy and change in the development of the law.[31] This is well captured in the original meaning of the Latin term *doctrina*, which refers to knowledge or learning which is passed on from one generation to the next. This sets the doctrinal approach apart from the historical and comparative method that are both geared towards the different goal of understanding how other legal systems than the positive law are best

[28] CALD Statement on the Nature of Legal Research (2005), www.cald.asn.au/docs/cald%20statement%20on%20the%20nature%20of%20legal%20research%20-%202005.pdf, at 3.

[29] Cf. See Ernest J. Weinrib, 'Legal formalism', in: Dennis Patterson (ed.), *A Companion to Philosophy of Law and Legal Theory*, 2nd edn., Oxford (Wiley-Blackwell) 2010, 327, at 335; and (in Dutch) H.C.F. Schoordijk, 'Het recht moeten wij niet denken als een systeem vooraleer wij er systeem in hebben gebracht', *Nederlands Juristenblad* 2008, 1720.

[30] Cf. Rolf Stürner, 'Die Zivilrechtswissenschaft und ihre Methodik', *Archiv für die civilistische Praxis* 214 (2014), 7, at 11: 'Allgemein gesagt liegt das Wesen rechtswissenschaftlicher Dogmatik in der systematischen Zuordnung des Einzelfalles zu Grundregeln und Grundprinzipien auf der Basis des geltenden Rechts.'

[31] CALD Statement, at 3. See Section 5.3; Bartie, 'The Lingering Core of Legal Scholarship', at 350.

understood. This does not mean that past or foreign elements cannot be taken into account in further developing the system of present-day law, but only as part of this prevailing system.

Any well-trained legal academic or lawyer will recognise these three common traits of the doctrinal approach. But this does not mean that there is clarity about its aims and methods. As I have argued elsewhere, the proper reaction to the asserted lack of 'academic level' of traditional legal scholarship (as sometimes expressed by outsiders[32]) should not be to give up this type of work, but to further develop its intellectual foundations. There is a dire need to do so, thus to be clear about aims and methods of the discipline. The doctrinal paradigm is intuitive, if not arcane, and this has severe consequences for the position of law among the other disciplines practised at universities that are better able to market their work to funding agencies and to the outside world.[33] The implicit knowledge that we have about legal doctrine should be made explicit.

5.3 The Aims of Legal Doctrine

What are the aims of the doctrinal approach towards law? I argue in the following that legal doctrine can serve three main goals:[34] description, prescription and justification. These aims are closely interrelated and even reinforce each other. It will become clear in this section that because doctrine aims to describe the existing law, it also has a prescriptive voice and, through this, can legitimise newly proposed solutions.

5.3.1 Description

The first aim of legal doctrine is to describe the existing law (the *lex lata*) in a certain field (such as tort law or administrative law) or concerning a certain institution (such as contractual remedies or constitutional review) in a way that is as neutral and consistent as possible in order to inform

[32] See on this Fiona Cownie, *Legal Academics: Cultures and Identities*, Oxford (Hart) 2004, 97.

[33] See (arguing for the same) e.g., Hutchinson & Duncan, 'Defining and Describing What We Do', at 85; Christian Bumke, 'Rechtsdogmatik', *JuristenZeitung* 69 (2014), at 642 ('implizite Wissens').

[34] Rubin, 'Legal scholarship', in Patterson (ed.), *A Companion to Philosophy of Law and Legal Theory*, at 550, distinguishes between description, prescription, and meta-description and meta-prescription.

the audience how the law actually reads.[35] Examples include the description of German private law in the *Münchener Kommentar zum Bürgerlichen Gesetzbuch*, of English constitutional law in Dicey's *An Introduction to the Law of the Constitution* and of American law in the big treatises. Von Savigny's monumental *System of the Modern Roman Law* (1840–1848) also belongs to this type of scholarship, as well as a majority of the articles published in today's European law journals.[36] These are all informed by a desire to place the prevalent sources of law (including legislation and case law) in a system and make this system intelligible to the reader. Jeremy Bentham designated this type of academic work as 'expository jurisprudence',[37] which nicely reveals the choices immanent in such systematisation: *how* the law is exposed is left to the doctrinalist, who is to decide how previously selected legislation and judicial decisions are fitted together into one working whole.[38]

It is difficult to see how the law could do without this systematising description. It is legal doctrine which creates the shared framework of concepts and categories, without which a debate about law is not even possible.[39] It provides a language for discussion.[40] Thus the question of whether a security right in a movable asset ('pledge' or 'charge') must be registered or when constitutional review should be possible cannot be answered without a legal framework which defines these concepts. In this respect, doctrine *creates* the legal reality. While knowledge about

[35] See also Smits, *Mind and Method*, no. 7. German scholars use the term 'durchdringen' (penetrate): see e.g., Bumke, 'Rechtsdogmatik', at 645.

[36] A brief survey of the tables of content of the French *Revue Trimestrielle de Droit Civil* and the German *Archiv für die civilistische Praxis* for 2013 and 2014 reveals that a majority of the articles are about doctrinal issues.

[37] Jeremy Bentham, *An Introduction to the Principles of Morals and Legislation* (ed. J.H. Burns & H.L.A. Hart), Oxford (Clarendon Press) 1970, Ch. XVII, 21.

[38] Cf. McCrudden, 'Legal Research and the Social Sciences', at 634.

[39] Smits, Mind and Method, no. 45; Tiller & Cross, 'What is legal doctrine?', 517: 'legal doctrine is the currency of the law'; Stephen D. Smith, 'In Defense of Traditional Legal Scholarship: A Comment', *University of Colorado Law Review* 63 (1992), 627, at 629: 'Indeed, to suggest that legal scholarship should be less obsessed with doctrine would be like suggesting that historians should not spend so much effort studying things that happened in the distant past, or that astronomers ought to worry more about earthly concerns.'

[40] See Marietta Auer, *Der privatrechtliche Diskurs der Moderne*, Tübingen (Mohr Siebeck) 2014; John C.P. Goldberg, 'Introduction: Pragmatism and Private Law', *Harvard Law Review* 125 (2012), 1640, at 1650; J.B.M. Vranken, *Algemeen deel*, Zwolle (W.E.J. Tjeenk Willink) 1995.

physics is usually conveyed by way of mathematical formulas, the law is communicated through doctrine.[41] Transfer of knowledge about the law is impossible without doctrine.

However, the underlying rationale of doctrinal description goes far beyond a mere theoretical interest. Legal doctrine can be seen as representing the normative complexity of the law: the thousands of rules and decided cases, each with their own nuances and organised as a system, show the many ways in which the law can deal with conflicting arguments. Doctrine thus reflects how subtle the law often can be and why a small change of the facts can lead to a wholly different outcome. To describe this is no easy task, and even if it may seem easy initially, a competent lawyer will *make* it difficult, not to keep himself busy but because he knows that subtle nuances are relevant. Singer put it like this: 'law is complicated because qualitative distinctions matter, and they matter at this level of detail'.[42] The elaboration of the doctrinal system is therefore not an etheric activity unconnected to reality, but an essential part of the legal activity aiming to capture the subtleness of the law.[43] Only doctrine can grasp the law's complexity, not for nuance's own sake, but because it helps to understand and solve practical problems.[44] A reduction of the law to principles, underlying policies or arguments could not sufficiently express this complexity, as is now also acknowledged again in the recent American movement of the 'New Private Law.'[45]

It can therefore be easily argued that the more complicated the law becomes, the greater the need for its systematic description. Doctrine rationalises and stabilises in order to keep the law intelligible.[46] It is no coincidence that in nineteenth century Germany the 'Juristenrecht' (as developed by, e.g., Von Savigny and Windscheid) almost *had* to

[41] Cf. Edwards, 'The Growing Disjunction', at 59: 'A lawyer is by definition skilled in the law, just as a doctor is skilled with the human body.'

[42] Joseph William Singer, 'Normative Methods for Lawyers', *University of California Los Angeles Law Review* 56 (2009), 899, at 938.

[43] Smits, *Mind and Method*, no. 45.

[44] Cf. Goldberg, 'Introduction', 1652: 'being nuanced about legal concepts can help us think through practical problems.'

[45] Goldberg, 'Introduction', at 1650, arguing that legal doctrine and conceptualism are highly useful.

[46] Jansen, 'Rechtsdogmatik im Zivilrecht': 'ordnende und stabilisierende Rekonstruktion.' Kelsen also saw description as a main aim of legal doctrine: Hans Kelsen, *Reine Rechtslehre*, 2nd edn., Wien (Verlag Osterreich) 1960, at 72 ff.

become a source of law in order for the law to function.[47] It was only through systematisation that it was possible to treat the like alike. This has remained an important function of legal doctrine: it helps to create coherence and, through this, to keep the law certain and predictable and make sure that similar cases are decided in the same way.[48]

This implies that to describe the system of the law in a new field,[49] or organise an existing field on basis of new principles,[50] can be a highly creative activity. It does not come as a surprise that to present the law as a coherent set of concepts, rules and principles by exposing contradictions, defining concepts and classifying rules and cases, has defined the history of legal scholarship. However, an important question is whether this way of looking at law also has a future. Rubin argues against this.[51] He claims that, with the rise of the administrative state, our concept of law has been fundamentally transformed. If law is used to implement government policy, it often comes in the form of separate regulations and rules that have no relationship with one another. This means that a search for coherence is doomed to fail. In addition, it means that the standard for judging the value of law is not whether it is coherent but whether it is effective in realising the policy goals of the modern state. This would call for a 'post-coherentist' methodology 'that can identify purposes, debate alternative purposes, determine measures for the attainment of those purposes and then investigate the law's actual operation'.[52]

Rubin's argument is an important one. But, as he submits himself, it does not make doctrinal work obsolete. The rise of the administrative state and the rules it produces does not, in my view, lead away from the descriptive aim of doctrinal work. To the contrary: the problem with many of the rules and regulations issued by the modern State is that they are often highly fragmented and difficult to find. This is exactly what a

[47] Raoul C. Van Caenegem, *Judges, Legislators and Professors*, Cambridge (Cambridge University Press) 1987. See on Germany Jan Schröder, *Recht als Wissenschaft*, 2nd edn., München (Beck) 2012.

[48] Stürner, 'Die Zivilrechtswissenschaft', at 11: 'Ohne solche Systematik kommt kein Rechtssystem der modernen zivilisierten Welt aus, ist es doch nur so möglich, dem wesentlichen Grundelement menschlicher Gerechtigkeit volle Geltung zu verschaffen, nämlich der Gleichheit mit ihrem Gebot "Gleiches gleich, Ungleiches ungleich" und Ähnliches adäquat modifiziert zu behandeln.'

[49] For an example, see Michael Martinek, *Moderne Vertragstypen*, 3 Vols., München (Beck) 1991–1993.

[50] An example is Peter Birks, *An Introduction to the Law of Restitution*, Oxford (Clarendon Press) 1985.

[51] Edward Rubin, Chapter 8 in this volume.

[52] Rubin, Chapter 8.

doctrinal description can remedy. The counterargument that the various rules are insufficiently interrelated does not hold: in any doctrinal description it is necessary to identify the principles and policies underlying a certain field. Which rules are interrelated only becomes clear by developing such a doctrinal framework. The present doctrinal systems in private law, criminal law and constitutional law are not any different: they tie together what, without a doctrinal system, would only be fragmented rules. This does not mean that all government regulations can be systematised under one heading, but this is not uncommon in legal doctrine. It is to the person making the systematisation to decide which rules should be tied together under which principles and policies. Descriptive legal doctrine can thus fulfil an essential function in presenting and understanding the legislative products of the regulatory state. Quite another question is how the prescriptive function of doctrine is affected by it. This will be discussed in the following section.

5.3.2 Prescription

Legal doctrine is not limited to a mere description and understanding of the existing law. It also comprises of a search for practical solutions that fit the existing system best. Description is always complemented by a more *prescriptive* approach directed towards legal decision makers such as legislatures, courts and, to a lesser extent, the executive.[53] There is a very good reason why legal doctrine can fulfil this role to establish the *lex ferenda*: it reflects the law's normativity. If law is about norms for human behaviour, doctrine articulates what these norms are. Doctrine is a source of information on how to behave.[54]

The essence of prescriptive legal doctrine is that it is not primarily extralegal considerations (such as economic or policy analysis) that guide the search for the best outcome, but the extent to which the outcome fits the system. Each argument must be led through the filter of the legal system before it can be accepted: the legal activity consists in *feeling out* the system. This meaning of legal doctrine was well captured by the Dutch law professor Herman Schoordijk who claims that the system forces the legal actor to 'bring his value judgements, that can never be

[53] Cf. Minow, 'Archetypical Legal Scholarship', 65.

[54] See Smits, *Mind and Method*; as well as Atias, 'Ce que savent les jurists', 315, no. 1: 'Riche et complexe, il se compose de multiples informations sur ce qui convient aux êtres humains dans leurs relations entre eux' and Goldberg, 'Introduction', at 650.

based completely on the existing legal system, in harmony with judgements previously given in practice or theory'.[55] Dependent on whether the solution is accepted as binding law or not, this exercise can have a positive or a negative result.

This ability of doctrine to guide (judicial) decision making naturally does not mean that the outcome follows automatically from the system. The doctrinal approach is not similar to a mechanical application of determinate rules.[56] But the well-known criticism of Legal Realism and the Critical Legal Studies movement[57] that a doctrinal system has no other value than to disguise underlying considerations that 'really' guide the decision maker is too far-fetched.[58] Even though the doctrinal system will never provide certainty about how to decide, judges are in fact led by doctrine.[59]

There is one exceptional element of prescriptive legal doctrine that merits separate attention.[60] Legal systematisation differs in one important respect from description in other disciplines: it influences the actual application of the law. Because legal academics work on a system that is also used in practice, important normative consequences can follow from their work. Anyone making use of a coherent system will propagate a change of the law if this fits in with the system itself. Koopmans describes this as follows:[61]

> If biologists classify a whale as a mammal instead of as a fish, nothing changes in the world of facts ... But if jurists qualify a barstool as a movable object and not as an immovable, they mean to say that in case of insolvency of the pub owner, it is not the bank that as mortgagee is entitled to the stool, but the brewery.

Any decision to systematise the law in a certain way can thus have practical consequences. This means that, at least in the continental legal

[55] H.C.F. Schoordijk, *Oordelen en vooroordelen*, Deventer (Kluwer) 1972, at 15.

[56] See Weinrib, in Patterson (ed.), *A Companion to Philosophy of Law and Legal Theory*, 327.

[57] See in detail Neil Duxbury, *Patterns of American Jurisprudence*, Oxford (Oxford University Press) 1995, 65.

[58] Roberto M. Unger, *The Critical Legal Studies Movement*, Cambridge, MA (Harvard University Press) 1986; and Duncan Kennedy, 'Form and Substance in Private Law Adjudication', *Harvard Law Review* 89 (1976), 1685.

[59] Tiller & Cross, 'What is legal doctrine?', at 527, concluding that 'there is ample empirical support for a general claim that doctrinal choices in fact matter in judicial decisionmaking'.

[60] On what follows: Smits, *Mind and Method*, no. 9.

[61] T. Koopmans, 'Denken en doen in het recht', in *Juridisch stippelwerk*, Deventer (Kluwer) 1991, 67, at 68.

tradition, norms are produced autonomously within the legal system itself.[62] This view is today mostly associated with the work of Luhmann and Teubner,[63] but it has always been an essential element of the doctrinal approach to law. In law as a system, the whole is greater than the sum of its parts.

The doctrinal approach can also be useful in evaluating the products of the modern administrative state. It is true, as Rubin argues, that the effectiveness of an intended policy is today often a much more relevant criterion for evaluation than the extent to which a policy is doctrinally coherent with other statutes.[64] But it is wrong to assume that the assessment of effectiveness cannot be part of the doctrinal approach. Underlying principles and policies are part and parcel of the doctrinal system and can thus be used to evaluate newly proposed solutions and government actions. To borrow an example from Rubin:[65] if the administration takes away private property for public purposes against reasonable compensation, such action can be evaluated under the doctrinal system governing such action (which could be made up of rules of private law, administrative law or fundamental rights, or a combination of all three). If there is not further rule controlling the government's selection of a specific property, the doctrinal system will reflect this: any rule on this will be absent. However, if there is a government policy in place which only allows the taking of property in certain cases because only then it is seen as effective, the rules reflecting this will be part of the doctrinal system. Effectiveness can thus be part of the doctrinal system itself, allowing doctrinalists to enter into a dialogue with decision makers.

5.3.3 *Justification*

The third, and least known, aim of legal doctrine is that it can also serve as a justification for the existing law. Succinctly put: if a rule does not fit into the system, it is not law. Here, the essence of the internal perspective comes out best: if the law is presented as a self-contained system of mutual reference, the validity of norms can be justified by reference to

[62] No better term to describe this phenomenon than the German 'Systemproduktivität': cf. Jestaedt, 'Wissenschaft im Recht', at 7.

[63] Niklas Luhmann, *Law as a Social System*, Oxford (Oxford University Press) 2004 (orig. 1993); Gunther Teubner (ed.), *Autopoietic Law: A New Approach to Law and Society*, Berlin (De Gruyter) 1987.

[64] Rubin, Chapter 8.

[65] Rubin, Chapter 8.

this system. In particular, Weinrib argues that formalism is therefore also a theory of legal justification.[66] He emphasises that formalism presupposes a view of law as an 'immanently intelligible normative practice'. This means that a legal system is already justified by its own coherence that will have to be permanently readjusted on the basis of new judicial decisions and legislation: 'Justificatory coherence points not outward to a transcendent ideal but inward to a harmonious interrelationship among the constituents of the structure of justification'.[67] These elements are the principles, rules, cases and concepts that together express the coherence necessary for the legal system to function.

This idea of legal doctrine as an independent justification of the law is probably strongest in the Germanic legal tradition, where doctrine (in any event, in private law) is seen as an activity independent from the work of democratic legislators and courts.[68] This allows to justify law through the system, turning law into an apolitical entity. Just as the truths of physics or chemistry are not dependent on some political viewpoint, the doctrinal approach would offer a rational and objective account of the law. This is an echo of the Historical School and its 'law as science', but it also fits in with recent accounts of how private law is legitimised in practice: norms derive their validity not necessarily from the enactment by official institutions, but can also be based on their acceptance by legal practice.[69] Legal doctrine then allows to legitimise the new solution because it fits in with the system that is accepted and used by the legal community.

But one does not need to regard doctrine as a science in order to use it as a justification for the existing law. Systematic thinking is always based on the ideal of integrity: it requires legal solutions to be constructed in a way that best fits and justifies the law as a whole.[70] Indeed, much high-quality doctrinal work is about justifying a given or proposed legal

[66] Ernest J. Weinrib, 'Legal Formalism: On the Immanent Rationality of Law', *Yale Law Journal* 97 (1988), 949.

[67] Weinrib, *The Idea of Private Law*, 339–340. See also Jaap Hage, 'The Justification of Value Judgments', in B. Akkermans et al. (eds.), *Who Does What? On the allocation of regulatory competences in European private law*, Cambridge-Antwerp (Intersentia) 2015, 15, at 32.

[68] This is to a lesser extent also true for other civil law jurisdictions. See for France, e.g., Jestaz & Jamin, *La doctrine*, 245.

[69] See Nils Jansen, *The Making of Legal Authority*, Oxford (Oxford University Press) 2010.

[70] Mathias Siems, 'Legal originality', *Oxford Journal of Legal Studies* 28 (2008), 147, at 150. The obvious reference here is to Ronald Dworkin, *Law's Empire*, Cambridge, MA (Harvard University Press) 1986.

solution to a problem by testing its acceptability within the system. An informative example of recent date is the discussion about the binding nature of corporate social responsibility codes. Such codes contain voluntary guidelines that companies say they will respect with regard to labour, human rights and the environment. An important societal and legal question is to what extent such codes can be interpreted as containing enforceable obligations and, if so, towards whom. In the doctrinal approach this question must be answered by a meticulous investigation of how such obligations would fit in with the existing systems of contract and tort law.[71] This also illustrates the close connection between the prescriptive and the justificatory function of doctrine: if it follows from the doctrinal analysis that such guidelines should be binding, this conclusion can also be justified by reference to its acceptability within the system. This does of course not mean that a legal rule *needs* to be justified by reference to legal doctrine: empiricists will use a different criterion.

5.4 The Methods of Doctrinal Work

Having identified three aims of the doctrinal approach towards law, the next question is which methods can be used to achieve these goals. It was already emphasised that there is little attention for the methodology of doctrinal research.[72] With a lack of an authoritative textbook on the legal academic method or a fundamental discussion about it, it remains a 'methodological minefield'[73] or at best a 'black box'.[74] It has even become a truism that most jurists know how to do doctrinal work but are not able to tell how they do what they do. The famous comparatist Ernst Rabel is even supposed to have said that a good jurist has his method, but does

[71] See Anna Beckers, *Enforcing Corporate Social Responsibility Codes*, Oxford (Hart) 2015.

[72] See, however, recently (on German administrative law) Eberhard Schmidt-Assmann, *Verwaltungsrechtliche Dogmatik*, Tübingen (Mohr Siebeck) 2013; on Dutch private law, the discussion between Pauline Westerman and Jan B.M. Vranken and Jaap Hage, 'The Method of a Truly Normative Legal Science', in Mark Van Hoecke (ed.), *Methodologies of Legal Research*, Oxford (Hart) 2011, 19; Rob van Gestel & Hans Micklitz, 'Revitalizing Doctrinal Legal Research in Europe. What about Methodology?', in Ulla Neergaard et al. (eds.), *European Legal Method: Paradoxes and Revitalisation*, Kopenhagen (Djoef) 2011, 25; and the special issue of *Archiv für die civilistische Praxis* 214 (2014), 1.

[73] See Carmine Conte, 'From Only the "Bottom Up"? Legitimate Forms of Judicial Reasoning in Private Law', *Oxford Journal of Legal Studies* 35 (2015), 1, at 2.

[74] See Bumke, 'Rechtsdogmatik', at 645.

not speak about it.[75] This raises the question whether we are able to 'unpack' the method of doctrinal reasoning implicit in much traditional legal research.[76] Is it possible to uncover the choices that are usually only made implicitly? I do not claim that the following provides a full overview of the necessary choices, but it does give insight into some of the main options that remain usually hidden in the doctrinal literature as if there is only one doctrinal method. Although I will make some suggestions as to how these choices could be made, the aim of this contribution is not to provide definite answers as these are highly dependent on the exact research topic and question.

The proper approach to identifying methodological choices is surely not a generic one, in which no distinction is made between the different types of activities involved in doctrinal work. Otherwise, one is not able to go beyond the stereotype that one does 'desktop research', or is involved in 'rigorous analysis and creative synthesis, the making of connections between seemingly disparate doctrinal strands, and the challenge of extracting general principles from an inchoate mass of primary materials'.[77] Instead, I wish to identify three consecutive choices that need to be made when doing methodologically sound doctrinal work. Before I do so, some attention must be paid to identifying the appropriate research question.

It is not difficult to see what is the research question in doctrinal work. The three previously distinguished aims all lend themselves to serve as such: description, prescription and justification are all legitimate aims of legal doctrine.[78] This means that the researcher who wishes to describe or legitimise the existing law, or wants to indicate which solution fits the system best, can make use of the doctrinal approach. This does not mean that the doctrinal method is *the only one* to reach these goals. Thus, if the research question is how the French law on liability for animals reads, it is also possible to describe the law in economic or sociological terms. Likewise, normative economic analysis could prescribe the desired

[75] Wolfgang Fikentscher, *Methoden des Rechts in vergleichender Darstellung*, vol. 1, Tübingen (Mohr Siebeck) 1975, at 10.

[76] See Hutchinson & Duncan,'Defining and Describing What We Do', at 99: 'Unfortunately the doctrinal method is often so implicit and so tacit that many working within the legal paradigm consider that it is unnecessary to verbalise the process.'

[77] CALD Statement, at 3.

[78] I do not rule out that the method can still to some extent be dependent on the aim of the research: when the aim is description, the test is more coherence; when it is prescription, it is more the acceptability of the solution and its consequences.

outcome if one's question is how the law should read, while the legitimation of the positive law can also be found in the democratic legitimacy of legislature and courts that have created the main rules in this area. This defines the realm of legal doctrine as an important approach to the law, but certainly not the only one that is conceivable.

It is important to know whether the question that one seeks to answer in doctrinal research is the same as the one being answered by practitioners – in particular, judges. This is often implicitly assumed, as has been made clear by Vranken, arguing that the role model of the judge is also guiding the doctrinalist. It is indeed wrong to assume that the method of judicial application is the same as the academic method.[79] Judge and jurist may both be working in the same garden, but they have profoundly different tasks. While the judge primarily looks inductively for what he can use to solve the case under consideration (*taking* what he finds useful), the jurist has a more fundamental role to play in *developing* the system, ideally bound by methodological constraints. In addition, the scholar can freely choose his topic and make all kinds of recommendations for future law, while the judge cannot. Posner also contrasts these two distinct tasks,[80] while the German literature distinguishes between *Gebrauchsdogmatik* and *wissenschaftlicher Dogmatik.*[81] Practice and theory use the same language, but have a different purpose and serve a different audience.

The first methodological choice that academics face is about the materials to be used in developing the doctrinal system.[82] Most present-day doctrinal work is focused on the more recent official national sources (legislation and case law) within a confined area (such as contracts, family law, criminal procedure, or a part thereof) without even making explicit that this is a choice at all. Why the focus on tort law or on a specific part

[79] Vranken, 'Exciting Times for Legal Scholarship', at 43–44: 'legal researchers approach their work as judges do' and id., *Algemeen deel: een synthese*, Deventer (Kluwer) 2014.

[80] Richard A. Posner, 'In Memoriam: Bernard D. Meltzer', *University of Chicago Law Review* 74 (2007), 435, at 437: 'The messy work product of the judges and legislators requires a good deal of tidying up, of synthesis, analysis, restatement, and critique. These are intellectually demanding tasks, requiring vast knowledge and the ability … to organize dispersed, fragmentary, prolix, and rebarbative material.' See also Aleksander Peczenik, Scientia Iuris in Enrico Pattaro (ed.), *A Treatise of Legal Philosophy and General Jurisprudence*, vol. 4, Dordrecht (Springer) 2005, at 2.

[81] See, e.g. Rolf Stürner, 'Das Zivilrecht der Moderne und die Bedeutung der Rechtsdogmatik', *JuristenZeitung* 67 (2012), 10, at 11 ff. See also Hutchinson & Duncan, 'Defining and Describing What We Do', at 107.

[82] On which Jestaz & Jamin, o.c., 218.

of this field,[83] and not on developing an overall system of private law?[84] Why not involve also private regulation such as codes of conduct? Why not consistently consider law of supranational origin? The present tendency in Europe to look at law as a multilayered[85] or pluralist system is in itself already a choice *not* to integrate rules coming from different levels of governance. It keeps national private, criminal and constitutional law apart from the European rules. But why? Would it not be more fertile to bring these norms coming from different lawgivers under one systematic heading, and is this not where the more creative doctrinal work can be done? A different choice was made in the Global Administrative Law movement, in which universal principles of administrative law are sought by considering not only national laws, but also fundamental rights, values of good governance and private regulation.[86] To continue, why not organise the law more in terms of particular types of parties, such as consumers, landowners and road drivers, or particular subject matters, such as the environment and higher education?[87] Asking these questions also leads to a recently much-debated issue: how to involve findings on the effect of law? Today, everyone accepts that a true understanding of the law necessarily involves insight into its working.[88] But should this remain apart from doctrinal work, or can it be part of it? As explained in Section 5.3.2, the fact that certain rules are part of the doctrinal system can already be evidence of their effectiveness, but this is not true for all rules. To sum up: a methodologically sound doctrinal description requires many choices to be made.[89]

How these choices should be made is largely dependent on the question the researcher is asking, making it difficult to generalise. Any more

[83] Jan B.M. Vranken, 'Methodology of Legal Doctrinal Research', in Van Hoecke, *Methodologies of Legal Research*, at 111: 'In contract and tort law alone, there are hundreds of systems'.

[84] For an effort to reorganise the law of contract, torts and restitution along common principles, see P.S. Atiyah, *Promises, Morals, and Law*, Oxford (Oxford University Press) 1981, at 138 ff.

[85] See for private law e.g. Beate Gsell, 'Zivilrechtsanwendung im Europäischen Mehrebenensystem', *Archiv für die civilistische Praxis* 214 (2014), 99.

[86] See e.g. Carol Harlow, 'Global Administrative Law: The Quest for Principles and Values', *European Journal of International Law* 17 (2006), 187.

[87] Lamond, 'Analogical Reasoning in the Common Law', at 577.

[88] See, instead of many others, Roger Cotterell, 'Why Must Legal Ideas be Interpreted Sociologically?', *Journal of Law and Society* 25 (1998), 171 and Rubin, Chapter 8.

[89] Cf. William Twining, *Blackstone's Tower: The English Law School*, London (Stevens & Sons) 1994, at 131: 'even the lowest forms of exposition involve interpretation, selection and arrangement.'

general statement on how to answer the above questions necessarily involves a choice for one preferred research topic over another. For example, there is nothing methodologically wrong with a study on how the Dutch Supreme Court dealt with the insanity defence in its case law of the last sixty years. The definition of the topic already excludes discussion about the materials and sources that have to be taken into account. Quite another matter is of course whether this is a sufficiently original research topic. If, on the other hand, the study is about whether the insanity defence should be abolished, the methodological questions mentioned above are in urgent need of an answer.

A related, more technical, question about the choice of materials is how to make the selection *within* each of the relevant sources. All case law, or only that of the highest court? To what extent are explanatory memoranda to legislative texts part of the relevant materials? Should all literature written within one jurisdiction be looked at, or is it fine to limit oneself only to textbooks? What is the role of foreign literature?[90] My own take on this matter is that the present selection of literature is often too random. Although it will depend on the exact research question being asked, the chosen sample of materials can often be extended.

Once it is clear what the scope of the system and of the choice of materials should be, a second question emerges: which techniques are used to describe the existing law? Does one search primarily for common principles or is there also place for diversity? If so, what is the right mix between the two? What is the place for induction, deduction and synthesis, and which other legal argumentation techniques are used? What is the exact role for analogy[91] and for policy goals in developing the system? On basis of which criteria does one establish a principle and why is it that *these* resemblances are relevant and others are not? These are questions on which not even a debate takes place among doctrinalists.

The third choice to be made is which conception of a 'system' is used. Next to the elements that make up the system and the techniques used to describe it, one needs an idea of when this combination of elements and techniques actually forms a system. There is general consensus that the

[90] Books that consider these questions are scarce. See, e.g., Michael McConville & Wing Hong Chui (eds.), *Research Methods for Law*, Edinburgh (Edinburgh University Press) 2007; Terry Hutchinson, *Researching and Writing in Law*, 3rd edn., London (Thomson Reuters) 2010; D. Watkins & M. Burton, *Research Methods in Law*, London (Routledge) 2013. See also Marnix V.R. Snel, 'Source-usage within doctrinal legal inquiry: choices, problems, and challenges', *Recht & Methode in onderzoek en onderwijs* 2014-06.

[91] On analogy, see Lamond, 'Analogical Reasoning in the Common Law', 567.

legal-doctrinal system refers to the 'inner system' of rules, concepts and principles that keeps the law together,[92] but such a system can be organised in many different ways. In particular in the German literature, there is therefore a wide-ranging debate about the requirements the materials must meet in order to qualify as a system.[93] This is discussion about, for example, the relationship between principles and rules, about how to solve conflicts among contradictory principles, about the role of concepts within the system and about the degree of consistency and coherence that is required. Many different theories were developed in this respect[94] and we still lack an accurate comparative overview of all possible variations. It is not the aim of this contribution to develop such an overview, only to make clear that many choices need to be made in a more explicit way when carrying out valuable doctrinal work.

The point made in the above is that methodology matters much more to legal-dogmatic research than is usually assumed. Only a better methodological awareness in standard legal scholarship will reveal the many choices immanent in carrying out doctrinal work. A modern doctrinal legal methodology must reflect the changes that the law itself went through in the last decades. A doctrinal study on some aspect of modern law which does not consider nonnational sources or the relevance of private ordering does not meet today's standards. In my view, truly creative doctrinal work can be done on developing new doctrinal systems that take these elements into account. As explained earlier, findings about the effectiveness of existing or newly proposed rules can also be part of such systems. Perhaps even more important is that current doctrinal scholarship suffers from the distinction between the main substantive fields of law. Now that problems can increasingly be solved using different legal frameworks (e.g., private law and fundamental rights, administrative law and tax law, criminal law and fundamental rights), it makes much more sense to develop a doctrinal system for a certain problem

[92] Karl Larenz, *Methodenlehre der Rechtswissenschaft*, 6th edn., Heidelberg (Springer) 1991, at 474.

[93] Claus-Wilhelm Canaris, *Systemdenken und Systembegriff in der Jurisprudenz*, 2nd edn., Berlin (Duncker & Humblot) 1983; Robert Alexy, *Theorie der juristischen Argumentation*, 7th edn., Frankfurt (Suhrkamp) 2012, 331; and for a discussion of different positions, Karl Riesenhuber, *System und Prinzipien des Europaïschen Vertragsrechts*, Berlin (De Gruyter) 2003, at 5 ff.

[94] See for the common law also Neil MacCormick, *Legal Reasoning and Legal Theory*, Oxford (Clarendon Press) 1978.

(protection of personal guarantor, taking of property, rights of the suspect) instead of for a whole field.

5.5 Conclusion

This chapter has shown that there is a dire need for a better understanding of doctrinal research. I identified three main aims and various methodological choices to be made when carrying out such research. This conclusion highlights two findings of this investigation.

Probably the most important finding from the above is that it is too easily forgotten that legal doctrine reflects the normative complexity of the law. It offers highly detailed and sophisticated information about how to deal with conflicting arguments. Stripping the law from this practical knowledge by reducing it to general principles or policies, or by trading it in for economic or empirical analysis, is not helpful.[95] This does not mean that alternative approaches to the law are not relevant, but they all have to take the doctrinal description of the existing law as a starting point and are in that sense dependent on legal doctrine.[96] Valuable economic, empirical or behavioural analysis of law would be impossible without first knowing what the existing law says *and* without using legal doctrine at the end as a justification for the proposed novel solution that follows from these alternative approaches. In this respect, legal doctrine is the Alpha and the Omega of the law.[97]

The second finding is that, despite the importance of legal-doctrinal work, its bad reputation is not entirely undeserved. Doctrinalists pay too little attention to the choices they make when creating or developing a legal system. Doctrinal research can be highly original,[98] but too often it is not. This calls for a change in attitude. It seems inevitable that legal doctrine must search for new foundations if it wants to compete with

[95] Goldberg, 'Introduction', at 1650: 'reality is complex and . . . it will not advance the cause of knowledge to assume that one comes to understand reality by stripping away superstructure to get to base.'

[96] Cf. CALD Statement, at 3: 'If doctrinal research is a distinctive part of legal research, that distinctiveness permeates every other aspect of legal research for which the identification, analysis and evaluation of legal doctrine is a basis, starting point, platform or underpinning.'

[97] See on this point looked at from a different perspective: Jan M. Smits, 'Law and Interdisciplinarity: on the Inevitable Normativity of Legal Studies', *Critical Analysis of Law* 1:1 (2014), 75.

[98] The same conclusion is reached by Siems, 'Legal originality', 147, at 149, who describes different ways in which doctrinal work can offer something 'more.'

newer types of research in law. In the end, this is a matter of how attractive it is for academics to engage in doctrinal work. The above shows that the three main objections against doctrinal work (too provincial, too narrow and not creative enough[99]) can be easily discarded, provided one is willing to take the methodological effort. Doctrinal research is worth it.

[99] See Section 5.1.

6

Making Doctrine for European Law

NILS JANSEN

6.1 Introduction

A central issue of modern European scholarship is the making of European legal doctrine, i.e., the intellectual and conceptual basis of the common language of European law. Apparently European jurists and legislatures assume (again) that there is such a common legal language; it is used, e.g., when the European Commission drafts new legislation or when academics design principles of European (private) law. Unfortunately, the language of European private law seems to be still a kind of pidgin – its terms derive from many national legal systems; its grammar is not sufficiently complex; and many of its concepts are vague. This poor state of European legal language is not surprising, however; it would be surprising if it were otherwise. The conceptual basis of modern national legal systems did likewise not simply evolve by itself, and it was not part of the furniture of the empirical world. Legal concepts were *made* by those who administered the legal systems. In modern legal systems these concepts are tools that are designed by professional jurists. Such tools may be more or less appropriate in view of their purpose. It follows that European scholars should not and cannot simply rely on the present language of European law when analysing and describing the elements of private law. Rather, European jurists should thoroughly reflect the present terminology and reconstruct fitting conceptual tools.

European scholars have long been active in the making of a European legal doctrine. Since the 1980s, an increasing number of scholars have engaged in many projects aimed at developing such a legal language and thus have participated in the making of a common European legal doctrine.[1] Most noteworthy among those projects are textbooks on European Contract or Tort law (such as the books by Kötz, von Bar or

[1] An early pioneer was E. Rabel, *Das Recht des Warenkaufs* (1936/1958).

van Dam)[2] and the many non-legislative codifications[3] in this field (Principles of European Contract Law [PECL];[4] UNIDROIT Principles of International Commercial Contracts [PICC];[5] Acquis-Principles [ACQP];[6] Draft Common Frame of Reference [DCFR];[7] Principles of European Tort Law [PETL]).[8] Many of those projects, however, focussed more on rule making than on the intellectual conceptual and doctrinal basis of European private law. Not all of them were based on a consistent methodology or only on a clear method. Methodological reflection is rare in such projects;[9] and, indeed, there is no strong tradition in Europe to reflect on the making of legal doctrine. Many jurists regard doctrine as unimportant; others seem to assume that doctrine develops organically in legal discourse and ultimately finds an expression in legal rules. But this misstates large parts of the history of learned law in Europe and of the achievements of civilians, of natural-law scholars and of common-law scholars such as Blackstone or Peter Birks.

Much has been said about the project of 'restating' European private law and in particular about scholars engaging in rule making rather than

[2] H. Kötz, *European Contract Law* (T. Weir, tr., 1997); C. von. Bar, *The Common European Law of Torts*, 2 vols. (1998/2000); C. van Dam, *European Tort Law* (2006).

[3] On the concept of a non-legislative codification, see Jansen, *The Making of Legal Authority: Non-legislative codifications in Historical and Comparative Perspective* (2010).

[4] Principles of European Contract Law: O. Lando, and H. Beale (eds.), *Principles of European Contract Law*, Parts I and II (2000); O. Lando, E. Clive, A. Prüm, R. Zimmermann (eds.), *Principles of European Contract Law*, Part III (2003).

[5] UNIDROIT (ed.), *UNIDROIT Principles of International Commercial Contracts 2010* (2011).

[6] The Research Group on the Existing EC Private Law (Acquis Group), *Principles of the Existing EC Contract Law (Acquis Principles). Contract I* (2007); *Contract II* (2009).

[7] C. von Bar, and E. Clive (eds.), *Principles, Definitions and Model Rules of European Private Law: Draft Common Frame of Reference (DCFR), Full Edition* (6 vols., 2009).

[8] European Group on Tort Law, *Principles of European Tort Law* (2005).

[9] Most of these non-legislative codifications contain an introductory part that provides readers with information about the respective working group and its structure; furthermore, those introductions explain the purpose of the texts and occasionally give an indication about the 'method' used by the group; the most explicit example seems to be G. Dannemann, 'Consolidating EC Contract Law: An Introduction to the Work of the Acquis Group', in ACQP II (no. 6), xxxvi–xlix. But those explanations are meant to validate and add authority to the result; they are not meant to provide the reader with information about eventual methods of research applied. Indeed, these non-legislative codifications, though drafted primarily by legal scholars, do not usually explain the rules with scholarly arguments; hence, they would be misunderstood, if they were seen as contribution to scholarly discourse. See, more detailed, N. Jansen and R. Zimmermann, '"A European civil code in all but name": Discussing the Nature and Purposes of the Draft Common Frame of Reference', (2010) 69 *CLJ* 98–112, 104–107.

in scholarship.[10] In this chapter, I wish to present – and reflect from a methodological point of view – the idea of a commentary on European contract law; it is a project, on which I am currently working in collaboration with Reinhard Zimmermann. I will present the methodological approach employed for this project with specific examples taken from the law of assignment. The assumption underlying this chapter is that methodology should be treated as a reflective, rather than a prescriptive issue. There is no 'ideal' method to be applied universally; it is simply not helpful to formulate methodological guidelines that are to be applied by other scholars: There is no uniform path leading to appropriate answers for quite different research questions. Whether a particular methodological approach is convincing depends on the actual research question, or legal problem, on the one hand, and on the shared knowledge and beliefs of a scientific community on the other. The purpose of methodological explanation can hence only be to elucidate a particular piece of scholarly work and thus enable others to assess its results.

My example is taken from the law of assignment. This choice of topic is based primarily on three abstract considerations: First, the law of assignment is beyond the parties' choice of law, as it concerns not only the interests and rights of the parties to the assignment, but also those of the debtor as well as of the assignor's and assignee's creditors. Hence, the idea of a competition of legal systems and rules cannot be used as a device to further legal development and discovery. Second, this field of law seems to be particularly tricky and interesting both from a methodological and from a doctrinal point of view: The law of assignment concerns the interests of many parties; and the rules and the language used in national laws exhibit a particularly high degree of divergence. Furthermore, this field of modern law is based on metaphorical ideas that are quite different from those taken for granted by the Roman and medieval jurists who coined the doctrinal language of modern law. Further problems arise from the fact that there is neither European legislation in this

[10] N. Jansen and R. Zimmermann, 'Restating the *Acquis Communautaire*? A Critical Examination of the "Principles of the Existing EC Contract Law"', (2008) 71 *MLR* 505–534; Jansen and Zimmerman, '"A European civil code in all but name"'; H. Eidenmüller, F. Faust, C. Grigoleit, N. Jansen, G. Wagner, and R. Zimmermann, 'The Common Frame of Reference for European Private Law – Policy Choices and Codification Problems', (2008) 28 *OJLSt* 659–708; H. Eidenmüller, N. Jansen, E.-M. Kieninger, G. Wagner, and R. Zimmermann, 'The Proposal for a Regulation on a Common European Sales Law: Deficits of the Most Recent Textual Layer of European Contract Law', (2012) 16 *Edinburgh LR* 16 301–357.

field of the law nor any such legislation to be expected in the near future; hence, European lawyers and legal scholars cannot relate their research to formally binding legislative authorities. All this makes this field of the law a particularly tricky issue also from a methodological perspective. And finally, the law of assignment is economically important. Rules on assignment are of preeminent significance for modern forms of receivables financing such as factoring. Clearly, European markets would profit immensely by a unification of the law.[11]

Before explaining this project more specifically, however, it seems appropriate to address some general issues of legal methodology. They concern similarities and differences between legal and other forms of scholarship, on the one hand, and between the judge's and the doctrinal scholar's methods on the other.[12] The purpose of this part is to make explicit and explain the methodological assumptions implicitly underlying the project of a commentary on European contract law.

6.2 Doctrinal Legal Scholarship

During recent years, legal scholarship and legal education have become the object of fierce debate, first in Germany and then in Europe and the United States. Is there a 'proprium' of legal scholarship?[13] Or do legal scholars have to work interdisciplinarily in order to treat their subject in a 'scholarly' way?[14] Should legal scholars accept scholarly standards that are long established in other professions such as peer review? I do not want to

[11] Legislative unification is, of course, beyond the horizon of this paper. Yet unifying legislation can only be convincing and successful, if it grows from a common legal language that develops in professional legal discourse and in particular in legal scholarship.

[12] These remarks have been prompted by the stimulating recent paper of R. van Gestel, H.-W. Micklitz, and M. Poiares Maduro, 'Methodology in the new legal world', *EUI Working Papers* Law 2012/13; cf. also J. Vranken, 'Exciting Times for Legal Scholarship', (2012) 2 *Recht en Methode in onderzoek en onderwijs* 42–62, 44–49.

[13] C. Engel and W. Schön (eds.), *Das Proprium der Rechtswissenschaft* (2007).

[14] This, in particular, is part of the current debate in Germany on the status and future development of legal scholarship; see Wissenschaftsrat (ed.), *Perspektiven der Rechtswissenschaft in Deutschland: Situation, Analysen, Empfehlungen* (2012), and the contributions to the debate in the *Juristenzeitung* 2013: S. Grundmann, 'Ein doppeltes Plädoyer für internationale Öffnung und stärker vernetzte Interdisziplinarität', 693–697; T. Gutmann, 'Der Holzkopf des Phädrus: Perspektiven der Grundlagenfächer', 697–700; C. Hillgruber, 'Mehr Rechtswissenschaft wagen!', 700–704; S. Lorenz, 'Forschung, Praxis und Lehre im Bericht des Wissenschaftsrats "Perspektiven der Rechtswissenschaft in Deutschland"', 704–708; S. Rixen, 'Juristische Bildung, nicht leicht gemacht:

address those controversial issues directly – although I am convinced that legal scholarship profits from interdisciplinary open-mindedness, I do neither believe that there is no genuinely legal (doctrinal) scholarship nor that the application of interdisciplinary methods alone ensures high quality of legal research.

My concern here is rather with the fact that law is different from most other objects of human research in that it is not only the object but also the product of scholarship. Indeed, the object of legal research – concepts like 'contract', 'assignment', 'property', 'obligation', 'duty', or 'right' – are not empirical objects in the world, which exist independently of legal scholarship and which legal scholars could simply observe, describe and analyse like an apple or a social institution. Rather, these concepts are *made* by jurists and in particular by legal scholars.[15] True, from the perspective of most jurists, those concepts and doctrines are devices which they inherit from former generations of jurists. From their perspective, those concepts are the furniture of a legal system; they have no less reality than an apple on the tree. And yet, jurists, and in particular scholars, constantly engage in the making, rethinking, and reconstructing of those concepts and doctrines.[16] They do so by employing them in judicial practice and professional teaching. It follows not merely that legal scholarship *influences* its object – such a phenomenon would be well-known in other disciplines such as microphysics and social sciences. Rather, the point is that legal scholarship is even *constitutive* of its object: There cannot be a scholarly legal system unless its conceptual and doctrinal basis is built and reconstructed by professional jurists rethinking and reorganising the law in a scholarly way. There is no European legal system that does not build on such elements of legal scholarship.[17] The following comments on the concept of 'assignment' (6.4.1) may be read as an example illustrating this point: They are not simply a – more or less

Die "Perspektiven der Rechtswissenschaft" des Wissenschaftsrats', 708–712; M. Stolleis, 'Stärkung der Grundlagenfächer', 712–714.

[15] See H. L. A. Hart, *Definition and Theory in Jurisprudence* (1953), 5–7.

[16] N. Jansen, '"Tief ist der Brunnen der Vergangenheit": Funktion, Methode und Ausgangspunkt historischer Fragestellungen in der Privatrechtsdogmatik', (2005) 27 *Zeitschrift für Neuere Rechtsgeschichte* 202–228, 213–216.

[17] Z. Bankowski, D. N. MacCormick, R. S. Summers, and J. Wróblewski, 'On Method and Methodology', in D. N. MacCormick and R. S. Summers (eds.), *Interpreting Statutes* (1991), 9–27, 19 f.; R. S. Summers and M. Taruffo, 'Interpretation and Comparative Analysis', in *Interpreting Statutes*, loc. cit., 461–510, 465; Zweigert/Kötz (German) 1996, 95 ff., 145 ff., 262 ff.; H. P. Glenn, *Legal Traditions of the World* (2000), 132–135, 226–228.

correct – description of the institute of assignment. Rather, those comments concern the issue of *legal definition*[18] in that they contribute to the making of what may once be a European assignment – and what may be quite different from what is today termed 'assignment' in national legal systems.

6.2.1 *Methodology and the Law*

These observations are highly significant also for a correct understanding of legal method and of discussions concerning methodology in legal research. Methods are techniques of research. In accordance with the original meaning of the Greek concept,[19] they may be described metaphorically as a path leading from available knowledge to an answer to a research question.[20] In the law, however, it is often not only unknown, but moreover undetermined, where the path will eventually lead to. In hard cases, which are the object of judicial decisions and of scholarly argument, there is quite often no objectively 'right answer': There is neither reasonably clear legislation or precedent, nor a clearly better argument. Hence, the answer given by a scholar will *add* an element to the legal system, if it is accepted by the legal community; often it changes, by implication, other parts of the law as well. 'Right answers' to legal questions are therefore different from what other professions conceive of as a 'true answer'. Of course, in all sciences, 'truth' relates to general research paradigms acknowledged in the respective scientific community. In the law, however, the 'rightness' of a scholarly proposition cannot even be verified or falsified by objective criteria. Its rightness depends on its ultimate acceptance in the legal community.

In most other sciences, the proper design of method is therefore primarily a technical issue: It should be as easy and cheap as possible and it should allow other scholars to falsify or otherwise assess the result of research. In doctrinal legal scholarship, in contrast, the status of method and methodology is different: As in other sciences, the method chosen shall make it possible for other scholars to assess the result of legal research. Yet the assessment will not be based on the idea of the answer given being 'true', but rather on whether it is convincing or plausible. To a large degree (though never fully), this depends on the sources, on which

[18] On the concept of legal definition, see Hart, *Definition and Theory.*

[19] S. Martens, *Methodenlehre des Unionsrechts* (2013), 6.

[20] Van Gestel, Micklitz, and Poiares Maduro, 'Methodology', 1.

the research is based, and on the method employed. Yet, the assessment of a legal method can never be completely separated from the results which it generates. Thus, legal methodology, even if not prescriptive, unavoidably becomes a normative issue:[21] Legal systems are not least defined by generally recognised methodological standards and shared methodological assumptions. Those standards, which are often habitually observed, rather than explicitly discussed, help to integrate and stabilise legal systems.[22]

An illustration of this proposition is the doctrine of the legal 'sources'. Sources in the technical sense are basic elements that constitute a legal system,[23] such as legislation and – in most legal systems – precedents. From the judge's perspective, those sources are the starting points of legal argument: the point of departure, on which the judgement shall ultimately be based. Their authority consists in the legal profession accepting such texts as a basis of legal argument without requiring further reasons to do so.[24] From the scholar's perspective, those sources may be regarded as 'data' on which research is based. Neither scholars nor judges, however, can base their argument or their research solely on the 'official' sources of a legal system; moreover, it may be unclear what the relevant sources are. In many civilian legal systems, it was long disputed whether judicial precedents should be assigned the status of a source of the law. And in all developed legal systems, texts written by learned jurists were, and are, treated as important sources of information and thus became informal authorities. Often, learned texts of authority acquired an even greater authority than legislation or precedent.[25] Historical examples are non-legislative codifications such as the *Decretum Gratiani*, the *Corpus Iuris Civilis*, or the Saxon Mirror,[26] or scholarly commentaries such as the standard glosses to the *Corpora iuris*,[27] or even the *Summa theologiae* as the prime textual reference of sixteenth century natural-law discourse. In

[21] See, most recently, Martens, *Methodenlehre*, 6, 92–132.

[22] Jansen, 'Methoden, Institutionen, Texte. Zur diskursiven Funktion und medialen Präsenz dogmatisierender Ordnungsvorstellungen und Deutungsmuster im normativen Diskurs', (2011) 128 *Zeitschrift der Savigny-Stiftung für Rechtsgeschichte (germanistische Abteilung)* 1–71, 12–31.

[23] Martens, *Methodenlehre*, 123.

[24] For this concept of authority, see Jansen, *Making Legal Authority*, 41.

[25] cf. Martens, *Methodenlehre*, 127–131, criticising a sharp antithesis of 'binding' and 'nonbinding' sources of law.

[26] Jansen, *Making Legal Authority*, 20–41.

[27] See, on the *Glossa ordinaria* to the *Corpus iuris civilis*, Arthur Duck (1580–1648), *De Usu et Authoritate Juris Civilis Romanorum, in Dominiis Principum Christanorum Libri Duo*

the twentieth century, comparable authority was assigned to the American restatements;[28] likewise, the PICC and the PECL are beginning to become legal authorities in transnational law.[29] In all legal systems, moreover, judges, lawyers and scholars increasingly rely on standardised literature such as the German commentaries or *Chitty on Contracts*, when conducting legal research or making an argument.

From a naïve methodological point of view, the choice of sources may be seen primarily as a technical question. According to such a view, guiding criteria should be the reliability and objectivity of the relevant source. As a matter of scholarly principle, preference should be given to (more reliable) primary than to (less reliable) secondary sources. Scholars should rely on the original contributions to doctrinal discourse: on innovative scholarly work, on judicial precedent and, first of all, on the relevant legislation. Commentaries and textbooks would be treated merely as supplementary tools to find those primary sources. Unfortunately, however, such an approach misses the very point of legal argument. It assumes a descriptive perspective *vis-à-vis* the legal system and thus does not take into account that legal scholars, like judges, are *participants* in legal systems; this is both true for the academic jurist who writes a scholarly paper and for the authors of commentaries and textbooks that are designed for the legal practice. The task of all these jurists is not to describe, but rather to reconstruct their legal system.[30] The form of legal research is hence legal argument rather than a descriptive depiction of a legal system's primary sources. If description was used

(Leipzig 1668), lib I, cap VIII, § 6: 'tantaque est Accursii Authoritas, ut ex ejus Sententia Causa judicanda sit quoties insignis aliquis Interpres ei adhaeret'; Antonius Maria Coratius Cortonensis (Corazzi), *Tract. (Tractatus) de communi v.i. (utriusque iuris) doctorum opinione, constituenda, attendenda & poenis recendentium ab ea* (Perugia 1572) tit III, [2] f.: '. . . duo doctores maximae autoritatis, ut est glosa, & Bartolus faciant communem opinionem'; cf. P. Weimar, 'Accursius', in M. Stolleis (ed.), *Juristen, Ein biographisches Lexikon, Von der Antike bis zum 20. Jahrhundert* (1995), 18–19; more generally, Jansen, *Making Legal Authority*, 22, 25, 37, 113–121.

28 R. Michaels, 'Restatements', in J. Basedow, K.J. Hopt, and R. Zimmermann (eds.), *The Max Planck Encyclopedia of European Private Law* (*MaxEuP*) (2012), 1464–1468.

29 Jansen, *Making Legal Authority*, 59–76; cf. R. Michaels, 'Umdenken für die UNIDROIT-Prinzipien. Vom Rechtswahlstatut zum Allgemeinen Teil des transnationalen Vertragsrechts', (2009) 73 *Rabels Zeitschrift für internationales und ausländisches Privatrecht* 866–888.

30 See (critically) on the prevailing praxis of 'proving' foreign law in court proceedings, N. Jansen and R. Michaels, 'Die Auslegung und Fortbildung ausländischen Rechts', (2003) 116 *Zeitschrift für Zivilprozeß* 3–55, 13–22.

as a method to restate the law, it would deeply misunderstand the nature of legal argument and also of legal systems.

Yet, even from the descriptive perspective of a legal historian or a comparative lawyer, the primary sources of a legal system cannot be a sufficient basis for research. The reason is not only the abundant mass of – often contradictory – primary information, which jurists cannot completely take into account. This could merely be a pragmatic reason to rely on secondary sources restating the relevant arguments. The more important factor is the relevance of the weights of arguments made by courts and other participants in a legal system. As long as there is neither an objectively right answer to a doctrinal question, nor a 'forceless force of better arguments',[31] this weight cannot be determined appropriately without information concerning the argument's recognition by the courts and within the academic community. The law is not simply contained in the primary sources; rather it is the object of, and emerges in, the discussions in a legal system. The law is more than norms and arguments; it cannot be fully understood when ignoring the informal processes of *recognition* of arguments. The information about those processes can be gathered only from secondary sources which thus may become even more important than the primary ones.[32] It makes a big difference to a legal system whether or not an argument or a 'theory' proposed by a scholar makes its way into a leading commentary, such as the German *Palandt*, the English *Chitty on Contracts* or into a new restatement.

In making choices between different sources of information, jurists – judges like scholars – assign authority to these sources and thus contribute to the making of legal authorities. Indeed, jurists never simply happen upon informal authorities in the law: Legal authority is not simply present but is ever newly created, and consequently is subject to ongoing processes of legal change. Thus, every jurist contributes to the formation of informal authority with his or her professional conduct and expectations of the conduct of fellow jurists.[33] The more lawyers

[31] cf. J. Habermas, 'Wahrheitstheorien', in *Vorstudien und Ergänzungen zur Theorie des kommunikativen Handelns* (1995), 127–183, 161.

[32] D. Kästle, 'Juristische Kommentare: Theologische Kommentare. Von der Farbe des Chamäleons', in Kästle and Jansen (ed.), *Kommentare in Recht und Religion* (2014), 393–450, in particular 330 f., 335 f., 440–442, 445–448; N. Jansen, 'Informal Authorities in European Private Law' (2013) 20 *Maastricht Journal of European and Comparative Law* 482–505, 493–496, also with empirical data on the citation praxis of supreme courts.

[33] cf. on such processes, G. Essen and N. Jansen (eds.), *Dogmatisierungsprozesse in Recht und Religion* (2011); Jansen, 'Methoden, Institutionen, Texte'.

who focus their attention, for example, on the case law and a few standard commentaries, the more stable a legal system becomes – yet it also threatens thereby to ossify. This applies all the more where commentaries restrict themselves to reproducing case law and – actual or anticipated – leading doctrine, and thereby uncouple legal practice and innovative legal research. Likewise, by referring to foreign or transnational authorities, judges and scholars open up their legal systems and may make them participate in a transnational discourse.[34] It should not be surprising that the methodological selection of a data basis may thus become a contested political issue; a contemporary example is the debate in the United States on the citation by courts of foreign judgements.[35]

Similar considerations apply as far as the method of interpretation of legislation is concerned: Quite clearly, it makes a great difference to a legal system, whether the aim of legal interpretation is seen to reconstruct the meaning given to a norm by its historical legislator, or whether an additional normative criterion, such as the *effet utile*, becomes the decisive aspect in the construction of legislation, or whether statutes are expected to be constructed narrowly where they interfere with the common law – as was not only the position prevailing in England during large parts of the nineteenth and twentieth centuries, but also under the elder *ius commune*.[36] Likewise, it makes a big difference whether European legislation is interpreted in the light of the European conceptual heritage or cut off its common roots. The expectations prevailing in a legal community on the sources and methods to be employed in judicial and also in scholarly argument fundamentally determine the normative structure of a legal system.

Nothing of these remarks is meant to suggest that methodological issues in the law were totally different from those in other sciences. Thus, the idea of testing hypothetical general propositions about the law with

[34] This is commonplace in particular in human rights adjudication; see A.-M. Slaughter, *A New World Order* (2004), 65; C. McCrudden, 'A Common Law of Human Rights?: Transnational Judicial Conversations on Constitutional Rights', (2000) 20 *OJLSt* 499–532, 506–510; R. Bader Ginsburg, '"A Decent Respect to the Opinions of [Human]kind": The Value of a Comparative Perspective in Constitutional Adjudication': (2006) 64 *Cambridge L.J.* 575–592 (= (2006) 1 *Florida International University LR* 27); A. Nußberger, 'Wer zitiert wen? – Zur Funktion von Zitaten bei der Herausbildung gemeineuropäischen Verfassungsrechts', (2006) *Juristenzeitung* 763–770, 765–767.

[35] F. Schauer, 'Authority and Authorities', (2008) 94 *Virginia LR* 1931–1961.

[36] R. Zimmermann, 'Statuta sunt stricte interpretanda?', (2007) 56 *Cambridge LJ* 315–328.

specific basic propositions (i.e., certain basic data on specific issues) may often be helpful.[37] Yet even here, there are obvious differences. In particular, it is always possible (though often unlikely) to reconsider even a basic elementary legal proposition in the light of a new theory.[38] Even in civilian legal systems, theory often seems to be based more on the ideal of a reflective equilibrium than on the abstract interpretation of legislation and deductive reasoning. In any event, these observations suffice to show that methodological choices in the law are not identical with methodological issues in other sciences – they are more complex and not simply the best way to the 'truth'. In particular, they should not be reduced to the idea of a scientifically most appropriate approach to describing a legal system existing independently of its reconstruction in judicial practice on the one hand and academic teaching and scholarship on the other.

To sum up: doctrinal legal scholarship is characterised by a tension between the search for truth and innovative research, on the one hand, and the active participation in legal development, i.e., in the conservation of present and the making of future law, on the other hand. Where scholars contribute to doctrinal debates, they are actors not only within the *academic system* of scientific research, but also within their *legal systems*; they have to live with, and should make explicit this tension. Unavoidably, they cultivate the law's culture of authorities; and they constantly build, or rebuild, their legal systems by doing so. This is particularly important for an emerging legal system such as present European private law, where basic methodological issues are not yet determined: It obviously makes a big difference, whether comparative information is expected to be based directly on national scholarly articles and monographs, or on leading national commentaries and textbooks, or on the International Encyclopedia of Comparative Law and other comparative literature. And where reference is made to the DCFR or to the PECL in order to support a statement on the present state of European law, those texts are made an authoritative basis of emerging European contract law.

[37] A. Peczenik, 'Empirical Foundations of Legal Dogmatics', (1968) 3 *Études de Logique Juridique* 32–64; C.-W. Canaris, 'Funktion, Struktur und Falsifikation juristischer Theorien', (1993) *Juristenzeitung* 377–391, 385–388; Jansen, 'Dogmatik, Erkenntnis und Theorie im europäischen Privatrecht' (2005) *Zeitschrift für Europäisches Privatrecht* 750–783, 771–774. cf. further Martens, *Methodenlehre*, 68 f.

[38] Jansen, 'Dogmatik', 772.

All this can be seen particularly well in the discussion of the two innovative rules in the law of assignment discussed below. The question of whether the rule on the debtor's additional costs (6.4.2) and the rules on unauthorised modifications of the contract (6.4.3) should be recognised as European principles depends on what counts as the relevant authorities and sources of European contract law (European restatements, national laws, comparative literature) and what counts as a relevant and convincing argument. It would be inappropriate, however, to assume that European lawyers should in a first step agree on the relevant authorities before then discussing the doctrinal issues. Rather, European lawyers contribute to the making of European authorities by making doctrinal arguments of this sort.

6.2.2 *Scholars and Judges*

Are scholarly research methods different from those applied by judges? Or should they be different? Is there a scholarly perspective on legal systems that is different from the judicial point of view?[39]

Clearly, the appropriate choice of method depends, first of all, on the specific research question. Here, it seems obvious that the spectrum of possible questions to be asked by legal scholars is far broader than the questions to be answered by judges. Scholars are concerned not only with doctrinal questions but also with the social, economic and historical contexts of legal systems; moreover, scholars of legal theory (jurisprudence) analyse basic conceptual issues in the form of abstract theories of legal systems. Large parts of legal research do not concern normative, but rather empirical issues; jurists may then employ the methods of economists, of social scientists or of historians. As far as such forms of legal research are concerned, scholars face no difficulty accepting the usual standards of scholarly work: They may be expected to (and do) subject their work to peer review; and they are very explicit about their methods of research. In legal history, to take just one example, there is a long tradition of fundamental methodological debate;[40] many journals in fields such as law and

[39] Van Gestel, Micklitz, and Poiares Maduro, 'Methodology', 3, 20 with further references on this discussion.

[40] cf. R. Zimmermann et al. (eds.) *Rechtsgeschichte und Privatrechtsdogmatik* (1999); J. Eckert (ed.), *Der praktische Nutzen der Rechtsgeschichte: Festschrift Hattenhauer* (2003); and the contributions to the debate 'Wozu Rechtsgeschichte?' ('why legal history'), in (2003) 3 *Rechtsgeschichte* 12–76; 4 (2004) *Rechtsgeschichte* 12–81.

economics, legal history or jurisprudence are peer reviewed. All this, however, is of little interest for the methods of doctrinal legal scholarship.

It is often said that scholars should *explain* legal rules, whereas judges should *apply* them. Scholars hence should raise 'why' – questions, which do not need to bother the judge.[41] The problem of the latter distinction is not primarily its unwanted scent of an alleged intellectual superiority and the ambiguity of 'why' – questions: Indeed, the answer given to such a question may be a historical or an economic explanation; it may refer to the purpose which is assumed to underlie a norm or to the legislative programme. The main problem of this distinction is rather that it is difficult to see why 'why' – questions should be irrelevant for judges and lawyers. Of course, all those issues may attract the scholar's attention; but why should they be irrelevant for the judge? Quite clearly, judges and other practitioners can argue much more convincingly if they base their argument on the purpose of a norm; in this respect, there cannot be any difference between judicial and scholarly argument. Of course, scholars are in a better position to address questions as to the historical, economic and social background of a norm. Yet again: why should their answers not likewise interest the judge? If not: why would the research be important? Judges can much better and much more reasonably analyse the purpose of a norm, if their argument is based on deep knowledge about its social and economic relevance and about its historical development. It is difficult to see why judges (and other practitioners) *should not* be interested in, or pay attention to, 'why' – questions and to foundational legal knowledge. Indeed, the purpose of the commentary on European contract law shall be to make available for judges and other practitioners the historical, intellectual and comparative foundations of European contract law. The contributors to this commentary regard it as inappropriate to keep those issues locked in the prison cell of legal academia and thus make them irrelevant for the judicial development of the law.

Another difference between the scholar's and the judge's doctrinal method might be constructed relying on the idea that scholars should adopt an analytic and descriptive perspective on a legal system rather than engage actively in normative legal debate. Or it might be suggested that scholars should primarily be interested in general propositions about the law, whereas the task of judges would be seen to decide specific cases

[41] Van Gestel, Micklitz, and Poiares Maduro, 'Methodology', 5 f.

at hand. Those differences, however, concern more the institutional standing and influence of judges and academics in a legal system than a methodological issue.[42] Where scholars take a distant view on doctrinal debates and see their task in explaining the authoritative judgements of judges, those judges, rather than the scholars, will become the 'oracles of the law'. Where scholars listen to and follow judges formulating general rules and principles, rather than deciding specific cases, they may completely lose control of the legal system. Scholars may, however, also assume a more self-confident role in a legal system; their – often habitual – professional self-image may be to develop the legal system and to explore its way to the future. This is, *inter alia*, a purpose of the commentary on European contract law. The success of this kind of scholarship depends on the reaction of the other participants to the legal field, in particular of judges and legislatures. And it depends, of course, on the institutional structure of the legal and of the academic system: Recent comparative analysis suggests that the influence of legal scholars may weaken if scholars commit themselves too much to the scholarly standards of other sciences and thereby produce literature which is of little help or not accessible for practising jurists.[43] Again, the methodological approach to legal scholarship turns out to be a deeply normative and even political issue. Quite clearly, scholars would overestimate their role in the legal system, if they thought they could objectively delineate the 'correct' roles of scholars and judges in this respect. Rather, they may engage and become party in such a struggle for influence. It would then be a task for contemporary comparative lawyers and for future historians to describe the shifting influence of judges, practitioners and academics in different legal systems.[44]

There is one point, however, which does everywhere distinguish the scholar's perspective, and hence the scholar's method, from the judge's

[42] The classical references are J.P. Dawson, *The Oracles of the Law* (1968), and R. van Caenegem, *Judges, Legislators and Professors. Chapters in European Legal History* (1987). More recently, P. Grossi, *Das Recht in der europäischen Geschichte* (2010) 9, 71–205. For a comparative survery, see W. Twining, W. Farnsworth, S. Vogenauer, and F. Tesón, 'The Role of Academics in the Legal System', in P. Cane and M. Tushnet (eds.), *The Oxford Handbook of Legal Studies* (paperback edn. 2005), 920–949.

[43] cf. the reports on developments in common law systems by Twining and Farnsworth in Twining, Farnsworth, Vogenauer and Tesón, 'The Role of Academics'.

[44] For an analysis on the basis of sociological theory of the shift of influence from scholars to practitioners in the field of the modern 'lex mercatoria', see the study by Y. Dezalay and B.G. Garth, *Dealing in Virtue, International Commercial Arbitration and the Creation of a Transnational Legal Order* (1996).

point of view: Whereas the judge is indeed expected to apply, and thus not fundamentally question, a valid legal rule at hand, it is part of the scholars' professional business to take a critical, evaluative perspective on their legal system. Arguments of this sort may well be found in a scholarly commentary on European law. Scholars are expected to rethink the law: to identify rules as dysfunctional and to suggest alternative solutions. This is why times of legal change are particularly challenging for legal scholars, and why so many of them have become actors in the process of building European private law. True, judges are similarly engaged in reinterpreting and thus – at times even fundamentally – reconstructing the rules of their legal systems. In doing so, however, they have to apply the existing rules; they cannot decide not to apply valid legal rules; and it is does not make much sense for a judge to criticise a valid legal rule. (Where judges are asked to give opinion as legal experts at an issue of legal reform, they may, of course, suggest changing their system; but they will not do this in the role of judges, but of legal experts.)

6.3 A Commentary on European Contract Laws

It is not exactly easy to describe and analyse the present state of European private law scholarship; yet it seems safe to say that it appears rather complex and shows no particularly high degree of coherence. There is a lot of literature on the impact of European law on national laws, and there is literature specifically addressing the European Union's legislation and the European Court of Justice's case law. Articles and textbooks address issues of European consumer law, European company law, European procedural law, and so forth; and there are even textbooks on EU contract law.[45] At the same time, many lawyers are busy analysing (drafts of) European directives and regulations critically; furthermore, many scholars do a lot of advisory work with bureaucrats in Brussels. Comparative lawyers described the similarities and differences between European legal systems; they wrote historical and comparative textbooks on the European law of obligations (Zimmermann, Ranieri)[46] and they even tried to identify common rules and principles of European contract

[45] B. Heiderhoff, *Europäisches Privatrecht* (3rd edn., 2012); K. Riesenhuber, *EU-Vertragsrecht* (2013).
[46] R. Zimmermann, *The Law of Obligations: Roman Foundations of the Civilian Tradition* (1996); F. Ranieri, *Europäisches Obligationenrecht* (3rd edn., 2009).

law (Kötz),[47] of European tort law (van Dam, von Bar)[48] and of a European law of unjustified enrichment.[49] At the same time, however, much academic effort not only by well-established professors but also by doctoral and postdoctoral researchers has been invested into prestigious projects of rule making; these efforts find expression in the many non-legislative codifications in this field of the law.[50] Other scholars analysed and criticised those proposals. It is not surprising that all those groups of scholars employed different methods: They were obviously concerned with different questions and tasks – indeed, not all these tasks are easy to qualify as academic research. It would be astonishing if we would observe one common method emerging in this process.

As a result of all these different approaches, there is not yet a genuinely European scholarship on contract law; rather, there are a number of isolated discourses and perhaps even contract laws. Much of the research and knowledge produced by one group of authors seems to be irrelevant for others: While comparative scholars have often ignored European legislation, EC-scholars often regard comparative work as irrelevant. And the effort put into the critical evaluation of non-legislative codifications and of proposals by the European Commission seems to have had only little impact on later reformulations of such rules. Hence, it is high time to integrate those discussions, to relate them with one another and thus to provide comprehensive information about the present state of European contract law. This must be the purpose of a commentary on European contract law.

Modern commentaries usually provide information about a legal system by interpreting its authoritative sources (normally the text of a codification). The approach of these commentaries may hence be characterised as exegetical: Such commentaries present legal knowledge and also case law in the form of interpretations of legislation.[51] In European

[47] Kötz, *Contract Law*. [48] van Dam, *Tort Law*; von Bar, *Law of Torts*.

[49] P. Schlechtriem, *Restitution und Bereicherungsausgleich in Europa: Eine rechtsvergleichende Darstellung*, 2 vols. (2000/2001).

[50] 'Further Academia dei giusprivatisti Europei', *Code Européen des contrats*, www.eurcontrats.eu/site2/; Association Henri Capitant, Société de Législation Comparée, *Projet de Cadre Commun de Référence – Principes contractuels communs* (2008); for an English version (black letter rules only) see B. Fauvarque-Cosson and D. Mazeaud (eds.), *European Contract Law: Materials for a Common Frame of Reference: Terminology, Guiding Principles, Model Rules* (2008), 573–614.

[51] For a detailed and nuanced picture, see Kästle, 'Juristische Kommentare: theologische Kommentare', 409–417, 426 f.

contract law, however, such an approach appears to be less plausible as there is simply not sufficient authoritative legislation. True, European contract lawyers may refer to the many directives in this field of the law, and they may even hope for a *Common European Sales Law* (CESL) to come into force in the near future; such an instrument could be taken as an authoritative reference text. Indeed, a first traditional commentary on the draft European Commission's proposal for such an instrument has already been published;[52] others are about to follow.[53] Yet, the CESL will not cover important aspects of general contract law such as representation, set-off, or assignment. As far as those aspects of contract law are concerned, it will not be possible to present legal knowledge in the form of an interpretation of legislation

Furthermore, even within the scope of the CESL, lawyers will not only need information about the meaning of the respective provisions. First of all, they will need the information which is necessary to make choices about opting in or out of this body of rules. They will therefore wish to know whether the instrument's rules and concepts are identical with or differ from the rules and concepts found in national legal systems; and they will also wish to know whether European jurists regard those rules as convincing. And finally, even as far as the meaning of the rules in an instrument like the CESL is concerned, it may be unwise not to consider other authorities in European contract law. Most provisions in the CESL are reformulations of elder versions of the same norms in the PECL, in the ACQP or in the DCFR; the most recent formulation of a rule is thus a contribution to an ongoing discussion of European contract law. The meaning of those rules will therefore often become much clearer when the most recent formulation is contrasted with earlier versions of the rule.[54]

The purpose of a European commentary shall be to provide comprehensive information on European contract law in view of the segmented state of European scholarship and in view of a plurality of textual authorities. It should hence be based on all relevant reference texts and has to explain and critically evaluate those authorities. The guiding question will always be: Which is the state of law with respect to this

[52] R. Schulze (ed.), *Common European Sales Law* (2012).

[53] D. Staudenmaier (ed.), *Common European Sales Law*, announced to come out in 2016.

[54] See already N. Jansen and R. Zimmermann, 'Contract Formation and Mistake in European Contract Law: A Genetic Comparison of Transnational Model Rules', (2011) 21 *OJLSt* 625–662.

question? Are there differences between diverging authorities? Is it possible, in view of a plurality of authorities, to state with sufficient certainty a rule for the issue in question? Where does it derive from? It is suggested that such a commentary may be particularly helpful, if it employs the method of historical and comparative critical doctrinal scholarship: It should compare the texts with one another and reconstruct the genesis of those texts. Moreover, the commentary should make accessible to the reader the existing literature and learning on those texts and provide basic comparative and historical information about the present state of national laws. Such a commentary gives expression to the conviction that legal systems develop over time and that they cannot be fully understood if they are cut off their roots.

Quite clearly, such a commentary on European contract laws is a Herculean project: not only for its authors, but possibly also for the readers. Thus, it would be make no sense to collect all available comparative and historical information on a specific issue – nobody could write, or only read, such a book. Likewise, not all texts can be analysed in equal detail. Hence, decisions are necessary as to the relative relevance of the respective texts and information. Such decisions are important: It is necessary to identify relevant and important information. The purpose of a commentary is not only to provide the reader with an answer to the question at hand, and to offer a concise overview of the relevant research literature. One of the most important aspects of a good commentary is the information which is not included.

More specifically, a genuinely European commentary cannot be expected to do more than refer readers to the often detailed relevant comparative literature and to central national authorities such as leading textbooks or commentaries. Here, preference should be given to comparative literature written in English, as this language is best accessible to most European jurists. Yet, in view of the complexity of European scholarship, it would be inacceptable to disregard contributions solely because of their language. Reference to national laws, by contrast, should normally be made on the basis of national contributions (see the references in the notes to Section 6.4). In this respect, it is neither possible nor helpful to provide the reader with – often boring – reports on all legal systems; comparative reports should primarily inform the reader about the different approaches to a legal problem found in different legal systems. Thus, a commentary on European private law should depict – and thereby reconstruct – a *European* discussion; it shall not present a picture of the state of law in the *Member States*. In that approach, the commentary follows a model, which has already been employed by scholars such as Hein Kötz:[55] It contributes to the making of European contract law; indeed, European contract law may be argued to emerge in this type of scholarship.[56] The genuinely European literature, i.e., the literature relating to the European Union's legislative acts and to the non-legislative codifications, should therefore comprehensively be taken into account: These contributions are the most important data in the process of making European contract law; hence, serious scholarship has to take all these contributions into account. A commentary could not provide comprehensive information about European contract law if it neglected relevant contributions to these discussions.

6.4 Assignment

In the field of assignments it seems to be particularly difficult to determine the relevant authorities: The picture is quite complex, and the authority of relevant texts is difficult to assess. Despite the economic significance of receivables financing, a future CESL will most likely not provide for rules on assignment. There is, however, uniform law, in particular the UN Convention on the Assignment of Receivables in International Trade of 2001 (CARIT)[57] and the UNIDROIT Convention on International Factoring of 1988 (Factoring Convention).[58] The

[55] Kötz, *Contract Law*. [56] *MaxEuP*/N. Jansen, 'European Private Law', 637–640.

[57] www.uncitral.org/uncitral/en/uncitral_texts/security/2001Convention_receivables.html. This instrument was adopted after six years of negotiations; cf. M.E. Trager, 'Towards a Predictable Law on International Receivables Financing: The UNCITRAL Convention', (1999) 31 *NYU Journal of International Law and Politics* 611–643, 616–624, 637–640. See on this convention in particular S.V. Bazinas (one of the drafters of the CARIT), 'Key Policy Issues of the United Nations Convention on the Assignment of Receivables in International Trade', (2003) 11 *Tulane Journal of International and Comparative Law* 275–301; cf. also, on an earlier version of this Convention, ibid., 'Lowering the Cost of Credit: The Promise in the Future UNCITRAL Convention on Assignment of Receivables in International Trade', (2001) 9 *Tulane Journal of International and Comparative Law* 259–294; further, H.C. Sigman, F. Garcimartín and I. Heredia Cervantes, 'The United Nations Convention on the Assignment of Receivables in International Trade: A Comparative Analysis from Spanish and United States Perspectives', (2006) *ZEuP* 236–282; E.-M. Kieninger, 'Vereinheitlichung des Rechts der Forderungsabtretung – Zur United Nations Convention on the Assignment of Receivables in International Trade', in *Raum und Recht. Festschrift 600 Jahre Würzburger Juristenfakultät* (2002), 297–317.

[58] www.unidroit.org/instruments/factoring. See F. Mestre, 'Rapport explicatif sur le projet de convention sur l'affacturage international', (1987) *ULR* 85–149. The report provides the reader also with information concerning the historical background of the Convention.

CARIT has not yet come into force, however, not least because of alleged differences to the European Union's conflicts-of-laws rules.[59] Nonetheless, it seems to be the most important instrument in this field.[60] Its basic policies have been met with approval and are supported by a *Legislative Guide on Secured Transactions* adopted by UNCITRAL in 2008; indeed, this instrument is based, as far as assignments are concerned, on the CARIT. All these instruments give likewise expression to market-liberal principles; they are meant 'to promote low-cost credit by enhancing the availability of secured credit' and 'to allow debtors to use the full value inherent in their assets to support credit'.[61] Nevertheless, the authority of these instruments is not obvious as only the Factoring Convention has come into force, and even this convention has been ratified only by few European states. Moreover, the CARIT was not designed as a reference text for a European commentary; its technical and overly detailed style on the one hand and the numerous decisions to leave a particular issue to national laws on the other hand are an expression of the difficulties to find an international political consensus on the matters in question.

Looking to the non-legislative reference texts, the picture does not become much clearer: On the one hand, there are the PECL and the PICC, both of which have strongly been influenced by the CARIT. The DCFR's provisions on assignment, in contrast, quite significantly depart from the international state of the debate; and they have hence been met with severe criticism.[62] It follows that the PICC and the PECL are the most appropriate and natural starting points for the purpose of this commentary and future development of European law. Yet there are significant divergences also between those two latter texts; hence, it is not possible simply to rely on one of those two texts to 'find' a European rule or doctrine. Furthermore, it is always necessary to consider the Factoring Convention and the CARIT, on which the

[59] E.-M. Kieninger, 'Das Abtretungsrecht des DCFR', (2010) *ZEuP* 724-746, 726; for the status of the convention, see www.uncitral.org/uncitral/en/uncitral_texts/security/2001Convention_receivables_status.html.

[60] H. Eidenmüller, 'Die Dogmatik der Zession vor dem Hintergrund der internationalen Entwicklung', (2004) 204 *Archiv für die civilistische Praxis* 457–501, 458–460.

[61] UNCITRAL, *Legislative Guide on Secured Transactions* (2010); the terminology and recommendations have also been published separately: UNCITRAL, *Legislative Guide on Secured Transactions. Terminology and Recommendations* (2009; www.uncitral.org/uncitral/en/uncitral_texts/security/Guide_securedtrans.html), Recommendation 1.

[62] Kieninger, 'Abtretungsrecht'.

non-legislative rules are often based. All this, it is hoped, will become clear from the following three examples.

6.4.1 *Defining a New Concept: 'Assignment'*

All instruments under consideration characterise or define assignments as 'transfers' of obligations: 'An "assignment" of a right is the transfer of the right from one person (the "assignor") to another person (the "assignee")' (Art. III.-5:102 (1) DCFR); 'An assignment of a contractual claim is a transfer of a right to performance' (Art. 11:101 PECL, Comment A); '"Assignment of a right" means the transfer by agreement from one person (the "assignor") to another person (the "assignee"), including transfer by way of security, of the assignor's right to payment of a monetary sum or other performance from a third person ("the obligor")' (Art. 9.1.1 PICC). Or: '"Assignment" means the transfer by agreement from one person ("assignor") to another person ("assignee") of all or part of or an undivided interest in the assignor's contractual right to payment of a monetary sum ("receivable") from a third person ("the debtor")' (Art. 2 (a) CARIT).

A traditional commentary would select one of those provisions as its reference text and then comment upon it on a word-by-word basis.[63] Of course, such an explanation may be useful for many jurists; and, indeed, some information like this will be expected in every commentary. It would be unwise to dismiss the inclusion into the comments of such information as 'unscholarly'. Thus, as far as the requirement of 'agreement' (in all authorities but the DCFR) is concerned, readers will expect comments on the fact that transfers by operation of law are excluded from the scope of the relevant provisions, and on the applicable provisions. Do, for instance, the general provisions on contract law apply, although international authorities do not qualify assignments as contracts? Furthermore, the inclusion into the definition of 'transfers by way of security' raises difficulties – under many legal systems, it seems difficult to qualify as a 'transfer' assignments that are made for purposes of security. This leads to the more fundamental question of the idea of a 'transfer of claims'. A commentary as presented above shall elucidate this

[63] cf. the commentary by F. Mazza on Art. 9.1.1 PICC in S. Vogenauer and J. Kleinheisterkamp (eds.), *Commentary on the UNIDROIT Principles of International Commercial Contracts* (PICC) (2009).

highly metaphorical idea from a historical and comparative perspective and thus clarify its meaning.

Now, the idea of a transfer of obligations is not a necessary or natural element of legal systems. Roman jurists as well as medieval civilians and English common lawyers started from the opposite assumption that an obligation was a highly personal relation binding the debtor to the creditor by means of a legal bond (*vinculum iuris*). For those jurists, it was obvious that obligations could not be transferred to a third person.[64] The closest equivalent to assignments under Roman law was hence the *procuratio in rem suam*; here, the creditor of a claim authorised a *procurator* to sue the debtor in the name of the creditor.[65] Nevertheless, the idea of a transfer of obligations has become part of the common conceptual heritage of European private law. It emerged when lawyers conceptualised obligations as property rights (*dominium*) and thus constructed assignments of claims in analogy to transfers of (other) property rights.[66] Today elements of this conception are established in all European legal systems.[67] Its use in the international instruments' definition therefore seems to be unproblematic; why bother about it?

The reason is the many problems connected with this idea. Thus, the concept of a 'transfer' seems to be stretched over its limits as far as assignments of future claims are concerned: How could one 'transfer' a 'thing' which does not yet exist? But the possibility of assigning future rights is a central policy of international and European contract law; modern forms of receivables financing would simply be impossible if future claims could not be assigned.[68] More importantly, the proprietary allusions of this idea of a transfer of claims seem to tie with one another the effects of an assignment between the parties and *vis-à-vis* the debtor

[64] Zimmermann, *Obligations*, 58–67; F. Schulz, *Classical Roman Law* (1951) 628; H. Kötz, in *International Encyclopedia of Comparative Law* (*IECL*), chapter VII-13, [61] f.

[65] Gaius, Inst. 2.39; cf. also Gaius, Inst. 4.83 f. As a consequence, the 'assignor' remained in the position of the creditor; he could therefore revoke the authorization (Paulus D. 3.3.16) or require performance to himself; see Schulz, *Classical Roman Law*, 626 f.; Zimmermann, *Obligations*, 60 f.

[66] See, very clearly, S. Pufendorf, *De iure naturae et gentium libri octo* (cum integris commentariis *Io Nic Hertii* atque *Io Barbeyraci*, Frankfurt/Leipzig 1759), lib IV, cap IX, § 2; C. Wolff, *Institutiones iuris naturae et gentium* (Halle 1750) § 338; cf. already L. Lessius, *De iustitia et iure* (Paris 1618), lib. II, cap. III, dub. II, n. 16.

[67] *IECL* VII-13/Kötz [58].

[68] See Art. 5 Factoring Convention; Art. 8 (1) CARIT; Art. 9.1.5 PICC; Art. 11:102 (2) PECL; Art. III.-5:106 (1) DCFR.

and other third parties. Yet, from a functional perspective, it is not obvious why the transfer of an item of wealth between the assignor and the assignee should be parallelised with the effects of this transfer against third parties and in particular with the substitution of creditors.[69] In this respect, the international authorities opted for different, innovative rules, according to which the agreement between the assignor and the assignee does not as such effect a genuine transfer of the obligation or of any other item of wealth, but rather 'vests in the assignee a power to effect substitution of the creditor'.[70] The assignee can thus acquire the obligation by giving notice to the debtor in case the assignor does not. If the debtor, after the assignment, performs his obligation towards the assignor, he will be discharged as long as he has not received notice of the assignment.[71] The assignee has a claim for those proceeds against the assignor;[72] yet the assignment does not give to the assignee an equitable right in the proceeds.

This international model of assignment is in accordance with most civilian legal systems,[73] though not with the common law.[74] Under

[69] On what follows, see G. Lubbe, 'Assignment', in H. MacQueen and R. Zimmermann, *European Contract Law: Scots and South African Perspectives* (2006), 307–330, 312–321. Some legal systems, in particular Nordic countries, have replaced the traditional 'unitary' approach to the passing of ownership with such a 'functional', fragmentary approach. For a critical evaluation of advantages and disadvantages of this approach, cf. L. van Vliet, 'Acquisition and Loss of Ownership of Goods – Book VIII of the Draft Common Frame of Reference', (2011) *ZEuP* 292–334, 293 f.

[70] Lubbe, 'Assignment', 327; cf. also P. Nienaber and G. Gretton, 'Assignation/Cession', in R. Zimmermann, D. Visser, and K. Reid (eds.), *Mixed Legal Systems in Comparative Perspective* (2005), 787–818, 790 f, 796; *MaxEuP*/H. Kötz, 'Assignment', 76, describing the 'effects of assignment' as an entitlement of the assignee against the assignor 'to deliver to him all documents evidencing the debt assigned and provide the information needed for its collection'. See also UNCITRAL, *Legislative Guide*, Recommendations 115 and 119.

[71] Art. 9.1.10 PICC; Art. 17 (1) and (2) CARIT; Art. 11:303 (1) and (4) PECL; Art. III.-5:119 DCFR.

[72] Art. 14 CARIT; Art. 9.1.15 PICC. cf. also Art. 11:203 PECL; Bazinas, 'Key Policy Issues', 289. In the DCFR, the issue is relegated to the law of unjustified enrichment; see Art. III.-5:122, Comment.

[73] Under German law, the assignee has in such a case a claim against the assignor under § 816 (2) BGB, which does not, however, automatically enjoy priority in insolvency proceedings; §§ 47, 51 no. 1 German Statute on insolvency (*Insolvenzordnung*) gives priority to the assignee, yet only in cases where the debtor paid after insolvency and into a clearly separable account; see *Münchener Kommentar HGB*/C Schmidt (2009), § 354a HGB, [27].

[74] Under English law, equitable assignments do not require a notice given to the debtor to become effective. If a debtor after the agreement between assignor and assignee, but before receiving a notice, pays to the assignor, it seems 'beyond doubt' that the assignor

international law, there is no serious authority for the assignment as such to vest the assignee with anything like an equitable right. Only Art. III.-5:122 DCFR provides for a kind of constructive trust.[75] Furthermore, the 'transfer' of an obligation by assignment does not by itself make the assignee the owner of an asset which could be attached by his or her creditors; in this respect the international and European model rules depart quite significantly from what is normally assumed in most legal systems. Despite the definition of assignments as 'transfers', international law treats this proprietary aspect of assignment as a different matter to be regulated elsewhere – either in a different provision or by national laws.[76] The prevailing view is that the effect of an assignment *vis-à-vis* the debtor depends on the latter's notification,[77] and that other third-party effects should be regulated on the basis of a public filing system.[78] To establish such a public system, however, is an issue for future legislation.

Summing up, it must be concluded, contrary to what the PICC's official commentary suggests and what is hence assumed by some writers,[79] that the 'transfer' does *not* leave 'the assignor's assets to become

holds the money on constructive trust for the assignee; see *GE Crane Pty Ltd* v *Federal Commissioner of Taxation* (1971) 126 CLR 177 (High Court of Australia); R. Goode, 'Contractual prohibitions against assignment', (2009) *Lloyd's Maritime and Commercial Law Quarterly* 300–318, 306; M. Smith and N. Leslie, *The Law of Assignment* (2nd edn., 2013), [26.14]. cf. also *Barclays Bank Plc v Willowbrook International* [1987] Butterworth Company Law Cases 717.

[75] Art. III.-5:122 DCFR. Quite strangely, however, the DCFR bases its rule not on common law authority; the Notes rather refer to Art. 24 CARIT (Art. III.-5:122, Note 2 DCFR; cf. also Art. III.-5:108, Comment B) DCFR. But this norm gives priority to the assignee only in cases where the parties have agreed upon the assignor receiving payment on trust for the assignee.

[76] See Art. 11:202 (1), 11:401 (3), (4) PECL. The CARIT does not regulate priority conflicts between the assignee and other creditors of the assignor (Art. 4 (5) (ii)); neither do the PICC; see Art. 9.1.1, Comment 4 PICC; M.J. Bonell, 'Unidroit Principles 2004: The New Edition of the Principles of International Commercial Contracts adopted by the International Institute for the Unification of Private Law', (2004) *ULR* 5–40, 25.

[77] See reference above, n. 71.

[78] See UNCITRAL, *Legislative Guide*, Recommendations 1 (f) and 54–76; Kötz, *Contract Law*, 275 f.; cf. Eidenmüller, 'Dogmatik der Zession', 477–479. For the American filing system (based on Art. 9 UCC), which has become a model for modern filing systems, see H.C. Sigman, 'Security in movables in the United States – Uniform Commercial Code Article 9: a basis for comparison', in E.-M. Kieninger (ed.), *Security Rights in Movable Property in European Private Law* (2004), 54–80, 59, 76–78.

[79] cf., e.g., C. Rudolf, *Einheitsrecht für internationale Forderungsabtretungen: UN-Abtretungsübereinkommen, UNIDROIT-Factoringübereinkommen, PECL, UNIDROIT-Principles* (2006), 55–57: 'Wechsel der Rechtszuständigkeit'; see also 217 f. on the PECL and PICC.

part of those of the assignee'.[80] In the context of international and European law of assignment, 'transfer' is a very innovative, highly technical concept which must be constructed independently of the national laws' metaphorical allusions of a transfer of ownership.

What can be learned methodologically from this analysis?

(1) It is possible and indeed helpful to develop a European private law doctrine on the basis of quite different and diverging international instruments. The European legislature may then rely on concepts coined on the basis of the emerging European legal doctrine. For instance, there *is* a European concept of assignment emerging in the present discussions of European contract law even though there is no European legislation on receivables financing.

(2) New European concepts may significantly differ from the inherited concepts in national legal systems. However, new European concepts should not be introduced as a scholar's arbitrary invention; rather they have to be based on European and international authorities. It follows that such concepts may give expression to policies, which a scholar does not need to share from a moral or political point of view, but which jurists accept as the basis of modern international law.

Thus, the new European concept of assignment differs significantly from the inherited concepts in most national legal systems. The European concept of assignment favours the interests of financial markets more than the rules of many national legal systems.

(3) Traditional commentaries refer exegetically to a legislative authority; they interpret the provisions of a codification and present also relevant judge-made law as an interpretation in this sense. European private law cannot in the same sense be based on a single reference text. Rather, modern European scholarship has to find the law on the basis of a critical comparison of a number of authorities. Such a comparison has to reconstruct the genetic relationship of the different rules in question; thereby, it has to take into account the regulatory assumptions underlying those texts. It is hence necessary to take a more distant approach to those authorities.

[80] Art. 9.1.1, Comment 3 PICC; Vogenauer and Kleinheisterkamp/Mazza, Art. 9.1.1, [3] f. cf. also Art. 9.1.14 (a) PICC. The official comment 1 to this provision makes clear, however, that it does not concern the time at which the transfer becomes effective (contract of assignment or notice), but rather the 'scope of the assignment', i.e., the question, which rights under the contract are ultimately transferred to the assignee.

(4) Historical analysis may help to free modern concepts from historical burdens.[81] Often, the historical and comparative analysis will reveal that modern instruments rely on terms that are inherited from the national laws' traditions. Such terms may be burdened with conceptual implications or metaphorical allusions, however, which fit in badly with modern regulation. Conceptual implications and metaphorical allusions of this sort are particularly problematic in times when legislatures hope to avoid misunderstanding by exactly defining basic concepts and yet face difficulties to leave behind the conceptual heritage of the European private law tradition.

Thus, the international instruments' rules on the effects of assignments of claims appear to be much more innovative than their rather naïve legislative definitions of 'assignments'. Basic elements of this definition were coined in natural-law discussions when jurists conceived of claims as items of property. But this conception does not fit in well with the modern international laws' functional conception of assignments.

(5) European legal scholarship may identify the limits of present European contract law and thus raise important questions for future development.

For example, there is no international authority, yet, according to which the assignment would vest in the assignee an equitable right in the proceedings. Why this should be so, however, is not obvious. Scholars and legislatures are invited to think about such a right.

6.4.2 *Developing a New Rule: The Debtor's Additional Costs*

According to Art. 9.1.8 PICC, '(t)he obligor has a right to be compensated by the assignor or the assignee for any additional costs caused by the assignment'. It seems that this provision is a generalisation of Art. 11:306 PECL (= Art. III.-5:117 DCFR), according to which 'the assignor is liable to the debtor for any increased costs which the debtor incurs by reason of any change in the place of performance', and of Art. 11:103 PECL, according to which the assignor is liable to the debtor for any increased costs which the debtor incurs as a result of a partial assignments (very similar is Art. III.-5:107 (3) DCFR).

[81] See Jansen, '"Brunnen der Vergangenheit"'.

These provisions are quite remarkable for a variety of reasons: In particular, there seems to be only a weak comparative basis in national laws for these rules. In fact, only § 270 (3) German *Bürgerliches Gesetzbuch* (BGB) and § 3 (3) Danish *Gjeldbrevlov* (Promissory Notes Act, 1939) provide for rules that resemble Art. 11:306 PECL;[82] and there is no similar national rule in national laws for partial assignments.[83] Similarly, convention law is silent as far as such a claim for recovery of costs is concerned.[84] Nonetheless, it would be wrong to conclude that this provision should not be regarded as an expression of European private law. There *is* a lot of authority that allows for partial assignments[85] and regards assignment as effective even though they result in a change of the place of performance.[86] Both those rules are

82 The Notes to Art. 11:306 PECL moreover refer to Dutch law. Dutch law, however, does *not* provide for a claim for increased cost; rather the debtor may withhold payment until a more appropriate place has been chosen, if as a consequence of the change of place of payment 'the performance of the obligation would become considerably more onerous': Art. 6:117 BW; see L.P.W. van Vliet, in D. Busch, E. Hondius, H. van Kooten, and H. Schelhaas (eds.), *The Principles of European Contract Law (Part III) and Dutch Law: A Commentary* II (2006), 119 f. (also for the translation).

83 No references in the Notes to Art. 11:103 PECL and Art. III.–5:107 DCFR.

84 The Notes to Art. 11:306 PECL allege the CISG as authority for their rule; yet under the CISG, it is disputed whether the provision on a change of the seller's place can be applied analogously to cases of assignment of claims for payment. Here, however, the question is not whether the solution under Art. 57 (2) CISG seems appropriate, but rather, whether this question is to be determined by the law applicable to the assignment; see, for this position F. Mohs, in I. Schwenzer (ed.), *Schlechtriem and Schwenzer: Commentary on the UN Convention on the International Sale of Goods (CISG)* (3rd edn., 2005), Art. 57 [21]. The prevailing opinion, however, holds that the decisive arguments can be found, as general principles, in the CISG itself; a recourse to the otherwise applicable law is hence unnecessary; see O.L.G. Celle, *CISG-online* 507 (11.11.1998); *Münchener Kommentar*; and P. Huber (2012) Art. 57 CISG, [23]; *Staudinger*/Magnus (2013), Art. 57 CISG, [18] with a comprehensive overview of the discussion.

85 See Art. 9.1.4 PICC; Art. 8 (1) CARIT; further Art. 11:103 PECL; Art. III.-5:107 DCFR; UNCITRAL, 'Explanatory note by the UNCITRAL secretariat on the United Nations Convention on the Assignment of Receivables in International Trade', in: *United Nations Convention on the Assignment of Receivables in International Trade* (2004; www.uncitral.org/uncitral/en/uncitral_texts/security/2001Convention_receivables.html), 27–45, [9], [40]. Most national legal systems tend to allow for partial assignments, though not without reluctance; see *IECL* VII-13/Kötz [72]; *Jauernig*/Stürner, § 398, [12]; J.M. Milo, in Busch, Hondius, van Kooten, Schelhaas, and Schrama, *Dutch Law* II, 87 f.; Sigman, Garcimartín, and Heredia Cervantes, 'Comparative Analysis', 252; Smith and Leslie, *Assignment* [16.21]–[16.23], [21.37]–[21.39]; Nienaber and Gretton, 'Assignation/ Cession', 807–809.

86 Under most legal systems, however, the debtor cannot be obliged to make performance in a different country; Art. 15 (2)(b) CARIT (= UNCITRAL, *Legislative Guide*,

difficult to explain, however, on the basis of the traditional idea of a transfer of claims. According to this idea, the assignment *cannot* modify the debtor's obligation as the assignment is a transfer of an (incorporeal) thing. It seems to follow that neither partial assignments nor assignments resulting in a new place of performance should be possible. Where national doctrinal literature discusses partial assignments or the change of place of performance, writers therefore describe these cases as exceptions to the basic rule without providing for an explanation of these exceptions, however.[87] The reason is obvious: Partial assignments and even changes of the place of payment cannot be explained on the basis of prevailing doctrinal assumptions. Nevertheless, modern receivables financing would be impossible if debtors could not be asked to make payment at a different place; and partial assignments of claims for money are a common practice in many countries. Lawyers tend to avoid questions to which no convincing answer is visible.

European private law allows for a fresh look at these problems from a new, less conceptual and more functional point of view. From this perspective, there is no good reason anymore why assignments should not modify the obligation. In fact, a change of place of payment occurs regularly, where monetary claims are assigned. The problem is no longer a conceptual difficulty, but rather the normative question of the limits of acceptable modifications. It is not surprising, therefore, that the differences between the PECL's and the PICC's rules and the Illustrations given for those rules primarily concern this question. Moreover, the idea to allow for a modification of the debtor's obligation, as long as possible disadvantages on the debtor's side can easily be compensated, quite obviously overcomes the limits of the traditional approach. Under national legal systems, it was not possible to address directly the interests involved. European doctrinal scholarship will have to develop this rule in more detail; in particular, scholars will have to explore whether there are convincing criteria to draw a boundary between acceptable – if compensated – and inacceptable modifications of the rule. Arguments for this question can arguably be found in other

Recommendation 117 (b)(ii)) provides an apt restatement of European law: "A payment instruction may change the person, address or account to which the debtor is required to make payment, but may not change . . . The State specified in the original contract in which payment is to be made to a State other than that in which the debtor is located."

87 cf. *Münchener Kommentar*/G.H. Roth (2007) § 398, [93]; van Vliet, in Busch, Hondius, van Kooten, Schelhaas, and Schrama, *Dutch Law* II (n 82) 119 f.

international rules on assignment; yet this is not the place for those issues.[88] The question is rather, again, the methodological assumptions implied in such an approach to European scholarship.

(6) European private law doctrine is not in the same way determined by its conceptual heritage as the private-law doctrines in many national legal systems. This does not mean, however, that European scholarship may be less exact; to the contrary: One of the most important tasks of our time is to sharpen the conceptual tools of European private law. This type of scholarship may often help to identify blind spots in traditional private-law doctrine.

6.4.3 *Rejecting a New Rule: Unauthorised Modifications of the Contract*

It was a well-established, fundamental principle of European law that debtors, who are bound by notice of the assignment, have to make performance to the assignee and can no longer renegotiate the agreement with the original creditors: 'The basic rule is that after the debtor's notice of the assignment he and the assignor can do nothing to prejudice the assignee's rights.'[89] In Europe, this rule applies without exceptions; and it has been confirmed also by recent legislation on receivables financing.[90] Indeed, it is so basic that most authorities do not even state it explicitly. Nevertheless, Art. 11:308 PECL adds an 'interesting exception to this rule',[91] which is based on US authority (§ 9-405 UCC) and on Art. 20 (2)(b) CARIT:

> **Art. 11:308 PECL: Unauthorised Modification Not Binding on Assignee:** A modification of the claim made by agreement between the assignor and the debtor, without the consent of the assignee, after a notice of assignment, whether or not conforming to Article 11:303 (1), reaches the debtor does not affect the rights of the assignee against the debtor unless the modification is provided for in the assignment agreement or is one which is made in good faith and is of a nature to which the assignee could not reasonably object.

[88] See my comments on this rule; forthcoming.

[89] *IECL* VII-13/Kötz [95]; see also the Note to Art. PECL 11:308.

[90] See, as an example, Art. L313-27 (2) French Code monétaire et financier.

[91] *IECL* VII-13/Kötz [95].

This latter exception seems to be quite plausible in view of the fact that readjustments of commercial contracts may sometimes indeed be reasonable. Under a construction contract, it is not unusual that such adjustments are even necessary, in view of unexpected circumstances, to continue the performance of the contract. Nonetheless it is doubtful, whether this exception should be stated as a good rule of European law. It is backed by no further international or European authority;[92] and the rule makes sense only if the assignor's right to payment 'has not been fully earned by performance'.[93] In such a situation, a reasonable renegotiation of the contract will usually be – and under the respective provisions has to be! – in the interest of the assignee as well who would otherwise have to expect the debtor rescind the contract in future. Also the advocates of this rule admit that the assignee's consent will normally not be difficult to obtain.[94] Moreover, the parties to the assignment are of course competent to grant to the assignor a power to modify the contract. Thus, a rule such as Art. 11:308 PECL makes courts decide about an issue which would better be provided for by the parties to the assignment; as a result, it weakens the assignee's position in negotiations, where he disapproves of the modification of the claim by the parties to the contract. It seems that weightier arguments would be necessary to impose upon new creditors a nonconsented modification of their contract and their claims.

Why should a European commentary recognise this rule – or why should it not do so? The reason cannot be found on the basis of policy considerations alone; otherwise, every solution will seem arbitrary in view of contravening pros and cons. Law is more than practical argument: it is practical argument based on authorities. Hence, a basic methodological principle applies:

[92] But see Art. III.-5:112 (4) DCFR addressing the issue in the context of the assignor's undertakings. It does not make sense, however, to allow the assignor to modify the contract without also granting to the assignor a legal power to do so. See Eidenmüller, Faust, Grigoleit, Jansen, Wagner, and Zimmermann, 'Policy Choices', 688.

[93] § 9-405 (b)(1) UCC; similarly Art. 20 (2)(b) CARIT.

[94] *IECL* VII-13/Kötz, [95]. But see Art. 11:204 PECL, Comment E: 'commercial inconvenience'; similarly Eidenmüller, 'Dogmatik der Zession', 486 f.; cf. also Eidenmüller, Faust, Grigoleit, Jansen, Wagner, and Zimmermann, 'Policy Choices', 687 f. But the existence of transaction costs alone is no sufficient argument to dispense with the other party's consent; otherwise, it is not clear why the debtor should negotiate the modification with the assignor rather than decide about it on a discretionary basis.

(7) In cases, in which European legal systems are based on similar principles, recognition of an innovative rule requires arguments of considerable authority.

Of course, this rule cannot mean that European scholars should count authorities – there are two international authorities (PICC and PECL) on the rule for a claim for additional costs and two (PECL and CARIT) on the rule for unauthorised modifications. The question whether there is sufficient authority for a rule may often require legal argument. A comparison between the rule on unauthorised modifications and the rule on additional costs (see Section 6.4.2) may illustrate the difference: Both rules likewise seem to be highly innovative. Yet, the rule on additional costs resulting from the assignment relates to a blind spot in many legal systems, in which partial assignments and assignments resulting in a change of the place of performance have long become a daily practice. Despite its innovative nature, this rule does hence find a basis in national laws. No such authority exists, however, for the rule on unauthorised modifications of contracts. It is based on policies, which are not acknowledged in any European legal system. Scholars may well argue that such a rule should be introduced for reasons of public policy or because of economic consideration. They should not pretend, however, that such a rule adequately depicts European law.

6.5 Conclusion

The purpose of this chapter is to illustrate, by way of example, the historical and comparative method that seems appropriate when developing elements of European legal doctrine on the basis of a plurality of diverging non-legislative authorities. This method makes it possible to describe principles of European private law doctrine even if there are no binding rules yet.

It has become apparent that the methodological issues involved in the making of European private law doctrine are quite different from those of most other sciences. They involve a commitment to the making of European private law. And they involve the recognition of authorities that are not yet firmly established. European scholars do not only make European contract law, but moreover contribute to the recognition of authorities in this field of law. This does not categorically distinguish European legal doctrine from other forms of doctrinal scholarship: There is no European legal system working without informal authorities. Yet, it cannot and should not be denied that the landscape of European authorities is still being formed. Its contours are not as clearly fixed as those of most national legal systems; hence European scholarship significantly contributes to the making of legal authorities in this field of the law. The important point is to make those methodological decisions transparent and to show that they are all based on plausible, convincing argument.

At the same time, it has been seen that the making of European contract law requires new methods as explained above. Most importantly, European jurists have to take a more constructive approach to legal doctrine. Of course, most national civil-law theory is formulated, today, within the framework of a codification and established doctrine. It is hence *applicative* in that it is meant to apply and further develop a legislative framework. Hence, it must be based primarily on conceptual argument and logical deduction. European legal doctrine, in contrast, is predominantly *constructive*.[95] Scholars are called upon to design new categories and concepts and make explicit the underlying values and policies. Yet, they should do so as jurists, rather than as legislatures: they have to reconstruct, rather than simply create, a new European law; hence, they have to base doctrinal argument on established rules and authorities. Altogether, this approach may be described in the form of the seven propositions which have been stated above:

(1) It is possible and indeed helpful to develop a European private law doctrine on the basis of quite different and diverging international instruments. The European legislature may then rely on concepts coined on the basis of the emerging European legal doctrine.
(2) New European concepts may significantly differ from the inherited concepts in national legal systems. However, new European concepts should not be introduced as a scholar's arbitrary invention; rather they have to be based on European and international authorities. It follows that such concepts may give expression to policies, which a scholar does not need to share from a moral or political point of view, but which jurists accept as the basis of modern international law.
(3) Traditional commentaries refer exegetically to a legislative authority; they interpret the provisions of a codification and present also relevant judge-made law as an interpretation in this sense. European private law cannot in the same sense be based on a single reference text. Rather, modern European scholarship has to find the law on the

[95] See for this distinction Jansen, '"Brunnen der Vergangenheit"', 223–227.

basis of a critical comparison of a number of authorities. Such a comparison has to reconstruct the genetic relationship of the different rules in question; thereby, it has to take into account the regulatory assumptions underlying those texts. It is hence necessary to take a more distant approach to those authorities.

(4) Historical analysis may help to free modern concepts from historical burdens.[96] Often, the historical and comparative analysis will reveal that modern instruments rely on terms that are inherited from the national laws' traditions. Such terms may be burdened with conceptual implications or metaphorical allusions, however, which fit in badly with modern regulation. Conceptual implications and metaphorical allusions of this sort are particularly problematic in times when legislatures hope to avoid misunderstanding by exactly defining basic concepts and yet face difficulties to leave behind the conceptual heritage of the European private law tradition.

(5) European legal scholarship may identify the limits of present European contract law and thus raise important questions for future development.

(6) European private law doctrine is not in the same way determined by its conceptual heritage as the private-law doctrines in many national legal systems. This does not mean, however, that European scholarship may be less exact; to the contrary: One of the most important tasks of our time is to sharpen the conceptual tools of European private law. This type of scholarship may often help to identify blind spots in traditional private-law doctrine.

(7) In cases in which European legal systems are based on similar principles, recognition of an innovative rule requires arguments of considerable authority.

[96] See Jansen, '"Brunnen der Vergangenheit"'.

7

A European Advantage in Legal Scholarship?

HANS-W. MICKLITZ*

'To put it provocatively: the continental European approach to law is an epistemological anachronism while US-American jurisprudence has moved on to the present' (M. Reimann, 2014 p. 33).

'Europe is a success story. Why is it not told? Why are Europeans so defensive? Why are they not proud of their achievements?' (Barry Eichengreen, lecture at the European University Institute)[1]

7.1 The Contribution of European Legal Scholarship

In the thirteenth Ernst Rabel lecture 2012, M. Reimann stressed the 'American Advantage in Global Lawyering'.[2] His argument is that continental legal systems in Europe remain bound to a classical understanding evinced through national uniformity, systematic structure, clear demarcations, authoritative rules, autonomous law and law as decision-making rules. The American advantage in global lawyering is said to result from, first, conceptions of law and the realities of transnational practice (handling pluralism, tolerating incoherence, working with fuzzy categories, using rules in multiple ways, employing law for policy goals and creating solutions for concrete problems) and, second, from operating in the digital world (Westlaw and Lexis). Reimann leaves unexplored possible advantages of 'the classical approach's superior ability to maintain order, clarity and certainty in the law'.[3]

* The research leading to these results has received funding from the European Research Council under the European Union's Seventh Framework Programme (FP/2007–2013) / ERC Grant Agreement n. [269722].

[1] Based on B. Eichengreen, *The European Economy since 1945: Coordinated Capitalism and Beyond*, Princeton University Press, 2008. I remember neither the exact words nor the exact date, but it must have been around 2010. But I took notes.

[2] M. Reimann, 'The American Advantage in Global Lawyering, Dreizehnte Ernst-Rabel-Vorlesung', 78 *RabelsZ* 2012, 2–36.

[3] Reimann, 'The American Advantage', 36.

Taking seriously the consequence of his findings would trigger the need for a different kind of legal education, a different kind of legal methodology and a different kind of legal scholarship. As I share most of his findings, I will not try to defend the 'continental advantage' or engage into an analysis of the common law as a potential bridge between the American and the continental way of global lawyering. However, my argument is that Reimann overlooks the changes which have occurred in the European legal order and which might serve as an object of legal scholarship and as a blueprint for comparing EU and US law in what he terms 'global lawyering'. In this sense, his view on the American advantage is incomplete. Whether or not there is an American advantage in global lawyering should include a close analysis of the European Union, of EU law and of EU legal scholarship. I would go so far as to state that the European legal order can be understood, today more than ever, as a 'laboratory'.[4] Due to its openness and its incomplete – perhaps never to be completed – federal structure, the European Union, EU law and EU legal scholarship could serve as a counterpart to the American advantage, apt to trigger a mutual learning process as to the advantages and disadvantages of a distinct American and European style of what Reimann calls 'global lawyering'. One might ask whether the European advantage is a current reality or a promising potential. Its potential lies in the disclosure of its reality, but this requires a different view on Europe, one which changes perspective. Such a perspective would focus on the achievements of this unique construct called the European Union which is not a state, which more than likely will never be a state or a federation of states in the Westphalian sense, but which is at the same time much more than an international organisation.

Therefore, my intention is to demonstrate where the European legal order offers perspectives for a postclassical order, a perspective that requires a particular form and understanding of European legal scholarship. In this sense, Reimann's paper and his forceful critique of the dominant 'epistemological anachronism' in the continental European

[4] This term was already used by M. Cappelletti in M. Cappelletti, M. Seccombe and J.H.H. Weiler, 'Integration Through Law: Europe and the American Federal Experience' in M. Cappelletti, M. Seccombe and J.H.H. Weiler (eds.), *Integration Through Law*, de Gruyter, 1986, vol. 1, Book 1, at 10 (with a view to future progress); H.-W. Micklitz, 'The European Union Project', in J. Dickson/P. Eleftheriadis (eds.), *The Philosophical Foundations of European Union Law*, Oxford University Press, 2013, 538–554. In the US context see Brandeis's dissent on the states as laboratories: *New State Ice Co. v. Liebmann*, 285 U.S. 262, 52 S.Ct. 371, 76 L.Ed. 747 (1932), http://biotech.law.lsu.edu/cases/pp/new_state_ice.htm.

approach serve as a starting point for a debate which would require, in a second step, a clarification of what global lawyering means and what the yardstick of comparison between the two legal orders should be. Global lawyering refers to legal practice: to what law firms around the world are doing and to the role of dispute settlement in arbitral bodies outside courts. The question would then be whether the European legal order and European legal scholarship properly understood could compete with the American advantage. For the time being, my objective is more modest; this chapter places emphasis on the postclassical character of the European legal order and the type of scholarship it requires to disclose that particular European, although largely neglected, advantage. It is this 'success story' (Barry Eichengreen) which has to be retold through the lenses of law and legal scholarship.

I subscribe to most elements of the postclassical conception of law. In fact most of my writings in the last years on the European legal order in general and the European private legal order in particular could be grouped around the categories Reimann uses to identify the postclassical character of European law. Unity in European law is not possible. European law remains fragmentary.[5] The doctrines of supremacy and direct affect have their limits. European law is not a 'system' in the traditional sense of a coherent and pyramid-like state-made legal order.[6] On the contrary, European law is constantly blurring categories and questions rules and Member State practices.[7] This is done through the autonomous interpretation of its foundational rules. The search for 'autonomy' implies two things: the need for disconnecting from traditional meanings of law in the Member States and the attempt of European identity-building. However, this does not mean that EU law is institutionally autonomous because it has to rely on national law for gap-filling purposes and on national institutions for its implementation and enforcement. Moreover, it seems as if the European Union is gradually turning into an institution builder outside the Treaty, via

[5] Th. Wilhelmsson, 'Private Law in the EU: Harmonised or Fragmented Harmonisation', 10 *European Review of Private Law* 2002, 77.

[6] I deliberately avoid speaking of a European legal system; see for the difference the discussion between J. Dickson and K. Cutler, M. Giudice in J. Dickson and P. Eleftheriadis (eds.), *The Philosophical Foundations of European Union Law*, Oxford University Press, 2013, at 25, respectively at 54.

[7] On rationalisation see Ch. Joerges, 'The Europeanisation of Private Law as a Rationalisation Process and as a Contest of Legal Disciplines – an Analysis of the Directive on Unfair Terms in Consumer Contracts', 3 *European Review of Private Law* 1995, 175–192.

agentification[8] and via out-of-court settlement mechanisms.[9] European law more than any other national continental law is multilayered; it is law in a constant and dynamic process, developing via legislation, the European Commission and European agencies. Herein lies a resemblance to the common law. The flow of the European Court of Justice (ECJ) judgements provides ample evidence for the capacity of the European legal order to generate new principles, new remedies and emphasise diverse values.[10]

However, is there a downside in the move from classical to postclassical law, a downside and disadvantage detrimental for 'law'? R. Dworkin[11] drew the attention of legal scholarship to the fragile 'integrity of the law'. Reimann highlights the instrumentalisation of American law, which he regards as a strength and constitutive element of the postclassical American legal order.[12] His analysis goes hand in hand with D. Kennedy[13] who explains the American instrumentalism through the paradoxical strong belief *and* the strong distrust of American society in law. When it comes to instrumentalisation of law for political purposes, alarm bells are ringing in continental Europe, in particular in Germany. This might be due to the legacy in Europe of the traumatic experience of fascism. Yet the whole integration process of the European Union is characterised by the instrumentalisation of law, visible in the European Union in the sheer quantity of rules, first with regard to the Internal Market and now aimed at building a Banking Union.[14] It might well be that the deep cultural

8 M. Scholten/M.v.Rijsbergen, 'The Limits of Agentification in the European Union', 15 *German Law Journal* 2014, 1123.

9 Alternative dispute resolution (ADR) and online dispute resolution (ODR) are a new institutional layer of enforcement; H. Eidenmüller and M. Engel, 'Against False Settlement: Designing Efficient Consumer Rights Enforcement Systems in Europe', 29 *Ohio State Journal on Dispute Resolution* 2014, 261; G. Rühl, 'Die Richtlinie über alternative Streitbeilegung: Handlungsperspektiven und Handlungsoptionen', 127 *Zeitschrift für Zivilprozess* 2014, 61; R. Caponi, 'Just Settlement of Just About Settlement? Mediated Agreements: A Comparative Overview of the Basics', 79 *RabelsZeitschrift* 2015, 117.

10 T. Tridimas, *The General Principles of European Law*, 2nd edn., Oxford University Press, 2006; N. Reich, *General Principles of EU Civil Law*, Intersentia, 2014.

11 R. Dworkin, 'Law as Integrity, Law's Empire', 1986, http://theoryofjurisprudence.blogspot.it/2007/12/ronald-dworkin-law-as-integrity.html; see also L. Fuller, '8 desiderata in the Morality of the Law', 1964.

12 Reimann, 'The American Advantage', 13.

13 D. Kennedy, 'The Paradox of American Critical Legalism', 3 *European Law Journal* 1997, 359–377.

14 H.-W. Micklitz, 'The Internal Market and the Banking Union', on file with the author, to be published in St. Grundmann and H.-W. Micklitz (eds.), *The European Banking Union*

resistance against the politicisation of the law hindered European legal scholarship to realise the liberating effect that results from instrumentalisation. Perhaps this is what Reimann has in mind when he refers to the 'epistemological anachronism' (a highfaluting circumscription of continental legal positivism) of the continental European approach. The herd behaviour in European legal scholarship, the unquestioned preparedness to follow the changing integration paradigms of the European Union, however, is much more apt to enhance old European fears than to expose the promising reality and potential of the European legal order as a postclassical exercise.[15]

Two remarks might help to understand the different attitudes towards instrumentalisation of the law. The United States benefits from 200 years of federal experiences. It is an established federal state. All the phenomena that are characteristic for the move from classical to postclassical law in the United States occurred within a closed system. The European Union, however, is not even sixty years old, it is not a federation and its future is uncertain, especially in the current stage of crisis with respect to the problems of the Eurozone, the handling of the problem of migration and the separate status that certain EU Member States seem to strive for. Europe is at the very best to be understood as a constitution in the making, as a constant open-ended process.[16] The second remark concerns the different approaches in legal scholarship. In the United States the politicisation and instrumentalisation of law throughout the last century has been accompanied by an equally strong deep-going academic debate on the chances and risks of such a use of law. There is no (not yet) such forceful counterpart in European legal scholarship that might compensate for the potential risks that lie in the instrumentalisation of law. Pushing the European advantage entails the need to revitalise the critical tradition in European legal scholarship; this means a more encompassing reflection on law, examining its interdisciplinary embeddedness.

Why has European legal scholarship never gained the necessary intellectual distance to the European integration project and why it has

and Constitution Beacon for Advanced Integration or Death-Knell for Democracy, Hart Publishing, 2016.

[15] See my analysis in R. van Gestel and H.-W. Micklitz, 'Revitalising Doctrinal Legal Research in Europe: What About Methodology?', in U. Neergard and R. Nielsen (eds.), *European Legal Method – Paradoxes and Revitalisation*, 2011, in particular pages 35–56.

[16] Most outspoken for more than twenty years now is Ch. Joerges, 'What Is Left of the European Economic Constitution? A Melancholic Eulogy', 30 *European Law Review* 2005, 461–489, inspired by F. Hayek, N. Luhmann and G. Teubner.

become much easier for European legal scholarship to take such a distance today? The 'spiritual dimension' (Azoulai) of the self-explaining and self-legitimising integration project might help us to understand the reluctance in European legal scholarship. For nearly five decades the instrumentalisation of law served a double purpose: law was turned into a tool to achieve and promote integration (the surface level) and law was meant to support European identity-building (the foundational level).[17] The self-explanatory and self-legitimising purpose of an ever-deeper 'integration', however, has been put into question,[18] long before the UK referendum of 23 June 2016 or the Greek referendum of 5 July 2015, most visibly through the French and the Dutch referenda against the European Constitution in 2005. The shaky foundations of building a political transnational community through and with the help of 'law' were brought to public attention across Europe by these events. It is now back on the agenda. The future of Europe will largely depend on whether Europe can define its identity outside and beyond the 'ever-deeper integration' paradigm since it is becoming increasingly clear that a growing number of Member States do not want an ever-deeper integration at this stage. Turning the unstable political situation into an intellectual opportunity means focusing on the achievements of European integration and to highlight – not to hide – the consequences of the fading of the vision that ever-closer integration will one day almost naturally lead to 'the United States of Europe'. It is only through such a shift in perspective that the European advantage can be given shape and focus.

In sum: in the United States the instrumentalisation of the law does not need legitimacy beyond its use as a tool embedded in the US constitution (surface level); in Europe, instrumentalisation of the law necessarily cuts the boundaries of the open-ended constitution and reaches the

[17] See for the attempts of the ECJ to build a European identity and a European Society through the preliminary reference procedure, G. Comandé, 'The Fifth European Union Freedom: Aggregating Citizenship. . .around Private Law', in H.-W. Micklitz (ed.), *Constitutionalisation of European Private Law*, Oxford University Press, 2014, 61–101; K. Carr, Regulating the Periphery – Shaking the Core, European Identity Building through the Lenses of Private Law, MS 2015 on file with the author (to be published as an EUI-ERC Working Paper 2015).

[18] JHH Weiler, 'Deciphering the Political and Legal DNA of European Integration: An Exploratory Essay', in J. Dickson and P. Eleftheriadis (eds.), *Philosophical Foundations of European Union Law*, Oxford University Press, 2012, 137–158. See also N. Walker, 'After finalité? The Future of the European Constitutional Idea', EUI Working Paper, LAW No. 2007/16.

political community. There are two lessons to be drawn from the differences in the move from classical to postclassical law in the United States versus the European Union. First, the instrumentalisation of law in the United States does not touch upon the political community, at least not as directly as in the European Union. Market (private ordering) and state (legal intervention for policy purposes) are treated as separated,[19] whereas in the European Union, such a homogenous socioeconomic and political setting is not present and is, therefore, subject to political contestation. Second, the double instrumentalisation of law (promoting integration and building a European identity) could be regarded as an opportunity for European legal scholarship to engage into how global lawyering should and must look like in a transnational legal order beyond the boundaries of a nation-state. The underlying assumption of the European advantage is that the European use of law as an instrument and the instrumental use of the law on a global level are somehow comparable, at least in the sense that the European legal order might provide input into the debate on 'transnational law'. However, in the following section I will limit myself to develop the argument of the 'European advantage'. I will, in a second step, and another publication, link the European advantage to the blossoming, but nevertheless stagnant, discussion on transnational law.

7.2 European Integration and the Role of Law

I will place emphasis on European legal scholarship and its socioeconomic and sociopolitical context, on the role of legal research and the methods legal research applied in promoting European integration during the first five years of European integration. There is no sharp line between EU law, EU legal scholarship and EU legal methodology, primarily owing to differing understandings on what EU law stands for, what legal scholarship encompasses and what legal methodology means. In the idea of the European advantage, all three merge into a European approach to postclassical law. It is here where the potential lies for developing a European way of global lawyering and of competing with the American advantage. This process documents the European move towards a postclassical conception in European law. It is not my

[19] I will not go into the debate in the United States on the role of the federal government and its intervention in the market versus market individualism, which is a huge political debate dividing right and left, leading to 'culture wars'.

intention to reiterate what has been written on the genuine character of the European legal order. Quite to the contrary, I take it for granted that the esteemed reader enjoys a basic understanding of the particularities of the European Union and of the role of law in the European integration process. The genealogy of the European Union could be reconstructed around the interplay of 'integration' and 'law'. Walter Hallstein famously and influentially stated in 1969: 'The European Community is a remarkable legal phenomenon. It is a creation of law; it is a source of law; and it is a legal system'.[20] There is a direct line from Walter Hallstein to the formula Mauro Cappelletti, Monica Seccombe and Joseph H. H. Weiler so powerfully coined in their vast project on *Integration Through Law: Europe and the American Federal Experience.*[21] This project took a comparative stance, and the idea was to engage in a mutual learning process by using the United States as a blueprint and benchmark for the federalisation of Europe. It was 'revisited' in 2012 by Augenstein[22] and 'rethought' in 2014 by way of a conference organised by the European University Institute and the University of Florence on 'The Heritage of Mauro Cappelletti'.[23] The overall conclusion seems to be that the European Union suffers from a lack of 'orientation'.

What matters is the politics behind the formula of 'integration through law' and its connection to European legal scholarship. Three stages could be distinguished, each of them will be analysed in light of 'the integration through law paradigm' and the variations it had to undergo in the last sixty years due to the changing economic, social and political environment. Each of them affected EU law, European legal scholarship and European legal methodology, and each stage constituted a further building block in the development of a genuine postclassical understanding of European law. What ties the different stages of integration together is the approach, at first rather cautious but then stronger, to liberate the European legal order from its 'epistemological anachronism'.

[20] W. Hallstein, *Europe in the Making* (originally published in German under the title *Der unvollendete Bundesstaat, ECON 1969*), George Allen & Unwin Ltd., 1972, 30.

[21] Cappelletti, Seccombe and Weiler, 'Integration Through Law', Book 1, at 4; hereinafter 'ITL'.

[22] D. Augenstein (ed.), *'Integration through Law' Revisited. The Making of the European Polity*, Ashgate, 2012.

[23] L. Azoulai gave a keynote speech, titled 'Integration through Law and US', published in ICON 2015. The special issue also covered a selected number of papers presented. All papers are published by the University of Florence in Italian.

The 'integration through law' formula reached its peak in the 1986 project on the completion of the Internal Market, which was to be achieved through 'regulation'. Correctly speaking, the Internal Market project should be equated with 'integration through regulation'. The argument is that the first four decades helped to establish the European legal order and yielded European legal scholarship, largely distinct from national legal scholarship, questioning the classical in the continental European tradition and laying the foundations for the postclassical move. It turned out to be an instrumental result-orientated ex post legitimating scholarship, in the main championed by pro-European lawyers and a pro-European legal community meant to justify and to promote integration through competition and regulation (market regulation and social regulation).[24] This explains the lack of intellectual distance between European law and European law scholarship. Europe and European integration were regarded not only by European scholars as 'good', a promising exercise to overcome the legacy of the world wars. Needless to say, the move towards politicisation of the law through its instrumental use raised much concern in the classicist community of national continental lawyers – not from a theoretical or even a philosophical point of view, but from the proclaimed fear that too much regulatory intervention would jeopardise the economic constitution of Europe.[25]

The next move occurred around the millennium and can be captured by the formula 'integration without law' or less provocative 'integration through governance', enshrined and condensed in the 2002 White Paper on Governance.[26] European legal scholarship had to open its doors towards political science. Political science placed emphasis on the multi-level governance structure of the European Union.[27] The link towards federalism is obvious but the emphasis shifted from the 'constitutional

[24] A. Vauchez, *Brokering Europe, Euro-Layers and the Making of a Transnational Polity*, Cambridge University Press, 2015.

[25] See E.-J. Mestmäcker, 'Auf dem Wege zu einer Ordnungspolitik für Europa', in E.-J. Mestmäcker, H. Möller and H.P. Schwartz (eds.), *Eine Ordnungspolitik für Europ:. Festschrift für Hans v.d. Groeben*, Nomos-Verlagsgesellschaft, 1987, 9–49, in the aftermath of the adoption of the Single European Act (not available in English); twenty years later in opposition against two grand projects, the European Constitution and the Civil Code. Interestingly enough the French voted against the Constitution and raised the most outspoken critique against the European Civil Code project.

[26] Ch. Joerges, 'Integration durch Entrechtlichung? Ein Zwischenruf', *ZERP-Diskussions*, papier 1, 2007.

[27] M. Dawson, *New Governance and the Transformation of European Law: Coordinating EU Social Law and Policy*, Cambridge University Press, 2011.

architecture of the EU' (the federalist outlook) to the 'administrative structure' (multilevel governance).[28] In the aftermath of integration through governance, legal scholarly research lost its monopoly on drafting and shaping forward-looking market and social regulation. The potential impact of new market and social regulation had to be tested against the EU governance structure. In essence, the two forms of integration existed side-by-side: integration through law (through regulation) and regulation without law (through new modes of governance). European legal scholarship had to learn the lesson of the 'law and . . .' saga and the nonexistence of clear-cut legal boxes; however, not in form of sociolegal research run by legal sociologists, which left room for all the intricacies of legal complexity, but through the broad brush of political scientists that successfully set the different boxes of classical national traditions to one side, thereby delivering the most interesting research on law and legal institutions. This is the moment where the consensus among European scholars for the European integration project began to fall apart. The result was a divided intellectual community, divided into the 'sceptics' and the 'believers'.

This is not yet the end of the 'integration through or without law' saga. Less visible at the turn of the millennium, but stronger since 2000, are two new paradigms that gained ground in European integration: economic efficiency and fundamental/human rights. They are tentatively caught in the 'integration beyond law' formula. Both parameters had a strong impact on European legal scholarship, and both initiated and promoted a transnationalisation of European law. I understand them as the European variant of 'global lawyering'. The first – economic efficiency – brought law and economics, institutional economics and behavioural economics to the European forum.[29] Whilst the intellectual origins go back to World War II, economic efficiency had difficulties gaining ground in national politics beyond the United States and the United Kingdom because of its perceived neoliberal orientation.[30] For the first time, European legal scholarship is obliged to take account of the three

[28] On the administrative state see Chapter 8 in this volume.

[29] See on the origins of the three different strains St. Grundmann, Kapitel 3. Privatrecht und (Institutionen-) Ökonomik, in Mit Stefan Grundmann, Moritz Renner, Autoren und Herausgeber, Privatrechtstheorie 2 Bände, Mohr Siebeck, 2015, 167.

[30] The move has been strongly criticised as being neoliberal and downgrading, if not eliminating, matters of social justice, e.g., W. Streeck, 'The Crises of Democratic Capitalism', 71 *New Left Review* 2011, 5; F.W. Scharpf, 'The Eurocrisis as a Victory of Neoliberalism?', in J.E. Fossum and A.J. Menéndez (eds.), *The European Union in Crises or the*

approaches of economic efficiency (law and economics, institutional economics and behavioural economics) and to critically reflect on, in particular, the success and failures of the Internal Market project. The rise of behavioural economics in both the United States and the European Union allows scholars to link the current discourse back to socio-legal research undertaken in the 1970s and 1980s. The second paradigm is more familiar to European legal scholarship. Constitutionalisation of the European legal order through fundamental and human rights provides for a comfortable escape route for European legal scholarship to avoid the transatlantic, or better the global, irritations resulting from the overall rise of economics and of economic thinking, of the economisation of law. There is a lot of ambivalence in the European legal scholarship that focuses on fundamental rights and human rights, in that constitutionalisation entails the risk to fall back to a classical understanding and to set aside the transnational dimension of constitutionalisation. It is classical in its often very doctrinal outlook; it is postclassical in its instrumental approach and its transborder dimension. This will have to be shown later.

The move to efficiency and constitutionalisation, from inward looking to outward looking, from the building of a genuine Internal Market to a European polity that is recognised in the outside world,[31] added economics to European scholarly research and the overall debate on transnational law,[32] as to whether and to what extent the European legal order is, and remains, distinct from transnational law despite the institutional change (efficiency and constitutionalisation) it is suggested EU law has undergone. In less ambitious language one might say that the human rights turn in EU legal scholarship has emphasised the transnational outward looking focus of European legal scholars, the turn from Internal Market thinking towards the European Union as a global market

European Union as Crises? ARENA Report Series 2, ARENA, Centre for European Studies University of Oslo, 2014, 143–154.

[31] See the new research on *Europe in the World*, Robert Schuman Centre for Advanced Studies, European University Institute, run by U. Krötz.

[32] It is difficult to mention even a list of the key books. My own view on the different approaches is laid down in *Cahier à Thème, Les Grandes Théories du Droit Transnational*, with contibutions from K. Tuori, B. Kingsbury, N. Krisch, R.B. Stewart, H. Muir Watt, Ch. Joerges, F. Roedel, F. Cafaggi, R. Zimmermann, G.-P. Calliess, M. Renner, A. Fischer-Lescano, G. Teubner and P. Schiff Berman, Revue Internationale de Droit Economique 2013, 1–2, 1–256.

player and an international polity.[33] We move away from politics to the abstractions of 'rights' because this 'conceals' the political, where there is sharp division as to values. The same argument can be made for economic reasoning, which tends to obscure value choices as to distributions and turns potentially political questions into ones about consumer choice – i.e., let the market decide. If reflected in scholarship, this is symptomatic of sharp disagreements as to the ends we want to achieve, so we retreat into language that avoids or conceals discussions as to ends.

7.3 European Legal Scholarship: Revitalising Critical Legal Thinking

A clarification on the meaning of the European dimension in legal scholarship is needed. Reimann uses European legal scholarship as a term which designates Europe as contrary to the United States. In this sense European legal scholarship might be both: national legal scholarship from within Europe or European legal scholarship, and legal scholarship that focuses on the European legal order and on European law. Quite often the two perspectives are not clearly enough separated. National European legal scholarship might be classical or postclassical; the same is true for European law scholarship. I identify the European advantage in European law scholarship, which I equate with postclassical, and national European legal scholarship, which I equate with classical. Maybe an example is needed to clarify what I mean. The European constitution or the European Civil Code could be studied through the lenses of the national constitution or the national codification. The consequences of such an approach are well known, and they are condensed in the proclaimed democratic deficit or the incoherent and unsystematic European private law. The perspective I prefer is to use is the newness of the European legal order, both in its 'constitutional' and in its 'private law' dimension. Whilst such a distinction might sound simplistic and overstated, the confrontation helps to focus on the particularities of the European legal order which yield, or are about to yield, the 'European advantage'. In the following, I will build on the distinction, introduced earlier, between the surface and the foundational level of the instrumentalisation of EU law, to show the type of question European

[33] G. Majone, *Europe as the Would-be World Power: The EU at Fifty*, Cambridge University Press, 2009; W. van Gerven, Cover of The European Union by Walter van Gerven, The European Union A Polity of States and Peoples, 2005.

legal scholarship has to raise to be able to exploit its advantages. The surface level stands for the unquestioned use of law for whatever political purpose, and the foundational is being equated with raising deeper and more far-going questions on the role and function of law.

In the United States, legal scholarship has strongly promoted and supported the shift from classical to postclassical law through legal realism and the 'law and ...' movement.[34] This is at least how I understand Reimann's analysis of the American advantage. Continental legal scholarship remained bound, by and large, to the classical categories despite the irritations brought about in the aftermath of the 1968 revolution/*révolte* and despite all the Europeanisation rhetoric that could have paved the way for a deeper reflection, whereas the US law schools with the Ivy League universities to the forefront accelerated the move from classical to postclassical up to a point where US practitioners, judges and lawyers voiced strong critique against the legal education in US top law schools.[35] This is not the correct occasion to discuss whether the critique is right or wrong. In defence of US legal scholarship, I would argue that a postclassical conception of 'law' – not only of American law or European law or continental law or common law, but of law *per se* – requires a strong and deep multitheoretical and multiphilosophical (political and moral philosophy) education which empowers the law student to master fragmentation, incoherence, opaque legal categories and the enormous amount of rules (public in statutory acts and international conventions, private ordering and hybrid forms of rules). What is needed in addition, however, is a legal methodology that allows the postclassical lawyer to bring down big theories to concrete cases, rules, and regulations[36]: as Ludwig von Wittgenstein wrote, '*Recht ist alles, was Fall ist*' ('Right is everything that is the case').

National European legal scholarship has not yet reached that stage. The European continental legal systems remain unaffected, by and large, by US developments. In 2012, the German *Wissenschaftsrat* strongly criticised German legal education for not taking the postclassical move

[34] V. Nourse and G. Shaffer, Varieties of New Legal Realism: Can A New World Order Prompt a New Legal Theory?, *Cornell Law Review* 95 (2009), 61–139.

[35] See for a European view on this development R. Van Gestel, 'Evaluating Legal Research, About the Good, the Bad and the Ugly', in T. Tanquerel and A. Flückiger (eds.) *Assessing research in law: Stakes and methods*, Bruylant, 2015, 27–55.

[36] H.-W. Micklitz, 'An Essay on the Bifurcation of Legal Education - National vs Transnational', in R. Huang (ed.) *Legal Education in the Global Context: Opportunities and Challenges*, Ashgate, 2015.

into consideration and putting more emphasis on deeper theoretical and philosophical questions behind the law,[37] with little consequences on the curricula so far. There are but a few universities in Europe where similar phenomena as in the United States can be observed – i.e., a certain disconnection from legal practice.[38] The Universities of Tilburg and Maastricht offer genuinely European undergraduate studies. The European University Institute provides for a doctoral programme in a genuinely European environment. The disconnection results in Maastricht and Tilburg from the missing foundation of the legal education in one particular national legal system and consequently an uncertainty in how to apply the law (which law) to concrete cases. At the European University Institute, the vast majority of researchers are grounded in their national legal tradition. However, they are gradually disconnected from their home countries, mainly through the strong emphasis on the European and international legal order backed through legal theory and legal philosophy. That is why it does not suffice to start a methodology debate in Europe with what separates legal scholars from practitioners. In light of the extremely heterogeneous legal landscape in the European Union, there is more to be taken into account because EU law is, like 'global law', something more than, and something different from, state-made law or classical international public law.

The genuine European 'scholarly deficit' is different and it cuts across the few institutions that offer genuinely European education and the vast majority of national institutions focusing on the classical conception of law. I see it in the focus and often limitation on the surface level, whilst downplaying or simply neglecting the foundational level. All too often European legal scholarship simply follows the 'trials and tribulations' of the changing European integration paradigms, here presented through integration through law, integration without law and integration beyond law. The critical thinking of the 1970s did not find its way into European legal scholarship. This attitude produces shortcomings at the two levels of instrumentalisation: there is not enough emphasis on whether and to what extent the policy paradigms can be made compatible with the

[37] Perspektiven der Rechtswissenschaft in Deutschland. Situation, Analysen, Empfehlungen, www.wissenschaftsrat.de/download/archiv/2558-12.pdf.

[38] There have even been some scholarly writings on how to develop European education. See, e.g., Jan Smits, 'European Legal Education: How to Prepare Students for Global Citizenship', http://papers.ssrn.com/sol3/papers.cfm?abstract_id=1719118 slightly biased in favour of how it is done in Maastricht though.

existing legal order (surface) and, secondly, there is not enough theory which would allow for testing the implicit assumptions behind the policy paradigms and the research which follows suit to forge a European identity (foundational). This deficiency and the lack of distinction between the two levels unfortunately results in a lot of 'wishful thinking', 'advocacy' and often unconscious 'ideology' that has little to do with critical legal scholarship.

Are we asking the right questions in regards of disclosing the European advantage in legal scholarship?[39] Are we too much focusing on the surface level which entails the risk to fall back to legal thinking in classical categories? What sort of new ideas, perspectives, theories and methods can legal scholars generate if they do not simply follow law and policy makers but think about why EU law is developing as it did and does over the last fifty-eight years and why law is so heavily instrumentalised at the EU level, and what it implies with regard to the move from classical to postclassical? But is what is useful also true? Is that the zeitgeist?[40] Interesting questions emerge in that case. They may have a surface as well as a foundational dimension. What exactly is the relationship between law, legal research and European integration? What is the role of law and how is the role of law changing within and over time in the three paradigms? Why is European legal research so overwhelmingly policy driven? Why is there no 'halt', no moment of rethinking, just moving and moving towards an ever-closer Union without knowing what that could, or perhaps should, mean? Why are there so many implicit assumptions in scholarly legal publications, such as: harmonisation of laws is good and legal diversity is bad (or vice versa); fundamental and human rights are a blessing for EU law but economic rights are a curse; consulting stakeholders over new EU laws and policies is right but listening to lobbyists is wrong; statutory (EU) legislation is superior to biased co-regulation, which does not take stakeholders into account; transparency in decision making is good, secrecy bad; and so on. Is it not an important academic responsibility for legal scholars studying EU law to test these implicit assumptions instead of taking them for granted?

[39] L. Vicente and H.-W. Micklitz (eds.), 'Interdisciplinary Research: Are We Asking the Right Questions in Legal Research?', EUI LAW Working Paper 2015/04.

[40] This comes close to the definition of science by the German Constitutional Court that defines science as: 'serious and systematic attempt to gain new insights capable of' external review and criticism, 'and guided by the regulative ideal of truth'. See BVerfG 35, 79/113 (2004) and BVerfG 90, 1 (13/14).

Again, it seems as if there is a difference between the United States and the European Union. In the United States the postclassical move is deeply embedded into theoretical and philosophical training which works as a shield against dominating ideologies, perhaps not in the short run, as the rise of the efficiency doctrine demonstrates, but in the long run and in the fierce debate between the different camps. The reason might be that law is, predominantly, an undergraduate course in Europe. The European focus is narrow as lawyers, and the Europeans lack the tools of other disciplines.

In the last couple of years the European market for academic legal books and law journals is flooded with contributions on legal methodology, not necessarily on a European legal methodology.[41] What does the rise of legal methodology contribute to the postclassical challenge? The projects sailing under that flag range far and wide, from more theoretical conceptual reflections on whether law is a science and, if so, what kind of science and where has it be grounded in humanities and/or in social science,[42] to the influence of law and economics on legal doctrine[43] and the new wave on comparative law[44] towards *Gesetzgebungslehre*,[45] the art of legislation.[46] This is indicative because not even in Europe – or even narrower, not even in continental Europe – does a common understanding of what might be meant by legal methodology

[41] There are exceptions; see the special issues in 209 *Archiv für Civilistische Praxis* 1 (2009); K. Riesenhuber, *Riesenhuber, Europäische Methodenlehre, Handbuch für Ausbildung und Praxis, Methodenfragen des Europarechts - für Ausbildung und Praxis* (3rd edn.), C.H. Beck, 2014.

[42] M. van Hoecke (ed.), *Methodologies of Legal Research: Which Kind of Method for What Kind of Discipline*, Hart, 2011; J. Smits, *The Mind and Method of the Legal Academic*, Edward Elgar, 2012; R. van Gestel and H.-W. Micklitz, 'Why Methods Matter in European Legal Scholarship', 20 *European Law Journal* 2014, 292–316.

[43] Today, mainly law and economics, behavioral economics; in the 1970s, sociolegal research. See, for instance, T. Ulen, 'A Nobel Prize in Legal Science: Theory, Empirical Work, and the Scientific Method in the Study of Law', 4 *U. Ill. L. Rev.* 2002, 875.

[44] M. Siems, *Comparative Law*, Cambridge University Press, 2014; M. Adams and D. Heirbaut (eds.), *The Method and Culture of Comparative Law, Essays in Honour of Marc van Hoecke*, Hart Publishing, 2014.

[45] G.F. Schuppert, *Governance und Rechtsetzung, Grundfragen einer modernen Regelungswissenschaft*, Nomos, 2010; H.-P. Schwintowski, 'denn sie wissen nicht, was sie tun!- Warum Politik und Gesetzgebung so oft irren. Ein Plädoyer für die Neue Analytische Regelungswissenschaft', NAWI, Nomos, 2015.

[46] S. Emenegger, *Gesetzgebungskunst: Gute Gesetzgebung als Gegenstand einer legislativen Methodenbewegung in der Rechtswissenschaft um 1900 - Zur Geschichte der Gesetzgebungslehre (Grundlagen Der Rechtswissenschaft)*, Mohr Siebeck, 2006.

exist. The stream of publications seem to be guided by a common message: by the search for 'appropriate tools' that allow lawyers to handle the postclassical challenge. This is, of course, my interpretation. Usually, the authors do not openly address the postclassical challenge. Instead, they unfold the broad range of 'law and disciplines', law and sociology, law and social sciences, law and economics in all variations, and comparative law. I cannot see any other explanation for the rise of legal methodology than deep irritation on the future positioning of 'law' in democratic societies. Most of the publications point in that direction, so far with little or no impact on legal education. There are few voices who openly address the postclassical move and defend the role and place of doctrinal research. J. Smits belongs to them. In his book on 'the Mind and the Method of the Legal Academic' he pleas for legal scholarship that maintains its (normative) identity vis-à-vis neighbouring disciplines.[47]

It looks as if there is too much surface level and not enough foundational scholarship. Where has the academic tradition gone in Europe that led scholarly research and legal scholarship to discuss and reveal the relationship between '*Vorverständnis und Methodenwahl*' – between preconception and choice of legal methods – as developed by Josef Esser more than forty years ago, whose work on this subject has unfortunately never been translated into English.[48] Josef Esser's work is paradigmatic of a particular 'Zeitgeist'[49] that questioned the 'apolitical' character of law. He stands for a series of academics worldwide in the late 1960s and early 1970s who highlighted that law and legal systems cannot be disconnected from all sorts of implicit preconceptions that determine ones perspective, including, e.g., the prevalence of Western democracy over any other political system; the need to guarantee private property; to secure freedom of contract; and to maintain personal responsibility. These theorists did not advocate for a particular role that law and the legal function should meet. But they require us to draw a clear distinction between the surface and the foundational level and to review and discuss constantly the interlink between the two. They left us with a strong message

[47] Smits, *The Mind and Method.*

[48] J. Esser, *Vorverständnis und Methodenwahl in der Rechtsfindung*, 1972, but it has been translated into Italian.

[49] G.W.F. Hegel, *Vorlesungen über die Philosophie der Geschich*te, Band 18, Frankfurt am Main, 1979.

succinctly encapsulated by the 'poet of the tramps', William Henry Davies:[50]

> What is this life if, full of care, We have no time to *stand and stare*, A poor life this, if full of care, We have no time to *stand and stare*. (emphasis added)

The challenge to stand and stare requires self-reflection and self-control of the premises from which we start our research activities. This does not only mean to defend the identity of legal scholarship as an autonomous discipline. Methodology can assist in getting a hold of one's own preconceptions, by challenging us to make our implicit (assumptions) explicit, by raising awareness such that do not only look for confirmation of what we (unconsciously) expect to be the outcome of the research, and by warning us to keep an open eye for alternative explanations and counterevidence.

Disclosing preconceptions does not mean to limit oneself to doctrinal research. However, it means to reexamine and relocate the role and function of doctrinal research in a postnational environment. There is no way back from postclassical to classical, from postnation-state to nation-state, independent from the fate of the European Union even after a Grexit and/or a Brexit. Although it seems as if not only politicians and men and women on the Clapham omnibus (the men and women in the streets),[51] but also legal scholars like to turn the clock back to what A. Somek calls constitutionalism 1.0, stressing the superiority of the 'good old 19th or early 20th century democracy' over the messy and opaque 'cosmopolitan constitutionalism 3.0'.[52] The European Union and the European legal order, as long as it exists and in all probability

[50] 1871–1940; I borrowed this wonderful metaphor from our colleague Roger Brownsword, who used the poem as a paradigm for what he misses in the current debate on the theoretical foundations of European private law; see R. Brownsword, The Theoretical Foundations of European Private Law: A Time to Stand and Stare in R. Brownsword, H.-W. Micklitz, L. Niglia and St. Weatherill (eds.), *The Foundations of European Private Law*, Hart Publishing, 2011, 159–176.

[51] See the wonderful note of A. MacPherson and R. Zimmermann, 'The Clapham Omnibus – Revisted', *Zeitschrift für Europäisches Privatrecht* 2015, 685.

[52] Alexander Somek, *The Cosmopolitan Constitution*, Oxford University Press, 2014, reviewed by D. Patterson, 'The Dark Future of Constitutionalism', *Constitutional Commentary* 2015, http://papers.ssrn.com/sol3/papers.cfm?abstract_id=2580783; the same melancholic undertone is in Luigi Corrias, Opinion, Between Grexit and Utopia: EU Legal Theory in the Mirror of los indignados, 44 *Netherlands Journal of Legal Philosophy* 2015, 1–7.

even beyond, will continue to serve as the perfect laboratory not only for global lawyering, or maybe for lawyering beyond the nation-state, but also, in particular, for studying the impact and effect of the instrumentalisation of law for political purposes, for using law as a substitute for the political (*das Politische*).[53] Therefore, the European Union could and should serve as a blueprint to study the inherent political deficits of a transnational legal order.[54] The transnational community has produced an enormous amount of rules to justify and to legitimate transnational law. However, transnational law suffers from a lack of a political community that ties law to 'the people (a demos)'.[55] This is exactly the problem of the European Union since the beginning – its lack of democratic legitimacy. The history of the European Union and EU law could be read as a story on the search for legitimacy. One might therefore study the European Union as a blueprint for the future of the transnational legal order, in which the transformation of the nation-state can be studied in a nutshell.[56] Nearly sixty years provide for solid material. In simple terms: European legal integration has moved faster than the building of European citizenship, a European polity, and a European identity. This experience, the constant confrontation between the differentiated pace of development and the lessons that the European Union learnt over time in its constant fight to close that gap is the still largely 'undiscovered treasure chest' of EU law that could enrich legal scholarship. And this is what I dare to call the 'European advantage'.

7.4 The (Missed) European Potential and the Need for its Rediscovery

The genuine European contribution to the postclassical instrumentalisation of the law, and the possible distortions it might entail, differs in its origin from the much earlier and much deeper move in the American legal system. It needed the failure of the two grand projects – the European Constitution and the European Civil Code – to open space

[53] The long shadow of Carl Schmitt can still be felt.

[54] J. Zeitlin (ed.), *Extending Experimentalist Governance? The European Union and Transnational Regulation*, Oxford University Press, 2015.

[55] See Azoulai, 'Integration through Law and US'.

[56] H.-W. Micklitz and D. Patterson, 'From the Nation State to the Market State: The Evolution of EU Private Law, EUI Working Paper 2012/15', in B. van Vooren, St. Blockmans and J. Wouters (eds.), *The EU's Role in Global Governance: The Legal Dimension*, Oxford University Press, 2013, 59–78.

to view the European Union as a *postclassical* legal order, an order which cannot be caught in either constitutional language along the line of nineteenth century nation-state building or in nineteenth century civil code building in continental Europe.

M. Reimann provides two reasons as to why American law is ahead of the European Union:[57] (1) 'dumb luck' – the advantage of global lawyering fell into the American lap – and (2) much deeper and much more sophisticated, the move from classical to postclassical law, which is claimed to be in harmony with broader intellectual trends. The continental European tradition is still deeply rooted in universalism and rationalism which stands behind the classical concept of law and which goes back to scientific and philosophical developments from the seventeenth century onwards. In this intellectual climate, knowledge is objective, absolute, universal and consistent. Over the twentieth century this conception of knowledge was overtaken in natural science through Einstein and Heisenberg,[58] and in philosophy through Nietzsche and Heidegger. Knowledge is not hierarchical, is the result of flat networks. In law this is best presented, according to Reimann, by Sousa Santos[59] who denies the existence of one objective truth (or law) and instead advocates for pluralism of competing orders and values. It is in this context where Reimann coins the rather provocative statement on the anachronistic character of continental legal tradition, quoted at the beginning of this chapter.

The cracks in the classical continental systems were visible and voiced before World War I and even more forcefully in the twenty years between the two world wars. Raymond Aron, the French sociologist, and Fritz Stern, the great legal historian agreed in a public debate held in 1979 that at the turn of the twentieth century one could have expected that Germany would leave its footprint on the twentieth century, though not through two world wars.[60] This would have implied that Germany

[57] Reimann, 'The American Advantage', 32–33.

[58] H.-P. Dürr (ed.), *Physik und Transparenz, Die Großen Physiker unserer Zeit über ihre Begegnung mit dem Wunderbaren*, with Beiträgen von D. Bohm, N. Bohr, M. Born, A. Einstein, W. Heisenberg, P. Jordan, W. Pauli, M. Planck, E. Schrödinger, C.F. v. Weizsäcker, Scherz Verlag, 1st edn. 1986, quoted from the 2010 edn.

[59] Buonaventura de Sousa Santos, 'A Map of Misreading: Toward a Postmodern Conception of Law', 14 *Journal of Law and Society* 1987, 279–299.

[60] Eberhard Jäckel: Das deutsche Jahrhundert. Eine historische Bilanz. Deutsche Verlags-Anstalt, Stuttgart 1996: Rezension, www.faz.net/aktuell/feuilleton/politik/rezension-sachbuch-wem-gehoert-das-jahrhundert-11304465.html. Why this title ('The German Century')? The book starts with a conversation between Raymond Aron, a French sociologist who had studied in Germany, and the American historian Fritz Stern, who was born in

might and could have been at the forefront of the move from the classical to the postclassical law. Indeed, Reimann's references to key figures in natural sciences and philosophy seem to be in line with the statement. Two tentative remarks may be allowed. Taking Germany as paradigmatic for the development in other continental European legal systems, it seems safe to argue that the subterranean and surface cracks in the classical tradition, exploded by 1968, shattered the classical continental legal tradition – but did not lead to its collapse. The move from the classical to the postclassical occurred silently and less dramatically via and through the building of Europe – through law (and regulation). The second remark has to be treated with even greater caution. Udi Greenberg[61] has shown how the ideas of the Weimar Republic travelled to the United States and influenced the ideological foundations of the Cold War. The mostly Jewish emigrants who left Germany early enough and ended up in US universities have left their traces in the American legal system and might have contributed to, and accelerated, the development of the postclassical legal system in the US. Simply look at Hermann Kantorowicz's influence on empirical legal realism, Fritz Kessler's on freedom of contract[62] or Julius Stone's on legal education in Australia.

Europe and European legal scholarship did not reconnect to the early beginnings of the postclassical move after World War II. In the search for a European future, Europe looked into its past, into the deeper cultural foundations that united the legal systems not only of the continent but also of the common law. One might term this a form of revitalisation of the classical understanding. Franz Wieacker's work *Voraussetzungen*

Wroclaw but was expelled from his home already in the 1930s. Aron observed melancholically that the twentieth century could have been Germany's century. Stern agreed with him: in the modern history of Europe there was always just one country – first Spain, then France, then the Netherlands, then the United Kingdom – that did not only rule over a period, but shaped it: 'Hence, one could have expected, in the beginning of the century, that Germany would take such a supreme role.' Jäckel continues by saying that the title of his book is not a contradiction: 'It was the German century. No other country put its mark on Europe and the world so deeply in the 20th century like Germany did.' (translated from the original text by myself)

61 U. Greenberg, *The Weimar Century, German Émigrés and the Ideological Foundations of the Cold War*, Princeton University Press, 2014.

62 Ch. Joerges, 'Demos vs. Ethnos in Private Law: Friedrich Kessler and his German Heritage', 104 *Yale L. J.* 1995, 2137; although Kessler was not a pioneer here. The assault on the classical was already underway from Holmes; see B. Leiter, Holmes, *Nietzsche and Classical Realism*, U Texas School of Law Pub., Law Working Paper No. 003 available at http://papers.ssrn.com/sol3/papers.cfm?abstract_id=215193, who calls the affinities between Holmes and Nietzsche 'classical realism'.

europäischer Rechtskultur (Foundations of European Legal Culture)[63] sums up many decades of research condensed in his masterpiece: *Privatrechtsgeschichte der Neuzeit* (History of Private Law in the Modern Age)[64] focuses on a common European legal culture. The title implies a community of Europe with roots in history and in law. Thus, Wieacker adheres to the tradition of *ius commune*, to a concept of law uniting legal history and comparative law – in the European legal culture. On the occasion of the 28th German Historians' Day, Reinhard Zimmermann made a powerful plea for the importance of the *ius commune* as a basis and source of knowledge of European private law, codified in continental law *and* common law:[65] 'In defiance of all differences of modern legal dogmatics, European contract law is at the end of the day from the same mould. Over centuries lawyers have worked/operated on the basis of the same rules, institutions and ways of thinking, and everywhere the profession has been shaped by the same values and philosophical currents . . . England has to be considered as a part of Europe as well.'[66]

The community of European culture represents the deeper foundation for European integration, as stated briefly and convincingly in the Schumann Declaration of 9 May 1950.[67] J. H. H. Weiler describes the political and cultural conviction behind the Declaration as 'European messianism',[68] as an attempt to strongly recall both pillars of the European civilisation after the disaster of World War II: 'the enlightenment and the heritage of the French Revolution and European Christian tradition'.[69] The grounding in the common past, the century old European culture, helped Europe to overcome the trauma of two world wars, to build an Internal Market, and to invent the language of an ever-deeper

[63] Publisher Göttinger Tageblatt, 1985, translated into English by Edgar Bodenheimer with the title 'Foundations of European Legal Culture', 38 *The American Journal of Comparative law* 1990, 1–29. The quotes of the text derive from the English and not from the German version.

[64] Translated by Tony Weir.

[65] 'Heard melodies are sweet, but those unheard are sweeter.' Condicio tacita, implied conditions und die Fortbildung des europäischen Vertragsrechts, Archiv für civilistische 193 Praxis 1993, 121.

[66] 'Heard melodies', 173.

[67] http://europa.eu/about-eu/basic-information/symbols/europe-day/schuman-declaration/index_de.htm.

[68] J.H.H. Weiler, 'Deciphering the Political and Legal DNA of European Integration: An Exploratory Essay', in J. Dickson and P. Eleftheriadis (eds.), *Philosophical Foundations of European Union Law*, 2012, 137, 151.

[69] Weiler, 'Deciphering the Political and Legal DNA', 147.

integration, and it fits the European nationalist tradition of creation myths. The culmination of this backward-looking perspective to shape the future was the project to build a European Constitution after the fall of the Berlin Wall in 1989 and, not for all, but for many private lawyers the European Civil Code project in the first decade of the new millennium. This is backward-looking to the 'classical' as the model of the legal order is taken from the nation-state – Europe as federation, a United States of Europe, private law as codified law in the continental tradition. Both projects therefore form building blocks of a 'European State'.

I certainly do not insinuate that there was no resistance against the unidirectional move throughout the last sixty years, in particular against a European Constitution or even more so against a European Civil Code. The resistance unites very different strains of debates – political, legal and theoretical ones – covering a broad range of positions from left to right. The purpose of this contribution, however, is to show and to disclose the postclassical in the European legal order. Such an exercise refers back Josef Esser's plea and steps back from political and policy trends; in a way, it is also a plea to revitalise critical legal thought in the best tradition of the European and the American 'left'. Such an exercise is not possible without generalisations. The rest of the chapter is built in the following way. First, I will discuss/examine the deadlock which the European legal scholarship has reached, gaining more and more distance from questioning the role and function of legal scholarship and following, instead, the mainstream ideology: the strive for European integration, overusing and overemphasising the role and function of law. Second, this kind of stock taking serves as a bridge to what is the real concern of this chapter, to analyse and to reconstruct in the three waves of integration through law, without law and beyond law what I believe should be recognised as the European potential to contribute to the postclassical legal order. My intention is to identify in each of the waves a particular set of postclassical elements – more or less visible, more or less contradictory – which drawn together demonstrate the gradual liberation of the classical approach and might hopefully attract the attention of US legal scholarship.

7.5 The Instrumental Use of Law: Stuck in Transition

The instrumentalisation of law for political purposes in the European Union that unites so much of today's legal scholarship is somehow related to the developments that occurred in and around 1968, the year of what the French call a 'revolution', the Germans remember as a '*Studentenrevolte*' (the revolt of the students), and the Dutch associate with the '*opstand van arbeiders en studenten*' (the riot of workers and students). The events of May 1968 initiated a change in the way the law was perceived not only in states where political turmoil led to visible changes, but even more so, in Europe and the European Union.[70] What happened is that European legal scholarship, in the slipstream of law and policy makers, gradually drifted away from a critical 'stand and stare approach' of Esser and others and slowly became more engaged with the idea that law is a political project and a vehicle for social and societal change. For legislatures all over Europe, the latter resulted in a shift from *codification* (capturing in laws what grew bottom-up from society) towards *modification* of human and corporate behaviour (legislation as a policy instrument).[71] It soon became clear, though, that it is impossible to steer a highly complex society with a rational, central rule approach and detailed instructions.[72] As a consequence, legislatures started to leave the judiciary with more and more discretion by reverting to open texture, legal principles and delegation of lawmaking powers to the executive. Some have even argued that Montesquieu's concept of the *Trias Politica* transformed into a *Duas Politica* in which the executive and the judiciary took over much of the power of the legislature resulting in a more partial and policy-orientated way of lawmaking.[73]

Much has been written about all this, but what has not been researched thoroughly is what the effects of these fundamental changes in lawmaking, in particular the move from *Trias Politica to Duas Politica* have been on doctrinal legal scholarship, on the missed opportunities to pick up the thread of the prewar debate on the postclassical character of the law.[74]

[70] There is an astonishing similarity between Walter Hallstein's concept of the EU and post-1960 left wing instrumentalism.

[71] T. Koopmans, De rol van de wetgever, in *Honderd jaar rechtsleven, Nederlandse Juristen-Vereniging, 1870–1970*, Tjeenk Willink, 1970, 211–235.

[72] H.R. van Gunsteren, *The Quest for Control: A Critique of the Rational-Central-Rule Approach in Public Affairs*, John Wiley & Sons, 1976.

[73] M.G. Rood, Heeft de rechter een taak in zogeheten politieke zaken?, Zwolle: Tjeenk Willink 1975, p. 32, A.F.M. Brenninkmeijer, 'De plaats van de rechter in onze constitutionele rechtsorde', in J.M. Polak e.a., De rechter als dictator? Dynamiek in de trias. Verschuivingen in de verhouding regelgeving, bestuur en rechtspraak, Lochem: Van den Brink & Co 1987, 51–70; T. Koopmans, *Courts and Political Institutions*, Cambridge University Press, 2003, 247.

[74] H. Kantorowicz, Der Kampf um die Rechtswissenschaft (under the pseudonym Gnaeus Flavius), 1906.

Since legal research in Europe has always remained close to legal practice – much closer than in the US – is it not likely that at least some of this policy orientation rubbed off on the surface level of doctrinal legal research? I think this is the case, and I believe, in particular, that those scholars studying European law were affected by it because European law had and still has no strong doctrinal roots that could have functioned as a barrier against the ongoing instrumentalisation of law through European integration. It suffices to recall how communist countries with strong classical roots were able to shield their legal order against ideological communist influences.[75] Maybe more importantly Europe and European lawyers lacked the necessary postclassical theoretical and philosophical arsenal – or preparedness – to question and counterbalance the political instrumentalisation of the law.[76] Implicitly, it was taken for granted that the European legal order could be construed and founded in the philosophical foundations of the seventeenth century: universalism and rationalism. It seems as if they were 'stuck in Weimar', in realising the social projects developed prior to World War II in France and in Germany, now in the good times of the rapidly growing capitalist economies in the 1950s, 1960s and 1970s at least until the 'oil crisis' in 1973. This handicap survived in the political discussions on the feasibility of a European constitution and a European private law. Both are missed intellectual opportunities of engaging into deeper debates of the genuine foundations of the European legal order. It needed the failure of the two grand projects as well as the current and permanent stage of crisis to open a debate in two directions, one backward looking with a nostalgic eye to the safe harbour of Constitution 1.0,[77] the other forward looking about to strip off the remains of the classic continental tradition.[78]

[75] See the contributions in M. Bobek (ed.), *Central European Judges under the European Influence: The Transformative Power of the EU Revisited*, Hart Publishing, 2015.

[76] Or the willingness? This seems to be what M. Reimann suggests, in crude language to Locke, Hobbes, Kant and Hart, and not enough F. Nietzsche and M. Heidegger (and I would add from my perspective P. Sloterdijk). See the somewhat helpless attempt to seek the philosophical foundations of EU law, J. Dickson and P. Eleftheriadis (eds.), *The Philosophical Foundations of European Union Law*, Yearbook of European Law, 2013.

[77] Somek, *The Cosmopolitan Constitution*; Streeck, 'The Crises of Democratic Capitalism'; Scharpf, 'The Eurocrisis as a Victory of Neoliberalism?'; Joerges, 'What Is Left'.

[78] K.-H. Ladeur, 'The Evolution of General Administrative Law and the Emergence of Postmodern Administrative Law', Osgoode Hall Law School, Comparative Research in Law & Political Economy, Research Paper Series, Research Paper No. 16/201; G. Teubner, *Constitutional Fragments Societal Constitutionalism and Globalization*, Oxford University Press, 2012.

Mainstream surface-level European legal scholarship, pushing and fighting for ever-deeper integration, does not question the preconceptions on which these choices rest and does not realise the importance of taking an autonomous approach that calls for a justification of the topical choice and for the development of a research design expressing what is new about the research, which methods will be applied and how the project can be anchored in legal theories (the foundational level). There is an endless list of dissertations, books, articles and so forth that simply follow mainstream ideas and ideologies, often developed by policy makers or judges, without questioning them. In many cases, the authors do not even bother to explain on whose shoulders they stand, where they deviate from fellow researchers or from mainstream beliefs in practice or, in general, to what extent they add something to the body of knowledge. In the following, I will demonstrate via three examples – European values, European regulatory techniques and European research policy – how surface-level research might miss opportunities that would allow for exploring the postclassical move. The first example is taken from antidiscrimination, one of the prominent and strongly promoted values in the European legal order.

Think of, e.g., the current conflict around the scope of antidiscrimination rules. The European Union heavily contributed to making antidiscrimination one of its – perhaps even *the* – 'guiding' principle in which a genuine European dimension becomes clear and reaches beyond its application in the Member States.[79] The consequence is an endless stream of publications which point in one direction only: the extension of the principles to each and every event, to the public sphere and ever-stronger to the private sphere.[80] A conservative, though highly contested

[79] D. Kennedy, Three Globalisations, Three Globalisations of Law and Legal Thought: 1850–2000, in: D. Trubek and A. Santos (eds.), *The New Law and Economic Development: A Critical Appraisal*, Cambridge University Press, 2006, 19–73, where he demonstrates that the nation states exempted family law from the scope of application of the antidiscrimination principle. It was for the European Union to enlarge the principle and to penetrate via citizen rights into national family law regimes.

[80] Request for a preliminary ruling from the Cour de cassation (France) lodged on 24 April 2015 — Asma Bougnaoui, Association de défense des droits de l'homme (ADDH) v Micropole Univers SA (Case C-188/15) OJ 2015/C 221/03 Parties to the main proceedings, Applicants: Asma Bougnaoui, Association de défense des droits de l'homme (ADDH) Defendant: Micropole Univers SA Question referred 'Must Article 4(1) of Council Directive 78/2000/EC of 27 November 2000 establishing a general framework for equal treatment in employment and occupation, (1) 'be interpreted as meaning that the wish of a customer of an information technology consulting company no longer to

reading of the antidiscrimination principle tends to reduce its scope of application to keep the private legal order free from a concept, which is said to be alien to the idea that contracting partners can freely choose the contracting partner, whatever the motives and reasons behind the choice might be.[81]

What many scholars on both sides of the debate tend to forget is that arguments can be brought forward in both directions. The reform-orientated approach is identified with an attitude of 'the more equal treatment and the less discrimination, the better for the society'. The conservative autonomy-based approach is regarded as backward-looking and outdated. The protection against, for example, unequal treatment on the basis of sex by insurance companies, which was recently at stake in case C-236/09 of the CJEU, is claimed as a success by one camp and criticised as dysfunctional by the other.[82] What kind of consequences for the legal system results from the extension of the antidiscrimination principle into private law relations, in the example insurance contracts? What are the standards under which the extension *de lege lata* within the framework of the legal doctrine can be justified? Unfortunately, these sorts of questions are seldom brought to the foreground.[83]

An important lesson for legal scholarship is that one may sympathise with either position depending on our preconceptions and political preferences. What Esser had in mind, however, even reaches far beyond this. He did not argue in favour of the neutrality of the law or something similar. He was concerned with the question behind the question. Is discrimination really always bad? What is the relationship between autonomy and discrimination? Do we also need discrimination, for example, in order to stimulate competition or shall that be abolished because 'fair' competition is the order of the day, the logical consequence of public policy interfering into competition?[84] What exactly constitutes

have the information technology services of that company provided by an employee, a design engineer, wearing an Islamic headscarf, is a genuine and determining occupational requirement, by reason of the nature of the particular occupational activities concerned or of the context in which they are carried out?'

81 See e.g., J. Basedow, 'Grundsatz der Nichtdiskriminierung', *ZEuP* 2008, 230; F.-J. Säcker, 'Vertragsfreiheit und Schutz vor Diskriminierung', *ZEuP* 2006, 1.

82 ECJ, Case C-236/09 – Test Achats, ECR 2011 I-773.

83 See now for a balanced and rather sophisticated analysis, N. Reich, 'General Principles of EU Civil Law', *Intersentia* 2014.

84 In sports, for example, we do discriminate on the basis of sex on many occasions in order to make sure that men and women have their own competition in order not to discourage

discrimination (is age, for example, a relevant criterion since we are all aging?), and can (shall?) law impose antidiscrimination on deeply rooted social behaviour touching upon the foundations of a society or can it only deal with some of the symptoms of unequal treatment that appear at the surface level of the legal system? A. Somek[85] has convincingly demonstrated how the widespread antidiscrimination principle is undermining the integrity of the law, in the name of the law. Why does all the activist research not take this deeper layer of the debate into account? Maybe with the argument that antidiscrimination reaches beyond law and that politics instead of law is needed to implement it?

My second example concerns the insistence on a particular regulatory technique. The need for (further) harmonisation of national laws and policies is often an implicit assumption in the work of those writing about European law ('harmonisation is good, diversity is bad').[86] It is deeply enshrined in the 'integration through law' rhetoric, in particular after the adoption of the Single European Act, which was meant to complete the Internal Market, mainly through secondary community law. There is a direct line from the early harmonisation of consumer laws through the EU towards the European Civil Code project. All these measures were justified and legitimised by reference to set aside barriers to trade and complete the Internal Market at 'a high level of consumer protection' (Art. 114 TFEU). Currently the wind seems to turn, but only after the European Commission ran into a deadlock with its project to revise the consumer law acquis and the draft regulation on a Common European Sales Law. The new European Commission is undertaking serious steps to question the value of ever more harmonisation as a means to promote European integration. In legal scholarship the Euro sceptics are gaining ground. Harmonisation tends to become a foul word for market-driven European integration.[87]

the members of the different groups. We even discriminate on many occasions in terms of payment between male and female athletes.

[85] A. Somek, *Engineering Equality: An Essay on European Anti-Discrimination Law*, Oxford University Press, 2011.

[86] See, e.g., the contributions in Genevieve Helleringer and Kai Purnhagen (eds.), *Towards a European Legal Culture*, Beck/Hart/Nomos, 2014.

[87] The trendsetters are again on the left side of the spectrum. I shy away from mentioning names. It seems, however, as if particular European legal journals play a prominent role, just as the Kritische Justiz in Germany in the 1970s and 1980s.

Katherina Sideri[88] and James Scott[89] stand for a methodological approach towards lawmaking that raises serious questions with respect to legislative policies that call for harmonisation of different legal orders. However, they do not have the European Union alone in mind, they have a much larger view. Sideri's argument is that instead of top-down harmonisation in the European Union more bottom-up thinking is needed, which tries to link EU policy to local practice. The same argument has been made earlier by sociologist James Scott. He has shown that most legal systems working with blueprint plans and unification models, such as the former USSR, have dramatically failed in the end because they neglect the importance of *metis*. This is a type of knowledge that cannot be reduced to formulaic instructions. The word contrasts with the Greek word *techne*, which describes that knowledge and practice that 'may be logically derived from initial assumptions'. Why is there no research questioning the endless success stories the European Commission is publishing on, for example, the completion of the Internal Market? There is always 'progress', the aim has not 'yet' been achieved, but 'provided this and that harmonisation measure is taken', 'we' – meaning the people of Europe – are coming one step 'nearer' to the ultimate goal: but what is it? The critical turn against market-driven integration would gain substantive credit, if the 'socialist language' of the European Commission, the plans, unification models and time predictions would be contrasted against serious impact studies and linked to the 'administrative state' or the critique raised against authoritarian liberalism already in the 1920s.[90] It would allow for raising uncomfortable questions like those on possible similarities between the failures of socialist bureaucratic projects and the European market-building exercise, and last but not least, on the European Commission itself. If European legal scholarship shows a blind eye to all these type of questions, US researchers or European researchers who moved to the United States in the last decades will fill the gaps.[91]

[88] K. Sideri, *Law's Practical Wisdom, the Theory of Law Making in the New Governance Structures of the European Union*, Ashgate Farnham, 2007.

[89] J. Scott, *Seeing it Like a State: How Certain Schemes to Improve the Human Condition Have Failed*, Yale University Press, 1998.

[90] H. Heller, 'Autoritärer Liberalismus?', 44 *Neue Rundschau* 1933, 289–298.

[91] E.G.D. Kelemen, *Euro-legalism The Transformation of Law and Regulation in the European Union*, Harvard University Press, 2011, who shows how the EU is stuck in the pros and cons of class actions overlooking the deeper changes that have already occurred in the European legal order; J. Coffee, Entrepreneurial Litigation, Its Rise Fall and Future, 2015.

My last example is taken from the role and importance of the European Commission as the major funder of (legal) research, perhaps not only in the European Union. The European Commission is setting the research agenda, is prioritising particular methods, on matched funding of contract research, and in general, by the strong emphasis on the transfer of knowledge from one party (scholars) to another (business or government) for economic purposes (e.g., the direct link in the Seventh Framework Programme of the EC with the Lisbon agenda of becoming the most competitive economy in the world,[92] now Horizon 2020[93]).

There is little or no research on how the centralisation of funding resources in the hands of one single transnational institution that enjoys a particular mandate and a monopoly in initiating lawmaking within the limits of the principle of enumerated powers under the EU Treaties affects legal scholarship. Since 1986, the mandate has been to complete the Internal Market; since 2012 the mandate is to set up a banking union, which according to some scholarly research comes close to reshaping the European Economic Constitution. Right now, the Digital Single Market (DSM) is on the agenda. Whatever the mandate might be, the European Commission holds the power and enjoys the necessary resources to seek advice through legal (and more often than not nonlegal) scholarship. There is some nonrepresentative evidence that the European Commission seems at times ready to 'guide' the outcome of scholarly research into the predefined political direction, e.g., in the strongly promoted project of the Common European Sales Law, the slim version of the original European Civil Code project.[94] The funding culture has deeply impacted universities in Europe. Scholars are expected to raise money. Those who do not raise money, those who are not engaged in policy-driven research, may be downgraded, less respected and less well paid. Those who are not ready to follow the mainstream feel pressured (by research foundations, faculty managers, publishers, etc.) to justify and explain why they are not ready to accept the overwhelming wisdom that law and hence legal research should have societal relevance. There is even a new buzzword for this. It is called 'valorisation'. One needs to be able to explain the results of scholarly research to business and society and show

[92] See: http://cordis.europa.eu/fp7/understand_en.html.
[93] www.forschungsrahmenprogramm.de/horizont2020.htm.
[94] R. van Gestel/H.-W. Micklitz, 'Comparative Law and EU-Legislation: Inspiration, Evaluation or Justification?', in M. Adams and D. Heirbaut (eds.), *The Method and Culture of Comparative Law, Essays in Honour of Marc van Hoecke*, Hart Publishing, 2014, 301–319.

the 'return on investment'. This neglects that the history of science shows that what the actual 'added value' of scientific research for society is often hard to predict in advance. Moreover, serendipity plays an important role. Are we still prepared to accept this reality?

Taking the three examples together, there might be good and valid reasons why the instrumental use of law is justified in many situations and why surface level research is needed. The most obvious could be to demonstrate that there are deficiencies in the legal systems calling for a solution, although not necessarily through law. However, provided the inherent preconceptions and the reasons lying behind such assumptions are not disclosed, surface-level European scholarship risks losing its major asset: the often less visible undercurrent of the postclassical move in the building of Europe through law. After all, the history of science shows that 'opting out', 'swimming against the tide'[95] and 'picking the fruits of serendipity' have often resulted in deeper knowledge than pre-programmed surface-level research that one can see everywhere today. This is true for the debate around genuine European values and on the central role of the antidiscrimination paradigm in a supranational legal order; it is true with regard to the regulatory technique of harmonisation that is often substituted via regulation through harmonisation. Most importantly, however, centralising legal research in the hands of an institution which has a self-interest in the outcome to legitimise its own policy of an ever-deeper integration; maybe even its existence can certainly not be regarded as the appropriate institution to finance research that takes a critical stance, that looks into the postclassical potential of the European legal order. It is somewhat ironic that the European Commission, which is at the centre of the three examples chosen, is trapped by the spiritual dimension of the 'ever-deeper integration', which renders it impossible to reap the benefits of its success (Barry Eichengreen).

M. Reimann has outlined what he believes to be the key elements of postclassical law. I would propose to add three further elements which I understand as the genuinely European contribution to postclassical law: (1) the social in the law; (2) law and the nonlaw; and (3) institution building beyond law. In the following, I will develop all three through the lenses of the integration through, without and beyond law rhetoric. As it stands, the analysis looks tentative and premature. It is meant to be an

[95] E. Flaig, Gegen den Strom, Für eine sekuläre Republik Europa, 2013. Unfortunately it exists only in German but it tells us wisdoms that do not fit into mainstream thinking.

invitation for scholarly discussion, a start for a transatlantic dialogue. What should become crystal clear is that all three elements demonstrate and underpin the postclassical character of EU law.

7.6 First European Contribution: The Social in the Law

The social in the law relates to the major achievements of Europe, the notion and concept of the welfare state, the idea and concept to use law as a means to improve distributive justice. The materialisation of the law (Max Weber) fits into what M. Reimann identifies as the common characteristic of the postclassical approach to law. The move away from formalism implies that the classical concept of the law is gradually shattered. There is a direct line between Weimar in the 1920s, the student revolt or revolution in 1968 and the 1986 European Internal Market program that added social regulation to European market integration. Europe's contribution consists in demonstrating that an ever-larger market cannot be achieved without social minimum standards.[96] There is a price to pay for market building and this is the integration of the social. The European 'social' looks different from established distinction of distributive or corrective justice. Europe is yielding its own pattern of justice, which I term access justice.[97] It stands side-by-side with the many faces of social justice in the various Member States, but it shows that a common platform is essential for market building. In order to drive my argument home, I will have to sketch the history of the twentieth century. This requires a self-restriction.

The events of 1968 constituted the break-even point in the European postwar society, the year that became the start of a new era driven by a new generation that expected from the nation-state more than simply securing a flourishing economy. It demanded from the state the establishment of a 'just society'.[98] In retrospect, it seems as if the clock was turned backward. Once again, the formalist character of (doctrinal) legal scholarship was attacked. Again Julius von Kirchmann,[99] Rudolf von Jhering,[100]

96 Which constitutes a variation of K. Polanyhi, Grand Transformation, 1944.

97 See K. Tuori, *European Constitutionalism*, Cambridge University Press, 2015.

98 At least this is what could be regarded as a common denominator for France and Germany.

99 Ibid.

100 Der Kampf ums Recht, alluding to Darwin; see F. Wieacker, Privatrechtsgeschichte der Neuzeit, 2. neubearbeitete Auflage, 1967, 566.

Max Weber[101] and Hermann Kantorowicz[102] served as witnesses for considering the societal role and function of law afresh. Law, this was the overall message after 1968, should serve to redistribute wealth, to domesticise economic power and to secure liberty and justice for the weakest in society. This approach after 1968 nourished the welfare state. F. Scharpf coined the term of the social-democratisation of Member States, whatever their political regime looked like and whatever their legal order looked like.[103] The post-1968 society should be a better society, a more just society, and law was the means to achieve this aim.

In Germany between the two wars, Otto Sinzheimer conceptualised the economic constitution which was meant to be a labour constitution; Ludwig Raiser investigated the economic and political role and function of standard contract terms, Fritz Naphtali developed the concept of a '*Wirtschaftsdemokratie*' (economic democracy); and Herman Heller developed the foundations of the social welfare state.[104] The ideas of the 1920s and 1930s were revitalised by the socioliberal coalition (two political parties, the social-democrats and the liberal party remained in power for ten years, from 1972 to 1982). Basic legislation was adopted post-1968 in all areas of the society, in industrial relations and in the nascent environmental and consumer policy. Similar developments occurred to varying degrees in all European states. France deserves to be highlighted. France developed the *droit social* in the first decades of the twentieth century, and France heavily influenced social regulation after World War II. The underpinning ideology of all these policy projects was that law and legislation should produce social change. However, by the early 1980s the decline of the social welfare state had already become pretty obvious. The legal reform projects in the Welfare States had to overcome all sorts of difficulties: resistance in the society, failures of implementation and enforcement, capture of administrative agencies involved in the new policies and budget restrictions.

The rise of the social in the European Union started with the 'White Paper on the Completion of the Internal Market'[105] and eventually led in 1986 to the adoption of the Single European Act, which dramatically

[101] Wirtschaft und Gesellschaft. Grundriß der verstehenden Soziologie, 1922.

[102] Herrmann Kantorowicz, Der Kampf um die Rechtswissenschaft (unter dem Pseudonym Gnaeus Flavius), 1906.

[103] F.W. Scharpf, *Crisis and Social Democracy in Europe*, trans. R. Crowley and F. Thompsen, Cornell University Press, 1991.

[104] Otto Sinzheimer, Ludwig Raiser, Fritz Napthali, Herrmann Heller.

[105] COM (1985) 310 final.

changed the foundations on which the European construct was built. The Treaty of Rome from 1957 was built on a clear division of responsibilities: the market for the European Union and the social for the Member States. The Single European Act empowered the European Union to adopt secondary community law on health and safety at work, and consumer and environmental protection. Europe took over the social at the 'right' moment in time. The foundation of the Centre for European Legal Policy (*Zentrum für Europäische Rechtspolitik*) at the University of Bremen is paradigmatic. The Centre was established in 1982.[106] It turned into a trend-setter for social welfare–inspired European legal scholarship and provided an intellectual home for left-wing scholars not only from Germany.[107] The ideology of the Internal Market with a 'social face' held the research community together and formed its direction, sponsored and promoted by the European Commission. European integration was 'good' *per se*, and there was no space for questioning the sentiment of the project. An important by-product of 1986 was an increase in the status of European law and European legal scholarship. Those scholars were all self-taught lawyers. European legal scholarship was an unchartered territory with no or little foundational training underneath and with a blue sky to dream of new perspectives.

All that has dramatically changed between 1986 and 2016. The 'social' is said to be on the decline; the European Union is being attacked from the left for dismantling the welfare state and of promoting a neoliberal economy through the strong prioritising of economic efficiency, of downgrading worker rights[108] and of compromising democracy – in short, of suffering from a deep 'Justice Deficit'.[109] Two observations deserve to be highlighted as they underpin the postclassical move in EU law. Despite all the ups and downs, the modest successes in strengthening the social and the more obvious failures, it should not be overlooked that all Treaty amendments after 1986 gradually extended the social dimension in the European Union. Before the economic crisis triggered through the Lehman Brothers crisis and the Euro crisis, some

[106] www.jura.uni-bremen.de/institute/zentrum-fuer-europaeische-rechtspolitik/.

[107] See in particular Ch. Joerges and D. Trubek (eds.), Critical Legal Thought: An American German Debate, 1988.

[108] D. Schiek, (ed) *The EU Economic and Social Model in the Global Crisis: Interdisciplinary Perspectives*, Ashgate, 2013.

[109] All the critique against the claimed neoliberal outlook of D. Kochenov, G. de Búrca and A. Williams (eds.), *Europe's Justice Deficit?*, Hart Publishing, 2015.

scholars even proclaimed the emergence of a European social model.[110] One way of reading the move from integration through law to integration through governance is to promote the Social even in areas were the European Union has not been given competences through the new modes of governance, the Open Method of Coordination (OMC) and through 'social dialogue'.[111] Integration beyond law is characterised by an ever-stronger constitutionalisation of EU law via the Charter of Fundamental Rights to balance the efficiency paradigm proclaimed in the Lisbon Council in 2000. As such, there is a strong continuity in completing the Internal Market with a social face, but the role and function of the law is changing, from hard law-making guided by the conviction that laws could change society, to new forms of governance outside or at the periphery of law, to judicial balancing in Luxembourg. One may easily disagree as to whether this has been achieved, but the more important message is that the European Union sticks to the social and experiments with actors, modes and institutions.

This brings me to my second observation. The scholarly landscape has changed dramatically over time. The *soixante-huitards* and their disciples have, by and large, withdrawn their support from the European project and switched camp, from proponents to opponents. The bright side of this behavioural turn is the opportunity to get back and to 'stand and stare'. However, what is often missing in the rising critique against the claimed neoliberal outlook of the European Union, the claimed lack of solidarity and the claimed missing social justice in the aftermath of the Lehman Brothers and the Euro crises is that the yardstick against which the European Union is measured is taken most of the time implicitly from a transfigured (classical) vision of the national 'just' welfare state. Such an approach overlooks that the degree to which European states were willing and are willing to transform the welfare state very much depends on the particular national economic, social and political

[110] With a rather positive undertone D. Damjanovic and B. de Witte, 'Welfare Integration through EU Law: the overall Picture in the Light of the Lisbon Treaty', in U. Neergaard, R. Nielsen and L.M. Roseburry (eds.), *Integrating Welfare Functions into EU Law – From Rome to Lisbon*, DJOF Publishing 2009, 53–96.

[111] The European social dialogue refers to discussions, consultations, negotiations and joint actions involving organisations representing the two sides of industry (employers and workers). It takes two main forms – a tripartite dialogue involving the public authorities, and a bipartite dialogue between the European employers and trade union organisations. It has resulted in over 300 joint texts by the European social partners, which are included in a database.

situation in the respective countries. More important in our context is that it sets aside the postclassical achievements of the European Union, which I have identified in the emergence of a genuine pattern of justice – access justice – that is no longer bound to a particular intellectual history of a Member States but that takes into account the particular character of the European Union as a postnation-state entity.[112] I call the EU model of justice *access justice/Zugangsgerechtigkeit* (justice through access, *not* access to justice), i.e., that it is for the European Union to grant access justice to those who are excluded from the market or to those who face difficulties in making use of the market freedoms. European law has to make sure that all parties have and maintain access to the market – and to the European society insofar as this exists. Access justice/*Zugangsgerechtigkeit* is a ground-level mechanism inherently linked to the Internal Market.[113] For more than thirty years now the European Union is experimenting in how to best realise the self-set but deeply rooted social dimension of the Europeanisation of the market. One might wonder whether and to what extent transnational law and transnational legal regimes for sectorial global markets could benefit from these insights.

7.7 Second Key Element: The Law and the Nonlaw

Integration without law through governance constitutes the second genuine European characteristic. 'Governance' could only emerge in the European construct, in a supranational entity equipped with limited enumerated powers, where competence conflicts between the Member States and the European Union on the law-making side and on the law enforcement side are in-built into the legal order. Herein, the similarities to the overall debate on 'transnational and/or global law' are even more obvious. The development in the European Union over the last couple of decades, but in particular since the adoption of the Internal Market programme, now being accomplished by the decision to forge a European Banking Union, is paradigmatic of the uncertainties as to whether it is still 'law'. These rules produced within a rather lose legislative framework that delegates law-making power to private standard bodies or sometimes even without such a legislative framework which, when the

[112] H. Micklitz, 'Introduction: Social Justice and Access Justice in Private Law', in H.-W. Micklitz (ed.), *The Many Concepts of Social Justice in European Private Law*, Edward Elgar, 2011, 3–57.

[113] Tuori, *European Constitutionalism*, ch. 7, at 227.

European Union or its agencies are engaging in rule making at the international level, resembles much more politics than law. It seems as if D. Kennedy is right in his characterisation of the third globalisation that 'politics is law by other means'.[114]

The European Commission has to monitor the implementation process of the Internal Market programme at the Member State level. It requires a thorough management of who should be responsible for what in the Internal Market or European polity.[115] The most visible sign of the changing paradigm, away from integration through law via the Internal Market project, is the White Paper on Governance adopted in 2002.[116] At the surface level it seems as if the Internal Market programme yielded 'European Governance'. However, both concepts emerged more or less simultaneously. European governance has deeper and older roots (see, for example, hereafter the so-called 'new approach') than the white paper suggests.[117] The structural deficit in the capacity of the European Union to promulgate rules and its lack of capacity and competence to enforce them were brought to the limelight through the huge regulatory projects triggered by the Internal Market programme.[118] From the mid 1980s onwards, one might therefore identify a growing reliance of the European Commission on the use and testing of regulatory techniques which do not simply copy national instrumental laws, but introduce new modes of lawmaking and enforcement which fit into the category of multilevel governance.

It all started with the 1984 New Approach to Technical Standards and Regulations which eventually led to the adoption of 'comitology'

[114] D. Kennedy, 'Three Globalisations of Law and Legal Thought: 1850–2000', in D. Trubek and A. Santos (eds.), *The New Law and Economic Development: A Critical Appraisal*, Cambridge University Press, 2006, 19–73, at 72.

[115] W. van Gerven, *The European Union: A Polity of States and People*, Hart Publishing, 2005.

[116] European Governance, COM(2001) 428 final.

[117] See H.-P. Ipsen, Europäisches Gemeinschaftsrecht 1972, die EG als Zweckverband funktionaler Integration.

[118] There is considerable discussion of the roots within the doctrine; see Ch. Joerges and M. Everson, 'The European Turn to Governance and Unanswered Questions of Legitimacy: Two Examples and Counterintuitive Suggestions', in Ch. Joerges, B. Strath and P. Wagner (eds.), *The Economy as Polity: The Political Constitution of Contemporary Capitalism*, UCL Press, 2005, 159; O. de Schutter, 'The Implementation of Fundamental Rights Through the Open Method of Co-ordination', in O. de Schutter and S. Deakin (eds.), *Social Rights and Market Forces: Is the Open Method of Co-ordination of Employment and Social Rights the Future of Social Europe?*, Bruylant, 2005, 279; Dawson, *New Governance*.

in 1987.[119] The former document and its interplay with 'comitology' are paradigmatic in the coming together of Internal Market policy and what was later termed 'governance'.[120] The New Approach and 'comitology' served as a blueprint for similar concepts, the 2001 Lamfalussy procedure, the OMC, co-regulation in 2002 and since 2012 the Banking Union.[121] The new economic approach dates back to 1999,[122] but it had a deep impact far beyond competition law, on shifting the focus from minimum harmonisation to maximum harmonisation in economic relations, including private law matters, institutionally on testing measures against the competition paradigm.[123]

For the community of legal scholars throughout Europe, however, all these attempts remained for a long time widely unnoticed, as they took place in rather remote areas of EU law and did not (yet) reach the higher level of a more general debate on implementation and enforcement. The launch of the White Paper on Governance, 2002, changed not only the political landscape but also reshaped the research agenda. Governance led to a far-reaching politicisation of lawmaking and enforcement, politicisation understood as circumventing or overruling 'law' as the decisive means for shaping the European integration process, not publicness and open political debate in democratic fora. Traditional legislation became less popular to the advantage of self-regulation,[124] co-regulation[125] and 'new' modes of governance.[126] Politics and political scientists 'replaced'

[119] Directive 99/468/EC, OJ L 184, 17.7.1999, 23.

[120] E. Vos, 'The Rise of Committees', 3 *European Law Journal* 1997, 211.

[121] Th. M.J. Möllers, Lamfalussy-Verfahren und Europäisches Wirtschaftsrecht, ZEuP 2008, 480.

[122] N. Forwood, The European Commission's More Economic Approach, in C.-D. Ehlermann/M. Marquis (eds.), *European Competititon Law Annual 2009*, Hart Publishing 2010, available online, www.eui.eu/Documents/RSCAS/Research/Competition/2009/2009-COMPETITION-Forwood.pdf.

[123] www.europeanvoice.com/article/imported/draft-laws-to-be-put-to-eu-competitivity-test/69238.aspx.

[124] F. Cafaggi (ed.), *Reframing Self-Regulation in European Private Law*, Kluwer Law, 2006.

[125] A. Héritier/S. Eckert, *New modes of governance in the shadow of hierarchy: self-regulation by industry in Europe*, RSCAS 2007/20.

[126] Colin Scott has argued that many of the new modes of governance are not really new and as far as they are new, they are often not all that innovative; C. Scott, 'Governing Without Law or Governing Without Government? New-ish Governance and the Legitimacy of the EU'. 15 *European Law Journal* (2),160; see more comprehensively F. Cafaggi and H. Muir Watt (eds.), Making of European Private Law: Governance Design, 2008; F. Cafaggi and H. Muir Watt (eds.), The Regulatory Functions of European Private Law, 2009.

law and lawyers in many of these new areas. Legislative studies (*Gesetzgebungslehre*), once dominated by jurists/public lawyers, lost terrain to new disciplines, such as regulation and governance,[127] where political scientists now rule the game.[128] New subfields emerged, such as risk regulation, information and communications technology regulation, energy and transport regulation, and so on. Instead of one Internal Market, many separate sectorial markets were built, on telecommunication, energy, transport, financial services and banking services, most of them with a strong reach beyond the EU territory. In these fields doctrinal legal research has lost ground and is replaced by multidisciplinary 'law and . . .' approaches requiring different methods and theories, but all putting emphasis on 'practice'. The 'legal character' (the normative dimension) of these sectorial rules produced under the various new governance schemes can only be disclosed through looking into their practical importance. K.-H. Ladeur is about to analyse the key role of 'legal practice' in the understanding of 'law' beyond national boundaries. He questions the 'imperialism of legal theory' against legal practice. The key to understanding legal practice is claimed to be the 'textuality of the law'.[129]

In pursuit of the rise of the governance paradigm, political scientists were upgraded and lawyers were downgraded. Unfortunately, little has been written on the relationship between law and political science.[130] More and more legal research projects were and are undertaken by legal scientists or formulated by nonlawyers. The repercussions for legal practice can be demonstrated by referring to the involvement of political scientists in the lawmaking process. A key element of the White Paper on Governance, 2002, is the better regulation programme, now being renamed and adjusted by 'smart regulation'.[131] An important part of this

[127] See the journal *Regulation & Governance* that mentions political scientist as its first target group.

[128] See, e.g., the ECPR standing group on regulatory governance: http://regulation.upf.edu/, or the research group in Copenhagen on Judicial governance run by M. Wind.

[129] I would like to thank K.-H. Ladeur for letting me know of his recent book project. It will be a theory on legal practice, based on poststructuralists such as Giorgio Agamben, Jacques Derrida, Jean-Luc Nancy and Christoph Menke.

[130] But see K.J. Alter, R. Dehousse and G. Vanberg, *Law, Political Science and EU Legal Studies: An interdisciplinary Project?*, European Union Politics, 2002, 113.

[131] S. Weatherill, *Better Regulation*, Hart, 2007. There is a huge academic debate in this area; see more generally Weimar, 2007 as well as various publications from Joerges, inter alia with Everson, in Joerges, Strath and Wagner (eds.), 2005, 159 et seq.; and on the legitimacy of soft law, L. Senden, Soft Law in European Community Law, 2006. The

programme is the introduction of ex ante evaluation and impact assessments, which should forestall the adoption of new rules. Impact assessments are in practice often executed by political scientists (or economists), whereas lawyers play an auxiliary role only. Their competence is needed to fill in templates designed by political scientists and economists. Also the task of the legal service of the European Commission in the legislative drafting process is changing more and more into a role of offering technical-legal assistance. Similar developments occur on the enforcement side. The research on how rules are implemented and by whom are more often undertaken by political scientists and economists. What happened? Why are lawyers outsourced? Or did they outsource themselves by keeping to a strict and narrow research paradigm? It is pretty obvious that only a minority of lawyers engaged in a discourse on the relationship between governance and law – for example, on the interpretation of codes of conducts, on certification schemes, on covenants or other hybrid forms of governance, on the 'rule of recognition',[132] on the function of impact assessments, internet consultations and other better regulation tools for the CJEU in the interpretation of directives and regulations once a conflict arises about how EU law has to be applied or enforced.[133] The majority of legal scholars left the field to political scientists without realising the long-term, far-reaching implications for legal scholarship.

The new modes of governance raise, first and foremost, a problem of legitimacy. How can the drift away from established lawmaking procedures, from traditional sets of regulatory instruments, from seeking new

EU has its own website on better/smart regulation http://ec.europa.eu/smart-regulation/index_en.htm.

[132] Ch. Joerges and Yves Meny, 'Mountain or Molehill', EUI Jean Monnet Working Paper 6/2001 available at www.eui.eu/Documents/RSCAS/Research/OnlineSymposia/Amstrong.pdf; Dawson, *New Governance*, on the constitutionality of the OMC method, and Rob van Gestel's question about what agentification, soft law and standardisation meant for the primacy of the EU legislature in www.ingentaconnect.com/content/hart/tpl/2014/00000002/00000001/art00003. Stijn Smismans, St. Smismans, 'From Harmonisation to coordination? EU Law in the Lisbon Governance Architecture', 18 *Journal of European Public Policy* 2011, 502; Paul Verbruggen, *Enforcing Transnational Private Regulation, A Comparative Analysis of Advertising and Food Safety*, Elgar, 2014 on the making and the enforcement of soft law in the field of advertising and food law.

[133] See A.C.M. Meuwese, *Impact Assessment in EU Lawmaking*, Kluwer Law International, 2008; A. Alemanno, 'The Better Regulation Initiative at the Judicial Gate: A Trojan Horse Within the Commission's Walls or the Way Forward?', 15 *European Law Journal* 2009, 396, versus R. Munday, 'In the Wake of "Good Governance": Impact Assessments and the Politicisiation of Statutory Interpretation', *Modern Law Review* 2008, 385–412.

links between the classical and the postclassical, from hard judicial and/ or administrative enforcement to softer forms be given democratic legitimacy? The normative side of this academic debate is whether governance may only be democratically legitimated if basic procedural requirements, such as transparency, participation and accountability, are safeguarded and if the enforceability of these parameters is secured via individual or collective rights.[134]

Integration through governance, much more than integration through law, should be understood as a 'wake-up' call addressed to classical legal scholarship. Integration through law, in particular the Cappelletti/Seccombe/Weiler project, bears an undertone. Europe could and should learn from the United States, from a fully fledged federation that could provide deep insights on how the European Constitution and the European Market could be built. When the Berlin Wall fell in 1989, there might have been a short political moment to realise the old dream of a United States of Europe. However, the struggle over the enlargement and the disagreement between the Member States eventually led to the elaboration of the European Constitution, which, however, was never meant to establish a federal Europe, modelled after the United States. Looking back, it seems as if the 'White Paper' constituted the swan song on any political project to transform the European Union into some sort of a supranational state. Linking this insight to the transformation of nation-states into market states, with the European Union being at the forefront of the development, the European legal order serves indeed as a fertile ground for studying the postclassical approach under two perspectives, the shaky future of the classical approach within the Member States and the potential of the postclassical move within the European Union through the move from 'law' to 'governance'.

7.8 Third Key Element: Institution Building Beyond the Nation-State

Why 'integration beyond law'? Where is the 'beyond'? Where is the postclassical move? What is meant by institution building? The hypothesis is that the current integration paradigm can no longer be associated with one dominant ideology, although the new paradigm shares a common direction. 'Beyond' points beyond the boundaries of the

[134] This is the argument Hans-W. Micklitz made in *The Politics of Judicial Co-operation in the EU*, Cambridge University Press, 2005, 479 et seq.

European Union; 'beyond' means Europe in the world, but does this suffice to justify the postclassical move proclaimed? When it comes to institution building, one might, first and foremost, think of new governance, of all the hybrid institutions that have emerged in the aftermath of the white paper on 'governance', on the OMC, of the Lamfalussy procedure and its followers in the Banking Union. This is a relatively well-researched phenomenon. Therefore, my focus will be on the aim of the European Union to become 'the most competitive and most dynamic knowledge-based economy' in the world (Lisbon agenda 2000) and the obvious need to counterbalance integration by nonlegal means via constitutionalisation through the EU judiciary. Both characterise the third key element, and both bear a substantive and an institutional dimension.

The shift towards economic efficiency in 2000 lies at the core of all those who criticise the European Union for its neoliberal turn, but it is equally the opening up of the European Union towards the globalisation of the economy. Theoretically, it would allow the European Union to test the whole Internal Market programme against the efficiency paradigms that dominates globalisation. The Transatlantic Trade and Investment Partnership negotiations between the European Union and the United States might be interpreted as such an attempt. The European Union is not able to start a serious self-assessment out of its own intellectual resources; it needs the external extension to engage into such an exercise. Constitutionalisation of the European Union, in particular via fundamental rights and human rights, is an ongoing process ('creeping constitutionalisation'[135]). The integration of the Charter of Fundamental Rights into the EU legal order, however, has accelerated the process. In light of the move towards governance, constitutionalisation links the nonlaw back to law, the executive (the European Commission) back to the judiciary (the ECJ in Luxembourg).

The Lisbon Council Declaration in 2002, although not an official legally binding document, heavily affected the spirit of the lawmaking process in the European Union, in its content, its procedure and its institutional design. Despite its soft character, the Declaration remains the backbone of the economic efficiency doctrine, at least the one which is favoured and advocated for by the European Commission, whilst traces of it can also be

[135] G. Teubner, 'Societal Constitutionalism: Alternatives to State-Centred Constitutional Theory?', in Ch. Joerges, I.-J. Sand and G. Teubner (eds.), *Constitutionalism and Transnational Governance*, Oxford Press, 2004, 3–28.

found in the case law of the CJEU.[136] In the presidential conclusion of the Lisbon Council decision the following statement can be found:

> An effective framework review and improvement based on the Internal Market Strategy endorsed by the Helsinki Council, is essential if the full benefits of market liberalization *are to be reaped* (emphasis added). Moreover, fair and uniformly applied competition and state aid rules are essential for ensuring that business can thrive and operative effectively on a level playing field in the internal market.[137]

The increasing importance of economic efficiency led to major changes in legal scholarship and legal research in European law. Europe legal scholarship seen as a whole has been relatively reluctant to integrate law and economics into its research design, at least until recently. It is fair to assume that contrary to the United States, law and economics still does not represent the mainstream thinking in European scholarly research. The inner reason might indeed be that legal doctrine in Europe is traditionally anchored much deeper in legal science and scholarly research than in the United States.[138] However, here again the wind seems to shift. The European Commission is shifting the focus more and more towards using law and economics–type thinking for shaping and testing the feasibility of European rule making.[139] However, it is not the hard version of law and economics, but behavioural economics, which is promoted ever more strongly by the European Commission.[140] Politically, it might even strengthen integration through nonlegal means as the tool box of behavioural economics is not necessarily linked to legal means.[141] European legal scholarship comes under pressure. Economists and, in particular, empirical economists are gaining ground in core areas of legal scholarship. Today, good scholarly research requires familiarity with law and economics. In the final analysis, the Lisbon Council

[136] St. Smismans, 'From Harmonisation to coordination? EU law in the Lisbon governance architecture', 18 *Journal of European Public Policy* 2011, 502.

[137] See www.europarl.europa.eu/summits/lis1_en.htm, at p. 5.

[138] K. Grechenig and M. Gelter, 'Divergente Evolution des Rechtsdenkens – Von amerikanischer Rechtsökonomik und deutscher Dogmatik', 72 *RabelsZ* 2008, 513.

[139] See G. Wagner (ed.), *The Common Frame of Reference, A View from Law and Economics*, Sellier, 2009.

[140] See for a first stock taking A. Alemanno and A.-L. Sibony (eds.), *Nudge and the Law*, Hart, 2015.

[141] But see E.J. Mestmäcker, *A Legal Theory without Law: Posner v. Hayek on Economic Analysis of Law*, Mohr Siebeck, 2007; H.-W. Micklitz, 'The Politics of Behavioural Economics', Manuscript, 2015, on file with the author.

Declaration in 2000 paved the way for European legal scholars to catch up with the development in the United States.

Where is the institutional dimension beyond? What are institutions? A strong legalistic understanding of institutions does not suffice to get an understanding of the impact of the Lisbon Council Declaration. Institutions are not only courts and administrations, or hybrid bodies in charge with the production of technical standards like ISO/CEN, IEC/CENELEC or ETSI, accreditation and certification bodies or its counterparts in the Banking Union. I use institutions in the meaning given to the term in institutional economics.[142] It is only through such an understanding that the far-reaching consequences become clear. The Lisbon credo is strongly embedded in the better regulation approach. The better regulation approach triggered the impact assessment approach. The European Commission felt the need to set up its own website, to adopt rules and regulations on what better regulations are and how the impact assessments should be designed.[143] In a much narrower understanding of institutions the European Union is currently discussing the often promoted need to formally separate the unit which is in charge of the impact assessments from those units within the European Commission that has to transplant the impact assessment into particular regulatory projects. The consequences of the better regulation approach is the emergence of a new network of institutions, in between the European Union but also beyond that focus to the political requirements set out first in the Lisbon strategy in 2000, which are continuously updated.

On the surface, there is a link between the increasing attention given to new forms of governance in the European Union, the initial project to adopt a European Constitution and the drift towards constitutionalisation via fundamental and human rights. Today constitutionalisation is beginning to dominate legal scholarship in whatever area of the law, including private law which in the ordoliberal thinking should be kept separate from the constitutional order.[144] Questioning the use and

[142] 'Institutions: The rules of the game: the humanly devised constraints that structure human interaction. They are made up of formal constraints (such as rules, laws, constitutions), informal constraints (such as norms of behaviour, conventions, self-imposed codes of conduct), and their enforcement characteristics', www.coase.org/nieglossary.htm.

[143] http://ec.europa.eu/smart-regulation/index_en.htm.

[144] E.J. Mestmäcker, E. Böhm, W. Canaris and the recent research in Constitutionalisation of Private Law; O. Cherednychenko, *Fundamental Rights, Contract Law and the Protection of the Weaker Party: A Comparative Analysis of the Constitutionalisation of the*

usefulness of human rights and fundamental rights, for the purpose of having a deeper look into the impact on the legal system and the political implications of stretching human rights and fundamental rights beyond all boundaries, has become a politically highly sensitive question.[145]

The CJEU started speaking of a constitutional charter in *Les Verts* in 1986.[146] However, it never used the word Constitution with a big 'C'.[147] The White Paper on Governance enhanced a scholarly debate on how the constitutionalisation process should and might look like. Azoulai[148] distinguishes four forms of constitutionalisation: (1) federalisation; (2) multipluralism; (3) conflictual constitutionalisation; and (4) dualistic constitutionalisation in an attempt to structure the current debate. Tuori uses the metaphor of the many constitutions of Europe very much in line with constitutional pluralism but going beyond that debate in looking in the substance of the different constitutions, e.g., the political, the economic and the social constitution.[149] The big 'C' was introduced via the political debate in the constitutional assembly – and failed. The constitutionalisation via human rights and fundamental rights come in two waves. The first refers to the social dimension, now very much and more than ever about the 'social' in a transnational dimension;[150] the second touches upon the foundations of the European legal order: what is law,

Contract Law with Emphasis on Risky Financial Transactions, Sellier, 2008; Ch. Mak, *Fundamental Rights in European Contract Law: A Comparison of the Impact of Fundamental Rights on Contractual Relationships in Germany, the Netherlands, Italy and England*, Wolters Kluwer, 2008; A. C. Ciacchi, G. Brüggemeier and G. Comandé (eds.), *Fundamental Rights and Private Law in the European Union, Volume I and II, Comparative Analysis of Selected Case Patterns*, Cambridge University Press 2010.

145 There are exceptions to the rule. A. Sen, 'Elements of a Theory on Human Rights', *Philosophy and Public Affairs*, 2004, 315; H. Collins, The Constitutionalisation of Private Law as a Path to Social Justice in H.-W. Micklitz (ed.), *The Many Faces of Social Justice in Private Law*, Elgar, 2011, 133.

146 ECJ, 26.9.1984, Case 294/83 [1986] ECR 1339 at 23.

147 N. Walker, Big 'C' or small 'c', *ELJ* 2006, 12.

148 Intégration juridique et légitimité, in L. Fontaine (dir.), *Droit et légitimité*, collection "Droit et justice", Bruylant, 2011.

149 K. Tuori and S. Sankari (eds.), *The Many Constitutions of Europe*, Routledge, 2010.

150 Still hidden in Mohamed Aziz, see H.-W. Micklitz, 'Mohamed Aziz: Sympathetic and Activist, but Did the Court Get it Wrong?', in A. Sodersten and J.H.H. Weiler (eds.), *Where the Court got it Wrong, Publications of ICON*, forth-coming, www.ecln.net/florence-2013.html; outspoken in later cases, see F. Della Negra, 'The Uncertain Development of the Case Law on Consumer Protection in Mortgage Enforcement Proceedings: Sánchez Morcillo and Kušionová, *CMLR* 2015, 1009–1032.

what is politics, the notion of a person, the notion of state, the notion of contract and property, the notion of remedies.[151]

The first wave goes very much along with what I termed the 'social' in the law. However, in a trans-European perspective, fundamental and human rights may easily gain a new dimension when they are referred to in order to question the legitimacy of the European Union and the Member States to impose austerity measures on Euro-Member States which are in economic trouble.[152] The second wave might be even more important with a view to the postclassical move. Here the ECJ is entrusted with the responsibility to balance integration through nonlaw against fundamental and human rights implications that urge the Court to draw a line between law and politics, or to transform politics (nonlaw) into enforceable law. What the ECJ might be doing, for the right of the wrong, is to eliminate the residuals of the classical and to shape and entrench the postclassical legal order. Thus, the third key element bears strong conceptual and institutional implications.

Institutionally, it is to be highlighted that courts, or the European court, continue to be institutions of which the public are aware, more often than before in conflict with the highest courts of the Member States. From an institutional perspective two observations deserve to be highlighted: the key role of courts as institution builders and the emergence of new forms of cooperation/interaction between the ECJ and the Member States courts under the preliminary reference procedure, between the ECJ and non-EU courts, whenever the constitutionalisation leads to conflicts with courts that take a different, less human and fundamental rights – orientated approach. A full picture of the new institutional setting would require research that is not yet under way.

[151] H.-W. Micklitz, 'Person, Contract, Property: The Foundations of Private Law Constitutionally Revisited', presented at the Secola conference 2015 in Oxford, MS, 2015, on file with author.

[152] Legal Brief prepared for the Special Committee of the Hellenic Parliament on the Audit of the Greek Debt (Greek Debt Truth Committee), 15 June 2015, Economic Policy, Conditionality, Socio-Economic Rights and International Legal Responsibility: The Case of Greece 2010–2015 by Olivier De Schutter, PhD Centre for Philosophy of Law and Institute for Interdisciplinary Research in Legal Sciences University of Louvain, and Margot E. Salomon, PhD Centre for the Study of Human Rights and Law Department London School of Economics and Political Science available at http://cadtm.org/Legal-Brief-Prepared-for-the.

7.9 Preliminary Conclusion

This chapter introduced the hypothesis that there is a European advantage in legal scholarship. Such a reading presupposes to understand the European legal order as 'postclassical'. Thus, European legal scholarship might wish to engage in competition with US legal scholarship on who contributes what to 'global lawyering'. Roughly speaking, this chapter was broken down into two parts. The first part was devoted to the argument that EU law and European legal scholarship – meaning the scholarship which is devoted to the genuinely European dimension of EU law sloughing off (as far as possible) the respective national bias/perspective on EU law – is gradually moving away from, in the past sixty years, the long integration process from its classical roots. This is already complicated enough. Most of the legal scholarship, implicitly or explicitly, measures the European legal order against the national blueprint, or what is even more problematic, against the hidden dream of a United States of Europe. Such a perspective overlooks the newness of the European legal order and the potential it yields in the postclassical debate. It needed the failure of two grand projects, the European Constitution and the European Civil Code, to focus on the achievements of the European Union, of EU law and of EU legal scholarship, which are unique and which stand apart from the US federal state and from the postwar European nation-states. Such a change in perspective is only possible through the revitalisation of a critical and distant stance against the ups and downs of the constantly changing integration paradigm. The European Union is constantly in the making; it is a laboratory. Its strength is its unfinished character in an open-ended process that leaves room for experimentation, for the development of a legal order that is no longer coherent and no longer systematic. Only such change in perspective allows for setting free what I dare to call the European advantage.

The second part of the chapter is trying to give shape to the European advantage. Against the sixty years of European integration I have tentatively identified three constitutive elements in which the European advantage is condensed and which might contribute to the debate over the future of global and transnational law: (1) the social dimension, which differs from the national welfare state and which allows for a new understanding of the social dimension in a transnational legal order, in substance through a new paradigm of justice and in form through its multigovernance structure; (2) the law–nonlaw distinction, which has led the European Union to produce ever more new forms of lawmaking and of law enforcement, in a multilayered system under integration of public and private players; (3) the institution building not only within and through governance but in the new millennium in the overall attempts of striking a balance between economic efficiency in a globalised market and the rising importance of human and fundamental rights.

Once European legal scholarship is ready to embark on the unknown journey, new constitutive elements may be referred to and defended. What is more important and what I could not really develop in this chapter is the potential crucial importance of the necessary interaction between the classical and the postclassical legal order and of, as Reimann presumes, the common law as building a bridge between the two. Currently, I assume that the postclassical legal order is not self-standing – that it needs some reconnection to the classical legal order. Once again, Europe might benefit from the experience of a century-old classical legal order in most, but not all, EU Member States. One may wonder whether a fruitful starting point for a transatlantic discourse could be that the supposition that US legal scholarship has placed too much emphasis on the 'law and . . .' disciplines and on the somewhat helpless search for a legal method, which allows for the integration of nonlegal disciplines into the legal system;[153] whereas national European scholarship is in its major parts looks backward to the classical too much. What has become somewhat lost in US scholarship is the role and function of classical legal doctrine in EU legal scholarship and the critical stance towards a positivist order, or in the EU context, the instrumentalisation of law for integration purposes.

Things have come full circle. EU legal scholarship may benefit from the postclassical move in US scholarship and realise the shaky dreams of a still-coherent legal order. In the plea for sound doctrinal legal scholarship the US debate on the role and function of doctrinal legal research might want to look at 'good old Europe'.[154] All this needs to be developed.

[153] See the analysis of V. Nourse and G. Shaffer, 'Varieties of New Legal Realism: Can A New World Order Prompt a New Legal Theory?,' 95 *Cornell Law Review* 2009, 61–139.

[154] Edwards, Harry T. 'The Growing Disjunction Between Legal Education and the Legal Profession', 91 *Michigan Law Review* 1992, 34–78.

8

From Coherence to Effectiveness

A Legal Methodology for the Modern World

EDWARD L. RUBIN

The basic problem with legal methodology, in both the United States and Europe, should be apparent. During the past 200 years, the Western world's conception of government has been transformed; that transformation, as is well known, is the advent and development of the administrative state. Law, however one defines it, has clearly been transformed as well. A plausible starting point for any effort to construct a methodology of legal scholarship must take this transformation into account. If we wanted to understand the law of the Hittites or the Aztecs, we would need to begin with their conception of law. To begin by saying, "We can assume that the Hittites and the Aztecs had the same conception of law that we do," would be obviously wrong. In fact, it would be risible. But when scholars analyze the law of our own society, they generally assume that the same concept of law that prevailed in premodern times is equally applicable to the very different society, and different form of government, that exists today. That may not be quite as risible, but it is just as wrong.

To document the many ways in which our current conception of law differs from its premodern predecessor would require a discussion of our entire legal system. This chapter will be concerned with the most basic one: the idea that the legal system of a particular jurisdiction consists of a coherent set of rules, that is, a set of rules that derive from general principles. In both the common law and civil law jurisdictions of the premodern West, this idea was virtually definitional. Governmental actions that could not be described as being derived from identified or implicit principles, and were therefore not consistent with other actions that were so derived, were not regarded as law. Rather, they were seen as acts of will. By the simple process of exclusion, the claim of legal coherence was sustained.

A modern administrative state, whether democratic or dictatorial, uses law – or more precisely the rules regarding citizen behavior, resource allocation, and the physical environment that apply within the boundaries of the state – as a means of implementing the policies that it adopts. The rules that are declared, and the statutes that enact them, have no necessary relationship with one another; they are all individual and separate acts of will. Regulations enacted by administrative agencies that the legislature or elected chief executive has authorized are related to the authorizing statute, but have no necessary connection with each other or to regulations promulgated under a different exercise of legislative or executive authority. In other words, there is simply no law in the premodern sense. Of course, statutes and regulations often borrow particular techniques from one another, and default statutes, such as an administrative procedure act, state generalized techniques that will apply unless explicitly countermanded by the lawmaking body. But these are matters of convenience, not the necessary features of the prior age that enabled enactments to qualify as law. Similarly, the surviving legal remnants of that prior age – the Codes on the European Continent and the common law in Britain and its former colonies – are retained as matters of convenience, on the basis of their familiarity, but can be, and often are, displaced by legislation or regulation that pays no attention to their quondam regularities.

To be relevant and useful, legal methodology must be rethought in light of this momentous change. Approaches derived from premodern conceptions of law may provide legal scholars with the conceptual basis for general condemnations and jeremiads about our current legal system, but they will not provide any useful ways to understand that system or to advance pragmatic recommendations for its improvement. In other words, we need a modern methodology of legal analysis that comports with the legal system that we actually possess. In terms of the specific topic that this contribution addresses, we need a methodology that dispenses with the concept of legal coherence and confronts the particularized nature of law in the modern administrative state. The regularities that serve as the substance of this methodology will be matters of technique and moral judgment, rather than the defining principles of a coherent system.

Section 8.1 of this chapter discusses legal coherentism. Its first section explains how the idea of law as a coherent system that was derived from principles dominated premodern thinking about law, and how inconsistent rules were explained or explained away. Section 8.2 shows how this approach serves as the basis for much contemporary legal scholarship. It then describes, in its first section, the way in which the modern administrative state eliminates the concept of legal coherentism and, in its second section, how legal scholarship about modern law needs to stop relying on this outmoded notion and develop a new methodology. Finally, Section 8.3 addresses two important objections to abandoning coherentism: first, that it would mean abandoning the rule of law, and second, that it succumbs to the loss of meaning that accompanies the modern's world's lack of a unified value system.

8.1 Legal Coherentism

8.1.1 The Coherentist Approach to Law

In the West, the concept of law as a coherent system, a set of rules that are connected by some sort of logical relationship to each other, derives from the belief in natural law. Like so many of our concepts, this originated in Greco-Roman thought. While it is not explicitly present in Aristotle, it owes much to his notion of a *telos*, the inherent purpose that an entity possesses as either a cause or a result of its nature.[1] The idea that there exists a natural law, or law of nature, was fully developed by Cicero. It probably evolved independently in Western (i.e., Medieval and Early Modern) thought, but it owes it specific contours to Cicero's enormous influence, greatly aided by the fact that he wrote in Latin, which every educated person in the Western world could read.[2]

As a Stoic, Cicero believed that a creator God, who acts in accordance with reason, also endows human beings with reason. Humans and God thus belong to the same community, that is, the community of reasoning entities. Natural law consists of rules governing behavior in this community. As such, it is derived from reason, and reflects the *telos*, or nature of humans as reasoning creatures. Because it is a particular feature of human life, however, not life in its entirety, natural law must also have a *telos* of its own, that is, an inherent purpose that defines and shapes it. That *telos* is justice, the quality that a reasoning person demands of law. Natural law, the law that divine reason reveals to us, therefore establishes

[1] Aristotle, Nichomachean Ethics (W.D. Ross, trans.), in II, *The Works of Aristotle* (Chicago: Encyclopaedia Britannica, 1952), p. 339.

[2] On Cicero's influence upon Western thought, see, e.g., Bernard Bailyn, *The Ideological Origins of the American Revolution* (Cambridge, MA: Belknap, 1992), pp. 22–26; Antony Black, *Political Thought in Europe, 1250–1450* (Cambridge: Cambridge University Press, 1992), pp. 9, 19–20, 24–28, 129–142; Peter Gay, *The Enlightenment: The Rise of Modern Paganism* (New York: W.W. Norton, 1966), pp. 105–110; John Addington Symonds, *The Renaissance in Italy* (New York: Modern Library, 1935), p. 575

and embodies the principles of justice.[3] Unlike other concepts borrowed from the Greco-Roman world, which required all the ingenuity of the scholastic philosophers to integrate with Christian doctrine, Cicero's idea of natural law could be almost effortlessly applied, and was part of Western jurisprudential thought from its beginnings. The classic statement of Western natural law doctrine is found in St. Thomas Aquinas' *Summa Theologica*, which argues that natural law is one of five kinds of law. It takes its place with eternal law and divine law as being created directly by God, but governs people's relations with each other, rather than their path to salvation (divine law) or the structure of the universe (eternal law). All laws, no matter who originates them, must be promulgated to count as law; natural law is promulgated through reason, and thus available to everyone, whether they have received Christ's revelation or not. A fourth kind of law, human law, is not promulgated by God, but it must fit within the boundaries of natural law or it is not law at all. A ruler who enacts human purported law that violates natural law is a tyrant, and his subjects are justified in overthrowing him.[4]

Both the origin and operation of natural law require it to be a coherent system of rules, that is, a system of rules that fit together in a consistent, logically elaborated pattern. Because natural law originates with reason, it must be the product of reason, rather than of will or whim. That is, it must emerge from a dispassionate thinking process that contemplates the nature of human beings and of the societies that their nature leads them to create.[5] In addition, the operation of natural law requires it to be a coherent and consistent system because it must be accessible to the reason that all human beings possess. As it was not inscribed on stone tablets, or even recorded in Scripture, reason is the only means by which the natural law can be discerned, and the only way it can claim universality. As Aquinas argued, even though salvation depends on Christ, and

[3] Cicero, *The Laws, in Cicero, The Republic, The Laws* (Niall Rudd, trans.) (Oxford: Oxford University Press, 1990), I. 16–35 (pp. 102–109), II.7-17 (pp. 23–28).

[4] St. Thomas Aquinas, *Summa Theologica* (Fathers of the English Dominican Province, trans.) (Notre Dame, IN: Christian Classics, 1981), I–II, QQ. 90–97 (pp. 993-1025). The fifth form of law, according to Aquinas, are the forms of sin, ibid., Q. 91, art. 6, p. 1000, an unusual argument that seems to have had little influence.

[5] The medieval debate about whether God necessarily creates a realm of reason (Aquinas), or whether His will is absolute and He has chosen reason as an act of will (Occam) does not affect natural law doctrine, because the principles that God communicates to humans will be reason-based by either account.

thus is limited to those who receive and accept His revelation, natural law is accessible to all people in all times through their ability to reason.

Belief in natural law theory thus leads to the idea that the legal system of a legitimate regime must consist of a coherent body of rules. Cicero, Aquinas, and other natural law theorists were of course aware that many rules or enactments ordinarily described as law could not be attributed to natural law, in the sense that they employed this concept. Because natural law is established by God, in either its Christian or Stoic version, or by the inherent nature of law or humans, in its more secular versions, it is, in all its forms, beyond the power of human beings to alter. But in a real society, humans create law all the time. Two categories of human law that were well recognized in premodern times and discussed at length by legal thinkers were the pronouncements of the ruler and the customs of the society. A third category, also well recognized in its particular manifestations but not as clearly identified or discussed as a category, were resource allocations, that is, the ruler's deployment of the material resources at his disposal. This last category overlaps with foreign relations, another body of actions by the ruler whose fit with natural law was somewhat difficult to determine.[6]

The most obvious category of human law is positive law, that is, binding commands enacted by the ruler of the polity, or subsidiary officials authorized by the ruler. Rulers of any sizable polity, even if they are charismatic in Weber's sense,[7] issue rules, that is, general orders governing the behavior of their subjects. It is possible to insist that they are actually magistrates rather than lawmakers, that the rules that enact are simply interpretations of the natural law that apply it to the specific features of the polity. But all serious legal theorists recognize that many of the rules needed to govern personal and commercial relations are too detailed or arbitrary to be derived from general principles and thus must be established by human law. For example, natural law may demand punishment for theft, but the precise calibration of the punishment must be determined by positive enactment; natural law may provide that contracts be enforced, but it cannot specify the particular rules that signal contractual validity. Natural law theorists generally responded to this

[6] For a more extended discussion of these points, see Edward L. Rubin, *Beyond Camelot: Rethinking Law and Politics for the Modern State* (Princeton, NJ: Princeton University Press, 2005), pp. 191–213.

[7] Max Weber, *Economy and Society* (Claus Wittich and Guenther Roth, eds.) (Berkeley, CA: University of California Press, 1978), pp. 1111–1157.

situation by emphasizing consistency with natural law rather than direct derivation. That is, they held that positive enactments can be recognized as part of the legal system so long as they are consistent with natural law principles. As such, these enactments can be regarded as elaborations or specifications of natural law principles, and there can be a range of such elaborations. But these law theorists also insisted that if positive enactments violate those principles, they are not law. Thus, Cicero, Aquinas, and most other natural lawyers solved the problem of positive enactments that are inconsistent with natural law principles by simply excluding such enactments from the category of law, and thus from the legal system.

Custom is a second category of human law, an important one in the premodern, pre-administrative polities of the Western world. Like positive law, it is too detailed to be plausibly derived from general principles accessible to universal reason. In the Middle Ages, for example, every country, and often every manor or castellany, had its own law, consisting of rules specifying things like the number of days that farmers could graze their livestock on the village common. Once again, the way natural law theorists integrated these rules into the legal system was to judge them by their consistency with natural law, rather than by whether they could be directly derived from it. In this case, however, the standard justification for doing so enabled them to make a stronger empirical claim about the coherence and consistency of law. Custom, they correctly observed, is built up over time. As a result, it is necessarily shaped by reason, the one human quality that remains a constant as behavior changes. Using a sort of wisdom-of-crowds argument, natural law theorists held that the illogicalities, errors and caprices that they necessarily conceded to be widespread among human beings would move in differing directions and thus cancel out as time went on. What would be left –as a sort of substrate that could be perceived through the mists of momentary variation – would be a body of law shaped primarily by reason. Sharing the same source as natural law itself, custom would thus be consistent with that law, and often a logical extension of it to address specific circumstances. It is on this basis that St. Thomas Aquinas declares customary law as preferable to statutory enactments.[8] Of course, natural law theory stands ready to condemn any customary provisions that violate natural law, and to banish them outside the boundaries of

[8] Aquinas, *Summa Theologica*, note 4, I-II, Q. 97, arts. 2–3 (pp. 1023–1024).

law; the claim is simply that this is less likely to occur when the provisions are the product of custom, rather than of positive enactment.

A third type of enactment that potentially challenges the coherence of the legal system can be described as resource allocation. It consists of decisions about the expenditure of funds or the disposition of land and chattels that lie within the direct control of the ruler. Decision procedures for these resources, which are generally extensive, will depend, of course, on the type of governmental system that prevails in the polity. In the absolutist monarchies of the Early Modern Era, the king, either directly or through delegates, made the decisions, with relatively little constraint. In constitutional monarchies or modern democracies, the legislature typically allocates funds and makes major decisions about other property, with the chief executive retaining varying amounts of discretion in implementing legislative commands. However the decision is made, is it clearly an act of will, like the positive enactment of a rule. Even if the allocation is the result of a reasoning process, like a carefully considered decision about the best place to build a road, it will generally be too particularized to be plausibly derived from the general principles of natural law, or to fit within a coherent system of humanly created rules.

Natural law theorists and legal theorists in general dealt with these resource allocations by ignoring them. However important they were, and whatever the proportion of public officials' time and energy they consumed, these decisions were simply not regarded as law, and therefore did not need to be explained or taken account of in one's account of the legal system. Far from being antediluvian, this approach, so obviously inconsistent with the realities of the administrative state, continues to this day. H. L. A. Hart, in a book that is often regarded as the most important work of legal theory in the postwar era, defines law as rules governing human conduct. Such rules, which he describes as primary, are not a complete description of the legal system; there are also secondary rules, specifying the way that the primary rules are formulated and administered.[9] What is striking, however, is that resource allocations, which would fit into Hart's primary rather than the secondary category, are excluded by this formulation. This is particularly striking because modern nations generally use the exact same secondary rules, such as the legislative process, to allocate resources as they do to control human

[9] H.L.A. Hart, *The Concept of Law* (Oxford: Clarendon Press, 1961), pp. 89–96.

conduct. The U.S. Congress is not trying to control human conduct when it buys land to protect as a wilderness area, or when it sends a space probe to Neptune, or even when it funds disability benefits (which are intended to ameliorate disabled people's plight, not to encourage healthy people to become disabled). A jurisprudential theory that excludes these important statutes from the category law is not a particularly good theory. An assertion that the legal system consists of a coherent body of rules is less than convincing when it can only be plausibly maintained by ignoring an entire body of enactments that are created by the same procedure as the rules that the theory purports to explain.

Governmental actions involving relations with other nations bear a certain resemblance to resource allocations in that they are often particularized and unrelated to the natural law principles which provide the legal system with its claimed coherence. Like such allocations, and like positive rules, they are often acts of will by the ruler. As a result, they are also typically excluded from the category or the concept of law, either by affirmative statement or, more often, by simply ignoring them. Here, however, the exclusion can be more readily justified. In contrast to resource allocations, which are often intertwined with conduct-guiding rules, the distinction between foreign and domestic relations is reasonably clear. Second, while it is obviously wrong to say that resource allocations are lawless, in the sense of being ungoverned or reverting to a presocial state of nature, one can conceivably make this statement about international relations. Nonetheless, excluding treaties, trade accommodations and international custom from the category of a nation's laws is awkward. It becomes more awkward still when treaties establish quasi-governmental institutions, such as the World Trade Organization (WTO)[10] or when they establish truly supranational governmental institutions, such as the European Union.[11] As this process proceeds, the nation is subject to overlapping rules from distinct, and differently motivated rule makers, rendering claims about the coherence of that nation's legal system still more problematic.

[10] See Anna Lanoszka, *The World Trade Organization: Changing Dynamics in the World Political Economy* (Boulder, CO: Lynne Rienner Publishers, 2009); Amrita Narlikar, *The World Trade Organization: A Very Short Introduction* (Oxford: Oxford University Press, 2005).

[11] John McCormick and Jonathan Olsen, *The European Union: Politics and Policies* (Boulder, CO: Westview Press, 2014); John Pinder and Simon Usherwood, *The European Union: A Very Short Introduction* (Oxford: Oxford University Press, 2013).

8.1.2 *The Coherentist Approach to Scholarship*

The traditional methodology of legal scholarship, in both common law and civil law jurisdictions, relies heavily on the asserted coherence of their respective legal systems. This is not simply a matter of homologous structure, but reflects a much deeper relationship between the conceptual foundations of the methodology and its subject matter. If legal scholarship were a purely descriptive discipline, then its coherence would depend, at least in part, on the coherence of the phenomena it was attempting to describe. Consider, for example, the difference between describing the fauna of a given territory and describing a recognized category of animals like birds or mammals. In the first case, the description would possess limited internal coherence because the animals in a given area bear no internal relationship to one another; there would be some mammals, some birds, some insects, and so forth. In the second case, however, the subject matter is defined in terms of internal features, such as mammary glands, fur, warm-bloodedness, and so forth, and a description of this subject matter would be a more organized account, focusing on similarities of function and variations within those similarities, rather than descriptions of separate, unrelated organisms. In both cases, however, the methodology, being descriptive, would be largely the same, with the difference in coherence being determined by the difference in the coherence of the subject matter. More important, the greater coherence of the second subject would be unrelated to the scholarly methodology employed to describe it. Mammals resemble each other because of the process of evolution, the radiation of different adaptations from a primordial ancestor through the mechanism of natural selection. This source of coherence has no relationship to the descriptive methodology that scholars employ in describing that more coherent category.

Legal scholarship, however, is a different matter because, as is widely recognized, it is normative as well as descriptive.[12] Descriptions of different legal systems will display differential levels of coherence based

[12] See Paul Brest, The Fundamental Rights Controversy: The Essential Contradictions of Normative Constitutional Scholarship, 90 *Yale L.J.* 1063, 1067–1081 (1981); George Fletcher, Two Modes of Legal Thought, 90 *Yale L.J.* 970 (1981); Edward L. Rubin, The Practice and Discourse of Legal Scholarship, 86 *Mich. L. Rev.* 1835, 1847–1853 (1988); Pierre Schlag, Normativity and the Politics of Form, 139 *U. Pa. L. Rev.* 801 (1991); Jan M. Smits, *The Mind and Method of the Legal Academic* (Cheltenham, UK: Edward Elgar, 2012), pp. 35–48

on the underlying coherence of the system being described, as in the case of descriptive biology. But in addition to this homologous structure, legal scholarship strives to achieve coherence through the same source as its subject matter, namely, human reason. Reason makes the law coherent in the traditional, premodern view, and reason provides the methodology by which legal scholars analyze the law and advance normative judgments about it. In other words, the methodology of traditional legal scholarship displays unity of discourse with its subject matter; both law and legal scholarship are conceived as systems for deriving specific rules governing society from general principles that fit together into a coherent conceptual framework.

This unity of discourse prevails in both common law and civil law jurisdictions. Common law is more accurately described as judge-made law. In earlier times, the general principles on which judges based their decisions were regarded as either natural law or customary law; as time went on and law became more secular, these dual origins merged into the idea of the society's in-dwelling legal principles. Scholars base their judgments on precisely the same source and use it for the normative evaluation of judicial decisions.[13] A typical work of common law scholarship might argue that the well-known case of *Smith v. Jones*, which held the defendant liable when the dinner that the plaintiff served him made him ill, was incorrectly decided because tort liability should follow only from foreseeable events, and in this case the food was washed in water that was contaminated by an unprecedented case of upstream pollution. Here, the scholar is not only using the same method as the judge, namely deriving a particular result from general principles through the use of reason, but relying on the same underlying belief that the law is a coherent system that allows such reasoning to be employed.[14] In a civil law system, the same unity of discourse would occur, except that both the

[13] See Paul Chynoweth, Legal Research, in Andrew Knight and Les Ruddock, eds., *Advanced Research Methods in the Built Environment* (Oxford: Wiley-Blackwell, 2008), p. 30; Rubin, The Practice and Discourse.

[14] US Supreme Court Justice Antonin Scalia believed that judges should use a coherentist approach to interpreting modern statutes even when they know that the statutes were not drafted on the basis of this principle. *Green v. Bock Laundry Mach. Co.*, 490 U.S. 504, 528 (1989) (Scalia, J., concurring in the judgment); Antonin Scalia, *A Matter of Interpretation: Federal Courts and the Law* (Princeton, NJ: Princeton University Press, 1998), p. 16; see William W. Buzbee, The One-Congress Fiction in Statutory Interpretation, 149 *U. Pa. L. Rev.* 171 (2000).

judge and the scholar would be deriving their conclusions from the principles embedded in the civil or criminal code.[15]

The deeper relationship or regularity between the coherence of legal scholarship and its subject matter in law, as opposed to animal physiology, derives from its normative character. The legal scholar is not only describing the court's decision in *Smith v. Jones*, but evaluating the reasoning process that the court employed and, if possible, proposing a preferable decision on the basis of the scholar's superior ability to reason. It would be possible to use this same methodology in animal physiology. To do so, however, the scholar would not only need to suggest that different adaptations would lead to adaptively superior organisms, but reach that result by duplicating the evolutionary process in her laboratory (or, perhaps, by simulating it with a computer program). Biologists generally do not typically engage in scholarship of this nature, but traditional legal scholars do.

Unlike the common law systems of Britain and its colonies, the civil and criminal codes of Continental legal systems are positive law, of course. While this difference has some effect on traditional scholarship, it is muted by the two systems' shared commitment to legal coherentism. The civilian codes are not regarded as either unrelated collections of provisions nor as acts of will by the legislature; rather, they are seen as legislative enactments of a coherent body of law derived from the customs of the society that have developed through the operation of human reason. Conversely, English common law was originated by the positive enactment of a sovereign, Henry II, as a solution to a specific problem of governance, namely, conflicting land grants issued by Stephen and Maude during their contest for the throne.[16] By the sixteenth century, to be sure, this origin had been forgotten and common law judges were maintaining the historically absurd but politically potent position that the common law was derived from customs that originated in pre-Roman times. In an odd convergence, this pseudo-customary law was then seen as politically acceptable in Early Modern England, and later the United States, because the legislature had acquiesced in its continued development and enforcement by the courts. Thus, in both England and the Continent, the myth of coherentism was maintained in

[15] R.A.J. van Gestel and Hans W. Micklitz, Revitalising Doctrinal Research in Europe: What about Methodology?, in Ulla Neergaard and Ruth Nielsen, eds., *European Legal Method* (Copenhagen: DJOF Publishing, 2011), p. 25.

[16] W.L. Warren, *Henry II* (Berkeley, CA: University of California Press, 1977), pp. 317–361.

the era of democracy through the claim that the elected legislature was either enacting or approving a set of laws derived from rationally generated custom.

8.2 Beyond Coherentism

8.2.1 The Administrative State and the End of Legal Coherentism

Legal coherentism is an attractive notion, but it emerged in premodern times and remains bound to the conception of government that prevailed in those times. The most obvious development that has rendered coherentism obsolete is the advent of the administrative state and its frequent, although obviously not inevitable linkage to democratic governance. To focus on the Western world, the monarchies of the Medieval and Early Modern periods were primarily concerned with establishing civil order within their areas of jurisdiction, and with maintaining or expanding those areas, first through marital alliance and conquest, and later through conquest and colonization. Both goals relied heavily on policy and political mechanisms, such as military force and financial resources. The legal aspect of civil order consisted primarily of prohibitions, declarations that political disloyalty, feuding, impulsive violence, disruption of commerce, and interference with travel were all crimes punishable by royal officials. Those laws needed to implement this could readily be cast as normative prohibitions and attributed to divine or reasoned principle.

With the decline of traditional village life and the concurrent advent of industrialization and urbanization, the role of government expanded. It was perceived as necessary for public authorities to move beyond the maintenance of civil order and provide for the welfare of citizens who were as cut off from the traditional sources of support and protection – and thus dependent on larger, public structures – as they were from supplies of food and water. Even authoritarian regimes responded to this situation, often in the interest of maintaining their own survival or fielding effective military forces in the era of general conscription. But the democratic regimes that developed during the industrial era, in part due to parallel changes in ideas and in part due to the greater ability of urbanized, nontraditionalist populations to mobilize politically, responded at a different level as their electorates demanded government intervention in areas such as workers' wages, workers' health, consumer protection, investor protection, and later, environmental protection and civil rights.

The policies implemented by an administrative are necessarily established by positive law. Each one is conceived as an effort to address a specific social problem and to design new governmental mechanisms for that purpose, most often a specialized administrative agency. Each one requires coordinated planning and the expenditure of resources that are quite obviously beyond the authority of judges to establish or the capacity of judges to implement. These administrative policies thus exceed the boundaries of code or common law; not only can they not be incorporated into those existing structures, but in fact they are often consciously and explicitly designed to displace those structures with a new and qualitatively different set of rules. They are particularized remedies for the problems that modernity presents or assurances of the promises and possibilities it offers.

A recent study of legislative drafting in the US Congress by Abbe Gluck and Lisa Shultz Bressman attempted to determine the extent to which the drafters, whether on committee staff or in Congress' centralized drafting unit (the Office of Legal Counsel) are actually thinking in terms of the canons of interpretation that courts use to determine the meaning of enacted statutes.[17] For example, a court confronted with a list of items in a statute (all chickens, turkeys, ducks, and fowl) will often use the rule of *nocitur a sociis* (the meaning of a word can be determined from the company it keeps) to construe an ambiguous term (because the specific items in the list are birds raised for food, "fowl" would add a domesticated goose to the list, but not a Canada Goose). The study found that the drafters pay varying levels of attention to different canons of construction, but the one that they entirely ignore is the "whole code" cannon – that the meaning of a term should be informed by the way the word is used in other statutes enacted within the same jurisdiction.[18] This is not surprising; the drafters are presented with a task, set for them by the elected representatives, of translating a policy directive into statutory language. They will naturally focus on that task, particularly if a complex, administrative statute is involved; other statutes will simply not seem

[17] Abbe R. Gluck and Lisa Schultz Bressman, Statutory Interpretation from the Inside: An Empirical Study of Congressional Drafting, Delegation, and the Canons, Parts I, 65 *Stan. L. Rev.* 901 (2013).

[18] Ibid., p. 936 ("our respondents also vigorously disputed that . . . the "whole code rule," under which courts construe terms *across* different statutes consistently – reflects how Congress drafts or even how it *tries* to draft. Specifically, only 9% of respondents told us that drafters often or always intend for terms to apply consistently across statutes that are unrelated by subject matter"; emphasis in original).

relevant to the difficult mission that confronts them.[19] In parliamentary systems, where the government typically drafts all the important statutes, the drafting process is often carried out by specially assigned staff in the Ministry of Justice, although it might also be parceled out to subject-specific ministries. This may well produce more professional work than the American system, but it seems likely that drafters given instructions from modern political authorities will be equally task oriented.

As positive enactments, administrative policies are clearly acts of will, rather than derivations from a normative order established by God or custom. In the Medieval and Early Modern periods, the monarch was the source of such enactments. The political legitimacy that he possessed supported their legality, but was counterbalanced by the concept of the king as magistrate, who had the authority to elaborate but not alter natural law. In modern democracies, the people, acting through their elected representatives, generate the acts of will that constitute the positive laws of the administrative state. The political legitimacy of these laws is greater than their premodern predecessors because there is no countervailing force.[20] Democracy, in part because it has been aligned with secularization in the Western world, is premised on the notion that the people are supreme, that their choices – their will – is the only test of political legitimacy. As Blackstone, a royal appointee and certainly no radical, famously said as early as the 1760s, "Parliament can do everything except making a woman a man or a man a woman."[21] To be sure, constitutionalism, subsequently developed in the United States and a feature of virtually every modern democracy except Britain, places limits on the legislature's range of action. But the validity of the constitution derives from the same source, namely the people,

[19] This is even true when different committees draft different parts of the same statute, an increasingly common situation these days; see Barbara Sinclair, *Unorthodox Lawmaking: New Legislative Processes in the U.S. Congress* (Washington, DC: CQ Press, 2007), pp. 12–16, 42–45, 116–118. As Gluck and Bressman, Statutory Interpretation from the Inside, p. 936, observe, "congressional committees are 'islands' that limit communication between committees drafting different parts of the same statute."

[20] In fact, I believe that the term "legitimacy" is an anachronistic misnomer when applied to modern government, and that the real issue is the level of compliance that a particular decision maker is able to achieve. Rubin, *Beyond Camelot*, pp. 144–178. Since this raises additional issues about modern government that are not directly germane to the topic of this chapter, I have retained the traditional terminology.

[21] Jean Louis de Lolme, *The Constitution of England; Or, an Account of the English Government* (David Lieberman, ed.) (Indianapolis, IN: Liberty Fund, 2007) [1794], p. 102. Presumably, it could now do this as well.

although acting in a different modality, and the constitution authorizes legislative action as well as limiting it.

Modernity not only detaches legislation from natural law and general principle, but also detaches it from custom. In part, this is the result of changes in the material conditions of society that are external to the legal system. The Scientific Revolution of the seventeenth century produced the world's first theoretical understanding of the physical world, and thereby generated enormous technological advances. A great deal of modern law is designed to deal with these changes; the regulation of automobiles, airlines, broadcasting, pharmaceuticals, industrial safety, industrial pollution, and a wide range of other administrative laws represent efforts to limit the risks, and increase the advantages, of developments that are too new and too rapid to be controlled by custom. A second feature of these developments, as basic to them as their novelty, is their sophistication and complexity. This places them beyond the understanding of the ordinary people who generate customs over time and demands the organized efforts of experts.[22] Finally, and more closely connected with the nature of the legal system, customary law is produced by stable, partially autonomous communities – the village culture of premodern society. Once people are detached from such communities and mixed together in large urban agglomerations, their mode of action, including their mode of generating law, will almost inevitably be political rather than customary. That is, they will consciously form political alliances whose purpose is to induce the government to enact positive law, rather than gradually generating patterns of behavior that crystalize into customary law.[23] This decline of customary law eliminates the form of human law that is most amenable to a coherentist position, at both the theoretical and pragmatic levels.

[22] See Jacques Ellul, *The Technological Society* (John Wilkinson, trans.) (New York: Vintage, 1964); Jürgen Habermas, *The Theory of Communicative Action: vol. 2: Lifeworld and System: A Critique of Functionalist Reason* (Thomas McCarthy, trans.) (Boston: Beacon Press, 1987), pp. 153–197; Don Ihde, *Technology and the Lifeworld: From Garden to Earth* (Bloomington, IN: Indiana University Press,1990); Henri Lefebvre, *Everyday Life in the Modern World* (Sasha Rabinovitch, trans.) (New Brunswick, NJ: Transaction Publishers, 1994).

[23] Social movement theory studies this modern process of collective action. See, e.g., Manuel Castells, *The Information Age: Economy, Society and Culture, vol. II: The Power of Identity* (Malden, MA: Blackwell Publishers, 1997), pp. 68–221; Donatella Della Porta and Mario Diani, *Social Movements: A Introduction* (Malden, MA: Blackwell Publishers, 1999); Sidney Tarrow, *Power in Movement: Social Movements, Collective Action and Politics* (Cambridge: Cambridge University Press, 1994).

Conversely, the form of human law that is least amenable to the coherentist position, namely resource allocation, is a particularly common and distinctive feature of administrative government. The primary task of premodern governments, which was to maintain order within their jurisdictions, finds a parallel in modern regulatory law, although that law is of a qualitatively different character. But modern administrative governments also carry out two basic functions that have virtually no premodern equivalent. First, they provide direct benefits to citizens: welfare, disability payments, unemployment compensation, education, housing, health care, and a variety of other services. Second, they operate large nonmilitary institutions that in some cases, such as schools and hospitals, serve as mechanisms for the provision of services, and in other cases, such as national parks, research laboratories, airlines, and prisons, serve separate purposes. Both the provision of services and the maintenance of institutions were performed by private organizations, largely religious in character, or were not performed at all, during the Medieval and Early Modern Eras. Their transfer to public authorities, and their vast expansion, is a characteristic of the modern administrative state.

Benefit distribution and the operation of domestic institutions require resource allocations, that is, they use funds that the government obtains – typically by traditional means such as taxation – to implement domestic programs that are directly administered by public authorities. Such programs must be authorized, designed, and structured by specific legislation. Even if the purpose of the program could be derived from generalized principles – which is itself unlikely – this implementing legislation is necessarily particular to the program's distinctive necessities. Moreover, these resource allocations are clearly acts of will by the ruling authority. This is not only because they are specific legislation, but also because they generally involve the use of public funds raised by taxation. Throughout Western history, taxation has always been regarded as an act of will, in part because of traditional concepts regarding private property, in part because finance is seen as a secular activity that possesses only an instrumental relationship to norms. It is this combination of specificity and political will which explains why resource allocation legislation is typically excluded from definitions of law formulated by people who remain committed to coherentism.

With respect to treaties and other legal aspects of globalization, the trajectory of legal developments is more complex, but the ultimate effect of these developments is equally antipathetic to legal coherentism. During the High Middle Ages, all legal activity in Europe was conducted in the same language, and most was based on the same Roman sources; all relied on a generally agreed-upon conception of underlying principles (natural law) and much of the substantive law was either promulgated or influenced by the Catholic Church, a truly international organization. The growth of nation-states in the Early Modern period, the integration of national law within each state, the growth of vernacular languages and, of course, the Protestant Reformation, combined to fracture the previous integration or unity of European law. Modern treaties, and most notably the legal structure of the European Union, move back in the direction of integration but now operate on a foundation of national law. If an adopted treaty has any domestic implications – and most do – it will constitute the law of the adopting nation, but will necessarily reflect the legal conceptions and pragmatic policies of at least one decision maker external to that nation. In the case of the European Union, the external decision maker is a complex, multinational process which will almost inevitably produce new legislation that conflicts with the domestic law of the constituent nations As a result, the treaties and other agreements that are central to modern globalization will generally pose a challenge to any effort to treat national law as a coherent totality.

Underlying the changes in the content of the law that result from the administrative state is a profound conceptual change in the normative framework from which the law emerges. In the premodern era – that is, before the simultaneous advent of industrialization and the administrative state – the prevailing worldview was that the state is a moral entity that exists independent of its subjects and serves as a higher purpose for their secular activities.[24] According to this view, law, as a feature of the state, consists of the norms that the sovereign establishes to guide human behavior. Because the sovereign rules by divine right and acts in conformance with natural law, these norms are reflections of the divine order, and are thus parallel to the higher purpose of achieving salvation that guides religious activities. This perspective, for reasons described above, produced the idea that the law is a coherent whole, based on enduring principles. The pragmatic effects of law were not ignored, but they were generally treated as subsidiary to the law's normative significance. To be good or proper law, a judicial decision, a legislative enactment or a customary practice needed to fit into the coherent structure of the legal system.

[24] For further explication, see Edward L. Rubin, *Soul, Self and Society: The New Morality and the Modern State* (Oxford: Oxford University Press, 2015), pp. 69–112.

The administrative state that has developed during the last two centuries replaces this premodern concept with the alternative idea that the purpose of the state is to serve its citizens. It is a response to mass industrial society, and to the secularization that both causes and results from that society. The underlying moral concept is that people's goal in life is not to achieve salvation or serve a higher purpose, but to experience the most rewarding or fulfilling life that is possible for them.[25] This concept imposes both negative and positive obligations on the state. Negatively, it means that the state must not interfere with people's life choices and must abandon its premodern demand that people serve the state. Positively, it means that the state must protect people from the rigors and dangers of industrial society and provide them with at least the minimal resources, including subsistence, housing, health care, and education.

This shift forges the connection between the administrative state and democracy. If the recognized goal of government is to serve the citizens' needs, there is likely to be an insistent demand among the citizenry that they express those needs by choosing government officials through election. Conversely, if the government is based on a normative ethos of serving citizen needs, choosing leaders by election is the best way to design the government so that the citizens' needs serve as its guiding principle. It is thus no accident that the first national democracies in the Western world evolved simultaneously with the administrative state. The result is that the citizenry's preferences, not developed over time like custom but expressed at the relatively brief intervals of the electoral cycle, determine public policy. Those preferences take the place of natural law and custom as a means of constraining the actions of the ruler, a democratic, administrative government takes the place of the divine ordering itself.

I have previously suggested that a useful way to think about governance in a modern administrative state is to bracket the term law and replace it with the concept of policy and implementation.[26] That is, the democratic process, generally by means of elected representatives, establishes policies, and then those policies are implemented by their appointees, sometimes courts but more often administrative agencies. There is no need to use the term "law," in the premodern sense, in describing or analyzing this process; more specific terms such as statutes, regulations,

[25] Ibid., pp. 113–168. [26] Rubin, *Beyond Camelot*, pp. 191–226.

and binding rules can be used instead. The purpose of such verbal manipulation is to counteract the implication, so firmly embedded in our concept of law, that these actions need to fit together into a coherent whole or to be justified in terms of general principles. Another way to achieve the same result is simply to acknowledge that law means something different in the administrative state than it did before, that it refers to nothing other than the policy and implementation process.

In either case, the standard for judging the value of law is not whether it is coherent but rather whether it is effective, that is, effective in establishing and implementing the policy goals of the modern state. In a democratic administrative state, the policy goals are determined by the citizens whose needs the administrative apparatus serves. As a result, the law's previous connection to doctrine is decisively sundered. All legal enactments are regarded as pure acts of will, choices made by the citizens to express their policy desires at a particular time. Questions of doctrinal coherence are not ignored, but they become subsidiary to the purpose-driven effectiveness analysis. In other words, the basic question about doctrinal coherence is whether it serves some identifiable social purpose, such as controlling government arbitrariness or increasing legal predictability. Coherence has been transformed from an underlying, deontological principle into an instrumental device that is deployed only when it can be effective.

8.2.2 Legal Scholarship and the Limits of Doctrinal Analysis

Legal methodology is regularly criticized for its traditionalist character, its emphasis on courts in the United States and Britain, or its emphasis on legal codes on the European Continent. But the essential step in developing a new, truly modern methodology of legal research is not simply to go beyond the court-centered approach of English language scholarship, and the code-centered approach of European scholarship, but to shift from a focus on legal coherence to a focus on legal effectiveness. The basic issue in legal scholarship should be the exploration of the way that public policy, once established through the political process, is implemented by governmental institutions, primarily administrative agencies. That policy will typically involve the essentially administrative goals of serving the interests of the citizens, that is, protecting them from the dangers of modern industrial society and providing them with benefits so that they can lead fulfilling lives. Democratic processes are not as reliable in ensuring that people will be able to seek self-fulfillment in the manner that they themselves choose; as a result, most Western regimes have established judicial as well as democratic controls on government policy. The implementation of these controls, or the design of programs that incorporate them, may be regarded as an aspect of effectiveness.

A legal methodology that focuses on effectiveness would differ from one based on coherence in a number of ways. To begin with, it would remedy the most obvious lacuna in American legal scholarship by directing attention to governmental institutions other than courts. Courts remain important, both in the small but still significant areas which continue to be governed by common law, and as a means of controlling other institutions. But most modern law is generated by either legislative enactment or administrative rulemaking and then implemented by a range of administrative action. To give just two examples, there is an extensive literature on the way courts interpret statutory law, but most of the statutory interpretation that matters is carried out by administrative agencies.[27] A great deal of work remains to be done on the way agencies interpret statutes, particularly since the Supreme Court, in recognition of this reality, instructed federal courts to defer to agency interpretation.[28] Second, although legal scholarship is predominantly normative, framing recommendations to the relevant institution, nearly all the existing scholarship advises courts about the best way to frame common law rules. There is simply no normative scholarship directed to legislatures about the best way to draft regulatory statutes, and very little directed to agencies about the best way to draft regulations. But it is these statutes and regulations, not common law rules, that constitute the substance of modern American law.

[27] See Jerry L. Mashaw, Norms, Practices and the Paradox of Deference: A Preliminary Inquiry into Agency Statutory Interpretation, 57 *Admin. L. Rev.* 501 (2005); Kevin Stack, Purposivism in the Executive Branch: How Agencies Interpret Statutes, 109 *Nw. U. L. Rev.* 871 (2015); Kevin Stack, Agency Statutory Interpretation and Policy Form, *Mich. St. L. Rev.* 225 (2009); Interpretation Peter Strauss, When the Judge is Not the Primary Official With Responsibility to Read: Agency Interpretation and the Problem of Legislative History, 66 *Chi.-Kent L. Rev.* 321 (1990).

[28] *Chevron, U.S.A., Inc. v. NRDC*, 467 U.S. 837 (1984). There is a vast scholarly literature on this case in the United States, but – significantly, and despite the holding of the case itself – most of it involves the judicial formulation of the doctrine or the role of courts in general. Although the decision made clear something that should have been apparent all along, scholars have, for the most part, not accepted its invitation and shifted their focus to the way agencies actually do interpret statutes. See Mashaw, Norms, Practices and the Paradox of Deference.

A second and more conceptual feature of a postcoherentist methodology is that it must employ a different method of analysis. If law is supposed to be coherent, then any given legal action, whether by a court or other institution, should be judged on the basis of its fidelity to the underlying principles of the legal system and its consonance with other contemporaneous actions. But if law is supposed to be effective, then the crucial question for legal scholarship is whether the law is achieving its intended purpose in real-world situations. This requires a scholarly discourse that can identify purposes, debate alternative purposes, determine measures for the attainment of those purposes, and then investigate the law's actual operation.

The arguments about general legal principles that occupy so much attention in traditional and even current legal scholarship are simply irrelevant in this more modern context. When Ronald Dworkin, after writing extensively about the common law method, realized that modern law is primarily statutory, he attempted to rescue his theory from its diminished relevance with the assertion that statutes should be judged on the basis of their "integrity" with other legal rules.[29] The absurdity of this claim, which his commitment to coherentism forced upon him, is apparent. There is simply no reason, in the modern world, why statutes need to fit together, or even resemble one another. A legislature may adopt one strategy for reducing air pollution and a completely different strategy for ensuring the financial stability of banks. This variation might not only be based on the nature of the subject matter, but also on the existing state of knowledge. Regulation of a known technology might look quite different from regulation of something new, even in a closely related subject area; we might have one approach to prenatal care, and another to the genetic modification of human beings. It might also be based on the perceived quality of the agency; a trusted agency might be given only a general

[29] Ronald Dworkin, *Law's Empire* (Cambridge, MA: Belknap Press, 1986), pp. 176–184. Dworkin bases his argument on the claim that a "checkboard" statute, such as one that criminalized abortions for women born in even numbered years, but not odd numbered years, would be deemed unacceptable. Far from supporting his position, the argument serves only to demonstrate his total lack of comprehension of modern administrative government that his position implies. Of course, we would reject such a statute, not only because it violates equal protection, but because it would be virtually insane from the perspective of effective public policy, the basis on which modern statutes are judged. Instead of constructing such a far-fetched hypothetical, all Dworkin needed to do is to consider two real statutes, such as the Federal Reserve Act and the Federal Trade Commission Act (passed within a few years of each other by the same political coalition) and he would have realized that his position was unsustainable.

authorization, whereas an unreliable one might require an elaborately detailed statute. Similar considerations (with subagencies in place of agencies) would govern the design of agency regulations. Scholarship that discusses the effectiveness of these enactments should base its analysis on a recognition of these variables, the way that each enactment functions in its particular area of operation, and its particularized use of language.

Both the institutional and conceptual features of administrative, post-coherentist legal discourse demand a further change in legal methodology from doctrinal analysis to empirical research. With respect to the institutional concerns of the scholarship, courts are relatively simple institutions, and relatively small ones. Much of their decision process is publicly disclosed through published opinions, and the effect of their decisions depends largely on the language of these opinions. Legislatures are more complex and opaque, and extensive empirical investigation is required to determine both their decision processes and the effect of their decisions. This is, of course, even more true of the administrative apparatus; in the United States, the executive branch (consisting largely of agencies) is two orders of magnitude larger than the judiciary; eleven of the fifteen Cabinet Departments have substantially more employees than the entire federal court system. Their structure is highly complex, and most of their decision process is not publicly disclosed or even fully documented. To determine what legislatures and agencies are deciding, and to understand the way the effectiveness of their decisions might be improved, requires extensive empirical investigation.

The need for a shift to empiricism is even more apparent on the conceptual level. Doctrinal coherence can be determined from an examination of a judicial opinion itself; the only research required to make this determination is the examination of other judicial opinions. The entire concept of coherence depends on the idea that the law is a self-contained system whose component parts can be judged by their relation to the whole. In contrast, the effectiveness of law depends upon its real-world effects; to determine those effects, we cannot rely upon an examination of its text but must determine the way it alters human behavior and the physical environment.

Such an inquiry demands extensive empirical investigation and a different set of academic tools than those traditionally used by legal scholars to explore questions of coherence. At the most basic level, it demands the partial integration of law and social science, a natural connection that has been severely underemphasized because the current approach to legal education, in both the United States and Europe, was designed before the advent of empirical social sciences as university disciplines.[30] Social science can be roughly defined as the systematic study of human society and its structures. When people believed that much of human law could be derived from natural law, they would have said (had social science existed at the time) that the overlap between the fields was only partial. But now that we recognize law as a human artifact, it fits securely within the subject matter of social science.

It seems apparent that this is precisely the trend that legal scholarship is taking at the present time. Empirical studies of law have become increasingly prominent in legal scholarship, particularly with the increase in the number of faculty members who have academic degrees in social science fields, as well as – or sometimes instead of – professional degrees in law.[31] Often, these studies involve the systematic use of survey data and statistical analysis.[32] To this might be added the laboratory studies that constitute an essential methodology of behavioral economics.[33] Much of the methodological debate regarding this approach focuses on whether such studies are being done well, not whether they should be done at all.[34] These data collection efforts are striking, but, as David Trubek has suggested,[35] they reflect an even more important conceptual

[30] See Edward Rubin, What's Wrong with Langdell's Method, and What to Do About It, 60 *Vand. L. Rev.* 609, 635–39 (2007)

[31] Legal Realist scholars in the United States had recognized the possible uses of empirical data, but their lack of training, and amateurish approach to the enterprise in general, doomed this earlier enterprise to failure. See John Henry Schlegel, *American Legal Realism and Empirical Social Science* (Chapel Hill, NC: University of North Carolina Press, 1995).

[32] See, e.g., Michael Heise, *The Past, Present and Future of Empirical Legal Scholarship: Judicial Decision Making and the New Empiricism, Ill. L. Rev.* 819, 821 (2002); Tracey George, An Empirical Study of Empirical Legal Scholarship: The Top Law Schools, 81 *Indiana L.J.* 141, 141 (2006).

[33] See, e.g., Daniel Kahneman and Amos Tversky, *Judgment Under Uncertainty: Heurisitics and Biases* (Cambridge: Cambridge University Press, 1982); Amos Tversky and Daniel Kahneman, The Framing of Decisions and the Psychology of Choice, 211 *Science* 453 (1981).

[34] See, e.g., Lee Epstein, Andrew Martin and Matthew Schneider, On the Effective Communication of the Results of Empirical Studies, Parts I and II, 59 *Vand. L. Rev.* 1811 (2006), 60 *Vand. L. Rev.* 801 (2007); Lee Epstein and Gary King, The Rules of Inference, 69 *U. Chi. L. Rev.* 1 (2002).

[35] David Trubek, Where the Action Is: Critical Legal Studies and Empiricism, 36 *Stan. L. Rev.* 575, 579–588 (1984). See also David Trubek and John Esser, Critical Empiricism in American Legal Studies: Paradox, Program or Pandora's Box, 14 *Law and Soc. Inquiry* 1 (1989).

departure. It constitutes a truly new approach to the legal system itself, rather than merely being new methodology for studying that system. From this perspective, empirical legal studies is different from the empiricism of the past and represents a truly transformative insight for legal scholarship and the legal system.[36]

The transformative effect of modern empiricism does not mean that legal scholarship would be absorbed into social science, however. The basic reason is that this scholarship remains a normative enterprise; it does not merely describe the actions taken by government decision makers – although such descriptions are certainly a common and valuable part of legal scholarship – but also evaluates those actions. Just as traditional scholarship regularly argues that the judge made an error in *Smith v. Jones* in imposing liability for an unforeseeable result, modern scholarship is called upon to assess whether an agency made an error in implementing the Smith-Jones Act by imposing fines for occasional lapses by the regulated parties rather than demanding systematic improvements. The standard by which such normative judgments are made, however, is not the decision's coherence with other decisions, but its effectiveness in producing the desired results. This approach is sometimes described as New Legal Realism in the United States.[37] In Europe, Jan Smits refers to it, somewhat more descriptively, as the empirical-normative method.[38]

In identifying the integration of legal scholarship and social science as an empirical-normative approach, a certain amount of epistemological caution is required. Very little legal scholarship is entirely normative; with the possible exception of highly theoretical jurisprudence, works of legal scholarship generally involve some description of existing legal provisions, even if they then proceed to criticize or condemn those

[36] For a survey of empirical scholarship involving law, see Chapter 11 in this volume.

[37] Howard Erlanger, Bryant Garth, Jane Larson, Elizabeth Mertz, Victoria Nourse, and David Wilkins, Is It Time for a New Legal Realism?, 2005 *Wisc. L. Rev.* 335, 337; Daniel Farber, Toward a New Legal Realism, 68 *U. Chi. L. Rev.* 279 (2001); Stewart Macaulay, Contracts, New Legal Realism, and Improving the Navigation of *The Yellow Submarine*, 80 *Tul. L. Rev.* 1161 (2006); Thomas J. Miles and Cass R. Sunstein, The New Legal Realism, 75 *U. Chi. L. Rev.* 831 (2008); Victoria Nourse and Gregory Shaffer, Varieties of New Legal Realism: Can a New World Order Prompt New Legal Theory?, 95 *Cornell L. Rev.* 61 (2009); Symposium, New Legal Realism, 31 *Law and Soc. Inq.* 797 (2006). On the relationship between the empirical legal studies movement and New Legal Realism, see Mark Suchman and Elizabeth Mertz, Toward a New Legal Empiricism: Empirical Legal Studies and New Legal Realism, 6 *Ann. Rev. Law Soc. Sci.* 555 (2010)

[38] Jan M. Smits, *The Mind and Method of the Legal Academic* (Northampton, MA: Edward Elgar Publishing, 2012) pp. 73–99.

provisions. Conversely, most theorists of social scientists recognize that the field cannot possibly consist of value-free description and analysis. As Weber observed, values serve as a necessary structuring device for social science, setting the agenda, guiding the collection of data, and defining the terms of analysis.[39] In addition, as Weber also noted, social science studies the way people construct meaning, and an understanding of this process requires the investigator to participate in it along with the people being studied, rather than merely observing them from afar.[40] What distinguishes law from social science, then, is not normativity per se, but the conscious effort to frame recommendations to actual or imagined decision makers. In the modern state, however, those decision makers are typically administrative agencies, and the task which they are assigned is to implement public policy in an effective manner. Framing recommendations to such decision makers requires the understanding of empirical effects that social science provides, not the elaboration of coherent legal doctrine.

The normative character of modern legal scholarship, moreover, need not be limited to the implementation of previously established policy. To begin with, there is no clear division between policy-making and policy-implementing institutions in a modern administrative state. While the legislature rarely implements programs directly, due to both time limitations and due process considerations, administrative agencies are often granted extensive policy-making functions in conjunction with their implementation role. This will clearly be true when the legislature is uncertain about the most effective strategy because the necessary information is unavailable – or because the members cannot agree – and writes an authorizing statute in vague or general terms.[41] Normative

[39] Max Weber, *The Methodology of the Social Sciences* (Edward A. Shils and Henry A. Finch, trans.) (New York: Free Press, 1949). See also Peter L. Berger and Thomas Luckmann, *The Social Construction of Reality: A Treatise in the Sociology of Knowledge* (New York: Anchor Books, 1966); Nelson Goodman, *Ways of Worldmaking* (Indianapolis, Ind.: Hackett Publishing, 1978); Peter Winch, *The Idea of a Social Science and its Relationship to Philosophy*, 2nd edn. (London: Routledge, 1990); cf. Arthur Danto, *Narration and Knowledge*, 2nd edn. (New York: Columbia University Press, 2007) (historical accounts).

[40] Weber, *Economy and Society*, pp. 8–11. See also Clifford Geertz, *The Interpretation of Cultures* (New York: Basic Books, 1977); Michael Polanyi, *Personal Knowledge: Towards a Post-Critical Philosophy* (Chicago: University of Chicago Press, 1974); Alfred Schutz, *The Phenomenology of the Social World* (George Walsh and Frederick Lehnert, trans.) (Chicago: Northwestern, 1967).

[41] Two well-known doctrines established by the US Supreme Court recognize the frequency and necessity of such uncertainty. The first is the Court's consistent refusal to strike down

scholarship addressing the agency's regulatory strategy will often need to discuss policy choices in this context. The epistemologically simplest way to understand such scholarship is to recognize that a second-best policy that can be effectively implemented might be superior to an optimal policy that cannot be, with effectiveness measured against the larger and perhaps extremely general policy that motivated the statute.[42]

That is not the limit of empirical-normative legal scholarship, however. Weber articulated a basic distinction between instrumentally rational (*zweckrational*) and value-rational (*wertrational*) action.[43] Although he defines the latter as "determined by a conscious belief in the value for its own sake . . . independently of its prospects of success," Habermas points out that if the consideration of value is indeed rational (as opposed to traditional, for example, which is one of Weber's other categories of action) then it is subject to thoughtful debate on the basis of its merits.[44] Such debate, which he refers to as communicative action, is open to scholarly consideration; in fact, Habermas's theory of communicative action is more convincing as a definition of scholarly discourse than as the framework for social emancipation or the justification of democracy to which he aspires.[45] The criteria for judgment would be normative, of course, but that hardly precludes scholars from contributing to the debate. Moreover, since someone who is willing to discuss her normative beliefs in a rational manner must necessarily consider

regulatory statutes, no matter how broadly drafted, as excessive delegations of legislative authority. Whitman v. American Trucking Assns., Inc., 531 U.S. 457 (2001); Industrial Union Dep't, AFL-CIO v. American Petroleum Inst., 448 U.S. 607 (1980) (Benzene Case), see Jerry Mashaw, *Greed, Chaos and Governance: Using Public Choice to Improve Public Law* (New Haven, Conn.: Yale University Press, 1997), pp. 146–155; Edward L. Rubin, Law and Legislation in the Administrative State 89 *Colum. L. Rev.* 369, 388–392 (1989). The second, of course, is the Chevron doctrine, *Chevron, USA, Inc. v. NRDC*, 467 U.S. 837, 865 (1984) (there are several reasons why Congress might not want to legislate with specificity, and all are to be understood as valid delegations of authority to the agency charged with implementation of the statute).

42 See Maxim Boyco, Andrei Schleifer and Robert Vishny, Second- Best Economic Policy for a Divided Government, 40 *Eur. Econ. Rev.* 767 (1996); Deborah Stone, *Policy Paradox: The Art of Political Decision Making*, rev. edn. (New York: W.W. Norton, 2002).

43 Weber, *Economy and Society*, pp. 24–25.

44 Jürgen Habermas, *The Theory of Communicative Action, vol 1: Reason and the Rationalization of Society* (Thomas McCarthy, trans.) (Boston: Beacon Press, 1984), pp. 273–337.

45 For Habermas's argument for social emancipation, see Habermas, supra note 22, pp. 374–403. For his theory of democracy, see Jürgen Habermas, *Between Facts and Norms: Contributions to a Discourse Theory of Law and Democracy* (Boston: MIT Press, 1996).

trade-offs, the debate is likely to involve empirical elements that scholars may be uniquely qualified to address. It is only when such debate has reached its end, and the legislature must make a decision by counting votes, that is, as a pure act of will, that empirical-normative legal scholarship comes to an end, and empirical political science scholarship about voting patterns must take over.[46]

An administratively oriented legal methodology need not abandon the study of courts, of course, or even the analysis of legal doctrine. There remains a considerable space for doctrinal analysis, and a significant space for coherentist methodology within the framework of a legal effectiveness approach. To begin with, an agency's most effective implementation strategy may consist of or include case-by-case adjudication of disputes. In this situation, doctrinal coherence serves several important functions, such as providing notice of the law to private parties (not necessary when rules are stated in advance by regulation) and allowing the incremental development of new legal rules. Second, there remain areas where implementation of policy is assigned to courts, rather than agencies. Because courts employ case-by-case adjudication, doctrinal coherence serves the purposes specified above. In addition, because courts are not monitored by elected officials, doctrinal coherence serves the additional purpose of controlling arbitrary behavior by them. In all these areas, however, doctrinal coherence is desirable if it achieves particular identifiable public purposes. It is not an end in itself, as it was in the pre-administrative era. Consequently, its value becomes an empirical question, thus further indicating the integration of the new legal methodology with social science.

Still another area where legal doctrine remains relevant, and coherentism plays an important role in Western legal systems, is constitutional law. Constitutions are positive enactments, not natural law, and many of

[46] But this is the way decisions are commonly made in modern democracies, which is the reason why the rationale for democracy that Weber derives from his theory is not convincing. Many political theorists, independently of Habermas, argue forcefully for a related approach, which is generally described as deliberative democracy. See, e.g., Amy Gutmann and Dennis Thompson, *Democracy and Disagreement* (Cambridge, MA: Belknap Press, 1996); James Fishkin, *Democracy and Deliberation: New Direction for Democratic Reform* (New Haven, CT: Yale University Press, 1991); Cass Sunstein, *The Partial Constitution* (Cambridge, MA: Harvard University Press, 1993). I argue that the approach reflects an a priori commitment to (or emotive nostalgia for) the Greek concept of direct democracy, and has little relevance to modern politics in Western democracies. Rubin, *Beyond Camelot*, pp. 117–119; Edward Rubin, Getting Past Democracy, 149 *U. Pa. L. Rev.* 711 (2001).

their provisions display the particularized, instrumental quality of other modern positive law enactments. There is no general principle, for example, that determines the relationship between the chief executive and the legislature or the timing of elections. But in addition, modern constitutions impose normative limits on governmental action, and while these are also positive enactments, they have strong normative components, usually grounded on modern concepts of human rights. Moreover, for a variety of institutional reasons, these limits are implemented by courts, through the development of legal doctrine that is equivalent, in many ways, to the development of common law in Anglo-American law. Clearly, the validity of this process depends upon the coherence of the doctrine, that is, the judges' ability to justify their decision to overturn democratically enacted legislation by demonstrating that the decision is derived from normative principles in a manner consistent with other such decisions.[47]

Even in this case, however, the essentially instrumental quality of modern law should often play a role that distinguishes the mode of justification from the one that would have been used in premodern times. It can do so through the same methodology that is essential to designing positive law in nonconstitutional situations, namely, empirical social science. To take one highly charged example, consider the current exclusion of child pornography from free speech protection in American constitutional law. No one doubts that the state has the authority to punish people who use children to produce this material. In *New York v. Ferber*, however, the Supreme Court has also allowed the state to punish people who simply watch it, an exception to the general right to receive information.[48]

Premodern people would have resolved a difficult case of this sort, involving the conflict between two powerfully felt norms, by appealing to Scripture, or to natural law, or to some other purely normative mode of analysis. The sexual abuse of children is so horrific that there is a tendency to revert to this mode of analysis, which is what the US Supreme Court did when it decided *Ferber*. But a modern approach to

[47] See David A. Strauss, *The Living Constitution* (2010).

[48] 458 U.S. 747 (1982). See also *Osborne v. Ohio*, 495 U.S. 103 (1990) (upholding statute that criminalized mere possession of child pornography). The decisions are based on *Miller v. California*, 413 U.S. 15 (1973) which held that obscene speech as defined in that case, could be regulated in a manner forbidden for nonobscene speech. In *Ashcroft v. Free Speech Coalition*, 535 U.S. 234 (2002), the Court struck down parts of the subsequent Child Pornography Prevention Act, 18 U.S.C. § 2252.

law would blend normative analysis, which clearly remains important in this situation, with empirical considerations. It would construct the question in more instrumental terms – not whether watching child pornography is an inherent wrong, or sin, but whether criminalizing it serves as an effective way to protect children. Surely, one relevant question, from the modern perspective, is whether the criminal prohibition actually reduces the amount of child pornography that is produced. A second question is whether those who watch it are themselves more or less likely to engage in sexual abuse. These are empirical questions which can be addressed, even if not definitively answered, through social science research. Sometimes the litigants will provide such research, but they cannot be depended upon to do so, particularly if the court does not indicate that it will entertain such considerations. In any event, the neutrality of the research they provide will be open to question. Courts should be able to rely on social scientists, perhaps with joint degrees or perhaps working in conjunction with colleagues from law, to provide data of this sort. The current incapacity of most Western courts to commission such research when deciding complex cases is an atavism, a failure to comprehend the character of law in the modern administrative state.

8.3 The Irrelevance of Contemporary Arguments for Coherentism

8.3.1 The Rule of Law

The changes in law and governance described in Section 8.2.1 have certainly not gone unnoticed; in fact, it seems fair to say that the majority of legal scholars would agree that the Western world's approach to law has changed in the matter described. It also seems fair to say that a majority of legal scholars who have observed this change do not like it. Far from embracing the reality of modern government and developing a new approach to legal scholarship that would simultaneously provide an illuminating account of that government and enter into an effective dialogue with its decision makers, scholars often adopt a stance of bemused or outraged condemnation. Writing from a wide range of political and normative positions, from conservative to progressive and from ancient natural law to modern discourse theory, scholars such as Ronald Dworkin, John Finnis, Richard Epstein, Gary Lawson, Theodore Lowi, Anthony Kronman, Robert Nozick, Brian Tamanaha, and many others have not only resisted shifting to the new methodology described above, but have centered their scholarship on its rejection.[49]

There are at least three major problems with this widely adopted stance. First, unless one rejects the moral status of democracy, modern government is legitimate. Urging acceptance of the modern administrative state is not a reversion to the quiescent belief that "whatever is, is right."[50] Rather, it simply acknowledges the fact that administrative governance is what every Western democracy has chosen for itself, using processes that few modern scholars would challenge. Second, the modern administrative state, in addition to being the product of a democratic process, is, quite simply, the government in place, and will be, as all its critics concede, for the foreseeable future. It is always salutary to criticize the regime in power, but one must regard that regime as supremely evil to advocate blanket condemnation as opposed to incremental improvement. Administrative government is the government we have, and it is the scholar's task to live with it and make it better.

Little more need be said about these first two problems in the present context, but the third problem with contemporary criticism of the modern administrative state is central to the question of scholarly methodology. That problem is that the criticisms are undertheorized, in the sense of being grounded on unjustified assumptions. The most common basis of the criticism is that administrative governance's repudiation of legal coherence violates the rule of law. But this assumes that coherentism and the rule of law are equivalent, which is only true if one embeds premodern ideas about law into the concept. In other words, the blanket condemnation, and even many of the specific concerns about modern administrative government are tautological; they argue that the new mode of governance employed by Western democracies is defective because it is a new mode of governance.

[49] See Dworkin, *Law's Empire*; John Finnis, *Natural Law and Natural Rights* (Oxford, Eng.: Clarendon Press, 1980); Anthony Kronman, The Lost Lawyer: Failing Ideals of the Legal Profession (1993); Gary Lawson, The Rise and Rise of the Administrative State, 107 *Harv. L. Rev.* 1231 (1994); Theodore Lowi, *The End of Liberalism: The Second Republic of the United States*, 2nd edn. (New York: W.W. Norton, 1979), pp. 92–126; Robert Nozick, *Anarchy, State and Utopia* (New York: Basic Books, 1974), pp. 88–119; Brian Tamanaha, *On the Rule of Law: History, Politics, Theory* (Cambridge: Cambridge University Press, 2004); Brian Tamanaha, *Law as a Means to an End* (Cambridge: Cambridge University Press, 2006).

[50] Alexander Pope, *An Essay on Man, Epistle I, in Alexander Pope, Selected Poetry and Prose* (New York: Holt, Rinehart and Winston, 1965), l. 294, p. 137.

The rule of law has two different meanings, both of them important. First, it can mean that government must be subject to rules that constrain its actions.[51] Second, it can mean that government must act through rules, that is, it must apply coercive force on a general basis, rather than against individual citizens.[52] Neither of these salutary principles depends on law being a coherent system of rules derived from overarching principles, however. Coherentism has a role in the implementation of these principles, largely because we rely on courts to implement some aspects of them. But this makes coherentism a subordinate element within the rule of law, not an essential feature. If the connection between legal coherence and the two rule of law principles sounds necessary or even logical, that is because the scholars who make this connection are relying on premodern modes of thought.

Premodern people tried to use the coherentist concept of law to achieve the rule of law in the first sense, which is subjecting government action to rules. That was natural law doctrine, which held that the ruler must obey a set of rules that could be derived from either the nature of God or the nature of humans, as discerned by human reason. The first difficulty with this approach is that it simply did not work because it did not lead to the creation of an enforcement mechanism. The solution that John of Salisbury, St. Thomas, and various other scholars offered, which is that God would punish the evil ruler in the afterlife, is an admission of defeat.[53] The second difficulty, at least from our perspective, is that natural law theory failed to condemn slavery, social inequality, gender

[51] Anthony Babington, *The Rule of Law in Britain From the Roman Occupation to the Present Day* (Chichester: B. Rose, 1978), pp. 257–290; Lon Fuller, *The Morality of Law*, rev. edn. (New Haven, CT: Yale University Press, 1969), pp. 33–41; Antal Orkeny and Kim Scheppele, Rules of Law: The Complexity of Legality in Hungary, in Martin Krygier and Adam Czarnota, eds., *The Rule of Law after Communism* (Aldershot: Ashgate, 1999), p. 55; Margaret Radin, Reconsidering the Rule of Law, 69 *Boston Univ. L. Rev*, 781 (1989); Geoffrey Walker, *The Rule of Law: Foundation of Constitutional Democracy* (Carlton, Victoria: Melbourne University Press, 1988), pp. 31–32.

[52] A.V. Dicey, *Introduction to the Study of Law and the Constitution*, 10th edn. (London: Macmillan, 1987), pp. 202–203; Frederich Hayek, *The Road to Serfdom*, 15th edn. (Chicago: University of Chicago Press, 1994), pp. 80–81; Mortimer Kadish and Sanford Kadish, *Discretion to Disobey: A Study of Lawful Departures from Legal Rules* (Stanford, CA: Stanford University Press, 1973), pp. 40–45; Antonin Scalia, The Rule of Law as a Law of Rules, 56 *U. Chi. L. Rev.* 1175 (1989); Robert Summers, A Formal Theory of the Rule of Law, 6 *Ratio Juris* 127 (1993).

[53] St. Thomas Aquinas, *On Kingship to the King of Cyprus* (New York: Hyperion Press, 1990), § 51; John of Salisbury, Policraticus (Cary J. Nederman, trans.) (Cambridge: Cambridge University Press, 1990), pp. 209–211.

inequality, punitive torture, interrogative torture, suppression of speech and suppression of religious belief. On reflection, this should not be surprising, because the theory relies on the underlying concept of nature, or naturalness, which tends to endorse the status quo, and the indeterminacy of natural law – people hear the voice of God in distinctly different ways – provides little resistance to this conventionalist tendency.

The process of actually subjecting the government to rules involves the positive enactments characteristic of the modern state. These began with various statutes passed by the English Parliament, but achieved their modern form with the adoption of the US Constitution, followed by written constitutions in nearly all other democratic nations. Not only does a written constitution limit, although of course does not eliminate, the indeterminacy of the controls that are placed on government, but it generates a pragmatically viable enforcement mechanism, namely constitutional courts. Some of the rules imposed by modern constitutions, and enforced by these courts, are obviously particular and thereby non-coherentist, such as the distribution of authority among different government institutions, or the procedures for enacting statutes. Even human rights guarantees, which seem to derive from general principles, were in fact established by specific political reform movements: freedom of conscience, protection against self-incrimination, the abolition of torture, and the abolition of slavery were separate and only tangentially related efforts.[54] These rights have been unified by scholars into a general theory of human dignity that is now elaborated by scholars through a coherentist theory, and implemented by courts through coherentist doctrine, as discussed above. But that only provides the content for some of the rules to which governments are subjected. The general process of subjecting government to rules – the rule of law itself, in the first sense of the term – is established by positive law, as an act of will by the citizenry.

With respect to the second meaning of the rule of law – that the government must act through general rules – the role of coherentism is similarly subordinate. To begin with an important, although secondary

[54] See Lynn Hunt, *Inventing Human Rights: A History* (New York: W.W. Norton, 2007); John H. Langbein, *Torture and the Law of Proof* (Chicago: University of Chicago Press, 2006); Leonard Levy, *Origins of the Fifth Amendment* (New York: Macmillan, 1986); Rubin, *Beyond Camelot*, pp. 260–268; Edward L. Rubin, Rethinking Human Rights, 9 *Int'l Legal Theory* 5 (2003); Hugh Thomas, *The Slave Trade: The Story of the Atlantic Slave Trade: 1440–1870* (New York: Touchstone, 1997), pp. 449–557.

point, the government's obligation to act through general rules applies only when those rules have negative consequences for individuals, and perhaps only when those consequences involve life or liberty. The apparently universal character of the general rules requirement ignores the expanded functions of the modern administrative state and, in particular, its resources allocations. Government research grants are awarded to specific individuals, yet no one regards this feature as unfair, and it is arbitrary to declare that such grants are not legal actions. Similarly, the modern state can authorize a specific private company to build a public facility, provide a public service, or carry out a research program. Such allocations can be analyzed by scholars, but the only relevant questions are whether they are effective in carrying out an intended policy, or whether the policy is advisable; it simply does not make sense to ask whether they are doctrinally coherent with other statutes. Moreover, the modern state regularly takes away specific people's property for public purposes; it might pass a law, for example, that the farms belonging to John Smith and Joe Jones shall be taken for construction of a military base. Our sense of fairness, which is embodied in the principle of due process but can equally be described as the rule of law, does not forbid such seizures of private property. The only requirement is that the government must pay Smith and Jones the market value of their property. Here again, there may be questions about whether the government is using this authority properly or effectively, but unless one wants to argue that the authority in general violates the rule of law – and virtually no one does – these questions cannot be explored through doctrinal analysis because there simply is no doctrinal principle that controls the government's selection of particular property under this authority.

The claim that this second meaning of the rule of law can be equated with coherentism suffers from an even more basic conceptual difficulty, however; it simply misunderstands the nature of modern legal enactments, in the sense described above. We no longer think of lawmakers as magistrates, adapting the enduring principles of natural law to the pragmatic circumstances of our times. Rather, major administrative laws are separate enactments, justified by the citizenry's election of the lawmakers and designed to address a particular issue, using whatever legal instrumentalities will be the most effective. Would any member of a modern legislature say that the use of incentives to encourage research, while it seems like the most effective strategy, should not be used because the legislature had previously used command and control regulation to discourage pollution? In the modern administrative state, as the

Bressman-Gluck study indicates, each major legislative initiative is evaluated separately. This does not mean that scholars cannot advance general theories about legislation. Of course they can; a scholar might argue that command and control regulation is always effective, or never effective, or, more realistically, that it is effective under certain conditions and not others. But the criteria for this determination would be effectiveness, not doctrinal coherence, and the methodology would be empirical-normative, not doctrinal-normative.

8.3.2 *The Need for Unity*

Weber offers an argument against the abandonment of coherentism that is considerably more formidable than the arguments of legal scholars and political scientists who rely on rule of law claims. According to Weber, modernity establishes autonomous spheres of value, which include empirical truth, normative validity, and aesthetic beauty. This process fractures the preexisting unity of belief, the persuasion that what is true must be moral, that what is moral must be beautiful, that what is beautiful must be true, and so forth. He describes this as modern polytheism, akin to the Greco-Roman practice of praying to different gods for different purposes.[55] The general problem that it poses for modernity is loss of meaning, a loss reflected in the inability to resolve conflicts that inevitably occur in arenas where these mutually incompatible value spheres collide. For example, the conflict between morality and aesthetics in the realm of visual art deprives morality of the support it previously obtained from pictorial representation, while simultaneously reducing art to the abstract and abstruse aestheticism that leaves museum-goers bewildered and forces government architects into the hands of street-corner muralists for their decorative schemes.

More central to Weber's concerns, and of course more relevant to this discussion, is the conflict between empirical and moral validity in the area of law and public governance.[56] Because the separation of the value sphere is the result of rationalization, it can only be resolved, in modern society, by rational processes. But with the connection between empirical

[55] Max Weber, Science as a Vocation, in H.H. Gerth and C. Wright Mills, eds., *From Max Weber: Essays in Sociology* (New York: Oxford University Press, 1946), pp. 129, 147–149.

[56] Habermas describes this as a "switching station . . . between the cognitive-instrumental and the normative complexes of rationality." Habermas, supra note 44, p. 250. See also his illuminating chart, fig. 11, p. 238.

and moral validity severed in the realm of law (and elsewhere, of course), the instrumental rationality of bureaucratic governance loses its connection with the values rationality of normative argument. The spirit of capitalism, and the closely associated development of the bureaucratic state, then generate an overwhelming tendency to elaborate and institutionalize instrumental rationality for its own sake, that is, without any agreement or even understanding of the purposes, necessarily normative in character, that capitalism and bureaucracy should serve. This is Weber's famous iron cage.[57]

Weber offers two escape routes from the iron cage that closes in on us in the political arena. First, he suggests that the instrumental rationality of bureaucratic government can be legitimated, that is, rendered normatively valid, by procedure, that is, formal rules operating within the legal system that determine when laws are properly enacted.[58] This is, of course, a positivist concept of law; Hans Kelsen's *grundnorm* and H. L. A. Hart's rule of recognition can both be characterized as procedural rules of this sort.[59] Second, and more broadly, Weber suggests that the fractured unity of society in general can be restored by the private efforts of individuals, as an aspect of their own life experience.[60] His pessimistic assessment of modernity, however, offers little hope that either of these methods will succeed. Procedure may be an adequate means of maintaining social order, but it will not provide true normative validity for government. Personal efforts condemn individuals to lonely isolation that places extreme demands on their capacity for action.

Jürgen Habermas greatly expands on the weakness of these two strategies for escaping from the iron cage before offering his own solution. Procedure, he incisively points out, can never legitimate a legal order; Weber's characterization of legal domination as a form of legitimate

57 Max Weber, *The Protestant Ethic and the Spirit of Capitalism* (Talcott Parsons, trans.) (New York: Routledge, 2001), pp. 123–124. Parsons' translation is now recognized as inaccurate; a more recent version renders this phrase (*stahlhartes Gehäuse*) as "a steel-hard casing." Max Weber, *The Protestant Ethic and the Spirit of Capitalism* (Stephen Kalberg, trans.) (Los Angeles: Roxbury Publishing, 2002), p. 123. This seems convincing, since Weber is contrasting the situation he is describing with Baxter's statement that material goods "should lie on the shoulders of his saints like 'a lightweight coat that could be thrown off at any time." See ibid., p. 245, n. 129 for Kalberg's additional arguments. But the Parsons translation has become too well-entrenched to be abandoned.

58 Weber, *Economy and Society*, pp. 36–38, 215–226.

59 Hart, *The Concept of Law*, pp.94–117; Hans Kelsen, *Pure Theory of Law* (Berkeley, CA: University of California Press, 1967), pp. 2–7.

60 Weber, Science as a Vocation, pp. 148–156.

domination is an outright error:[61] "From whatever angle one views it, legality based on positive enactment alone can *indicate* an underlying legitimacy, but never replace it."[62] Individual efforts to achieve unity not only place excessive demands on modern people, but are rendered futile by what Habermas vividly describes as the colonization of the lifeworld, the control exercised over modern people's lives by political and economic forces that are too large and complex for them to understand. Habermas's solution is the emancipatory force of communicative action, mutual efforts to achieve understanding that he derives from the inherent nature of language.

There are a number of grounds for skepticism regarding this proposed solution. Despite Habermas' effort to ground it in the institutional structures of the democratic state, communicative action sounds like the guiding principle of academic scholarship, not political or social interaction. It is simply unrealistic to expect the citizens of a nation to subject their political behavior to such severe constraints, and 200 years of democratic experience in Britain and the United States reveals no discernable movement toward this goal. The theoretical problem that underlies this empirical objection is that communicative action underemphasizes the role of emotion in human decision making, not only as an observed fact but as a necessary precondition to any form of human action.[63] The problems with Habermas' solution, however, should not be a cause for despair, or for abandoning the project of modernity, because there is also a defect in his statement of the problem. He simply fails to demonstrate that the unification of action spheres is required for either human flourishing or governmental legitimacy. For all his efforts to grapple with modernity, he has in fact imported a premodern criterion

[61] Habermas admits to some astonishment that Weber would have missed this point, see Habermas, *The Theory of Communicative Action*, p. 253. I am not certain that he did. It is at least one possible interpretation of his argument to see the fact that procedure legitimates the bureaucratic state, in the eyes of its citizens, as an aspect of the iron cage. This would make his late essay, "Parliament and Government in a Reconstructed Germany," Weber, Economy and Society, p. 1381, an extension of his earlier thought, rather than a revision of it, and seems more consistent with Benedix's account of Weber's feelings about the subject; see Reinhard Bendix, *Max Weber: An Intellectual Portrait* (Berkeley, CA: University of California Press), pp. 450–457.

[62] Habermas, *The Theory of Communicative Action*, p. 267 (emphasis in original).

[63] See Anthony Damasio, *Descartes' Error: Emotion, Reason and the Human Brain* (New York: Penguin, 2005); Daniel Goleman, *Emotional Intelligence: Why It Can Matter More than IQ* (London: Bloomsbury, 2005).

into the modern world. One reason is that neither Weber nor Habermas defines modern morality, at either the individual or the political level.

To begin at the level of individuals, the moral system that prevailed in the premodern West has no name at present and cannot be called Christian morality because Christianity went through at least two major transformations prior to the Medieval–Early Modern period. I have characterized it as a morality of higher purposes, a system of normative beliefs based on the principles that individual behavior should be directed to the salvation of one's soul and that political behavior should serve the state.[64] A moral system of this sort depends heavily upon, and contributes heavily toward, cultural or conceptual unity for several reasons, one of which is that it is inherently hierarchical. Everything stands in relation to other things, and the hierarchical pattern is reiterated at each level. Thus, the family is a hierarchy with the father at its head, the state is a hierarchy with the king at its head, and creation is a hierarchy with lower animals at its base and God at its head. This conception was called the Great Chain of Being.[65] The hierarchies it identified then fit together; humans occupy the middle part of the Great Chain, with animals below and angels above. Within human society, the family hierarchy is at the base, manors and counties are in the middle and the king is at the top. These ideas inspire literature and visual art, which in turn depicts and strengthens them.

Modern morality, I argue, centers on the distinctly different notion of human self-fulfillment.[66] In essence, it is a secular, individualized and narrative conception of life, where people construct their own identities as their life proceeds. There is no higher purpose, only happiness or pleasure in the here and now, but this morality is distinguished from vulgar hedonism because people are aware that their future will become their here and now, so that they must plan, develop skills, save money, and defer present gratification. Self-fulfillment, morality's mechanism of internalizing its demands, is neither shame nor guilt, as in previous moralities, but regret– regret that one has not lived a fulfilling life. This is a genuine morality because, like the morality of higher purposes, it is universal in its application. All members of the society are entitled to

[64] Rubin, *Soul, Self and Society*, pp. 69-112.

[65] See Arthur Lovejoy, *The Great Chain of Being: A Study in the History of an Idea* (New York: Harper and Row, 1960). See Keith Thomas, *The Ends of Life: Roads to Fulfillment in Early Modern England* (Oxford: Oxford University Press, 2009), pp. 13–20, 110–119.

[66] Rubin, *Soul, Self and Society*, pp. 113–158.

fulfill themselves, which places strict limits on human behavior; one may not act in a manner that interferes with other people's efforts to fulfill themselves. Well-established features of modern morality flow directly from this general conception. Thus, slavery, never condemned under the morality of higher purposes, is forbidden; women, consigned to the higher purpose of childbirth and child care by the previous morality, must have full career opportunity; sex is for pleasure, so it is moral if based on consent, not because it serves the higher purpose of procreation.

One distinctive feature of self-fulfillment morality, as opposed to the preceding morality of higher purposes, is that it is compartmentalized. The previous conception is that moral behavior was a basic character trait; one was either a good person, and a good subject, or one was not. Good people went to Heaven, while bad people went to Hell; it was an entirely dichotomous determination (Purgatory, a controversial addition to Scripture, is not an exception, being part of Heaven).[67] In modern morality, however, people construct their own grounds for self-fulfillment as they proceed along their life path, and can do so with differential success in each area. Thus, we can say, and we commonly do, that a person has a fulfilling career but an unfulfilling family life, or that a person was unfulfilled in her early adulthood but found fulfillment later.

Thus, Weber and Habermas are right to say that the unity of substantive values that characterized the belief system of the premodern West has been shattered in modern times, but wrong to say that this results in existential isolation, a dismal divide between the individual and the surrounding culture. The search for self-fulfillment in each area of one's life, and the different ways in which one might characterize those different areas and achieve fulfillment in each, is the dominant belief system of our culture, and that culture endorses and supports those taxonomic and aspirational efforts. To be sure, it provides people with a variety of resources, rather than substantive prescriptions, but that is precisely the difference between modern morality and its predecessor. Can one say that one is better than the other? Each is better from its own perspective, and immoral from the other, but there is no Archimedean place on which to stand. Does modern morality make increased and unachievable demands on individuals? Who knows; who can say whether the difficulty premodern individuals felt in complying with a defined, substantive

[67] To go to Purgatory was to be saved, the only difference being that one needed to go through a process of expiation. A colloquial way to explain the doctrine is that one can't flunk Purgatory; the teacher there is God, who is perfect in this role as He is in all others.

standard of a moral life, is greater or less than the difficulty modern individuals feel in obeying more procedural limits and constructing their own substantive values? The criteria for making such comparative judgments are entirely unclear, and neither Weber nor Habermas even attempts to provide them. What they do, instead, is to project modern morality back into premodern times and assert that life was more fulfilling when there was a unified belief system. This not only creates a grass-is-greener problem at the empirical level, but involves a theoretical contradiction. If we could ask premodern people what they thought of our present morality, they would probably not say that we are less fulfilled, because that is our morality. They would say that more of us are going to Hell, a judgment we would tend to dismiss as irrelevant or jejune.

Proceeding to the realm of government, modern morality demands that the state serve its citizens, that is, insulate them from the potential oppressions of industrialism and provide them with the opportunity to construct fulfilling lives for themselves. But because this guiding principle focuses on the results that government action achieves, rather than the hierarchical form it adopts, translating it into action is heavily dependent on empirical relationships. That does not make it any less a norm, but only a different kind of norm. It derives from, and supports, the personal morality of self-fulfillment. Due to the nature of its goals, and the empirical demands to which it must respond, this public morality demands an administrative state. Conversely, the political development of the administrative state generates this norm and its related personal morality.

Thus, modern political morality establishes both a criterion for governmental action and a structure by which such action is to be instantiated. The criterion is that the government must serve the interests of the people, and must do so effectively because – unlike its premodern predecessor – the morality dictates that it actually achieve results, and not simply maintain order and appearances. Thus, the instrumental rationality by which the government achieves real-world effect is not the iron cage, but a direct consequence of the new morality's demands.[68]

[68] Moreover, to underscore its moral character, it finds just as much support in Scripture as its predecessor. See, e.g., James 2:15–17 ("If a brother or a sister is naked and destitute of daily food, And one of you says to the, 'Depart in peace, be warmed and filled,' but you do not give them the things that are needed for the body, what does it profit? Thus also faith by itself, if it does not have works, is dead.")

The structure by which these effects are achieved is the administrative state, whose characteristic features include the designation of a specific subject matter as their jurisdiction, and a staff of credentialed employees trained in that subject matter. In other words, instead of divided functionally, into executive, rulemaking, and adjudicatory institutions like the general government, agencies combine all three functions but are limited to a particular substantive area of operations.

In other words, administrative government carries out its moral obligation to serve the citizens by establishing effective programs in specific subject areas. Here, as in the personal lives of the citizens, the totality is divided into separate spheres, and each sphere has its own rules and its own criteria for success. Each agency has a separate authorizing statute, which represents a positive and individualized enactment by the legislature. Each agency has its own area of expertise, its own methodologies, and its own practical experience. There is no overarching unity, no necessary correspondence among the separate areas. There is an overarching morality – the modern morality of self-fulfillment – but that morality demands that the laws governing each agency and the regulations each agency produces must be conceived to achieve effectiveness in each specific area. An agency acts wrongfully when it strives for doctrinal unity with other agencies; its moral obligation is to develop and act upon its own criteria for effectiveness.

The task of modern legal scholarship is to engage in empirical-normative evaluation of the programs in each specific field. This does not mean that it need abandon the effort to identify general principles, but rather that those principles must be empirical, not doctrinal. A scholar might argue, for example, that cooperative enforcement should replace command and control regulation in all, or many, areas, but that argument would need to be supported by empirical evidence, not doctrinal coherence, and it would need to be demonstrated in each separate field, not assumed to be a universal principle on an a priori basis. The unity of values whose loss Weber and Habermas bemoaned in fact exists, but it resides in a new morality of self-fulfillment, and that morality demands that each governmental agency establish, and be evaluated on, its own set of substantive rules designed to function as effectively as possible.

8.4 Conclusion

Legal scholarship must wake from its coherentist reveries. The world has changed, and the legal system has changed with it. Law is no longer limited to a system of normatively grounded rules designed to maintain public order. Rather, it is now a means by which democratic society carries out the varied and extensive purposes that are characteristic of an administrative state. As a result, internal or doctrinal coherence is no longer a sufficient criterion for law. If legal scholars cling to their past practices, if they continue to analyze law in terms of its coherence, they will condemn themselves to a marginal role in the modern legal world. They will be able to speak to the normative constraints that the nation's constitution imposes on the lawmaking process, and to the increasingly limited areas where that process makes use of older methods of implementation such as common law and codes. But they will not be producing academic work that addresses the basic legal structure of the society, the regulatory and administrative process that now dominates every modern national government. To do so, legal scholars will need to relinquish their commitment to coherence and concern themselves with the effectiveness of law and its ability to achieve our democratically determined purposes. That requires a new methodology, one focused on empirical results and pragmatic strategies.

The transition, to be sure, is not necessarily an easy one. It will require the development of new methods, new techniques, and new forms of training. It will also require that we relinquish the vision of a doctrinally coherent, normatively structured legal system. Such a system has undoubted appeal; many people seem to prefer being watched by even a vengeful or a jealous god to living in an empty universe. But the price of conceptual or social nostalgia is increasing irrelevance. We owe ourselves, and our society, a different outcome.

9

Ranking, Peer Review, Bibliometrics and Alternative Ways to Improve the Quality of Doctrinal Legal Scholarship

ROB VAN GESTEL

'There are two things wrong with almost all legal writing. One is its style. The other is its content. That, I think, about covers the ground.'[1]

9.1 Quality and Methodology

A lot has changed since Rodell's famous 1936 article 'Goodbye to Law Reviews', but what has remained is the critique towards the quality and relevance of scholarly legal publications in law journals. As far as relevance is concerned, my impression is that the debate in the United States and Europe is partly headed in different directions.[2] A lot of the criticism in the United States, especially after the 2008 credit crunch, runs against the alleged gap between legal scholarship and legal practice.[3] Much research flowing from the elite law schools is accused of being too esoteric and useless for legal practice. Newton even claims that the collapse of the market for legal services has shown that if law schools continue their trend of hiring tenure-track faculty members whose chief mission is to produce theoretical and interdisciplinary scholarship for law

[1] F. Rodell, Goodbye to Law Reviews, *Virginia Law Review*, 1936, p. 38.

[2] See also the observations by Ralf Michaels: www.verfassungsblog.de/law-as-the-study-of-norms-foundational-subjects-and-interdisciplinarity-in-germany-and-the-united-states/#.UwT2QF5kIfs.

[3] For an overview, see B. Tamanaha, *Failing Law Schools*, Chicago: University of Chicago Press, 2012; www.aals.org/wp-content/uploads/2014/08/OnLegalScholarship-West-Citron.pdf; Report and Recommendations of the American Bar Association Task Force on the Future of Legal Educations, www.americanbar.org/content/dam/aba/administrative/professional_responsibility/report_and_recommendations_of_aba_task_force.authcheckdam.pdf.

reviews rather than prepare their students to actually practice law, law students will increasingly lack the skills necessary to become competent, ethical practitioners.[4] Even US Supreme Court Justice Roberts criticized the alleged trend towards impractical legal scholarship in the United States. In a controversial and much discussed 2011 interview, he stated:

> Pick up a copy of any law review that you see, and the first article is likely to be, you know, the influence of Immanuel Kant on evidentiary approaches in 18th Century Bulgaria, or something, which I'm sure was of great interest to the academic that wrote it, but isn't of much help to the bar.[5]

It is up for debate whether American legal scholarship in the majority of the top-tiered law schools has drifted too far off from legal practice. What is more interesting, though, is that in many European countries the debate now seems to go in the opposite direction. According to Smits, traditional (doctrinal) legal research in Europe is in a state of 'identity crisis'.[6] Not only do scholars from other social sciences accuse legal scholars of being unacademic, but lawyers themselves also appear to have growing doubts about the methodologies they apply and about the theoretical relevance of traditional legal research. In Germany, for example, the *Wissenschaftsrat* has argued that in view of the close ties between legal scholarship and practice,[7] the future success of the discipline will depend on the ability to recognize and understand crucial changes in the structure of law, such as the juridification of society, the emergence of new forms of nonstate law making, and the Europeanization and internationalization of law. To this end, structural changes are deemed necessary. These include a shift from specialist and applied knowledge to more comprehensive and foundational knowledge and far greater attention for interdisciplinary approaches and international cooperation.[8] Similar debates can be found in other European countries.[9]

[4] B.E. Newton, Preaching What they Don't Practice: Why Law Faculties' Preoccupation with Impractical Scholarship and Devaluation of Practical Competencies Obstruct Reform in the Legal Academy, *South Carolina Law Review*, 62, pp. 105–156 (2010).

[5] www.nytimes.com/2013/10/22/us/law-scholarships-lackluster-reviews.html?_r=0.

[6] J. Smits, *The Mind and Method of the Legal Academic*, Cheltenham: Edward Elgar, 2013, pp. 4–6.

[7] The German Council of Science and Humanities (Wissenschaftsrat) provides advice to the German Federal Government and the State (Länder) Governments on the structure and development of higher education and research. See www.wissenschaftsrat.de/en/about.html.

[8] Wissenschaftsrat, Prospects of Legal Scholarship in Germany, Hamburg, 2012, p. 39.

[9] See for an overview: C. Stolker, *Rethinking the Law School*, Cambridge: Cambridge University Press, 2014.

What legal scholars on both sides of the Atlantic do not seem to realize yet is that the debate about the prospects of legal scholarship also determines the way we think about the quality of our research. After all, quality assessment always presupposes a standard of something as measured against other things of a similar kind to serve a certain purpose. Hence one first needs to select units for comparison that are sufficiently similar in order to be compared (e.g., are doctrinal and empirical legal research sufficiently similar?) and required is at least some sort of agreement on the purpose of scholarly legal research (e.g., is it first and foremost to serve legal practice or to add something to the body of knowledge?) before being able to find quality indicators and assessment methods suitable to measure whether this purpose is served by the publications under scrutiny. Moreover, we need to realize that research quality is a relative concept. We expect more from an experienced scholar from an elite law school than from a starting scholar of a much lower-ranked school, we set higher standards for the methodological rigor of a PhD dissertation than for a case note, and we (hopefully) have higher expectations about the English writing skills of an American legal scholar, who is a native speaker, than from the same skills of a European law professor for whom English is not his/her mother tongue.

But if quality of legal scholarship is such a relative concept, then how should we measure or assess it? Several answers can be given here. One possible answer would be to let the best scholars decide what counts as good scholarship because ultimately 'good scholarship is what good scholars do'. However, this could easily end up in circular reasoning since one would first need to know who the best experts are. In other words, this presupposes that we already have a yardstick to decide how we can discern between good and mediocre legal scholars. Another possibility could be to look at rankings in order to determine which scholars publish in the 'best' journals but, as we will see hereafter, this is problematic as well since there are hardly any rankings of law journals in Europe, and in the United States, scholars frequently complain about the fact that rankings do not actually measure quality of legal scholarship.[10] A third way could be to count citations, downloads or other signs of research impact, but this runs the risk of replacing quality based on substance with measuring what can be counted on the basis of proxies.

[10] See, for example, the thorough study by T. Eisenberg and M. Wells, Ranking Law Journals and the Limits of Journal Citation Reports, *Economic Inquiry*, 52, 4, pp. 1301–1314 (2014).

Therefore, it is necessary to explore different methods to assess the quality of traditional legal publications in order to see to what extent we can capture quality based on substance via ranking, peer review, and bibliometric indicators.

9.2 Object of Study

This chapter will focus mainly on traditional legal publications. There are several reasons for this. First, doctrinal legal research is probably the type of legal research that is most heavily intertwined with language, legal culture and national legal practice. With regard to this type of research, the differences in form, style and tradition across jurisdictions are most likely the biggest, which makes it all the more challenging to look for common ground with regard to the quality and methodological accountability of this research. Second, doctrinal legal researchers usually do not seem to make their implicit methods explicit. As Terry Hutchinson and Nigel Duncan describe for the common law situation:

> The doctrinal research methodology developed intuitively within the common law – a research method at the core of practice. There was no need to justify or classify it within a broader research framework. Modern academic lawyers are facing a different situation. At a time when competition for limited research funds is becoming more intense, and in which interdisciplinary work is highly valued and non-lawyers are involved in the assessment of grant applications, lawyer-applicants who engage in doctrinal research need to be able to explain their methodology more clearly.[11]

My hypothesis is that this observation also applies to doctrinal legal research in the civil law tradition because the basic methodological challenges for doctrinalists are quite similar. They use the same 'data' (legislation, case law and literature) and are grounded in the same (hermeneutic) tradition, which relies heavily on the interpretation of texts. If this is true, then how does the fact that doctrinal methodologies remain implicit affect the quality of legal scholarship? Third, doctrinal legal research is the oldest form of scholarly legal research. It has managed to survive over centuries,[12] while the attention for empirical

[11] T. Hutchinson and N. Duncan, Defining and Describing What we Do: Doctrinal Legal Research, *Deakin Law Review*, 17, 1, p. 83 (2012).

[12] See for a history R.C van Caenegem, *Judges, Legislators and Professors: Chapters in European Legal History*, Cambridge: Cambridge University Press 1992.

approaches and 'law and . . .' research is much younger and has been subject to far greater fluctuations. Feldman has even argued that, although law as a discipline has had several 'misguided love affairs with science', legal scholars have over the last two centuries always returned to the same doctrinal well.[13] Fourth, doctrinal legal publications are sometimes considered to be old fashioned, inward-looking, preoccupied with technicalities, and relying too much on practical wisdom and common sense.[14] This raises the question: how can we recognize any quality in these publications?

9.3 Aim, Research Question and Order of the Argument

The main aim of this contribution is to show that law has the advantage of lagging behind other disciplines when it comes to assessing the quality of scholarly legal publications. Therefore, the forum of legal scholars both in the United States and in Europe needs to discuss how to move forward since there is a danger that if we do nothing, other (social) sciences will sooner or later impose their assessment methods on us, which might leave little room to take the particularities of traditional legal research into account[15]; whereas I believe that doctrinal legal research is certainly not dead, although it might need to be revitalized.[16] Apart from that, copy and pasting the assessment methods from other sciences could very well lead to a crowding out of quality by quantity as Binswanger has argued:

> In the current system, scientific knowledge is replaced by measurable outputs. Not the content of an article or a project counts, but the number of published and cited articles or the number and the amount of money of the acquired projects. Since the measurable output is considered to be the indicator of quality, the true quality is more and more crowded out. The need to publish constantly leaves no time to worry too long about

[13] R. Feldman, *The Role of Science in Law*, Oxford: Oxford University Press, 2009.

[14] Among many others: D. Vick, Interdisciplinarity and the Discipline of Law, *Journal of Law and Society*, 31, 2, p. 164 (2004); D. Rhode, Legal Scholarship, *Harvard Law Review*, 115, pp. 1327–1361 (2002); P. Schlag, Spam Jurisprudence, Air Law, and the Rank Anxiety of Nothing Happening (A Report on the State of the Art), *Geo. L. J.*, 97, 803, pp. 821–823 (2009).

[15] One of these particularities is, of course, that doctrinal legal publications are usually not exclusively aimed at the forum of legal scholars but also address practitioners.

[16] R.A.J. van Gestel and H.W. Micklitz, Revitalising Doctrinal Legal Research in Europe: What about Methodology? in U. Neergard and R. Nielsen (eds.), *European Legal Method: Paradoxes and Revitalisation*, Copenhagen: DJŐF publishing, 2011, pp. 25–73.

> the progress of knowledge, although this should be the real purpose of scientific activity.[17]

The risk of crowding out quality based on substance is linked to the idea that university managers increasingly seem to believe that organizing competition will almost automatically lead to innovation via a race to the top. Rankings, for example, are often seen as a method to organize a status competition between journals, but one easily forgets that the best publications are not necessarily published in the highest-ranked journals or with the most reputable publishers, especially in an era where authors have far more possibilities to spread their ideas via open access platforms, social media and the Internet more generally. Besides, if we want to use rankings as a yardstick for research quality we first need to know more about how they are construed. Most journal rankings are based either on bibliometric indicators or peer review by experts, which makes them dependent on the strengths and weaknesses of these assessment methods. That is why this chapter tries to answer the following research question:

> To what extent can ranking of law journals, introduction of peer review and the use of bibliometric indicators contribute to the substantive quality of doctrinal legal publications, or do we need to think of alternative ways to improve the quality of these publications?

In order to answer this question, we first need to go into the advantages and disadvantages of a ranking of law journals in order to see whether a European ranking could contribute to the assessment of scholarly legal publications. In the humanities, establishing such a European ranking has been tried before. What could law as a discipline learn from this? And what about US law journal rankings? To what extent do these accurately reflect the substantive quality of scholarly legal publications? After this, the focus will shift to peer review. Here the situation is reversed. In the United States, peer review is still the exception to the rule, whereas in Europe, and in particular in the UK, one can find more and more peer-reviewed journals. The question remains, though, to what extent external peer review is an effective method to prevent the publication of substandard research or to recognize research excellence. Is external peer review really so much better than, for example, assessment

[17] M. Binswanger, Excellence by Nonsense: The Competition for Publications in Modern Science, in: Sönke Bartling and Sascha Friesike (eds.), *Opening Science: The Evolving Guide on How the Internet is Changing Research, Collaboration and Scholarly Publishing*, Heidelberg: Springer, 2014, p. 66.

by a professional editorial board, and how about the time and resources that peer review cost? Next, the attention will shift to the use of bibliometrics to assess research quality in order to see to what extent research impact can serve as an indicator for substantive quality in law. My hypothesis is that neither rankings, metrics nor peer review, are capable of fully reflecting substantive research quality in terms of originality, thoroughness and profundity.[18] That is why the last part of this contribution will be devoted to some possible alternatives.

9.4 Journal Rankings

Ranking of law journals is a relatively new phenomenon that is gaining influence, most of all in the United States but also in other countries, such as Canada,[19] the United Kingdom,[20] Australia,[21] Israel,[22] and China.[23] Behind this is a growing need for cross-national scholarly legal communication and a simultaneous rise of the number of specialized law journals depending on a broader reader audience than can be found in individual countries, which increases the need for transnational comparison.[24] Ranking is a way to make differences between law reviews more tangible. This can be done for a variety of reasons ranging from providing guidelines for authors with respect to where to submit their papers to decisions concerning promotion on the basis of publication track

[18] I have developed this thesis more in-depth in R.A.J. van Gestel, Kwaliteit van juridische publicaties: Over ranking, peer review, sciëntometrics en vertrouwen in alternatieve evaluatiemethoden, in. R.H. de Bock, P.J.P.M. van Lochem and R.A.J. van Gestel, *Kwaliteit als Keuze: Kwaliteit (Sbeoordeling) van Rechtspraak, Wetgeving en Rechtwetenschap, Preadviezen Nederlandse Juristenvereniging*, Deventer: Kluwer, 2015, pp. 243–378.

[19] Canadian scholars have ranked law journals according to the Washington and Lee rankings in the United States. See www.acpd-calt.org/?p=1589.

[20] See http://siemslegal.blogspot.nl/2012/10/uk-law-journal-ranking-rae-2008-data.html.

[21] See http://research.unsw.edu.au/excellence-research-australia-era-outlet-ranking. Ian Ramsay and G.P. Stapledon, A Citation Analysis of Australian Law Journals, *MELB. U. L. REV.*, 21, 676 (1997); Dennis Warren, Australian Law Journals: An Analysis of Citation Patterns, *AUSTRL. ACAD. & RES. LIBR.*, 27, 261 (1996).

[22] R. Perry, Ranking Hebrew Law Reviews: Theoretical Foundations and a Preliminary Empirical Study, *HAIFA L. REV.*, 1, 401 (2004).

[23] There are a number of formal journal ranking systems in China, one example that includes law journals is the Chinese Social Science Citation Index ('CSSCI'), see at: http://cssrac.nju.edu.cn/.

[24] R.A.J. van Gestel, Sense and Non-sense of a European Ranking of Law Schools and Law Journals, *Legal Studies*, 35, 1, pp. 165–185 (2015).

records. The underlying mechanism that is used is almost always a status competition on the basis of the reputation of the authors that publish in the journal,[25] on the basis of rejection rates by the journal, or on downloads or number of citations.[26]

Law journal rankings can be expert-based, metrics-based or combinations of both. Expert-based rankings are time consuming and often rather subjective, since a proper assessment of the quality of a journal would imply reading the contributions to the journals and deciding on the basis of majority voting. This offers an advantage for general law journals because specialized law reviews can only be assessed by specialists, who will normally be underrepresented in committees responsible for setting up journal rankings. With metric-based rankings, such as the Washington & Lee ranking, this problem does not exist but other problems arise instead. The citation counts used in these sorts of rankings tell us little about the actual quality of individual publications in the journal or about the quality of the editing and publication process. A high-impact factor certainly does not guarantee that the most innovative publications will automatically be published in these journals. It could even work the other way around in the sense that a high-impact factor makes journal editors and peer reviewers overcautious with respect to publishing innovative but controversial papers that challenge mainstream thinking.

Combinations of expert-based and metrics-based journal rankings are rare.[27] In the United Kingdom, Campbell, Goodacre and Little tried to come up with such a ranking by looking at which journals the submission made to the research assessment exercise (RAE 2001) had been published in, but this method also has major shortcomings. To mention just one: a journal that is very selective in what is publishes may receive a low score in the RAE, but this will not reflect the reputation of the journal. The Harvard Law Review and Yale Law

[25] T. George and C. Guthrie, An Empirical Evaluation of Specialized Law Reviews, *Florida State University Law Review*, 26, p. 813 (1999). R. Jarvis and P. Coleman, Ranking Law Reviews: An Empirical Analysis Based on Author Prominence, *Ariz. L. Rev.*, 39, 15 (1997); and R. Jarvis and P. Coleman, Ranking Law Reviews by Author Prominence - Ten Years Later, *Law Library Journal*, 99, 3, pp. 573–588 (2007).

[26] For an overview. R. Korobkin, Ranking Journals: Some Thoughts on Theory and Methodology, *Florida State University Law Review*, 26, pp. 851–876 (1998–1999).

[27] For an example: http://siemslegal.blogspot.co.uk/2011/03/world-law-journal-ranking-2011.html.

Journal, for example, did not receive a single score in the RAE 2001.[28] This does not, of course, imply that both law reviews should be regarded as substandard. Far more likely is that these journals are not included because British scholars do not submit papers to these journals and editors of these US law reviews are biased against publications written by foreigners.[29]

9.4.1 *What Do Law Journal Rankings Measure?*

Law journal rankings are meant to stimulate competition, which may improve the quality of scholarly legal writing because the best journals will receive the highest ranking, which will normally lead to more submissions, enabling the editorial board to come to a better selection of publishable papers, which will on its turn offer prestige, both to the authors of these papers and to the editors of the journal.[30]

Well-designed rankings may also serve as a quality control mechanism for the editors in the sense that they provide a mechanism for self-evaluation. If a law review drops on the ranking scale, this could indicate flaws in the editorial policy, the (peer) review process or in the selection of research topics and the way these are valued by the reader and so on. The other way around, a rise on the ranking probably corresponds with a more positive appreciation of the journal's quality.

However, ranking of law journals should not be confused with a direct appreciation of the quality of the content of the journal. Even in case the content of law reviews is assessed by an expert committee or a user survey it is impossible for the assessors to have a deep knowledge about the quality of the content of more than just a couple of journals over more than a couple of years. Moreover, there is no objective way to determine how possible differences of opinion between experts about the

[28] K. Campbell, A Goodacre, and G. Little, Ranking of United Kingdom Law Journals: An Analysis of the Research assessment Exercise 2001 Submissions and Results, 26, 470–501 (1999).

[29] See for instance R. Dibadj, Comparative fashions in legal research, in: T. Tanquerel and A. Flückiger (eds.), *Assessing Research in Law*, Brussels: Bruylant 2015, pp. 218–219. If one looks at the journal ranking M. Siems made on the basis of the UK 2014 REF, one notices that it is heavily dominated by UK and EU law journals. See http://siemslegal.blogspot.nl/2015/01/law-journal-ranking-based-on-ref-2014.html.

[30] An elaborate list of advantages can be found in R. Perry, The Relative Value of American Law Reviews: A Critical Appraisal of Ranking Methods, *Virginia Journal of Law & Technology*, 11, 1, pp. 4–6 (2006).

quality of the content of a journal should be reconciled for the purpose of setting up a ranking.[31]

In case of journal rankings relying on citation scores, it is even more evident that these are proxies of substantive quality at best. After all, the number of citations that a journal receives only tells something about the *average* interest of readers in what the journal publishes and nothing about the content of individual publications. Besides, if one gives more weight to citations in prestigious journals, one would first need to know exactly why these journals are prestigious, which presupposes some sort of informal ranking.[32] Empirical research shows that citation is not only highly influenced by the rank of the review in which a work is published but also by the law school from which the author graduated.[33] Even if one takes the number of citations at the article level into account, Korobkin has outlined that there are at least ten different scenarios where citation has nothing to do with quality.[34] Other metrics-based rankings using rejection rates, downloads and/or actual use of journals all have similar problems; they do not necessarily correlate with the quality of the content and the data can be manipulated.

Last but not least, different law journal rankings come up with different lists of top journals. If one compares the Washington and Lee ranking,[35] for example, with the ranking of international top journal from Google Scholar, one finds different outcomes, in particular when other than US journals are included.[36] The same applies if one compares these outcomes with a ranking of law journals based on the UK REF.[37] The more rankings of journals we compare, the more difficult it is going to be to decide which one should be taken the most seriously. One soon ends up in a 'you have your ranking, I have mine' situation.[38] In order to avoid a ranking of rankings, we should first try to reach consensus on what the purpose should be of a truly international law journal ranking:

[31] J. Svantesson, International Ranking of Law Journals – Can it be Done and at What Cost?, *Legal Studies*, 29, 4, p. 685 (2009).

[32] Ibid., p. 683.

[33] J. Harrison and A. Mashburn, Citations, Justifications, and the Troubled State of Legal Scholarship: An Empirical Study, SSRN working paper, February 24, 2014. See http://papers.ssrn.com/sol3/papers.cfm?abstract_id=2569499.

[34] Korobkin, Ranking Journals, p. 866.

[35] http://abovethelaw.com/2014/02/americas-next-top-law-review-new-rankings/.

[36] http://opiniojuris.org/2013/03/20/google-rankings-of-the-most-cited-international-law-journals/.

[37] http://siemslegal.blogspot.nl/2015/01/law-journal-ranking-based-on-ref-2014.html.

[38] See http://guides.library.harvard.edu/content.php?pid=68282&sid=512184.

is it to organize more transnational competition between law journals in the United States and Europe, do we want to use rankings as a tool to discern between professional and academic publications or do we, for instance, want to rank journals in order to keep the number of publication outlets under stricter control in order to avoid spreading submissions too thin across a wide range of periodicals?

9.4.2 *Conclusion*

Law review rankings can be a helpful transparency tool for different groups of users. A ranking may, for instance, provide guidelines for starting researchers showing in which (international) journals to publish in order to build an academic CV or to librarians which journal they should buy for their library collection.

Any international law journal ranking would, however, require a classification of law journals across national borders. If one is unable to do this on the basis of a comparison of the content of the different journals, the only alternative is relying on quantitative performance indicators, such as citation scores, h-indexes, rejection rates and so on. This can be done but it presupposes a truly international database containing relevant and reliable bibliometric data. Such a database does not yet exist for the field of law. Even if it would exist, though, scoring journals against performance indicators must not be confused for a professional judgment of the quality of the content of the journals. That would require an assessment by peers, which is extremely difficult in case of an international ranking because it presupposes deep knowledge about the legal systems being studied and the differences in academic culture.

An international ranking or classification of law journals only makes sense if we keep in mind the limited value it can have in promoting research quality. That is why journal rankings should never be used as a stand-alone tool to monitor and evaluate the research performance of individual scholars. In particular with regard to decisions concerning tenure and promotion, it is extremely important that assessors actually read and analyze what a scholar has been writing. At the same time, European law schools should realize that as long as there are no European citation databases, established European law journals, such as the European Journal of International Law (EJIL), will be ranked low on US law journal rankings since these predominantly rely on citation counts in US journals. The EJIL has been the highest-ranked journal on the Washington and Lee journal ranking but it never belongs to the top 100. This should not come as a surprise, though, since the Washington and Lee ranking mainly depends on citation counts in US law journals, while it is more than likely that the EJIL has more readers in Europe than in the United States.[39] It might also explain why other prestigious European law journals, such as the Modern Law Review or the Common Market Law Review, are ranked so low on the Washington and Lee ranking.

9.5 Peer Review

Especially in the United States, a lot of criticism has been raised against student-edited law reviews. Not only is it hard to explain to scholars in other disciplines that students are supposed to assess the quality of scholarly publications since students are in training to become expert practitioners, which does not necessarily make them qualified as academic peers who are able to critically evaluate scholarly work of their teachers.[40] Student editing also has a number of other well-known disadvantages. Probably the most important one is the focus on author reputation and affiliation instead of substantive quality.

As a consequence it is not surprising that an empirical inquiry by Yoon, evaluating over 25,000 articles from nearly 200 general interest law reviews in the United States, revealed that, with few exceptions, law reviews publish more articles from faculty at their own institution than from faculty from other law schools.[41] In general, these in-house publications are significantly less cited, though, than publications from outside faculty. According to Yoon, this disparity is even more pronounced at the higher-ranked law reviews. This appears to be in line with a study by Kotkin of the top ten US law journals, for which she studied 777 articles between 2005 and 2008. The outcome was that, 42 per cent (325) of the authors came from the top *ten US News and World Report* schools, 64 per cent (500) from the top twenty-five and 75 per cent (580) from the top fifty. Authors from schools ranked above fifty account for only 14 per cent (110) of the total.[42]

[39] See J. Weiler Impact Factor: The Food is Bad and What's More There is Not Enough of It, *EJIL*, 23, 3, pp. 607–612 (2012).

[40] L. Friedman, Law Reviews and Legal Scholarship: Some Comments, *Denver University Law Review*, 75, 1, pp. 661–669 (1998).

[41] A. Yoon, Editorial Bias in Legal Academia, *Journal of Legal Analysis*, 5, 2, pp. 309–338 (2013).

[42] M. Kotkin, Of Authorship and Audacity: An Empirical Study of Gender Disparity and Privilege in the 'Top Ten' Law Reviews, *Women's Rts. L. Rep*, 31, 385 at 406 (2010).

These publications signal both protectionism and editorial bias, which may undermine research quality because it elevates lower-quality publications from in-house staff into a faculty's own journal at the expense of higher-quality publications by authors from other faculties.[43] This protectionism is fuelled by the fact that most US law journals are student edited. Since students have a hard time deciding whether a paper presents facts and concepts accurately and demonstrates appropriate knowledge of the existing research in the field, it is a public secret that they rely on formalities, such as uniformity in citations (the 'Bluebook') and footnote checking, but even more so on the reputation and affiliation of the authors. Therefore, it is no wonder that a recent survey in the United States of 1,325 law professors, 338 student editors, 215 attorneys and 156 judges showed that the vast majority of the respondents indicated reforms are needed and that the introduction of (blind) peer review was on top of the list of priorities.[44] The question that needs to be discussed hereafter is, however, to what extent peer review is the solution for problems of selection bias, lack of research experience from student editors and a formalistic way of deciding about quality.

In Europe, and in particular in the United Kingdom, there are far more peer-reviewed law journals, but in most countries there is no unified tradition of peer review. Student editing, editorial screening and assessment by external referees coexist.[45] Quite often, peer review of books and journal articles is done by the people who decide about the publication of manuscripts, whereas in modern variants of peer review in other disciplines than law, editorial decisions and peer review are deliberately separated,[46] as is today common practice in the beta

[43] Yoon, Editorial Bias in Legal Academia, p. 336.

[44] R.A. Wise et al., Do Law Reviews Need Reform? A Survey of Law Professors, Student Editors, Attorneys, and Judges, *Loy. L. Rev.*, 59, 1, pp. 1–75 (2013).

[45] A major survey among 3040 senior scientists from a range of academic disciplines shows that the vast majority of the addressees (93 per cent) believe that peer review is a necessary evaluation method and 90 per cent of the interviewees think that peer review directly contributes to the quality of scholarly publications. See M. Ware, *Peer Review: Benefits, Perceptions and Alternatives*, London: Publishing Research Consortium, 2008, www.publishingresearch.org.uk/documents/PRCsummary4Warefinal.pdf.

[46] One of the first examples of prepublication peer review is often attributed to Henry Oldenburg as founding father of the British journal 'Philosophical Transactions of the Royal Society', which was established in 1665. As Porter has noticed the introduction of peer review by Oldenburg was meant to stress that is was about: 'a more truly scientific periodical ... excluding legal and theological matters, but including especially the accounts of experiments conducted before the [Royal] Society'.

and gamma sciences.[47] That is why Michaels has noticed about peer review that:

> While it has many manifestations, peer review generally involves a review of materials by experts who are thought to have adequate knowledge and technical expertise to judge the material's quality, while being sufficiently impartial and disinterested to provide judgment free of conflict of interest.[48]

In law we are not that far yet. In the United States this is due to the dominance of student-edited law journals, but in many European countries it is because there is no clear distinction between professional publications and academic publications. Scholarly books and articles are not only written by academics but also by judges, legislators, attorneys and so on. As a consequence, it is often hard to tell who the scholarly legal forum is and what standards are supposed to apply to academic legal publications. This makes the competition for external funding from research foundations increasingly difficult for lawyers because doctrinal legal scholars are also not used to make their implicit methods explicit, which makes the quality of these publications hard to understand for outsiders. In such a situation, the introduction of some form of peer review could be applied as a procedural mechanism to show to the outside world that guarantees are built into the publication process to warrant the academic value of scholarly legal research. The question we have to ask ourselves, though, is to what extent peer review is actually a guarantee for research quality from a substantive perspective. This probably not only depends on the expertise of the peer reviewers, but also on the standards they should apply and the way in which the peer review process is organized and monitored.

The latter already indicates how important it is to have a policy about referee selection and instruction with regard to the quality indicators they are supposed to apply and about the demarcation between the duties of referees in the peer review process and the responsibilities of editorial

[47] The journal *Nature* introduced peer review not earlier than 1967. See www.nature.com/nature/history/timeline_1960s.html. The international Committee of Medical Journal Editors describes peer review as: 'the critical assessment of manuscripts submitted to journals by experts who are usually not part of the editorial staff.' See the Uniform Requirements for Manuscripts Submitted to Biomedical Journals, International Committee of Medical Journal Editors, www.icmje.org/.

[48] D. Michaels, Politicizing Peer Review: The Scientific Perspective, in: W. Wagner and R. Steinzor (eds.), *Rescuing Science from Politics: Regulation and the Distortion of Scientific Research*, New York: Cambridge University Press, 2006, p. 219.

boards. For example, a decision about the likely relevance of a contribution for the readers of a journal is, in general, not a decision for a referee to make but is something that should be left to editors. Editorial boards on their turn need to think about how they want to deal with contradicting quality judgments made by independent referees. Is this reason to bring in an extra referee, does one give the author the benefit of the doubt, is the precautionary principle applicable here (e.g., do not publish in case of doubt?) or does the editorial board itself need to step forward in case of conflicting peer review judgments and, if so, how are the editors going to decide between conflicting peer review judgments? The answer that deliberation is required then is not really satisfying as long as there is not at least some shared concept of what determines research quality.

9.5.1 For Which Problems is Peer Review Supposed to be the Solution?

It is often not immediately clear for which problems the introduction of peer review is supposed to be the solution. This is nevertheless an important question since peer review comes in different shapes and sizes. There is, for example, prepublication peer review used by scholarly journals and academic publishers, but there is also ex post peer review in the form of book reviews, assessment of publications in tenure procedures and internal or external research assessment exercises, such as the UK REF. Nevertheless, what all the forms have in common is that it is about trust-building. Gould formulates it as follows:

> As noted, in the best of all worlds, academic peer review acts as a barrier to poor scholarship, assuring researchers that what they are reading has been fairly judged and published based on a certainty that the work is sound. In theory, academic scholars – typically three – dispassionately review research produced by cohort members of the academy, almost all of whom are assistant, associate, or full professors. Part of the promise of peer review is that the best works are published after being judged by dispassionate scholars focused solely on the value of the work itself. In a way, this is a protocol in which the academic field regulates its members: An accumulation of success in publishing results in successful promotion and tenure. This is the ideal state and most hoped for outcome.[49]

[49] T. Gould, *Do We Still Need Peer Review?*, Landham/Toronto/Plymouth: The Scarecrow Press, 2013, p. 3.

Although peer review can be seen as a form of academic self-regulation, assessment by three independent reviewers is certainly not standard practice in the field of law. Confusing is that the label 'peer reviewed' is used for quite different things. Sometimes it refers to an assessment of manuscripts by anonymous independent external experts on the basis of a set of guidelines or quality criteria, but just as often, peer review is used to describe a screening of papers by journal editors or book editors who are directly responsible for publication. Even prestigious journals are often unclear about the criteria these assessors should apply and to what extent the adversarial principle is applied to the exchange of arguments between authors and referees. What seems fairly clear, however, is that peer review is supposed to detect cases of fraud, prevent errors, inaccuracies and unwarranted assertions. On the other hand, peer review is also meant to improve the quality of publications through a dialogue with the authors and, more in general, ensure compliance with academic standards of validity and methodological rigor.[50] Next to this, blind peer review is seen as a mechanism to avoid prejudice and selection bias from the side of journal editors and book publishers. In case journals, where editors or publishers are confronted with a supply of manuscripts that outweighs the demand and exceeds the available journal space, peer review can be a mechanism to select only the best articles for publication.

Finally, peer review can also be used as a procedural mechanism to separate professional publications from academic publications. In particular when certain types of professional publications (e.g., case notes, commentaries and textbooks) are threatened to become banned from internal or external research assessments, pressure will mount to stretch the category of academic publications. If one cannot reach consensus over substantive criteria to discern between professional and academic publications, the only thing left to do is to introduce a procedural selection mechanism in order to avoid that everything may be called an academic legal publication. Otherwise the distinction between academic and nonacademic research gets blurred. This is particularly important for doctrinal legal publications because these are in practice being written by practitioners and scholars alike and often hard to distinguish on the basis of the research methodologies being applied.

[50] These are perceived to be the major advantages of peer review in our discipline. See N. McCormack, Peer Review and Legal Publishing: What Law Librarians Need to Know about Open, Single-Blind, and Double-Blind Reviewing, *Law Library Journal*, 101, 1, 60 (2009).

9.5.2 *For Which Solutions Is Peer Review a Problem?*

Experiments with dummy articles and papers with intentionally added errors and flaws prove that prepublication peer review is far from perfect in filtering out substandard publications.[51] Even with respect to the detection of research fraud, peer review does not appear to be very effective. Informal 'peer pressure' and a culture in which criticism among scholars inside research groups is stimulated is probably more important in the prevention of plagiarism and other forms of fraud than organized peer review.[52] Individual referees, for example, will often not be alert on the possibility of fraud and will not become suspicious by dubious publications patterns since they are only asked to look at one particular manuscript.[53]

Because the process of selection and instruction of peer reviewers is often not very transparent, it is uncertain whether referees actually are what they are supposed to be, namely: independent, unbiased, qualified experts, who have deep knowledge about the topic of the publication they are to assess, and score high themselves on the quality indicators they have to apply on others. History shows that external referees, who are used to screen manuscripts, suffer from the same sort of biases as the authors of the publications they are hired to assess. Schatz discerns between four major types of biases: (1) ad hominem bias (a personal preference for or disapproval of certain authors due to friendship, competition or jealousy between the referee and refereed); (2) affiliation bias (a certain favouritism for or prejudice against a certain research institute or law school where the author is employed); (3) ideological bias (a preference for or prejudice against a certain school of thought, theory, paradigm or methodology); (4) aesthetic bias (a preference for or disapproval of a certain form, style or presentation of research that is not

51 J. Bohannon, Who's Afraid of Peer Review?, *Science*, 342, 6154, 60–65 (2013), DOI: 10.1126/science.342.6154.60W; G. Baxt, J. F. Waeckerle, J. A. Berlin and M. L. Callaham, Who Reviews the Reviewers? Feasibility of Using a Fictitious Manuscript to Evaluate Peer Reviewer Performance, *Annals of Emergency Medicine* 32, 310–317, (1998), DOI:10.1016/S0196-0644(98)70006-X. PMID 9737492 ; D.P. Peters and S.J. Ceci, Peer-Review Practices of Psychological Journals: The Fate of Published Articles, Submitted Aging, *Behavioral and Brain Sciences*, 5, 187–255 (1982).

52 KNAW-adviescommissie Integriteit, beleid en vertrouwen in wetenschap, Vertrouwen in wetenschap, Mei 2013, pp. 50–51.

53 W. Stroebe, T. Postmes and R. Spears, Scientific Misconduct and the Myth of Self-Correction in Science, *Perspectives on Psychological Science*, 7, 6, 670–688 (2012).

based on substantive quality).[54] This list can be extended with all sorts of other biases regarding sex, age, origin and so forth.

It is important to realize that peer review is not an effective medicine against all biases. If organized properly, (double) blind review may work to fight ad hominem bias but it is not capable of preventing aesthetic or ideological bias from the side of referees because these prejudices are directly linked to the form and content of a publication. In smaller jurisdictions and in highly specialized fields, organizing a truly anonymous peer review process is often virtually impossible because referees will recognize the work of authors through the style in which it is written or through the references in footnotes.

Authors of publications with a multidisciplinary character face additional problems when confronted with peer review comments because the expertise of the referees often does not fully match with the theories or methods applied in their research project. This makes that referees are only capable of assessing part of the research, but referees are not always willing to openly admit this.[55] It depends on the integrity of the referee and whether he is prepared to explain the limits of his expertise to an editorial board. Moreover, we know that peer review comments by different referees often do not correlate and, even if they do, they do not automatically have predictive value when it comes to future impact scores on the basis of citation counts.[56] Recurring complaints can also be heard that peer reviewers tend towards conservatism in their assessments. In particular, publications which deviate from mainstream thinking would often be assessed too critically. Some studies even reveal that publications of later Nobel Prize winners were confronted with highly critical comments made by referees who did not recognize their revolutionary nature.[57]

Peer review has also practical disadvantages, such as delaying the publication process by adding an extra assessment layer.[58] Besides, it is

[54] D. Schatz, *Peer Review: A Critical Inquiry*, Oxford: Rowman & Littlefield Publishers 2004, ch. 2.

[55] KNAW-commissie Kwaliteitszorg, Kwaliteitszorg in de wetenschap, Amsterdam, Maart 2008, p. 26.

[56] Among many: A. Eyre-Walker and N. Stoletzki, The Assessment of Science: The Relative Merits of Post-Publication Review, the Impact Factor, and the Number of Citations, *PLoS Biol*, 11, 10, e1001675 (2013). doi:10.1371/journal.pbio.1001675.

[57] J. Campanario, Rejecting and Resisting Nobel Class discoveries: Accounts by Nobel Laureates, *Scientometrics*, 81, 2, 549–565 (2009).

[58] See http://scholarone.com/media/pdf/peerreviewwhitepaper.pdf.

expensive in terms of time and recourses because referees cannot use the time they spend on assessing other people's work on their own research. It is needless to say that this becomes even more problematic if the process of review and rejection repeats itself several times. The time the review process takes may even hinder authors to keep their publication up to date with new developments in practice, which can easily harm the societal relevance of publications. One may even wonder whether multiple revisions of manuscripts to satisfy the criticism of referees with sometimes almost contradictory comments and preferences always contributes to the quality of publications. Perhaps the most devastating critique against peer review, however, is that there is little evidence that peer review generally leads to a higher quality of scholarly publications both at the bottom and the top of the publication ladder.[59] On the one hand, peer review has not been very successful at preventing fraud in the past because referees usually do not focus on detecting, for example, plagiarism because they normally have no reason to suspect it. Even if they would be instructed to pay more attention to this, the question would probably still be if referees are prepared to invest the amount of time and energy needed to really check the validity of the research findings as long as peer review is a matter of academic courtesy for which they are not financially compensated.[60] On the other hand, we have seen that referees are also not always willing or able to recognize research excellence.

In terms of ability, the number of submissions is an important precondition for selectivity. Journals or publishers with difficulties to attract enough manuscripts for publication cannot afford the luxury of a high rejection rate. But even in case of abundant submissions it is not easy to select the most promising manuscripts for publication. Hereafter, it will be shown that the most highly cited papers are certainly not always published in the highest-ranked journals or with the most reputable publishers. Research with regard to the selection of candidates for research grants offered by the Dutch national research foundation have furthermore proven that peer reviewers often have difficulties to distinguish between good and excellent researchers. Quite often those who were offered a grant later appeared to score lower on citation indexes

59 House of Commons Science and Technology Committee, Peer Review in Scientific Publications, London, 18 July 2011, p. 88.

60 W. Stroebe, T. Postmes and R. Spears, Scientific Misconduct and the Myth of Self-Correction in Science, *Perspectives on Psychological Science*, 7, 6, 670–688 (2012).

than those who just missed a grant.[61] Moreover, towards the end of the selection process the criteria usually become softer and softer.[62] From an initial assessment of past performance on the basis of the content of publications and quantitative indicators, the selection criteria transform into rather fluid categories, such as enthusiasm, persuasiveness and perseverance. Assessment panels, for example, asked themselves: is this someone who can inspire and lead a research group?

Serious doubts are possible about whether it is possible to answer these sorts of questions on the basis of a single interview. Apart from that, appearances may be deceiving here. Brilliant minds certainly do not have to be good communicators capable of presenting themselves in the most appealing manner. Peer reviewers should be made aware of the fact that it is dangerous to rule out the odd man or woman because history has shown that ground-breaking research has often come from strange characters.

9.5.3 Peer Review Presupposes Consensus over Quality Indicators

Perhaps the most fundamental problem to overcome with regard to the application of peer review in the assessment of research quality is the lack of consensus on what constitutes quality of legal research from a substantive perspective. Without an assessment of publications against well-chosen quality indicators, peer review can easily result in a subjective 'I know it when I see it' approach,[63] which will not be able to explain why different reviewers see different things as a sign of (lacking) quality. Here, the main problem is that most law journals and publishers do not explicate the indicators they require their referees to apply in the peer review process. As far as one does find criteria these are usually formulated as very broad and open categories, as can be found in the UK REF, where 'originality, significance, and rigor' are the main criteria for the assessment of submissions. These are linked to five levels ranging from 'quality that is world leading' to 'quality that falls below the

[61] P. van den Besselaar and L. Leydesdorff, Past Performance, Peer Review and Project Selection: A Case Study in the Social and Behavioral Sciences, *Research Evaluation*, 18, 4, 273–288 (2009).

[62] P. van Arendsbergen, Talent Proof: Selection Processes in Research Funding and Careers, Dissertation VU 2014. Zie: http://dare.ubvu.vu.nl/handle/1871/51588.

[63] This approach is not limited to the assessment of legal scholarship, we can also witness it in judicial law-making. See for instance: *Jacobellis v. Ohio*, 378 U.S. 184 (1964) with the famous concurring opinion by Justice Steward Potter.

standard of nationally recognized work'. In Belgium, Luxembourg and the Netherlands, the scholarly legal research community by and large seems to agree that scholarly legal publications should at least be 'original, thorough, and profound'.[64] These criteria show great resemblance to the indicators used by the expert panels in the UK REF.

Unfortunately, such criteria are rather vague and open to multiple interpretations. Originality, for instance, can mean lots of different things, including asking new questions with regard to old legal problems, contributing to theory building by taking a different look at existing doctrines, and even charting a field of study for the first time in a systematic way.[65] Although originality is closely connected to theory building, this does not imply that scholarly legal publications must always contain a completely new theory. In fact, this is probably rarely the case. The more usual approach taken by scholarly legal research is probably to criticize a doctrinal position, or to reveal inconsistencies in legislation, case law or literature. Something similar applies to thoroughness, profundity and significance. Thoroughness is associated with visible competence and methodological rigor. Unlike attorneys, legal scholars may not be one-sided in their use of sources to deal with a legal dispute and leave the counterevidence to others. Profundity describes the extent to which authors try to find underlying explanations or theories for developments in law (e.g., answering why-questions instead of how-questions) and significance is closely related to societal and scientific impact.

Societal relevance, of course, has to do with the added value that legal research has for practice. For doctrinal legal research this can mean many different things. Researchers may, for instance, develop a theory capable of predicting how judges will deal with new legal questions or try to fit emerging legal problems into existing doctrines and precedents. Scholarly impact, on the other hand, is about the way in which research contributes to the body of academic knowledge. This does not have to result in practical legal solutions but may also be about explaining why the law develops as it does or lead to alternative ways of thinking about legal problems by comparing different approaches to similar problems in multiple jurisdictions. The way in which these alternative ways of

[64] R.A.J. van Gestel and J.B.M. Vranken, Assessing Legal Research: Sense and Nonsense of Peer Review versus Bibliometrics and the Need for a European Approach, *German Law Journal*, 12 3, 901–929 (2011).

[65] M. Siems, Legal Originality, *Oxford Journal of Legal Studies*, 147–164 (2008).

thinking about legal problems should be evaluated in terms of plausibility can never be purely objective but, as Rubin has argued, the more work of other scholars encourages doubts about one's own beliefs or to elicit anxiety that those beliefs are incorrect, the more one should also be careful about possible biases.[66]

As far as quality indicators are concerned, an essential question is finally to what extent the same criteria should apply to different types of publications. The methodological rigor of empirical legal research, for example, requests other things when it comes to data collection, falsifying hypothesis and generalization of research findings, than doctrinal legal research. Similar remarks can be made with respect to different publication types. One can probably not copy and paste the requirements for a solid PhD dissertation to a text book or a commentary. This already implies that the scholarly legal forum should reflect on the necessity of standardization with regard to the quality criteria for different types of publications. Roux has, for example, argued with respect to the situation in Australia that:

> The very notion of a PhD in law also assumes that some kind of cross-disciplinary standard must be met. Even when annual review panels are composed entirely of legal academics and where examiners are themselves academic lawyers, the criteria they are expected to apply are framed in cross-disciplinary terms. In effect this means that, however intuitive, and however resistant to specification in social science terms, the criteria for good doctrinal PhD research must be recast in terms that fit, or at least are not antithetical to, the standard elements of a sound doctoral research dissertation, viz.: a clear and confined research question, a comprehensive and targeted literature review, an appropriate methodology that is rationally related to a governing theoretical framework, and a plausible statement of the project's research significance. Two features of doctrinal research in particular make these standard elements difficult to apply: (1) the fact that doctrinal research is often presented in a highly rhetorical style; and (2) the fact that the criteria for sound doctrinal research as a whole, quite apart from doctrinal PhD research, are rarely articulated.[67]

Here, we immediately see the dilemmas one faces when dealing with standardization of quality criteria for doctrinal legal research. On the one

[66] E. Rubin, On Beyond Truth: A Theory for Evaluating Legal Scholarship, *California Law Review*, 80, 889–963 (1992).

[67] T. Roux, Judging the Quality of Legal Research: A Qualified Response to the Demand for Greater Methodological Rigour, SSRN, 9 September 2014, p. 7. See http://papers.ssrn.com/sol3/papers.cfm?abstract_id=2499258.

hand, it seems unacceptable when the quality criteria for every field of law can be different, especially with respect to PhD dissertations, because otherwise the difficulty of getting a doctoral degree would depend entirely on the lenience of individual law faculties. On the other hand, this leaves us with the question: who decides when and how quality criteria should be harmonized and how much leeway should be given for differentiation between various types of publications? Furthermore, it is important to note that the building of quality concepts and quality criteria is a normative process, which is therefore highly debatable and hence needs to be conducted in close cooperation with the forum of legal scholars since they are the most important stakeholders.

9.5.4 Conclusion

Peer review is a well-known and broadly accepted method to scrutinize the quality of scholarly publications in numerous other disciplines than law. It has the advantage of a natural link with the argumentative nature of doctrinal legal research, and if anonymity can be guaranteed, it may serve as an effective warrant against certain forms of prejudice and selection bias, at least if the identity of authors cannot be traced via the content or the style of writing. Attractive also is that peer review can be applied both ex ante (e.g., assessments of submissions to journals) and ex post (e.g., tenure decisions or national research assessment exercises) and to different types of publications (e.g., books, articles, essays) without serious adjustment.

A positive feature of peer review is also that it can be a nuanced way of research assessment, in particular when referees keep enough professional distance to the object of study. Peer review comments may be used to improve the quality of legal publications via an exchange of arguments with authors about the content of the research. Besides, peer review can deal with a broad range of quality-related issues (e.g., research question and methodology, use of sources, theoretical and societal relevance, etc.).

Unfortunately, there are also well-documented and generally recognized problems with peer review. For starters, the intersubjectivity of peer review as shown by the correlation of comments is often low. As we have seen, biases are hard to rule out completely, and both shared interests (e.g., peer review cartels) and conflicts of interests (e.g., competition between referees and refereed) may negatively influence the outcomes. In particular, in case of open (nonblind) review all kinds of cognitive biases may affect the assessment outcomes (e.g., so-called halo-effect, which makes that researchers with a good reputation are scrutinized in a less critical way than less well-known scholars).

More in general, multi- and interdisciplinary research is often difficult to assess because of mismatches between the expertise of referees and refereed. We also know that peer review can easily lead to conservatism, for example, because referees are overly concerned with protecting the reputation of 'their' journal or publisher. This may also explain why critical peer review comments are not necessarily a good indicator for later research impact as measured via citation counts or other bibliometric indicators.

9.6 Bibliometric Assessment of Legal Publications

Since the introduction of the Science Citation Index in 1961, bibliometrics have become increasingly popular in the evaluation of scientific research.[68] Quantitative evaluation methods using metrics basically focus either on 'output' or 'impact'. Output can be the number of publications in certain outlets, awards and prizes for research or variety in the sort of publications being produced. Impact concerns the reception of research by other scholars (scientific relevance) or social actors (societal relevance). Some bibliometric indicators represent a combination of both, such as the Hirsch index, which is based on a combination of a scientist's most cited papers (productivity) and the number of citations (impact) that they have received in other publications.

> A scientist has index h if h of his/her Np papers have at least h citations each, and the other (Np − h) papers have no more than h citations each.[69]

Not only citations of journal articles are measured but also the number of downloads of papers, the rejection rate of manuscripts by editorial boards or the references to publications on social media. Popular is, for instance, the journal impact factor (JIF), which stands for the average number of citations that articles in a certain journal receive during a fixed period of usually two years until the date of measuring. The JIF tells nothing about the number of citations that an individual article in a journal gets

[68] For an overview: B. Cronin and C.R. Sugimoto (eds.), *Beyond Bibliometrics: Harnessing Multidimensional Indicators of Scholarly Impact*, Cambridge, MA: MIT Press, 2014.

[69] J. Hirsch, An Index to Quantify an Individual's Scientific Research Output, *PNAS*, 102, 46, 16569–16572 (2005).

but is a yardstick for journals. Journals that publish more issues a year and select papers on popular topics will normally have a higher JIF than highly specialized journals focused on a smaller audience of readers. This of course does not imply that the latter journals publish lower-quality papers.

What applies, not only to the h-index and the JIF, but to all bibliometric indicators, is that they measure what their architects want them to measure. In that sense, metrics are never 'objective' but always represent a certain perspective on, or theory about, quality. By themselves, metrics can never take all possible relevant differences between, for example, the size of a (sub)field of study, the aging of knowledge, and the national or international orientation of researchers, fully into account. These limitations have not prevented that evaluation of research via bibliometric indicators has grown more popular especially in the fields of science, technology and medicine (STM).

9.6.1 Law and Bibliometrics

In the social sciences and humanities (SSH), including law, the use of metrics is still lagging behind. According to Van Leeuwen, this is primarily caused by five fundamental differences in publication culture with STM.[70]

First of all, the pace of conducting research, and the way academic knowledge ages in time differs between SSH and STM. In STM knowledge often becomes obsolete within a range of three to four years, whereas in SSH this may take even up to ten years or more and certainly books (monographs) often have a longer life-span than articles. Second, the STM disciplines are usually more focused on transnational cooperation than SSH, which is certainly true for law. Third, the research teams in STM are normally bigger than in SSH where much of the research is still conducted individually, which has a strong influence on the role of coauthorships. Fourth, the diversity of publication types in the SSH (e.g., academic and professional publications, articles and books, case notes and commentaries) is much bigger than in STM where journal articles in international journals are the most important. Because the large majority of the journals in STM can be found in electronic databases, such as Web

[70] T. van Leeuwen, Bibliometric research evaluations, Web of Science and the Social Sciences and Humanities: a problematic relationship?, Bibliometrie – Praxis und Forschung, Band 2 2013, pp. 8-1 t/m 8-18.

of Science and Scopus, they are more accessible for bibliometric evaluations. Moreover, scholars in the SSH domain are also more focused on the public debate with other actors than academics. Fifth and finally, the variety of languages in which publications are being written in the SSH, including law, is much larger than in STM where English serves as the lingua franca. This makes comparisons on the basis of bibliometric indicators more difficult.

In the eyes of Van Leeuwen, all this leads inevitably to the conclusion that quality assessment via traditional bibliometric indicators is in law highly problematic, if not impossible.[71] This is not the end of the story, though. More and more, law schools start to use metrics as a tool for internal assessments. They look for things like: what is the JIF of the publications of young scholars who are in a tenure track? How many research grants or prizes did the staff of our law school generate, which we can show in external research assessment exercises? How many downloads on the Social Science Research Network (SSRN) did our staff receive in comparison to the staff of other law schools? These kinds of questions are becoming increasingly important in many law schools. Sometimes bibliometric evaluation methods are imposed upon law faculties. In 2008, for example, the Council of Australian Law Deans (CALD) was surprised by an initiative of the Australian Research Council to introduce a journal classification based on bibliometric indicators with strong resemblance to the Washington and Lee ranking. Bowry who was involved in this process on behalf of CALD writes about it:

> I was left with the strong impression that release of the law list was a provocative step designed to force law to accept the overall concept of ranking journals, through being forced to engage in 'modifying' a list. If so, this objective was achieved: from this time on there was no longer any real discussion of rejecting rankings but rather only discussion of how to 'improve' a bad situation. I felt senior bibliometrics staff were indifferent to law's concerns because we were a small and self-contained discipline and were taking up too much of their time, when they were subject to very tight time pressures within the department. Peer review was generally distrusted, at least in part because it was a process largely opaque to their own research expertise and because their bibliometric expertise was not really necessary to conduct it. In recourse terms, they felt peer review as inefficient as it involved duplication of effort to subject an already peer-reviewed publication to further additional peer review. In bibliometric terms, assessing the overall journal reputation and preferably also

[71] Ibid., pp. 8–17 and 8–18.

> citations was felt to be sufficient, and more objective . . . I was told that the Washington and Lee based list 'stood up' to scrutiny according to bibliometric criteria of validity. There was no attempt made at all to justify the methodology as appropriate for Australian legal research or for the purpose it was to be put. The presumption was that as the ERA was to involve an international comparative assessment, it was inappropriate to take local concerns about local publications too seriously, lest it be pandering to domestic insecurities and self-interest.'[72]

After lots of protest and several revisions, the Australian law list was officially abandoned in 2011 because there was clear and consistent evidence that the ranking was being deployed inappropriately by law school managers. They were increasingly setting targets and introducing bonus schemes for publication in A and A* journals for promotional purposes, while neglecting that publishing on certain categories of topics in certain preferred fields made publication in high-ranked journals much easier than in others.[73]

In the United Kingdom one has also witnessed repeated attempts to introduce the use of metrics in the national research assessment because of the time consuming and costly nature of the peer review process that is currently (still) being used in the field of law. Despite the fact that the law panel already in 2001 declared that internationally recognized excellence was found in a wide range of outlets and both in prestigious and little-known journals, that did not put the debate about metrics to a stop. In 2009 a pilot project was undertaken to explore the possibilities of using bibliometric indicators in the RAE because the peer review process was considered too time consuming and expensive, but the outcome was the existing metrics were not yet sophisticated enough to replace peer review by expert panels. More recently, however, the Higher Education Funding Council for England (HEFCE) started a new investigation to see what role metrics could play in future national research assessments. Before the outcomes of that project were presented, the academic leader of the project already suggested that it might be time to come to a national research assessment exercise every ten years with a 'light touch midterm review' on the basis of citation scores, altmetrics and other quantitative

72 K. Bowry, Audit Culture: Why Law Journals Are Ranked and What Impact this Has on the Discipline of Law Today, *Legal Education Review*, 23, 2, 291–312, 2013, at 302.

73 D. Svantesson, Truisms About the Australian Publishing Climate for Law Journal Articles, and Some Strategies to Cope; or a Feminist Perspective on the Human Rights of Vegetarian Child-Soldiers in Outer Space, *Canberra Law Review*, 10, 3, 11 and 7 (2011).

indicators.[74] This leaves the impression that HEFCE wants to reduce the peer review burden one way or the other and prefers the use of metrics as the cheapest way of doing this.

In Germany, France and Switzerland, there is much more scepticism towards the use of metrics in the assessment of legal research. The German *Wissenschaftsrat* has argued that bibliometric methods are not sufficiently capable of measuring research performance in legal scholarship. Citations would not necessarily measure the importance of a publication or the degree to which an author's thought is original. Besides practitioners commentaries are probably among the most frequently cited legal publication genres but that does not necessarily indicate their scientific relevance.[75] In France there seems to be a general aversion against quantitative research evaluation in the field of law, not in the least because it would limit academic freedom.[76] In Switzerland an interesting survey was conducted by the universities of Bern and Geneva among 397 law professors, 873 attorneys and 98 law journals with regard to research evaluation methods.[77] One of the outcomes was that more than 90 per cent of the professors and 83 per cent of the attorneys declared to find 'substantive quality' very important citation scores and rejection rates score much lower in both groups.[78] The finding of the Swiss survey correspond with a study by the Swiss Science and Technology Council in which the Council also pointed towards the risks of 'metrics informed peer review'. The Council claimed that there is a real danger that peer reviewers will base their conclusions about the quality of individual publications too much on general bibliometrical information generated on an aggregated (group) level. Apart from that, the Council warned for a crowding out of intrinsic motivation to undertake high-risk

[74] See www.timeshighereducation.co.uk/news/overhaul-of-metrics-usage-could-cut-frequency-of-ref/2012436.article.

[75] Wissenschaftsrat, Prospects of Legal Scholarship in Germany: Current Situation, Analyses, Recommendations, Hamburg, 9 November 2012, p. 54.

[76] Ciuca, Richevaux, Roussel, Wailly, Évaluation de la recherce en droit: L'impossibilité de quantifier le qualitative, in Tanquerel and Flückiger (eds.) *L'Evaluation de La Recherce en Droit*, Bruxelles: Bruylant, 2015, pp. 307–333.

[77] The results of the survey have not been published yet but they are on file with the author, who was a member of the expert panel that served as an advisory body to the researchers.

[78] Citation scores are deemed important (40 per cent) and very important (6.67 per cent) by the professors compared to 54.17 per cent and 9.38 per cent of the attorneys. The rejection rate of journal submissions is considered important (32.65 per cent) and very important (5.1 per cent) by the professors, whereas these numbers are 31.08 per cent and 0.68 per cent for attorneys.

and border-crossing research if researchers start orienting themselves more on the scoring on indicators than on following their curiosity.[79]

All in all, one might perhaps conclude that there is (still?) more attention for quantitative research evaluation methods in the Anglo-Saxon world than there is in continental Europe. One of the more pragmatic reasons for this could very well be the availability of digital repositories, such as LexisNexis, HeinOnline, and Westlaw, in which publications are stored full-text. This makes citation analysis much easier. For most European countries such centralized databases do not exist yet and due to differences in language, formats and style of publications, one may wonder whether it is likely that a European-wide database of legal publications is going to emerge anytime soon.

9.6.2 *Advantages and Disadvantages of Bibliometrics*

About the advantages of bibliometrics one can be relatively brief since these more or less mirror the earlier-mentioned disadvantages of peer review. Compared to peer review, research assessments using metrics are relatively cheap, quick, and applicable in multiple (sub)disciplines without major adjustments. Bibliometric indicators can be used to assess individual publications, research groups, faculties, and even complete universities. Moreover, the evaluations do not require cooperation from the side of the scholars who are getting evaluated and can be kept up to date relatively easy via repeated electronic surveys, which has the benefit that evaluations become less of a still photograph. In some cases, when open access databases such as Google Scholar are used, the outcomes of the evaluations can even be monitored and criticized by the general public.

A positive side-effect of evaluation via bibliometric indicators is that one can obtain information that would otherwise be hard to get from authors or referees.[80] Citation analysis, for example, can be used to supplement peer review by comparing decisions from referees with later citation rates in order to see whether referees selected high-impact papers for publication. Next to relevant information regarding publications patterns, data gathered via bibliometric evaluations is often used to

[79] SWTR, Leistungsmessung und Qualitätssicherung in der Wissenschaft, SWTR Schrift 3/2013, p. 40.

[80] H. Moed, *Citation Analysis in Research Evaluation*, Dordrecht: Springer, 2004, p. 33.

develop successful research policies. What type of publications lead to research grants, prizes or contract research?

With the rise of article-level metrics ('altmetrics') through which the social impact of scholarly legal research can be measured via social media such as Facebook and Twitter, evaluators can gain a lot of new information about the effects of legal research on a wide variety of actors. Altmetrics possess the advantage, compared to traditional impact measurements that need a much longer incubation period, of almost instant information about the impact of legal research on both scholarly for and nonscholars.

Without doubt the most important disadvantage of the application of bibliometric indicators is that these are always proxies of quality that should not be confused with judgments directly based on content concerning the originality, thoroughness or profundity of research. Telling is perhaps that the director of one of the most influential institutions in the world on scientometrics (CWTS) declared in 2013 that:

> Indicators, such as the journal impact factor and h-index, have become too much the standard for everything. Journals and scholars have started to see them as a goal in itself. They adjusted their behavior to it. Some indicators, however, can be manipulated, in order to score high and be eligible for promotion and receiving grants. One may question whether this leads to good research. [translation RvG][81]

More recently, Nature published the 'Leiden manifesto for research metrics'. This manifesto signals that scientometricians increasingly feel that metrics are misused to govern science in a way that has counterproductive effects.[82] One of the complaints is that research evaluation is increasingly led by raw data rather than by professional judgment and implemented by organizations without proper knowledge of, or advice on, good research evaluation practices. Similar criticism can be found in a report from the International Joint Committee on Quantitative Assessment of Research in which the committee notices that bibliometric evaluation methods are often overrated due to a misplaced faith in their accuracy, objectivity and simplicity.[83] The San Francisco Declaration on Research Assessment stresses there is a pressing need to improve the

[81] P. Wouters, Wetenschapsmeter wil niet meer botweg wetenschap meten, NRC, 7 December 2013.

[82] See www.nature.com/news/bibliometrics-the-leiden-manifesto-for-research-metrics-1.17351.

[83] See www.iciam.org/QAR/.

ways in which the output of scientific research is evaluated. It complains against the misuse of the JIF to evaluate the 'quality' of individual scholars, whereas this indicator is not suited for this.[84] One may even doubt whether the JIF is always a good indicator on the aggregate level of innovation and research impact. An interesting study by Google employees focused on citation patterns in Google Scholar over the period 1995–2013, for instance, shows that with regard to the ten most cited journals in a broad range of disciplines, the 1,000 most cited articles are today less frequently published in these highest-ranked journals:

> Our analysis indicates that the number of top-1000 papers published in non-elite journals for the representative subject category went from 149 in 1995 to 245 in 2013, a growth of 64%. Looking at broad research areas, 4 out of 9 broad areas saw at least one-third of the top-cited articles published in non-elite journals in 2013. All broad areas of research saw a growth in the fraction of top-cited articles published in non-elite journals over 1995–2013. For 6 out of 9 broad areas, the fraction of top-cited papers published in non-elite journals for the representative subject category grew by 45% or more.[85]

The problems with quantitative research evaluation methods is not that they do not steer output, but that indicators get a life of their own. This is sometimes referred to as 'Goodhart's law'.[86] It says that as soon as a measure becomes a target, it ceases to be a good measure. What this means in practice is that researchers will focus on how to score on the indicators presented to them instead of on the concepts of quality behind them, which will blur the outcomes of the evaluation.[87] In other words, scholars will start developing their own tactics to game the assessment method. We have, for example, seen in the past that if the number of publications becomes an important indicator in evaluation schemes, researchers will develop all kind of 'salami tactics' to slice publications

84 See www.ascb.org/dora-old/files/SFDeclarationFINAL.pdf.

85 A. Acharya, A. Verstak, H. Suzuki, S. Henderson, M. Iakhiaev, C. Chiung Yu Lin, N. Shetty, Rise of the Rest: The Growing Impact of Non-Elite Journals, 9 October 2014, http://arxiv.org/pdf/1410.2217.pdf.

86 Goodhart applied his 'law' to governmental policy in the sphere of economics: 'As soon as the government attempts to regulate any particular set of financial assets, these become unreliable as indicators of economic trends.' The reason behind this would be that investors are going to anticipate on the intended effects of governmental policy. For more information: http://cyberlibris.typepad.com/blog/files/Goodharts_Law.pdf.

87 D. Colquhoun and A. Plested, Scientists Don't Count: Why You Should Ignore Altmetrics and other Bibliometric Nightmares: www.dcscience.net/2014/01/16/why-you-should-ignore-altmetrics-and-other-bibliometric-nightmares/.

in the smallest publishable units to increase their output. This gaming comes in different shapes and sizes. It varies from enlarging the number of coauthors in publications to lift one's h-index or to get more citations as a group, to editorial boards that cite large numbers of authors from their own journal or encourage contributors to do so in order to increase the JIF, thereby improving the reputation of the journal.

Closely related to this last point is the fact that when faculty managers and funding bodies misuse bibliometric information to increase certain forms of research production, this could lead to a 'publish or perish' culture that encourages doubtful research practices, such as self-plagiarism. For example, when past performance is considered an important indicator, even for early-career grants, this might stimulate PhDs to exploit their thesis topic as much as possible since this is probably the fastest way to generate 'new' publications. It could be seen as an open invitation to recycle parts of a PhD dissertation, perhaps with minor adjustments, into journal articles. Even if that would not result in unethical behaviour, the question remains whether it fosters scholarly innovation. Therefore, one should not underestimate the steering power of performance indicators on scholarly behaviour or overestimate the self-regulatory capacity of the scholarly legal forum in the prevention of gaming.

The latter is why movements, such as 'science in transition', are trying to mobilize scholars in the battle against the growing influence of managerialism, steering on output and governing by numbers in academia to the detriment academic freedom, curiosity driven blue-sky research and reliance on serendipity.[88] In the field of law there does not seem to be much concern yet about the possible adverse effects of quantitative research evaluation but this could easily be the result of the fact that law is lagging behind other disciplines where the influence of bibliometrics is much stronger. It might be a matter of time before law will be forced by other (social) sciences to show accountability in terms of how the quality of scholarly research is being evaluated and presented to the outside world.

9.7 What Does this Mean?

That the external pressure to introduce quality control mechanisms is mounting can already be witnessed in the humanities where several

[88] See www.scienceintransition.nl/english.

projects have been started to develop quality indicators and journal rankings. In 2001 the European Science Foundation, for example, tried to come to a European Reference Index for the humanities to increase the visibility of the research taken place in this field in different countries. The plan was to introduce a classification of journals from different countries in three categories: A, B, and C. A lot of effort was put into this, but in 2009 around fifty editorial boards wrote a manifesto in which they declared to step out of the project:

> The ERIH depends on a fundamental misunderstanding of conduct and publication of research in our field, and in the humanities in general. Journals' quality cannot be separated from their contents and their review processes. Great research may be published anywhere and in any language. Truly ground-breaking work may be more likely to appear from marginal, dissident or unexpected sources, rather than from a well-established and entrenched mainstream. Our journals are various, heterogeneous and distinct. Some are aimed at a broad, general and international readership, others are more specialized in their content and implied audience. Their scope and readership say nothing about the quality of their intellectual content. The ERIH, on the other hand, confuses internationality with quality in a way that is particularly prejudicial to specialist and non-English language journals.[89]

These arguments also apply to the field of law. Especially in Europe there is a huge variety of law journals, written in different languages for often a mixture of scholars and practitioners. Moreover, books, case notes, commentaries, and the like, are still very important in law. Nevertheless, what legal scholars could learn from the experiences in the humanities is that even organized resistance has not prevented that a classification of journals was pushed through and that even in national evaluations, articles in English language journals are now often considered to push more weight than publications in domestic journals and with national publishers. That is why certain experts in the field of the humanities have warned lawyers to stay in charge of the process of research evaluation in their own field and keep the forum of legal scholars involved instead of leaving quality management to administrators. Some social scientists add to this that preference should be given to peer review over bibliometrics and rankings. Or as De Swaan has put it:

> Trust less on counting and measuring and more on words and values. Do not only quantify, but pay more attention to deliberation. Hundreds of

[89] H. Cook et al., Journals Under Threat, *Medical History*, 53, 2 (2009).

> doubts and counter-arguments may be given. How many papers of what kind should somebody produce every year? How do we compare articles to a book? Who can tell us what an original contribution entails? How do we know that an article is not only read and cited, but also generating ideas for other authors? All these questions are pertinent but now comes the great and novel insight: about all the questions one can argue with each other. [translation RvG][90]

Although this might sound sympathetic at first, the problem that remains is that as long as (1) there is no consensus within the forum of legal scholars about what constitutes quality in scholarly publications; (2) there are no proper procedures for the selection of peer reviewers or for dispute settlement in case peer reviewers disagree among each other or with the editorial board; and (3) there is no clear separation between professional and academic publications, doubts may be cast whether peer review will contribute significantly to the quality of legal research. Hence, before prescribing a one-size-fits-all procedure for peer review, it might be better to think about the quality criteria that referees need to apply and how the peer review process should be organized and experiment with different forms of peer review on a small scale first.

It could very well be that double-blind peer review works relatively well for journals or publishers in larger jurisdictions with a fierce international competition between scholars to achieve publications in the highest-ranked journals and the most reputable publishers, but that it will not work in smaller jurisdictions where journals and publishers suffer from a shortage of submissions and where the scholarly community is so intimate that peers will recognize the work of their colleagues, who may also be their competitors, even if manuscripts are anonymized. It would, for instance, be interesting to compare the outcomes of assessments of publications by external referees of journals with the citations scores of the same papers after they have been published to discover whether the peer review process succeeded in filtering out manuscripts with the potential of generating a high number of citations. In case certain referees are constantly critical about papers that are later published in other journals and have received high citation scores there, editors should investigate what is actually going on in the peer review process.

[90] A. de Swaan, Oordeel en voordeel, Over Verantwoorde Beoordeling van Onderzoek, in J.W. Duyvendak, G. Engbersen, M. Teeuwen and I. Verhoeven (eds.), *Macht en Verantwoordelijkheid: Essays Voor Kees Schuyt*, Amsterdam: Amsterdam University Press, 2007, p. 271.

Similar checks and balances can be developed for PhDs who increasingly graduate on articles published in peer-reviewed journals. It might be interesting to compare the referee reports from the journals with the ones from PhD committees responsible for granting the doctoral degree. If there are major differences between the reports it is important to find out why this is the case. Finally, gathering all sorts of quantitative data, such as citation scores, abstract views, download numbers, length of successful articles and so on, could generate a lot of relevant information for authors to take into account in their publication strategy. For instance: what we could learn from this type of research is that if one wants to publish a paper on the legal scholarship network on SSRN that attracts attention, what should be the total length of the article and the size of the abstract and what sort of titles get the most downloads?[91]

9.8 Alternatives?

A seemingly obvious conclusion to be drawn from the foregoing is: let us compare existing evaluation methods, such as rankings, bibliometric evaluation and peer review to combine the strengths of each method while tempering the shortcomings. Although this may appear as an attractive solution, the trouble is that it can easily create a new problem of over-evaluation or 'evaluitis'. It could undermine the 'return on investment' from evaluation and increase bureaucracy. Apart from that, emphasizing the importance of monitoring and evaluation could also contribute to an academic culture of distrust in which scholars are supposed to be incentivized constantly because they would otherwise fail to produce the best possible research.[92] This attitude towards scholars and scholarly research is not only devastating for a serendipitous scholarly environment in which creativity can thrive, but it can also have a serious negative impact on public confidence in academic research. That is why it is important to think about possible alternatives.

[91] M. Siems, Legal Research in Search of Attention: A Quantitative Assessment, *King's Law Journal* (forthcoming, on file with the author).

[92] H. Schissler, Qualitätsmessung: H. Schissler: Rezensionsartikel, What the Hell is Quality?, in: H-Soz-Kult, 12.05.2009, pp. 5–6. See Http://hsozkult.geschichte.hu-berlin.de/forum/id=1099&type=diskussionen.

9.8.1 *Improving Input Quality by Training, Trust and Socialization of Future Legal Scholars*

A first alternative way of thinking about (assessing) research quality is to shift our focus from monitoring and evaluating research output to improving the quality of the input. Just like top football clubs, which invest heavily in youth training programmes to stimulate talent, law schools could pay much more attention to filtering out students with a 'taste for scholarship' early in the law school programme. The purpose would be to train them more systematically to do proper academic legal research, accustom them with the ethics and best practices of scholarly legal writing, and develop a critical scholarly attitude.

Currently, many law schools in the United States and Europe still pay relatively little attention to the training of students in conducting independent academic research, for example by focusing on a variety of research methods (doctrinal, comparative, empirical, etc.), on philosophy of science (where does scholarly legal research differ from professional research?), on research ethics (where does creative interpretation and borrowing stop and research fraud begin?), on academic legal writing and on peer reviewing the work of others. In addition, law schools should make students aware of the fact that an academic legal education requires something more than being prepared for the bar or the bench. Even students primarily interested in normative questions should be taught that doctrinal legal research can go far beyond 'solving' cases on the basis of existing legislation, case law and literature. We sometimes seem to forget that doctrinal research can also be evaluative (e.g., does a new anti-terrorism bill comply with international treaties), explanatory (e.g., why has the Supreme Court changed position on a certain fundamental rights issue) or predictive (e.g., what are the possible consequences for the right to privacy of big data science?), and so on. In addition, doctrinalists can apply more and other research methods than judges do and they are not bound by positive law. This means they can criticize courts and legislatures in a valid way for getting it wrong as long as they are able to explain which normative framework is used for evaluation with what kind of criteria and why these should apply in the case at hand.[93]

Next to changes in the regular law school curriculum, it would be interesting to (further) develop research master programmes in law.

[93] J.B.M. Vranken, Exciting Times for Legal Scholarship, *Recht en Methode*, 2, 2, pp. 42–62 (2012).

These are LLM programmes focused on academic writing skills, methodology, theory building and so forth. Part of some of these programmes is that students develop their own PhD proposal. This enables law faculties to use research masters to filter out the most talented students for a PhD trajectory. In such a trajectory, students are supervised by experienced scholars to deliver a dissertation as a proof of academic quality. In the United States and Canada, a normal step after a PhD/SJD trajectory for the best doctoral students is to offer them a tenure track in which they need to prove to be worthy for an academic career at the highest level (professorship). Part of a tenure-track procedure is normally that the candidate independently demonstrates his or her scholarly abilities by writing articles for the better journals, attract funding, develop and provide courses for students, exhibit certain administrative or managerial skills and so forth. Ideally, an impartial committee of experts in the particular field decides at the end of the tenure-track whether tenure is granted, which will lead to a (semi-)permanent senior position.

Sceptics will probably argue that this merely replaces one problem (how to determine the substantive quality of scholarly legal writings) for another (why does scholar A receive tenure and scholar B not?). This is only partly true, though, because committees deciding over tenure will need to read and assess the publications of the candidates, but these publications no longer have to be studied in isolation. Prepublication assessments by peer reviewers or editorial boards can be compared with an evaluation ex post by studying a sample of publications, and observe postpublication impact, for instance, by studying book reviews. Since the tenure-track will cover at least several years, a committee that takes its job seriously can observe how someone developed over a number of years and take different aspects of research quality into account. Did the candidate succeed in developing and carrying out a research agenda? Is a scholar invited to (inter)national conferences to present his or her research? Are there other signs of scholarly recognition and appreciation, such as prizes and rewards?

Someone who has gone through several selection procedures to become a legal scholar and received tenure has shown to be willing and able to produce high-quality work over a longer period of time, deserves trust from the scholarly community. This is why tenure should be the start of a period of deevaluation. After all, it is unlikely that scholars who have been granted tenure will suddenly cease to perform as may be expected. Besides, the idea behind the tenure system is also to limit the number of years that someone can remain employed on a temporary contract in order to protect academic freedom of teachers and researchers when they dissent from prevailing opinion, openly disagree with authorities of any sort or spend time on unfashionable topics. While these threats to academic freedom may have reduced, new threats have emerged. Especially in Europe, the system of public funding of universities is now under pressure and has tightened the grip of managers on academics. In such a climate, research evaluation and funding are tools to steer academic research in a certain direction as is clearly the case in much of the funding schemes for applied research. These are often driven by the agendas of public policy-makers instead of by the curiosity of academics and their desire to add something to the body of knowledge. To provide counterweight to these developments, it is crucial to protect academic freedom.

9.8.2 Reducing Publication Pressure and Increasing Methodological Accountability

Another way of thinking about enhancing the quality of scholarly legal research and changing existing evaluation practices is a reduction of the pressure to publish, while lifting the level of methodological accountability in doctrinal legal publications.

One of the major problems that is threatening peer review today and explains the growing popularity of bibliometrics is the enormous increase in the amount of scientific publications in general. This makes it increasingly difficult for scholars to keep reading and commenting upon each other's work. In 2007, Thomas Smith calculated that of all the articles in LexisNexis about 43 per cent of law review and journal sources, such as articles and case notes, are never cited even once, and 79 per cent get ten or fewer citations.[94] What does this mean? Are all these articles of poor quality and do they add nothing to the state of the art? Even if there is a core of 'top' articles and books that attract most of the readers and gathers most of the citations, we may wonder for whom all the other papers are written, why they are written, and what their effect is on research evaluation. Paradoxically, because of the increase in research output, existing evaluation methods are reaching their limits. In Australia, for example, where the number of scholarly publications was, in the 1990s, considered important, a steep increase in the number of journal

[94] T. Smith, The Web of Law, *San Diego Law Review*, 44, 309–354 at 336 (2007).

articles in the Science Citation Index (25 per cent between 1993–2003), was matched by a sharp decrease in the average number of citations per article.[95] And in Section 9.6.2 in this chapter, I referred to research showing that on Google Scholar the most cited articles are now less frequently published in top journals. This can undermine the whole idea that journals with the highest impact factor publish the most important papers. It puts current evaluation practices into perspective.

Especially in countries where national research assessments play a major role, it might be better to introduce a maximum number of publications allowed to be submitted to the research assessment exercise than working with a minimum number. Research evaluation mechanisms in which scoring a minimum amount of credits is essential tend to overlook that this easily becomes an incentive to publish more 'risk-free' papers in order to fulfil the target instead of pushing the boundaries of the body of knowledge. The other way around, if researchers may only submit a few publications to a research assessment exercise and their performance is judged on the basis of these self-selected publications, scholars will realize they have to produce a few pieces every three to five years that are really innovative instead of a lot of 'middle of the road' work.[96] One could, of course, object that this does not solve the problem of how to recognize creativity and originality but a pragmatic answer that could help to solve a part of this problem is to ask scholars themselves to be more explicit and open about where *they* think their publications offer new information or a change of perspective. Many research foundations require this in case of rewarding research proposals with a grant. Why could journals and publishers not also set a higher standard here where it comes to the sort of explanation that is required about what is added to the state of the art?

With regard to doctrinal legal scholarship, Tiller and Cross have argued that legal researchers have extensively dealt with doctrine as a normative matter but have given little attention to the manner in which doctrinal research actually functions.[97] An important reason for this is that doctrinal scholarship has been focused on the traditional legal model

[95] L. Butler, Explaining Australia's increased share of ISI publications: The Effects of a Funding Formula Based on Publication Counts. *Research Policy* 32, pp. 143–155 (2003).

[96] My proposal is, of course, not to prohibit legal scholars to write more publications than may be submitted for review in the research assessment exercise, but only to limit the number of publications that are subject to review.

[97] E. Tiller and F. Cross, What is Legal Doctrine, *Northwestern University Law Review*, 100, 1, 518 (2006).

of judicial decision making based on 'reasoned response to reasoned argument'.[98] As a consequence, conducting doctrinal legal research has often been identified with applying the methods of legal practitioners. Of course there is overlap between the type of interpretation methods that judges, attorneys, and scholars may use (e.g., textual, historical and teleological) but doctrinal legal scholars can and should do more and other things in their research. This already starts with the 'legal research problem', which is, for the judge, the problem that is brought before him by the conflicting parties, whereas the legal scholar is fully free to choose whatever research problem he wants to study. Moreover, the judge is restricted in his research by the limits of the law and by rules of procedure and evidence which determine how the investigation should proceed. In the end, he needs to take a decision and cannot refuse to do so. A scholar on the other hand is not bound by positive law but can argue that the law should be changed, and he may also conclude that he cannot find an answer to the research question or that he found out during the research that he raised the wrong question.

As far as attorneys are concerned, the parallel with legal scholarship is even more problematic. Spitzer has argued that legal education is currently too much focused on the 'art of persuasion' and 'winning debates'.[99] In scholarly legal research, however, there is no real opposite party to fill in the lacunae an author has left in the selection and analysis of legal sources or to come up with counterevidence or counterarguments, at least not prior to publication. It is the responsibility of the legal scholar to present the full picture with an open mind and a willingness to challenge one's assumptions, always keeping open the possibility that one might be wrong. In particular for doctrinal research this is crucial because one can almost always find some facts and arguments to defend a certain position. This makes the risk of 'advocacy scholarship' and 'instrumentalization' of legal rules and principles to defend the most desirable legal solution for a doctrinalist real and present,[100] which is also why methodological accountability is so important. After all, the research skills, the research community and the methodological rules of law as an academic discipline together can:

[98] D. Shapiro, In Defense of Judicial Candor, *Harvard Law Review*, 100, 731, 737 (1987).
[99] R.J. Spitzer, *Saving the Constitution from Lawyers. How Legal Training and Law Reviews Distort Constitutional Meaning*, Cambridge: Cambridge University Press, 2008, pp. 22–27.
[100] B. Tamanaha, *The Perils of Pervasive Legal Instrumentalism*, Nijmegen: Wolf Legal Publishers, 2006, 54.

> act as a mediator between the researcher's subjective beliefs and opinions and the data and evidence that he or she produces through research. If this domain is functioning properly, it acts as something like a filter which prevents bad research from passing through.[101]

Even though methodological rigor may not help to prevent plagiarism and other forms of research fraud, raising the standards for accountability could help to prevent tunnel vision (e.g., looking for confirmation), herd behaviour (e.g., ignorantly following other researchers mistaken ideas) and outright sloppy research (e.g., overlooking relevant sources), if law journals, legal publishers and law faculties would join forces in demanding from researchers to explain better what they are doing in doctrinal research and how they are doing it. Epstein and King have given some illustrative examples of things that can easily go wrong in doctrinal analysis, such as researchers attempting to make an inference about the 'state of law' by focusing on a few exemplary or key cases without explaining why these particular cases are exemplary or whether they fairly represent any cases other than those selected by the author.[102] Something similar applies to the use of legislation when determining or interpreting 'legislative intent'. In that case doctrinal analysis usually involves the consideration of the parliamentary debates but authors rarely explain how they have selected the relevant governmental and parliamentary documents and what the analytical framework has been to analyze these documents.[103] Finally, doctrinal scholars often make recommendations for law reform, suggesting that their 'solutions' to existing legal problems are better than the ones that exist in today's law. Hardly ever, though, do authors explain what their normative framework is for determining what 'better' means and how we can recognize the improvement.

The question is whether doctrinal scholars could not learn something here from other social sciences where it is, for example, common to start one's research with an explicit research question, which identifies what the author intends to add to the state of the art of the research with regard to a certain topic. This can, for example, be done by:

> (1) asking a question that the legal community may view as important but that no other scholar has tackled; (2) attempting to settle a question that

[101] M. McConville and W. Hong Chui (ed.), *Research Methods for Law*, Edinburgh University Press: Edinburgh 2007, p. 22.

[102] L. Epstein and G. King, The Rules of Inference, *University of Chicago Law Review*, 69, 1–209 (2002) at 32.

[103] Ibid., p. 42.

> has evoked conflicting responses; (3) raising an "old" question but addressing it in a unique way; (4) collecting new data on the same observable implications or different implications altogether; or (5) applying better methods to reanalyze existing data.[104]

Working with an explicit research question enables editors and peer reviewers to determine what the focus of the research is and whether the author does more than merely describe positive law. It also helps them to assess if the conclusion of the research matches with the initial question and whether the question is really answered in the end. All this facilitates criticism and control.

Something similar holds true for the use of sources. Traditionally, doctrinalists have done relatively little to explain their use of 'data'. Law journals and legal publishers, on their turn, often seem to worry more about style requirements and footnote checking than about how sources have been collected, selected, analyzed, and synthesized. Besides, there are no international standards for referencing, while citing other authors, court decisions or legal rules either in an approving or disapproving manner is often (implicitly) seen as a sign of scholarly impact and quality. On a higher level of abstraction we might agree to some extent that it is important to cite the most authoritative sources, to pay tribute to the *auctor intellectualis* of a certain idea or concept, and that it is not allowed to leave aside opinions that one dislikes, but on a more concrete level, there is no consensus on when citing is (not) necessary or how to deal with findings from previous research (e.g., to what extent do these findings need to be double checked before one may rely on them?). Alarming is that empirical research shows that citation by other authors is highly influenced by the rank of the journal in which the article is published and the law school from which the author graduated. One of the rare studies that tries to look what is behind citations concludes that a minority of scholars citing a work do so for anything related to the content of the ideas, the way of reasoning, the research methodology or the conclusions found in the cited works.[105] If this is actually true, we desperately need clearer international methodological conventions on how to deal with sources. These conventions should not only indicate

[104] Ibid., p. 59. Data can also be read as 'sources' in this case because it does not have to concern empirical data.

[105] J. Harrison and A. Mashburn, Citations, Justifications, and the Troubled State of Legal Scholarship: An Empirical Study, *SSRN* (2015): http://papers.ssrn.com/sol3/papers.cfm?abstract_id=2569499.

when citations are appropriate, but also in which case reference to one source will suffice or when multiple references are required, what the order should be of sources to which one refers in case several authors have made the same claim or used similar arguments, and when reference to one's own previous publications is (not) in order.

More in general, we perhaps need more tailor-made guidelines in doctrinal legal research concerning how to deal with the growing plurality of legal sources in the legal world of today in which the boundaries between international and national law, and hard law and soft law, become increasingly blurred. While we are doing this, we might also take a look at what could be learned from other disciplines when it comes to writing a systematic literature review, for example by using coding schemes to analyze large amounts of text or case law. I do not want to argue that we need to simply copy and paste these methods to the field of law but why could we not learn something from how other disciplines, such as medicine, psychology and sociology, conduct comprehensive literature reviews? Furthermore, would it not benefit the internationalization of law and legal research if we could come to a more uniform international format for law journal articles with certain basic methodological requirements that each scholarly article in every country should be able to fulfil in order to enhance cross-border academic publishing?[106]

9.8.3 Theory and Methodology

It would be a mistake to believe that methodological rigor alone could turn each and every piece of doctrinal legal scholarship into high-quality work. As mentioned above, it probably works the other way around, methodological scrutiny might prevent poor research from passing through. This, however, raises an important question, namely: how do we recognize excellent doctrinal work? One answer might be: by the level of theory building that takes place in a doctrinal legal publication, which elevates the analysis beyond merely describing positive law or purely prescribing what the author sees as 'desirable' law.

Unfortunately, many doctrinal legal scholars feel uncomfortable with labelling themselves as theorists,[107] probably because in doing so they

[106] This has been proposed before by Stolker. See C. Stolker, Legal Journals: In Pursuit of a More Scientific Approach, *European Journal of Legal Education*, 2, 2, 77–94 (2005).

[107] R. Cryer, T. Hervey and B. Sokhi-Bulley, *Research Methodologies in EU and International Law*, Oxford: Hart Publishing 2011, p. 5.

run the risk of distancing themselves too much from legal practice. On the other hand, Posner has claimed that traditional 'black letter' research is lacking: 'penetrating and rigorous theories, counterintuitive hypotheses that are falsifiable but not falsified (and so are at least tentatively supported), precise instrumentation, an exact vocabulary, [and] a clear separation of positive and normative inquiry'.[108] Especially the last part of his argument – the intertwinement between positive and normative inquiry – is typical for doctrinal research. Peczenik has given the following example, derived from Dreier:

> Consider two competing theories in contracts, the will theory and the declaration (reliance, trust) theory. According to the first, a party is in principle not bound by declared contract terms that unintentionally end up conflicting with the real will expressed when concluding the contract. According to the second, the declared will takes precedence over factual will, because the other party must go by what was stated. How does one test which theory is right? If the theories are descriptive, the test is in their coherence with the words of the statute and with factual judicial practice. If the theories are normative, the ultimate test lies in the justice and reasonableness of their consequences. In practice, both kinds of testing take place.[109]

The problem is that in doctrinal research these two types of theory building are often mixed up. Sometimes doctrinal scholars apply normative (interpretation) methods to answer questions that are essentially empirical, such as how can we improve the impact of legislation or the problem-solving features of judicial law making? Or they present their arguments and analysis as purely descriptive, while they are actually making normative propositions about which legal solutions are considered desirable. In case normative arguments are used to answer empirical questions, doctrinal theories are stretched beyond their limits. The fact, for example, that a certain 'solution' seems to fit better in the legal system – which requires some sort of theoretical argument – does not have to say anything about whether it will actually help to solve the underlying practical problem. The other way around, one needs a normative theory to make choices between different possibly applicable doctrines to tackle a practical legal problem. To give an example:

[108] R. Posner, *The Problems of Jurisprudence*, Harvard: Harvard University Press 1993, p. 69.

[109] See A. Peczenik, *Scientia Iuris. Legal Doctrine as Knowledge of Law and as a Source of Law*, Dordrecht: Springer 2005, p. 5.

> In 2012 the Dutch Supreme Court had to decide whether a reference to private (technical) standards in the Dutch Building Decree (DBD) transfers these private norms into public regulations. This was highly relevant since the Dutch Copyright Act rules that there can rest no copyright on laws, decrees or ordinances issued by public authorities. Two theoretical viewpoints were defended in the literature. The first one might be a called the 'usurpation theory', which basically claimed that if a public bill refers to private standards for the interpretation of open texture in the law, the private standards transform into public regulations. The other theory, which can be labelled as the 'competence theory', approached the status of the standards as a question of delegation. Since the organization responsible for the drafting of the standards (the Dutch Standardization Institute) had not received any competence to draft public regulations for the legislature, the technical standards must have remained private, which meant that the copyright stayed with the Standardization Institute.[110]

Which doctrinal theory (usurpation or competence) should prevail in the given example? The letter of the law or the legal system as such does not provide the answer here, since both theories are defendable and could be fitted in easily. One usually needs to find the answers to conflicting positions in the purpose of the rules (why does the legislature refer to private standards?), the normative values behind legislative choices (everybody should be able to know the law versus intellectual ownership deserves legal protection), and legal rights and principles (e.g., legality, legal certainty and right to property). Research excellence in doctrinal publications therefore often lies in the theoretical justification of the choices an author makes between different normative positions and the extent to which the social context is taken into account. The trouble is, though, that how this social context should be taken into account cannot be found in any methodological handbook for doctrinalists.

What would help tremendously is when doctrinalists were asked to explain the theoretical relevance of their research more explicitly to the reader. Where does the author deviate from existing doctrines and why? To which scholarly debate does he/she want to contribute? What new insights or perspectives did the research deliver and for whom might that be important: scholars and/or practitioners? Information about these sorts of questions would enable editors, peer reviewers and readers to make a better judgment about the scholarly value of a publication and enable others to criticize the author on the theoretical relevance of the research. Information about this could be requested in electronic

[110] R.A.J. van Gestel, Hoge Raad is Duur, *RegelMaat*, 27, 4, 249–295 (2012).

submission forms or as information that needs to be included in abstracts of journal articles or in the preface of academic books. It would also make clear to what extent the author is capable of discerning between main issues and side issues and to what extent his or her contribution has made a novel contribution to the debate in a certain field. This could enhance the credibility of doctrinal legal research and show to the outside world that there is more to 'black letter research' than lawyers just arguing with each other.

9.9 Conclusion

As mentioned in the introduction, law as a discipline has in a certain sense the advantage of lagging behind other social sciences when it comes to research assessment and quality management. It enables the scholarly legal community to learn from the mistakes that other disciplines have made before. Perhaps the most important mistake over the past decades has been the increasing focus on output control, ranking, and scoring on quantitative performance indicators, which has led to increasing complaints about a disregard for the research content and advancement of knowledge. Although peer review is as such more suitable to assess the quality of the content of research, it is far from flawless. Studies have shown that peer review is not a very effective remedy against research fraud or gross misconduct. At the same time, external referees often behave too conservatively to recognize ground-breaking research because it deviates from mainstream thinking. Moreover, even though (double) blind peer review is meant to avoid bias from the side of the referees, certain types of bias by referees themselves cannot be ruled out by blinding the review process. Perhaps even more important is that successful peer review presupposes a certain agreement on the quality criteria that scholarly publications need to fulfil and on how referees are selected and instructed by journals and publishers. With regard to traditional legal research there is no consensus on this. It seems fair to say that current peer review practices depend too heavily on the intuition and experience of those assessing the quality of publications.

As a consequence, it might seem logical to opt for a combination of ranking, peer review and metrics-based research assessment in order to attenuate the disadvantages of individual research evaluation methods. This could, however, easily result in 'evaluitis' or a bureaucracy, which will overshoot the mark and lead to a culture of distrust and lack of confidence in academics. Therefore a fundamental change in the current practice of research assessment is necessary. I have proposed three alternative lines of thinking to move forward with improving the quality of scholarly (doctrinal) legal publications.

The first one shifts the emphasis from output control to the input side of training and socialization of research talent. Both in Europe and in the United States, more attention could be paid to the training and education of young scholars with a taste for science. This is of particular importance for students who have not received much prior education in research methods, philosophy of science, academic writing, research ethics, and so on. For those students it is important to learn what the differences are between the research that legal practitioners undertake that is focused on finding out what the law says on a certain topic and academic legal research that is supposed to add new knowledge to a scholarly debate. Students need to be taught how academic doctrinal legal research may differ from what judges and attorneys do. Law students with a taste for scholarship could be filtered out early in the law school curriculum in order to get extra training on how to set up and carry out small-scale research projects. For those who want to pursue an academic career, the first experience with doing independent research could be followed up by a research master or PhD programme, which enables talented students to further develop their research skills under the supervision of experienced scholars. Other than in the regular law school curriculum, the focus with regard to doctrinal research in these programmes should shift from answering 'how' questions to 'why' questions and from a purely black letter approach to a study of the law in its sociopolitical and global context.

If one can provide law students with academic ambitions special training programmes – which start early in the law school curriculum and are followed through until a PhD trajectory with individualized supervision and a few years of tenure afterwards – before one receives a permanent position as a legal scholar, law schools should be able to give a tremendous boost to the quality of doctrinal legal scholarship. This would even be more so if we add the other two alternatives discussed earlier, namely: reducing publication pressure and increasing the attention for methodological accountability and theory building in doctrinal legal scholarship. So far doctrinalists have mostly kept their methods and research techniques implicit, and theory building is often hidden behind technical jargon. This is, however, not something that needs to remain like this. There is no reason why doctrinal legal publications could not entail a well-formulated research question that explains what it is that the researcher wants to add to the state of the art. Especially in the digital age we are living in, in which more and other (foreign) legal sources are available for scholars, it is increasingly important that authors explain how they have collected, selected, analyzed and synthesized their 'sample' of legal sources in order to show the validity of the research findings. On other methodological issues, traditional legal scholarship might also learn from other social sciences, such as with regard to the question of how to write a truly *systematic* literature review.

The same goes mutatis mutandis for theory building. There is no reason why doctrinal research could not have theoretical relevance, but doctrinalists could do much better in, for instance, explaining the theoretical framework they use on which they base their normative recommendations. More in general, a sharper distinction between fact finding and normative considerations is essential to enhance the trustworthiness of doctrinal work. Law journals and book publishers could stimulate this process of methodological and theoretical exposition by developing clearer guidelines for both authors and referees with regard to what is expected in terms of originality, thoroughness and profundity and how these abstract values can be translated into more practical requirements, such as formulating proper research questions, applying a responsible use of legal sources and conducting a systematic literature review that reduces the risk of overlooking relevant information.

Building consensus with regard to what quality of legal scholarship entails and how we can recognize it is probably a never-ending story. This should not withhold us from starting and continuing the debate. Debating what quality is and how we can grasp it is more like a morality of aspiration, which requires continuous effort. The worst thing we could do is just choose one or more quality monitoring systems in order to get rid of the debate.

PART III

The Interaction of Legal Scholarship with Other Disciplines

10

The Logic of the Law

The Analytical Foundations of Methodology

NEIL KOMESAR

10.1 Introduction

Law is vast and complex. To explore it and to understand it requires a mode of organizing what we know and what we need to know. That means establishing a way to determine what is important and why. In other words, we need an analytical framework. For the multidimensional world of intellectual inquiry captured in phrases like legal methodology, this analytical framework should be insightful, accessible and adaptive. It should be powerful enough to yield insights across all legal areas and yet be understandable to analysts of different backgrounds and inclinations. It should be able to speak to what law is, what it will be, and what it should be.

Like many others, I have been pursuing an analytical framework for understanding law. For me, such an analytical framework must focus on society's decision making processes, their behavior, and, most importantly, the choices between them. I have referred to these decision making processes as institutions, the choice among them as institutional choice and the analysis of this choice as comparative institutional analysis. Although the term institution has several conventional meanings, when I use it, I mean institutions as decision making processes. These decision-making institutions can be divided into three broad categories: the market, the political process, and the adjudicative process (the courts).

In its most common form, law can be seen as the product of a decision making institution: the courts. Public law, such as constitutional law and administrative law, involves the choice between decision making by the courts and the political process and private law, such as contract and tort law, involves the choice between the courts and the market as well as the choice between these institutions and the political process. Law evolves as courts decide whether they or some other institution will decide important issues of public policy. For reasons that will become obvious, courts will usually allocate decision making elsewhere. More broadly, public policy involves fundamental questions of institutional choice dominated by the choice between the market and the political process and between various aspects of the political process, such as the choice between state political processes and national political processes and the choice between national political processes and international political processes. The question of who decides is pervasive and profound in both law and public policy.

I have used economic analysis to construct comparative institutional analysis. In the process, I have sought to differentiate those aspects of economics that are critical and those that just get in the way. Both legal analysis and the economic analysis of law and public policy share a serious defect. They both rely on single institutional analysis rather than comparative institutional analysis. That is, they examine institutional choice by focusing on only one alternative. In this connection, I have used comparative institutional analysis to reform economic analysis as well as legal analysis.

In the first part of this chapter, I set out some basic tools of comparative institutional analysis. In the second part of this chapter, I explore the role of institutional choice and comparative institutional analysis in defining the basic intuitions of law. Here I examine equal protection law, property law, class action law, contract law, and corporate law through the lens of comparative institutional analysis. This broad set of applications shows the range of comparative institutional analysis and reveals the parallels across areas of law often considered unconnected. In the third part of the chapter, I consider the role of economic analysis in understanding and constructing comparative institutional analysis and the role of institutional choice and comparative institutional analysis in unlocking the potential of economics for the analysis of law and public policy. Here I will consider the role and limits of goals such as resource allocation efficiency, the intellectual costs of single institutional analysis, and the central place of the dynamics of participation. I will close by drawing implications for the reform of legal education, legal scholarship, and the economic analysis of law and public policy.

10.2 Basic Tools

This part of the chapter briefly summarizes three of the most important tools employed in the comparative institutional approach to law and public policy: the participation-centered approach, the two-force model of politics, and the basic parameters of the adjudicative process.

10.2.1 The Participation-Centered Approach

I recognize that my call for comparative institutional analysis must be accompanied by a strategy for identifying and comparing institutional capabilities. To that end, I provide an analytical approach – the "participation-centered approach" – that should permit analysts of law and public policy to organize studies of institutional choice in the various areas of law or public policy that interest them. The resulting analytical framework provides, minimally, a place to start – a way to organize data, intuitions, and arguments and to focus further inquiry. It attempts to capture as much detail as possible given the desire that the framework be portable.

In the participation-centered approach, variation in the performance of an institution is tied to the participation of important institutional actors common to all the institutions. The focus is bottom-up, emphasizing the activities of consumers, producers, voters, lobbyists, and litigants. At least initially, official actors in the political process and the judiciary legislators and judges play a secondary role. The conception of institutional participation is a basic economic one. The character of institutional participation is determined by the interaction between the benefits of that participation and the costs of that participation. The benefit side focuses on the characteristics of the distribution of benefits or stakes across the relevant populations. Here the central determinants are the average per capita stakes and the extent to which per capita stakes vary within the population. The cost side focuses on the costs of participating in the institutions – transaction costs, litigation costs, and political participation costs. These costs generally fall into one of two broad categories: the cost of information and the cost of organization. The cost of information is the more important category – in good measure, organization costs are primarily information costs. Here the central determinants of cost include the complexity or difficulty of understanding the substantive issue and the institutional processes in question, the numbers of people on one side or the other of the interest in question, and the formal barriers to access associated with institutional rules and procedures.

The dynamics of participation are central in the approach to institutional behavior employed throughout this chapter. We will see them laid out in the brief discussion of the political process and the courts that immediately follow, employed in the discussion of legal doctrine in the next section and connected to the economic analysis of law and public policy in the section that closes the chapter.

10.2.2 The Two-Force Model of Politics: Fear of the Few and the Fear of the Many

We can see the power and dexterity of the dynamics of participation by examining the political process. Focusing on the dynamics of participation produces a broader and more powerful economic analysis of politics. Much of what economists and other social scientists have contributed to the analysis of politics, especially the work that has found its way into law, is based on a simple but powerful image of the dynamics of participation: small, concentrated interest groups are active and large dispersed groups are passive. In this scenario, small interest groups made up of individuals with high per capita stakes have greater political influence than groups larger in number but with smaller per capita stakes even when the total stakes for the larger group may significantly exceed that for the smaller group. For simplicity, I lump this body of work into the interest group theory of politics (IGTP) and refer to the disproportionate influence of the concentrated few as "minoritarian bias."

Despite the power of this traditional conception of the political process, there are two sources of doubt about its adequacy. First, too much legislation seems to be broad-based and even public interested to justify complete reliance on the IGTP. Second, and more important for my purposes, the IGTP omits another and opposite political malfunction with as much tradition and historical pedigree as minoritarian bias – the overrepresentation of the many over the few (majoritarian bias). The fear of this political malfunction was paramount in the framing of the US Constitution[1] and animated much of twentieth century constitutional law, especially equal protection law.

Fortunately, a closer look at the dynamics of participation allows the IGTP to be broadened to integrate majoritarian and minoritarian

[1] Neil Komesar, *Constitutions As Basic Structure, Oxford Handbook of the United States Constitution*, Mark Tushnet, Mark Graber, and Sanford Levinson, eds., (New York, Oxford University Press, 2015) [hereinafter cited as *Constitutions*] and Neil Komesar, *Imperfect Alternatives: Choosing Institutions in Law, Economics, and Public Policy* (Chicago, University of Chicago Press, 1994) at 217–221 [hereinafter cited as *Alternatives*].

influences and their interaction into a single analytical framework capable of generating a continuum of political outcomes. Majoritarian influence represents a countervailing force to minoritarian influence. The power of this majoritarian force will vary from the dormant force imagined by the IGTP to a dominant, even oppressive force captured in phrases like "tyranny of the majority." Once again, it comes back to the dynamics of participation.

The IGTP is clearly a participation-centered view of the political process with political participation and influence dependent on the costs and benefits of that participation. Effective political participation requires that people recognize their interests and understand the political process and its various channels of influence. The more complex the social issue, the more difficult or expensive it is to recognize one's position. The more complex and extensive the political process, the more difficult it is to understand its channels of influence. High per capita–stakes players have the incentive to understand both their interests and how to influence the political process. When the combination of low per capita stakes and high participation costs makes dispersed majorities dormant, the only voice heard is that of the high-stakes minority.

But there can be significant variation in the determinants of the dynamics of participation (the distribution of the stakes and the costs of political participation) and, consequently, significant variation in the dominance of the few and the dormancy of the many. As the absolute per capita stakes for the majority increase (even holding constant the ratio between majoritarian and minoritarian per capita stakes), members of the majority are more likely to expend the resources necessary to understand an issue. Variation within the distribution of the per capita benefits of political action – the degree of heterogeneity – also affects the probability of collective action on behalf of the majority by subgroups of higher-stake individuals. Those with higher stakes can sometimes operate as a catalytic subgroup, activating the more dormant members. In turn, the costs of political participation vary depending on the size and population of the jurisdiction, the number of legislators, the frequency of election and the size and scope of the legislative agenda. Smaller polities and, therefore, smaller numbers of voters and fewer issues increase the probability of majoritarian response by lowering the costs of information and organization. Complexity and, therefore, the cost of information also vary with the subject matter of the issue in question, the endowment of general information determined in part by cultural symbols and the coverage of the press and media. Simpler issues or those involving familiar symbols and media coverage increase the probability of majoritarian response.

Thus, the political influence of concentrated minorities varies depending on the complexity of the issue involved, the absolute level of the average per capita stakes of the larger group, the unevenness of the distribution of the larger group along with the chance that this heterogeneity will produce catalytic subgroups, and the availability of free or low cost information to the larger group. Voting provides large groups with a form of political action that, in some instances, can be a powerful substitute for the organizational advantages of special interest groups. Taken to its logical conclusion, this analysis suggests that there are instances in which the larger group may dominate.

The two-force model offers a straightforward way to understand the broader range of political behavior and political outcomes through variation in the strength of the two influences, which in turn is linked to variations in the costs and benefits of participation. As the majoritarian influence grows, we can get a countervailance between the two forces and, with it, political outcomes that are more "balanced" than predicted by a model that focused on only one force. Broad-based legislation can occur even in the context of strong, narrowly selfish motivation on the part of either elected officials or interest groups. Moreover, the two-force model also recognizes and integrates a political evil beyond the purview of one-force models – overwhelming majoritarian influence leading to majoritarian bias.[2]

10.2.3 The Adjudicative Process: General Parameters

The working of the adjudicative process raises three broad institutional considerations: the competence or substantive ability of adjudicative decision makers such as judges and juries, the dynamics of litigation, and the physical capacity of the adjudicative process. These three considerations interact with each other and with factors like numbers and

[2] Although my analysis is stated in the form of two forces, it could be generalized to more. One can imagine a whole range of interest groups varying in size, heterogeneity, per capita impact, endowed knowledge, or any of the other factors that have been suggested in the two-force model. Casting the analysis of the political process at least initially in terms of the tradeoff between two forces – minoritarian and majoritarian – mirrors the significant historic role of these forces. It also provides a simple spectrum that pulls together and dramatically points up the juxtaposition of factors emphasized elsewhere.

complexity[3] to determine the performance of the courts and the characteristics of law and rights.

These interactions are played out against the background of the structure of the adjudicative process. Compared to the political process and the market, the judicial or adjudicative process exhibits three distinctive structural elements. First, the adjudicative process is more formally defined and has more formal requirements for participation than do the other two institutions. Second, the adjudicative process is much smaller – its physical resources and personnel are far fewer – than the political or market processes and, more importantly, it is far more difficult to increase in size. Third, judges, the central officials of the judicial process, are more independent from the general population than either their market or political counterparts. These three basic characteristics – higher threshold access cost, limited scale, and judicial independence – are related.

The independence of judges stems primarily from their terms of employment. The connection can be seen most dramatically in the US federal judiciary. Federal judges serve for life and cannot be removed except by a cumbersome impeachment process. Compensation is set for judges as a class, and Congress cannot single out the compensation of individual judges. In addition, federal judges traditionally come to the bench as a final vocation. The longevity and high average age of federal judges attest to a limited interest in job mobility. Although judges are not completely indifferent to alternate job opportunities, the range of alternatives attractive to judges appears to be more limited than for political and market actors. Job security and the general disinterest in other positions makes it difficult to influence judges by replacement or inducement. Replacing judges is a longer term strategy than replacing legislators. Financial inducement of judges is more difficult to arrange than with elected officials both because elected officials have a more pressing need for campaign contributions and because contributions to elected officials carry fewer sanctions.

Juries are similarly walled-off from outside influence or at least more so than comparable decision makers in the market and political processes. They are chosen at random from the population and serve for only short periods – in general, for only a few trials or indictments. Their

[3] When I use the term "numbers," I am referring to the number of individuals impacted by a given transaction or societal decision. Complexity is meant to pick up difficulty of understanding a given transaction or societal decision.

anonymity and continuous turnover as well as the difficulty of predicting which case any individual juror may hear makes them a difficult target for influence. Unlike bureaucrats who hear many cases of a specialized type, a given juror will hear only one or two cases. Any long-term or subtle efforts aimed at gaining favor with jurors – such as educating them to favor a given position – would have to be aimed at the general population. Jurors are a vast, diffuse, and moving target.

Independence, or at least insulation from unequal influence, is also increased by the manner in which information comes to judges and juries. Information reaching both judge and jury is largely funneled through the courtroom and the adversarial process. Obviously, neither judge nor jury is immune to pretrial sources of information; they were not born on the day of trial. But ex parte discussion is at least formally precluded and is, in reality, much more difficult to accomplish than in the informal political process, let alone in the highly informal market. The requirements of written complaints, service, and notice along with pretrial discovery and the rules of evidence are designed to give all parties to a lawsuit equal access both to information and to official decision makers.

These features of the adjudicative process lend support to the popular image that the judicial process is more even-handed and its officials more independent than political officials. However, the same structural elements and safeguards that produce independence and even-handedness raise the cost of participation – the costs of litigation. There is a trade-off between equality of participation and amount of participation. The resulting differences in the costs of participation cause significant differences in the range of issues seen by the courts relative to these other institutions. It also can cause significant differences between formal equality of participation and actual equality of participation as the increased costs of litigation preclude certain groups and issues.

Before any trial is held, litigants can expect contests before judges testing the sufficiency of the complaint or of its service as well as raising issues such as standing, jurisdiction, choice of law, justiciability, and ripeness. Litigants can also expect to spend a long period before trial in a process of discovery used to elicit information and evidence. Unlike fact gathering in the political process, this factual investigation is funded primarily by the parties, not the public. If trial follows, the arguments and the evidence presented to judges and juries must fulfill extensive rules of procedure and evidence. These rules are complex and, therefore, expensive to understand and fulfill. This expensive presentation is again made and funded primarily by the litigating parties.

The cost of participation in the adjudicative process, like the cost of participation in the market and political processes, is dominated by the cost of information. In the adjudicative process, the formalities and complexities of the process itself require such a significant accumulation of knowledge and experience that the virtually universal manner of dealing with them is to hire an expert – the lawyer. Thus, although litigants can, in theory, represent themselves in court, few litigate their interests without the significant, indeed often dominating, presence of a hired lawyer with expertise in the particular area of law. Lawyers are hired as the least expensive (but certainly not inexpensive) way to deal with the daunting information costs of litigation.

From a social standpoint, the greater insulation of judges from the various pressures, produced in part by the presence of all the formalities, provides an important source of comparative advantage for the adjudicative process. This independence provides judges with the opportunity to shape social decisions without some of the systemic pressures that distort other institutions. The dynamics of participation through direct influence of judges is restrained when compared to such forces in the political process and the market. The insulation of judges also creates a greater formal equality in which all litigants are forced to influence the decision in the controlled environment of the courtroom.

But the dynamics of participation are clearly at play in the adjudicative process through the dynamics of litigation. The threshold costs of litigation, interacting with the distribution of stakes, can keep the courts from a given social issue and even from large sets of social issues and the dynamics of participation in litigation may turn the high costs of litigation into serious inequality as low stakes players and those with limited experience with adjudication are systematically disadvantaged. The high threshold costs associated with the formal requirements of the adjudicative process will not preclude all issues nor do they mean that the cost of participation in the adjudicative process will necessarily be higher than the cost of participation in other institutions. That depends on the setting. The point here is that the judicial independence that distinguishes the adjudicative process from other institutions comes at a significant cost that will affect the number and type of issues handled by the judiciary.

The dynamics of litigation is the feature of the adjudicative process that is linked most directly to the participation-centered model of institutional behavior emphasized in the economic approach to the market and in my two-force model of the political process. But there are two other facets of the adjudicative process that impact its role: competence and scale. By competence, I mean the ability of trials (the adversarial process) and of triers (judges and juries) to investigate, understand, and make the substantive social decisions that may come to them. By scale, I mean the resources or budget available to the judiciary and the constraints on the expansion of the size of the adjudicative process. Scale and competence interact with each other and with the determinants of litigation (stakes and costs) to determine the institutional ability of the adjudicative process.

Various concerns have been raised about the competence of judges and juries as decision makers: concerns about the competence of juries to understand highly technical issues and evidence in complex, large-scale litigation; concerns about the ability of judges to handle complex and sensitive issues concerning subjects such as foreign affairs or national defense; and concerns about the ability of the adjudicative process to deal with large-scale social-policy issues where there are many conflicting interests and a continuing need for implementation and oversight. There is little doubt that juries have limited technical expertise. They are randomly chosen from the general population, and individual jurors are often chosen in the *voir dire* explicitly to avoid expertise in the specific issues of the case. These inexpert juries are often asked to listen to the technical and complex testimony of conflicting expert witnesses and decide difficult substantive issues. Similarly, trial and appellate judges formally trained only as lawyers and coming from a wide variety of practice backgrounds are regularly asked to judge the facts in and fashion the rules and remedies for complex litigation involving a wide range of human activity. These judges, both trial and appellate, usually are not asked to specialize in one type of controversy and, therefore, do not obtain the expertise that such frequent exposure would bring.

In theory, the implications of increasing or decreasing the physical capacity (the scale) of any institution are significant in determining the ability of that institution. However, the constraints on the size of the adjudicative process and the implications of these constraints on judicial choices are more obvious and dramatic than any comparable constraints on the size of the market and political processes. In fact, it is the relative ease with which the market and political processes expand that creates the demands that strain the physical capacity of the adjudicative process. It is the output of these larger institutions that the courts are called upon to review. As numbers and complexity increase, the functioning of these alternative institutions deteriorate and the demand on the courts increases.

The most important constraint on the expansion of the adjudicative process stems from the central role of judges, particularly of appellate judges. The main bottleneck here is the appellate court structure. Each judicial system within the United States has at its apex a Supreme Court meant to articulate the rules under which adjudication takes place and to define the rights that trigger litigation. These courts are staffed by a small set of judges. The most obvious reform, increasing the number of judges on these high courts, does not easily or even necessarily increase the output of this court. Although an increase in judges would decrease the per-judge load of opinion writing, it would likely increase the time and effort necessary to reach a collective decision by this body. In fact, increasing the numbers would probably make such collective decisions more difficult and time consuming.

Because judges are given so much power without the discipline of lost profits or lost office, we constrain this power by more formality and especially more prescribed layers of review. Formality means increased cost and the formal hierarchy of review constrains growth. It is by no means impossible to expand the judiciary. The US judiciary has grown significantly. But, as the US experience indicates, this growth is far less rapid than the growth in the alternative institutions. It is difficult to imagine the judiciary growing at the same rate as these other institutions without eradicating most of the attributes we associate with the adjudicative process.

It is common to imagine idealized courts as obvious substitutes for defective markets and political processes. But, like the real-world market and the real-world political process, the real-world adjudicative process is neither frictionless nor costless. More importantly, analogous to the market and the political process, its frictions and costs increase as numbers and complexity increase in the form of the numbers of litigants, size of individual damages, disparity of interests, and the complexity of the substantive issues. For example, air pollution covering a considerable area is likely to be characterized by a large social loss dispersed over many victims, each of whom suffers relatively low loss and, therefore, has relatively low stakes in any subsequent litigation. These impacts, as well as the sources of pollution, are complex, subtle, and difficult to recognize. These circumstances significantly encumber market and political processes in dealing with these issues.

But they raise similar problems for courts. Even if victims recognize these losses and their cause, the low stakes may not justify the significant threshold costs of litigation. Litigation has significant economies of scale; one does not buy any serious lawyering for the expenditure of $100, $1,000, or even $10,000. The point is simple and familiar but important: the strength of judicial protection depends on the reality of adjudicative remedies, these remedies depend on the dynamics of litigation, and the dynamics of litigation are a function of the factors of the participation-centered model – in particular, numbers and complexity. The character of law and rights and their implications for the welfare of society are determined by institutional and systemic factors like the dynamics of litigation. We will see these forces at play in the subsequent discussion of class actions.

10.3 Institutional Choice and the Law: Taming Terminology and the Determinants of Doctrine

It is common for most nonlawyers (and even some lawyers and judges) to think of law as fixed and the learning of the law as something analogous to learning anatomy or the chemical tables. Read carefully and it is all there. Commit that body of doctrine to memory and you are a lawyer. In reality, however, law is constantly in motion. Changes sometimes are obvious such as when precedent is overruled. But most of the change is more subtle and is forced when standard and seemingly unchanging doctrine is applied to constantly varying and often unforeseen settings. Life overwhelms fixity.

Law schools do a good job of teaching future lawyers the lesson that law is not fixed. But legal education offers no analytical framework to fill the resulting void. That is its great failing. The emphasis in legal education is still on careful reading of opinions and statutes combined with vaguely defined ad hoc skills and stabs at explanations that vary from legal subject to legal subject and law teacher to law teacher. When added to the continuing fiction that law can be determined by the mechanical application of external sources ranging from the canons of interpretation to the Oxford dictionary, the result is far less clear than it pretends to be or needs to be.

It is my belief that there are important insights to be gained in every area of the law by focusing on institutional choice (the allocation of decision making) and employing comparative institutional analysis. When lawyers and legal scholars use the term "law," they commonly mean court-made or court-interpreted law. Here law is the product of a decision making process – the adjudicative process – filled with limits and trade-offs. Defining a role for law means defining a role for the adjudicative process and that requires recognizing its limits. To use a simple economics metaphor, this is the supply side of law.

Allocating these limited judicial resources appropriately, however, means considering demand as well as supply and that necessitates looking at more than courts. Courts are most needed where alternative decision makers like political processes and markets work least well. If we focus solely on questions of supply and, therefore, solely on the characteristics of the courts, we waste the courts by using them where they work well but are least needed. On the other hand, if we focus solely on demand and, therefore, on the failings of these other institutions, we set tasks for law and courts that far exceed their capacity. These conflicting pressures of supply and demand form the law. Understanding what the law is or ought to be requires understanding these conflicting pressures.

Because this analytical approach works across all areas of the law, it allows its users to see important parallels. Unconscionability, unconstitutionality, and the business judgment rule all raise the same issues. Little governments and, therefore, issues of political malfunction appear in condo associations, labor unions, and corporations as well as conventionally defined political processes. The problems associated with judicial review exist in a similar fashion whether we are dealing with constitutional doctrine, contracts doctrine, or torts doctrine.

Seeing the pervasive role of institutional choice and comparative institutional analysis breaks down barriers inherent in distinctions such as common law–constitutional law (private-public). Legislation, regulation, constitutional law, and common law can all be examined using the same analytical framework. Focusing on institutional choice and comparative institutional analysis also recasts ideological debates in new lights. There are seldom easy answers to the most relevant institutional choices and that means that conventional ideologies that attempt to hardwire institutional choice are subject to doubt.

In this part of the chapter, I want to show the power of comparative institutional analysis as an analytical framework by examining legal doctrine. Doctrine – established legal formulation– has always been cast as the linchpin of legal analysis and legal method. The law is filled with doctrinal constructs that appear to determine who decides without any need for comparative institutional analysis. In the common law context, constructs like unconscionability in contract law and physical invasion in property law appear to define the form and extent of judicial protection. US constitutional law is replete with constructs like the taking of private property, suspect classification, and fundamental rights that seem to determine the extent of serious constitutional judicial review. From this vantage point, legal analysis appears straightforward: if institutional choice defines legal analysis and institutional choice is defined by these doctrinal constructs, then legal analysis is really about doctrine and, therefore, legal analysis is simply a matter of understanding the meaning of terms like physical invasion, suspect classifications, fundamental rights, and the taking of private property. This is what conventional doctrinal analysis and, more generally, conventional legal analysis seem to do.

As most legal analysts know, however, this approach is frustratingly unavailing. Viewed in context, these doctrinal thresholds are, to say the least, not straightforwardly defined. Physical invasion sounds like a scientific construct definable by recourse to notions of physics. But, at least at the defining margins of property law, it doesn't work that way. In application, the notion of suspect classifications is related to suspicion of the political process, but there is much more going on. Fundamental rights is a construct with no intrinsic meaning. Similarly, private property and taking are concepts of virtually unlimited plasticity.

But there is a way to understand these elusive terms. These terms ostensibly meant to define institutional choice are in fact defined by institutional choice and, therefore, by the variables of comparative institutional analysis. When doctrinal formulations contain thresholds for institutional choice, the sophisticated legal analyst reverses the causality: institutional choice determines doctrine rather than doctrine determining institutional choice. It is time now for me to show how this works.

10.3.1 Constitutional Law: Equal Protection, Fundamental Rights, and Suspect Classifications

Constitutional law seems straightforwardly about institutional choice – in particular, the choice between judicial and political decision making and, therefore, it should be directly accessible via comparative institutional analysis. Constitutions are primarily about institutional design and institutional choice. Even the most cursory examination of the US Constitution reveals its dominant concern with the design of the US decision-making process. The first three Articles of the US Constitution detail the characteristics of the Congress, the Presidency, and the Supreme Court. The greatest controversies in the framing of the Constitution surrounded the makeup of the Congress and the methods of choosing the Congress and the President. Although handled in vaguer terms, attention is also given to the issue of the allocation of responsibility among the branches of the federal government and between the federal and state governments.

No doubt, the US Constitution reflects important and controversial goal or value choices. These include those vague notions appearing in the Preamble plus the protection of a wide variety of other interests, including a time-limited protection of slavery. But enunciation of these values and interests tells us very little about the US Constitution and constitutional law. Realizing goals and values requires making tough institutional choices and that is where the action is.[4]

Consider the well-known concept of fundamental rights. Fundamental rights is a term thrown around by both lawyers and nonlawyers and by judges and politicians in every legal system. Its use by US judges and constitutional scholars is often maligned as arbitrary. It seems to be defined in strange and seemingly perverse ways especially when contrasted with its use in places like the European Union. In the European Union, the construct, as defined by documents like the Charter of Fundamental Rights, includes a broad menu of all that one might consider to be important to living such as housing, jobs, education, and health care. In Europe, fundamental means fundamental.

In contrast, the term fundamental rights in US constitutional law is narrowly defined and contains none of the subjects just listed. Why such a radical difference? We could look for the explanation in a more advanced European culture combined with a very conservative US Supreme Court. The first might be possible (although I doubt it), but the second seems weak given that many of the Supreme Court cases limiting the definition of fundamental rights were decided forty to fifty years ago, before the Rehnquist and Roberts courts.

There is a more straightforward mode of explanation. If you want to understand the meaning of a legal term, ask what function it plays. In US constitutional law, the term "fundamental rights" determines an important institutional choice. If legislation impinges on a fundamental right, then serious judicial review under equal protection or substantive due

[4] Komesar, *Constitutions.*

process follows and, therefore, decision making about the subject largely shifts from the political process to the courts.

If housing, jobs, food, and health care were declared "fundamental," the judiciary would have to take a serious hand in their effectuation. If fundamental rights are broadly defined and equated with importance, then the courts have the task of seriously reviewing and remaking public policy on a broad and massive basis. Although these issues are often handled badly by the political process, their scale, difficulty, and the basic need to tap the desires and needs of the populace generally make even the highly imperfect political process superior to the adjudicative process. These subjects are not excluded from the list of "fundamental rights" because they are socially unimportant. If anything, they are excluded because they are too important.

The analytic point is simple, straightforward, and yet, I suppose, surprising to those accustomed to conventional legal methodology. Form follows function. And function defines usage. If institutional choice is defined by the concept of fundamental rights, then the chances are that the realities of institutional choice are the key to understanding the constrained and seemingly paradoxical definition of fundamental rights in US law. The implications of shifting societal decisions from the political process to the adjudicative process shapes the definition of fundamental rights. Certainly, we do not want to allocate scarce judicial resources to totally unimportant issues. But we cannot, do not, and should not allocate the determination of all or even most fundamental issues to the courts. Thus, although it appears that the term "fundamental rights" defines institutional choice, in reality, the causation is reversed. Institutional choice defines "fundamental rights." When constitutional scholars look for the meaning of this constitutional construct in natural law and moral philosophy, they are looking in the wrong place.

The different and more generous treatment of the term fundamental rights in European Union law follows from the different institutional choice role played by the construct. In the European Union, the European Court of Justice has not yet decided which if any items from the EU Charter of Human Rights trigger serious judicial review. My prediction is that their usage of fundamental rights in that context will cover only a small subset of the menu contained in the Charter.[5]

[5] For an example, see Johanna Croon, *Reconceptualizing European Equality Law: A Comparative Institutional Analysis*, Thesis submitted for assessment with a view of

Fundamental rights is one of those constitutional terms that is relatively empty or counterintuitive unless we employ the lens of institutional choice. Other constitutional terms reflect features of institutional choice more directly. Consider the term "suspect classification," another constitutional construct which, like fundamental rights, triggers serious judicial review in the equal protection context. The notion of suspectness directly relates to the need for serious judicial review. The list of suspect classifications includes race, religion, and national origin. Historically, racial, religious, and national minorities have been severely mistreated in the political process. This is all standard lore that has been articulated often on the face of cases and by legal commentators.

But once we recognize that the construct of suspect classification serves the function of institutional choice, we are put on notice that the need for judicial review in response to serious political malfunction can only be part of the story. If we are really to understand or critique what we see in equal protection law, we need to integrate the supply side of rights – the limitations of the adjudicative process (the courts) – which we saw operate so strongly in confining the meaning of fundamental rights. We should not, therefore, be surprised if the equation between suspect classification and suspectness will also be influenced by supply-side considerations. There is something important to be learned by seeing these two tendencies together – situations where severe strains on the adjudicative process accompany instances of serious political malfunction. For reasons I will come to, there are many such cases.

Perhaps the most poignant such case is *Korematsu* – the Japanese relocation case.[6] After the outbreak of World War II, people of Japanese ancestry, among them US citizens, were forced to relocate from the West Coast to camps in the interior. The political malfunction was obvious. A racial and national minority was being forced to suffer significant hardship and to do so in a time rife with xenophobia. The potential for political malfunction was appreciable. But the courts were being asked to second guess the decisions of wartime military commanders and the political process that put them in place. This was and remains a difficult institutional choice with weighty consequences.

The difficulty of these institutional choices reveals the nature of law and legal analysis. It is often said that hard cases make bad law. And

obtaining the degree of Doctor of Laws of the European University Institute (Florence, February 2013).

[6] *Korematsu v. United States*, 323 U.S. 214 (1944).

Korematsu, which validated the relocation, was a bad decision. But even if the Supreme Court had decided differently and we viewed the decision as good, it would still have been a close call. Hard cases may sometimes make bad law. But they always show the real nature of law stripped of the extra verbiage of easier cases. Hard cases reveal law.

We can see these lessons in a less dramatic, but perhaps even more revealing, context in the *Cleburne* case.[7] In that case, a home for the developmentally disabled was denied permission to locate in Cleburne, Texas. The requirement to get permission embodied in Cleburne's zoning law singled out the developmentally disabled (along with a few others) for the additional requirement to obtain permission. The owners of the home brought action to overturn the refusal of permission as a violation of equal protection. It was clear to the plaintiff's lawyers, as it is to anyone familiar with US equal protection law, that a failure to come under the rubric of either strict scrutiny or intermediate scrutiny would likely doom the chance for serious judicial review and, therefore, its chance of overturning Cleburne's refusal of permission. As a general rule, minimal scrutiny is no scrutiny at all. As such they sought to have mental disability declared a quasi-suspect classification.

A US District Court in *Cleburne* declared that mental disability was not a quasi-suspect classification, gave the government's decision minimal scrutiny and found it valid. The plaintiff appealed and convinced a US Court of Appeals to declare that mental disability was a quasi-suspect classification. Using heightened scrutiny, the Court of Appeals invalidated Cleburne's decision. Now the government appealed to the US Supreme Court. The Supreme Court did not agree that mental disability was a quasi-suspect classification, but upheld the decision that Cleburne's action was unconstitutional. In doing so, the Supreme Court claimed it was applying minimal scrutiny.

From a comparative institutional standpoint, the invalidation of legislation under minimal scrutiny is puzzling. Real minimal scrutiny is and must be zero scrutiny. Or put more exactly, the spectrum of judicial scrutiny must be dominated by zero scrutiny. Check the cases. Justice Marshall's concurring-dissenting opinion does a good job of showing that, under the relevant precedent, real minimal scrutiny would have rubber-stamped the government's actions as valid and, therefore, the majority of the Court could not really be using minimal scrutiny. More

[7] *City of Cleburne v. Cleburne Living Center*, 473 U.S. 432 (1985).

importantly, from an institutional choice perspective, since virtually all governmental action involves some form of unequal treatment and the courts could not seriously review more than a minuscule percentage of that output, the great bulk of government action must receive no meaningful judicial review.

A simple teacher's image is useful here. Imagine a classroom blackboard and draw a small semicircle around one corner. (I usually use the upper right.) If the output of the political process were signified by all the spaces in the classroom – walls, ceiling, and floor – then the maximum subset of that output which courts could seriously review is represented by that small corner of the blackboard. The supply side of judicial review is severely limited by the capacity of courts to deliver that review. Thus, if minimal scrutiny is the residual category for judicial review of government actions not subject to strict scrutiny or heightened scrutiny, it must contain and indeed be dominated by zero scrutiny. Although, in theory, minimal scrutiny appears to have substance since it asks whether the government action has a legitimate purpose and the classification in question is rationally related to that purpose; in reality, real minimal scrutiny has to rubber-stamp most government action valid without any examination.

Yet every so often a different form of minimal scrutiny shows up. Effective constitutional law practitioners, judges, and scholars must be able to understand what is really going on and should be able to do so *before* the case is litigated. You can call it minimal scrutiny plus or secret heightened scrutiny, but it is simply an indication that the factors that drive serious judicial review are at a tipping-point – a true decisional margin.

The opinions in *Cleburne* show various Justices struggling with this issue. As is common, the concurring or dissenting opinions are freer to reveal their thinking. In *Cleburne*, this meant the declaration of one or another continuum of judicial review reflecting gradations of political malfunction and, therefore, gradations in judicial review not captured by the three categories of strict scrutiny, heightened scrutiny, and minimal scrutiny. The issue of course is what drives these gradations and what the configuration of the continuum looks like.

For example, Justice Marshall's continuum was based on gradation in the suspectness of the classification and fundamentalness of the interest harmed. Applying this to the developmentally disabled and to the refusal to allow the use of the home, he saw a long history of mistreatment by government and a serious loss imposed by denying the developmentally disabled an ability to live independently. Indeed, it isn't very difficult to see a serious form of political malfunction in the form of majoritarian bias or, more exactly here, a NIMBY (not in my backyard) problem.[8]

Justice Marshall is correct when he suggests that the majority isn't using minimal scrutiny and his suggestion that suspectness (and indeed fundamentalness) has gradations. But, from an institutional choice perspective, there is still something obviously missing from Justice Marshall's analysis. The degree of political malfunction and the seriousness of the harm done by the government action define the demand side for judicial review. But there is also a supply side and, therefore, a need to consider the ability of the courts to remake the associated decisions.

As it turns out, it is not difficult to find supply-side considerations in the *Cleburne* opinions. In explaining its reasons for rejecting the conclusion that developmental disability is a quasi-suspect classification, the majority opinion emphasized that the classification has many legitimate uses, some of which advantage as well as disadvantage the developmentally disabled; that it was difficult for courts to determine which are the correct and incorrect instances of the use of the classification and that if a court gets it wrong, it can harm not only the general public but also the developmentally disabled themselves. In addition, they worried that if judicial review is extended to this large and diffuse group other classifications such as the aging, the disabled, the mentally ill, and the infirm which are equally large and involve similarly complex substantive issues can make claim for serious judicial review. Put succinctly in institutional analysis terms: the extension of an invitation for judicial review to the developmentally disabled whatever the need for that review will strain both the competence and the capacity of the adjudicative process.

Yet, despite these serious supply-side strains, the majority in reality employed serious scrutiny, treated the developmentally disabled as a quasi-suspect classification albeit a secret one and invalidated the government action. *Cleburne*, like *Korematsu*, is a close case and because of that a hard case. The law articulated in the case is strained by the majority's insistence that it is only doing minimal scrutiny. But, as with other hard cases, *Cleburne* shows the underpinnings of the tough institutional choice it raises and clarifies what the courts are doing.

[8] I explore this issue and the reasoning in *Cleburne* in more detail in Neil Komesar, *Law's Limits: The Rule of Law and the Supply and Demand of Rights* (Cambridge, Cambridge University Press, 2001), ch. 4. I will explore the underpinnings of political malfunction in general and majoritarian bias in particular in Section 10.3 of this chapter.

Hard cases are not all that unusual for two reasons. Clear cases are unlikely to be litigated, appealed, and decided by the highest courts. That is a product of the dynamics of litigation and settlement. More broadly, institutional choices are likely to be close cases because institutions tend to move together. The same factors that cause malfunction or problems in one are likely to cause parallel problems in the institutional alternatives. This is a point we will come back to in more detail when we examine the analytical underpinnings of comparative institutional analysis in the third part of this chapter.

10.3.2 Contract Law and Corporate Law: Unconscionability and the Business Judgment Rule

I am not a contracts or corporate law scholar. Yet the comparison between institutional choice in the constitutional law and contracts/corporate settings is too fascinating and useful to allow my ignorance to stand in the way. We are once again dealing with judicial review, but in this case judicial review of market decision making.

Contract law involves the interaction between two institutions: the courts as the engine of contract law and the market (transactional process) as the engine of transactions. On one level, these institutions are complements: Courts enforce contracts and, thereby, facilitate transacting. Without some means of assuring enforcement, long-term complex transactions would be severely limited. Courts are one such enforcement mechanism. Transacting is basically a form of participation and subject, therefore, to the dynamics of participation. Information and the costs of information are once again central. In such a setting, facilitating transactions may paradoxically require substituting court decision making for problematic transactional decision making. For example, insufficient or asymmetric information may make parties leery of long-term and complex arrangements. In such a setting, courts might promote transacting by providing the assurance that transactions gone wrong may be later corrected in the courts. Thus, even in the pursuit of better transacting and resource allocation efficiency, courts and transacting (the market) are also substitutes.

It is easy enough to see concerns about institutional behavior and institutional choice in contracts doctrine. The demand side for the judicial review of transactions is explicit. Concerns about market malfunction are manifest in doctrines like incapacity, fraud, and duress. Market malfunctions in the contracts context commonly involve problems with information and understanding. Information is costly. The incentive to obtain costly information depends on the per capita stakes of the contracting parties. Information is also less costly for some people. The resulting skewed information is commonly called "asymmetric information" by economists. Contracts with minors or with the insane are presumptively unenforceable because there are significant doubts about the ability of children and the insane to obtain information and even understand what is in their best interests. Fraud is an extreme example of the manipulation of one-sided or asymmetric information. There is also a problem with market transactions when one of the parties has no or severely limited choices. Duress – the gun at the head – is an extreme example of contracts under limited choice. All these concerns about market malfunction are most broadly represented in the unconscionability doctrine. The threshold for judicial review under the unconscionability doctrine is articulated in terms of unequal bargaining power parsed into asymmetric information and understanding (one side understands the implications and the other does not) and something like the absence of choice or competition.

Thus, contract law, like constitutional law, focuses on problems or malfunctions in an institutional alternative to the courts. Constitutional judicial review focuses on the political process and political malfunction, and contracts judicial review focuses on the market and market malfunction. Here is the demand side for the judicial review of transactions, and as with constitutional judicial review the demand side is strongly represented in contracts law.

However, unlike constitutional law, there seems to be little attention to supply-side considerations such as limited resources and substantive ability of the courts. The absence of supply-side concerns in the articulation of these contract doctrines seems odd. The presence of these important institutional choices and the apparent absence of one side of the balance tells us that we need to look harder at the law.

This institutional choice trade-off, its consequences and the mystery of the missing supply-side elements are most dramatically seen in the context of unconscionability. The contracts in these cases involve complex substantive issues. Judicial review of these issues can strain judicial competence. Moreover, if the courts get these issues wrong, they can harm the very parties they mean to help. If courts wrongly deny enforcement, they may deny the weaker parties access to the market and, therefore, to goods and services and beneficial business arrangements.

More importantly, the number of transactions potentially covered by an unconscionability doctrine defined only by the demand side of market malfunction could create a strain on judicial resources even greater than that presented by sweeping constitutional judicial review. Market malfunction, even serious market malfunction, is a condition too easily and often met. When economists use the term market malfunction, they are referring to deviations from ideal conditions – from perfect competition. In that case, every transaction is the product of market malfunction because no market is ever perfect. If the unconscionability doctrine is defined solely by market malfunction, then the implication is that virtually all contract terms will potentially be subject to serious judicial review. But this result would not only be foolish but impossible. Remember the corner of the blackboard. Courts simply could not review all or even a small fraction of all contract provisions. And even if they could, in most instances, the ability of courts to know which contract provisions were reasonable seems in general inferior to even imperfect markets (the only kind of markets that exist).

From an institutional choice perspective, the unconscionability doctrine as articulated is an incomplete threshold. Something must be controlling the sizable potential demand in a doctrine that announces that courts will reassess any provision contracted for in the presence of serious market malfunction. How are supply-side considerations – issue of the constraints on judicial scale and substantive ability – worked out in unconscionability?

There are several possibilities. First, I may be wrong about the absence of supply-side factors in court-made doctrine. Contracts or unconscionability scholars may be aware of instances in which courts have articulated limits to the market malfunction threshold analogous to the machinations of defining suspect classifications in the equal protection context. In that case, institutional choice and comparative institutional analysis should help these scholars recognize, organize, and explore these constraints. Second, the intuition of lawyers and judges may implicitly recognize that claims of market malfunction must be very severe and that difficult determinations of substantive elements like price or rent are likely to receive a cold reception from the courts. Here there would be no articulation in the cases. The results would be the product of lawyering or judicial instinct. If so, then institutional choice and comparative institutional analysis are valuable in explicating these instincts and making them available and clear to law students.

It is entirely possible, however, that most of the supply-side concerns are handled by the dynamics of litigation and, therefore, never forced on the consciousness of judges nor reflected in doctrine or lawyering. The dynamics of litigation may be operating here in two ways. First, the actions may not be brought because there is a superior alternative to litigation to solve the imperfections in the original transaction – adjustments through ongoing relationships. Here, present transactions are the corrective mechanism for problems in past transactions; problematic provisions are corrected within ongoing relationships without the expense of litigation. Here we have an institutional choice of a different variety. Transacting parties are choosing to work out their differences by continuing negotiation thereby avoiding the costs of working them out in the adjudicative process via litigation, including the cost of disrupting ongoing business relationships.

Second, and more relevant to the common context of unconscionability, the dynamics of litigation may preclude many unconscionability claims because the costs of litigation are too high. Where the victims of one-sided clauses suffer low per capita losses or have insufficient funds, litigation is not an option. As a general matter, the adjudicative process has a small claims problem. We will return to this subject in the section on class action.

I do not have the expertise to pick the correct reason or set of reasons. Most likely, the factors will vary with setting. What is important here, however, is the role of comparative institutional analysis in revealing the existence of an incomplete and untested threshold inherent in the common articulations of contracts doctrines like unconscionability and to understand the institutional choices at work. There is either a more complete and balanced doctrinal reflection of institutional choice implicit in unconscionability lawyering and judging or the dynamics of participation and the substitution of institutional alternatives control the demand on the courts without recourse to any analytical efforts by judges. Either way, institutional choice and comparative institutional analysis can ferret out the issue, point to viable hypotheses, and suggest potential reforms.

These same issues surface in several other important contracts doctrines under which courts are asked to substitute their judgment on the reasonableness of contracts. As a property teacher, I have seen the changed circumstances doctrine operating in the enforcement and interpretation of private land-use contracts. Private land use imposed by transaction often have very long durations, and circumstances can change over time, making a restriction sensible when first imposed and unreasonable later. Restricted parties may come to courts for relief from these supposedly unreasonable restrictions.

The changed circumstances doctrine presents the choice between a *past* transactional process and a *present* adjudicative process. Here, present courts have the advantage of hindsight. But they have the familiar issues of judicial competence and capacity (scale). One only needs to realize how many private land-use restrictions exist and that the removal of restrictions involves parties with significant per capita stakes to see that there could be potentially serious strain on judicial resources in broad-based judicial review of these contract provisions.

The pattern of cases shows that courts tend to demand quite dramatic changes before they will enter into serious consideration of the reasonableness of restrictions. But this area of contract law is also interesting because of the presence of institutional choices that go beyond past markets and present courts. For example, there is always the possibility that any problems with the foresight of *past* markets can be corrected by *present* markets. If the restriction is onerous, the party restricted can bargain for its removal. Present transactions like present courts have the advantage of hindsight, and in two-party settings where transaction costs are low, this market mechanism has clear advantages over the adjudicative process.

But of course the subsequent transactions can vary in their ability to correct outdated restrictions, and the major source of variation is the number of parties. Most land-use restrictions are initially imposed in two-party transactions between the developer of a multi-unit housing development and the initial buyer of each parcel of land or unit of housing. The developer eventually sells all the parcels or units and then leaves the scene. Now enforcement rights pass to all the purchasers. When restrictions are imposed by the developer of a large development, the parties that can enforce this restriction eventually include all the other land owners in the development, and there can be hundreds, even thousands, of such owners. The transaction costs of bargaining for the removal of the restrictions with so many parties involves overcoming serious collective action problems. In this setting, transactions to correct outdated restrictions become far less tenable. Courts are more likely to be called upon to correct outdated restrictions.

When it comes to these large developments, however, there is yet another decision making alternative: the homeowners association. Aware of the potential problems of changed circumstances, a developer may establish a little government to deal with the problem. Homeowner or condominium boards elected by a majority of the homeowners can now decide whether a restriction should still be enforced. These are present-day decision makers with the advantage of hindsight, and their constitutions allow decision making that is not constrained by the need for unanimity that is required in multiparty transactions.

But little governments, like the big ones we saw in the context of constitutional law, face problems analogous to the political malfunction we discussed in connection with constitutional law. These could involve issues of overrepresentation of special interests (minoritarian bias) or of the tyranny of the majority (majoritarian bias). Given the presence of these political malfunctions, it would not be odd to see a form of judicial review analogous to constitutional law appear. These malfunctions form the demand side for judicial review of the decisions of the homeowners association. Such review has been sought and sometimes given. But if there is a demand side for judicial review of the determinations of these private governments, there is also a supply side. Indeed, the pervasive use of private land-use restrictions and of homeowner associations creates the potential for a significant amount of litigation. Homeowners have relatively high stakes and, therefore, may turn to litigation. At least one important state court has emphasized supply-side considerations in declaring a form of hands-off minimal scrutiny associated with the review of homeowner association determinations about private restrictions.[9]

An even more challenging example of the quandary posed by judicial review of private governance comes in the context of corporate law. Corporate law, like contract law, raises issues about judicial review of market decision making. Corporations, especially large, publicly held corporations, are complex decision making structures, and like all complex decision making structures, they are imperfect. Decisions by corporate management can favor management over ownership (stockholders) or one group of stockholders over another. There are a number of mechanisms to deal with these problems. The buying and selling of stock can put pressure on managers and corporate takeover can replace the managers. But these mechanisms are themselves problematic. Some of these problems occur when, like public officials, corporate executives take steps to make takeovers more difficult, thereby blocking their own removal.

[9] This distinction will again be picked up in the difference between the behavior of potential and actual victims in the analysis of tort reform in Section 10.4 of this chapter.

Given this situation, it is hardly surprising that courts are called upon to review the decisions of corporate management. But there are again supply-side problems as courts face issues of competence and scale. The pressures and problems of judicial review of corporate decision making have manifested themselves in the so-called business judgment rule. Under the business judgment rule, the issue is whether and when the courts will second guess corporate determinations. As with unconscionability, the institutional choice is between the courts and the market. Like unconscionability, the business judgment rule explicitly reflects institutional choice aspects in its basic articulation, but unlike unconscionability, the business judgment rule's articulation gives explicit attention to the supply side – the courts are seen as, in general, less able decision makers than corporations.

As always, there are both supply and demand sides to this story. Courts do sometimes, if rarely, seriously review corporate business judgments. For the lawyer or the judge faced with a specific situation, there is always the issue of whether they have before them that rare instance. Understanding this possibility requires an analysis that looks both for severe forms of market or corporate malfunction and instances in which courts might feel more comfortable substantively or where courts can control the number of cases that might follow.

The emphasis on supply-side considerations in the business judgment rule relative to unconscionability may signal a difference in the dynamics of litigation and more broadly the dynamics of participation in the business judgment rule and corporate context. The dynamics of corporate decision making, especially for large, publicly held corporations, may not display as many continuing relationships as business contracting in general, and therefore, an uncontrolled invitation from the courts to review these decisions might receive a more robust litigation response. The number of parties in a corporate dispute is far larger than in most contract settings. When a dispute arises, injured parties would need to bargain with vast numbers of other stockholders in order to resolve the question internally. Moreover, unlike the consumers or apartment renters in the unconscionability setting, these injured shareholders are more likely to have stakes high enough to justify the cost of litigation.

Contract and corporate law are filled with challenging issues of institutional choice. The immense scale of transacting and corporate decision making requires that the courts play only a small role as a substitute. In the context of unconscionability, the dynamics of litigation may serve to control the demand for judicial review to such an extent that courts are not forced to consider their own limitations. In the context of corporate decision making, the demand for judicial review is not so neatly controlled and, therefore, courts, in the form of doctrines like the business judgment rule, are forced to make the supply side of judicial review explicit. I can only sketch the challenging analytical issues raised by institutional choice framework in contract and corporate law and leave it to those with more expertise and an adventurous spirit to work them through.

10.3.3 On Property

The concept of property so important in philosophy and social science plays a wide variety of roles in US law. It triggers judicially controlled just compensation and due process. It forms the background of the common law manifested in judicially formed property doctrines like trespass and nuisance. Conceptually, the term property can cover everything and anything. More exactly, everything can be translated into the concept of property without violating its conceptual boundaries. One might think of property as limited to land or physical capital. But that would at the least ignore intellectual property. It would also ignore the expansion of the term capital to include, first, human capital and second, social capital, and by now versions of capital without end. Human capital largely removes the old distinction between labor and capital. Conceptually, anything which produces returns can be considered capital and anything that is capital can be considered property. Don't trust my word for it. Prompted by a Supreme Court seemingly focused on property rights, legal scholars have been rediscovering and expanding the notions of capital and property.

Given this sophisticated understanding of property and given that the concept of property defines both constitutional and common law rights, it would then seem easy to know when courts must require just compensation and due process and dole out common law remedies like injunctions. Always. But anyone with even a passing knowledge of law knows that this isn't even close to true. The problem with a construct that can mean anything is that it usually means nothing or, more exactly, has no analytical bite.

How then do we make sense of those constitutional and common law property-based thresholds that trigger judicial enforcement? The answer is to begin by remembering that *judicial* enforcement is the operative term and then to follow the familiar trails of institutional choice and comparative institutional analysis. I have followed this trail many times and do not have the room to follow all its branches here.[10] So let me summarize them by an abbreviated walk through just compensation law and the notion of the taking of property.

Under US law, the taking of private property triggers judicially enforced just compensation. But supply-side concerns quickly set in. The administrative costs, especially for courts, of determining who the winners and losers are and the extent of loss is so great that we know that property (and its taking) will have to be narrowly defined. Just compensation law is filled with the sort of strange distinctions that delight law professors and, in turn, torture law students: fly-over, fly-by; up the creek, down the creek; and so forth. These are simply arbitrary cut-offs, analogous to the famously torturous doctrine of proximate cause in tort law. These cut-offs control the demands on judicial decision making. They will change depending on the cost of and need for judicial review and the view on these issues can vary among judges. The able lawyer will know when a case would have a chance of moving these cut-offs by organizing the facts and his or her sense of the judges according to supply-side institutional factors like the potential strains on judicial capacity and competence and demand-side factors like the need for judicial review of political process decision making on compensation.

The doctrine of regulatory takings is particularly illustrative. Over the past three decades, the US Supreme Court has expanded the range of judicial review of political process decision making on land use by expanding the requirement that, when public land-use authorities want to restrict private land use, they do so by eminent domain, not by regulation. The present Supreme Court has coined the concept of total takings to determine when eminent domain will be required.

But total takings is itself a slippery concept because the list of traditional private property forms is quite broad and includes, as forms of property interests, private restrictions variously called negative easements, equitable servitudes, restrictive covenants, or negative covenants. These private restrictions do the same job as governmentally imposed regulations of land use. Thus, conceptually, every regulation *could be* a total taking of a property interest. Does this mean that every regulation *will be* a taking and trigger the need for just compensation? Conceptually, yes. Analytically, impossible. If you think about it, you will see why.

[10] Komesar, *Law's Limits*, is, beginning to end, a book about property and institutional choice and much of Komesar, *Alternatives*, is also about property. Both follow the trail.

(Hint: the corner of the blackboard.) How does a practitioner, judicial clerk, or judge determine how far the concept would or should go? You will hardly be surprised to find out that I see the answer in comparative institutional analysis. The present Supreme Court obviously distrusts political process determinations on land use at least on the issue of compensation. But even a Supreme Court that severely distrusts public land-use decision making could not expand this doctrine very far because of the strains on judicial competence and capacity inherent in the need to remake land-use choices and determine the validity and extent of the losses to be compensated.[11]

The construct of property is strewn across the law. In the abstract, it is a concept of virtually infinite elasticity. But in reality, its meaning is constrained by the roles it plays. It portends a judicial role and that itself severely limits its meaning. Whether and when this limited judicial role is triggered depends on the degree of strain it places on judicial ability and capacity and on the need for that judicial decision making. In the crucible of this institutional choice lies the meaning (or, more exactly, meanings) of property. Once again, it is not the meaning of a doctrinal construct like property which determines institutional choice; it is the character of institutional choice that determines the meaning of doctrinal constructs. Here is where lawyers and judges will find the character of both common law and constitutional property rights and the meaning of constructs like total taking and physical invasion.

10.3.4 Civil Procedure: Class Actions

In theory, class actions provide a potential cure for a serious difficulty in the dynamics of litigation and, therefore, in the workings of the adjudicative process. Where a serious societal injury is broadly distributed over a large number of people, the dynamics of litigation for standard individual litigation may preclude participation in the adjudicative process and, therefore, keep important issues from the courts. A classic example is the litigation of issues like air or water pollution where, although the total societal injury may be enormous, it is distributed among millions of households with per capita stakes too small to justify the expenses of litigation. The class action mechanism promotes litigation in these settings by providing a way to cover litigation expenses from a source other

[11] I have discussed the subjects of just compensation in general and regulatory takings in particular in Komesar, *Law's Limits*, ch. 5 and Komesar, *Alternatives*, ch. 8.

than the pocket of a single member of the plaintiff group. Thus, all those injured by the air pollution could bring one action, represented by one set of lawyers paid from one pot of damages. Even where there is only injunctive relief, the courts are often empowered to order the losing defendant to pay the plaintiffs' litigation expenses.

Although in theory the class action mechanism could solve the problems caused by the dispersion of stakes, there are inadequacies in the class action system, and these inadequacies, like the inadequacies in the individual litigation it is meant to replace, increase as numbers and complexity increase. We have a familiar story. Institutions move together. The result is that class actions may function least well when they are most needed and best where they are least needed. We are in the world of close calls and difficult choices.

There are of course doctrinal thresholds that supposedly determine the availability of class actions. These include terms like representativeness, numerosity, commonality, and typicality. But in practice the use of these vague terms cannot be understood unless we ask familiar sorts of institutional choice questions. Moreover, the institutional choice between individual and class action has a more global institutional choice lurking in the background – the choice between the adjudicative process and the political process. This second layer reflects a common feature of comparative institutional analysis: there may be several levels of institutional choice at play.

The class-action mechanism tends to improve the dynamics of litigation at the expense of decreasing the substantive competence of the adjudicative process. In individual litigation, judges and juries are informed by a contest between two opposing viewpoints. Each one-sided view is tempered by an opposing one-sided view. Although hardly perfect, this competition of views has value as a decision making device. It is a far less credible system, however, if judges and juries hear only one side.

Class actions offer a greater possibility of one-sided or at least distorted representation than would be the case with most individual litigation, and this possibility again increases as numbers and complexity increase. The issue is representation, and the problems with representation relate to differences in the participation of various parties on the dispersed plaintiff side. First, we have the tension between active plaintiffs and passive plaintiffs. Frequently, passive plaintiffs may be those who have been exposed to a danger but whose injury has not yet manifested. Active plaintiffs may not care about preventative measures if they are no longer exposed to danger even though a significant portion of the passive plaintiffs are still in harm's way. Active plaintiffs may, therefore, accept awards for their damages and allow less tangible or less manifested injuries to be far less completely remedied.

As the number of victims (potential class members) increases and the substantive issues become increasingly complex, even named plaintiffs may have little role in determining what is litigated and how. Here the class-action lawyer takes center stage. As numbers and complexity increase, and there is a greater need for class actions, the prospect of client monitoring decreases. Put simply, the very problems that make individual litigation unlikely make client monitoring unlikely.

Here the dynamics of participation add a perverse wrinkle. The active client-lawyer team will be on the defendant side. Defendants are able to exploit the passivity on the plaintiff's side by offering settlements favorable to active plaintiffs but unfavorable to passive plaintiffs, or favorable to plaintiffs' lawyers but unfavorable to plaintiffs. High per capita stakes defendants are even able to choose the plaintiff's counsel most amenable to settlement on the defendant's terms. By strategically expending resources in opposition to certification, concentrated defendant groups may be able to select opposing counsel with an eye to those who will be most amenable to accepting settlement arrangements favorable to defendants.[12] There is even the possibility of fraudulent actions in which would-be defendants manufacture a plaintiff class that generously settles the action in the defendant's favor and precludes real plaintiffs from subsequent action. The usual safeguards of the adversarial process weaken in the face of the dormancy of dispersed interests.

Courts have responded to these distortions in representation by scrutinizing class actions more carefully than individual litigation. Much of this scrutiny centers on the certification of the class where courts address the issues of representativeness, numerosity, commonality, and typicality. These thresholds in part attempt to establish the correlation between the interests of active and passive members of the class before the litigation begins. Courts also can impose extensive notice requirements on the class representatives again as an attempt to protect passive plaintiffs. Even if these various devices help to lessen concerns about the competence of

[12] See John C. Coffee, Jr., Class Wars: The Dilemma of the Mass Tort Class Action, 95 *Colum. L. Rev.* 1343, 1371–1373 (1995) and Jonathan R. Macey and Geoffrey P. Miller, The Plaintiffs' Attorney's Role in Class Actions and Derivative Litigation: Economic Analysis and Recommendation for Reform, 58 *U. Chi. L. Rev.* 1, 63 (1991).

class representation, however, they do so by raising the costs and difficulty of bringing class actions which, in turn, has adverse effects on the dynamics of litigation.

We are faced with a familiar quandary. The larger the number of people injured and the more complex and difficult to discern the form, extent, and source of this injury, the more likely it will be that the injury and the problem that created it will not be represented in individual litigation. High numbers and complexity create a need for class actions. But the same variables also cause difficulties for class action litigation and certification. Greater numbers increase the likelihood of heterogeneity in the class and, therefore, increase the chance of problems with representativeness. Class action certification – and, therefore, the meaning given factors like representativeness, numerosity, commonality, and typicality – reflect tough institutional choices.

As the air pollution setting makes clear, however, the institutional choices associated with class actions are not limited to the choice between class action and individual action. If it were simply a choice between individual and class action, then the air pollution setting would call for class action largely by default because the chances of air pollution cases reaching the courts via private individual actions is virtually nonexistent. The limits on air pollution class action, however, also raise the choice between the adjudicative process and the political process. To the extent that government regulation is seen as a viable institutional alternative, courts do not have to strain the adjudicative process by expanding the possibility of private law class action.[13]

With rare exceptions, the courts have turned away from a significant role as a controller of air pollution, and they have done so primarily by refusing to certify class actions. The pattern of decisions as well as the greater success of certification of water pollution cases over air pollution cases seems to reflect supply-side concerns – in particular, the number of class members and the substantive complexity of the issues. With the exception of occasional "public interest" actions, widely dispersed interests seem largely absent from the courts at least in the context of common law air pollution.[14]

[13] The reluctance of courts to face these issues is reflected in the famous *Boomer* case which I have written about many times. See Komesar, *Alternatives*, ch. 1 and *Law's Limits*, ch. 1 and throughout most of the book.

[14] Coffee, Jr., Class Wars, 1371–1373.

The certification of class actions again involves close calls on at least two levels of institutional choice. Anyone seeking such certification – or opposing it – needs to understand that certification involves choices between decision making processes that are imperfect and how and why these imperfections vary. These are the pressure points of legal analysis and advocacy. Courts are regularly choosing what they (the adjudicative process) will and won't decide. As we have seen, they do this in the formation of substantive legal doctrines such as equal protection scrutiny and just compensation. But they also regularly make the decision of what they will decide when they craft procedural doctrines like class action and standing. Comparative institutional analysis makes it possible to better understand the meaning of the doctrinal terms and thresholds that appear to control these procedural devices and to better assess the choices made by courts.

10.3.5 The Rest of Law

I have only scratched the surface of the potential for the use of comparative institutional analysis as an analytical framework across areas of law. Quite clearly, administrative law parallels constitutional law. Administrative law scholars have responded to issues of institutional choice and comparative institutional analysis much sooner and more frequently than their constitutional law counterparts.[15] Various areas of law that involve government oversight of the market like securities law and consumer protection law raise questions that involve both the market/courts choice of contracts and corporations and the political process/courts choice of constitutional and administrative law. Little governments abound in labor law and condominium law as well as corporate law and with them are choices between markets, courts and political processes. I have shown that tort law and tort reform are dominated by issues of institutional choice.[16] And so one assumes is the parallel field of criminal law and administration. Recently, Wendy Wagner showed that environmental law and administrative law are replete with institutional

[15] For a sampling of this work on administrative law, see the recent symposium on comparative institutional analysis in the Wisconsin Law Review; 2013 *Wisc. L. Rev*, Issue 2. For an idea of the range of legal subjects that have been analyzed using comparative institutional analysis, see the appendix to my article in the symposium. Neil Komesar The Logic of the Law and the Essence of Economics: Reflections on Forty Years in the Wilderness, 2013 *Wis. L. Rev*. 265. (2013)

[16] Komesar, *Alternatives*, ch. 6.

choice issues,[17] and Bill Eskridge showed the same for statutory interpretation.[18] Nor are we speaking solely of US law. European scholars such as Miguel Maduro[19] and Johanna Croon[20] have shown the power of comparative institutional analysis in understanding European Union law, and Greg Shaffer has shown its value in understanding international law in general and WTO law in particular.[21] In fact, scholars have revealed the power of comparative institutional analysis across virtually every area of law and across multiple jurisdictions. Much has been done but far more remains.

10.4 Comparative Institutional Analysis and Economic Analysis

This part of the chapter explores the connection between economic analysis and comparative institutional analysis and, in turn, of both to legal analysis. It examines the attractions and distractions of economic analysis and the role of economic analysis in constructing a participation-centered approach to understanding institutions[22] and institutional behavior. It then addresses a fundamental flaw in the

[17] Wendy Wagner, The Participation-Centered Model Meets Administrative Process, 2013 *Wis. L. Rev* 671.

[18] William N. Eskridge, Jr., Comparative Institutional Analysis, Agency Interpretation, and Judicial Deference, 2013 *Wis. L. Rev.* 411.

[19] Miguel Poiares Maduro, *We, the Court: The European Court of Justice and the European Economic Constitution: a Critical Reading of Article 30 of EC Treaty* (Oxford, UK, Hart Publishing, 1998).

[20] Croon, *Reconceptualizing European Equality Law*.

[21] Gregory Shaffer, Recognizing Public Goods in WTO Dispute Settlement: Who Participates—Who Decides: The Case of TRIPS and Pharmaceutical Patent Protection, 7 *J. Int'l Econ. L.* 459 (2004); Gregory Shaffer, Power, Governance, and the WTO: A Comparative Institutional Approach, in *Power in Global Governance* 130, Michael Barnett and Raymond Duvall, eds. (Cambridge, Cambridge University Press, 2005); Gregory Shaffer, A Structural Theory of WTO Dispute Settlement: Why Institutional Choice Lies at the Center of the GMO Case, 41 *N.Y.U. J. Int'l L. & Pol.* 1 (2008).

[22] The term "institution" has two general meanings in economics. Commonly, institutions are defined as the rules of the game – laws, regulations, and constitutions – and, more broadly, also including norms, customs, and mores. These rules of the game provide the environment for economic activity. The major debate between neoclassical and institutional economists is over the analytical importance of these rules of the game. Institutional economists believe them central; most neoclassical economists give them lip service, but little attention. However, all economists, including neoclassical economists, shower attention on institutions as decision-making processes. It is institutions as decision-making processes that concern me. I have discussed these two views of institutions more extensively elsewhere. See Neil Komesar, The Essence of Economics: Law, Participation and Institutional Choice (Two Ways), in *Alternative Institutional*

economic analysis of law and public policy – its focus on single institutional rather than comparative institutional analysis – and the problems created by this flaw.

10.4.1 *The Role of Economic Analysis in Comparative Institutional Analysis*

Economic analysis has several attractive attributes. It is focused on trade-off. Benefits are always accompanied by costs. If something appears to be free, look a little closer. In turn, these trade-offs generate continua. There is almost always a range of possibilities, and variation within this range is driven by a small set of variables – basically, costs, benefits, and budget constraints.

This focus on the same small set of variables allows more to be internal to and determined by the same analytical framework. In other words, there is a tendency to make more relevant issues and factors endogenous rather than exogenous to the analysis. Thus, instead of supposing that there is or is not deterrence or at best supposing deterrence is at some particular externally determined level, we can speak about deterrability and see its variation as variations in factors like the costs and benefits of information.[23] We have already seen the same sort of analysis of our discussions of the dynamics of litigation. Whether and when an interest will be represented in the courts is a function of the same set of variables that determine whether and to what extent potential injurers can be deterred, whether and to what extent dispersed majorities will be politically dormant or active, or whether and to what extent consumers will be misled by advertising. We have also seen this analysis in the two-force model of the political process. There, the costs and benefits of political participation determine the likelihood of minoritarian bias, majoritarian bias, and no bias. This is the tip of the analytic iceberg – a small sample of the questions pertinent to law and public policy that can be seen as subject to variation based on the same small set of variables. The only limit to this sort of exploration is the ability and creativity of the analyst.

Indeed, here lies a mode of understanding the controversial subject of rational choice. Knowledge, information, and sophistication are not free and the cost of information and understanding matters. And so do its

Structures: Evolution and Impact, Sandra Batie and Nicholas Mercuro, eds., (London, Routledge, 2008).

[23] See Komesar, *Alternatives*, ch. 6.

benefits. We can expect that high-stakes players will know more and that low-stakes players are easier to fool. That does not mean that low-stakes players are fools. The same parties who are high stakes players and sophisticated in one area will be low-stakes players and unaware in another. Using these insights creatively is the way to open inquiry about and access to subjects as seemingly different as the present state of electioneering in the US and the elasticity of demand for products and services in the market.

Last but not least, the economic vision of institutional behavior is bottom-up. Institutional decisions are the product of the atomistic interaction of many parties such as buyers and sellers in the market, special interests and dispersed majorities in the political process, and litigants in the adjudicative process. The actions of these parties are, in turn, related to the basic variables. The costs and benefits of participation in these processes matter and these costs and benefits vary significantly both across the population, across issues, and over time. Societal participants such as producers and consumers, special interests and the mass of citizens and plaintiffs and defendants react to these costs and benefits – including by not reacting.

To many proponents and opponents of the economic analysis of law and public policy, economics is, by its nature, politically to the right – promarket, antipolitical process. But if economic analysis is about institutional behavior and the economic analysis of law and public policy is about institutional choice, then economic analysis of law and public policy done correctly cannot be by nature promarket or antimarket. If institutional choice is the essence of economic analysis, and I believe it is, then these institutional choices are the object of study and, therefore, cannot be presumed or hardwired a priori. As we have seen, institutional choice is often a close call and is likely to vary with basic factors like numbers and complexity. From this perspective, any ideological position that attempts to hardwire institutional choice becomes highly suspect – whether that position is promarket or antimarket, prorights or antirights. Economists in general or those who do law and economics in particular may be more promarket than the average academic. I really don't know. But I do know that those preferences are not inherent in economic analysis and indeed, if they are too rigidly held, they violate the basic instincts of economics.

Far more interesting and analytically tricky is the common belief that the analytical focus of the economic analysis of law and public policy is defined by a social goal: resource allocation efficiency. The attachment of economic analysis to resource allocation efficiency seems a given. For law and economics, resource allocation efficiency is the defining characteristic of law – at least, common law. I find resource allocation efficiency a useful component in the analysis of law and public policy. It is a general way to recognize the inherent need to balance impacts.

But efficiency is neither necessary nor sufficient to define the economic analysis of law and public policy. It is not sufficient because the goal of resource allocation efficiency standing alone tell us nothing about law and public policy. The link between any social goal and law and public policy is institutional choice. Depending on the circumstances, resource allocation efficiency may be consistent with regulation or no regulation, with rights or no rights, with market decision making or with nonmarket decision making. Moreover, a focus on resource allocation efficiency is not necessary for economic analysis to be useful. The essence of economics is institutional behavior and institutional choice and these issues are central whatever the perceived social goal. Economic analysis as a study of institutional behavior and institutional choice is applicable to law and public policy associated with equality, liberty, and justice as well as resource allocation efficiency.

10.4.2 Economics and Participation

We can see the central place of institutional behavior and institutional choice in economic analysis by focusing on the role of the dynamics of participation in the economic analysis of institutional behavior. Although the term is not used by economists, the concept of participation is the core of the economic analysis of market, political process, and adjudicative process behavior. Participation lies at the heart of key economics concepts such as externalities, transaction costs, and resource allocation efficiency. Transaction costs are the costs of market participation and, as Ronald Coase showed, externalities are failures of market participation – a failure of representation via transaction.[24] Because some transactions are missing, allocative decisions do not reflect all costs and benefits and, therefore, the market mechanism is an imperfect indicator of resource allocation efficiency. Resource allocation efficiency is defined by transaction costs and benefits and violated by externalities. The basic economic version of the market and transacting is a participation story. The same

[24] Ronald H. Coase, *The Problem of Social Cost*, 3 *J.L. & Econ.* 1 (1960).

inherent emphasis on participation is also present for the economic analysis of nonmarket institutions such as the political process and the adjudicative process. Both economic and noneconomic models of the political process emphasize representation. Failures of political representation, just like externalities in the market, are failures of participation associated with variations in the costs and benefits of participation. Some interests have more active political participation and are, therefore, better represented in the political process. Sophisticated models of politics like the interest group theory and the economic theory of regulation are defined by these dynamics of participation. As we have also already seen, the dynamics of participation underlies the analysis of the adjudicative process in the form of the dynamics of litigation where once again certain interests– commonly concentrated interests – are better represented.

The dynamics of participation already lie at the core of basic economic concepts and analysis both in neoclassical economics and institutional economics. By generalizing these concepts into the dynamics of participation, it becomes easier to compare institutions and to integrate, generalize, and evaluate insights about market malfunction from welfare economics and political malfunction from public choice economics into comparative institutional economics. It creates a more explicit and generally applicable economic analysis of institutional behavior and choice.

Once one sees that the dynamics of participation underlie the behavior of all the institutional alternatives, it is easier to understand why institutional behaviors tend to move together. Participation is a function of the costs of participation and the distribution of per capita stakes. In turn, these elements are a function of systemic variables like numbers and complexity. Where there are many people impacted it becomes more likely that we will have broadly distributed social impacts which are consistent with high total impact, but low per capita stakes. Greater numbers and complexity also mean that there will be higher cost of information and organization – higher participation costs.

The problems created by high participation costs and low per capita stakes haunt all the institutional alternatives. It creates dormancy for political majorities and, therefore, a bias in favor of concentrated minorities – minoritarian bias. It creates a similar dormancy in the adjudicative process through the dynamics of litigation, which we saw earlier in the discussion of class actions. As I have shown elsewhere, it creates a parallel problem in the market for items like safety and raises the chance of asymmetric information which can either cause market dormancy (the lemons problem) or produce the harmful transactions that we considered in the discussion of unconscionability.[25] The existence of similar movement in institutional alternatives warns analysts to watch for parallel problems in institutional alternatives. It also helps to understand why a badly functioning institution will often be the best available alternative.

Focusing on the dynamics of participation also expands the tools of economics beyond resource allocation efficiency. Participation is the key to the workings of all decision making institutions and the functioning of these institutions determines the achievement of any social goal, not just resource allocation efficiency. Constituting a society based on liberty or equality involves the same challenging questions of the design of and choice between decision making processes that challenge the achievement of resource allocation efficiency. This makes an economic analysis of institutional behavior based on the dynamics of participation a valuable tool no matter what the vision of goals.

Because institutions move together, the institutional choices associated with any goal are close calls dependent on variations in the dynamics of participation. This makes formulaic associations of goal and institution suspect. It is not evident which highly imperfect institutional alternative is best to produce fairer income distribution (commonly assumed to be the political process), better protection of individual liberty (commonly assumed to be the courts), or greater resource allocation efficiency (commonly assumed to be the market). Contrary to common assumptions, these are the crucial and open questions that define law and public policy analysis.

Moreover, in addition to aiding in the determination of the correct institutional choice to go along with any goal choice, participation also defines many goals. Diverse views or philosophies emphasize the importance of participation and the detriments of inadequate, incomplete, or unequal participation. As we have seen, the basic intuition of resource allocation efficiency is participation and representation. But efficiency isn't the only conception of the good that is defined by the representation of impacts and the dynamics of participation. John Rawls' theory of justice – most well-known for its theory of distributive justice – is derived from an idealized mechanism for representing all interests.[26] In turn, communitarianism places emphasis on the representation of interests and the dynamics of participation. The object is to construct a society where the incentives for communication and long-term participation

[25] See Section 10.3.2 of this chapter.

[26] John Rawls, *A Theory of Justice* (Boston, Belknap Press, 1971).

produce (or perhaps define) a higher social good. Scratch the surface of most societal goals and you will find concerns about participation. These goals and their concerns about participation are not always the same, but the concept of participation gives us a way to integrate, understand, and debate these goals as well as determine how to translate each into law and public policy.

10.4.3 Economics Impaired: The Price of Single Institutional Analysis

I have thus far discussed the role of economic analysis in creating a valuable approach to institutional behavior and, therefore, to comparative institutional analysis. Viewed correctly, economics (whether it is neoclassical economics or institutional economics) is the study of institutional behavior. In turn, the economic analysis of law and public policy is the study of institutional choice. Welfare economics focuses on the choice between the market and the political process (the regulatory choice) and law and economics focuses on the choice between the market and the courts. It would seem to follow that the sensible and correct way to analyze institutional choices and, therefore, to make use of the economic insights about institutional behavior is through institutional comparison. From the standpoint of both logic and relevance, comparative institutional analysis must be the basis of the economic approach to institutional choice and, therefore, the economic analysis of law and public policy. But it seldom is. The economic analysis of law and public policy sets off on the right track and then veers off at the last and most important step.

In the welfare economics tradition, most economic analyses of law and public policy ask whether there has been a market failure. They then explain, criticize, or justify responses, usually government interventions or, in the case of law and economics, decision making by courts, according to the character and extent of this market failure. Similarly, public choice is used to address institutional choices such as deregulation or increased judicial review of legislation by focusing on the political process and its malfunctions. Both of these analyses are single institutional. In the context of market malfunction, there is no parallel examination of the intervening political process or courts and, in the case of political malfunction, there is no parallel examination of the substituted markets or courts. Often there is no examination of the institutional alternatives at all. At most there is a superficial recognition that alternatives have costs without the recognition that the same conditions that produce imperfections in the institution of interest produce parallel problems in the alternatives.

As I have shown elsewhere, single institutional analysis of institutional choice is bad analysis.[27] But it is especially bad *economic* analysis. Single institutional analysis is inconsistent with the most accepted aspects of the notion of rational choice. Although there is considerable debate both within economics and between economists and others about the degree of rationality and knowledge assumed by economics, it is unassailable that choice involves more than one alternative. The meaning of "rational" may be in doubt. But that "choice" involves alternatives is not.

Moreover, single institutional analysis violates the logic of such basic economic constructs as opportunity costs and the role of complements and substitutes and ignores the fundamental economic concern for tradeoffs as the basic determinant of value. The concept of opportunity costs defines cost in terms of alternatives and, in turn, opportunity costs define supply curves. Similarly, the price of substitutes, which is to say the price of alternatives, is a basic parameter of the demand curve. The parallel existence of welfare economics, with its focus on market malfunctions, and public choice economics, with its emphasis on political malfunctions, underlines the need to integrate these fields into a larger field of comparative institutional economics.[28]

The argument against single institutional analysis seems so obvious that its continued prevalence in the economic analysis of law and public policy requires examination. Perhaps the attraction of single institutional analysis lies in the economics of economics. Single institutional analysis is easier and cheaper than comparative institutional analysis. Since, others things being equal, cheaper is better, perhaps there is a basis for a single institutional approach to institutional choice. At the least, the single institutional analysis of welfare economics sets out a necessary condition – in the form of market malfunction or political malfunction – for institutional choices such as government regulation or deregulation. Moreover, the degree or extent of market failure or political malfunction would seem critical in assessing the case for regulation or deregulation

[27] Komesar, *Alternatives.*

[28] Susan Rose Ackerman, Progressive Law and Economics – And the New Administrative Law, 98 *Yale LJ* 341 (1988); Douglas North, *Structure and Change in Economic History* 47–48 (1981); Joseph P. Kalt and Mark A. Zupan, Capture and Ideology in the Economic Theory of *Politics, 74 Am Econ Rev* 279 (1984); Daniel A. Farber and Philip P. Frickey, The Jurisprudence of Public Choice, 65 *Tex L Rev* 873, 893–900 (1987).

and, therefore, single institutional analysis would seem a good first approximation of comparative institutional analysis.

Upon closer inspection, however, these arguments for single institutional analysis are weak. Yes, market failure or political malfunction are necessary conditions. But they are trivial necessary conditions with little analytic value. They are always fulfilled and, in a complex world, always significantly fulfilled. The best functioning market or political process is always far from perfect.

More importantly, a single institutional approach cannot be justified even as a first approximation of comparative institutional analysis because institutions tend to move together. The same conditions that cause one institution to deteriorate also cause its institutional alternatives to do so. In particular, all institutions deteriorate as numbers and complexity increase, creating a similar movement of institutions and ruling out a role for single institutional analysis. That institutions tend to move in a similar direction does not mean that they move identically. As numbers and complexity increase and, therefore, transaction costs and other participation costs increase, institutions can vary in the rate if not the direction of their movement. It is here that comparative advantages and superior institutional choices lie. I have used comparative institutional analysis to explore the case for and against various institutional choices in longer works.[29] For present purposes, however, the central point is both simple and fundamental: *Institutions move together and that makes single institutional analysis irrelevant and comparative institutional analysis essential.*

Collective action problems and participation costs haunt all institutions and collective action and participation costs are haunted by numbers and complexity. Parades of horribles tell us little because, at high numbers and complexity, all institutional alternatives are severely strained and, therefore, a severely malfunctioning market, community, political process, or court will end up as the best choice. As a matter of theoretical symmetry, the same sort of analysis operates at low or even no participation costs. The conventional view is that, at zero transaction costs, the market is the superior resource allocation mechanism. This view seems to follow from the existence of a perfect market. But, in fact, institutional choice at zero transaction costs is indeterminate because the same conditions that underlie zero transaction costs underlie frictionless

[29] Komesar, *Alternatives*, 177–195, 250–255; Komesar, *Law's Limits*, 116–122.

political and adjudicative processes. The gist of the zero transaction costs world is costless with complete information and understanding. In such a world, government officials can easily aggregate public preferences and a perfectly aware populace can curb any official transgressions. Even problems created by unweighted voting would be avoided by vote trading and political transacting – all done costlessly. This parallel impact is a corollary of the fact that institutions move together: deteriorating as numbers and complexity increase and improving as numbers and complexity decrease.

Single institutional analysis asks the wrong questions. Moreover, it asks the wrong questions in the wrong contexts. In general, deviations from ideal, zero-cost states – such as the presence or absence of perfect information – are irrelevant for institutional choice. The relevant margin of inquiry is the choice among highly imperfect institutions at high numbers and complexity. Institutional alternatives must be compared in the same context, and that means at the same level of numbers and complexity. The comparative institutional approach refocuses the economic analysis of law and public policy on relevant contexts. It moves economic analysis away from useless debates about deviation from perfect conditions to the relevant if difficult comparison of highly imperfect institutions.

We can see the problems created by single institutional analysis by examining a renowned maxim of law and economics: the assertion that the common law – but not the law produced by the legislature – tends toward efficiency. Law and economics scholars attempting to establish the efficiency of the common law look at common law decisions, where judicial decision making is substituted for market decision making, point to a serious market malfunction and conclude that the judicial substitution for the market that ensued was, therefore, a move toward efficiency. Similarly, where the courts refuse to substitute for the market, the analysts argue that the market was working and that the judicial decision that deferred to the market was also a move toward efficiency.

But this analysis is single institutional. Whether a decision to substitute for or defer to the market is a move toward efficiency depends not on whether or how well the market is working in the abstract but on how well the market is working relative to the institutional alternative, which in these instances is common law courts. When the correct question is asked, it is often difficult to know whether the judicial decisions in question increase or decrease resource allocation efficiency. Because institutions tend to move together, these institutional choices will commonly be close calls. Therefore, we can expect that judges (or legal scholars) interested in efficiency would have conflicting views on which strategy – substitution or deferral – is best and, in turn, it will be difficult to say whether the common law in particular cases or in general moves toward or away from resource allocation efficiency.

I have examined prominent examples of common law decision making in the property rights and torts context and I have found it easy to make out a plausible case that quite opposing judicial decisions on institutional choice would both be consistent with efficiency. I have opened two books and innumerable courses with an analysis of the famous *Boomer* case using institutional choice and examining efficiency. The combination provides a powerful set of insights about the issues raised there. But it is virtually impossible to say a priori whether the position of the majority or that of the dissent in *Boomer* was more consistent with efficiency.[30] In general, institutional choices correctly understood (i.e., compared in the same context) are close calls because as one institution becomes increasingly defective as numbers and complexity increase, so do its institutional alternatives.

That brings me to the other half of the assertion about the efficiency of the common law: the relative merits of the common law versus legislative process as a means of achieving resource allocation efficiency. The efficiency of the common law principle not only asserts that the decisions of the adjudicative process tend toward efficiency, but that those of the political process do not. A little reflection on this proposition shows that it is an example of the fallacy of comparing noncomparables or more exactly comparing institutional alternatives from noncomparable contexts.

In general, common law judicial decision making involves law and public policy issues where numbers and complexity are lower, most often much lower, than in most legislative decision making settings. All institutions look less attractive as numbers and complexity increase and, therefore, comparing institutions at noncomparable margins of numbers and complexity will almost always favor the institution from the lower numbers and complexity setting. The problem is that this is a comparison of noncomparables.

The comparison between the political process and the courts inherent in the conventional law and economics view is even more suspect when

[30] See Komesar, *Alternatives*, pp. 14–30; Komesar, *Law's Limits*, ch. 2.

one realizes that, for most of the range of societal decision making where the political process prevails, the courts are not even plausible alternatives. The issue is judicial capacity or scale. As we have seen, the adjudicative process is simply far smaller than the political and market processes it is called upon to review. The adjudicative process cannot – not just should not – be substituted for the political process on most issues. At the very least, the adjudicative process simply does not have the size or scale to do the job. Thus, as an obvious example, few would argue that reallocating all decisions about national defense from the political process to common law courts would be a move toward efficiency, even though government decision making on national defense is subject to serious political malfunction. At this level of numbers and complexity, the courts are not a viable alternative, at least not on a general level.

The political process generally operates at high levels of numbers and complexity. This decision making process and its results may be unattractive and very far from perfect or ideal, but a perfect alternative is not available and, at high numbers and complexity, attractiveness is seldom an attribute of even the best decision maker. To the extent that common law decision making occurs at lower numbers and complexity than legislative decision making, observed common law decisions are quite likely less subject to institutional malfunction than observed legislation. As such, they may in some visceral sense be more attractive. But, because this analysis involves comparing noncomparables, it tells us nothing about whether these outputs tend more or less toward efficiency (or any other goal).

10.5 Conclusion: Legal Education, Legal Scholarship, and Law Reform

My message is simple: Institutional choice and comparative institutional analysis are central in understanding law of all sorts. This message is reflected in hundreds of works. These works span virtually every area of law and reach across and beyond national boundaries.[31]

This analytical framework is not just for legal scholars. It captures the essence of what judges and lawyers do. Through the lens of comparative institutional analysis, lawyers can see the determinants of law and therefore understand which facts in a given setting are strengths or weaknesses

[31] I have listed some of these works in the "Appendix" to Komesar, The Logic of the Law.

for their client's case. These lawyers can then wisely counsel their clients and effectively negotiate and advocate on their behalf. Comparative institutional analysis allows judges and the lawyers who appear before them to understand the implications of the decisions that they are about to make and to see those decisions as part of a larger context.

The tools of comparative institutional analysis should be part of the law school curriculum. Law schools exist to train lawyers and the tools of comparative institutional analysis are well adapted for that purpose. It is an analytical approach that is accessible to law students. This hardly means that it is simple to learn or to teach. But these costs are not overwhelming and the benefits are great. Those benefits are enhanced because of the vast range of subjects and uses where this analytical framework is valuable. A law student or law teacher who learns this approach can then move to unfamiliar areas of law and still have a strong sense of the important factors at play.

Comparative institutional analysis can be integrated into any course without much change in the basic materials in use and it aids curricular reform by highlighting the similarities in subject matters and, even more importantly, the source of these similarities. It provides a simple but powerful set of tools to understand and teach legal analysis. Moreover, comparative institutional analysis does not require the acceptance of any ideology. It does not force any program of law and public policy. Instead, it provides the tools to assess, debate, and choose such programs. It is a reform of legal education that is plausible and powerful.

What is true for legal education is true for legal scholarship and law reform. Certain basic questions must be addressed whatever the legal issue or reform in question. In addressing these questions, it is intellectually dangerous to ignore the allocation of decision making or to treat it as trivial. Anyone who believes that legal analysis or reform is straightforward and does not require taking comparative institutional analysis seriously will produce unsupportable gaps in their work. A critic who understands comparative institutional analysis can just accept all their arguments in this work and show that these arguments still do not justify the conclusions. One can wander across legal areas and various suggested approaches and without much effort see the linchpins of the underlying arguments and the weaknesses created by the failure to appreciate some fundamental aspect of institutional choice.

To some reformers, comparative institutional analysis may be unattractive because it does not easily dictate policy prescriptions or, more exactly, dictate the policy prescriptions preferred by the reformer.

As the use of comparative institutional analysis expands and empiricism fills in the gaps, it will be easier to make the tough institutional choices. But at base the inability to easily prescribe policy stems from the stubborn fact that institutions move together and, therefore, the institutional choices and policy choices are close calls and, therefore, inherently difficult. As numbers and complexity increase, all institutional alternatives will deteriorate. In this circumstance, single institutional analysis will appear to yield easy answers because it will be easy to trot out parades of horribles. But because all the institutional alternatives will likely suffer from similar problems, this single institutional analysis is empty. Its easy answers are the illusion of faulty analysis. Most real policy choices are and will remain close calls.

The failure to come to grips with these hard facts has wasted valuable intellectual talent. In the US legal academy, we seem to expect our young scholars to come up with a sweeping solution in every publication. We should know better. The resulting sweeping solutions are always defective and we are forcing creative minds to cut off intellectual inquiry in order to hide these defects. Society is confronted with serious policy issues and we cannot wait until everything is known to decide what we think is right. In this world, comparative institutional analysis will have to make do with plausible guesses in lieu of better empiricism. But testing the plausibility of these guesses and improving the empiricism about institutional choice are the realistic building blocks to better policy analysis, and these steps are suppressed by papering over the challenges of comparative institutional analysis and pretending that the answers are easy and obvious.

Related here is the question of how comparative institutional analysis accommodates new institutions – in particular, institutional reforms. One of the normative objectives of comparative institutional analysis is the discovery of real institutional reforms. But new decision making processes like old ones require careful scrutiny. In too many cases, reforms are simply old institutions in new dress. All reforms have attributes that parallel those of old institutions. Being able to recognize real reform from cosmetic reform and to assess how reforms will actually work in the relevant setting stems from the ability to see all institutional alternatives in the same terms by using the dynamics of participation.

Empiricism and comparative institutional analysis need to work together. There is a crying need for empiricism about institutional behavior and institutional choice. But as anyone who has attempted serious empiricism knows, it is expensive. These costs need to yield benefits, and that means empiricism needs to be focused on pertinent margins of inquiry and hypotheses that have already been vetted by sound analysis. When empiricism is used to debunk an assertion derived from single institutional analysis, it is a waste because good analysis should already have done that job. Empiricism is needed to examine the close calls that stand at the vortex of law and public policy not the showy nonsense produced by defective analysis. The interaction between empiricism and comparative institutional analysis must be iterative: analysis focuses empiricism and empiricism reforms analysis.[32]

Economics has provided me a set of tools that have allowed me to follow my analytical instincts. The economic analysis of law and public policy is, however, trapped by the fallacies of single institutional analysis. The economic analysis of law and public policy already recognizes the central place of institutional choice. Without understanding that the next logical step is comparative institutional analysis, however, the economic analysis of law and public policy continues to ask the wrong questions and focus on the wrong margins of inquiry.

When the right questions are asked and addressed, legal analysis, as well as economic analysis, can throw off the bad habits that have limited their effectiveness. Although much more needs to be done, there exists a firm foundation for future legal analysis. Armed with a framework constructed with an appreciation for the central place of institutional choice and comparative institutional analysis, legal analysis and legal method have a base from which lawyers, judges, and scholars can construct a deeper appreciation of the meaning of law.

[32] For a skillful melding of empiricism and comparative institutional analysis, see Victoria Nourse and Gregory Shaffer, Varieties of New Legal Realism: Can a New World Order Prompt a New Legal Theory?, 95 *Cornell L. Rev.* 61 (2009).

11

The Role of Empirical Legal Studies in Legal Scholarship, Legal Education and Policy Making

A US Perspective

DEBORAH R. HENSLER AND MATTHEW A. GASPERETTI

11.1 Introduction

Law is both normative and positive. Ideally, legal rules and standards instantiate normative values and promote normative goals. Foundational to legal rules and standards are positive assumptions about individuals' knowledge, attitudes, and behavior – assumptions about what normative values citizens share and about how to incentivize behaviors that will maximize the likelihood of achieving society's normative goals. Legal scholarship, however, has long focused on normative analysis and paid relatively little attention to the validity of the positive assumptions that justify the adoption and application of statutes, regulations, and procedural rules.[1] Empirical legal research investigates the validity of these assumptions. Viewed from this perspective, the question for students of legal methodology is not "why should empirical legal studies be a component of legal scholarship and legal education?" but rather "why don't legal scholars view empirical research as an essential component of legal analysis and legal education?"

11.2 What Is Empirical Legal Research?

Empirical legal research is the investigation of legally relevant facts using diverse methods and theories derived from the social sciences. The time

[1] John A. Ferejohn and Barry R Weingast, "A Positive Theory of Statutory Interpretation," *International Review of Law and Economics* 12, 2 (1992): 263–279; Robert A. Kagan, "What Socio-Legal Scholars Should Do When There Is Too Much Law to Study," *Journal of Law and Society* 22, 1 (1995): 140–148; Richard A. Posner, "The Present Situation in Legal Scholarship," *Yale Law Journal* 90, 5 (1981): 1113–1130.

frame of the research may be historical, contemporary, or prospective. The goals of empirical legal studies include theory building, theory testing, and identifying and answering legal policy questions.

Contemporary empirical legal scholarship, particularly in the United States, is largely quantitative and focuses on causal investigations. Scholars adopting a quantitative approach often apply statistical techniques to large datasets in search of causal relationships.[2] But quantitative causal analyses are only one component of empirical legal research, which properly defined also includes quantitative descriptive analyses and qualitative inquiry. Descriptive quantitative studies that answer questions about the prevalence of legal phenomena often have more immediate practical import than causal analyses, which are usually hedged with caveats. Questions about prevalence are central to many contemporary public policy controversies. For example, empirical research has identified the types of class actions that are most prevalent in the United States today,[3] as well as the number of consumer complaints resolved by alternative dispute resolution procedures in Europe.[4] Other research has focused on the juridical process in order to determine if individual holdout jurors undermine jury trials;[5] if punitive damage awards are unduly large,[6] unpredictable,[7] or reflective of biases;[8] and if an explosion in US litigation[9] is undermining judicial efficiency.[10]

[2] Lee Epstein and Andrew D. Martin, *An Introduction to Empirical Legal Research*. Oxford: Oxford University Press, 2014.

[3] Deborah R. Hensler, "Goldilocks and the Class Action," *Harvard Law Review Forum* 126 (2012): 56–60; Deborah R. Hensler, M Susan Marquis, Allan Abrahamse, Sandra H. Berry, Patricia A. Ebener, Elizabeth Lewis, Edgar Lind, et al., *Compensation for Accidental Injuries in the United States*. Santa Monica, CA: RAND Corporation, 1991; Robert H. Klonoff, "The Decline of Class Actions," *Washington University Law Review* 90, 3 (2013): 729–837.

[4] Christopher Hodges, Iris Benöhr, and Naomi Creutzfeldt-Banda. *Consumer ADR in Europe*. Oxford: Bloomsbury Publishing, 2012.

[5] Harry Kalven and Hans Zeisel, "The American Jury and the Death Penalty," *The University of Chicago Law Review* 33, 4 (1966): 769–781.

[6] Stephen Daniels and Joanne Martin, "Myth and Reality in Punitive Damages," *Minnesota Law Review* 75, 1 (1990): 1–64.

[7] Theodore Eisenberg, John Goerdt, Brian Ostrom, David Rottman, and Martin T. Wells, "The Predictability of Punitive Damages," *The Journal of Legal Studies* 26, S2 (1997): 623–661.

[8] Neil Vidmar, "Empirical Evidence on the Deep Pockets Hypothesis: Jury Awards for Pain and Suffering in Medical Malpractice Cases," *Duke Law Journal* 43, 2 (1993): 217–266.

[9] Marc. Galanter, "The Day after the Litigation Explosion," *Maryland Law Review* 46, 1 (1986): 3–39.

[10] Arthur R. Miller, "The Pretrial Rush to Judgment: Are the Litigation Explosion, Liability Crisis, and Efficiency Cliches Eroding Our Day in Court and Jury Trial Commitments," *New York University Law Review* 78, 3 (2003): 982–1134.

While quantitative research can both describe and explain certain legal phenomena, qualitative inquiries, including descriptive case studies,[11] often shed more light on the nature of legal processes than quantitative analyses. For example, the inception and progression of complex civil litigation,[12] the process of adopting new statutory and procedural rules, and the barriers to implementing new legal policies have proved susceptible to qualitative inquiry.

Contemporary empirical legal studies draw heavily on economic theory.[13] While useful for understanding legal behavior, economic theory is by no means the only helpful theoretical perspective. A broad range of theories, drawn from cognitive and social psychology,[14] sociology,[15]

[11] John M, Conley and William M O'Barr, "Fundamentals of Jurisprudence: An Ethnography of Judicial Decision Making in Informal Courts," *North Carolina Law Review* 66, 3 (1987): 467–508; Carol J. Greenhouse, *Praying for Justice: Faith, Order, and Community in an American Town: The Anthropology of Contemporary Issues.* Ithaca, NY: Cornell University Press, 1986; Sally Engle Merry, *Getting Justice and Getting Even: Legal Consciousness among Working-Class Americans.* Chicago: University of Chicago Press, 1990; William M. O'Barr and John M Conley, "Litigant Satisfaction Versus Legal Adequacy in Small Claims Court Narratives," in Judith N. Levi and Anne Graffam Walker, eds., *Language in the Judicial Process*, 97–131. New York: Springer, 1990.

[12] Peter Schuck, *Agent Orange On Trial: Mass Toxic Disasters In The Courts.* Cambridge, MA: Belknap Press, 1987; Deborah Hensler, William Felstiner, Patricia Ebener, and Molly Selvin, *Asbestos In The Courts: The Challenge Of Mass Toxic Torts.* Santa Monica, CA: RAND, 1985; Thomas Burke, *Lawyers, Lawsuits And Legal Rights: The Battle Over Litigation In American Society.* Berkeley, CA: University of California at Berkeley, 2002.

[13] Christine Jolls, Cass R. Sunstein, and Richard Thaler, "A Behavioral Approach to Law and Economics," *Stanford Law Review* 50, 5 (1998): 1471–1550; William M Landes and Richard A. Posner, "The Influence of Economics on Law: A Quantitative Study," *Journal of Law and Economics* 36, 1 (1993): 385–424; Richard A. Posner, "Rational Choice, Behavioral Economics, and the Law," *Stanford Law Review* 50, 5 (1998): 1551–1575; Thomas S. Ulen, "Behavioral Law and Economics: Law, Policy, and Science," *Supreme Court Economic Review* 21, 1 (2013): 5–42; Joshua D. Wright and Douglas H. Ginsburg, "Behavioral Law and Economics: Its Origins, Fatal Flaws, and Implications for Liberty," *Northwestern University Law Review* 106, 3 (2012): 1033–1090.

[14] E. Allan Lind, Tom R. Tyler, and Yuen J. Huo, "Procedural Context and Culture: Variation in the Antecedents of Procedural Justice Judgments," *Journal of Personality and Social Psychology* 73, 4 (1997): 767–780; Jeffrey Z. Rubin and Bert R. Brown, *The Social Psychology of Bargaining and Negotiation.* New York: Academic Press, 1975; Michael J Saks and Reid Hastie, *Social Psychology in Court.* Oxford: Van Nostrand Reinhold, 1978.

[15] Pierre Bourdieu, "Force of Law: Toward a Sociology of the Juridical Field," *Hastings Law Journal* 38, 1 (1986): 805–813; Eugen Ehrlich, *Fundamental Principles of the Sociology of Law*, Vol. 5. Cambridge, MA: Harvard University Press, 1936; Lawrence M. Friedman, "Borders: On the Emerging Sociology of Transnational Law," *Stanford Journal of International Law* 32 (1996): 65–90.

history,[16] anthropology,[17] and political science,[18] as well as from economics,[19] help explain legal behavior.

In sum, the empirical legal method, properly understood, encompasses more diverse theoretical perspectives and methodological approaches than many believe. Both quantitative and qualitative approaches are *empirical* in that they seek to investigate the world as it is rather than as we might wish it to be.

11.3 "Everything Old Is New Again"

In some quarters, empirical legal studies are hailed (or denigrated) as a new approach to legal analysis and as quintessentially American.[20] Some commentators trace the inception of empirical legal studies in the United States to the early 1980s,[21] while the fact that the eponymous flagship *Journal of Empirical Legal Studies* is only eleven years old is also often construed as evidence that the field is a recent phenomenon. However, the roots of modern empirical legal research in the United States stretch

[16] Robert W. Gordon, "Critical Legal Histories," *Stanford Law Review* 36, no. 1/2 (1984): 57–125; Christopher Tomlins, "History in the American Juridical Field: Narrative, Justification, and Explanation," *Yale Journal of Law & the Humanities* 16, 2 (2004): 323–398; Mark Tushnet, "Interdisciplinary Legal Scholarship: The Case of History-in-Law," *Chicago-Kent Law Review* 71, 3 (1995): 909–936.

[17] William M. O'Barr and John M Conley, "Litigant Satisfaction Versus Legal Adequacy in Small Claims Court Narratives," in Judith N. Levi and Anne Graffam Walker, eds., *Language in the Judicial Process*, 97–131. New York: Springer, 1990; Annelise Riles, "Representing In-Between: Law, Anthropology, and the Rhetoric of Interdisciplinary," *University of Illinois Law Review* 3 (1994): 597–650; Simon Roberts, *Order and Dispute: An Introduction to Legal Anthropology*. 2nd edn. New Orleans: Quid Pro Books, 2013.

[18] Frank B Cross, "Political Science and the New Legal Realism. A Case of Unfortunate Interdisciplinary Ignorance," *Northwestern University Law Review* 92, 1 (1997): 251–326; Emilie M. Hafner-Burton, David G. Victor, and Yonatan Lupu, "Political Science Research on International Law: The State of the Field," *American Journal of International Law* 106, 1 (2012): 47–97; Anne-Marie Slaughter, Andrew S. Tulumello, and Stepan Wood, "International Law and International Relations Theory: A New Generation of Interdisciplinary Scholarship," *The American Journal of International Law* 92, 3 (1998): 367–397.

[19] Christine Jolls, Cass R. Sunstein, and Richard Thaler. "A Behavioral Approach to Law and Economics," *Stanford Law Review* 50, 5 (1998): 1471–1550.

[20] Michael Heise, "The Past, Present, and Future of Empirical Legal Scholarship: Judicial Decision Making and the New Empiricism," *University of Illinois Law Review*, 4 (2002): 819–850.

[21] Roger A. Fairfax Jr., "Wielding the Double-Edged Sword: Charles Hamilton Houston and Judicial Activism in the Age of Legal Realism," *Harvard Blackletter Law Journal* 14 (1998): 17–44.

back at least to the beginning of the twentieth century.[22] The advent of the "legal realist" school of jurisprudence, Roscoe Pound's calls for the collection and analysis of data to support more efficient court administration, and the introduction in 1908 of what became known as the "Brandeis brief" – which popularized citing factual data, both economic and social, in support of a legal argument – all helped to create an environment in the United States that encouraged empirical studies of legal phenomena.[23]

More importantly, Americans were scarcely the first to use social science research methods to study legal structures and institutions. Positivism emerged as an academic discipline as European theorists such as Auguste Comte, who were well versed in the English Newtonian and Lockean empirical traditions, applied scientific methods to the study of society in an attempt to effect normative change.[24] Comte's work significantly influenced many of his contemporaries, including Emile Durkheim, whose pioneering sociological scholarship on crime and social deviance led to the creation of the field of criminology.[25] Durkheim viewed criminality as an essential component of society that reflected social arrangements and could be studied through comparative legal analyses.[26] His ideas would prove influential in law in the early twentieth century. Equally influential were cross-cultural legal analyses, which were in the process of being refined in the late nineteenth century,[27] when Sir Henry Maine published the groundbreaking *Ancient Law* and Lewis Henry Morgan published *Ancient Society*. Although both men were later

[22] Fairfax Jr., "Wielding the Double-Edged Sword"; Heise, "The Past, Present, and Future of Empirical Legal Scholarship"; Thomas J Miles, and Cass R. Sunstein, "Do Judges Make Regulatory Policy? An Empirical Investigation of Chevron," *The University of Chicago Law Review* 73, 3 (2006): 823–881.

[23] Fairfax Jr., "Wielding the Double-Edged Sword"; Tanenhaus, Joseph. "Supreme Court Attitudes toward Federal Administrative Agencies: 1947–1956—an Application of Social Science Methods to the Study of the Judicial Process," *Vanderbilt Law Review* 14, 2 (1960): 473–502; Russell R. Wheeler, "Roscoe Pound and the Evolution of Judicial Administration," *South Texas Law Review* 48, 4 (2006): 943–968.

[24] Carol Berkenkotter, "The Legacy of Positivism in Empirical Composition Research," *Journal of Advanced Composition* 9, 1/2 (1989): 69–82; Célestin Bouglé, "Emile Durkheim," in Peter Hamilton, ed. *Emile Durkheim*. London: Taylor & Francis, 1995.

[25] Berkenkotter, "The Legacy of Positivism in Empirical Composition Research"; Bouglé, "Emile Durkheim."

[26] Steven Spitzer, "Toward a Marxian Theory of Deviance," *Social Problems* 22, 5 (1975): 638–651.

[27] John M. Conley and William M. O'Barr, "Legal Anthropology Comes Home: A Brief History of the Ethnographic Study of Law," *Loyola of Los Angeles Law Review* 27, 1 (1993): 41–64; Spitzer, supra note 26;

criticized for "Orientalizing" non-Western societies, both works mark early examples of comparative qualitative research and together they provided an important theoretical foundation for future scholars.[28]

In the nineteenth and early- to mid-twentieth century, many Western theorists believed that social control was maintained by the command of a sovereign who coerced compliance by means of sanctions.[29] However, as anthropologists, including Bronislaw Malinowski,[30] began to study non-Western cultures by undertaking ethnographic fieldwork, they discovered that in many "primitive" societies, social order was maintained even though these societies lacked formal legal structures as understood by scholars of Western civilization.[31] Recognition that all societies have law and that law can be studied through ethnography marked a conceptual awakening.[32] Malinowski, along with Alfred Radcliffe-Brown, posited that traditional societies were bound together by complex systems of norms and were regulated by social sanctions that compelled compliance.[33] Other ethnographers, including E. E. Evans-Pritchard,[34] noted horizontal enforcement of normative values through threats of retributive violence and witchcraft. Ethnography continues today as an important element of empirical legal studies.[35]

As social scientists continued to study law in a comparative context, it became clear to many that, as Malinowski famously wrote in 1934, "law ought to be defined by function and not by form" and scholars ought to study "the sociological realities [and] the cultural mechanisms" of legal systems.[36] These ideas began to permeate mainstream legal thought and

[28] Conley and O'Barr, "Fundamentals of Jurisprudence"; Max Gluckman, *The Judicial Process among the Barotse of Northern Rhodesia (Zambia)*. Manchester, UK: Manchester University Press, 1967.

[29] John Austin, *Province of Jurisprudence Determined*. London: John Murray, 1832; Hans Kelsen, *The Pure Theory Of Law*. Vienna: Verlag Franz Deuticke, 1934.

[30] Bronislaw Malinowski, *Crime and Custom in Savage Society*. London: Kegan Paul, 1926.

[31] Roberts, Order and Dispute.

[32] John M. Conley and William M. O'Barr. "Back to the Trobriands: The Enduring Influence of Malinowski's Crime and Custom in Savage Society," *Law & Social Inquiry* 27, 4 (2002): 847–874.

[33] Stuart Piddocke, "Social Sanctions," *Anthropologica* 10, 2 (1968): 261–285.

[34] E. E Evans-Pritchard, *The Nuer: A Description of the Modes of Livelihood and Political Institutions of a Nilotic People*. Oxford: Clarendon, 1940.

[35] Conley and O'Barr, "Legal Anthropology Comes Home."

[36] Roberts, Order and Dispute (quoting Herbert I. Hogbin, *Law and Order in Polynesia: A Study of Primitive Legal Institutions*. London: Christophers, 1934. See also John L. Comaroff and Simon Roberts. *Rules and Processes: The Cultural Logic of Dispute in an African Context*. Chicago: University of Chicago Press, 1986.

scholars started to reject the definition of law as a system of commands enforced by a sovereign in favor of a definition encompassing the variety of social rules that maintain order.[37] This conceptual shift inevitably changed the theoretical focus of those researchers who used social science methods to examine legal structures from attempting to determine "what law *does*" to attempting to determine "what law *is*."[38] By the mid-twentieth century, this change was also reflected in the burgeoning field of legal realism.

In 1940, Karl Llewellyn, one of the fathers of legal realism, demonstrated that quantitative and qualitative research methods could be used to improve the normative efficiency of the United States' juridical system.[39] He expanded this work in the seminal text, *The Cheyenne Way*, in 1941.[40] Although early legal anthropologists derived knowledge about law's function and normative effects from comparative studies of non-Western cultures, their theories and tools continue to be used to analyze contemporary Western legal structures today, including the United States' legal system.[41] The research that has resulted is as diverse as it is innovative. Qualitative research methods were used by Brickey and Miller to examine the operation of traffic courts;[42] by Conley and O'Barr to study judicial decision making;[43] by Cromwell and colleagues to learn about burglar target selection;[44] by Spradley to detail interactions between "urban nomads" and the criminal justice system;[45] by Gray to investigate the relationship between workplace culture and health and safety;[46] by Kohm to identify perceptions of law in American culture and

[37] Michel Foucault, *The History of Sexuality: An Introduction*, Robert Hurley. trans. New York: Vintage Books, 1980; H. L. A. Hart, *The Concept of Law*. Oxford: Oxford University Press, 1961.

[38] Roberts, Order and Dispute.

[39] Karl N. Llewellyn, "The Normative, the Legal, and the Law-Jobs: The Problem of Juristic Method," *Yale Law Journal* 49, 8 (1940): 1355–1400.

[40] Karl N. Llewellyn and Edward A. Hoebel, *The Cheyenne Way: Conflict and Case Law in Primitive Jurisprudence*. Buffalo, NY: W.S. Hein & Company, 1941.

[41] Conley and O'Barr, "Legal Anthropology Comes Home."

[42] Stephen L. Brickey and Dan E Miller. "Bureaucratic Due Process: An Ethnography of a Traffic Court," *Social Problems* 22, 5 (1975): 688–697.

[43] Conley and O'Barr, "Fundamentals of Jurisprudence."

[44] Paul F. Cromwell, James N Olson, and D'Aunn Wester Avary. *Breaking and Entering: An Ethnographic Analysis of Burglary*. Newbury Park, CA: Sage Publications, 1991.

[45] James P. Spradley, *You Owe Yourself a Drunk: An Ethnography of Urban Nomads*. Long Grove, IL: Waveland Press, 1999.

[46] Garry Gray, "A Socio-Legal Ethnography of the Right to Refuse Dangerous Work," in Austin Sarat and Patricia Ewick, eds., *Studies in Law, Politics, and Society*, 133–69. Bingley, UK: Emerald Group Publishing Limited, 2002.

media;[47] by Menjívar and Abrego to elucidate the effects of immigration laws on migrants;[48] and by Bourgois and Phillips to study the social effects the enforcement of drug laws have on the urban poor.[49] In sum, contemporary empirical legal research has been profoundly influenced by the work of late nineteenth and early twentieth-century scholars.

11.4 Empirical Legal Research in the Twentieth Century

In the late nineteenth century, American law schools replaced traditional apprentice models of legal training, while industrialization, immigration, and economic growth encouraged progressives to work to adapt the United States' legal system to combat emerging social problems.[50] This led to the rise of "sociological jurisprudence" in elite American law schools,[51] which ultimately extended beyond academia. By the early 1920s, American jurists Roscoe Pound, Felix Frankfurter, and colleagues were collaborating on an empirical analysis of the criminal justice system in Cleveland.[52] Prior to Pound and Frankfurter's study, beliefs about the criminal justice system were based on anecdotal evidence rather than empirical data, severely hindering reform efforts. Pound and Frankfurter used statistical methods to examine the functioning of the legal system and undertook qualitative fieldwork at prisons and in courts to determine how these institutions functioned. One of the most important contributions of this research was the popularization of the concept that the United States' legal system is a transmutable series of institutions that can be altered to operate more effectively. Arguably, this concept

[47] Steven A. Kohm, "The People's Law Versus Judge Judy Justice: Two Models of Law in American Reality-Based Courtroom TV," *Law & Society Review* 40, 3 (2006): 693–728.

[48] Cecilia Menjívar and Leisy Abrego, "Legal Violence: Immigration Law and the Lives of Central American Immigrants," *American Journal of Sociology* 117, 5 (2012): 1380–1421.

[49] Philippe Bourgois, *In Search of Respect: Selling Crack in El Barrio*. 2nd edn. Cambridge, UK: Cambridge University Press, 2003; Susan A. Phillips, *Operation Fly Trap: L.A. Gangs, Drugs, and the Law*. Chicago: University of Chicago Press, 2012.

[50] Michael Adler and Jonathan Simon. "Stepwise Progression: The Past, Present, and Possible Future of Empirical Research on Law in the United States and the United Kingdom," *Journal of Law and Society* 41, 2 (2014): 173–202.

[51] Ibid.

[52] Roscoe Pound, Felix Frankfurter, Reginald Heber Smith, Herbert Brutus Ehrmann, Alfred Bettman, Howard Fletcher Burns, Raymond Blaine Fosdick, Burdette Gibson Lewis, and Herman Morris Adler. *Criminal Justice in Cleveland: Reports of the Cleveland Foundation Survey of the Administration of Criminal Justice in Cleveland, Ohio*. Cleveland, OH: The Cleveland Foundation, 1922.

encouraged the development of empirical legal studies that were oriented toward legal reform.

11.4.1 The Flowering of Empirical Legal Research in the US in the 1960s and 1970s

Empirical research on legal institutions flowered in the post–World War II era,[53] led by interdisciplinary teams of social scientists and law faculty that focused on contemporary legal reform proposals. The most influential of these projects were housed in three law schools: the University of Chicago, Columbia University (New York), and the University of Michigan. This era also marked a methodological shift in empirical legal scholarship from predominantly anthropological to predominately sociological. Whereas the former favored intensive observation of single communities (supplemented by comparative analysis), the latter tended toward larger-scale data collection that supported quantitative analyses. Although the field of "law and economics" emerged during this era as well, it remained a largely theoretical discipline.

In the mid-1960s, Kalven and Zeisel published a groundbreaking sociological analysis of jury behavior, relying primarily on survey research methods and statistical analyses.[54] *The American Jury* was the product of a multiyear project, funded by the Ford Foundation, at the University of Chicago Law School. Relying chiefly on survey questionnaire and interview responses,[55] the authors explored patterns of jury

[53] Others have also commented on the development of empirical legal research during this era. See *e.g.*, Paul D Carrington, "Maurice Rosenberg," *Columbia Law Review* 95, 8 (1995): 1901–1910.

[54] Harry Kalven and Hanz Zeisel, *The American Jury*. Boston: Little, Brown & Co., 1966; an Austrian who received two doctorates, one in law and one in political science, Zeisel practiced law and conducted sociological research in Austria until the ascendance of the Nazis caused him to emigrate. He conducted media research in New York City prior to accepting a position as professor of law and society at the University of Chicago Law School. David S. Clark, ed., "Hans Zeisel," in *Encyclopedia of Law and Society: American and Global Perspectives*. Thousand Oaks, CA: Sage Publications, 2007. His collaborator on the jury project, Harry Kalven, was a preeminent torts and constitutional scholar.

[55] Kalven and Zeisel included videotapes of actual jury deliberations in their original study design. After one of these tapes was played at a judicial conference, a storm of criticism of this deliberate invasion of jury privacy ensued and the US Congress passed legislation forbidding future observation or recording of jury deliberations in federal courts. Shari Seidman Diamond, "Beyond Fantasy and Nightmare: A Portrait of the Jury," *Buffalo Law Review* 54, 3 (2006): 717–763.

verdicts and differences between these verdicts and judges' reports of how they would have decided the same cases. In contrast to popular portrayals of anomalous and legally unconstrained jury behavior, Kalven and Zeisel showed that judges would have reached the same conclusion as juries in the overwhelming majority of cases. Initially praised as innovative, the study's methodology later came under criticism. But it inspired a generation of jury scholars whose work has shaped reforms in trial procedures globally.[56]

Maurice Rosenberg's analysis of the consequences of judicial pretrial conferences provides a second example of reform-oriented, quantitatively driven, sociolegal research.[57] A product of Columbia University Law School's Project for Effective Justice, Rosenberg's research was inspired by the increased use of mandatory pretrial conferences to expedite dispute resolution. For several decades, civil justice reform committees of practitioners had promoted the use of such conferences with little evidence that they were effective. Rosenberg teamed up with sociologists at Columbia's Bureau of Applied Social Research[58] to conduct a randomized field experiment to empirically test the results of mandating pretrial conferences. Unfortunately for the reformers, the experimental results showed conclusively that such conferences had no measurable effects on trial court efficiency. Mandatory pretrial conferences did not reduce judicial time per case, nor did they reduce time to disposition. However, notwithstanding this, the survey results showed that lawyers and judges who participated in the conferences liked them. Randomized field experiments were later adopted by alternative dispute resolution (ADR) researchers with similar results: mandatory ADR programs generally have little effect on trial court

[56] Diamond, "Beyond Fantasy and Nightmare"; Valerie P. Hans and Neil Vidmar, "The American Jury at Twenty-Five Years," *Law & Social Inquiry* 16, 2 (1991): 323–352.

[57] Maurice Rosenberg, *The Pretrial Conference and Effective Justice: A Controlled Test in Personal Injury Litigation*. New York: Columbia University Press, 1964. Rosenberg served for thirty-nine years as a professor of law at Columbia University, where he received his law degree. He served as Assistant Secretary in the US Department of Justice and headed the short-lived Office for Improvements in the Administration of Justice during President Jimmy Carter's administration. On his death, he was memorialized as a "hero" of civil justice reform. See Carrington, "Maurice Rosenberg."

[58] An outgrowth of a World War II research project on mass communications, the Bureau of Applied Social Research was the leading university-based center for applied social research of its era. Its directors comprised the luminaries of applied social science during the 1960s and 1970s. See Judith S. Barton, ed., *Guide to the Bureau of Applied Social Research*. New York: Clearwater Publishing Company, 1984.

efficiency but garner relatively high marks for process quality from lawyers and the parties involved.[59]

A third line of empirical research, focused on evaluating compensation for and the costs of automobile accidents, burgeoned in the 1960s in response to an ongoing debate about substituting "no-fault" insurance schemes for traditional tort liability for automobile accidents.[60] The best-known examples of this research, which were funded by various government agencies and insurance companies, were the products of collaborations between social scientists and lawyers at the University of Michigan[61] and Columbia University.[62] As was true with regard to Kalven and Zeisel's jury research and Rosenberg's research on mandatory pretrial conferences, studies of patterns of tort recovery produced results that controverted popular perceptions: while many believed tort recoveries were grossly overcompensating plaintiffs, most recoveries were in fact shown to be relatively small, and individuals who had the most severe injuries and losses received a smaller fraction of their losses than those with more modest and less costly injuries. Furthermore, many individuals received no compensation and those who did shared a substantial fraction with their contingency fee lawyers. Unlike academic research that proverbially gathers dust on library shelves, research on automobile accident tort liability spurred decades of "no-fault" insurance reform proposals. Many of these reforms were implemented in substantial part due to the effort of law professor Jeffrey O'Connell, who devoted his academic career to this issue. O'Connell's contributions to the no-fault policy debate[63] were distinguished by his use of empirical data as well as statutory and jurisprudential analyses.

59 E. Allan Lind, *Arbitrating High-Stakes Cases*. Santa Monica, CA: RAND Corporation, 1990.

60 Robert E Keeton and Jeffrey O'Connell. *Basic Protection for the Traffic Victim: A Blueprint for Reforming Automobile Insurance*. New York: Little, Brown, and Company, 1965. The 1960s studies, however, were not the first of their kind: an earlier line of research traced its lineage back to the 1930s. James Fleming, "The Columbia Study of Compensation for Automobile Accidents: An Unanswered Challenge," *Columbia Law Review* 59, 3 (1959): 408–424.

61 Alfred E. Conrad, James N. Morgan, Robert W. Pratt, Jr., Charles E. Voltz, and Robert L. Bombaugh. *Automobile Accident Costs and Payments: Studies in the Economics of Injury Preparation*. Ann Arbor, MI: University of Michigan Press, 1964.

62 Marc A Franklin, Robert H. Chanin, and Irving Mark. "Accidents, Money, and the Law: A Study of the Economics of Personal Injury Litigation," *Columbia Law Review* 61, 1 (1961): 1–39; Maurice Rosenberg and Michael I Sovern. "Delay and the Dynamics of Personal Injury Litigation," *Columbia Law Review* 59, 8 (1959): 1115–1170.

63 Jeffrey O'Connell, "Operation of No-Fault Auto Laws: A Survey of the Surveys," *Nebraska Law Review* 56, 1 (1977): 23–50.

While no-fault researchers focused mainly on the outcomes of litigation, other sociolegal scholars were exploring legal claiming, lawyer–client interactions, and insurance claims resolution processes using a variety of methods. Carlin and Rosenthal both conducted interviews with lawyers and clients to investigate the relative roles of each in the litigation process.[64] Hunting and Neuwirth used police accident records, insurance claims files, and court files to investigate variations in claim rates by background and circumstances.[65] Ross conducted an intensive case study of how insurance claims adjusters negotiated settlements.[66] However, perhaps because these analysts worked independently rather than with teams of collaborators, or perhaps because their focus on process seemed less immediately relevant to the policy aims of the no-fault researchers, their studies garnered considerably less attention than the Chicago, Columbia, and Michigan studies.

Through the late 1970s the US empirical legal research landscape might be described as a vast expanse of unexamined territory interrupted by "islands" of intensive and increasingly sophisticated empirical inquiry, exemplified by the contributions of Kalven and Zeisel, Rosenberg and O'Connell (1977), and their cohorts in their respective fields. Although law schools provided homes for these leading scholars, the schools did not institutionalize empirical research. As a result, by the 1980s, there was little trace of these scholars' research at their home institutions, let alone outside of them, except among those who knew them personally. Perhaps this explains in part the belief of many contemporary empirical legal research scholars that they themselves are the true pioneers of empirical legal studies.

11.4.2 The 1980s: New Issues, New Centers of Empirical Legal Research

In the late 1970s, the research landscape shifted. Over the next couple of decades there was a proliferation of empirical research projects and public and private sector institutions dedicated to conducting empirical

64 Jerome E. Carlin, *Lawyers on Their Own: The Solo Practitioner in an Urban Setting.* New Orleans: Quid Pro Books, (1962, 2011); Douglas E. Rosenthal, *Lawyer and Client: Who's in Charge.* New York: The Russell Sage Foundation, 1974.

65 Roger Bryant Hunting and Gloria S Neuwirth. *Who Sues in New York City? A Study of Automobile Accident Claims.* Ann Arbor, MI: New York City Bar Association, 1962.

66 Hugh Laurence Ross, *Settled out of Court: The Social Process of Insurance Claims Adjustment.* Hawthorne, NY: Aldline Publishing Company, 1970.

studies of legal behavior. One of the most prominent of these was the Civil Litigation Research Project (CLRP), launched in the late 1970s.[67] CLRP followed in the footsteps of the University of Chicago, Columbia University, and University of Michigan scholars in that it was an innovative analysis of legal behavior conducted by an interdisciplinary team of political scientists and law professors, in this instance at the University of Wisconsin.[68] To this date it is the only large-scale study of civil dispute processing ever funded by the US Department of Justice.[69] The theoretical framework for the study developed by Felstiner, Abel, and Sarat[70] – "naming, blaming, and claiming" – remains one of the most influential paradigms for research on legal disputing not just in the United States but worldwide. As was true of earlier empirical legal studies, CLRP's findings, which were based on analyses of survey and case record data, controverted many popular perceptions of civil justice. In contrast to contemporary views of hyperlitigious Americans, many survey respondents reported problems for which they had not sought legal assistance and disputes that they had not litigated. Moreover, a majority of disputes that made it into court involved no discovery, and only a small fraction of cases reached trial.[71] Owing to its success, CLRP shaped the careers of some of the most prominent American empirical legal scholars of their generation.

In parallel with investigations of court processes and legal claiming, the late 1970s and 1980s saw the expansion of research on the legal profession, centered at the American Bar Foundation in Chicago. The Chicago Lawyers Survey, conducted in the mid-1970s by John Heinz and his colleagues, provided the first detailed investigation of lawyers' social

[67] David M. Trubek, Joel B. Grossman, William L. Felstiner, Herbert M. Kritzer, and Austin Sarat, *Civil Litigation Research Project Final Report*. Madison, WI: University of Wisconsin-Madison Law School, 1983.

[68] It is likely relevant to the quality and impact of academic empirical legal research projects that they were all conducted at universities that were leaders in applied social research. The iconoclastic legal scholars at these universities likely found it easier to identify partners for their investigations than they might have had they been situated at universities without such intellectual resources.

[69] Notably, it was the DOJ's Office for Improvements in the Administration of Justice, headed by Maurice Rosenberg, which funded this research.

[70] William L. Felstiner, Richard L. Abel, and Austin Sarat, "The Emergence and Transformation of Disputes: Naming, Blaming, Claiming," *Law & Society Review* 15, 3/4 (1980–1981): 631–654.

[71] Deborah R. Hensler, "Trends in Tort Litigation: Findings from the Institute for Civil Justice's Research," *Ohio State Law Journal* 48, 2 (1987): 479–496.

background characteristics, practice patterns, and the relationship between the two.[72] It provided a model for research on the profession that focused on lawyers as social and political actors, as well as professional practitioners. Like the work of Kalven and Zeisel, Rosenberg, and O'Connell before him, Heinz's research had a far-reaching effect on his field of study and on a generation of sociolegal scholars whose research on the legal profession now extends globally.[73]

The 1980s also saw an increase in the number of institutions conducting empirical research on dispute processing within and outside of the courts. Much of this research responded to debates in the public policy arena that used crisis rhetoric to describe the state of the legal system, while pressing for significant changes in substantive law and procedural rules. For example, the Federal Judicial Center (FJC),[74] the National Center for State Courts (NCSC),[75] the RAND Corporation's Institute for Civil Justice (ICJ),[76] and a host of national and state-based bar association task forces conducted empirical research on court congestion and delay that built on Rosenberg's and others' 1960s court-related research.[77] These projects laid

[72] John P. Heinz, and Edward O. Laumann, *Chicago Lawyers: The Social Structure of the Bar*. New York: The Russell Sage Foundation and American Bar Association, 1982.

[73] Yves Dezalay, and Bryant G. Garth, *Asian Legal Revivals: Lawyers in the Shadow of Empire*. Chicago Series in Law and Society. Chicago: University of Chicago Press, 2010; John P Heinz, Edward O. Laumann, Robert L. Nelson, and Ethan Michelson. "The Changing Character of Lawyers' Work: Chicago in 1975 and 1995," *Law & Society Review* 32, 4 (1998): 751–776; Robert L. Nelson, *Partners with Power: The Social Transformation of the Large Law Firm*. Berkeley, CA: University of California Press, 1988.

[74] The FJC is the research and educational arm of the US Federal Courts established by the US Congress in 1967. See Peter Graham Fish, *The Politics of Federal Judicial Administration*. Princeton, NJ: Princeton University Press, 2015. 1973; Russell R. Wheeler, "Empirical Research and the Politics of Judicial Administration: Creating the Federal Judicial Center," *Law & Contemporary Problems* 51, 3 (1988): 31–53.

[75] The NCSC is a nonprofit organization established in 1971 to provide research, education, and management consulting to state court judges and administrators. It was founded at the urging of then-Chief Justice of the US Supreme Court, Warren Burger.

[76] The RAND ICJ was established in 1979 at the urging of the insurance industry, which was seeking empirical research to support its lobbying efforts. To maintain its independence, RAND sought funding for the research from diverse private and public sources and established a board representing stakeholders including insurance and noninsurance corporations, plaintiff and defense lawyers, consumer advocates, judges, and academicians to oversee the ICJ's research agenda. Deborah Hensler was one of the founders of the ICJ and served as its director from 1993–1998.

[77] Patricia A Ebener, Jane W Adler, Molly Selvin, and Michael S Yesley, *Court Efforts to Reduce Pretrial Delay*. Santa Monica, CA: RAND Corporation, 1981; Steven Flanders, *Case Management and Court Management in United States District Courts*. Vol. 77, Washington, DC: Federal Judicial Center, 1977; John Goerdt, Chris Lomvardias, Geoff

the foundation for RAND's analysis of the consequences of the federal Civil Justice Reform Act of 1990.[78] The FJC and NCSC also spearheaded the systematization and publication of court filing statistics that now undergird investigations of court processes and litigation trends in the United States. The ICJ funded the creation of jury verdict databases that supported research on jury decision making,[79] which spurred the development of statistical research on jury decisions that continued on into the twenty-first century.[80] In turn, statistical analyses of jury verdict patterns stimulated further study of insurance settlements.[81]

In the 1990s and 2000s, the adoption of court-connected ADR programs in US federal and state courts elicited another line of empirical research, encouraged by funding from the Hewlett Foundation and the

Gallas, and Barry Mahoney, *Examining Court Delay: The Pace of Litigation in 26 Urban Trial Courts, 1987*. Williamsburg, VA: National Center for State Courts 1989; Wolf V. Heydebrand and Carroll Seron, *Rationalizing Justice: The Political Economy of Federal District Courts*. Albany, NY: State University of New York Press, 1990; Molly Selvin and Patricia A. Ebener, *Managing the Unmanageable: A History of Civil Delay in the Los Angeles Superior Court*. Santa Monica, CA: RAND Corporation, 1984.

78 James S Kakalik, Terence Dunworth, Laural A. Hill, Daniel F. McCaffrey, Marian Oshiro, Nicholas M. Pace, and Mary E. Vaiana, *Just, Speedy and Inexpensive? An Evaluation of Mediation and Early Neutral Evaluation under the Civil Justice Reform Act*. Santa Monica, CA: RAND Corporation, 1996.

79 Erik K. Moller, Nicholas M. Pace, and Stephen J. Carroll, "Punitive Damages in Financial Injury Jury Verdicts," *The Journal of Legal Studies* 28, 2 (1999): 283–339; George L. Priest, "The Current Insurance Crisis and Modern Tort Law," *Yale Law Journal* 96, 7 (1987): 1521–1590; George L. Priest, "Modern Tort Law and Its Reform," *Valparaiso University Law Review* 22, 1 (1987): 1–38; Michael G. Shanley and Mark A. Peterson, *Comparative Justice: Civil Jury Verdicts in San Francisco and Cook Counties, 1959–1980*. Santa Monica, CA: RAND Corporation, 1983.

80 Thomas H. Cohen, *Bureau of Justice Statistics Bulletin: Tort Trials and Verdicts in Large Counties, 2001*. Civil Justice Survey of State Courts, 2001. US Department of Justice, Office of Justice Programs, 2004; David A. Hyman, Bernard Black, Kathryn Zeiler, Charles Silver, and William M Sage, "Do Defendants Pay What Juries Award? Post-Verdict Haircuts in Texas Medical Malpractice Cases, 1988–2003," *Journal of Empirical Legal Studies* 4, 1 (2007): 3–68; Nicholas M. Pace, Daniela Golinelli, and Laura Zakaras, *Capping Non-Economic Awards in Medical Malpractice Trials: California Jury Verdicts under MICRA*. Santa Monica, CA: RAND Corporation, 2004; Seth A. Seabury, Nicholas M. Pace, and Robert T. Reville, "Forty Years of Civil Jury Verdicts," *Journal of Empirical Legal Studies* 1, 1 (2004): 1–25.

81 Charles Silver, David A. Hyman, Bernard S. Black, and Myungho Paik, "Policy Limits, Payouts, and Blood Money: Medical Malpractice Settlements in the Shadow of Insurance," *UC Irvine Law Review* 5, 3 (2015): 559–586; Kathryn Zeiler, Charles Silver, Bernard Black, David A Hyman, and William M Sage, "Physicians' Insurance Limits and Malpractice Payments: Evidence from Texas Closed Claims, 1990–2003," *The Journal of Legal Studies* 36, S2 (2007): S9–S45.

National Institute for Dispute Resolution.[82] Although dispute resolution professionals promoted mediation and conciliation as tools for preserving relationships in conflictual situations, judges and court administrators often championed court-annexed ADR programs as mechanisms for increasing dispute processing efficiency.[83] To the chagrin of the dispute resolution professionals and the dismay of court administrators, most empirical studies found no evidence of such efficiency benefits.[84] However, interest in (and funding for) ADR research encouraged the movement of procedural justice research from the laboratory to the field. Social psychologists Allan Lind and Tom Tyler used a combination of laboratory and field experiments and survey research to explore how disputants' evaluations of process fairness influence their evaluations of dispute resolution procedures and institutions.[85] Like Felstiner and colleagues' theoretically driven research on claiming, Lind and Tyler's theoretically driven research on procedural justice built a vibrant field that transcends national borders today.[86]

The American Law and Society Association (LSA), which was founded in the 1960s, connected many of these latter twentieth-century scholars to each other, bringing together legal anthropologists, legal historians, sociologists of the legal profession, social psychologists who focused on legal behavior and attitudes, and institutional political scientists who focused on courts.[87] Although originally theoretically and ideologically driven, by the mid-1980s the field had become more empirical.[88] Over time, the LSA also began to attract more law faculty to its annual

[82] Irving R. Kaufman, "Reform for a System in Crisis: Alternative Dispute Resolution in the Federal Courts," *Fordham Law Review* 59, 1 (1990): 1–38; Richard C. Reuben, "Constitutional Gravity: A Unitary Theory of Alternative Dispute Resolution and Public Civil Justice," *UCLA Law Review* 47, 1 (1999): 949–1104.

[83] Kakalik et al., Just, Speedy and Inexpensive?

[84] Deborah R. Hensler, "Our Courts, Ourselves: How the Alternative Dispute Resolution Movement Is Re-Shaping Our Legal System," *Penn State Law Review* 108, 1 (2003): 165–198; Montaigne Centre. "Procedural Justice: Reflections on Legal Practice," *Utrecht Law Review* 10, 4 (2014): 1–161.

[85] E. Allan Lind and Tom R. Tyler, *The Social Psychology of Procedural Justice*. New York: Plenum Press, 1988.

[86] Martin Gramatikov and Laura Klaming, "Getting Divorced Online: Procedural and Outcome Justice in Online Divorce Mediation," *Journal of Law & Family Studies* 14, 1 (2011): 97–120.; Allan Lind, Tom R. Tyler, and Yuen J. Huo, "Procedural Context and Culture: Variation in the Antecedents of Procedural Justice Judgments," *Journal of Personality and Social Psychology* 73, 4 (1997): 767–780.

[87] Richard L. Abel, *The Law & Society Reader*. New York: New York University Press, 1995.

[88] Ibid.

gatherings, which reflected the gradual incorporation of empirical findings into legal doctrinal scholarship and education.

In sum, there is at least a century-old tradition of noneconomic, empirical study of legally relevant phenomena within and outside the United States using quantitative and qualitative methods.[89] Over time, this work has infiltrated US legal scholarship and legal education as more traditionally trained legal scholars, such as George Priest (Yale Law School),[90] Gary Schwartz (UCLA Law School),[91] and Cass Sunstein (Harvard Law School and previously University of Chicago Law School),[92] have incorporated empirical results into their doctrinal and theoretical scholarship (and in some instances collaborated themselves on empirical studies). The result has been the emergence of law faculty with joint degrees in both law and a social science discipline at elite law schools in recent years who use these skills to meld normative and doctrinal legal analyses together with empirical research.[93]

11.5 But Is it any Good?

Ironically, Lee Eptstein and Gary King's 2002 article on the methodological weaknesses of much self-proclaimed "empirical legal research"[94] is sometimes cited by critics of the empirical legal studies movement as a rationale for rejecting such work, or at least limiting its inclusion in the

[89] Fairfax Jr., "Wielding the Double-Edged Sword"; Heise, "The Past, Present, and Future of Empirical Legal Scholarship"; Miles and Sunstein, "Do Judges Make Regulatory Policy?"

[90] George L. Priest, Modern Tort Law and Its Reform," *Valparaiso University Law Review* 22, 1 (1987): 1–38; George L. Priest, "Punitive Damages and Enterprise Liability," *Southern California Law Review* 56, 1 (1982): 123–132.

[91] Gary T. Schwartz, "The Beginning and the Possible End of the Rise of Modern American Tort Law," *Georgia Law Review* 26, 3 (1991): 601–702; Gary T. Schwartz, "Reality in the Economic Analysis of Tort Law: Does Tort Law Really Deter," *UCLA Law Review* 42, 2 (1994): 377–444.

[92] Miles and Sunstein, "Do Judges Make Regulatory Policy?"; Cass R. Sunstein, "Must Formalism Be Defended Empirically?". *The University of Chicago Law Review* 66, 3 (1999): 636–670; Cass R. Sunstein, "Empirically Informed Regulation," *The University of Chicago Law Review* 78, 4 (2011): 1349–1429; Cass R Sunstein, David Schkade, Lisa M. Ellman, and Andres Sawicki. *Are Judges Political? An Empirical Analysis of the Federal Judiciary*. Washington, DC: The Brookings Institution, 2006.

[93] Jeremy A. Blumenthal, "Law and Social Science in the Twenty-First Century," *Southern California Interdisciplinary Law Journal* 12, 1 (2002): 1–54; Heise, "The Past, Present, and Future of Empirical Legal Scholarship"; Michael Hiese, "The Importance of Being Empirical," *Pepperdine Law Review* 26, 4 (1998): 807–834.

[94] Lee Epstein and Gary King, "The Rules of Inference," *The University of Chicago Law Review* 69, 1 (2002): 1–133.

legal studies curriculum. This was scarcely their goal. Rather, they sought to persuade creators of such research to use more rigorous methods and to persuade the legal academic community to develop an infrastructure that would impose stricter standards for publication. The establishment of the peer-reviewed *Journal of Empirical Legal Studies* was to some extent a response to their critique. As more social science researchers with graduate-level training have entered the legal academy,[95] more sophisticated analyses have begun to appear.[96]

Although it is encouraging that legal academia is becoming increasingly interdisciplinary, legal relevance has sometimes been sacrificed in the process.[97] The search for databases that allow empirical legal scholars to show off their quantitative analytic skills has the potential to lead to empirical research in search of interesting questions to answer, rather than research in search of answers to significant questions.[98] Further, the effort to identify databases that allow for analyses of the consequences of different legal policies sometimes leads to exploration of these differences in nonrepresentative circumstances.[99] Empirical researchers whose training is limited to quantitative analytic techniques sometimes lack the skills – or interest – to interpret their findings,[100],falling back on the mantra "further research is necessary" to figure out what their findings mean or what they imply for legal policy making. Disciplinary training and

95 Hiese, "The Importance of Being Empirical."

96 Tom Ginsburg and Thomas J. Miles, "Empiricism and the Rising Incidence of Coauthorship in Law," *University of Illinois Law Review* 2011 (2011): 1785–1826; Lynn M LoPucki, "Disciplining Legal Scholarship," *Tulane Law Review* 90, 1 (2015): 1–35; Richard A. Posner,"The Decline of Law as an Autonomous Discipline: 1962–1987," *Harvard Law Review* 100, 4 (1987): 761–780.

97 LoPucki, "Disciplining Legal Scholarship"; Brent E. Newton, "Preaching What They Don't Practice: Why Law Faculties' Preoccupation with Impractical Scholarship and Devaluation of Practical Competencies Obstruct Reform in the Legal Academy," *South Carolina Law Review* 62, 1 (2010): 105–156; Richard A. Posner, "The Deprofessionalization of Legal Teaching and Scholarship," *Michigan Law Review* 91, 8 (1993): 1921–1928.

98 Theodore Eisenberg, "The Origins, Nature, and Promise of Empirical Legal Studies and a Response to Concerns," *University of Illinois Law Review*, 5 (2011): 1713–1738; Tracey E. George, "An Empirical Study of Empirical Legal Scholarship: The Top Law Schools," *Indiana Law Journal* 81, 1 (2006): 141–162 Michael Heise, "An Empirical Analysis of Empirical Legal Scholarship Production, 1990–2009," *University of Illinois Law Review* (2011): 1739–1752.

99 Harry T. Edwards and Michael A. Livermore, "Pitfalls of Empirical Studies That Attempt to Understand the Factors Affecting Appellate Decisionmaking," *Duke Law Journal* 58, 8 (2009): 1895–1989; D. James Greiner, "Causal Inference in Civil Rights Litigation," *Harvard Law Review* 122, 2 (2008): 533–598.

100 Hiese, "The Importance of Being Empirical."

incentives to prove one's bona fides in the academic environment also create barriers to multidisciplinary collaborations of the sort necessary to produce practically relevant findings.[101] Unfortunately, these weaknesses cannot be solved simply by better methodological training or peer-reviewed journals[102]

Garnering less attention from critics is the potential for legal academicians – like their colleagues in medicine – to be lured into serving the political goals of interested parties who can provide support for expensive empirical research or offer lucrative opportunities for expert testimony in high-stakes litigation.[103] The lack of a peer review tradition in student-led law reviews exacerbates these dangers.[104] Moreover, the tendency of interest groups to "cherry-pick" published research findings to support their positions in hot political debates may tend to discredit empirical research in the eyes of policymakers who all too often respond with the aphorism "there are lies, damned lies and statistics" when presented with contradictory findings.[105] Often these policymakers (and their staffs) are themselves lawyers with little or no training in empirical research methods who have no ability to independently assess the validity of inferences drawn from empirical studies.[106] Nor are jurists immune from such tendencies.[107] Judges are often suspicious of statistical data, rejecting strong empirical findings, like evidence of discriminatory patterns of jury verdicts in capital punishment cases[108] or

101 Ibid.

102 Leah M. Christensen, and Julie A. Oseid, "Navigating the Law Review Article Selection Process: An Empirical Study of Those with All the Power—Student Editors," *South Carolina Law Review* 59, 1 (2007): 175–224; Gregory Mitchell, "Empirical Legal Scholarship as Scientific Dialogue," *North Carolina Law Review* 83, 1 (2004): 167–204; David Monsma, "The Academic Equivalence of Science and Law: Normative Legal Scholarship in the Quantitative Domain of Social Science," *TM Cooley L. Rev.* 23, 1 (2006): 157–220.

103 Eisenberg, "The Origins, Nature, and Promise"; D. James Greiner, "Causal Inference in Civil Rights Litigation," *Harvard Law Review* 122, 2 (2008): 533–598; J. Morgan Kousser, "Are Expert Witnesses Whores? Reflections on Objectivity in Scholarship and Expert Witnessing," *The Public Historian* 6, 1 (1984): 5–19.

104 Mitchell, "Empirical Legal Scholarship."

105 David L. Faigman, "The Law's Scientific Revolution: Reflections and Ruminations on the Law's Use of Experts in Year Seven of the Revolution," *Washington and Lee Law Review* 57, 3 (2000): 661–684; Jennifer K. Robbennolt, "Evaluating Empirical Research Methods: Using Empirical Research in Law and Policy," *Nebraska Law Review* 81, 2 (2002): 777–804.

106 Faigman, "The Law's Scientific Revolution"; Robbennolt, "Evaluating Empirical Research Methods."

107 Faigman, "The Law's Scientific Revolution"; David L. Faigman, "Judges as Amateur Scientists," *Boston University Law Review* 86, 5 (2006): 1207–1226.

108 David C., Baldus, George Woodworth, and Catherine M. Grosso. "Race and Proportionality since McCleskey V. Kemp (1987): Different Actors with Mixed Strategies of Denial

pay and promotion in employment[109] in favor of intuitive individual judgments, being apparently unaware of or impervious to extensive evidence of the unreliability of such intuitions.

Ultimately, the contribution of empirical legal studies to theory building and policymaking depends on the quality of the research measured both by empirical methodological standards and legal relevance.[110] But just as we do not reject the efforts of physicists because claims of "cold fusion" are unsupported[111] or the efforts of molecular biologists because reports that human embryonic stem cells had been successfully cloned were based on fabricated experiments,[112] it is inappropriate to reject the entire empirical research project because of the methodological flaws of individual empirical studies.[113] Rather, such critiques illustrate the need to train law students in empirical research methods so that they are better positioned to assess the value of individual studies to legal education and legal policymaking.

11.6 Contributions of Empirical Legal Research

Notwithstanding its flaws, empirical legal research has contributed significantly to the development of legal theory and legal policy, touching virtually every area of substantive and procedural law.[114] Examining the contributions of empirical legal studies over the last century is beyond

and Avoidance," *Columbia Human Rights Law Review* 39, 2 (2007): 143–177; L. Randall Kennedy, "McCleskey V. Kemp: Race, Capital Punishment, and the Supreme Court," *Harvard Law Review* 101, 7 (1988): 1388–1443.

109 Joseph L. Gastwirth, "Statistical Reasoning in the Legal Setting," *The American Statistician* 46, 1 (1992): 55–69; Allan G. King, "'Gross Statistical Disparities' as Evidence of a Pattern and Practice of Discrimination: Statistical Versus Legal Significance," *The Labor Lawyer* 22, 3 (2007): 271–292, but see Kingsley R. Browne, "Statistical Proof of Discrimination: Beyond Damned Lies," *Washington Law Review* 68, 3 (1993): 477–558.

110 George, "An Empirical Study of Empirical Legal Scholarship"; Hiese, "The Importance of Being Empirical."

111 John Robert Huizenga, *Cold Fusion: The Scientific Fiasco of the Century*. Oxford, Eng.: Oxford University Press, 1994; William F. McComas, "The Principal Elements of the Nature of Science: Dispelling the Myths," in *The Nature of Science in Science Education: Rationales and Strategies*, Science & Technology Education Library, 53–70. Springer, 2002.

112 David Cyranoski, "Verdict: Hwang's Human Stem Cells Were All Fakes," *Nature* 439, 7073 (2006): 122–123; R. Saunders and Julian Savulescu. "Research Ethics and Lessons from Hwanggate: What Can We Learn from the Korean Cloning Fraud?," *Journal of Medical Ethics* 34, 3 (2008): 214–221.

113 George, "An Empirical Study of Empirical Legal Scholarship."

114 Hiese, "The Importance of Being Empirical."

the scope of this essay. Instead, we focus on selected examples of empirical research, conducted over the past few decades that have shaped academic discourse and legal policy debate. Single empirical studies rarely, if ever, produce significant change. Together, however, empirical studies in particular legal domains have helped to influence how legal academicians and policy makers think about legal phenomena and sometimes their decisions.[115] Research in many of the areas cited in this section has made its way into legal education through inclusion in case books or supplementary course materials. Additionally, the proliferation of such materials, and the increasing acceptance of the importance of empirical research[116] to theory development and policymaking has led to the inclusion of empirical research methods courses in the curricula of some elite US law schools.[117]

11.6.1 Theory Development

Empirical researchers have used social science methods to test hypotheses and develop theories that have added to understanding of legally relevant behavioral practices in diverse contexts. Recent research has contributed significantly to comprehension of negotiating behavior[118] and claiming behavior,[119] revealed how individuals experience the legal system,[120] and tested the efficacy of law as a deterrent to deviant

[115] Scott L. Cummings, "Empirical Studies of Law and Social Change: What Is the Field? What Are the Questions?," *Wisconsin Law Review* 2013, 1 (2013): 171–204; Heise, "The Past, Present, and Future of Empirical Legal Scholarship"; Miles and Sunstein, "Do Judges Make Regulatory Policy?".

[116] Epstein and King, "The Rules of Inference."

[117] George, "An Empirical Study of Empirical Legal Scholarship"; Heise, "The Past, Present, and Future of Empirical Legal Scholarship."

[118] Roger Fisher, William L. Ury, and Bruce Patton. *Getting to Yes: Negotiating Agreement without Giving In*. New York: Penguin Books, 2011; Rebecca Hollander-Blumoff, "Just Negotiation," *Washington University Law Review* 88, 2 (2010): 381–432; Carrie Menkel-Meadow, "Toward Another View of Legal Negotiation: The Structure of Problem Solving," *UCLA Law Review* 31, 4 (1983): 754–842.

[119] Theodore Eisneberg, "The Need for a National Civil Justice Survey of Incidence and Claiming Behavior," *Fordham Urban Law Journal* 37, 1 (2010): 17; Deborah R Hensler, M. Susan Marquis, Allan Abrahamse, Sandra H. Berry, Patricia A. Ebener, Elizabeth Lewis, Edgar Lind, et al., *Compensation for Accidental Injuries in the United States*. Santa Monica, CA: RAND Corporation, 1991; Herbert M Kritzer, *Lawyers at Work*. Contemporary Society Series. New Orleans: Quid Pro Books, 2015.

[120] Hollander-Blumoff, "Just Negotiation"; Sally Engle Merry, *Getting Justice and Getting Even: Legal Consciousness among Working-Class Americans*. Chicago: University of Chicago Press, 1990.

behavior.[121] For example, Hollander-Blumoff used empirical data drawn from social psychology to demonstrate that procedural justice has a significant influence on adherence to third-party decisions in bilateral negotiations and helps foster the perception that such systems are legitimate.[122]

More generally, negotiation theorists have used experimental methods to examine the effects of "fixed pie" thinking,[123] endowment effects,[124] and risk assessment under uncertainty on bargaining behavior and outcomes.[125] Survey researchers have studied who claims, for what, and under what circumstances,[126] while procedural justice researchers have used laboratory and field experiments to investigate the effects of different procedural dimensions (e.g., "voice," decision control, dignitary values, etc.) on perceptions of procedural fairness and the effects of perceived fairness on satisfaction and compliance with dispute resolution outcomes.[127] Finally, deterrence researchers have analyzed litigation,

121 Harold G. Grasmick and Donald E. Green, "Legal Punishment, Social Disapproval and Internalization as Inhibitors of Illegal Behavior," *Journal of Criminal Law and Criminology* 71, 3 (1980): 325–335; Dan M. Kahan, "The Secret Ambition of Deterrence," *Harvard Law Review* 113, 2 (1999): 413–500; Andrew F Popper, "In Defense of Deterrence," *Alabama Law Review* 75, 1 (2011): 181–204.

122 Hollander-Blumoff, "Just Negotiation."

123 Max H. Bazerman,"Negotiator Judgment: A Critical Look at the Rationality Assumption," *American Behavioral Scientist* 27, 2 (1983): 211–228; Carsten K. De Dreu, W., Sander L. Koole, and Wolfgang Steinel, "Unfixing the Fixed Pie: A Motivated Information-Processing Approach to Integrative Negotiation," *Journal of Personality and Social Psychology* 79, 6 (2000): 975–987; Robin L. Pinkley, Terri L. Griffith, and Gregory B. Northcraft, "'Fixed Pie' a La Mode: Information Availability, Information Processing, and the Negotiation of Suboptimal Agreements," *Organizational Behavior and Human Decision Processes* 62, 1 (1995): 101–112.

124 Daniel Kahneman, Jack L. Knetsch, and Richard H. Thaler, "Experimental Tests of the Endowment Effect and the Coase Theorem," *Journal of Political Economy* 98, 6 (1990): 1325–1348.

125 Hazel G. Genn, *Hard Bargaining: Out of Court Settlement in Personal Injury Actions.* Oxford Socio-Legal Studies. Oxford: Oxford University Press, 1987. Christine Jolls, Cass R. Sunstein, and Richard Thaler, "A Behavioral Approach to Law and Economics," *Stanford Law Review* 50, 5 (1998): 1471–1550.

126 Hensler et al., *Compensation for Accidental Injuries in the United States.*

127 Morton Deutsch,and Peter T. Coleman. "Some Guidelines for Developing a Creative Approach to Conflict," in Morton Deutsch and Peter T. Coleman, eds., *The Handbook of Conflict Resolution*, 355–365. San Francisco: Jossey-Bass Publishers, 2000; Deborah R. Hensler, Suppose It's Not True: Challenging Mediation Ideology," *Journal of Dispute Resolution* 2002, 1 (2002): 81–100; Rebecca Hollander-Blumoff and Tom R. Tyler, "Procedural Justice and the Rule of Law: Fostering Legitimacy in Alternative Dispute Resolution," *Journal of Dispute Resolution* 2011, 1 (2011): 1–20.

financial, and media data, and have interviewed business representatives and lawyers to assess the potential of tort law to deter injurious behavior.[128]

11.6.2 Legal Policy

Empirical legal research has added significantly to debate over tort law and legal procedural reform in the United States. Statistical data on trends in civil jury verdicts have been widely cited in federal and state legislative debates on introducing and amending automobile "no-fault" regimes[129] and restricting product liability,[130] medical malpractice verdicts,[131] noneconomic damages,[132] joint and several liability,[133] and punitive damages.[134] Empirical research on sanctions for frivolous

[128] Daniel S Bailis and Robert J. MacCoun, "Estimating Liability Risks with the Media as Your Guide," *Judicature* 80, 1 (1996): 64–67;. Michael L Rustad, "In Defense of Punitive Damages in Products Liability: Testing Tort Anecdotes with Empirical Data," *Iowa Law Review* 78, 1 (1992): 1–88; Gary T. Schwartz, Reality in the Economic Analysis of Tort Law: Does Tort Law Really Deter," *UCLA Law Review* 42, 2 (1994): 377–444.

[129] Nora Freeman Engstrom, "An Alternative Explanation for No-Fault's 'Demise,'" *DePaul Law Review* 61, 1 (2012): 303–382; Elisabeth M. Landes, "Insurance, Liability, and Accidents: A Theoretical and Empirical Investigation of the Effect of No-Fault Accidents," *Journal of Law & Economics* 25, 1 (1982): 49–66.

[130] A. Mitchell Polinsky and Steven Shavell, "The Uneasy Case for Product Liability," *Harvard Law Review* 123, 6 (2010): 1437–1492; W. Kip Viscusi and Michael J. Moore, "Product Liability, Research and Development, and Innovation," *Journal of Political Economy* 101, 1 (1993): 161–184.

[131] Henry S. Farber and Michelle J. White, "Medical Malpractice: An Empirical Examination of the Litigation Process," *The Rand Journal of Economics* 22, 2 (1991): 199–217; David M. Studdert, Michelle M. Mello, Atul A. Gawande, Tejal K. Gandhi, Allen Kachalia, Catherine Yoon, Ann Louise Puopolo, and Troyen A. Brennan, "Claims, Errors, and Compensation Payments in Medical Malpractice Litigation," *New England Journal of Medicine* 354, 19 (2006): 2024–2033; Neil Vidmar, Empirical Evidence on the Deep Pockets Hypothesis: Jury Awards for Pain and Suffering in Medical Malpractice Cases," *Duke Law Journal* 43, 2 (1993): 217–266.

[132] Mark J. Browne and Robert Puelz, "The Effect of Legal Rules on the Value of Economic and Non-Economic Damages and the Decision to File," *Journal of Risk and Uncertainty* 18, 2 (1999): 189–213; Joseph H. King Jr., "Pain and Suffering, Noneconomic Damages, and the Goals of Tort Law," *Southern Methodist University Law Review* 57, 1 (2004): 163–210.

[133] Howard F Chang and Hilary Sigman, *Incentives to Settle under Joint and Several Liability: Working Paper 7096*, 40. Cambridge, MA: National Bureau of Economic Research, 1999; Han-Duck Lee, Mark J. Browne, and Joan T. Schmit, "How Does Joint and Several Tort Reform Affect the Rate of Tort Filings? Evidence from the State Courts," *Journal of Risk and Insurance* 61, 2 (1994): 295–316.

[134] Theodore Eisenberg, Neil LaFountain, Brian Ostrom, and David Rottman, "Juries, Judges, and Punitive Damages: An Empirical Study," *Cornell Law Review* 87, 1 (2001):

litigation, the outcomes of court-mandated ADR programs,[135] pleading standards,[136] and class actions[137] have all shaped academic discourse and policy discussions of procedural reform as well.

At the same time, empirical legal research has contributed to the evolution of areas as diverse as family law,[138] environmental law,[139] and bankruptcy law.[140] Studies of the economic impact of divorce on

743–782; Jennifer K. Robbennolt, "Determining Punitive Damages: Empirical Insights and Implications for Reform," *Buffalo Law Review* 50, 1 (2002): 103–204; Rustad, Michael L., "In Defense of Punitive Damages in Products Liability: Testing Tort Anecdotes with Empirical Data," *Iowa Law Review* 78, 1 (1992): 1–88.

135 Hensler, "Our Courts, Ourselves"; Thomas J. Stipanowich, "ADR and the 'Vanishing Trial': The Growth and Impact of 'Alternative Dispute Resolution'," *Journal of Empirical Legal Studies* 1, 3 (2004): 843–912.

136 Jonah B. Gelbach, "Locking the Doors to Discovery? Assessing the Effects of Twombly and Iqbal on Access to Discovery," *Yale Law Journal* 121, 8 (2012): 2270–2348; Patricia W. Hatamyar, "The Tao of Pleading: Do Twombly and Iqbal Matter Empirically?," *American University Law Review* 59 (2010): 553–633; Lonny Hoffman, "Twombly and Iqbal's Measure: An Assessment of the Federal Judicial Center's Study of Motions to Dismiss," *The Federal Courts Law Review* 6, 1 (2012): 1–40.

137 Janet Cooper Alexander, "Do the Merits Matter? A Study of Settlements in Securities Class Actions," *Stanford Law Review* 43, 3 (1991): 497–598; Theodore Eisenberg and Geoffrey Miller, "The Role of Op-Outs and Objectors in Class Action Litigation: Theoretical and Empirical Issues," *Vanderbilt Law Review* 57, 5 (2004): 1529–1568; Theodore Eisenberg, and Geoffrey Miller, "Attorney Fees in Class Action Settlements: An Empirical Study," *Journal of Empirical Legal Studies* 1, 1 (2004): 27–78; Theodore Eisenberg and Geoffrey Miller, "Incentive Awards to Class Action Plaintiffs: An Empirical Study," In *Cornell Legal Studies Research Paper No. 05-037*, 2005; Deborah R. Hensler, Bonnie Dombey-Moore, Elizabeth Giddens, Jennifer Gross, and Erik Moller, *Class Action Dilemmas: Pursuing Public Goals for Private Gain*. Santa Monica, CA: RAND Corporation, 2000.

138 Barbara A. Babb, "An Interdisciplinary Approach to Family Law Jurisprudence: Application of an Ecological and Therapeutic Perspective," *Indiana Law Journal* 72, 3 (1996): 775–808; Margaret F. Brinig, "Empirical Work in Family Law," *University of Illinois Law Review*, 4 (2002): 1083–1110; Patricia J. Falk, "Lesbian Mothers: Psychosocial Assumptions in Family Law," *American Psychologist* 44, 6 (1989): 941–947.

139 Jason J Czarnezki, "An Empirical Investigation of Judicial Decisionmaking, Statutory Interpretation, and the Chevron Doctrine in Environmental Law," *University of Colorado Law Review* 79, 3 (2008): 767–824; Michael G. Faure, "Effectiveness of Environmental Law: What Does the Evidence Tell Us?," *William & Mary Environmental Law and Policy Review* 36, 2 (2012): 293–336; Scott R. Saleska and Kirsten H. Engel, "Facts Are Stubborn Things: An Empirical Reality Check in the Theoretical Debate over the Race-to-the-Bottom in State Environmental Standard-Setting," *Cornell Journal of Law & Public Policy* 8, 1 (1998): 55–88.

140 Robert M. Lawless, "An Empirical Analysis of Bankruptcy Certiorari," *Missouri Law Review* 62, 1 (1997): 101–134; Lynn M LoPucki, "Disciplining Legal Scholarship," *Tulane Law Review* 90, 1 (2015): 1–35; Jay Lawrence Westbrook, "Empirical Research in Consumer Bankruptcy," *Texas Law Review* 80, 7 (2002): 2123–2160.

women and children[141] emphasize the need to reform divorce law. Multidisciplinary environmental studies highlight the need for clean air and clean water policies[142] as well as clean technology and climate change policies.[143] Legal academicians also have built datasets on bankruptcy litigation that provide a basis for evaluating calls for reform.[144]

11.7 Conclusion

Although it continues to encounter skepticism, especially outside the United States, empirical legal research – as a method, rather than a "movement" – is an essential component of scholarly and public policy inquiry into legally relevant behavior. It is neither new nor peculiarly American: as long as societies have existed, they have created "law," and as long as positive social science has existed, law has been one of the topics of empirical inquiry. Like other empirical research disciplines, empirical legal research is susceptible to failures of methodological rigor – and unfortunately, to the suborning of some of its scholars by economic actors. To what extent and at what pace these weaknesses can be remedied is not clear, but the fact that they are the subjects of lively debate is a hopeful sign.

Over more than a century, the scope of empirical legal research has broadened to touch virtually every aspect of legal institutions and behavior in the United States and is becoming more common elsewhere. Even though empirical findings are often ignored or discounted in high-stakes

[141] Brinig, "Empirical Work in Family Law"; Eleanor E. Maccoby and Robert H. Mnookin, *Dividing the Child: Social and Legal Dilemmas of Custody*, Cambridge, MA: Harvard University Press, 1992; Tess Wilkinson-Ryan and Deborah Small, "Negotiating Divorce: Gender and the Behavioral Economics of Divorce Bargaining," *Law & Inequality* 26, 1 (2008): 109–132.

[142] Bruce A. Ackerman and Richard B. Stewart, "Reforming Environmental Law," *Stanford Law Review* 37, 5 (1985): 1333–1365; Thomas H. Tietenberg, *Emissions Trading: An Exercise in Reforming Pollution Policy*. Washington DC: Resources for the Future, 1985.

[143] David L Markell and J. B. Ruhl, "An Empirical Assessment of Climate Change in the Courts: A New Jurisprudence or Business as Usual?," *Florida Law Review* 64, 1 (2011): 15–86; David L. Markell and J. B. Ruhl, "An Empirical Survey of Climate Change Litigation in the United States," *Environmental Law Reporter* 40, 7 (2010): 10644–10655.

[144] Robert M. Lawless, Angela K. Littwin, Katherine M. Porter, John A. E. Pottow, Deborah Thorne, and Elizabeth Warren, "Did Bankruptcy Reform Fail? An Empirical Study of Consumer Debtors," *American Bankruptcy Law Journal* 82, 3 (2008): 349–406; Katherine Porter, "The Pretend Solution: An Empirical Study of Bankruptcy Outcomes," *Texas Law Review* 90, 1 (2011): 103–162.

political debates, calls for "data" to inform debates are increasingly common. It is not impossible to believe that sometime in the future leaders of the bench and bar will call for "evidence-based" recommendations whenever they consider legal reform.

Today, empirical legal research appears to be an accepted avenue of legal scholarship in US law schools and increasingly in law faculties outside the United States as well. The popularity of empirical scholarship among law faculty may fade over time as other perspectives become more popular, but because of the law's centrality to society, the study of legal behavior will continue in anthropology, economics, history, political science, psychology, and sociology. Hopefully, there will always be legal scholars who are ready to make use of such research whether or not they engage in it themselves.

12

A Behavioural Law and Economics Perspective

Between Methodology and Ideology when Behavioural Sciences Meet Law

ORLY LOBEL

12.1 Introduction

Perhaps more than any other recent development in the study of law, the incorporation of behavioural economics into law and policy has been received with overwhelming enthusiasm. In Europe, The European Commission for Applying Behavioural Sciences to EU Policy-making now considers the broad implications of this approach in nearly any area of policy, from smoking to recycling, from consumerism to tax, from energy policy to health care. In the United Kingdom and the United States, similar behavioural dream teams have been formed to aid in a myriad of regulatory areas. Regulators are eager to learn what the behavioural law and economics approach has to offer, and scholars within the field are tasked with offering further insights. Recently, an executive order issued by the White House solidified the commitment to identifying areas in which insights provided by the behavioural sciences can improve cost effectiveness, efficiency or functionality, and to implementing solutions based on those insights.[1] The methodological promise of the behavioural law and economics (BLE) approach is that it will give the legal community more realistic and effective ways to analyse the interface between human psychology, markets, and regulation.[2] Traditional economic approaches begin with the assumption

University Professor and Professor of Law, University of San Diego.

[1] Executive Order – Using Behavioral Science Insights to Better Serve the American People, 2015 WL 5334684, at *1 (hereinafter BSI Exec. Order)

[2] As this chapter will argue, it may well be more accurate and promising to use the term Behavioral Sciences and the Law (BSL) rather than the currently accepted BLE to surpass the current BLE tunnel vision and avoid losing sight of the breadth and richness of the approach. See also, Daniel Kahneman in his preface to *The Behavioral Foundations of Public Policy*, suggesting the term behavioural science in lieu of behavioural economics.

of *homo economicus*, the rational actor, but this stylized model proves fictitious. The assumption that market actors will consistently behave rationally with the single goal of profit maximization simply fails too frequently. BLE enlists contemporary social science to predict how actual humans will behave in real life. The selling point of BLE, which has led to its viral adoption as a primary method for twenty-first century law, is that it is both empirically grounded and normatively sound. BLE markets itself to the lawmaker as a toolkit that will achieve accurate results at a very low monetary and political cost: law can be embedded in private decision making efficiently, invisibly and sans controversy.

The key challenge for legal scholars is to avoid the tunnel vision and the imperialist push to collapse BLE to a narrow set of *prêt-à-porter* corrective measures for cognitive biases. The greater contribution, the one that must not be eclipsed by the watered-down nudge impulse, is the systematic integration of rich insights from behavioural sciences into law.

The paper proceeds as follows. Section 12.2 traces the neoclassical law and economics model and its discontent through both internal and external challenges to first generations of law and economics scholarship. As behavioural sciences dramatically expand the world of market failures, the research lends itself to the study of the role of law. Section 12.3 argues that the contemporary moment of opening law and economics to behavioural science must recognize the breadth of this integration. Behavioural approaches to law are explored in several schools of research on the economics and psychology of human behaviour. Even through the lens of divergence from the rational actor model, the meeting of social and cognitive psychology, and economics and policy provides a broad range of insights that can be divided into four categories: bounded rationality, bounded ethicality, bounded self-control and bounded self-interest. After canvassing the potential contributions of behavioural sciences to the study of law, Section 12.4 elaborates on the problems with a specific approach of BLE, one that collapses the broad canvas into the study of choice attitudes, debiasing and regulation-by-default. The section then suggests that BLE has been hindered by a tunnel vision and a conflation between BLE as methodology and as ideology.

12.2 From Law and Economics *Versus* Law and Society to Behavioural Law and Economics

Economists traditionally modelled human behaviour as fully rational, envisioning a regime where actors operate in markets as rational individuals with clear and coherent objectives. Market actors in this traditional model are self-interested and wealth maximizing; they process information in reliable ways; and they behave consistently with their stated goals and preferences. Therefore, unregulated markets are, as a rule, the best way to optimally aggregate individual preferences. As long as rights are allocated and policed with certainty, the market is the optimal system to satisfy varying self-interests in a social setting. According to first-generation law and economics, the role of economic analysis is to help the law identify the few places in which there are market failures. In this framework, the concept of market failure is quite narrow: namely, imperfect information, transaction costs, negative externalities, and, in some analyses, asymmetric information and bargaining power. In other words, the need for legal intervention in unregulated markets is limited and exceptional. Methodologically, then, the role of economic analysis in the field of law is to identify those exceptions to the rule that markets are better left unregulated. Legal intervention is justified only in those limited circumstances. For example, in the case of negative externalities, first-generation law and economics scholars reasoned that tort liability might be appropriate. To reduce transaction costs, default rules are needed. To correct for imperfect information, disclosure laws might be justified. Otherwise, once the allocation of rules is made, private market action is superior to public regulation.

Side by side with first-generation law and economics, multiple approaches in legal academia, ranging from sociolegal studies to critical theory, presented arguments about the many inadequacies of this analysis. These other interdisciplinary approaches positioned themselves in contrast to the economic analysis of the law. At the same time, setting the stage for the robust success of the behavioural approach to law and economics, the field of economics itself began to shift. New institutional economics, for example, underscored the fact that individuals are social beings whose preferences, reasoning and actions are, at least in part, constructed by their institutional settings.[3] As a result, second-generation law and economics scholarship began to shift from abstract application of neoclassic economics to more concrete institutional analysis.[4] Gary Minda described this second-generation law and economics scholarship

[3] Edward L. Rubin, 'The New Legal Process, the Synthesis of Discourse, and the Microanalysis of Institutions', 109 *Harv. L. Rev.* 1393, 1424–1433 (1996).

[4] Gary Minda, *Postmodern Legal Movements: Law and Jurisprudence at Century's End* 87–88 (1995).

as one in which 'only a small number of methodological issues appear to be settled ... Second generation [law and economics] scholars have retreated from the orthodoxy of "efficient" answers for nearly every legal question; instead, the second generation thinkers admit that "most law and economics questions are still open and likely to remain so for a long time".'[5]

As law and economics opened itself to more approaches from economic research, the critiques outside of law and economics continued to intensify. Martha Nussbaum wrote an influential article in which she provided a critique from a philosophical perspective.[6] Nussbaum listed among the central flaws of Chicago School law and economics the assumptions that individuals are merely self-interested preference satisfiers and that their preferences are fixed and exogenous. The critiques from Nussbaum and others reflected the same internal challenges that were being developed in the field of economics. In other words, time after time, the field of law and economics lags behind, and then adapts to ongoing conversations within economics, the primary field. It should thus be unsurprising that BLE was received with enthusiasm within legal research some years after behavioural economics established itself as a central intervention within economics research.

As the field of behavioural economics developed into a merger between economics and psychology, it became a frontier in studying judgement, decision making, motivation, ethics and incentives. In recent years, no scholarly field has commanded more attention in the public sphere than behavioural economics. The *New York Times* called Nobel Laureate Daniel Kahneman and his coauthor Amos Tversky 'the Lewis and Clark of the mind'. *The Guardian* referred to them as the 'Laurel and Hardy or Crick and Watson' of the humanities. This focus on the humanities is correct. Rather than understanding behavioural economics as a subfield of economics, it is more accurate to say that in its current form and breadth, behavioural economics is a window to the entire span of social science research. As I will later discuss, one of the distortions of BLE is the narrow focus on irrationality when in actuality, behavioural sciences include far greater insights than merely the set of cognitive failures that result in irrational choices.

5 Gary Minda, 'The Jurisprudential Movements of the 1980s', 50 *Ohio St. L.J.* 599, 607 (1989).

6 Martha C. Nussbaum, 'Flawed Foundations: The Philosophical Critique of (a Particular Type of) Economics', 64 *U. Chi. L. Rev.* 1197 (1997).

Against the background of external challenges to first-generation law and economics and internal changes in the field of economics, the field of law was ready for an integrative, multidisciplinary makeover. Instead of law being informed by a single field, BLE is especially appealing because it has a built-in triple perspective creating a triad of checks and balances: psychology, economics and law. Perhaps the biggest draw of behavioural economics as an approach to legal research is its partiality and recognition of fallibility. Its greatest strength is its commitment to modelling real-life choices and actions while continuously learning about and thickening the picture we have of ourselves. BLE is essentially a descriptive approach. Its mandate to the legal scholar is: find out what works in the interface between decision makers and their decision making environment. The decision making environment is what Roger Brownsword, in his article, 'Field, Frame and Focus', terms the 'regulatory environment'. Brownsword describes three generations of regulation, each shifting us from the command to the regulation-by-design.

If the study of law becomes primarily about how best to direct human behaviour, then it should not be surprising that behavioural economics has become central to legal research. It is in this setting that the two projects in law, directing behaviour and creating a normative system, collapse into one. Traditionally, law is measured for its success along two dimensions: effectiveness and legitimacy. The promise, and risk, of BLE is the *convergence* of legitimacy and effectiveness. Legitimacy stems from nonintervention, autonomy and self-direction; while effectiveness comes from constant movement toward a tighter-controlled policy environment that improves a person's choices on everything and anything, including health, finance and happiness.

12.3 Bounded Humanity: The Many Worlds of Behavioural Sciences

Behavioural economics as a field studies the realistic limits of a stylized *homo economicus*, a theoretical representation of rational human behaviour. The vast body of contemporary research demonstrates that humans deviate from this stylized model in at least four distinct ways. First, from a judgement and decision making perspective, human behaviour includes predictable patterns of cognitive failure, suggesting that we are boundedly rational. Second, from the perspective of our motivation and ability to carry out our intentions, we are limited by bounded self-control. Third, from an ethical perspective, humans are boundedly ethical. Fourth, from a social perspective, we are boundedly self-interested; our behaviour pervasively reveals a mix of self-regarding and other-regarding motivations.

12.3.1 Bounded Rationality

Nobel laureate Herbert Simon proposed early on that humans have limited capacities in processing information rationally.[7] Simon termed this concept 'bounded rationality'. Simon explained that while the field of economics (and by extension at the time, law and economics) presents models of decision making which assume that individuals are rational and consistently seek to maximize wealth, these models do not reflect reality. In reality, individuals often lack the processing and cognitive computing capacities to engage in perfectly optimal decision making. Since then, numerous studies in cognitive and social psychology, neuroscience, and judgement and decision making have demonstrated a myriad of mechanisms and processes that may generate biases in the way humans process information, form preferences, decide on courses of action and assess risk. Across most areas of life, from love to money and from work to health, humans are constrained in their capacities to act consistently and effectively with their own goals because of a range of systematic cognitive limitations.

The first frontiers of behavioural economics sought to identify systemic divergence from rational decision making. For example, in 1979, in one of the most influential works in behavioural economics, Kahneman and Tversky developed Prospect theory to explain how, in reality, people evaluate future risk.[8] If the processing method is indeed expected utility, risk processing should be constant and does not depend on subjective evaluation or framing. Prospect theory helps explain why people decide differently when outcomes are framed differently. It asserts that people compare losses and gains through heuristics, systematically using a reference point of a probable outcome and framing all deviations from that reference point as either losses or gains. Prospect theory directly challenges traditional theoretical models of expected utility, which assume rational actors consider every possible outcome in consistent probabilistic terms. It helps explain, for example, findings in behavioural

[7] Herbert A. Simon, *Behavioral Model of Rational Choice, in Models of Man, Social and Rational: Mathematical Essays on Rational Human Behavior in a Social Setting* (1957).

[8] Amos Tversky and Daniel Kahneman, 'Rational Choice and the Framing of Decisions', 59 *The Journal of Business* S4 (1986).

research that people ascribe greater value to things they already have – i.e., the endowment effect – and tend to be more averse to loss than to enjoy gain – i.e., loss aversion.[9] These related behavioural effects in turn present a great challenge to the Coase theorem, which has been incredibly influential for first-generation law and economics research, as they undermine its theoretical foundations that willingness to pay is necessarily equal to willingness to accept.

Other behavioural studies demonstrate ubiquitous shortcuts, or heuristics, beyond prospect theory. People use mental shortcuts to resolve questions more quickly and easily. For example, when facing a risk, a person might not calculate all the probabilities and collect data about the current statistics relating to the risk, but instead will think about a recently reported incident to judge the frequency and probability of the risk, a mental shortcut known as the availability bias.[10] Bounded rationality includes other cognitive errors such as being overly optimistic and systematically underestimating risk, known as the optimism bias, and the tendency to attach higher probability to events that actually happened, known as the hindsight bias. A bundle of context effects concern how people make choices according to the surrounding choices in the set. These effects include: the similarity effect, which is the introduction of an option that is similar to one of the other options affecting the choices between two other independent options; the compromise effect, which is the positioning of any three options as having a middle option, which like the similarity effect violates the independence from irrelevant alternatives because the positioning affects preference; and the attraction effect, which is the increased popularity of an option over the original subset when a less attractive option is introduced. In sum, rather than our preferences being fixed and consistent, they are shaped by the decision making environment and context in which the choices available to us are presented.

12.3.2 Bounded Self-Control

Human willpower is a limited resource that is frequently depleted. Despite our cognitive limitations in processing information and evaluating preferences and risk, humans often do know what is the right and

[9] Thaler, Richard H., 'Toward A Positive Theory of Consumer Choice', 1 *Journal of Economic Behavior and Organization* 39–60 (1980).

[10] Amos Tversky and Daniel Kahneman. 'Availability: A Heuristic for Judging Frequency and Probability', 5 *Cognitive Psychology* 207–232 (1973).

effective thing to do. And yet most of us are also flawed in our ability to live up to our ideals. We are too frequently tempted to overeat, to overspend, and to indulge in other behaviours with few short-term gains and multiple long-term detriments. Procrastination is the flipside of our inability to control immediate desires. Procrastination can lead to sub-optimal action in many circumstances. Additionally, procrastination can be more, rather than less, severe when the stakes are high because the anticipated difficulty of the task discourages immediate action.[11] Behaviourists explain this bundle of behaviours through the concept of bounded self-control, also known as ego depletion.[12]

Within this framework, an individual's impulse control is conceptualized as a finite resource, and with each decision throughout the day (especially decisions that run counter to one's impulses) the individual has less of this resource to use.[13] In this way, human self-control functions like a muscle, and just like a muscle the more it is used within a short period of time, the weaker and more tired it gets. As an example, translating this concept to the modern workplace, a recent study by Trugakos et al. measured organizational citizenship behaviour, or behaviour that benefits the organization through positive team involvement, throughout the course of the day; as the day wore on, the more a person faked emotions or hid their true emotion, the more exhausted they were at the end of the day, and the less likely they were to engage in organizational citizenship behaviour.[14] These workers' ability to control their behaviour effectively weakened throughout the day, indicating that self-control can be thought of as a renewable – but finite – resource. In short, human self-control is not boundless, and models of human behaviour must take this fact into account to accurately model outcomes.

12.3.3 Bounded Ethicality

The ethical world of humans is complex, and every discipline of study, from history to biology, from philosophy to neuroscience, has attempted

[11] Ted O'Donoghue and Matthew Rabin, 'Procrastination in Preparing for Retirement', in Henry Aaron, ed., *Behavioral Dimensions of Retirement Economics*. Washington, DC: Brookings Institution (1999).

[12] Thomas C. Schelling, 'The Intimate Contest for Self-Command', in *Choice and Consequence*. Cambridge, MA: Harvard University Press (1984).

[13] John P. Trugakos et al., 'Too Drained to Help: A Resource Depletion Perspective on Daily Interpersonal Citizenship Behaviors', 100 *Journal Of Applied Psychology* 1: 227–236 (2015).

[14] See ibid., at 228.

to enrich our account of it.[15] Behavioural ethics continues these inquiries by directly challenging traditional economic assumptions about illegality and norm violation. Research increasingly demonstrates that our judgements about what is the moral and right thing to do are governed by our bounded ethicality – humans are ethical beings within bounds[16] – and Behaviour demonstrates how decision making with regard to moral principles is impacted by the interface between the individual and the decision making environment. As will be discussed in this section, contextualization, incrementalism, role morality and compensatory behaviour all affect perceptions and actions related to one's ethical being.

In a series of studies I have conducted with my collaborator Yuval Feldman, we show how the decision to report or to ignore corruption is influenced by multiple factors linked to both the decision making environment and the individual's moral world.[17] These factors included the way the illegality was framed, the institutional setting in which the corruption was revealed, the background legal rules, and the incentives structure. We also found in our research that people tend to overestimate their own morality, which psychologists have termed the 'holier than thou' effect.

Relatedly, Bazerman and Tenbrunsel discuss the Goldman Sachs employee who blew the whistle on insider trading.[18] The employee regarded the victims of this illegal behaviour as part of 'a nameless' and 'faceless', until her own sister mentioned investments to her. Those

[15] For example, researchers have attempted to explain our ethicality in evolutionary terms, Mark Matousek, *Ethical Wisdom: The Search for a Moral Life* 99 (2011).

[16] Patricia Werhane et al., *Obstacles to Ethical Decision-Making: Mental Models, Milgram and the Problem of Obedience* (2013); Mary C. Kern and Dolly Chugh, 'Bounded Ethicality: The Perils of Loss Framing', 20 *Psychological Science* 378 (2009); Yuri Mishina et al., 'Why "Good" Firms Do Bad Things: The Effects of High Aspirations, High Expectations, and Prominence on the Incidence of Corporate Illegality', 53 *Acad. Mgmt. J.* 701, 703, 716 (2010); David De Cremer, ed., *Psychological Perspectives on Ethical Behavior and Decision Making* (2009); David De Cremer and Ann E. Tenbrunsel, eds. *Behavioral Business Ethics: Shaping an Emerging Field* (2012); Wray Herbert, *On Second Thought: Outsmarting Your Mind's Hard-Wired Habits* 94 (2010); Allan J. McDonald and James R. Hansen, *Truth, Lies and O-Rings: Inside the Space Shuttle Challenger Disaster* (2012); Brian Cruver, *Anatomy of Greed: Telling the Unshredded Truth from Inside Enron* (2003); David DeSteno and Piercarlo Valdesolo, *Out of Character: Surprising Truths about the Liar, Cheat, Sinner (and Saint) lurking in all of us* 50 (2011).

[17] Yuval Feldman and Orly Lobel, 'The Incentives Matrix: The Comparative Effectiveness of Rewards, Liabilities', 87 *Duties and Protections for Reporting Illegality Texas Law Review* (2010).

[18] Max H. Bazerman and Ann E. Tenbrunsel, *Blind Spots* (2011).

insignificant faceless investors of 401(k) pension plans suddenly became real individuals, and the employee contacted the regulators. This demonstrates the general principle that people tend to care more about harm when it is more visible and tangible.[19] When harm invokes emotions (our 'hot' state), for example, by presenting a picture of the risk rather than just numerical descriptions ('cold' state), people will act upon the information differently. In other words, the idea that people are 'good' or 'bad' in a fixed, acontextual way is proven false by the behavioural ethics literature.

Most strikingly, new research demonstrates that most people allow themselves to break the rules some of the time. As one researcher writes, 'the empirical evidence seems to point to the conclusion that we lie and cheat much more often than we care to admit. At the same time, we strive to maintain a positive image of ourselves, and moral values are a central component of our self-image.'[20] Most importantly, moves toward illegal behaviour happen in patterned and predictable ways as people tend to incrementally move toward unethicality. The process of incrementalism mitigates the self-perception of the problematic behaviour. Slowly, one starts getting used to a lower standard of behaviour, from minor transgressions to serious criminal behaviour.[21] Gino and Bazerman have referred to this incremental move to unethical behaviour as the 'boiling frog syndrome', based on experiments that demonstrate that when the water is incrementally raised, frogs do not realize they are boiling and do not jump out to save themselves. The human equivalent is found in those engaged in severe illegal activities who have often arrived at that level of criminality through small steps, each one gradually lowering their ethical bar until they reach the point of no return.[22]

Complementing incrementalism is the behavioural phenomenon of role morality, in which individuals allow themselves to engage in ethically questionable actions when wearing a specific hat. For example, a person might view themselves as ethical in all aspects of their private lives and yet become corrupt in their role as CEO or attorney. Relatedly, psychologists

[19] Margaret Heffernan, *Willful Blindness: Why We Ignore the Obvious at Our Peril* (2011)

[20] Francesca Gino, *Sidetracked: How Our Decisions Get Derailed and How We Can Stick to the Plan* (2013).

[21] Francesca Gino and Max H. Bazerman, *When Misconduct Goes Unnoticed: The Acceptability of Gradual Erosion in Others' Unethical Behavior*, 45 *Journal of Experimental Social Psychology* 708 (2009).

[22] Ibid.

observe the process of ethical fading, which occurs when individuals are too close to a problem to see the greater implications.[23] For certain actions, our minds allow moral disengagement, enabling a temporary and localized suppression of one's principled beliefs in a specific context.[24] Most people have a self-serving bias, a tendency to process information in ways that support preexisting beliefs.[25] In group settings, ethical demands can clash with our wish to please authority, to conform, to be part of a team, and to be complacent. This internal conflict is known as the conformity bias, which is the tendency to curb one's independent judgement in relation to the other people's judgement.[26] Relatedly, people often suffer from groupthink syndrome, where they find it very difficult to give their own opinion even when the group is suggesting something that is clearly wrong.[27]

A final set of examples of the lessons behavioural ethics offers is that of moral licensing and moral equilibrium. Humans tend to compensate for an unethical action by doing something good, though unrelated. Conversely, after performing a good or charitable action, there is a human tendency to give oneself license to do (an unrelated) wrong.[28] For example, people may allow themselves to eat particularly unhealthy food after a workout, offsetting the benefits of the workout. The mindset is that it all balances itself out, but the effects counteract the positive behaviour that is sought.

12.3.4 Bounded Self-Interest

The idea that self-interest is bounded is based on a set of insights in behavioural economics that challenge the neoclassical economics

[23] Ann E. Tenbrunsel and David M. Messick, 'Ethical Fading: The Role of Self-Deception in Unethical Behavior', 17 *Social Justice Research* 223 (2004).

[24] Albert Bandura, 'Mechanisms of Moral Disengagement', in *Origins of Terrorism* (W. Reich, ed., 1990).

[25] Emily Pronin and Kathleen Schmidt, 'Claims and Denials of Bias and Their Implications for Policy', in *The Behavioral Foundations of Public Policy* 195 (Eldar Shafir, ed., 2013).

[26] Irving L. Janis, *Victims of Groupthink: A Psychological Study of Foreign-Policy Decisions and Fiascoes* (1972); James K. Esser and Joanne S. Lindoerfer, 'Groupthink and the Space Shuttle Challenger Accident: Toward a Quantitative Case Analysis', 2 *Journal of Behavior and Decision Making* 167 (1989).

[27] Solomon E. Asch, Opinions and Social Pressure, in *Readings About the Social Animal* (1955).

[28] Robert A. Prentice, 'Moral Equilibrium: Stockbrokers and the Limits of Disclosure', *Wisconsin Law Review* 1059 (2011); Sonya Sachdeva et al., 'Sinning Saints and Saintly Sinners: The Paradox of Moral Self-Regulation', 20 *Psychological Science* 523 (2009); Uzma Khan and Ravi Dhar, 'Licensing Effect in Consumer Choice', 43 *Journal of Marketing Research* 259 (2006).

assumption that humans act solely for their own preference satisfaction and wealth maximization. Behavioural economics provides a wealth of research on the mixed motivations, self-regarding and other-regarding that coexist within humans. Far more often than rational economics would predict, we care about fairness and process beyond specific tangible outcomes.[29] We tend to cooperate far beyond what classic economic models predict,[30] with humans often engaging in prosocial behaviour unaccounted for by traditional economic analysis.[31] Moreover, people assess the fairness of others and tend to either reciprocate by rewarding the fair behaviour, or in the alternative, punishing the cheater by causing them to incur costs.[32]

At the same time that behavioural sciences vastly expand the world of market failures, there may be situations in which, because of our bounded self-interest, traditional market failures may be overstated. If people behave altruistically more often than the traditional model may predict, then it is possible that predictions about moral hazard or negative externalities are exaggerated. For example, perhaps we need less strict intellectual property laws to incentivize innovation when we understand that innovators operate for multiple reasons, rather than solely for monetary rewards.

Moreover, there exists what can be thought of as a market for altruism; a market in which charities, nonprofits, and other philanthropic organizations can patch the holes in the proverbial road created by market failures.[33] These organizations exist by virtue of their ability to occupy a niche in the market unfillable by most profitable enterprise – the opportunity to do genuine good in the world, and the existential reward that

[29] Matthew Rabin,. 'Incorporating Fairness into Game Theory and Economics', 83 *American Economic Review* 1281–1302 (1993).

[30] Richard H Thaler and Robyn M. Dawes, Cooperation, in Richard H. Thaler, *The Winner's Curse: Paradoxes and Anomalies of Economic Life*, 6–20 New York: The Free Press (1992).

[31] Edward L. Deci and Richard M. Ryan, 'Self-Determination Theory: When Mind Mediates Behavior', 1 *Journal of Mind and Behavior* 33 (1980); Myles I. Friedman and George H. Lackey, Jr., *The Psychology Of Human Control: A General Theory Of Purposeful Behavior* (1991); Shoham Choshen-Hillel and Ilan Yaniv 'Agency and the Construction of Social Preference: Between Inequality Aversion and Prosocial Behavior', 101 *Journal of Personality and Social Psychology*, 1253 (2011).

[32] Douglas A. Bosse, Robert A. Phillips, and Jeffery S. Harrison, 'Stakeholders, Reciprocity, and Firm Performance', 30 *Strategic Management Journal* 447, 448 (2009)

[33] M. Todd Henderson and Anup Malani, 'Corporate Philanthropy and the Market for Altruism', 109 *Columbia Law Review* 58 (2009).

Table 12.1 *Typologies of bounded humanity.*

Bounded rationality	**Bounded ethicality**
. Cognitive failures . Choice architecture . Default rules . Learning	. Expressive role of law . Disclosure regimes . Reputation and shaming . Priming with ethical stimuli . Crowding out . Institutional studies
Bounded self-control	**Bounded self-interest**
. Commitment mechanisms . Sticky defaults . Command regulation . Depletion	. The role of altruism and prosocial action in law . Participation and voice . Preference for process . Collaboration, sharing and motivation . Commons

provides. The end result is that models of human behaviour that hold to the outdated assumption that actors only engage in rational self-interested behaviour are fundamentally flawed, and instead must be reconceptualised taking into account the insights observed through the behavioural sciences to more accurately model and predict outcomes.

Table 12.1 contains a more comprehensive list of how boundedness plays a role in various aspects of human decision making. Some of these typologies have been discussed already, while others will be explained in greater detail later in this paper.

12.4 Implications for Legal Research

BLE has become a robust field of research. Legal scholars have suggested applying insights from behavioural economics to all fields of law, including contract, property, tax, employment, intellectual property and environmental regulation.[34] They regularly advocate an adjustment of legal rules to comport with these behavioural insights. For example, BLE

[34] On Amir and Orly Lobel, 'Stumble, Predict, Nudge: How Behavioral Economics Informs Law and Policy', 108 *Columbia Law Review* 2098 (2009); Nicholas Mercuro and Steven G. Medema, *Economics and the Law from Posner to Post-Modernism* (1997); Christine Jolls et al., 'A Behavioral Approach to Law and Economics', 50 *Stan. L. Rev.* 1471 (1998); Richard A. Posner, 'Social Norms, Social Meaning, and Economic Analysis of Law: A Comment', 27 *J. Legal Stud.* 553 (1998).

draws on the self-serving bias, the insight that individuals process information in a way that supports their previous assumptions, to advocate an adjustment to civil procedure rules. The self-serving bias in behavioural economics challenges the classic law and economics assumption that if adversaries receive full information, they will settle their case more easily because full information will lead to converging views about the merits of a case.[35] Instead, scholars advocate that limiting the information provided during those stages to adversarial litigants would induce rather than impede quick settlements. Can we draw these kinds of conclusions from experimental psychology and economics to inform the practice and shape of law as some of the research suggests? From a normative perspective, is behavioural engineering morally defensible? Or perhaps the implications are far more reaching than have been suggested thus far? And what about the inevitable problem that regulators are human too?[36]

12.4.1 *Playing Catch-Up with Behavioural Studies*

Having shown the great range and variety of bounded behaviour typologies, behavioural scientists have now turned much of their focus to identifying the mechanisms that lead to each type of human boundedness. A consensus emerges in the behavioural literature that we can describe decision making as based in two systems: reflexive or intuitive (System 1) and reflective or cognitive (System 2).[37] While there are competing names for this dual system – automatic/controlled, emotional/cognitive, reflexive/reflective – researchers largely share Nobel Laureate Daniel Kahneman's view about the

[35] Linda Babcock, George Loewenstein and Samuel Issacharoff. 'Creating Convergence: Debiasing Biased Litigants', 22 *Law and Social Inquiry* 913–926 (1997); Linda Babcock, George Loewenstein, Samuel Issacharoff and Colin Camerer, 'Biased Judgments of Fairness in Bargaining', 85 *American Economic Review* 1337–1343 (1995); Samuel Issacharoff and George Loewenstein, 'Unintended Consequences of Mandatory Disclosure', 73 *Texas Law Review*, 753–786 (1995).

[36] On this last question, see, 'Guided by the conviction that policy-makers can apply behavioural insights reflexively to develop better policies, the European Commission's Joint Research Centre established a "Summer School" in behavioural economics for EU policy-makers in 2012', http://ec.europa.eu/dgs/health_consumer/information_sources/docs/30092013_jrc_scientific_policy_report_en.pdf.

[37] Amir and Lobel, 'Stumble, Predict, Nudge' ("In lay terms, one may think about this as a distinction between biases that are caused by people not thinking carefully and those that are caused by people thinking, or indeed thinking too much . . . The distinction between System 1 and System 2 failures traces a plethora of dual-processes cognitive models, such as automatic-controlled, emotional-cognitive, reflexive-reflective, and many others, but the logic that manifests in all of them with respect to overcoming biases is almost the same").

dual reasoning structure: that humans think fast and slow.[38] Each system is associated with a different set of cognitive effects, strengths and weaknesses. For example, research shows that System 1 may be the best source for consistent performance related to visual tasks, while System 2 is superior concerning tasks requiring greater analytics.[39] The BLE focus on choice architecture – setting up the decision making environment in a deliberate way – is based on the insight that law can utilize cognitive failures to get people to reach the correct result. However, a pervasive problem for BLE is that it describes observations of many deviations from rational behaviour without adequately understanding whether the proposed solutions are adequate corrective measures. Understanding the source of the bias lends itself to understanding whether and how corrective approaches are available. While methods for 'debiasing' biases sourced in System 1 may be easier to implement through induced thinking, it may be more difficult to correct System 2 biases. Instead, the approach is through 'rebiasing' manipulation of outcomes while maintaining the bias.

Moreover, as the studies of bounded self-interest indicate the importance of process and fairness unrelated to outcome, how can law integrate these insights into policy? Insights derived from the behavioural sciences have already received the executive imprimatur, with these insights cited for improvements in Americans' ability to save for retirement and in streamlining the process of obtaining federal student aid.[40] To this end, an Executive Order has established a clear governmental priority not only to utilize insights from the behavioural sciences to improve public

[38] Daniel Kahneman, *Thinking, Fast and Slow* (2011); See also On Amir, A. Pocheptsova, R. Dhar, and R. Baumeister, *Deciding Without Resources: Psychological Depletion and Choice in Context Journal of Marketing Research* (2009); Keith E. Stanovich and Richard F. West, 'Individual differences in reasoning: Implications for the rationality debate?', 23 *Behavioral and Brain Sciences* 645–726 (2000); Evans J. S. T. 'In Two Minds: Dual-Process Accounts Of Reasoning', 7 *Trends In Cognitive Sciences* 10 (2003), 454–459, A.P. Dijksterhuis, Maarten W. Bos, N, Loran. F. Nordgren and Rick. B. van Baaren, 'On Making the Right Choice: The Deliberation Without Attention Effect', 311 *Science* 1005 (2006); Amir and Lobel, 'Stumble, Predict, Nudge'; A.P. Dijksterhuis and Loran F. Nordgren, 'A Theory of Unconscious Thought', 1 *Perspectives on Psychological Science* 95 (2006).; Daniel Kahneman, 'A Perspective on Judgment and Choice: Mapping Bounded Rationality', 58 *American Psychologist* 697 (2003); Timothy D. Wilson, and Jonathan. W. Schooler, 60 'Thinking Too Much: Introspection Can Reduce the Quality of Preferences and Decisions', *Journal of Personality and Social Psychology* 181 (1991).

[39] See. e.g., Zohar Rusou, Dan Zakay and Marius Usher, 'Pitting Intuitive and Analytical Thinking Against Each Other: The Case of Transitivity', 20 *Psychonomic Bulletin and Review* 608 (2013).

[40] BSI Exec. Order at 1.

welfare, program outcomes, and cost effectiveness, but also to hire behavioural scientists directly to go about achieving these goals.[41] Specific objectives include identifying individuals eligible for current federal programmes that are not participating and streamlining their ability to participate, structuring the way in which programme choices are presented to participating citizens in order to optimize their selections, and determining the frequency, presentation and labelling of programme options to facilitate participation in retirement or education programmes.[42]

However, if law serves an expressive role in forming our social norms, beliefs, and preferences, what are the inadvertent effects of hiding its presence?[43] With the current administrative priority on utilizing behavioural science to direct policy outcomes, it is especially important legal research contemplate the potential conflict between the need to direct outcomes and to allow autonomy, agency, and freedom of choice.[44] Legal scholars have been quick to adopt a simplified version of behavioural economics, but the long-term effectiveness and sustainability of the regulation-by-design approach is understudied.[45] Amir and Lobel critically argued that the key to using behavioural research as precursors to policy lies in identifying the root of the problem to be solved. Behavioural research reveals a 'vast maze of psychological mechanisms that may lead to bias'. In other words, 'if policymakers are to become consumers of the discipline of judgement and decision making, they must be wise consumers'.[46] Indeed, the behavioural insights that BLE has largely focused on often come from lab experiments, and behavioural economists recognize that the implications of these experiments in real-life settings cannot be translated seamlessly. These experiments are missing the rich social and organizational context of real market interactions, interactions that can only be understood when keeping the multidisciplinary promise of

[41] Ibid. [42] Ibid., at 1–2.

[43] On the expressive role of law, see Matthew D. Adler, 'Expressive Theories of Law: A Skeptical Overview', 148 *University of Pennsylvania Law Review* 1363 (2000) Elizabeth S. Anderson and Richard H. Pildes, 'Expressive Theories of Law: A General Restatement', 148 *University of Pennsylvania Law Review* 1503, 1506 (2000).

[44] Suzanne C. Thompson, 'Naturally Occurring Perception of Control: A Model of Bounded Flexibility', in *Control Motivation and Social Cognition* 74 (Gifford Weary et al. eds., 1993) [hereinafter *Control Motivation and Social Cognition*].

[45] Theresa M. Marteau, David Ogilvie, Martin Roland, Mark Suhrcke, and Michael. P. Kelly, 'Judging Nudging: Can Nudging Improve Population Health?', 342 *BMJ* 263 (2011).

[46] Amir and Lobel, 'Stumble, Predict, Nudge'.

the behavioral sciences alive.[47] In a new article that presents sets of tensions within the behavioural field, Feldman and Lobel (2014) argue that the breadth of the insights of social science inevitably presents challenges in how to operationalize these insights into the study of law.

12.4.2 Methodology as Strategy: Nudge and Broccoli as Complementary Mentalities

When the United States Supreme Court was deciding the constitutionality of Obamacare, broccoli served as a metaphor for market regulation, and the threat it poses to personal freedom and a warning against government intervention. During arguments, it was Justice Scalia who predictably made the seemingly naïve but potentially subversive inquiry, '[i]f Congress can require Americans to buy health insurance, could it force people to buy just about anything – including a green vegetable that many find distasteful?' On the steps of the Supreme Court, activists held up signs declaring, 'I hate broccoli'. A Republican senator asked Justice Kagan during her confirmation hearing if she would uphold the constitutionality of a bill that read: 'Americans, you have to eat three vegetables and three fruits every day', Kagan responded, '[s]ounds like a dumb law', but avoided answering further. Of course, the correct response to the broccoli question is that law can and does, as it always has, regulate consumption and well-being in multiple ways. The law governs these areas through mechanisms that range from traditional command-and-control regulation to new governance techniques of private–public collaborations, subsidization, taxation, production of research and basic knowledge, dissemination of information, education and the design of institutions.[48] Nonetheless, proponents of legislation are often reluctant to propose definitive

[47] Ibid. ('The bridge between new governance scholarship and behavioral economics points to future directions for interdisciplinary research. In order to continue applying behavioral insights to create smart and lean policy, more integrated research is required. Many of the groundbreaking behavioral economics studies are lab experiments, which lack the rich social and organizational context of real market interactions, and therefore have limited direct application to concrete social policy. Moreover, behavioral economics often neglects the institutional aspects of enforcement and compliance. Integrating lessons from both lab and field experiments, as well as from the various disciplines, including economics, psychology, sociology, and organizational behavior, into meaningful data is therefore a central challenge for regulatory agencies').

[48] *See* Orly Lobel, 'The Renew Deal: The Fall of Regulation and the Rise of Governance in Contemporary Legal Thought', 89 *Minnesota Law Review* 342 (2004). Ironically, specifically about broccoli, the *Washington Post* recently had statistics about how the significant

solutions, and thus BLE has proven seductive in this context. The broccoli metaphor is answered with a nudge metaphor: the threat to liberty of requiring people to eat their greens is appeased by the claim that all legal regulation can be an easy, gentle, nonthreatening nudge.

Here, the legal scholar comes to the aid of the regulator, who acts as an optical illusionist. The goal becomes discovering ways to create laws that are embedded in the decision making architecture. Probably the most popular example of a behavioural policy tool has been the setting of defaults. Thaler and Sunstein describe setting defaults as a primary method of law making which takes into account that most people stick with the a pre-set default choice in most decision making contexts, including savings, organ donations and online privacy.[49] Defaults are seductive as a regulatory method because they can be conceptualized as noncoercive. By definition, defaults are not mandatory and they allow exit.

To embrace this nudge mentality too fully is to approach research the way consumers approach products. BLE scholars want a product that they can readily incorporate for resale to policymakers, and policymakers want our laws to be offered up to us as produce. To belabour the broccoli image a bit longer, BLE scholars have become consumers of behavioural research as though these were veggies: we want studies to be available for us to digest easily and with flavour, just like we want our broccoli served to us alongside our grains and carbs – each part of a menu of options, served just on time and just in the right form and shape, available all seasons and all hours, safe from pesticides and child labour, packaged, labelled and neatly presented. We want to then offer law as everywhere and felt nowhere. Like an advertisement for feminine hygienic pads stated, we want 'to walk with and feel without'.[50]

increase in the consumption of broccoli in the past decade since the US Department of Agriculture declared it a super food.

49 Richard H. Thaler and Cass R. Sunstein, *Nudge: Improving Decisions about Health, Welfare and Happiness* (2009).

50 Both the activist/policymaker version and Thaler/Sunstein academic version of the libertarian paternalism soundbite are wrong conceptually. But it is entirely possible that strategically they have chosen the right rhetoric for their agenda, evidenced by the lure of nudge and the dynamic duo (one serving as the regulatory czar of the Obama administration; the other as the special consultant for the shift from regulation to governance in the UK government). Indeed, Thaler and Sunstein market their call for gentle policy nudges as appealing to 'conservatives, moderates, liberals, self-identified libertarians, and many others'. They are not unique in their desire to occupy the uneasy middle ground between conservative and liberal politics and to defy the conventional boxed camps that have long impeded policy reforms. But they are wrong in masking the normative choices that must be made in employing any regulatory mode. (the context: 'the era of big government is over'; 'neither left nor right.')

As should be clear from my previous writing, I share the commitment of other fellow BLE scholars to enhancing individual choice in regulatory design – a preference for diversifying regulatory approaches, such that they often leave a large degree of flexibility and agency for regulated parties.[51] Although I have argued in my own work that we use multiple techniques to promote regulatory compliance and social policy, and that regulators must become consumers of behavioural insights, it is a mistake when all of these goals are promoted under the guise of simply aiding private choice in a nonregulated market. BLE provides for the expansion of the policy-making toolbox in ways that integrate collaboration with control, process with coordination, design with incentives, information with data mining and reflexive regulation with monitoring and enforcement. People and societies will disagree on welfare goals, and public policy inevitably should and does attempt to objectively evaluate better individual choices pertaining to well-being. Legal scholarship ought to explicitly recognize these value judgements as a significant part of the legal process rather than to hide them by masking the intervention.

While human preference can be a moving target, one feature of individual preference is well established in the behavioural literature, namely that individuals value the ability to control their lives, paths and choices. Human beings come into the world and leave it with a passion for control, and research suggests that the loss of people's ability to direct their lives significantly influences their well-being. Further, while voluntariness, agency, and choice are matters of degree with no bright lines between coercive intervention and 'softer' guidance by the state, there are real and important differences among education, manipulation, and coercion.

While generally enthusiastic about the use of behavioural sciences to research ways in which law can be simultaneously more effective and is experienced as less interventionist than traditional command-and-control approaches, I have also argued against over-claiming the BLE contribution to such efforts, as is implied in the misleading term 'libertarian paternalism', which was widely popularized by Cass Sunstein and Richard Thaler in their book *Nudge*.[52] *Nudge* defines 'libertarian paternalism' as including 'actions, rules, and other nudges that can be easily avoided by opting out'. In contrast, Amir and Lobel argued that regulatory reforms under the umbrella of libertarian paternalism are neither libertarian nor paternalistic. Like Amir and Lobel's earlier critique of *Nudge*, Pildes and Bubb

[51] Amir and Lobel, 'Stumble, Predict, Nudge'; Feldman and Lobel, 'The Incentives Matrix'.
[52] Thaler and Sunstein, *Nudge*.

similarly argue that the insights emerging from behavioural economics often require much more forceful regulatory solutions than what dominant BLE scholarship has been willing to advocate. Moreover, the tools used by BLE are in fact stronger than they are willing to admit.[53] As will be further discussed in the next subsections, the pairing of the two concepts of libertarianism and paternalism to form a sound bite that represents the range of innovative solutions to address problems of both market and regulatory failures is distorting in several ways. First, it is underinclusive because it denies the full implications of behavioural research to strengthen traditional regulatory tools. Second, it is overinclusive, because it presents BLE as encompassing the entire body of legal studies, by collapsing methodology and ideology.

12.4.3 Distributional Implications

Traditionally, law and economics prefers to address any and all distributional questions through the tax system.[54] Kaplow and Shavell, for example, explain that using legal rules for distributive purposes is worse than income tax redistribution.[55] This works well in relation to traditional poverty economics, which assumed that the poor are either rational actors who direct their fate or that they are irrational in severely deviant ways that require strong paternalistic interventions. More recently, behavioural studies provide middle grounds that disrupt the way we understand social justice and resource distribution. The research shows that people living in poverty are neither more nor less inherently irrational than other human beings. Their circumstances and resources pattern the ways in which they will be prone to cognitive biases and suboptimal decision making. Moreover, it may be the very nature of their initial economic conditions that impairs their cognitive resources, perpetuating this condition, as the mere state of being poor seems to impair cognitive abilities and executive functions necessary in making sound

[53] Ryan Bubb and Richard H. Pildes, 'How Behavioral Economics Trims Its Sails and Why', 127 *Harvard Law Review* (2014): 'Moreover, somewhat ironically, the nudges recommended by BLE scholars are often not as light-touch as advertised . . . work in BLE has generally not subjected these tools to sufficient analysis to evaluate their effects'.

[54] Steven Shavell, 'A Note on Efficiency vs. Distributional Equity in Legal Rulemaking: Should Distributional Equity Matter Given Optimal Income Taxation?', 71 *American Economic Review*, 414–418 (1981).

[55] Louis Kaplow and Steven Shavell. 'Why the Legal System is Less Efficient Than the Income Tax in Redistributing Income', *Journal of Legal Studies*, 23:667–681 (1994).

judgements and decisions.[56] This results in a set of behaviours that exacerbate their financial conditions, such as over-borrowing or refraining from having bank accounts.[57]

Generally, the evidence is robust that people do not save enough and spend too much compared to their stated preferences and long-term goals.[58] This is the basis of the Save More Tomorrow (SMT) Programme, a popular BLE proposal for reform that allows employees to commit to contributing increasing portions of future salary increases to retirement accounts.[59] But beyond the greater consequences of flawed financial decision making displayed by those with fewer resources, an important line of research in the behavioural literature looks at the link between scarcity and the propensity for irrationality. Early studies had already shown that hunger affects the brain in profound ways, affecting capability to concentrate and to focus on more than one's next meal. Studies have shown this even in the context of people who normally have enough food on their plate. In their new book on scarcity (including scarcity of sleep, security, time, food, and money), Shafir and Mullainathan observe the price of poverty on psychological processes and decision making.[60] They use a series of behavioural studies to demonstrate how these conditions create tunnel vision of the mind. The price impoverished people pay goes beyond the physical. These studies show that the price includes by necessity the focus on the immediate day-to-day survival, with a limited ability to plan and think about the future, concluding that 'the poor are not just short of cash. They are short on bandwidth.' This research provides evidence that when poor individuals are reminded of their poverty, these individuals 'showed less flexible intelligence, and less executive control. With scarcity on his mind, he simply had less mind for everything else.'

This is a vicious circle with devastating implications on the ability to escape the cycle of poverty through savings, strategizing, training, and borrowing less. The conditions of poverty also lower self-control and the

[56] Anandi Mani et al., 'Poverty Impedes Cognitive Function', 341 *Science* 976–980 (2013).

[57] Anuj K. Shah et al, 'Some Consequences of Having Too Little', 338 *Science* 682–685 (2012).

[58] Shlomo Benartzi and Richard H Thaler, 'Save More Tomorrow: Using Behavioral Economics to Increase Employee Saving', 112 *Journal of Political Economy* S164–S187 (2004).

[59] Ibid.

[60] Sendhil Mulainathan and Eldar Shafir, *Scarcity: Why Having Too Little Means So Much* (2013).

ability to resist engaging in self-destructive and addictive behaviour. The authors call it the 'scarcity trap'; this framework is important to further explain why public interventions to create better capabilities to address health and financial well-being are so important. Deprivation of health and financial security is not only a harm in and of itself, but it is also a condition that further impacts the human mind in a self-struggle for human rights.

12.4.4 Methodology as Ideology: From Deviation Correction to Normative Insight

Arguably, the *raison d'être* of legal scholarship is to connect the world of practice with the world of theory, the descriptive with the normative. The general problem of the tension between the descriptive and normative projects, the theoretical and the empirical, which exists in almost all types of research and scholarship, is intensified in contemporary BLE. The problem with nudge mentality as the narrow dominant version of BLE is the conflation of methodology and ideology. People have limitations in their cognitive processing, but they are also more complex in their preferences and actions. This is not simply because they fail to comply with a theoretically perfect model of rationality, but because human decision making and morality are complex and rich. Indeed, it is behavioural science that provides us with the understanding that preferences are endogenously shaped and constructed by law. They are adaptive and generated by law itself. Inherently, then, BLE underscores the existence of a normative stance in any legal order. Legal research should not merely study behavioural economics as a how-to for correcting irrationality, but rather as insight into the normative world of social beings.

The challenge is to resist behavioural science technocracy as it translates into law. This means resisting the fantasy of upgrading nudge-style software that can input all the different terms that characterize, for instance, credit card offers, and translate them into a meaningful and comparable representation to a full-fledged behavioural software that would correct for all. Brownsword writes that the current moment in the study of law is witnessing a 'shift of focal interest from law and regulation' accompanied by 'a more "technological" approach to managing human conduct'. BLE takes a lead in this shift to the study of the regulatory environment/private individual interface. This is because BLE is interested in how people make decisions in the real world, and the real world includes all forms of ordering: from private ordering and the background social norms that surround individual decisions to the public ordering and the background legal rules. In other words, *context* is the most important contribution of behaviourism. It is the rejection of the abstract and celebration of the concrete and minute variances that shape our human perceptions and actions. The little 'tweaks' (not to be confused with nudges) make all the difference.

12.5 Conclusion

The integration of behavioural and psychological studies into the field of law and economics helps to create regulations and policies that aid individuals in maximizing their wealth and health. First-generation law and economics attempted to create the most efficient economic and legal regime for rational economic actors who consistently act in accordance to their stated goals of wealth maximization. The problem with the traditional approach, however, is that human nature is too complex to reduce to the traditional rational actor. Behavioural studies show that humans are messy and often act in ways detrimental to their stated goals. Humans suffer from biases that cloud their judgement and decision making, have limited self-control and overestimate their own morality. Understanding that humanity is not perfect, and examining the roots of those flaws, can help lawmakers and legal scholars craft rules that solve these problems. While BLE can be beneficial to society, dangers of over-control and paternalism loom. People enjoy the ability to control their own life, and while BLE should be used to create mechanisms that foster public welfare, the line between subtle choice architecture, and forcing Americans to consume broccoli with each meal is difficult to ascertain. Rather than assumptions about human behaviour in the abstract, BLE helps us understand how people make decisions in the real world and assists us in creating rules to improve public welfare without controlling how people live.

13

Freedom and Method

PAUL W. KAHN

As a professor of law and humanities, my methodological concerns are rather different from those that motivate scholars with a social science orientation. Still, method has been a subject of concern to me at least since I wrote *The Cultural Study of Law* almost twenty years ago.[1] There I proposed, and I have since pursued, an approach to the law that fits squarely within the humanist tradition of philosophical, literary, and historical inquiry. That tradition, not just in law but throughout higher education, is under threat today for reasons not unrelated to questions of method – or perhaps more accurately to a failure to understand the limits of method. In this paper, I will explain and defend the methodless character of the humanities. That does not mean inquiry is without order; rather, it means that there is no way to separate method from content. My defense must respond to a double challenge: first, without method, scholarship becomes nothing more than the expression of personal values; second, without method, teaching is not possible. I will respond to both challenges by arguing for interpretation as an ethical practice.

13.1 Setting the Problem

The humanist approaches law just as he approaches any other object of study: it is a matter of interpretation. Method is problematic in the humanities because interpretation is a free, creative act. Creation cannot be subject to rules, and without rules there can be no method. Yet the humanities must be taught. Pedagogy requires method, even when the subject is itself without method. Plato captures the idea of a method of the methodless in the *Republic*. He describes the method of a long course of study for those who would rule. At the very end of this training,

[1] Paul Kahn, *The Cultural Study of Law: Reconstructing Legal Scholarship* (Chicago: University of Chicago Press, 1999).

however, there is to be a moment of insight that is beyond words.[2] That which is most important to know is not the subject of any method. Plato calls that transcendent truth "the idea of the good." The suggestion is that inquiry is an ethical practice: interpretation puts at stake an idea of the good or, as we would say, the values of a community.

The exhaustion of method is an equally familiar point in religious inquiry: ritual has a method, but the ground of faith is without method. We might speak similarly of love: charity can have a method, but love is an openness to the infinite demand, which is always beyond method.[3] The point is familiar in the creative arts: technique can be taught, but creation of the beautiful requires a freedom beyond technique. We can extend the point still further: normal science has a method, but there is no method that accounts for the change of paradigm.[4] What then of politics? Ordinary politics may follow a method, but there is no method to revolution.

These examples give us a ready-to-hand sense of the limits of method. The very idea of method suggests routine or normalization. Beyond method there is an idea of a free subject who appears to us in the dimensions of knowledge, art, politics, religion, and love. In each domain, method exhausts itself, and still, a surplus remains. Contemporary accounts tend to speak of norm and exception.[5] They emphasize that the exception is the point of decision: we must decide for revolution, faith, beauty, love, or the good. The decision, as Carl Schmitt says, "[l]ooked at normatively . . . emanates from nothingness."[6] Such emanations are beyond method.

Surplus, decision, and exception are all ways of insisting on the freedom of the subject. Our experience cannot be fully accounted for by any form of determinism, whether that of cause and effect or that of formal proof. Thus, Kant had to write his *Third Critique*.[7] The *First* dealt with the understanding's ordering of all experience as the effect of a

[2] Plato, *Republic*, in *Complete Works*, (John M. Cooper, ed.) (Indianapolis: Hockett, 1977), 521c–533c.

[3] See Simon Critchley, *Infinitely Demanding: Ethics of Commitment, Politics of Resistance* (London: Verso, 2007); Emmanuel Lévinas, *Humanism of the Other* (Nidra Poller, trans.) (Urbana, Ill.: University of Illinois Press, 2003).

[4] See Paul Feyerabend, *Against Method*, 3rd edn. (London: Verso, 1993); Thomas S. Kuhn, *The Structure of Scientific Revolutions* (Chicago: University of Chicago Press, 1962).

[5] See, e.g., Giorgio Agamben, *State of Exception* (Kevin Attell, trans.) (University of Chicago Press, 2005).

[6] Carl Schmitt, *Political Theology: Four Chapters on the Concept of Sovereignty* (George Schwab, trans.) (Chicago: University of Chicago Press, 2005), pp. 31–32.

[7] Immanuel Kant, *Critique of Judgement*, (James Creed Meredith, trans.) (Oxford, Eng.: Oxford University Press, 2007).

cause: there is no phenomenon that cannot be explained as an effect determined by the conditions that preceded it.[8] The *Second Critique* dealt with the capacity of reason to determine the will by the form of law alone – the categorical imperative.[9] The *Third*, however, dealt with the freedom of the imagination, which is just where we find the activity of interpretation and the claims of judgment. Law, too, is a practice of freedom, relying upon interpretation and judgment.

A common view of law is that it is that part of politics that has been reduced to rules. If there are rules, there can be a method. But between the legal rule and its application, there must be a decision. The rule must be interpreted under the circumstances of the particular case. Much of the law is a process of persuading and being persuaded with respect to the correct interpretation of a rule. Legal persuasion advances through analogy and distinction. When we are persuaded by an analogy, we have not been determined by a rule or led through a proof. Instead, we have used our imaginations. Not just analogy, but all interpretation is persuasion without proof.[10] Conclusion follows from decision; we know what the law is only after we have decided, that is, after we have been persuaded.[11] On this point turns the possibility of law as a practice of freedom.

The humanist scholar also pursues analogies and makes distinctions in order to persuade. How we choose to persuade and how we are persuaded are all matters of ethos, that is, of character.[12] There is no such thing as a "neutral" interpretation, for there is no interpretation without a decision. Interpretation is never an innocent act. Judges, for the most part, flee from acknowledging this proposition. The scholar's responsibility is not to use

[8] Immanuel Kant, *Critique of Pure Reason* (Paul Guyer and Allen W. Wood, trans.) (Cambridge: Cambridge University Press).

[9] Immanuel Kant, *Critique of Practical Reason* (Mary Gregor, trans.) (Cambridge: Cambridge University Press).

[10] Bryan Garsten attributes this point to Rousseau. See Bryan Garsten, "Persuading Without Convincing: Rousseau," in Bryan Garsten, *Saving Persuasion: A Defense of Rhetoric and Judgment* (Cambridge, MA: Harvard University Press, 2006), pp. 55–83.

[11] I elaborate this point in my discussion of Schmitt and his critics in Paul Kahn, *Political Theology: Four New Chapters on the Concept of Sovereignty* (New York: Columbia University Press, 2011), pp. 76–85.

[12] Aristotle, *Rhetoric*, I.2.1356a5-20 in *Complete Works*, Jonathan Barnes, ed. (Princeton, N.J.: Princeton University Press, 1984). See also Eugene Garver, *For the Sake of Argument: Practical Reasoning, Character, and the Ethics of Belief* (Chicago: University of Chicago Press, 2004); James Boyd White, *Heracles' Bow: Essays on the Rhetoric and Poetics of the Law* (Madison, WI: University of Wisconsin Press, 1985), p. 34.

this point to criticize judges, but to think through the implications of the decision as an intersection of being and the good.

Belief that there is a relationship between interpretation and character is at the foundation of liberal education. This was exactly the point of Socratic pedagogy, which is why the dialogues so freely cross back and forth between descriptive and normative inquiry. This pedagogic model is hardly anachronistic. Only as long as we understand thinking to be an exercise in ethical responsibility can we justify the practices of a liberal education.[13] We want our students to make judgments and to have judgment; we want these two ideas of judgment to coincide in a lifetime of self-reflection. The failure to understand the connection of interpretation to character is a substantial part of the reason that colleges and universities are under such assault today. Even more importantly, this same failure undermines the possibility of a response to those critics who can see no actual benefit from investment in liberal education.

13.2 Against Method

The politics of interpretation are evident not just in the recent assaults on liberal education but also in the recurring critique of the interpretive character of American constitutional law. The absence of method leads critics to claim that interpretation is only a pretext for the imposition of the personal values of judges and scholars. The critic sees only two possibilities: either there is a method that grounds objectivity, or judgment is subjective and a matter of personal values.[14] On this view, authority without method must be circumscribed by strong, politically accountable institutions and neutral procedures.

Can that which is without method claim any kind of objectivity that can ground judgments of better and worse?[15] I approach this question in two steps. First, I explain my claim that there can be no method to

[13] On thinking and the other's point of view, see Hannah Arendt, *The Life of the Mind, vol 1, Thinking* (New York: Harcourt Brace Jovanovich, 1981).

[14] The leading proponent of the view that these are the only alternatives is Justice Scalia. See, most recently, Antonin Scalia and Bryan Garner, *Reading Law: The Interpretation of Legal Texts* (St. Paul, MN: Thomson/West, 2012).

[15] The legal realist response was to agree that there is no method to interpretation, but to measure legal results against consequences. The objectivity of law was to be located in means–end rationality. This approach was always subject to the response that policy planning is up to the legislature and administrative agencies.

interpretation because interpretation is a free act. Second, I use an example to explore what makes an interpretation more or less successful.

13.3 The Work of the Imagination

We can start with a Socratic puzzle. We can teach craft technique, abstract knowledge, and facts. In each case, we don't just teach a set of propositions that are to be memorized. Rather, we teach a method. A craftsman knows how to use his skills to address a range of demands, just as a geometrician knows all possible shapes, and a scientist knows how to study an entire range of phenomena. A craftsman does not know his craft if he knows how to make only one pot; a geometrician fails if he knows the properties of only one shape; a scientist fails if he knows only how to repeat a single experiment.

Acknowledging the link between discipline and method, Socrates is puzzled by the oracle's statement that he, Socrates, is the wisest man.[16] Yet he is not the master of any discipline – except perhaps stone cutting, which hardly seems a form of wisdom. What he knows is something about himself: his own ignorance. He knows that he does not know and he acts toward others on the basis of this knowledge. This point is important: knowing your ignorance is not the same as being ignorant. Socratic ignorance is not an absence that is to be cured; it is rather a practice.

Socratic engagement models the action of a free subject. Each dialogue begins with a set of beliefs and ends in that indeterminate surplus that indicates the capacity of the free subject to transcend his beliefs and practices. Socrates does not know beforehand where the conversation will come out. The conversation continues until it is interrupted by the ordinary necessities of daily life. One of those ordinary necessities is the decision of a law court, which condemns Socrates to death. We learn from these conversations not by finding a general proposition that unites them, but by seeing them as examples. To follow the Socratic example, then, is to let the discourse lead us wherever it might go. It demands commitment, not method. That we can commit to such an open-ended inquiry expresses our capacity to transcend whatever particular beliefs and practices we have at any moment.

By portraying the origin of inquiry in the ordinary pursuits of Athenians, Plato insists that this freedom is not exceptional. Indeed, just the

16 Plato, *Apology*, in Plato, *Complete Works*, 21a–b.

opposite: the Socratic inquiry normalizes the moment of freedom that is clearly visible in the exception. Focusing too much on the exception, we distort the nature of our own freedom, which is not exceptional at all. Freedom is realized wherever we think for ourselves. That begins with the commitment freely to engage each other. Because a free discourse requires commitment, thinking is an ethical act. Someone who refuses to engage in a conversation appears to be recalcitrant, stubborn, closed-minded, or just plain prejudiced. Someone who is not honest in his responses may be duplicitous, manipulating, or untrustworthy. Thinking freely, we realize the value, but also the virtues, of being a free subject. Virtues of character are important because real dialogue always poses substantial risk to one's settled beliefs and expectations. Even to begin requires a kind of courage. Character remains important as the dialogue continues because the engagement, as a free act, is unpredictable.[17] As old beliefs fall away, we can rely only on character – our own and that of our interlocutors. In this sense, character creates the conditions for inquiry. For this reason, Plato worried that philosophy was not a practice for the young: freedom without character can be dangerous.

Character is also important in the choices made in pursuing an interpretive practice. We show something about ourselves by the examples we draw, the analogies we make, and the questions we pose. The dialogue leads us, but not as a guide leads the blind. It leads by persuading and that is a function of what we value or can come to value.

In place of method, Socrates speaks of his "daimon."[18] Plato develops this point when he writes of spirits or muses that inspire poetry, by which he means the whole range of creative work. We know this idea still: there is a madness to creation. Thus, an artist cannot give an account of how he accomplished his work. There is no method to which he can point. We feel as if we are taken out of ourselves when we freely create. We are comfortable with this idea in the arts – we speak of "creative genius" – but the point extends to every interpretive practice.

Arendt is the modern philosopher most interested in the connection of freedom, creation, and thinking. She introduces a new language, distinguishing labor and work from action, in order to make the point.[19] Labor is that which we do by nature; work is production. Method makes work

17 In Plato's dialogues, Alcibiades represents the danger of freedom without character.

18 Plato, *Apology*, in Plato, *Complete Works*, 31d.

19 Hannah Arendt, *The Human Condition*, 2nd edn. (Chicago: University of Chicago Press, 1998).

"our second nature," for method allows for endless repetition. There is work in the factory, but there can also be work in the academy. When we send our research assistants out to run regressions on data, they are working. Just as the field worker can be replaced by a machine, the research assistant can be replaced by a computer. In contrast, action has no method. It is always new, always unpredictable. Politically, action is exemplified in revolution. The problem for constitutionalism, according to Arendt, is to design structures within which a free politics of action can continue after the moment of revolution.[20] This is exactly the problem of establishing a method for the methodless, and Arendt makes little progress toward the resolution of this paradox.

Arendt sees that the Athenian agora was the site of origin of both philosophical inquiry and democratic citizenship: Acting and thinking are overlapping ways of characterizing the activity of a free subject. The modern bureaucrat, according to her, stands opposed to both thinking and acting. One way to put the problem of the bureaucrat is that he follows a method instead of realizing the possibility of freedom. When politics becomes work without thought, it can lead to atrocity.[21]

Despite her book on Eichmann's trial, Arendt was not much of a jurisprudential thinker. She was more interested in revolution than law. Her contemporary, Carl Schmitt, however, focused his attention on the nature of freedom under law. Those inquiries took him, in the first instance, to a theory of the exception as the site of the unbound, free character of the sovereign decision. The sovereign decision is beyond method; it does not follow from any rule even though it is for the sake of a legal order. More importantly, although less noticed, that same concern with freedom's relationship to law took Schmitt to the problem of the judicial decision.[22]

Schmitt stood with the legal realists – and later the Critical Legal Studies scholars – in thinking that no legal rule applies itself. Between the legal rule and the judgment there is inevitably a gap that can only be crossed by a free act. The judge's role is to decide what the law means. There can be no method by which a judge determines the correct

[20] Hannah Arendt, *On Revolution* (New York: Viking Press, 1963). Arendt speculates unconvincingly on the usefulness of local soviets and town councils. Ibid., pp. 252–53.

[21] See Hannah Arendt, *Eichmann in Jerusalem: A Report on the Banality of Evil* (New York: Penguin, 2006). Eichmann, in turn, describes himself as following the Kantian rule. Ibid., pp. 135–36.

[22] Schmitt, *Political Theology*, ch. 2.

application of a rule in a contested case.[23] The very fact of contestation means that either outcome will rely upon the rule as its ground. In such a situation, the rule does not determine the judgment; rather, the judgment determines the meaning of the rule. We only know what the rule means after the act of judging. The legal rule does not eliminate the freedom of the judge; it requires that freedom for its own realization. Law is not a project of reducing the surplus, of bringing order to what had been disordered. To think this is to be in the grip of a misleading image. It is like thinking that because many novels have been written, there are fewer that remain. We always exercise our freedom against borders; the borders don't diminish our freedom.[24]

Judgment is not the exercise of method. For this reason, we speak of judgment not only as an act, but as a quality of character: someone who has judgment will make good judgments. Someone who lacks good judgment cannot substitute method for character. A person with poor judgment – a matter of character – will make bad decisions. She is not to be trusted. The same is true of other interpretive enterprises. Thus, the successful artist must have an "artistic disposition." We are unlikely to find instances of single, successful, creative productions – in law or art – because the creative act rests on character. The same is true of scholarly interpretation. We want to hear what the great scholar has to say not because we think he knows a lot, but because we are interested in the character of his interventions in the ongoing discourse of his discipline.

These examples show the relationship of character to interpretation. Interpretation requires judgment; judgment requires character. One has to become a person of judgment; one is not born into it. There are no child prodigies in law, just as there are no great novels, paintings, ballets, or films created by children.[25] Similarly, there are very few interpretive, critical texts written by young people that are worth reading.[26]

[23] See Stanley Fish, "Dennis Martinez and the Uses of Theory," *Yale Law Journal* 96 (1987): pp. 1773–1800; see also Kierkegaard's famous dictum, "the moment of decision is madness," discussed in Kahn, *Political Theology*, p. 49.

[24] The extreme example of this capacity is someone like Nelson Mandela, who remained a free subject even in prison. The history of the West is filled with monks, slaves, prisoners, and laborers who have demonstrated the same freedom.

[25] Music is the obvious exception: composition and performance. This exception, I suspect, has something to do with the mathematical quality of music, which may be related to the role of method in music.

[26] Occasionally, as in the case of Marx and Arendt, we recover early texts written by people who produced substantial work later. It is impossible to say whether the early texts would have stood on their own.

Because judgment is not the application of a rule, a judgment is not just an interpretation, but it must always be interpreted. Creation and reception point to one and the same process of interpretation. Interpretation always occurs within some sort of dialogue. This is no less true in law than in the arts. This dialogic character is visible in the judicial opinion: it must be interpreted even as it presents itself as an interpretation. Judges interpret precedents to create them. The judgment is not the conclusion of a private language, but a moment in an ongoing, public, interpretive enterprise. For this reason, no judgment is ever final; no opinion can be the last word. A legal system that closed down the possibility of reversal would no longer be one that expressed self-government.[27]

Because creative work is not an application of a method, it is beyond the purposive control of its creator. I can set out to write a novel, but I don't know what novel I will write until I write it. I cannot even know whether I will produce anything at all. The same is true of a painting: I don't first have a picture in my mind, which I then execute. I may set out with one idea and find myself actually producing something quite different. I will be surprised. Without method, the artist cannot explain how it is that he produces the work of art, nor can he even be sure that he can do it again. His statements of method can be no more informative than platitudinous admonitions to "work carefully" or "pay attention."

From the perspective of an account of causes, the work of art comes as if from nowhere. This is true of all forms of creativity. We cannot read the biography of Newton and understand the causes of *Principia Mathematica*. We cannot read Lincoln's biography and understand how he wrote the Gettysburg Address.[28] A judge who is completely predictable is a bad judge, for he gives us no evidence that he is thinking. The same is true of scholarly work in the humanities: if we engage our work freely and with commitment, we cannot explain where it comes from.

Of course, the artist knows rules of material production relevant to his creative act: how to mix paints, how to handle perspective, how to work from a sketch. The judge too knows the texts from which he is permitted to draw and the forms of argument that may be persuasive to his audience. In the absence of these forms of knowledge, the judge would

[27] *Stare decisis* – the Anglo-American legal principle requiring judicial respect for precedent – always comes with a doctrine of exceptions.

[28] Presidents are always learning that biography is not necessarily a good basis from which to predict judicial decisions. Consider Eisenhower on Justice Brennan or Nixon on Justice Blackmun.

not know what to say. But teaching these rules will not lead to a judgment, an opinion, or a scholarly interpretation. Both artist and judge must occupy the surplus, which is the domain of freedom.

Since a work of interpretation does not follow from a rule, the critic cannot evaluate it according to a rule.[29] To judge a creative work a success, we cannot say it realizes or comes close to realizing that which a rule sets forth as the ideal. Of productive processes (Arendt's category of work), this is exactly the way we evaluate them: products are better or worse realizations of an ideal. With respect to creative work, we don't measure, we interpret. Just as it was produced freely, we must receive it freely. We can be completely surprised, yet persuaded.

Modern reflection on the relationship of judgment to method began with Kant's *Critique of Judgment.* Kant approaches judgment as a capacity for aesthetic decision: what he calls a "judgment of taste."[30] Of work in the fine arts, he argues, there can be no method because creative work is not the product of any rule. Nevertheless, such work is not arbitrary; it is not merely a matter of subjective taste. If that were true, no judgments could be made about the quality of art, either by the artist or the critic. Creation has some relationship to rules, yet it does not follow from a rule. It is not an application, but it is not arbitrary.

The puzzling aspect of the work of art for Kant is its character as a unified whole. It may come into being step-by-step. We can watch the artist assemble the parts. Yet, we cannot account for the work by referring to these individual steps as parts. The work proceeds always as a whole: the parts exist only in reference to a whole. That whole is no more the end than the beginning of the process. The whole and the parts emerge together as if in a dialogue. The exploration of the relationship of part to whole is exactly what an interpretation offers. For this reason, every interpretation can put at issue an entire world.

Kant says that creative work is the product of "genius."[31] He does not mean by that someone of high intelligence. Rather, the emphasis is on the etymological root of the word in the idea a personal spirit – a daimon. Genius is a necessary element of any adequate account of our world with its free creative acts, which is why Kant sees genius as a category of nature.[32] Genius points to our own amazement at our capacity to create

[29] Kant, *Critique of Judgement*, Book 2, § 46.

[30] Kant, *Critique of Judgement*, Book I, §§ 11–22, Book II, §§ 31–38.

[31] Ibid., §§ 46–50.

[32] Ibid., § 46 ("Genius is the innate mental predisposition (*ingenium*) *through which* nature gives the rule to art.")

that for which we can give no causal explanation. Creating, the artist follows the idea that takes shape before him. There are any number of ways to express this point: he is led by his daimon; the spirit works itself out through him; he is possessed or mad; he has a kind of genius.[33] All refer to a kind of causation, a bringing into being, that has no method.

Kant makes a pedagogical point in response to this analysis when he argues that we learn of the beautiful only by studying examples.[34] We don't study rules, but rather we look to instances of accomplished, free creation. We form our own imaginations by living with these examples. This is character formation as the opening to beauty to which the artist then freely responds. The education of the critic follows the same pattern: he learns by studying examples. His expertise, upon which the judgment of taste relies, is the capacity to interpret by locating the work in a world of exemplars. If instead, the critic applies a theory and measures artistic creation by how well it meets that theory, he is no longer in conversation with the artist. Indeed, he is not in a conversation at all; his work is no longer interpretive.

We learn from examples. This is a familiar point in law, where argument often proceeds by analogy. The most basic legal rule is to treat like cases alike. This, however, is not a rule to be applied, but a conclusion we reach after we have been persuaded to see the case one way rather than another. We cannot follow any rule to determine what is like and what is different. We must reason from case to case. We start with an instance of which we are certain and then try to persuade each other of what is like this case. As we argue, we are offering interpretations of what it means to be alike or different.[35]

There are no rules for the production of analogies. Yet, just as with the production of works of art, some analogies are better than others. This generates the same puzzle that Kant faced when he thought about taste in art. How can we have better and worse taste, if there are no rules by which to measure success? As soon as there is a rule, judgment becomes a matter of measure. But there is no such thing as the perfectly beautiful. Nor is there a perfect realization of the concept of equality or of dignity. Is there a jurisprudential equivalent of taste? Are there lawyers, judges, or scholars who have what we might call a "taste for law?"

[33] Kant speaks of such alternative "causal" claims as referring to a "super-sensible" about which we can have no determinate concept. Ibid., Book II §57.

[34] Ibid., Book II, §47.

[35] I elaborate this argument in my book, Paul Kahn, *Making the Case* (New Haven, CT: Yale University Press, 2015).

13.4 An Example

Without rules, I can only demonstrate the excellence of interpretation by offering an example. The example must show how humanistic inquiry can resist method but nevertheless succeed or fail. Success is not a matter of personal preferences. I am not trying to persuade the reader to be like me. Rather, I am trying to persuade the reader to join in an inquiry into a shared world. Success means to be taken seriously, to be worth thinking about and thinking with. If I am persuasive, you will not be the same after you read the essay. I don't mean that you will no longer be "the same person" to friends and family. Legal interpretation is not therapy. The change will be in the horizon of understanding. If I persuade, you will see legal meaning differently – even if only at the margins.

I will use the example of a recent paper of mine on a subject of some relevance to this collection of essays: the relationship between domestic and international law.[36] My particular concern was to understand how the early American Supreme Court – the court of Chief Justice Marshall – made use of the law of nations.

The doctrinalist would approach this question by asking how US practice fit into a set of general categories: was the early Court monist or dualist? Were treaties self-enforcing? Were treaties and customary law treated differently? His ambition would be to find the formal rules that were applied – explicitly or implicitly – by the Court to reach these outcomes. The social scientist might approach the question by collecting all the cases that make a reference to the law of nations. Those cases would then be coded in order to produce data that could be quantified and manipulated. A social science researcher might want to plot changes over time or plot distribution over space. She would worry about whether the data could prove causation or only correlation. She reassures herself on this score by formulating a causal hypothesis that she then tests against the data.

The humanist makes no assumptions about either the application of formal doctrine or the competition of interests. What interests him is the way in which the opinions offer a point of access to a world of meaning. The legal world of the early nineteenth century was an imaginative construct that made it possible for jurists to see likeness and difference, history and progress, possibilities and actualities. This imagined world

[36] Paul W. Kahn, "The Law of Nations at the Origin of American Law," paper delivered at the University of Helsinki, May 13, 2013.

did not determine outcomes; rather, it provided resources for arguments along its multiple webs of significance.[37] The scholar's effort of interpretation tries to expose those webs to deliberate self-awareness.

The introduction to my essay frames a research agenda that is conceptual, historical, and cultural. The object of the inquiry is to learn something about the social imaginary at work in postrevolutionary American legal thought and practice.[38] As an interpretive enterprise, the inquiry advances by exploring the reciprocal relationship between parts and whole. If I am successful, the reader engages not as a passive recipient of information, but as a participant in a discourse. She reads the essay actively, by which I mean that she takes it as an invitation to think for herself. She will argue with my claims and see alternative directions that could have been pursued. She cannot prove me wrong by offering data or proofs. One interpretation can be displaced only by another interpretation. She may pursue her own interpretation, in which case she may persuade me to see differently.

Here, then, is how I begin.

> Before it was a political achievement, America was a technical achievement. It was also a social and economic achievement. Each characterization points to a line of inquiry: we want to know how those involved did it, what they thought about it, and how they organized themselves. What all these inquiries have in common is that they understand America as a project. It was so from the beginning and it remains so. Listen to Obama's Second Inaugural with its eloquent repetition of the phrase "our journey is not complete until . . ." He describes a collective project of self-formation directed at making "these words, these rights, these values – of Life, and Liberty, and the Pursuit of Happiness – real for every American."
>
> The idea of America as a project captures its special place in the history of modernity. America is to be a product of deliberation and choice, an exercise in applied political theory. Revolutionaries don't want only to arouse the crowd. They want to write books. The Republic of Letters and the political republic are intersecting communities. Our revolution produced *The Federalist Papers* – an important work in theory, published in newspapers as part of a democratic campaign of persuasion. The theoretical ambition of the founders remains startling. Jefferson's library formed the core of our national library; Adams and Madison studied classical political theory before attempting to draft a modern constitution; Hamilton studied economic theory.

[37] See Clifford Geertz, *The Interpretation of Cultures* (New York: Basic Books, 1973).

[38] On the concept of the social imaginary, see Charles Taylor, *Modern Social Imaginaries* (Durham, NC: Duke University Press, 2004).

> The modernism of the Founding is remarkable given that America actually begins with religious exiles. If a project is a practice informed by a theory, these exiles are not engaged in a project at all. The Puritans cross the ocean to preserve, not to invent. Their proof texts are not works of modern science – natural and political – but the Old and New Testaments. America has always offered refuge to religious exiles who want nothing to do with a scientific modernity. This, too, continues, producing some of our deepest political divisions – as well as some interesting syntheses in our civil religion.
>
> By the end of the eighteenth century, the political center of gravity had moved decisively in favor of science over faith. This is all the more remarkable given that the Second Great Awakening sweeps the country from 1790 to 1820. Yet, none of the founders is anchored in a traditional community of religious belief. None is a minister by training. Many are lawyers. Indeed, this is what makes them of special interest to us: the American project is uniquely bound up with law. We need, accordingly, to ask how they understood, imagined, and deployed law – both domestic law and the law of nations. They wanted to invent the former, but to accede to the latter. This double movement reflects the structure of sovereignty: self-government within a community of nations.

This introduction begins with an ordinary concept: the project. Imagining a project is an entirely familiar way of organizing our activities. By the second paragraph, however, I am trying to surprise the reader by suggesting the extraordinary range of this ordinary concept. We don't just have projects. We are a project both individually and collectively. If we can make of ourselves a project, then we are always located both within and beyond the project. There is a surplus. We are, for this reason, a never-ending project. This rapid movement from the ordinary idea of a project to the extraordinary reach of the concept should pull the reader slightly off balance. There is a suggestion already of self-reflection: is not this essay a project? What, then, is the position from which it is written and where does it locate the reader?

I use the familiar term "project" not just to introduce a new attitude toward the American founding, but a new attitude toward thinking. To think about the founding is not to record events or write biographies. It is to explore how a community occupies a world of meaning through the work of the social imaginary. An idea of interpretation should begin to come into view that takes as its object habits of thought, ways of seeing, and forms of discourse. What did they think they were doing? They thought they were pursuing a project.

The project will be my touchstone as I explore this era of American legal thought and action. It is a formation of the imagination and, in these opening paragraphs, I suggest that a formation of the imagination works through replication. The project is the social DNA of the era or what we might today call a "meme."[39] The imagination organizes experience according to a model: the idea that politics could be a project led to revolution and constitution. Of course, it also led to the modern conception of personal autonomy as the responsibility for constructing a life. Ben Franklin famously made his life a project. The personal and the political, the private and the public, intersect in the idea of the project.

This turn of the imagination toward the project, I suggest, is not simply an accident of American history – for example, its colonial origins. Instead, this turn is critical to modernity itself. The project is what the Enlightenment does to the imagination.[40] America is *the project* of modernity because modernity is the era characterized by the project. The surplus of human freedom is no longer conceived as the space of sin, but rather as an endless possibility for self-creation. With this, the moral valence of the project changes completely. The sin of pride is displaced by the virtue of taking responsibility for the self and the community. The project, accordingly, gives us a way of uniting inquiries into science (including the new science of politics), politics, education, morality, and law. Indeed, it offers a way of placing work in all of these fields into relationships with each other. It also introduces into the inquiry the idea that thinking itself has a history. Interpretation links the architecture of thought to its genealogy.[41]

If my essay is working, by the second page the reader should be vigorously questioning my claims. She should be asking whether the project is indeed so important and what are the alternative ways of organizing experience. I encourage that questioning by suggesting other possibilities in my juxtaposition of the sacred and the secular. The project succeeded ideas of sacred revelation and ritual obligation. Succession does not mean complete displacement. These ideas continue, just as the idea of the project was not absent before modernity. Mankind was, after all, a part of God's project of creation. The shift of the locus of the project from the sacred to the secular is a fertile subject for interpretation, and I hope my readers will pursue it.

[39] See J. M. Balkin, *Cultural Software: A Theory of Ideology* (New Haven, CT: Yale University Press, 1998).

[40] See Immanuel Kant, "What is Enlightenment?" in *Immanuel Kant, Foundations of the Metaphysics of Morals: and, What is Enlightenment?* (Lewis White Beck, trans.) (Upper Saddle River, NJ: Prentice Hall, 1997).

[41] See Paul Kahn, *The Cultural Study of Law: Reconstructing Legal Scholarship* (Chicago: University of Chicago Press, 2000).

An entire agenda of interpretive work should be opening up in an engagement with these first two pages – multiple explorations of the changing, master formations of the social imaginary as they produce and are produced by law. One wants to know what happens to the project once revolution has become an unimaginable possibility and the constitution has shifted from something to be made to something to be maintained.[42] Does it make sense to describe America as a revolutionary conservative project?

This agenda of interpretation demands a lot of the writer. To be in a position to make a persuasive argument, one has to be able to draw on diverse bodies of knowledge. The background knowledge of context is hardly limited to law, courts, and opinions. I have cast the interpretive effort against broader movements of empire, religious conflict, philosophy, and revolution. To decide to set out in this direction, I need to know about religious schism, about elite educational practices, and about the controversies that organized and informed early American politics as they touched on the law of nations. The essay will, for example, go on to explore the impressment controversy with Great Britain, the controversy over slavery and the slave trade, and the politics of Indian displacement. Did I know in advance that these would be the controversies around which to form the body of the essay? No. Only as I wrote did I come to see that otherwise dissimilar political crises offered mutually reinforcing points of access to the political imaginary. The whole only emerges with the parts, and vice versa.

My essay assumes a working familiarity with historical materials, but it is hardly antiquarian in its orientation. It introduces the very contemporary idea that forms of the imagination have a genealogy. How do I know that this idea can be useful in the interpretation of legal texts? I am inclined to think there might be something in this direction, but am I imposing an alien structure on the materials? All I can do is try to make the argument and ask myself whether it is persuasive. I have no privileged position from which to make the determination.

The opening of the essay also introduces the idea of an architecture of thought. I am searching for what we might call the master narrative structure of the era. I begin with the idea of the project because I think it will be a fecund source for exploring the structure of the modern imagination. The essay will have to make good on this promise. We may think of

[42] See Paul Kahn *Legitimacy and History: Self-Government in American Constitutional Theory* (New Haven, CT: Yale University Press, 1992), ch. 2.

the project as a "natural" resource for organizing practical experience, but it is not an obvious model for imagining law and politics. We might imagine law as emerging from time immemorial. In that case, we would be skeptical that law be can remade on the basis of theoretical expertise.[43] Similarly, models of natural law or of divine ordering are alternatives to the project. If we think that law is revealed in a sacred text, we might also think claims for a secular project of law to be not just wrong but heretical.[44]

I introduce this idea of project not as something obvious, but as itself posing a puzzle. How is it that communities so deeply entwined with religious beliefs and practices found their way to the imaginary of the project? Asking the question, I suggest that paradigms don't achieve dominance without contestation. I introduce this tension between the Enlightenment ideal and a theologically informed practice not because I am interested in who won, but in how the competition was imagined and managed. This will be important for the emergence of a civil religion in American politics, which continues to affect American attitudes toward the law of nations.

The puzzle of the relationship of faith to reason is an old theme of inquiry. The reader of my essay familiar with modern work on interpretation and culture will see that in these first two pages I am pointing toward Max Weber, while deploying a contemporary scholarly apparatus.[45] My essay will simultaneously be an imagined conversation with Chief Justice Marshall and a conversation with contemporary scholars. The idea that interpretation requires placing oneself within webs of significance is indebted to Clifford Geertz. The essay will be an effort at what he called "thick description."[46] I inflect this idea of thick description through work associated with Charles Taylor and Michel Foucault. With Taylor, I speak of the social imaginary and understand the interpretive burden as that of exploring the way in which a master narrative or an archetypal paradigm organizes practice and belief.[47] With Foucault, I insist that the imagination has a history.[48] I am not interpreting the

[43] Edmund Burke, *Reflections on the Revolution in France* (New York: Penguin, 1986) [1790] is the classic example of this skepticism toward a radical politics of the project.

[44] See Michael Walzer, *In God's Shadow: Politics in the Hebrew Bible* (New Haven, CT: Yale University Press, 2012).

[45] See Max Weber, *The Protestant Ethic and the Spirit of Capitalism* (Talcott Parsons, trans.) (London: Allen and Unwin, 1976).

[46] Geertz, *The Interpretation of Cultures*, ch. 1.

[47] Taylor, *Modern Social Imaginaries.*

[48] Michel Foucault, *The Birth of the Clinic: An Archaeology of Medical Perception* (A.M. Sheridan Smith, trans.) (New York: Pantheon Books, 1973); Michel Foucault, *Discipline and Punish: The Birth of the Prison*, (Alan Sheridan, trans.) (New York: Pantheon Books, 1977).

work of any of these scholars. Rather, I am interpreting early American legal thought. Yet, if someone were to interpret my work, they would want to situate it in its own historical moment.

These opening pages point to an inquiry that imagines itself as part of a larger investigation into the nature and origins of the modern. Much of the attraction of the essay lies in this direction. It promises not just to help us understand how early American jurists thought of themselves, but also how we continue to think of ourselves. We continue to live in a world deeply influenced by the imaginary forms that were taking shape then. Thus, President Obama's rhetoric appeals to cadences made possible by the transformation of a religious movement of exile into a secular project of law. In this way, an essay on judicial opinions from the early nineteenth century promises to say something about our post-9/11 world in which ideas of sovereignty, law, and national identity have all been very much at issue.

Because the imagination does not work by separation through categorical division, but by spinning webs of significance, an interpretation must have a similar quality of extending out in multiple directions. Again, think of a conversation, which can begin at any point but has the potential to expand indefinitely. A good interpretation goes "far enough" without being overwhelmed by endless possibilities. It has gone far enough when it has persuaded its audience. Persuasion is not a matter of checking an interpretation against the facts of the matter. The interpretation offers a map of what is otherwise without chart. The reader must trust that map. He will not trust it, if he does not trust me.

Accordingly, part of the persuasive burden is to show myself to be worthy of trust. This is not a qualification external to the interpretation, but internal to it. I have no other access to readers. I won't be trusted if I hide difficulties, if I misrepresent, if I push a personal agenda, if I appear to act on interests apart from those appropriate to the inquiry. I may start with a "hunch" about the direction in which to go, but I must self-consciously hold open the possibility that I may be wrong. Indeed, it is implausible that I will not find myself to be wrong at multiple points. For example, I set out thinking that the law of nations was a way of managing relations with other nations. I discovered that it was equally about managing moral contradictions within the nation.

I show my character – and whether I am to be trusted – in my presentation of the argument. This begins with the demand for honesty but extends to an acknowledged openness to my readers. I can only persuade if I show myself open to being persuaded. I must write in such a way that I invite arguments against my position, rather than close off criticism. I must, in other words, respect my readers as participants in an ongoing dialogue. No interpretation can ever claim to be more than a temporary resting point. Facts can be taught by lecturing, but an interpretation is successfully taught only when it is taken up in a free act of appropriation. To respect the readers' freedom means to create the conditions under which they can take up the challenge of persuading me to change my views. As a free act, interpretation is something that we do together.

Beyond demonstrating my own integrity, I must show myself sympathetic to those whose beliefs and practices are the object of my interpretation. I must be genuinely interested in them; I must not use them for my own ends. My interpretation will only persuade if the reader can imagine it being persuasive to those whose beliefs and actions are at issue. Of course, not everyone is a reliable interlocutor and people can have lots of reasons for misrepresenting themselves, but that cannot be true of most people most of the time.[49] The subjects of my interpretation, accordingly, put an ethical demand upon me to make sense of *their* world. A failure to sympathize with them, even when I disagree with their beliefs and practices, will cast doubt on my interpretation. This demand for a sympathetic imagination creates the appearance of a certain moral ambiguity in interpretation.[50] For example, I am interpreting the legal practices of a radically inequalitarian society. I cannot be a reliable interpreter if my approach is directed by my moral condemnation of their practices, including that of slavery.

There is, then, a threefold ethical demand upon the interpreter. First, the interpreter must show himself to be honest, which means transparent in his work on the materials. Second, he must respect his readers, by holding himself open to persuasion. Third, he must show sympathy for the persons and practices that are the object of his interpretation. An interpretation is better – objectively better – as it satisfies these ethical demands of honesty, respect, and sympathy. Conversely, an interpretation that strikes us as dishonest, disrespectful, or unsympathetic will fail

[49] By contrast, René Girard offers a social theory of the scapegoat that relies on a certain opacity to the participants. René Girard, *Violence and the Sacred*, (Patrick Gregory, trans.) (Baltimore: Johns Hopkins, 1977), pp. 23–24.

[50] Lawyers always confront this ethical problem in representing clients. See Anthony T. Kronman, *The Lost Lawyer: Failing Ideals of the Legal Profession* (Cambridge, MA: Belknap Press, 1993).

to persuade anyone. All three of these ethical demands are violated by any attempt of the interpreter to privilege his own personal opinions and political values. There can be no persuasion in that direction.

13.5 The Method of the Methodless: Pedagogy

If interpretation is unavoidably a matter of ethos, then so too is pedagogy. In teaching there is no escape from a self-reflection on ethics. To teach is to create a community of a certain kind. That community seeks to displace a natural hierarchy by reciprocal commitments among participants.

To the advanced student trying to learn how to interpret legal phenomena, I am inclined to say "do something like this," as I hand him my essay on the law of nations in early American judicial practice. If he persists in asking "but what is this?" I give him another example. Learning by example is hardly foreign to legal study – at least in common law jurisdictions. Earlier forms of legal education were literally forms of apprenticeship. The case method arguably has been an effort to move some part of that experiential learning directly into the classroom.[51]

Sometimes the pedagogy of the example is literally all that I can offer. I give graduate students my own work and demand of them that they produce. We then engage each other's work. They are to criticize and engage my work in the same way that I respond to their work. Method is no more than this reciprocal commitment to a community of discourse.

Teaching in the humanities is about thinking together, not about conveying knowledge. There is no difference between teaching and taking seriously, and ultimately between teaching and learning. This kind of teaching cannot be easily done in the lecture hall or over the Internet. It requires a community of dialogue. If there remains anything to the idea of mentorship, it is located here. Not in the willingness to advance the

[51] The origins of the case method lie in antiquated ideas of a formal legal science to be inferred from the opinions – the vision of Christopher Langdell who initiated the modern law school at Harvard at the end of the nineteenth century. His scientific aspirations could not survive the legal realists who expanded the method to include "materials" other than opinions: materials with which the modern lawyer engaged in the creation and reform of regulatory state must be familiar. See generally Thomas C. Grey, "Langdell's Orthodoxy," *University of Pittsburgh Law Review* 45 (1983): p. 3 (arguing that Langdell's "classical orthodoxy is the thesis to which modern American legal thought has been the antithesis").

career prospects of one's students, but in making it possible for students to take up the risky activity of thinking.

Nevertheless, to insist on the absence of method too early can be pedagogically self-defeating. There must be a pedagogical method of the methodless. That method has a negative and a positive aspect. The negative aspect is to break the student loose from his or her expectations of mastering a subject matter. Because the ambition is negative, I can speak of method in this respect as a series of rules of thumb. The positive aspect can have no such rules because its ambition is to begin the creative – that is, free – practice of interpretation.

13.5.1 Pedagogy as a Practice of Unlearning

When judges complain about the state of legal scholarship, they think of academics as adjuncts to legal practice. Scholarship, on the judges' view, should be directed at helping them to decide cases.[52] For some judges, this means exploration of the effects of different legal rules. For others, it means exploration of the doctrinal implications of past decisions. The former are broadly consequentalist; the latter think of law as an autonomous normative order that must meet standards of formal consistency and coherence. A humanistic pedagogy must break the hold of both these ideas on the student's imagination.

Students, of course, are not responding to the judges' demands. Both judges and students, however, share the naïve view that the forms of knowledge are twofold: either we trace causes, as in the empirical sciences, or we elaborate formal, conceptual relationships. Accordingly, the scholar who is doing neither lacks "objectivity." His or her work can be anecdotal at best and mere personal opinion at worst.

The interpretive practice I have described is neither a matter of tracing effects nor of charting doctrine. It has little place for truth claims – empirical or formal. More broadly, scholarly interpretation is not a means toward some other end, whether judicial decisions or regulatory reform. The humanist interpreter does not ask what should the law be,

[52] Chief Justice John Roberts, for example, suggests that the average law review article "isn't of much help to the bar," while Judge Harry T. Edwards complains of "academicians" who are indifferent to teaching to the "problems facing the legal profession." Roberts quoted in Adam Liptak, "The Lackluster Reviews that Lawyers Love to Hate," *New York Times*, Oct. 21, 2013; Edwards in "A Conversation with Judge Harry T. Edwards," *Washington University Journal of Law and Policy* 16 (2004): 74.

but rather what is the shape of the world of meaning within which legal claims are persuasive to particular communities.

Because belief in truth and a practice of reform are mutually supportive, humanist interpretation suspends the commitment to both at once. That we are capable of such a suspension of belief is the discovery of philosophy: we can always take ourselves as an object of our own inquiry. We can ask how and why we see the world as we do or pursue one set of practices over others. From the perspective of interpretation, law is a text; it is not a means to an end. The humanist scholar has no view on whether the law is trying to make us better or whether it is succeeding in such an effort. He has no view on whether the law is or should be logically coherent. He has no concern with the outcome of any particular case. Rather, he focuses on the variety of imaginative resources that are put in play by any case.

Advancing the ends of legal reform through scholarly activities is neither more nor less virtuous than other forms of legal practice. The point of humanist scholarship is not to disparage traditional legal scholarship, but to open up an alternative to legal practice in whatever form it takes. Pedagogically, this means a break must be made between the study and the practice of law. The student must be forced to make a choice, for without that moment of deliberate awareness, she will constantly fall prey to the question, "What should the law be?" She does not, after all, stop being a citizen with distinct interests, values, and opinions just because she has taken up the study of law. The break required for interpretation is a temporary suspension of belief; it is a pause, not a termination. Even such a pause, however, is difficult to achieve.

The student's belief in the naïve model linking truth and reform is likely to be as firm as the beliefs of a deeply religious person. If we ask a Christian fundamentalist why he puts so much stock in the written text of the Bible, what kind of an answer are we expecting? Can he respond other than "it is the word of God." He offers us a proposition about the truth of the matter. He does not explain his beliefs as a historically contingent formation of the imagination; he cannot offer a genealogy of his practices. Nor can he place those beliefs in an architecture of beliefs that would enable us to begin to trace the connections between his attitudes toward this text and his attitudes toward time, space, family, state, competing religions, and professional formations, as well as love, duty, responsibility, and sacrifice. To take up an interpretive attitude would require that he imagine the possibility of being other than he is. That might be quite unimaginable for the true believer.

The negative moment of methodology is designed to dislodge the student from a position similar to that of the fundamentalist. He must be "shocked" to take up a position of self-reflection. Method here can do no more than offer some rules of thumb by which the controlled explosion of beliefs can be brought about – controlled because of the danger of falling into cynicism or a casual relativism. This is a danger that attaches to all genealogical inquiry.

My first rule is to tell students I neither care about nor want to hear their opinions. Their opinions do not count any more than their interests. All political commitments must be suspended when they enter the classroom. Argument must be pursued wherever it goes, even if it moves in directions that are politically disconcerting. The free act of interpretation requires what Kant calls "disinterest,"[53] which I would describe as a willingness to engage without precondition. The focus is not on how to get to some predetermined end, but on responding to what has been said. Education should be disruptive without being ideological.

My second rule is to tell students that there is no right answer to any question, for there is no truth of the matter. Just as a practice of interpretation is not a matter of pursuing personal opinions or interests, it is not a matter of discovering some preexisting truth. It does not matter whether that truth is located in claims of efficiency or of justice. Interpretation is a practice of persuasion. Persuasion is a function of the social imaginary, of beliefs and practices that are in circulation and that make sense to a community occupying a particular time and a place. The measure of a successful interpretation is not whether it is true, but whether it is interesting. It is interesting when it surprises us, making us to think anew about the character of our beliefs and practices.

My third rule is that legal interpretation is not a matter of predicting how a particular case will come out. Even the most persuasive interpretation will not persuade everyone.[54] It certainly will not persuade a decision maker who chooses not to listen. Nothing turns on the particular outcome, for a controversial case is one in which substantial legal arguments are available on both sides. Interpretation goes to what both sides share: ways of imagining order and meaning. To worry about winners and losers is to fall back into the practice of law.

The net effect of these three rules, if they succeed, is that students are temporarily displaced from what they believe. They are disoriented

[53] Kant, *Critique of Judgement*, Book I, §§ 2–5.

[54] See Aristotle, *Rhetoric*, I.1.1355b.

because they have lost the markers of truth and authority. Told that there is no truth and that decision makers have no authority over them, they are on their own. They do not know what to do because they have been told that reform is not their object. They must offer an interpretation, to which I will offer a response.

13.5.2 Pedagogy and Interpretation

The absence of method can lead to a particular existential anxiety. Not knowing how we create, we can never be certain whether we will be successful. Past success does not guarantee future success.[55] While no one is ever free of this anxiety, work in the humanities does bring a countervailing sense of wonder at the fact of our own creativity. We try to teach our students a sort of humility before the power of creation that is revealed through the person, but is not possessed by him. We teach them this by asking them directly to take up the task of creation, with all of the risks that this entails.

Humanistic study is not simply the discipline in which creative work is the object of study; it is itself a discipline of creation. Asked to interpret some text, I cannot simply make the work speak in its own voice. Instead, I engage it in a kind of conversation; I think with it. As in any genuine conversation, I hold open the future and thus expose myself to risk. I do not know what will emerge. I may be surprised; I may even surprise myself. When successful, there is genuine wonder that something that had previously been unimagined comes into existence.

This is why we often ask students to compare two works. The assignment requires the student to create something new. Putting the texts in a common space is an act of creation: the student must say something in his own voice. He cannot look up the answer; he cannot simply repeat what the texts say. There is no truth to be discovered; rather, a common world is to be imagined. The student must make the works speak to each other, but can do so only by speaking to them. At that moment of his own speech, he experiences himself as free. As a free subject, he has something to say. He is no less an author than the authors of the works he is interpreting.

The student cannot get the works to speak to each other without first thinking about how each work is itself an intervention in ongoing conversation. The point is not that we can only understand Shakespeare

[55] We speak of "writer's block," but the same experience appears in all the arts.

by understanding Elizabethan politics, although surely we have a lot to learn in that direction. Rather, we cannot understand Shakespeare without considering the broad history of the Western imagination. Power, belief, family, state, and individual dignity, equality and citizenship are all deeply embedded in traditions that trace back to classical and Christian thought. Law is not so different in this respect. It too builds on ideas of power, belief, family state, and individual, dignity, equality, and citizenship, all of which have a history that is never completely absent.

Every imaginative formation relies upon a web of meaning: patterns and practices of intuiting likeness and difference. The student begins to explore the architecture of this web through a kind of triangulation. Juxtaposing two works, he is forced to feel his way toward a third perspective – his own. He tries to see likeness and difference, but to do so he must interpret what it is to be alike or different. He must identify the threads of meaning that he judges to be relevant. He must, in other words, think, for he must consider a range of possibilities, and then speak in his own voice.

Freedom requires detachment in the negative sense that I sketched in the last section, but it is fully realized only in this experience of creating a common world – what Kant called "free play."[56] Once we begin creating, there is simply no end to it. Every text creates the possibility of an endless conversation. The conversation never ends of its own; it ends because we can no longer sustain it. We learn, then, of the weight of the body on the soul, that is, we experience from within another version of the gap between our finite and our free selves.

This mysterious experience of free creativity, which goes to the heart of who we are, is as close to the sacred as many of us are ever likely to get. It was once explained by speaking of the muses, or inspiration, or grace. When we look at any great work, we simply cannot imagine how the artist did this. Or rather, we can imagine it, but can't explain it. We can imagine it because in our own way we are constantly discovering our own freedom. Shakespeare is a mystery, but so then is my writing this little essay. I did not know where it would lead when I began. I act with the faith that it will bring something new into the world. Indeed, it will recreate the world, for every conversation offers a new starting point from which to see the whole. I cannot have this faith in myself without having a similar faith in others. That is the foundation of a pedagogical practice that takes students as autonomous, free subjects.

[56] See Kant, *Critique of Judgement*, Book I, § 9.

13.6 Conclusion: Freedom and Interpretation

Interpretation is the epistemic method that corresponds to a metaphysics of freedom. Interpretation of law insists that law is a product of our freedom; it is neither caused nor proven. A free act is respected only when freely responded to. Indeed, we go wrong if we imagine freedom as the work of the singular subject. Freedom is something we do together as we engage each other as agents. Law in a democracy is a product of our freedom, even as it protects us in this freedom.[57]

We know we are free because we speak to each other. Speaking together, we bring something new into the world. Only a person speaks; only a person is free. When we speak to each other, we are not following a script, we are writing one. If we were all alone, we would have no way to answer the question of whether we are free or determined.

A humanistic pedagogy is an invitation to enter a conversation. There is nothing more risky for the student than setting off on such a course. The risk is no less for the teacher. This is a pedagogy without authority. It may fail as often as it succeeds. Maybe more often, for most students do not come to law school to learn how to think for themselves. Yet, the risk of philosophy has been evident ever since the Athenians turned on Socrates. The risk today is not that of execution. There is still, however, the same risk that political authority will ask for an accounting from the philosopher. Like Socrates, we have no external measure to appeal to in our defense, for the virtues of this practice do not translate into legal reform. The defense of philosophy is never anything other than the practice of philosophy itself.

We cannot make the teaching of free inquiry any easier or less risky than it is. All that we can do is insist that thinking is an ethical act, and that the ethics of thinking is a demand upon every free subject. We should not expect to succeed with most students, yet we must act with the faith that every student is capable of thinking for himself.

[57] See Jürgen Habermas, *Between Facts and Norms: Contributions to a Discourse Theory of Law and Democracy* (William Rehg, trans.) (Cambridge, MA: MIT Press, 1996).

INDEX

CPSIA information can be obtained
at www.ICGtesting.com
Printed in the USA
LVOW12*1753110417
530427LV00010B/151/P

9 781107 130920